CASS SERIES ON POLITICS AND MILITARY AFFAIRS IN THE TWENTIETH CENTURY

WAR, STRATEGY AND INTELLIGENCE

By the same author

Israel's Political-Military Doctrine (1973)

Weak States in the International System (1981)

The Diplomacy of Surprise (1981)

Clausewitz and Modern Strategy (Ed.) (1986)

Strategic and Operational Deception in the Second World War (Ed.) (1987)

Leaders and Intelligence (Ed.) (1988)

War, Strategy and Intelligence

MICHAEL I. HANDEL

U.S. Army War College
Carlisle Barracks, PA

Routledge
Taylor & Francis Group

LONDON AND NEW YORK

First published 1989 in Great Britain by
Routledge
2 Park Square, Milton Park, Abingdon,
Oxon, OX14 4RN

and in the United States of America by
Routledge
270 Madison Ave, New York NY 10016

Transferred to Digital Printing 2006

British Library Cataloguing in Publication Data

Handel, Michael
    War, strategy and intelligence.—(Cass
series on politics and military affairs in
the twentieth century)
    1. Military operations. Strategy
    I. Title
    355.4'3

    ISBN 0-7146-3311-9
    ISBN 0-7146-4066-2 Pbk

Library of Congress Cataloging-in-Publication Data

Handel, Michael I.
    War, strategy, and intelligence / Michael I. Handel.
        p. cm. — (Cass series on politics and military affairs in
    the twentieth century)
    ISBN 9-7146-3311-9 — ISBN 0-7146-4066-2 (pbk.)
    1. Strategy. 2. Military intelligence. 3. Munitions. 4. War.
    5. Military history, Modern—20th century. I. Title. II. Series.
    U162.H29   1989
355.4'3—dc19   88-38202
                                                        CIP

Publisher's Note
The publisher has gone to great lengths to ensure the quality of
this reprint but points out that some imperfections in the original
may be apparent
Printed and bound by CPI Antony Rowe, Eastbourne

THIS BOOK IS DEDICATED WITH LOVE TO
MY MOTHER ILSE HANDEL

Contents

Acknowledgments

I would as always like to thank my wife, Jill Handel, for the good counsel she offered and tough questions she asked while editing most of the essays in this book.

Chapter 6 is reprinted from *International Security*, Spring 1980; Chapters 7 and 9 from *Jerusalem Papers on Peace Problems* (Magnes Press, Jerusalem); and Chapter 10 is reproduced by permission of Duke University Press. Other chapters first appeared in *The Journal of Strategic Studies* and *Intelligence and National Security*.

Should theory leave us here, and cheerfully go on elaborating absolute conclusions and prescriptions? Then it would be no use at all in real life. ... The art of war deals with living and with moral forces. Consequently, it cannot attain the absolute, or certainty; it must always leave a margin for uncertainty, in the greatest things as much as in the smallest.

Clausewitz, *On War*, Book I, Chapter I, p. 86.

Before a war military science seems a real science, like astronomy, but after a war it seems more like astrology.

Rebecca West

War, Strategy and Intelligence:
An Overview

War, Strategy and Intelligence:
An Overview

The essays assembled in this volume investigate the logic, conduct, and nature of war on the highest political and strategic levels while placing decidedly less emphasis on its operational and tactical aspects. The logic of war and its paradoxical nature are best understood through the study of military history with cautious reference to personal experiences in the upper echelons of leadership in war. One of the first paradoxes of war is that 'there is no failure like success'. Most notably in the age of technology, the experience gained in one war may be counterproductive – that is, totally irrelevant or misleading – in the next. As Major General W.D. Bird noted, 'The exact conditions in which any campaign was fought are unlikely to be repeated, and reliance on the experiences of one war is therefore liable to lead to false conclusions.'[1] Knowing what *not* to learn from the past may now have become more critical than knowing *what* to learn. In order to extract lessons of universal and hopefully some lasting value from this study, I have therefore based my research on a comparative approach.

My basic assumptions concerning the study of war are Clausewitzian (i.e., that war cannot be studied as an accurate or scientific discipline – that it is an art and not a science). Clausewitz believed that although much could be learned from the systematic study of war, it would always be a highly unpredictable affair shaped by friction, uncertainty, and chance as well as by non-rational psychological, moral, and creative forces. 'In war everything is uncertain, and calculations have to be made with variable quantities.'[2] Unlike those who are convinced that the study of strategy will ultimately be transformed into an accurate, predictable discipline, Clausewitz axiomatically assumed that the theory – and hence the practice – of war could not exceed certain limitations. As he put it, 'a positive doctrine [of war] is unattainable'.[3]

The most elementary fact about war is that it cannot be governed by immutable laws. When both parties to a conflict are aware of such so-called laws, each can always be expected to anticipate the most logical and rational course of action that his opponent is likely to pursue. Major General Bird's observations on what we would now call the operational level of war are equally applicable to the domain of strategy. 'Success can never be attained by merely following a strategical formula. There is an effective answer to every maneuver, and for each example of successful strategical operation an instance may be cited of its failure.'[4] While the physical environment 'co-operates' with the scientist at least to the extent that it does not change in order to undermine his understanding, this is not true of the study of human affairs, in which conflict and stress give rise to adaptation and deception. *In fact, the greatest success in warfare is usually achieved by ignoring and circumventing the 'laws' of war.* For this reason, even the most rudimentary principles of war are seldom of much predictive value.

This simple truth has not been – and psychologically cannot be – accepted by most military professionals, who feel compelled to 'take action' and 'impose order' on their environment. Their daily vocabulary is replete with such 'take charge' words as *command, control, communication, management,* and *planning*, all of which connote a sense of mastery over the environment. They must find answers to immediate problems, and often lack the time to ask questions. The danger of this approach is that they may live under the illusion that they can be in command of events and operate according to predictable patterns of behavior, whereas in fact this is rarely possible.

It is the duty of the academic, the 'armchair strategist', to show why war is and will forever remain an often uncontrollable, unpredictable affair. He must reconcile the 'pathologies', 'failures', and discrepancies of the real world with the ideal conceptions of war. While the military leader has to 'think positively' in order to carry out his duties, the scholar can and should raise questions.

The so-called *principles of war* (such as economy of force, surprise, or the concentration of force); *maxims* of war urging commanders to 'always be very strong first in general, and then at the decisive point'; and *analytical concepts* (such as the culminating point of victory, constant tactical factor, or the dominant weapon) are in the end all truisms. In war, as Clausewitz said, 'different ways of reaching the objective are possible' and 'they are neither inconsistent, absurd, nor even mistaken'.[5] There is no single truth or law or even in most cases an obviously dominant solution. This does not mean that truisms should be ignored. As important tools for providing better insight into the complex phenomenon of war, they offer some general guidance for planning, set up ideals to be achieved in military operations, and establish criteria for the *ex post facto* evaluation of a strategy or the conduct of a war.

Clausewitz made the most successful original attempt to develop a comprehensive theory of war, yet it is now clear that many of his observations, although *correct for his own time*, are now obsolete (see Chapter 1 below). As I have argued elsewhere, modern conventional war has become so complicated that development of a single and elegant comprehensive theory would be extremely difficult.[6] Inasmuch as the chapters in this book are all theoretical, a word on the relevance and importance of theory in the study of strategy and war is in place. The theoretical study of war may not appeal to the pragmatic nature of military professionals, who sometimes fail to see its relevance to their world of action and dismiss theoretical work as irrelevant academic pilpul. This attitude is understandable but unfortunate, since it may have a very negative effect on their activities in the real world. Theory and practice are not only inseparable, they are in fact complementary. As G.K. Chesterton put it:

> 'I'm afraid I'm a practical man',
> said the doctor, with gruff humour,
> 'and I don't bother much about
> religion and philosophy.'
>   'You'll never be a practical man
> till you do', said Father Brown.

Actually, military men, particularly higher-ranking commanders, 'speak prose' without knowing it. Although their activities and decisions may be guided by tacit or intuitively grasped concepts rather than by formally developed ideas, they encompass theories all the same.

Clausewitz was, as mentioned earlier, convinced that the 'endless complexities involved' in the study of war make it impossible to formulate a positive theory of war. Elsewhere, he suggests that 'an irreconcilable conflict exists between this type of theory and actual practice'.[7] Nevertheless, he fully appreciated the value of theoretical reflection for the military profession even as he carefully called attention to its limitations.

> The primary purpose of any theory is to clarify concepts and ideas that have become, as it were, confused and entangled. ... It is precisely that inquiry which is the most essential part of any theory, and which may quite appropriately claim that title. It is an analytical investigation leading to a close acquaintance with the subject; applied to experience – in our case, to military history – it leads to thorough familiarity with it. Theory then becomes a guide to anyone who wants to learn about war from books; it will light his way, ease his progress, train his judgment, and help him to avoid pitfalls. ... Theory exists so that one need not start afresh each time sorting out the material and plowing through it, but will

find it ready to hand and in good order. It is meant to educate the mind of the future commander, or, more accurately, to guide him in his self-education, not to accompany him to the battlefield; just as a wise teacher guides and stimulates a young man's intellectual development, but is careful not to lead him by the hand for the rest of his life.

... A commander-in-chief need not be a learned historian nor a pundit. ...

The knowledge needed by a senior commander is distinguished by the fact that it can only be attained by a special talent, through the medium of reflection, study and thought: an intellectual instinct which extracts the essence from the phenomena of life. ... Any insights gained and garnered by the mind in its wanderings among basic concepts are the benefits that theory can provide. Theory cannot equip the mind with formulas for solving problems, nor can it mark the narrow path on which the sole solution is supposed to lie by planting a hedge of principles on either side. But it can give the mind insight into the great mass of phenomena and of their relationships, then leave it free to rise into the higher realms of action.[8]

Some additional points on the value of theory are worth noting.

(1) The understanding and practical knowledge of war cannot always be obtained by those who need it. Many soldiers will spend their entire careers preparing for war without ever having the opportunity to learn from practice on the battlefield. Others new to the profession of arms have not yet participated in action and can, therefore, only learn from the experience of others. Learning from others is by definition theoretical, not practical, and must be based on generalizations and lessons (i.e., theories) drawn from the experiences of many other soldiers (which involves comparison and selection of the most relevant lessons). The battlefield, like the operating table in the medical profession, should not be the beginning of learning but rather its culmination.

Furthermore, since recent wartime experience can be misleading or irrelevant in the age of accelerated technological change, theoretical insights into longer-range trends may be more reliable guideposts than the lessons of the last war (e.g., historical cycles in which the advantage moves back and forth between the offense and defense, or lessons learned from different wars concerning the introduction of new weapons technologies unaccompanied by specifically designed military doctrines).

(2) Many useful concepts of great practical value cannot be readily derived from experience alone (i.e., to extrapolate from a single case or a narrow statistical sample). Their conceptualization requires painstaking analysis and meticulous theoretical construction. Clausewitz could not have developed his innovative ideas about the role of friction, uncertainty, and chance in war without his theoretical study of war in the abstract, which he then compared and contrasted with war in the real world. It was the methodological device of the ideal type, when compared with war in practice, that led him to the formulation of his most creative ideas.

For example, the observation that successful deception is predominantly based on *reinforcing rather than changing the perceptions of the deceived* is not self-evident. It took the experience and genius of Brigadier Dudley Clarke to formulate this theoretical observation. He took what may have been done intuitively by many before him and made it explicit perhaps for the first time as a concept that could guide others to take more successful action (see Chapter 8, Appendix I, p.448 below). A sound theory is the most *effective and economical* way of distilling many years' experience and communicating it to others.

The idea that strategic surprise is inevitable was not self-evident either. Explanation of this problem required a careful comparison of many cases of strategic surprise, and systematic exploration of the tensions and contradictions inherent in intelligence work formulated as a set of 'paradoxes'. It had previously been assumed (and still is by some) that the problem of avoiding strategic surprise in the opening phase of a war could be resolved through such measures as the development of enhanced intelligence capabilities, the investment of more resources in intelligence work, and the institution of organizational reforms. In this case, however, theory indicates otherwise. Furthermore, the theory of the inevitability of strategic surprise supplies the strategist with a series of practical lessons that were not always obvious before. For example, if strategic surprise is accepted as virtually unavoidable, more attention should be directed to the development of a conventional second strike capability (e.g., the dispersion of command outposts, hardening of aircraft hangers). If increased budgets and access to more resources are not necessarily going to improve the chances of avoiding strategic surprise, then perhaps valuable resources can be saved or better allocated to deal with its aftermath. Moreover, the occurrence of such a surprise cannot usually be blamed totally or sometimes even partially on intelligence organizations. (It is futile to expect to avoid strategic – though *not* operational and tactical – surprise, and there are also other organizations and individuals who can be held equally accountable.) Finally, this theory makes it clear that basing a mobilization system on the assumption that the intelligence community will be able to give two weeks, one week, or 62 hours advance warning time may be unrealistic.

(3) As Clausewitz observed, a good education in theoretical thinking helps to develop a more critical-analytical mind. Even the best theory may not provide answers to every problem, but it can at least raise perceptive questions that might otherwise go unasked. A theory may therefore be of particular value in showing not so much what can be done as much as *what cannot be done*, for the limits of technology or intelligence are not readily discernible. The caveats resulting from theoretical examination of a problem are not always obvious to those men of action and practice who often have to learn through a costly trial and error process.

(4) A properly designed theory will also contain the criteria by which it can be tested; it will indicate the type of circumstances or new evidence that would necessitate its replacement or modification. A good theory therefore includes the elements of its own obsolescence. Thus, theories – more so than doctrines and tradition – attest to the inevitability of change and the dynamic nature of knowledge. This is particularly important in light of the military profession's traditional conservatism and the unceasing quest to identify permanent principles of war. On the other hand, military organizations in today's world have become so accustomed to rapid technological development that some may be *too* open to change. In this type of situation, theories can be useful in showing the value of continuity as well as of change and in pointing out the danger of expecting too much from technology or instituting change for its own sake.

Those military professionals who have little time for theoretical inquiries (normally left to civilian experts or retired military officers) must therefore make an extra effort to familiarize themselves with theories on war in order to cope better with the increased complexities of modern war. While this cannot be done in most routine or field positions, much more can be accomplished in military schools and war colleges.

*   *   *

The dimensions I focus on in this volume range from very general issues such as the impact of technology on conventional warfare, the politicization of intelligence, the problem of war termination, and the possible decline in the utility of power in international relations, to more narrowly defined issues such as strategic and technological surprise in war, quantity versus quality, the design of conventional force postures, and strategic and operational deception in war. In discussing these subjects, I have tried to provide a detailed comparative analysis of each, identify major past trends, and if possible indicate the direction of future trends. Although few of these issues received any attention in Clausewitz's *On War*, they are of the utmost concern to the modern strategist. Much more research must be completed on a variety of related issues before scholars attempt to construct a new comprehensive theory on war that would not so much replace as complement and update Clausewitz's study of war. Among the many subjects in need of further attention are the problem of attrition in war; changes in concepts of space and time since the early nineteenth century; offense and defense in modern war; how the role of the *military genius* has changed in modern war; whether the bureaucratization and the 'computerization' of war has diminished the value of the military genius; whether developments in modern intelligence have increased or decreased uncertainty in warfare; and the influence of the modern mass media and democracy on the political guidance of war.

The essays presented here have three broad common denominators: (1) the politics of waging war; (2) the limits of rational analysis in the study of war and strategy; and (3) the impact of technology on modern warfare.

I. THE POLITICS OF WAGING WAR

Politics, in the broader sense of the word, pervades and often dominates every important aspect of war from preparation to termination. This statement is not, however, an allusion to Clausewitz's well-known dictum that war, if it is to be rational or purposeful, must always serve a political goal and hence be dominated by it. ('... War is not merely an act of policy but a true political instrument, a continuation of political intercourse, carried on with other means. ... Politics is the womb in which war develops. ... The political object is the goal, war is the means of reaching it, and the means can never be considered in isolation from their purpose. ... War is only a branch of political activity; it is in no sense autonomous.')[9]

Quite to the contrary, the political influences I have in mind are those that can distort and subvert the political guidance or control to which Clausewitz referred. They are the political interests of individuals and/ or the parochial interests of military and non-military organizations alike that often determine the most important policies, strategies, and decisions governing actions before and during a war. While Clausewitz conveniently assumed that somewhere at the top of the political-military hierarchy there would be a single monarch or supreme commander to provide the political guidance in war, in reality almost all objectives in modern war are determined through a complicated *political process*. In this process, allied countries, competing organizations, and individuals negotiate and compromise until they come to an agreement on what strategy to follow and which goals to pursue. Those who disagree with the objectives or strategies selected and who feel that the decisions made do not support their own interests will at the very least continue trying to modify them and at worst act to subvert or circumvent them. From a military point of view, strategies or operational plans arrived at through this political process are not necessarily the most rational choice. They are instead the product of a search for consensus that reflects the relative influence of different individuals or organizations. Strategic and military choices, the selection and acquisition of weapons systems, intelligence recommendations and analysis, and the decision to terminate a war or negotiate are therefore mainly *political* in nature, not 'purely' military decisions. Given the nature of human beings, all major military-strategic decisions are political. Moreover, this is often true even on lower technical levels and can be related to other questions in which primarily technical or military solutions are possible. Thus Clausewitz was mistaken when he assumed that lower levels of military action can be governed solely by professional considerations in isolation from external and internal political influences. 'Policy', he said, 'of course will not extend its influence to operational detail. Political considerations do not determine the posting of guards or the employment of patrols. But they are more influential in the planning of war, and often even of the battle.'[10]

> If we keep in mind that war springs from some political purpose, it is natural that the prime cause of its existence will remain the supreme consideration in conducting it. *That, however, does not imply that the political aim is a tyrant*. It must adapt itself to a chosen means, a process which can radically change it; yet the political aim remains the first consideration.[11]

The political level is in fact a tyrant that does interfere frequently in *operational* considerations. In conventional warfare in the nuclear age, political interference will increasingly dictate operational and even lower level decisions. For Clausewitz, politics contained the external dominating force as well as logic of all military activity, but did not include the numerous other political processes that permeate all military affairs. The higher the level of decision-making (i.e., the strategic and operational as compared to the grand tactical and tactical), the more *political* the decisions become. These are the internal political kimensions that influence the conduct of war.

While there is a *homo politicus* out to maximize his own interests and relative power, much like the *homo economicus* whose objective is to maximize profit, there is no *homo militarus* or *homo strategicus* who exemplifies the logic of military action. The military man *is a subspecies of the political man, for both deal with power and influence.* He is, in other words, representative of a discipline which itself remains theoretically underdeveloped in comparison with economics. War, as Clausewitz put it so aptly, has 'its grammar ... but not its logic'.[12] Its logic, however we look at it, is always political. Unlike the economic man whose success is readily measured by the wealth he accumulates, the success of the political (or military) man is measured by the power and influence he acquires. Power and influence are far more difficult to measure than money and wealth. This may explain why economists have made such enormous conceptual progress since Adam Smith wrote *The Wealth of Nations*. Despite the economists' limits of understanding (they too deal with human nature), the body of theoretical literature in economics has continued to grow in depth and sophistication, whereas little progress has been made in our theoretical understanding of war and strategy since Sun Tzu, Thucydides, and Clausewitz. Most of the time, the majority of modern military leaders are not directly involved in either war or fighting; instead they must expend far more of their energy obtaining the funds and resources preparing for war, protecting their 'turf', and competing for scarce resources with each other as well as with non-military men and organizations. In order to be promoted – to acquire power and influence – they must also invest considerable time and energy in the 'politics' of their own careers.

On the strategic level we find that decisions are not necessarily dictated by the availability or effectiveness of weapons and troops but by many political needs and pressures. The British decision to begin a strategic bombing campaign against Germany in 1942 was not arrived at because strategic bombing was the most effective way to win the war or the best way to use scarce resources. Among other reasons, the decision was made because it was the most expedient way for political leaders to show that they were taking successful offensive action against Germany. Whether or not the strategic bombing was truly effective, Bomber Command was in a position to strengthen its case by finding the evidence to prove its success while suppressing any hint of failure and wasted resources. Much the same could be said of the US Air Corps at that time. The assessment of the effectiveness of strategic bombing was made to justify the establishment of an institutionally independent Air Force.

In much the same way, pressures to open a second front in Europe *as soon as possible* reflected the American President's need to garner popular support by taking forceful action. Similarly, Churchill's unrelenting insistence that Wavell and Auchinleck launch offensives prematurely in the Western Desert is well known. One major problem of the German high command and intelligence during the Second World War was that their professional military training caused them to predict Allied strategic and operational moves on the basis of 'objective' military logic. But rather than being governed by what was *militarily* the most reasonable course of action, the Allies' strategic and operational decisions were frequently dictated by political considerations.[13]

In order to receive credit for a decisive victory, military commanders almost always want to obtain more resources (inevitably on the account of other commanders) to launch a major offensive in their sector. Certainly, their actions are motivated by the desire for personal aggrandizement and the advancement of organizational and national prestige as well as by the objective military circumstances. They forget Clausewitz's dictum that in war there are many different ways of reaching the objective which 'are neither inconsistent, absurd, or even mistaken'. Intent on pursuing a certain course of action, they then produce elaborate arguments to prove that their strategy and operational plans are also the most rational ones.

The national, organizational, and personal considerations that are paramount in the conduct of war itself play an even more important role in peacetime. Haggling over budgets with government leaders and parliamentary authorities, fighting over scarce resources with *other* branches of the armed services and *within* each one, and deciding on weapons procurement all involve major political considerations such as coalition-building and trading favors. In fact, political and economic needs are apt to dictate the choice of weapons that make less sense (e.g., battleships instead of carriers; nuclear submarines instead of conventionally powered submarines; manned bombers over rockets; three types of fighter-bombers instead of one or two; light instead of heavy divisions; and a 600- instead of a 500-ship navy). Whatever the political or economic logic of weapons procurement happens to be, *ex post facto* rationalization will try to make it appear as the best military choice. Many of those who argue for or against an existing or proposed military doctrine address themselves to the underlying military logic when, in fact, the raison d'être of the doctrine is principally political and economic.

Although the political factor is discussed in many of the following chapters, it is the main subject of Chapter 4, 'The Politics of Intelligence'. The ideal intelligence community consists of cooperating organizations in search of the objective truth; the common objective is to arrive at an unbiased and neutral estimate of the enemy's intentions and capabilities. As Chapter 4 emphasizes, this ideal is seldom even approximated in real life. All intelligence work is not only riddled by non-political problems of perception, but is also distorted by the interference of political considerations and processes on all levels. Military intelligence organizations, whether consciously or not, tend to inflate the capabilities of the enemy in order to promote their own procurement plans. To justify their own existence they may exaggerate the aggressive intentions of the enemy in peacetime. Leaders seeking to rationalize their actions solicit the intelligence data that support their own policies while they ignore contradictory evidence. The need to secure funds and influence motivates intelligence organizations to make their analytical estimates as acceptable as possible to leaders and parent organizations. Few wish to be remembered as the bearers of bad news. Other political influences come into play when intelligence organizations must coordinate their reports, for the production of such estimates involves a 'political' bargaining process in which the relative strength and influence of each organization play a major role. Finally, individuals – whether leaders or analysts – distort intelligence in order to protect their interests, enhance their survival, or satisfy personal psychological needs.

The same type of systematic analysis can be applied to the formation of strategy on the highest levels, the preparation and creation of operational plans (though less so for their execution), the procurement of weapons, and the design of military doctrines.

Chapter 9 includes a discussion of how political considerations can interfere with the process of war termination. Many wars continue long after it has become evident that they cannot be won on the battlefield or that victory would be too costly. Leaders who have staked their political fortunes on a war are reluctant to admit that they have wasted their country's resources or weakened its position. Rather than admit a mistake in judgment, they may change their initial objectives. In order to extricate themselves from such a predicament, leaders also become willing to earmark far more resources for this cause than originally planned; or they may follow an indecisive mid-course between hawks and doves in order to maintain their power, even though they know full well that the war cannot be won no matter how long it continues.[14] Military leaders who were originally opposed to initiating a war may nevertheless become reluctant to call for its termination until they have succeeded in some measure on the battlefield. If an army and its leaders have not performed well, they might prefer to prolong the conflict until they have proven their worth and justified their continued existence in peacetime. Wars rarely end as soon as there is a deadlock on the battlefield.

In Chapter 10, 'The Future of War: The Diminishing Returns of Military Power', I explore how the evolution of democratic values in Western and developed societies combined with a gradual increase in the importance of domestic politics have restricted the capacity of modern developed states to wage prolonged and costly wars. The appetite for war in developed societies has steadily diminished with the unprecedented holocaust of the First World War, which extended to the civilian homefront during the Second World War; the inability to win or to justify the wars in Vietnam, Afghanistan, and Lebanon; the ability to view the brutality of war on the television screen at home; and the fear of nuclear war. For most citizens in the developed world, war has finally become the *ultima ratio*. In contrast to the age of nationalism, when the prevailing perception was that the individual existed to serve the State, the modern citizen in developed countries believes that the State exists chiefly to serve his own selfish ends. Domestic political conditions have therefore radically changed the ability of the modern state to wage war. Modern military and strategic doctrines (e.g., the so-called Weinberger Doctrine) will have to be determined not so much by the imperatives of modern technology but by the degree of domestic support for prolonged military operations within modern developed societies.

The impact of political considerations is also examined, for example, in Chapter 3 on 'Technological Surprise in War'. During the Second World War, the decision whether to use *Window* (metallic chaff), and, if so, at what point in the Allied bombing offensive on Germany to introduce it, was in the end political not technological. The effectiveness of *Window*, the quantities needed, and the optimal timing of its introduction were scientific problems that could be decided rationally; but the developers of radar and those responsible for Britain's air defense who were opposed to the early introduction of *Window*, invented elaborate arguments to demonstrate its ineffectiveness and possible risk to England should the Germans begin to use similar devices. Their stalling tactics and political bargaining delayed the introduction of *Window*, causing the unnecessary loss of many Allied bomber crews. In this way, even technical and scientific problems can be politicized when organizations and individuals feel threatened.

Political pressures can also lead to the premature introduction of new weapons or to the disclosure of highly classified weapons technologies at the wrong time. Israel's invasion of Lebanon in 1982 was, for instance, an unsuccessful exercise in personal aggrandizement for its leaders that needlessly exposed the workings of numerous recently developed weapons technologies. Most of the data (now obsolete) used in Chapter 2, 'Numbers Do Count: The Question of Quality versus Quantity', was released during the US presidential election campaign of 1980. Highly classified figures on the lack of readiness of US fighter aircrafts and severe shortages of ammunition were leaked to the press in order to undermine President Jimmy Carter's bid for re-election.

Another important political dimension that influences the formation of strategy is the military services' search for organizational independence. Often, institutional survival and organizational interests dictate the discussion of the future character of war, the choice of the preferred weapon, and the determination of the enemy's threat. Strategic planning is thus influenced as much by domestic and organizational considerations as by 'external' factors. Strategic plans and military doctrines that at first sight seem to be based on military logic alone are in fact quite likely to be based on parochial organizational interests. The preoccupation with organizational autonomy and obtaining budgetary support even further complicates attempts to enhance cooperation between the services.

Politics may give war a rational purpose on one level yet rob it of its own rationale on many others. Consequently, the pristine clarity of Clausewitz's dictum that war should be dominated by political guidance cannot escape the muddying influence of those whose competing political interests make war in the real world much more unpredictable. Even if a theory of strategic thought based on objective military logic could be developed, politics in all of its dimensions would negate the value and the feasibility of its practical application.

II. THE LIMITS OF RATIONAL ANALYSIS IN STRATEGY AND WAR

Carl von Clausewitz was perhaps the first major strategist to give full recognition to the influence of non-rational elements on warfare. Among the many elements he identified and discussed are: '*hostile feelings* and hostile intentions', and the 'instinctive passion of hatred'. From this inquiry he concluded that

> it would be an obvious fallacy to imagine war between civilized peoples as resulting merely from a rational act on the part of their governments and to conceive of war as gradually ridding itself of

passion so that in the end one would never really need to use the physical impact of the fighting forces – comparative figures of their strength would be enough. That would be a kind of war by algebra.[15]

The quotation continues: 'Theorists were already beginning to think along such lines when the recent wars taught them a lesson. If war is an act of force, the emotions cannot fail to be involved.' He discussed the *strength of will* in war as complementing and compensating for *material capabilities* and added that although 'will is equal in its importance to material capabilities ... the strength of ... will is much less easy to determine and can only be gauged approximately by the strength of the motive animating it'. Clausewitz then went on to evaluate the role of morale, noting that 'the passions that are to be kindled in war must already be inherent in the people.'[16] Above all, though, his strength lay in a thorough understanding of the psychological factors that fashion the role of the individual. Perceptive insights on the behavior of soldiers and commanders appear throughout his work, in which he recognized, for example, the tendency of higher level commanders to avoid risks and make worst-case assumptions in battle. 'Men are always more inclined to pitch their estimate of the enemy's strength too high than too low, such is human nature ... As a rule most men would rather believe bad news than good, and rather tend to exaggerate the bad.'[17] His vivid description of a soldier's reaction to the perils of fire and danger on the battlefield bears repeating. When rational behavior and cool calculations become difficult,

> the novice cannot pass through these layers of increasing intensity of danger without sensing that here ideas are governed by other factors, that the light of reason is refracted in a manner quite different from that which is normal in academic speculation. It is an exceptional man who keeps his powers of quick decision intact if he has never been through this experience before.[18]

More than anyone before or since, Clausewitz developed the role of the Genius, who *best expresses* the creativity, imagination, and intuition that allow him to operate on a higher plane. The Commander's *coup d'oeil* and creativity, like the inspiration of an artist, cannot be taught. If it already exists within the individual, it can, however, be cultivated through education and experience. The paradoxical natures of danger, risk, and boldness in war also defy rational analysis. Boldness in war, Clausewitz asserted 'has its own prerogatives. It must be granted a certain power over and above successful calculations involving space, time and magnitude of forces, for whenever it is superior, it will take advantage of its opponent's weakness. In other words, it is a genuinely creative force.'[19] Analysis of these higher-level, non-rational dimensions of war has been neglected since *On War* was written. The study of strategy on the higher level has focused on what we can refer to as the rational calculus of war (e.g., the measurement of power; the applications of power; planning, strategy, and military operations, the design of force postures; and the relationship between means and objectives). This does not mean that students of international crisis and human behavior have failed to investigate some non-rational elements; but most of these studies have been confined to lower levels – to questions such as individual and group behavior under fire, and group cohesiveness – without being integrated into the more general, higher-level theories.[20]

In recent years, much has been written on the limits of human perception, which can be defined as the inability of human beings to view their environment objectively. Clausewitz recognized the importance of the problem but referred to it only very briefly: 'The difficulty of *accurate recognition* constitutes one of the most serious sources of friction in war, by making things appear entirely different from what one had expected.'[21] Factors such as cultural bias, language differences, national historical experiences, ethnocentric bias, wishful thinking, a variety of 'collective defense mechanisms', the projection of one's own experience, doctrines or capabilities on the opponent, rigid concepts, and political influences all contribute to our misperception of reality.[22] Although good intelligence is of course intended to bring our subjective perception closer to the 'objective reality', even the best intelligence organization in the world can never guarantee an accurate perception of the opponent nor the acceptance of its analysis. As shown in all the chapters on intelligence (Chapters 3 to 8) and in the chapter on war termination, our inability to perceive the environment accurately is a major obstacle to the formation of a rational strategy and the improvement of all intelligence work.

Strategic analysts and most theoretical works on strategy mistakenly assume that our perception of the opponent is usually accurate, which therefore makes the design and selection of a rational strategy possible. American strategy in Vietnam; the Israeli strategy of reprisals and deterrence policy vis-à-vis the Arabs and the Arab strategy vis-à-vis Israel; the Allied overestimation of the success of strategic bombing in the Second World War; and the Japanese conception of what the American reaction to their attack on Pearl Harbor would be, all illustrate the extent of the gap between reality and perception and how this unavoidable gap sharply reduces the possibility of choosing a 'rational strategy'.

The chapters on deception further demonstrate how one side in war can manipulate the perceptions of its opponent in order to make him deceive himself. The fact that effective deception always *reinforces the enemy's existing perceptions* also explains why the use of strategem cannot really be exposed even in those instances where it fails. Differences in perception between opponents in war also explain why their readiness to terminate a war is unlikely to occur simultaneously, even in a deadlocked war of attrition (e.g., the First World War on the Western Front, the Korean War, the Iran–Iraq War). In retrospect, however, such a point of equilibrium at which it would have made sense for both to cease fighting is not usually difficult to identify (see also the discussion below, pp. 39–44).

The assessment of risk in war, also of central importance, is so complex that in fact it very often defies rational analysis. The evaluation of risk is paradoxical, as I discuss in Chapter 5 on 'Intelligence and the Problems of Strategic Surprise'. *The greater the risk and the less feasible the operation seems to be, the less hazardous it is in practice. Thus the greater the apparent risk, the smaller it becomes in reality.* This is one of the most fundamental paradoxes in the rational analysis of strategy. Was the invasion of Normandy instead of the Pas de Calais a greater or smaller operational risk? Was the landing at Inchon a 5000 to 1 shot as some have described it or in fact a lower risk operation? Was the Israeli raid on Entebbe a high or low risk operation? Why was the raid on Entebbe less risky than the American rescue operations in Iran? Are generals who take greater risks more successful than those who don't? What is the difference between a short-run high-risk strategy and a long-run high-risk strategy? Was it rational for Britain or the Soviet Union to continue fighting instead of suing for peace when the Germans defeated France and almost won the Battle of Britain or when they stood 20 kilometers away from Moscow? Under what conditions does it make sense to take greater risks and under what conditions does it not? These questions have no unequivocal or universally accepted answers. The best approach to a particular situation depends on specific conditions such as the creativity and imagination of commanders and political leaders; the availability of other less risky options; the quality of intelligence; the ability to achieve surprise; the probability of forthcoming help from allies; and the anticipated consequences of failure.

As the essay on strategic surprise shows, surprise is almost always unavoidable. As a result, high risks are actually reduced when associated with the achievement of surprise. It must, however, also be remembered that even very successful 'high-risk' strategic surprises achieved in the opening phase of a war can seldom guarantee victory in the long run (e.g., Barbarossa, Pearl Harbor). Too often leaders and strategists rely on short-range assessments, hoping against hope that initial strategic and operational success alone will somehow ensure the final outcome of a war in their favor: the choice of high-risk strategies that are successful in the short run is preferred to long-range calculations that necessitate evaluation of such factors as relative war potential, the attitude of other states, and the ability to achieve a quick and conclusive victory. This at least partially explains why there is no positive correlation between countries that initiate war and those that are ultimately victorious. Napoleon could not win the wars he initiated against the rest of Europe; the south did not win against the north in the American Civil War; and Germany lost two major World Wars it began. Iraq could not win the war it initiated against Iran; Israel did not win the war it launched against Lebanon in 1982; and Argentina could not win the war it started in the Falkland Islands. In all of these examples from modern history, something obviously went awry in the attacker's preliminary calculations and later in the conduct of the war. *States do not begin wars in order to lose*!

In game theory, the metaphor of the *prisoner's dilemma* suggests that under certain conditions, the most rational decisions could be more counterproductive than decisions that appear at first to be less rational. This further discredits the assumption that the formulation of strategy and the conduct of war can be infused with the spirit of rationality.

III. TECHNOLOGY AND MODERN WARFARE

The political nature of war as well as its non-rational dimensions have remained virtually unchanged throughout history. Individual and organizational politics were always part and parcel of war; inaccurate perceptions and problems related to risk assessment have always existed. Technology, however, in its ever-accelerating advancement since the Industrial Revolution, injected a major new element into warfare which greatly complicated an already complex area of human activity.

No dimension of warfare has escaped the influence of technological development. Increased mobility and the development of airpower 'shrank' space and time, changing the achievement of strategic surprise from a highly attractive idea in theory into a feasible alternative. What had formerly been possible only on the tactical level now became a major strategic element. The invention of the telegraph, telephone, and wireless communication created new opportunities to improve and centralize command and control, but also gave rise to new problems. The combined impact of improved mobility and modern communication drastically decreased the time available to make critical decisions even as it intensified the psychological pressures on all levels of decisionmakers. Irreversible changes took place in the balance between political and military control of war; the relationship between the offense and defense; the quality and type of manpower required; rates of attrition; and the relationship between the economy, civilians, and war. Rapid technological progress also blurred the distinction between the battlefield and the home front as well as between the civilian population and combatants. Modification of military doctrines became far more frequent in an effort to keep pace with new technologies. The invention of nuclear weapons led to a paradigm shift – a revolution in strategy; the art of war was transformed from the art of fighting and maneuvering on the battlefield to that of avoiding military conflict (i.e., deterrence). These changes are only a few of the myriad examples that could be cited to demonstrate the impact of modern technological developments on warfare.

Clausewitz fully apprehended the infinite complexity of war, which made the decisions 'faced by the commander-in-chief resemble mathematical problems worthy of the gifts of a Newton or an Euler'.[23] In war, all of the relevant factors are never known, and even if they were, their relative importance and interrelationship at each point in time would be difficult to comprehend and subject to unpredictable change. As a result, Clausewitz believed that the formulation of a positive or scientific theory of war would never be possible. It was clear to him *a priori* that all attempts to propose such a theory evinced ignorance of the essence of war since they were bound to fail.

All These Attempts are Objectionable

It is only analytically that these attempts at theory can be called advances in the realm of truth; synthetically, in the rules and regulations they offer, they are absolutely useless.

They aim at fixed values; but in war everything is uncertain, and calculations have to be made with variable quantities.

They direct the inquiry exclusively toward physical quantities, whereas all military action is intertwined with psychological forces and effects.

They consider only unilateral action, whereas war consists of a continuous interaction of opposites.[24]

Since Clausewitz's death, modern technology has added *a new dimension* of uncertainty to war, making contemporary attempts to develop an all-encompassing 'scientific theory' even more difficult than in the past. For example, the real-time transmission of information or orders made possible by modern technology might at first glance appear to have increased the reliability of intelligence. Instead of reducing uncertainty, however, it generated many new problems (e.g., the interception of signals, fresh opportunities for deception, and a flood of confusing and irrelevant information). Modern technology has thus given rise to new types of uncertainty that result from too much rather than too little information. The ratio of time available to the amount of information that must be processed may in fact have been reduced. Moreover, the general availability of new technologies to all participants in a war cancels out the advantages that might otherwise be realized from greater knowledge and control. When both sides have telephones, radios, radars, high-speed computers, or RPVs, no one has the advantage (that is to say, when all other things are equal). Far from being eradicated, uncertainty has only moved to a higher plane, although the *perception* that one is and can be in control may have been enhanced.

Technology has a logic and momentum of its own. Technological innovations consistently race ahead before their social or military doctrinal implications have been wholly grasped. Consequently, there is a perpetual time lag between the development of new weapons and the capacity to devise military doctrines for their optimal exploitation. The gap between technological innovation and the comprehension of its non-material social or doctrinal implications is much greater in military than in civilian affairs: unlike products in the civilian industrial and technological environments, new weapons technologies can seldom undergo realistic testing and evaluation in peacetime. Even during a war, the new dominant weapons or relative trends in the effectiveness of weapons are not readily identifiable. The impact of the machine gun, trenches, heavy artillery, and the like was not properly understood in the period from the American Civil War to the end of the First World War. By the end of the First World War, the effects of technology and trends in modern warfare had yet to be clearly identified, and while air power was *overestimated* before and during the Second World War insofar as strategic bombardment is concerned, its influence on naval warfare was *underestimated* before the war, and only gradually came to be appreciated during the war itself.

J.F.C. Fuller's concept of the *dominant weapon* is, for example, an interesting analytical tool but it offers little assistance in selecting the best weapons for the future. The accelerated rate of military technological developments makes each succeeding war in many ways radically different from the previous one. Experience may have been of the greatest importance for military commanders in Clausewitz's time, but today it is more often irrelevant or even misleading (at least as far as military technologies and their influence on the battlefield are concerned). The idea that *experience could become irrelevant or counter-productive* would surely have sounded alien to Clausewitz.

The endless number of military inventions is limited only by the imagination of the soldier and the scientist. The dizzying array of new and untested weapons and counterweapons, defensive and offensive weapons, precision and area weapons, more sophisticated communications equipment offset by better jamming capabilities and real-time surveillance – generate numerous contradictory trends whose ultimate synergistic influence on the battlefield is increasingly difficult to fathom. Estimates of how untested state-of-the-art weapons will shape the future battlefield are critical to the formulation and integration of strategic and operational doctrines. The key question that must be answered before a suitable combination of strategic and operational doctrines can be designed is whether the overall trend in weapons technology favors the defense or the offense. There are basically four possible combinations of strategic and operational doctrines, tabulated in the matrix below.

FOUR POSSIBLE COMBINATIONS OF OFFENSIVE OR DEFENSIVE STRATEGIC AND OPERATIONAL DOCTRINES

| | STRATEGIC DOCTRINES (OR POLICIES) | |
	OFFENSE	DEFENSE
OFFENSE	1. OFFENSIVE OFFENSIVE	2. DEFENSIVE OFFENSIVE
OPERATIONAL DOCTRINES		
DEFENSE	3. OFFENSIVE DEFENSIVE	4. DEFENSIVE DEFENSIVE

The choice of a specific combination involves political as well as technological considerations. Identifying the correct trends in weapons development is a formidable task in peacetime, for new weapons technologies can be tested only up to a certain point in war exercises. The correct choice could lead to a quick and decisive victory; the wrong choice to a military debacle. Far too often, the test of trial and error on the battlefield is the only way to arrive at a practical solution, but even then there is not always a definitive answer. A few examples will illustrate the problems encountered. All major governments and military organizations before the First World War chose the combination of an offensive strategy and an offensive doctrine on the operational and lower levels of war[25] (Box No. 1 in matrix). Machine guns, heavy artillery, barbed wire and trenches, and limited protected mobility, in fact gave a decisive advantage to the defense. As the war progressed, it gradually became apparent that the initially favored purely offensive strategy and operational doctrine had failed disastrously. Delay in recognizing the imperatives of military technology to a large extent explains the prolonged war of attrition that ensued. It is not surprising that after the Great War, the French – who learned the lessons of the previous war only too well – chose a purely defensive strategic and operational doctrine. Twenty years later, Nazi Germany once again selected an all-out offensive strategic and operational doctrine which this time led to major victories (Box 1). On the other hand, the French, who had invested heavily in the Maginot Line (Box 4), were beaten decisively. Having lost the First World War, the Germans were compelled to search for new solutions, while the 'victorious' French were content to fight the last war all over again. (What further complicates our understanding is the fact that the French defeat in 1940 does not necessarily prove that they adopted the wrong doctrine or employed the wrong weapons. It may only indicate that they improperly implemented the doctrine they chose.) In 1967, the Israelis were strategically on the defense (i.e., did not intend to initiate a war) but their geography and weapon technologies dictated an offensive operational doctrine, that is, heavy reliance on achieving operational surprise and maintaining the initiative (Box 2). By 1973, Egypt's decision to rely on an offensive strategy, in combination with a defensive operational doctrine, was perfectly matched to the latest developments in anti-tank and anti-aircraft technologies. Major military success was its reward (Box 3). Having succeeded in the 1967 war on the basis of a defensive, status-quo-oriented strategy and an offensive operational doctrine, the Israelis, on the other hand, suffered a serious setback because they saw no reason to modify their approach in 1973 (Box 2). For political reasons, they claimed that the newly acquired territories would allow them to adopt defensive strategic and operational doctrines, thus reducing the need for pre-emptive attacks in the future. Trends in weapons development favoring the defense combined with topographical improvements (i.e., the Suez Canal and Sinai Desert) that could better serve the defense indicated the wisdom of selecting a purely defensive military doctrine on all levels (Box 4); but psychologically and organizationally, the Israeli military could not bring itself to adopt a defensive military doctrine (i.e., it remained in Box 2). Consequently it continued to invest heavily in offensive weapons such as tanks and aircraft, despite their increased vulnerability since 1967. Once again, this shows that in modern war there is no failure like success and no success like failure.

Those responsible for weapons acquisition and the development of national force postures are now engaged in an intense debate over the nature of current and future trends in weapons technologies and their impact on the selection of strategic and operational doctrines. Modern weapons technology may have created the conditions under which the battlefield can be so heavily saturated by precision and area munitions, that maneuver will become impossible and heavy attrition will occur. If this indeed is the case, the best choice of strategic and operational doctrines will be Box 4 (purely defensive). If, however, maneuver remains possible and new technological and doctrinal solutions are found to reduce the rate of attrition on the battlefield, the best combination of a strategic and operational doctrine would be Box 2 (strategic defense–operational offensive) or even Box 1 (a purely offensive combination). Correct identification of trends is a problematic but crucial task, since the preparations for various types of war call for very different types of weapons procurement programs. Once the basic choices in weapons procurement have been made, rapid change is impossible.

Modern technology leads to a paradoxical interplay of the rational and non-rational elements in war. The very process of inventing new weapons is a creative and hence not necessarily rational phenomenon that depends on inspiration and imagination. In contrast, the scientific and technological development and testing of each weapons system and the comparison of similar competing weapons systems are predominantly rational (although as already argued, even on these levels non-rational economic, political, and personal considerations come into play.) The impossibility of testing all new weapons under realistic battle conditions in peacetime and the numerous contradictory trends in weapons development invariably limit the ability of the military to design suitable doctrines for new weapons. Therefore much has to depend on subjective perceptions of the future battlefield, which are in turn based on factors such as experience, lessons learned from other nations' wars, and political and organizational interests. Even though technology implies rationality to most people, and does indeed incorporate many rational dimensions, it has not made war a more rational activity. It has instead added new uncertainties, and made the theoretical understanding of war more important but also more difficult.

Despite the problems that have accompanied the introduction of new technologies since the end of the nineteenth century, the critical relationship between war and technology has yet to be the subject of a major theoretical work. This may reflect the formidable intricacy of the problems involved, be they scientific, social, or military, for completion of a comprehensive theoretical study would require equal familiarity with military history and strategy as well as with technology, engineering, and the natural sciences.[26]

Before technology can be assigned its due place in a general theory, however, we need to develop more specific lower level theories of technology's impact on war. For example, there are currently no specialized studies on the effect of radio communications or the combustion engine on war. I have attempted to do this in Chapters 1, 2, 3 and to a lesser extent also in Chapters 8 and 9, which explore such questions as how greater dependence on radio communications affected deception and how increased mobility and speed changed strategic surprise.

The Impact of Technology

The essays in this book are divided into three sections: (1) technology's impact on modern war; (2) intelligence and strategy; and (3) ending war. The first essay in Part I, 'Clausewitz in the Age of Technology', is also the broadest in scope. In it I examine Clausewitz's theoretical framework for the study of war in light of the revolutionary developments in military technology that have taken place since *On War* was written. Almost everything that Clausewitz wrote seems to describe accurately the nature of and conduct of war *for his time*. Yet technology has rendered some of his observations obsolete, while others require only minor adjustment or revision, and still others remain accurate.

Technology as we know it today or the connotation that it holds for the modern reader did not exist in Clausewitz's time. In today's world, the almost instinctive reaction when a problem is identified is to look for a technological solution. Technology has become a panacea. Most soldiers view it as the answer to their problems – not as a dimension that *generates* new problems of its own.

On the most fundamental level and in order to emphasize the decisive role played by technology in modern warfare, I suggest that were Clausewitz alive today, he would not only be unable to ignore the role of technology in war, but would actually incorporate it into his basic theoretical framework as an important independent force. I have therefore proposed 'squaring the triangle' (i.e., adding the technological and material aspects of war as a new qualitative dimension to his existing triangular framework of the *people*, the *military*, and the *government*). In the end, after all, war has always been a physical and material clash.

I then analyse the impact of technological developments on a select number of issues that are of key concern to Clausewitz in *On War*. Among these are the general impact of the technological-industrial revolution on war, and its effect on the speed of movement which, in turn, moved strategic surprise into the realm of viable and desirable alternatives. For Clausewitz strategic surprise was important in theory but largely impossible to achieve during his lifetime. I also examine the influence of technology on the role of intelligence in war. The reader may remember that Clausewitz discussed intelligence primarily as an *operational* battlefield problem, not a strategic one. He viewed intelligence essentially as an irrelevant nuisance – as 'noise' or a source of friction. Although, as I show in Part II, intelligence work is still beset by numerous problems and uncertainties, the obstacles that Clausewitz had in mind (on the whole communication problems) were largely overcome by the invention of the telegraph, telephone, radio, television, and other communication devices.

While Clausewitz axiomatically assumed that the defense is the strongest form of warfare on all levels, nowadays we cannot predict which will be stronger at any given time. *Dominant weapons*, to use J.F.C. Fuller's phrase, continuously change (his *constant tactical factor*), so the relationship between the offense and defense is cyclical and dynamic. Furthermore, even if the defense is still considered the stronger form of warfare on the battlefield, the offense can now be far more powerful in the opening phase of war because of the enhanced possibility of achieving strategic surprise. In other words, the offense and defense relate differently to each other on various levels at different times in the same war. As mentioned earlier, the many uncertainties now introduced by technology make it even more of a problem than in the past to predict the shape of future wars.

Rapid technological progress has created serious problems related to development of suitable military doctrines to match the new technologies; it has also fundamentally affected the various forms of political control and the role of the people in war (all of which are influenced by mass communication as well as by the expansion of war itself to include the civilian population). Specialized organizations were set up to manage diverse technologies, which in turn multiplied the number of agencies dealing with military matters (and with each other) and increased the bureaucratization of war. The bewildering complexity of modern weapons extended the dependence of armies on logistics and maintenance to the point where a *radical* change in the so-called tooth-to-tail ratio took place. (It has been estimated that over 50 percent of all American soldiers in Germany today work in positions that are in one way or another related to communication!) Reliance on sophisticated weapons has made the completion of adequate peacetime preparations all the more crucial, while the type of production that must be sustained during war itself has lent increased importance to economic strength and war potential as well as to the development of R&D. War, as I argue, is more often decided *not only* on the battlefield as Clausewitz assumed, but by the degree of economic strength and preparation preceding and during the war. The focus of decision has moved from the search for decision exclusively on the battlefield to the battle of wits and economic muscle on the home front.

Finally, increased rates of attrition, the mounting costs of war, and the advent of nuclear weapons may have rendered *every* victory Pyrrhic, thus diminishing the utility of power as an instrument of policy. This theme is explored in greater detail in the concluding chapter.

Chapter Two is a detailed examination of the relationship between quantity and quality in war. As is well known, all other things are never held equal, although they were, nevertheless, *more* equal in Napoleon's and Clausewitz's time, when both would have agreed that God favors the larger battalions. Indeed, during an age in which 'technology' was equally developed and relatively static, numerical superiority whether absolute or relative 'at the decisive point' was the key to success. The major qualitative elements, which were certainly of great importance, lay in the creative genius of the commanders and the morale and motivation of the troops – not in technology as is often the case today.

Technology has brought a new qualitative dimension to conventional warfare. As the quality of technology increases (e.g., the firepower, precision, range, 'lethality'), quantitative superiority becomes less critical; modern war is less labor-intensive and more capital-intensive. This trend in conventional war is likely to accelerate in the future. Superior weapons, technological surprise, and better maintenance can, as I show, compensate for numerical inferiority up to a point. Much depends on such factors as the type of warfare (e.g., conventional or guerrilla), the specific differences in technological development, and the relative size of the opposing armies.

Despite my emphasis on the importance of technology in modern warfare, I conclude that in most modern wars, technology alone *was not a decisive factor.* Short and decisive conventional wars were most often decided by *superior planning, superior leadership and motivation, strategic surprise, and the like. In longer wars what mattered the most was economic strength, war potential, or morale.* Since writing this essay I have somewhat modified my position in view of the 1982 Israeli–Syrian War in Lebanon. In air-to-air battles, close to 100 Syrian aircraft were shot down while no Israeli aircraft were lost. In addition, over 20 Syrian anti-aircraft batteries were destroyed in air-to-ground attacks.

In this instance, the two adversaries' unequal levels of sophistication did indeed lead to decisive results. Yet this was only one dimension of the war, for Israel's technological superiority was indecisive in land warfare. In other words, technological superiority is much more critical in air and sea warfare than in land warfare. The veracity of this statement was to a large extent borne out during the war in Vietnam. American technological superiority could not be translated into any decisive results in the war on the ground, where the stamina and morale of the North Vietnamese defeated both American technology and its superior war potential.

The rest of the chapter investigates why even the richest and most developed countries are finding it more and more difficult to obtain enough highly qualified manpower to operate sophisticated weaponry and/or pay for the increased cost of training soldiers. Much of the data used in the chapter may have changed during the Reagan Administration, but many of the fundamental problems remain unchanged. The chapter ends with an appendix detailing the short- and long-term trade-offs between quantity and quality in the design of a military force posture.

The first section of the book concludes with an in-depth essay on technological surprise in war. After defining this phenomenon, I distinguish between technological surprises that involve mass-produced weapons (e.g., tanks, gas warfare, new fuses, long-range rockets, new types of aircraft and ammunition) and those that make use of weapons produced on a small scale (e.g., the atom bomb, 'ULTRA' and 'Mulberry'). The former are hard to conceal and therefore make the success of technological surprise much less probable, while the latter are very difficult to expose and will almost always result in the attainment of surprise or a major advantage over the enemy.

I then discuss the conditions most favorable for the achievement of technological surprise. These include secrecy; a critical mass (adequate numbers); a suitable doctrine; the correct choice of weapons; and optimal timing in their introduction. The evidence presented led me to the following conclusion: *achievement of a critical mass* (i.e., the introduction of a new weapon in adequate numbers) *is much more important than the preservation of secrecy*. The introduction of a new weapon in small numbers leads to indecisive results while it prematurely discloses the weapon's existence. Such needless exposure simply gives the enemy valuable time to prepare a variety of technical and doctrinal countermeasures. On the other hand, waiting until sufficient quantities of a new weapon are at hand leads to superior results. Even though the enemy may learn of the new weapon's existence, he is unlikely to know how or when it will be first employed;

and if he hasn't yet captured any early examples of the weapon, he may not be fully aware of the technologies and scientific principles upon which it is based and thus will be unable to implement effective countermeasures in time. Once larger quantities of the weapon are introduced in combination with the proper doctrine, the outcome will be much more decisive. One way or the other, determining the best time to introduce a new weapons system is an extremely critical decision that should be approached logically and carefully. Unfortunately, both the military situation on the battlefield and competing political considerations persistently exert powerful pressures in favor of introducing new weapons prematurely – pressures which must be resisted as much as possible. Unlike strategic and diplomatic surprise, which are practically impossible to prevent, technological surprise has occasionally been avoided or effectively countered.

Since completing this essay, I have come across numerous additional cases of technological surprise, all of which confirm my original conclusions. If I were to rewrite the essay, however, I would further emphasize the following points. It is important to distinguish between technological surprise in a short war, which leaves no time for the opponent to design effective countermeasures, and technological surprise in a prolonged war, which allows for the development of countermeasures and counter-countermeasures. If a war is expected to be short and decisive (which frequently cannot be predicted), it would be most advantageous to introduce the largest possible quantity (a critical mass) and variety of new weapons right from the start without being overly concerned about countermeasures. This approach can be particularly effective when combined with strategic surprise in the opening phase of a war. If a war is expected to last longer, some new weapons technologies may be held in reserve and employed during its later phases. In this type of situation, careful thought would have to be given to second or even third generation weapons, enemy countermeasures, and the like.

This chapter makes it clear that political processes play as important a part in the design and fielding of weapons as in any other facet of war. Perceptual problems also play an important role in scientific intelligence. They are, for example, responsible for the common assumption that if 'we can't solve a technical problem, the enemy can't either'. Moreover, it is nearly impossible for intelligence to identify and search for a weapon when there is no concept of its existence. Still, in most instances, the state-of-the-art technology is well known to both sides and scientists share many concepts and perceptions. As a result, some technological surprises have been avoided in large part because it is easier to identify and understand material capabilities than it is to

evaluate intentions, which are of critical importance in attempting to
avoid strategic surprise.

Intelligence and the Problem of Strategic and Diplomatic Surprise

Avoidance of technological surprise is a major problem both in war and
in peace for any intelligence organization. This brings the reader to the
second section of the book, which analyses and relates the topics of
intelligence, deception, and strategic surprise.

I began my study of intelligence by examining the problem of
strategic surprise from a historical and theoretical perspective. Careful
consideration of the historical evidence soon indicated that strategic
surprise was inevitable. A number of years later and after much
intellectual resistance on my part, I finally concluded that intelligence
organizations were unable to anticipate an imminent strategic attack in
large part because of the politicization of the intelligence process. For
anyone who has served in the upper levels of an intelligence organization, the workings of such political influences must be obvious; but for
an academic who wanted to believe that the intelligence community
was engaged in a politically neutral search for the truth, it was not easy
to accept the fact that political considerations – personal as well as
organizational – might take precedence over determining the truth
about the enemy. The chapter on 'The Politics of Intelligence' therefore opens this section of the book even though it was the most recently
written of the essays on intelligence. To begin with, I tried to construct a
systematic conceptual framework that would help in classifying the
different forms of political interference in the intelligence process.
In the context of intelligence, politics can be defined as the protection
or enhancement of the interests of individuals and organizations; it
involves a *bargaining process among* and *within* intelligence and other
agencies in arriving at estimates acceptable to all. The intelligence
process is politicized in the sense that leaders inside and outside the
intelligence community interfere in the process in an effort to make the
analysis conform to their own positions and perceptions.

Although *ideally* intelligence estimates and reports ought to reflect
the truth, in *reality* this is rarely true. Some experts therefore concluded
that since intelligence in practice could never achieve the ideals of
neutrality and objectivity, the intelligence community should accept
this fact of life and deliberately enter the political arena in order to
more effectively influence the policy-making process. Although that
position is not without merit, the unattainable ideal of intelligence
work serves an important function and all intelligence organizations
must aspire to approximate it.

The intelligence process, unlike the natural sciences, is very susceptible to 'political' distortion and bias because it is an inexact and often intuitive discipline. The varying perspectives and parochial interests of individuals and organizations inevitably cause them to reach different and even contradictory conclusions on the basis of similar facts. This is why the politicization of intelligence is unavoidable.

Schematically all intelligence work can be divided into three levels: acquisition, analysis, and acceptance. The *acquisition* stage is, on the whole, the easiest and least political (as it often involves technical means). The level of *analysis* is much more complicated as problems of perception, preexisting concepts, and numerous political factors begin to cloud concepts of rationality and objectivity. The most problematic phase, though, is the level of *acceptance*. It is at this juncture that intelligence must run the gauntlet of a leader's political interests, experiences and wishful thinking. Suffice it to say that without the leader's acceptance, an intelligence estimate cannot survive unscathed regardless of its intrinsic worth. The relationship between leaders and intelligence agencies (as represented by their intelligence advisors) is therefore one of the most critical links in the whole intelligence process.[27]

When I first looked into the related problem of strategic surprise, there were few books and not more than half a dozen articles written directly on the subject.[28] Since 1975, when my first monograph on strategic surprise was published, the body of literature in this field has grown considerably.[29] Why has the subject of strategic surprise drawn so much attention in recent years? A few explanations are readily apparent: the disastrous consequences of a particular strategic surprise (much of the literature in the field was produced by Israeli scholars in reaction to the trauma of the Yom Kippur War); the fact that before the further development of the theory of deterrence and second-strike capability, nuclear weapons were seen as ideal for the achievement of strategic surprise; the problem of defending the central front in Europe; and the increasing interest in perception as part of the study of the theory of international relations. My own interest in the subject grew when my research indicated that strategic surprise in the opening phase of a war has always succeeded despite the availability of more than enough information to warn of an impending attack. This pointed to the erroneous nature of the widespread assumption that if only enough information were available, a careful, rational analysis would prevent strategic surprise. The subject of strategic surprise therefore proved to be an excellent forum for examination of certain non-rational and paradoxical dimensions of war and strategy. In addition, as in the study of medicine or psychoanalysis, deeper investigation of the pathologies of failures in the field was the best way to develop a better theoretical understanding of intelligence. The study of anomalies, apparently unexplainable phenomena that seem to contradict normal expectations, provides an outstanding opportunity to ask creative questions, challenge the accepted paradigm, and develop new theoretical insights.[30] The paradoxical fact that intelligence organizations fail to warn against a forthcoming attack despite the availability of all necessary information was apparently just such an anomaly.

The first two books to concentrate on the study of strategic surprise put forward some interesting concepts and theoretical explanations. In her seminal study, *Pearl Harbor: Warning and Decision*, Roberta Wohlstetter made the distinction between signals and noise, while in *Codeword Barbarossa*, Barton Whaley proposed deception as an alternative explanation. (In fact, deception can be viewed as a form of noise and therefore only complements but doesn't modify Wohlstetter's theory as Whaley thought.) Other explanations by Robert Jervis focused on the problems of perception and misperception and the psychological barriers to accurate comprehension of reality.

In my original monograph on strategic surprise, I synthesized many of these ideas and for the first time suggested that on the basis of historical evidence, strategic surprise in the opening phase of a war is in fact inevitable. A similar conclusion was independently reached by Richard K. Betts and published in his well-known *World Politics* article in 1978. While this conclusion may seem to be tautological in some respects, it has not yet been contradicted by events or seriously challenged by any theory.[31]

In the aforementioned monograph, I also developed five 'paradoxes' that explained why the contradictory nature of intelligence work as related to the problem of strategic warning essentially precludes the possibility of avoiding strategic surprise. Since that time, I identified four additional paradoxes and came to the conclusion that similar 'paradoxes' may also explain the nature of war and strategy in general. The nine 'paradoxes' (by no means an exhaustive list) are as follows:

> *Paradox No. 1*: As a result of the great difficulty in differentiating between 'signals' and 'noise' in strategic warning, both valid and erroneous information must be treated as uncertain. In effect, all that exists is noise, not signals.

> *Paradox No. 2*: The greater the risk and the less feasible an operation seems to be, the less hazardous it is in practice. Thus, the greater the apparent risk, the smaller it becomes in reality.

Paradox No. 3: The sounds of silence. A quiet international environment can act as background noise which, by conditioning observers to a peaceful routine, actually conceals preparations for war.

Paradox No. 4: The greater the credibility and reputation of an intelligence agency over time, the less its reports and conclusions are questioned; therefore, the greater the risk in the long run of over-reliance on its findings.

Paradox No. 5: Self-negating prophecy. Information predicting an imminent enemy attack leads to countermobilization which, in turn, prompts the enemy to delay or cancel his plans. Even in retrospect, it is rarely possible to know whether or not counter-mobilization was necessary.

Paradox No. 6: The greater the amount of information collected, the more difficult it becomes to filter, organize, and process the data in time to be of use.

Paradox No. 7: The greater the amount of information collected, the more noise there is to contend with.

Paradox No. 8: The higher the number of alerts, the less meaningful they become (alert fatigue).

Paradox No. 9: Increasing the sensitivity of working systems reduces the risk of surprise but increases the number of false alarms.[32]

In addition to these 'paradoxes' I also proposed a framework for analysis of the complexities associated with the estimation of capabilities and intentions. I showed why such an analysis cannot be made unilaterally but must take into account the estimates of both sides as they react to each other.

In the revised and expanded version of the original monograph, presented in Chapter 5, I examine the paradoxical problems of risk analysis in greater depth and trace the historical evolution of strategic surprise from its dismissal by Clausewitz as a practical impossibility to its more recent general recognition as an indispensable component of strategy in modern warfare. This is followed by a new discussion dealing with uncertainty, the processing of information, and the time factor. The chart presented in the text (p. 238) is of particular importance for an understanding of why the intended victim of surprise almost always lags behind his enemies in mobilizing his forces. I have by no means exhausted the theoretical insights that can be derived from this chart. For instance, it can be reconstructed for different historical cases of strategic surprise and provide ideas about the relative intensity of surprise attacks; it may be useful in demonstrating the problem of warning time in relation to the enemy's mobilization and the time necessary to mobilize one's own troops. In addition, it can throw light on the planning of strategic surprise from the attacker's point of view. The chart implies that it might be wiser for the attacker to launch his attack *not* when he is fully mobilized but at that point in time when the gap between his and the defender's readiness is the widest.

I close the chapter (as I did my original monograph) by noting that the only certainty about strategic surprise is that it will remain without a solution regardless of the sophistication of intelligence. This is because the root of the problem – the weakest link in the intelligence process – is human nature.

Having studied strategic military surprise in detail, I felt that one might be able to learn even more about it by comparing it with other types of surprise. Sadat's unexpected declaration of his intention to visit Jerusalem led me to examine surprise as a diplomatic tool. I found that major diplomatic surprises are much less common than strategic surprises – that in diplomacy, continuity and credibility predominate. I drew a distinction between *normal or routine diplomacy* and *revolutionary or surprise diplomacy*, which involves a radical change. Diplomatic surprise is particularly useful as a way of ending a diplomatic stalemate or prolonged period of hostility that no longer serves the interests of the parties involved. Diplomatic surprises such as the Ribbentrop–Molotov Agreement of August 1939, Nixon's China diplomacy, or Sadat's visit to Jerusalem are major vehicles for change.[33] I developed a typology of diplomatic surprise and showed that unlike strategic surprise, it requires cooperation between the two opposing sides to achieve a diplomatic breakthrough that surprises third parties. Diplomatic surprises call for careful preparations, a delicate signalling process, and detailed secret negotiations. Since diplomatic surprise does not involve major troop movements or material capabilities and the number of participants on both sides is very small, it is very difficult to anticipate, and much like strategic surprise, is virtually impossible to avoid.

In this book I have discussed three types of surprise: strategic-military, diplomatic, and technological. Each still poses serious problems for intelligence organizations despite heavy investment in the search for solutions. This is not likely to change. Some who hold the intelligence community responsible for the failure to warn of an attack – when the reason for the failure is not under its control – are simply looking for a scapegoat to take the blame for political blunders. Of the three types of surprise, military and diplomatic surprises by and large seem impossible to anticipate whereas technological surprise has frequently been avoided through good intelligence work. The best explanation for the exception of technological surprise may be that dealing with material and measurable phenomena allows for more objective evaluations and involves relatively less political interference. The more an intelligence organization has to deal with intangible factors such as enemy intentions, the greater the difficulties it faces. This explains why diplomatic surprise is the most difficult to avoid. In all areas of human activity, whether economic, political, romantic, or military, surprise can endow its initiator with an enormous, albeit temporary, advantage that will throw his adversary off balance. What the initiator must learn is not only to exploit fully the benefits of surprise once it has been achieved, but also to understand its limits. For unless its use is astutely combined with that of other elements such as military and economic strength, political vision, or diplomatic skill, surprise unaided may not be enough to accomplish the final results intended. Surprise very clearly is a means to an end, not an end in itself. If the initiator confidently assumes that an effective strategic surprise alone will guarantee the achievement of his ultimate goals, his success is indeed likely to be short-lived.

Deception is one of the most effective ways to secure the achievement of military surprise on all levels. This explains why deception, though part and parcel of war, is considered as a lesser function of surprise, while surprise has always been included as one of the basic principles of war. This book includes two essays on deception. The first essay, 'Military Deception in Peace and War', outlines a typology of deception based on two criteria: capabilities and intentions. While emphasizing the importance of deception in support of military operations, it concentrates primarily on strategic deception in peacetime. In contrast to strategic and operational deception in war, deception in peacetime is quite likely to be counterproductive, even self-defeating. This is primarily true of what I have called capability-oriented deceptions. If the deceiver exaggerates his capabilities, he might unwittingly motivate the intended victim to redouble his efforts: in an attempt to close the perceived – but fictitious – capabilities gap, the ostensibly weaker victim will 'go all out' to catch up with his opponent. In the end, the deceiver may find himself confronting a stronger enemy while he continues to entertain illusions about the superiority of his own strength. Conversely, a deceiver in peacetime may deliberately conceal his actual strength and appear weaker than he really is. Such cases are typically the by-product of a society that has become excessively secretive on matters related to military affairs. The unintended projection of weakness, which dangerously undermines the credibility of the deceiver's deterrence posture, may then tempt an aggressor to attack his 'vulnerable' enemy (e.g., the USSR 1941, Israel 1967).

Most successful deception operations *do not try to change the perceptions of the intended victim – they instead reinforce and capitalize on his existing perceptions*. This, to a large extent, explains why deception almost never fails and, in turn, why strategic and operational surprises are inevitable. When first writing about strategic and operational surprise, I tended to underestimate the importance of deception; but as my articles on deception show, this is no longer the case. Despite the fact that military deception may become more difficult to implement in the future, and will probably bear little resemblance to the pattern it followed during the Second World War, it will always play a major part in war.

Although the second essay on deception was originally written as a lengthy introduction to my book, *Strategic and Operational Deception in the Second World War*, I left the text unchanged despite its extensive references to the other authors' essays. The reason is that this introduction includes a discussion of some important theoretical issues as well as a summary of new evidence on Soviet and American deception operations during the Second World War. This subject is particularly interesting because it is not well known and has not been discussed elsewhere before. The most important theoretical issue dealt with in this section is the problem of evaluating the effectiveness of strategic and operational deception. While it is difficult, for analytical purposes, to isolate deception from the other factors that influence the outcome of military operations, I have nevertheless reached the conclusion that it can be done as suggested in the text below.

Another theoretical issue examined in the second essay stems from a comparison of deception before the twentieth century and deception in modern times, particularly since the Second World War. My main thesis here is that deception was radically transformed by modern technological developments (e.g., primarily the radio). No longer left to the *ad hoc* initiative of the inspired commander, deception depends on highly specialized organizations for its planning and execution (see pp. 380 ff. below). An extensive discussion is also devoted to the relationship between the intelligence and operations branches regarding the planning and implementation of deception operations.

Some of the observations on deception in both articles can be summarized as follows:

- The incentive to employ deception can be positively correlated with weakness. Those who use deception successfully while they are weak will continue to rely on it when they grow more powerful; those who don't use deception when they are strong will have difficulty in resorting to its use when they become weaker.
- The typical military commander shows little interest in deception, and is often wary of its use. The only way to change this attitude is to teach about the successful use of deception by using detailed historical case studies as the starting point.
- The success of deception can be correlated with (a) a feeling of vulnerability, (b) respect for the enemy, (c) understanding the enemy's style, language, culture, history, and military traditions. Racism, ethnocentrism, and a feeling of superiority will seriously impair the quality of all intelligence work and deception.
- Successful deception also depends on the ability to penetrate and, to a large extent, manipulate the adversary's intelligence. This is done by deciphering his coded messages and controlling his agents.
- Providing the enemy with as much correct, 'independently verifiable' information as possible is one key to effective deception. (This is one of the major reasons why military professionals are suspicious of deception operations.)
- All successful deception operations must design a type of bait that the enemy is known to be interested in swallowing, but that he must be made to work as hard as possible to catch. The greater the effort he invests in catching the 'bait', the more credible it will be.
- Strategic deception can succeed only if it is encouraged and supported at the highest levels of the political and military leadership (i.e., it is difficult to initiate deception from middle or low echelons).
- Although top political and military leaders must strongly support the systematic use of deception, they should not try to control it directly or intervene in its planning, management, and execution. Modern warfare is so complex that deception is best directed by experts who can give it their undivided attention.
- Deception operations must, whenever possible, be carried out on a *continuous basis*, and not merely as a single, short-term plan designed exclusively for a specific operation.
- Military deception is always designed to support military operations. Its *raison d'être* is derived from operations not intelligence.
- Deception operations, feints, and diversions can provide even greater support for military operations if they also acquire an importance of their own and pose a real threat to the enemy (their deceptive value must, however, take precedence over their value as an independent threat).

- Every deception operation must include plans to 'cover its tracks' and prevent disclosure of its successful methods after implementation in order to allow for its continued utility.
- It must always be remembered that if we can mislead the enemy, the enemy can mislead us.
- Even the most successful deception is not a panacea. It cannot substitute for any other military preparations, leadership, and hard fighting.
- In the majority of cases, the potential benefits to be derived from successful military deception and surprise are not fully exploited because of the average professional commander's lack of confidence in the use of stratagem and his aversion to taking risks (as Clausewitz noted). All deception plans should prepare the operational command to counteract these tendencies.

Although it is almost impossible to counter deception, it nevertheless pays to take the following precautionary measures:

- Diversify the sources of information and avoid over-reliance on one source. 'Reliance on one source is dangerous, the more reliable and comprehensive the source, the greater the dangers.'
- Never rely on agents who have not been seen or directly interviewed.
- Check and double-check all cases in which an agent's report on an important issue first appeared to be correct but turned out wrong and yet seemed to have a 'good explanation'.
- Since deception cannot be avoided, it is important to be able to respond quickly to unexpected developments, prepare a variety of contingency plans, and maintain adequate reserves that could rapidly be moved to different areas of operation.

A few more words about the future of deception are in place. The unusual success of Allied deception throughout the Second World War can be attributed to the convergence of many unique circumstances such as the length of the war; the development of ULTRA and the double-cross systems; the Allies' tremendous advantage in the air beginning in 1942; the particular doctrine and character of the German armed forces and their leader; and the innovative and unprecedented use of deception. It is highly unlikely that strategic and operational deception will ever again be employed on such an extensive scale. Nevertheless, while it would be very difficult to use the now-exposed methods again, deception will remain an inseparable part of war in the future. Taking into account the trend toward shorter wars, the new methods devised will need to ensure that much of the deception work has been completed *before* the outbreak of the war itself.

Nothing in the history of warfare since 1945 suggests that the importance of deception has declined, as some have asserted. Deception can still be positively correlated with better or more decisive results (e.g., Israel in 1956 and 1967, the Arabs in 1973, or the Soviets in the invasion of Czechoslovakia in 1968) whereas its relative absence has tended to correspond with prolonged wars of attrition (e.g., the Vietnam War, the Iran–Iraq War). Although it is likely that deception operations in the future will be characterized by the heavier use of sophisticated technological means, the use of stratagem itself should not be confused with electronic and counter-electronic warfare. It would be dangerous to believe that in the age of satellites, radars, infrared sensing devices, and sophisticated eavesdropping techniques, deception is becoming obsolete. After all, human nature cannot be expected to change; and since most deception operations are designed to reinforce the existing beliefs and perceptions of the deceived, successful deception will continue to be an important factor in war.

Ending Wars

The last section of the book is concerned with the question of how wars end. The first of the two chapters, 'The Problem of War Termination' (Chapter 9), analyses the decision-making processes that end military conflict and tries to determine why wars seem to last much longer than the interests of one or both adversaries would deem necessary. The final chapter, 'The Future of War: The Diminishing Returns of Military Power' (Chapter 10), identifies a number of general historical trends which indicate that war is beginning to lose much of its value as an effective instrument in international politics. My argument is not that violence or conflict will disappear, but that comparison of the costs and benefits of using military power will increasingly lead potential belligerents to the conclusion that war is no longer an effective way of achieving national objectives.

The simplest way to end a war is through a decisive military victory over the enemy's main body of military forces, thus rendering him 'incapable of further resistance'; once this has been accomplished, his country can be conquered and the victor can be expected – in Clausewitz's words – to compel the enemy to do his will. As Clausewitz realized, this was '*in theory* the true aim of war'[34] [my emphasis]. Nevertheless, he understood that *in reality*, most wars are not resolved through a quick and decisive victory on the battlefield and that even if they were, the results could not necessarily be considered final (i.e., in the long run, the winner might not succeed in imposing his will on the vanquished party, for whom the cessation of hostilities represents an opportunity to regroup his physical and mental forces and plan his continued resistance by military or other means). In one of the shortest but by far the most important sections of *On War*, he states:

IN WAR THE RESULT IS NEVER FINAL

Lastly, even the ultimate outcome of war is not always to be regarded as final. The defeated state often considers the outcome merely as a transitory evil, for which a remedy may still be found in political conditions at some later date. We may occupy a country completely, but hostilities can be renewed again in the interior, or perhaps with allied help. This, of course, can also happen *after* the peace treaty, but this only shows that not every war necessarily leads to a final decision and settlement.[35]

Although political and military leaders in the age of the *ancien régime* could still hope to impose their will on an opponent following a decisive victory on the battlefield, this has become much less likely in the age of nationalism and total war. The paradox of Napoleonic warfare was that while Napoleon continuously sought out the decisive victory on the battlefield, his own armies spread the concepts of nationalism, democracy, and total war which ultimately made it impossible to achieve a quick and conclusive victory. From that point onward, the total mobilization of national resources demanded by this new approach to warfare meant that wars could be won only through a prolonged series of battles involving entire populations.

Yet for so many military men who later tried to follow his example, Napoleon was the chief inspiration in their ceaseless quest of a formula for the ultimate decisive victory. Even Clausewitz could not completely rid himself of this idea. Although the most important parts of his book plainly show that such a victory would indeed be rare, Clausewitz nevertheless devoted much of *On War* to the search for ways to achieve it. To cite but one principal example, Chapter 9 of Book 8 is entitled 'The Plan of War Designed to Lead to the Total Defeat of the Enemy'. Such chapters surely drew more attention from his military readers than Chapter 1 of Book 1 or his discussion of the limited aims of war in Book 8.

A somewhat more extreme case is that of Count Schlieffen, who was still aspiring to achieve Hannibal's Cannae in the age of total war. Even if Hannibal could have hoped to conquer Rome in one decisive battle, to think that this was still possible in the age of mass mobilization, 'the nation in arms' and confrontations between huge economic resources, was a disastrous illusion.[36] Thus, modern statesmen and military leaders alike have too often ignored the simple truth that modern conventional wars do not usually come to a quick decision.

Clausewitz defined two basic conditions under which wars should be terminated. 'Inability to carry on the struggle can, in practice, be replaced by two other grounds for making peace: the first is the improbability of victory, the second is unacceptable costs.'[37] The criteria he established for the termination of war are eminently logical, but unfortunately they provide very little practical guidance. Those responsible for the initiation of war are normally very reluctant to admit that victory is unattainable. They may continue to hope that the latest in weapons technology will give them the desired advantage; or perhaps they expect that the intervention of a new ally, the opening of a new front, or the success of a major offensive will finally lead to the victory that has eluded them thus far. Often in contradiction to their own experience, they believe that the increased hardships being experienced by the enemy's population and military will cause imminent collapse instead of stiffened resistance. It is ironic that long after victory has become impossible or prohibitively expensive, *each* side assumes that if it can only endure a little longer, victory will be achieved. Ethnocentrism, misperception, hidden political costs, and many other non-rational elements explain why nations continue to fight much longer than it is in their interest to do so.

Most modern wars rapidly deteriorate into indecisive, prolonged wars of attrition. What may have encouraged political and military leaders in modern history to believe in the feasibility of quick and decisive victories were the wars of German unification, which, if anything, proved to be the exception. Far more typical of modern warfare than Moltke's victories or the more recent Six Day War is a long list of protracted, inconclusive conflicts including the American Civil War; the Boer War; the Russo-Japanese War; the First and Second World Wars; the Korean War; the Vietnam War; the Soviet War in Afghanistan; and the Iran–Iraq War. The final cost of war is always much greater than originally estimated during the preparatory or initial phases. With this eventuality in mind, Clausewitz argued that the unexpectedly high costs of war create a powerful incentive to make peace:

> Of even greater influence on the decision to make peace is the consciousness of all the effort that has already been made and of the efforts yet to come. Since war is not an act of senseless passion but is controlled by its political object, the value of this object must determine the sacrifices to be made for it in magnitude and also in duration. Once the expenditure of effort exceeds the value of the political object, the object must be renounced and peace must follow.

We see then that if one side cannot completely disarm the other, the desire for peace on either side will rise and fall with the probability of further successes and the amount of effort these would require. If such incentives were of equal strength on both sides, the two would resolve their political disputes by meeting half way. If the incentive grows on one side, it should diminish on the other. Peace will result so long as their sum total is sufficient – though the side that feels the lesser urge for peace will naturally get the better bargain.[38]

A schematic representation of this type of cost/benefit analysis is presented below.

THE CLAUSEWITZIAN RATIONAL CALCULUS OF WAR.

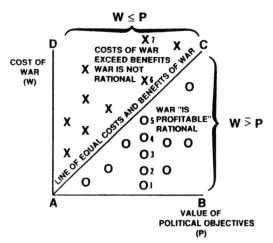

ALL POINTS (O) INCLUDED WITHIN THE AREA OF TRIANGLE ABC SUGGEST THE EXPECTED OR REAL BENEFITS OF WAR (W) EXCEED THE EXPECTED OR REAL COSTS (P). ON LINE AC THE COSTS AND BENEFITS OF WAR ARE EQUAL. ALL POINTS (X) IN TRIANGLE ADC INDICATE THAT THE REAL OR EXPECTED COSTS OF THE WAR (P) EXCEED ALL BENEFITS W.

The Clausewitzian *rational calculus of war* can rarely if ever be computed in reality. In the first place, there are no common denominators or criteria for measurement; hence no trade-offs can be established between the value of the political objectives and the costs of war. How can national independence, religious freedom, maintenance of the balance of power, or the value of assisting a friendly ally be compared with the economic resources and human lives wasted in war? It must also be remembered that the perceived value of the objectives and even more so of the costs of war continuously changes as events unfold.

A wise leader would always prefer that the projected benefits of war exceed its projected costs (e.g., any point below the Line of Equal Costs and Benefits in area ABC). In modern wars, though, both winners and losers are more likely to find themselves in area ADC, where the costs exceed any possible gains. Furthermore, even if the objectives of war are still worth fighting for (e.g., freedom or supporting an ally), in most cases the costs will turn out to be greater than expected, especially if the war is longer than anticipated (e.g., gradual move from point 1 to 7). While the expected benefits don't change, the cost almost always increases dramatically.

The very idea that the costs and benefits of war can be calculated in advance in fact contradicts Clausewitz's conclusion that most dimensions of war cannot be analysed in clear-cut, quantifiable terms. After the outbreak of hostilities, this approach is even less practicable because the more intense passions, political interests, and problems of perception frustrate attempts to ascertain with any degree of accuracy the costs and benefits of war. This task often remains impossible and controversial long after the war is over. The inability to determine the costs and benefits of war in a rational way is one important explanation for its unnecessary prolongation in most instances.

Even if one of the belligerent parties has finally decided that the cost of continuing a war exceeds any possible benefits, the termination of war itself can only take place if the other party is ready to negotiate. Clausewitz states that 'there can be no engagement unless both sides are willing'.[39] Likewise, the decision to terminate war hinges on mutual agreement. As is shown in Chapter 9, each belligerent's assessment of the other's ability to continue fighting, and hence their respective estimates of the war's outcome, seldom coincide.

In most prolonged wars of attrition, as soon as one side indicates either directly or through mediators that it is interested in negotiating an end to the war, his opponent sees such a move as a sign of weakening resolve. This then reconfirms the opponent's hope that victory is still within his grasp. *Thus, attempts to negotiate the termination of a war, can at times be self-negating, while the apparently stubborn refusal to negotiate may be perceived as an indicator of strength and hence can actually encourage negotiations.* This important paradox explains why both sides may feel compelled to project an image of strength and resolve while they continue to be locked in a war they would both like to end. The paradoxical nature of war termination was clearly recognized by Clausewitz in sections 12, 13, and 14 of Chapter 1, Book 1, in which he discusses such issues as the interruption of military activity and the principle of continuity. He observed that *in theory*, war should continue uninterruptedly because as soon as one side showed a desire to negotiate, the other would have an even greater incentive to press on to victory. Clausewitz assumed that in practice, insufficient information about the opponent as well as the asymmetry of the offense and defense would lead to the interruption of war; but in actuality, reality more frequently approximates Clausewitz's theoretical assumption because the opponents do not believe that they are indeed lacking any information. A nation's willingness to negotiate is usually seen by its opponent as *information* confirming its weakness – as an acknowledgement of faltering resolve. Moreover, while Clausewitz assumed that the defense was stronger than the offense (which might often lead to inaction), the uncertainty of the relationship between the offense and defense in today's world is, as discussed earlier, more likely to result in the continuation of action rather than its suspension.[40] Differences in timing between the two sides concerning the need to end the war and the appearance of weakness resulting from a unilateral peace offer explain the oscillations typical of the peace-making process. A state of equilibrium between opponents in terms of the readiness to negotiate can arise only when both simultaneously indicate a desire for peace. This can be facilitated either by third party mediation or by the total exhaustion of both sides.

The time when a single leader's decision could summarily end a war may be a thing of the past. The complexities of the decision-making process, numerous domestic participants, and the need to consult with allies all contribute to delays in the process (see flow chart, p.484). Thus, the best point at which to terminate wars is before they begin, by viewing them as a last resort and avoiding 'the common mistake in going to war, which is to begin at the wrong end, to act first and wait for disaster to discuss the matter'.[41]

The use of military power has become so costly and unrewarding that many nations will grow increasingly reluctant to consider it as a viable alternative. In the closing essay, 'The Future of War: The Diminishing Returns of Military Power', I identify five major long-range trends whose ultimate cumulative effect will be to discourage the use of military force in international relations. Some of these trends were evident in the past, and some became apparent recently, while others will be discernible only in the future; and their impact – although generally felt – may not be experienced in every region or in every country at the same time. The expected decline in the utility of military force is most applicable to the modern Western world, and least applicable to new Asian and African nations, for example, in which border disputes have not been resolved and in regions where many still aspire to self-determination. The five trends discussed are: (1) the spread of democratic values; (2) the primacy of domestic politics in the developed world; (3) the invention of nuclear weapons; (4) the increased costs of using military power; and (5) the relative decline in the importance of some raw materials.

The first two trends are overlapping. Once democracy was accepted as the real or declared norm for most states, the more powerful nations were hard pressed to justify their control of others who wished to assert their right to self-determination. Consequently, many former colonial states received their independence without a struggle. It had eventually become obvious that military power alone would never succeed in quelling the struggle for independence – a struggle that merely accelerated an inevitable trend. Citizens of the colonial powers were not, in the long run, ready to continue supporting wars that contradicted the values they cherished at home. The Second World War had drained the 'nationalistic energies' of the European states, while the actual or perceived threat from the Soviet Union overshadowed long-standing tensions within Europe (e.g., tensions between the Germans and French, or the French and British). Preoccupied as they were with their own national and economic progress, the populations of the developed nations, particularly those in Europe and North America, realized that even the most successful wars could not make a meaningful contribution to the welfare of their societies; therefore, they were unwilling to participate in wars in which there was no immediate threat to their national interests. Waging war without popular support has meant political suicide for the leaders of modern democratic states and political difficulties for their totalitarian counterparts. The absence of popular support in France for the war in Algeria; in the United States for the war in Vietnam; in the Soviet Union for the war in Afghanistan; in Israel for the war in Lebanon; and even in Iran for the continuation of the war with Iraq, provided at least some of the impetus for ending these protracted conflicts. The length of these wars also reflected the inability of the powers involved to justify an all-out effort. Thus, inadequate domestic support initially promotes indecision, which prolongs the war until public opposition becomes so widespread that leaders are forced to end the conflict through negotiation and withdrawal. Even in the Soviet Union, the glimmer of freedom and democracy recently afforded Soviet citizens has enabled public discontent concerning issues such as the war in Afghanistan to have some effect, however small, on government policies. If this trend is allowed to continue, the energy of the Soviet Government may be diverted more and more toward domestic matters; furthermore, growth in the influence of public opinion (even in a minor way) could make it increasingly difficult for Soviet leaders to use force against East European countries or to continue the traditional policy of repressing various national ethnic groups.

Perhaps for the first time in history, nuclear weapons have prevented a war between the hegemonic powers. The possibility of mutual destruction has made the superpowers and their allies much more cautious in challenging each other's vital interests. The danger of such confrontations became clear in the period from the late 1940s to the early 1960s, which culminated in the Cuban Missile Crisis. The only areas in which the superpowers could fight without risking a direct confrontation and nuclear escalation were those involving non-vital interests. This made it even more evident that the costs of war far exceeded any possible benefits.

The readiness to go to war has been further weakened by the tremendously high cost of combatting guerrilla tactics and the ever-greater price and lethality of weapons. The United States, the Soviet Union, Argentina, Iraq, Iran, Israel, China, and others had to learn the same lessons the hard way instead of learning from the experiences of others. While much more costly, the lessons learned through one's own experience are more enduring. The proliferation of nuclear weapons and even chemical and gas technologies may eventually give rise to regional balances of terror between, for example, the Arabs and Israelis, the Indians and Pakistanis, or the Iranians and Iraqis. Trends in low-intensity and conventional warfare have made war more expensive, less decisive, and less 'glamorous'. Resolve and stamina have been the mainstay of the guerrilla, who knows, as does Clausewitz's defender, that time is on his side. This, combined with the knowledge that prolonged wars of attrition were not popularly supported at home, worked in favor of the guerrilla fighters in Vietnam and Algeria. New weapons technologies and guerrilla tactics caused the super or great powers to invest far more resources than their opponents, who were backed by the other superpower. For a superpower, nothing could be more fortuitous than to provide relatively inexpensive support for a smaller nation that is engaged in an 'endless' war of attrition with the other superpower.

Even when losing a war against communist guerrillas, the United States and its allies – as it turned out – suffered minimal damage. It gradually became clear that what was formerly thought to be a monolithic communist bloc actually consisted of independent communist states plagued by conflict and tensions among themselves. Communist states, just like any other type of state, need peace for trade development and reconstruction. Therefore, a divided and under-developed world is perceived as less threatening to Western interests.

Other trends in the development of conventional weapons technology (not discussed in the original essay) are also heading in a direction that discourages the use of military power. Not only has the cost of conventional weapons soared, but rates of attrition for the more expensive weapons have increased as well, while the likelihood of fighting a quick and decisive war has decreased. The current cycles of conventional weapons development do much more than favor the defense over the offense: they may have produced such heavy, concentrated, and accurate firepower that the possibilities of maneuver on the contemporary – and especially the future – battlefield have been severely curtailed.

Finally, the desire to control markets and raw materials, which may explain some past wars, can no longer be justified when synthetic and composite substitute materials have been devised and world trade offers increased benefits. In the age of high technology, many raw materials are not as critical for economic growth, while peace, research, and development are indispensable.

An idyllic world free of strife is still an impossible dream. Much violence and conflict will continue to exist, though perhaps more in the guise of Lebanese-style civil wars in countries such as India, Korea, the Philippines, or Mexico. Wars between nations are, however, expected to decrease. A world more reluctant to engage in war is possible if not already here. *A world in which the future realist will argue against the use of military power based on the cold calculations of Realpolitik is inevitable.*

NOTES

1. Major-General W.D. Bird, *The Direction of War: A Study of Strategy* (Cambridge: Cambridge University Press, 1920), preface.
2. Carl von Clausewitz, *On War*, ed. and trans by Michael Howard and Peter Paret (Princeton: Princeton University Press, 1984), p. 136.
3. *On War*, p. 140.
4. Bird, *The Direction of War*, p. 188.
5. *On War*, p. 93; also pp. 94; 99; 139.
6. See Michael I. Handel, ed, *Clausewitz and Modern Strategy* (London: Cass, 1986), Introduction.
7. *On War*, p. 134.
8. Ibid., pp. 132; 141; 146; and 578.
9. Ibid., p. 87; 149; 605 (see also Book I., Ch. I, Section 27, p. 88).
10. Ibid., p. 606.
11. Ibid., p. 87.
12. Ibid., p. 605.

13. A sample of books that discuss the politics of waging war can include:
Allison, Graham T. *Essence of Decision*. Boston: Little Brown, 1971.
Bryant, Arthur. *The Turn of the Tide*. London: Collins 1957 and *Triumph in the West*. London: Collins, 1959.
Burns, James MacGregor. *Roosevelt: The Soldier of Freedom*. New York: Harcourt Brace Jovanovich, 1970.
Connell, John. *Auchinleck*. London: Cassell, 1959.
Craig, Gordon. *The Politics of the Prussian Army 1690–1945*. New York: Oxford University Press, 1956.
Hankey, Lord. *The Supreme Command 1914–1918*. 2 vols. London: Allen & Unwin, 1961.
Howard, Michael. *The Mediterranean Strategy in the Second World War*. New York: Praeger, 1968.
Kennedy, Major-General Sir John. *The Business of War*. London: Hutchinson, 1957.
King, J.C. *Generals and Politicians: Conflict Between France's High Command, Parliament and Government, 1914–1918*. Westport, Conn.: Greenwood Press, 1951.
Eric Larrabee. *Commander in Chief: Franklin Delano Roosevelt, His Lieutenants, and Their War*. New York: Harper and Row, 1987.
Maurice, Major-General Sir Frederick. *Statesmen and Soldiers of the Civil War*. Boston: Little Brown, 1926.
Roskill, Stephen. *Churchill and the Admirals*. New York: William Morrow, 1978.
Stoler, Mark A. *The Politics of the Second Front*. Westport, Conn: Greenwood Press, 1977.

It is not surprising that Clausewitz ignored what I call the politics of waging war. The political-military unity of command at his time considerably simplified the formulation of strategy in war. The separation of the political from the military leadership, the establishment of general staffs, and the bureaucratization of war during the second half of the 19th century marked the period when the politicization of the strategic decision-making process began to increase.

14. Leslie H. Gelb with Richard K. Betts, *The Irony of Vietnam: The System Worked* (Washington, D.C.: The Brookings Institution, 1979).
15. *On War*, p.76.
16. Ibid., pp.77, 89.
17. Ibid., p.117.
18. Ibid., p.113.
19. Ibid., p.190.
20. But see John Keegan, *The Face of Battle* (New York: The Viking Press, 1976), and Lord Moran, *The Anatomy of Courage*, 2nd ed. (London: Constable, 1966).
21. *On War*, p.117.
22. See Ken Booth, *Strategy and Ethnocentrism* (New York: Holmes and Meier, 1979); Robert Jervis, *The Logic of Images in International Relations* (Princeton: Princeton University Press, 1970); Robert Jervis, *Perception and Misperception in International Politics* (Princeton: Princeton University Press, 1976); Robert Jervis, 'Hypothesis on Misperception', *World Politics* 20: 3 (April 1968), 454–79.
23. *On War*, p.112; also pp.146, 586.
24. Ibid., p.136. 'It is even more ridiculous when we consider that these very critics usually exclude all moral qualities from strategic theory, and only examine material factors. They reduce everything to a few mathematical formulas of equilibrium and superiority, of time and space, limited by few angles and lines. If that were really all, it would hardly provide a scientific problem for a schoolboy.' Ibid., p.178.
25. See Jack Snyder, *The Ideology of the Offensive* (Ithaca, N.Y.: Cornell University Press, 1984).
26. The following books, however, address important aspects of technology and modern warfare:

Baxter, James Phinney. *The Introduction of the Ironclad Warship*. Cambridge: Harvard University Press, 1933.

Baxter, James Phinney. *Scientists Against Time*. Cambridge, Mass.: MIT Press, 1968.

Bloch, Ivan. *The Future of War*. Boston: Ginn, 1923.

Cipolla, C.M. *Guns and Sails in the Early Phase of European Expansion 1400–1700*. New York: Pantheon Books, 1965.

Dyster, Paul Albert. 'In the Wake of the Tank: The 20th Century Evolution of the Theory of Armored Warfare. Ph.D. dissertation, Johns Hopkins, 1984.

Fuller, J.F.C. *Armament and History*. London: Eyre and Spottiswood, 1946.

Howard, Michael. *War In European History*. Oxford: Oxford University Press, 1976.

Jones, R.V. *Most Secret War*. London: Hamish Hamilton, 1978.

Liddell Hart, B.H. *The Tanks*. Vol. 1. London: Cassell, 1959.

MacNeil, William H. *The Pursuit of Power*. Chicago: The University of Chicago Press, 1982.

Milward, Alan J. *War Economy and Society 1939–1945*. Berkeley: The University of California Press, 1977.

Morison, Elting. *War Machines and Modern Times*. Cambridge: MIT Press, 1966.

Parker, Geoffrey. *The Military Revolution*. Cambridge: Cambridge University Press, 1988.

Pearton, Maurice. *Diplomacy War and Technology Since 1830*. Lawrence: Kansas University Press, 1984.

Ranft, Bryan, ed. *Technical Change and British Naval Policy 1860–1939*. London: Hodder and Stoughton, 1977.

Smith, Merritt Roe, ed. *Military Enterprise and Technological Change*. Cambridge, Mass: MIT Press, 1985. The book includes a comprehensive bibliographical essay by Alex Roland, 'Techology and War: A Bibliographic Essay', pp. 347–79.

Van Creveld, Martin. *Technology and War*. New York: The Free Press. Forthcoming.

Wintringham, Tom, and Blashford-Snell, J.N. *Weapons and Tactics*. Harmondsworth: Penguin 1973.

27. See Michael I. Handel, ed., *Leaders and Intelligence* (London: Cass, 1989).
28. The three most important works were:

Wohlstetter, Roberta. *Pearl Harbor: Warning and Decision*. Stanford: Stanford University Press, 1962.

Whaley, Barton. *Codeword Barbarossa*. Cambridge: MIT Press, 1973, and

Stratagem: Deception and Surprise in War. Mimeographed. Cambridge, Mass: MIT Center for International Studies, 1969.

29. Michael I. Handel, *Perception Deception and Surprise: The Case of the Yom Kippur War*, Jerusalem Papers on Peace Problems, No. 19 (Jerusalem: The Hebrew University, 1976). This monograph includes a bibliography of the literature on strategic surprise as of 1975.
30. On the role played by anomalies see C. Kuhn, *The Structure of Scientific Revolutions*, 2nd ed., enlarged (Chicago: University of Chicago Press, 1970).
31. Richard K. Betts, 'Analysis, War and Decision: Why Intelligence Failures are Inevitable', *World Politics* (Oct. 1978): 61–89. Also Richard K. Betts, *Surprise Attack* (Washington, D.C.: The Brookings Institution, 1982).

For an unsuccessful attempt to challenge the thesis that strategic surprise is inevitable, see Ariel Levite, *Intelligence and Strategic Surprise* (New York: Columbia University Press, 1987). The author bases his study on a very small number of case studies (two to be exact) which provides an insufficient basis for the development of a more general theory; furthermore he confuses strategic with operational level surprises. For a detailed review, see Uri Bar-Joseph, 'Methodological Magic', *Intelligence and National Security* (Oct. 1988): 134–56.

32. The last 'paradox' is based on Betts, 'Analysis, War and Decision', pp.88–9.
33. See Michael I. Handel, *The Diplomacy of Surprise* (Cambridge, Mass: Harvard Center for International Affairs, 1981).
34. *On War*, p.75.
35. Ibid., p.80.
36. See Jehuda L. Wallach, *The Dogma of the Battle of Annihilation* (Westport, Conn.: Greenwood Press, 1986).
37. *On War*, p.91.
38. Ibid., p.92. This quotation demonstrates how wrong Liddell Hart was when he accused Clausewitz of advocating the limitless use of force regardless of the cost of war, and referred to him as the Mahdi of mass and mutual massacre. 'Clausewitz' principle of force without limit and without calculation of costs fits, and is only fit, for a hate-maddened mob. It is the negation of statesmanship – and of intelligence strategy, which seeks to serve the end of policy' (Liddell Hart, *The Ghost of Napoleon*, London: Faber & Faber, 1933, p.122). Clearly Liddell Hart either did not read *On War* carefully or read it as selectively as most other readers in order to reinforce some of his preconceived ideas.
39. *On War*, p.91.
40. Ibid., pp.84–5 (also Book 3, Ch. 16, pp.216–20).
41. Thucydides, *The History of The Peloponnesian War*, trans. Richard Crawley (New York: E.P. Dutton, 1959), Book I: 78.

PART ONE

Technology's Impact on Modern War

1

Clausewitz in the Age
of Technology

> As water has no constant form
> there are in war no constant conditions.
> — Sun Tzu, *The Art of War* (*c.* 500 BC)

I. CLAUSEWITZ AND THE STUDY OF WAR

Any early nineteenth-century textbook or theoretical work in chemistry, physics, or geology would be of little more than anecdotal value for the same profession's contemporary practitioners. It would certainly not be looked to as a source of important relevant insights, nor would it have value for the instruction of modern students, let alone be expected to represent the state of the art in an important profession. In many fields, in fact, the pace of change is so rapid that a major theoretical work can become obsolete within a generation or a decade, and textbooks must be updated or replaced every few years. Yet in the study of war – a subject of the utmost importance for the survival of modern civilization, and an area in which even one mistake can be disastrous for a whole society or generation – no theoretical work has yet surpassed Carl von Clausewitz' unfinished study, *On War* (1832), in its richness of wisdom and heuristic value.

This situation stems from the extremely complex nature of modern warfare with its seemingly infinite number of variables, ranging from the quantifiable to the intuitive, from the moral to the material. Since modern warfare therefore is not readily subject to scientific analysis, complete mastery of this subject is extremely difficult for a single scholar. Who can study, in depth, even a fraction of the topics considered relevant today for the understanding of modern war? Under the rubric of modern warfare, one can study psychology; anthropology; politics; political, military and economic history; the extremely wide variety of modern military technologies; measures and countermeasures of all sorts; intelligence;

arms control; civil–military relations; military–industrial potential; the origins and terminations of wars; bureaucratic behavior; management; leadership; and decisionmaking processes – to mention only a few.

Modern studies of war are often either specialized monographs (focusing on a particular, narrowly-defined subject area or historical period) and abstract 'transhistorical' studies of less than general scope, [1] or very broad encyclopedic surveys, such as Quincy Wright's *Study of War*,[2] which include every detail but often explain very little.

Clausewitz was fortunate to live during the last era in which it was still feasible for one person to create a comprehensive and *simplified* framework for the study of war; that is, to incorporate almost all the relevant knowledge existing in his time without being superficial. Consequently, he could reasonably limit his analysis of politics, strategy, and the essence of war to the actual conduct of war. For the most part, he ignored the origins of war, its moral and economic aspects, domestic or internal politics, and many other subjects now indispensable to a comprehensive theory: war has become too complicated to be studied in the methodological isolation of an *amoral, apolitical, 'non-economic', non-technological* 'black box'.

It is, then, not surprising to find that all recent attempts to capture the 'essence' of the conduct of war in a comprehensive and succinct form have not been entirely satisfactory. They have oscillated between contrived *simple* generalized formulas on the one hand and *encyclopedic surveys* on the other. Clausewitz avoided both extremes. He succeeded in being abstract without going theoretically overboard; in developing powerful concepts while avoiding the temptation to develop 'laws', 'rules', and 'practical' recommendations for action;[3] in providing apt examples to demonstrate his points while avoiding the quagmire of excessive trivial detail, including too many case studies. In his work there is not a single cliché to be found on a subject about which others cannot write without clichés.

One hundred and fifty years after his death, Clausewitz' contribution to the study and understanding of war remains unsurpassed. Still relevant today are his ideas on the primacy of political control in war; on the roles of friction, uncertainty, and chance; on danger and boldness; on historical examples; on war as an art; on the need to avoid dogmatic and positive theories, given the existence of several correct solutions to any military problem; and on the nature of war in general. Concepts such as tension and rest, the culminating point of victory, his critical discussion of maneuver, and the psychology of the defense and offense are perhaps even more relevant today than when they were written. Like that of other great men who were ahead of their time, Clausewitz' genius was not recognized by his contemporaries, although he had indeed, as he suggested in his note of 10 July 1827, '[brought] about a revolution in the theory of war' (p. 70).[4]

Despite the wealth of original ideas and concepts that make the most important aspects of Clausewitz' theory applicable today, many other facets of his theory have grown obsolete or remain valid only by virtue of modification and revision. Other dimensions that are important today, but which remained nascent during his lifetime, are simply not addressed in his writings.

Clausewitz' theories and observations on war that require modification can be classified in four major categories:

First, the differences in modern warfare resulting from technological innovations he could not have foreseen and therefore could not take into account;

Second, problems that existed in a relatively simple form in the nineteenth century but which are manifested today in a much more complicated form as a result of technological changes: for example, problems in strategic policy-making and in civil–military relations, and in improving the reliability of military intelligence (in which he had little confidence);

Third, topics such as the causes of war, moral/ethical questions related to war, and war's economic dimension. Clausewitz did not focus on these areas because he was concerned exclusively with the conduct of war itself. These topics are, however, of great interest to today's student of warfare, and are essential to any modern theory of war.

The fourth category consists of theories or observations that were wrong or inaccurate even for his own time. But my purpose is not to look for flaws in Clausewitz; rather, I will focus on those modifications required by the passage of time, primarily as a function of material changes, in order to give Clausewitz his proper place in the Age of Technology.

II. THE IMPACT OF THE INDUSTRIAL-TECHNOLOGICAL REVOLUTION ON WAR

With the benefit of hindsight it is apparent that Clausewitz lived and created during one of the most decisive transitional periods in the evolution of warfare — at the crossroads of two of the greatest revolutions in history, the French and Industrial Revolutions. The first revolution radically changed the nature of war from its formerly rather limited and moderate scope — in terms of both means and aims – into a matter of total mobilization and immoderate goals. After the powers of nationalism and revolutionary ideology were unleashed, war became, for the first time, not only the business of kings and the military, but also that of every citizen in the state. Democracy and nationalism released a large amount of heretofore latent energy for the pursuit of war. Although Clausewitz clearly identified this new trend in warfare, he was not completely sure that the change it had wrought was irreversible:

> Very few of the new manifestations in war can be ascribed to new inventions or new departures in ideas. They result mainly from the transformation of society and new social conditions. But these, too, while they are in the crisis of fermentation, should not be accepted as permanent. There can therefore be little doubt that many previous ways of fighting will reappear. (p. 515)

Ironically, at approximately the same time as Clausewitz' death, a new revolution which he could not have identified was in its formative stage: in combination with the trends established by the French Revolution, the Industrial and Technological Revolution changed the world in numerous irreversible ways. Since Clausewitz' time the military/technological environment has undergone at least two major revolutions, one in the conventional realm, the other in the nuclear realm, which have caused a paradigmatic shift in the nature of war. Numerous smaller military-technological and organizational revolutions have occurred as well (for example, the revolution in mobility, the revolution in firepower, the creation of war in the air as a third dimension of warfare, the revolution in communication from the invention of the radio and telegraph to that of 'smart weapons', computers and satellites).

Whereas in Napoleon's era, geography, time, and space were major environmental constraints on strategy, technology has to a large extent modified the imperatives of environment. The radio made distance irrelevant for the transmission of information; the submarine destroyed the British sense of geographic isolation; and ICBMs have threatened the security of 'Fortress America'. Technology has liberated the military strategist from some concerns of the past, while posing new problems in other areas.

The 'element of uncertainty' which – according to Clausewitz – dominates warfare has now been compounded by the introduction of a new dynamic variable. Many factors, including: the performance of new and untested weapons systems on the battlefield; these systems' interaction; their impact on military doctrines, tactics, strategy, as well as on the development of measures and countermeasures and on the military (and political) decision-making process – all have caused a quantum jump in the complexity of warfare.[5]

In war and its preparation, every technological change touches off a chain reaction that is not only technological, but also social, political, bureaucratic, managerial, and psychological. Such changes can be clear or subtle, short term or long term, critical or marginal – but they will occur with each technological innovation. When hundreds or thousands of changes occur simultaneously there is a corresponding increase in the uncertainty involved in predicting the shape of modern warfare and of the battlefield of the future.

Within less than a year following Clausewitz' death (16 November 1831), a major new element in warfare was introduced to Europe in the form of the first railways ('... the accelerator of nineteenth century warfare').[6] No sooner had the ink dried on the first edition of his *magnum opus, On War*, than the appearance of this new element of military technology began to render some dimensions of his theory obsolete.[7]

As early as 1833, a German by the name of Friedrich Wilhelm Harkort made 'the first definite proposals for the use of railways for strategical purposes'.[8] The first actual use of railways for a military operation occurred in 1846 when the Sixth Prussian Corps of 12,000 men with their horses, weapons, and ammunition, was dispatched by rail to subdue the independent Republic of Cracow.[9] By the time of the French campaign in Italy, the American Civil War, and the wars of German unification, railways constituted a major element of military mobility and were of decisive importance in warfare.

Clausewitz could still justifiably argue that 'today, armies are *so much alike* in weapons, training, and equipment that there is little difference in such matters between the best and worst of them' (p. 282) [my emphasis]. But the wars of the 1860s irrefutably demonstrated that a new force multiplier – to resort to modern jargon – had been introduced. Techno-logical innovation could now, when all other things were equal, make a decisive difference, a fact that could hardly have been recognized in Clausewitz' time. For instance, the battle of Koniggratz proved the superiority of the Prussian Dreyse rifle over the Austrian rifle, when 'the rate of fire of the Dreyse rifles inflicted appalling losses on the advancing Austrians: they suffered 45,000 casualties to the Prussians' 9,000'.[10]

The advent of the new technological age was unmistakable when European military observers during the American Civil War focused their interest not on the study of military doctrines or new tactics, but on the performance of new weapons.[11] This new emphasis on the study of weaponry would have made little sense to Clausewitz only fifty years earlier.

By the latter half of the nineteenth century, military technology was an autonomous force capable of influencing the shape of war in a decisive way. Man had created a Frankensteinian monster that could no longer be controlled. That battlefield decision, which Clausewitz made central to his theory, had rapidly shifted from the battlefield to the rear; from war to pre-war preparations in peacetime; from the soldier to the worker, inventor, and scientist. In the aftermath of the Industrial Revolution, the outcome of war was to be determined as much by the existence of an industrial base and war potential as by performance on the battlefield. As William James wrote: '... the intensely sharp competitive *preparation* for war by the nation *is the real war*, permanently increasing, so that the battles are only a sort of public verification of mastery gained during the "peace" intervals'.[12]

Correspondingly, for military leaders in the technological age, the destruction of the enemy's army – so central to Clausewitz' theory – became only as important as, or less important than, the destruction or occupation of the industrial centers necessary for the maintenance of enemy forces in the field.[13] In the American Civil War, the industrial superiority of the North, despite the equal or superior generalship of the Confederacy, was critical. Such a development would certainly have been strange to Clausewitz (unless of course industrial might could simply be translated to mean much larger armies, a quantitative advantage which his theory clearly recognized).

Although the foregoing changes took place rapidly after the 1860s, they were also difficult to perceive. The signals were still mixed. Prussia's rapid and clear victory over France in 1870 may have diverted attention from the growing importance of economic and industrial factors for performance on the battlefield. Even as late as the First and Second World Wars, the various general staffs and political leaders hoped to outflank material and economic imperatives by achieving quick and decisive results against the enemy's armed forces, as Clausewitz recommended. By devising brilliant new strategies, they hoped to escape the longer-term consequences of economic contraints.

Thus, although Clausewitz recommended a war of annihilation whenever possible, a strategy emphasizing the ultimate decisive clash between opponents, modern warfare is not only a clash between two armies, but also between the opponents' industries, economic resources, and entire populations. This situation has rendered the search for the decisive battle of annihilation futile – at least in the non-nuclear realm. In this respect Hans Delbrück's distinction between a strategy of annihilation (*Niederwerfungsstrategie*) and a strategy of attrition or exhaustion (*Ermattungsstrategie*) is an important theoretical addition to Clausewitz.

Modern conventional wars, when not decided in a single blow, tend to deteriorate into wars of attrition.[14] The German military which selectively extracted those passages in Clausewitz' work that emphasized the need for quick and decisive victories, thus misunderstood in two world wars the environment in which total modern warfare is conducted.[15]

As the two world wars demonstrated, the nature of war has altered irreversibly. While becoming more capital-intensive, war has changed materially at an ever-accelerating pace. Thus, while the modern student of warfare can certainly learn much from wars of the distant past, he will be better off concentrating on the immediate past and more so on the present. Clausewitz could still recommend, however, with much practical as well as theoretical benefit, that his readers study the eighteenth-century wars of Frederick the Great. Certainly, from the material and 'technological' points of view, these earlier wars resembled the wars of his own time. Until then, military-material and technological change had been slow and gradual. Continuity rather than change had been the norm. Because he expected all future wars to resemble these past wars, Clausewitz indeed had a good reason for drawing on the past to formulate his theories. He did recognize political, ideological, and social changes in his eras, but he viewed them as reversible.

Although Clausewitz could not and did not predict these imminent changes in the nature of war, his theory could accommodate change. After all, he did say that 'war is more than a true chameleon that slightly adapts its characteristics to the given case' (p. 89). The essence of war is change and adaptation to change.

Raymond Aron is unfair when he suggests that Clausewitz 'paints a fixed picture of the world'.[16] It was, in fact, Clausewitz' recognition of radical changes in the nature of warfare caused by the French Revolution which prompted him to develop a new theory of war:

> Clearly the tremendous effects of the French Revolution abroad were caused not so much by new military methods and concepts as by radical changes in policies and administration, by the new character of government, altered conditions of the French people, and the like .... It is true that war itself has undergone significant changes in character and methods, changes that have brought it closer to its absolute form .... They were caused by the new political conditions which the French Revolution created both in France and in Europe as a whole, conditions that set in motion new means and new forces, and have thus made possible a degree of energy in war that otherwise would have been inconceivable.
>
> It follows that the transformation of the art of war resulted from the transformation of politics. (pp. 609–10)

Clausewitz' theory emphasized the tendency of war to drive to extremes, to pursue immoderate unlimited goals. In fact, he developed an almost Marxist analysis in his sophisticated periodization of the history of warfare. He points out that warfare is conducted differently according to the

> nature of states and societies as they are determined by their times and prevailing conditions .... The semibarbarous Tartars, the republics of antiquity, the feudal lords and trading cities of the Middle Ages, the eighteenth century kings and the rulers and

peoples of the nineteenth century – all conducted war in their own particular way, using different methods and pursuing different aims. (p. 586)

Clausewitz' world was therefore far from fixed and unalterable. As we have seen above, change for him even worked in reverse. His very emphasis on uncertainty and dialectical method also implies change. But the sort of change he recognized was primarily political and social – not material. He also assumed a static world when he ignored the possibility of material and military technological changes which he could not have foreseen in detail but might have anticipated in a general way. His picture of warfare is as accurate as it could have been for his own time. In addition, those aspects of his theory which deal with human nature, with uncertainty and friction, with the primacy of politics, and with the need to conduct war in a calculated rational fashion, will remain eternally valid. In all other respects technology has permeated and irreversibly changed every aspect of warfare.

Technology has altered the nature of international politics by introducing destabilizing weapons systems and intense qualitative arms races; it has continuously affected the relationship between the defense and offense; it has transformed strategic surprise from a course of action 'highly attractive in theory' to an ever-present possibility. These developments in turn led to a rise in the importance of intelligence organizations and have increased the likelihood of preemptive attacks. They multiplied the number and types of special military branches and supportive organizations, thus triggering the unprecedented growth of military bureaucracies and the bureaucratization of military life, with all the attendant consequences. Technological developments also created the circumstances in which the 'military genius' may need to be replaced by a 'managerial genius'. Since greater professional knowledge and skills are required to comprehend military affairs, technology has undermined the capacity of political leaders to understand and control the military and the course of warfare. Technology created new opportunities for command and control and centralizing the conduct of war; it expanded warfare from the battlefield to the civilian rear; it blurred the differences between combatant and non-combatant – and it otherwise changed the shape and nature of modern war. All of these changes will be discussed in sections IV to XII below.

III. SQUARING THE TRIANGLE

In trying to construct the simplest possible analytical framework for the study of war, Clausewitz *reduced* the infinite number of variables and their complex interactions to the lowest common denominator. Thus he developed his famous triad – as he called it, his 'paradoxical trinity'. The three basic groups of variables were *the people* (or primordial violence, hate, and enmity – the blind natural forces); *the military* (the commander and his army who must manage the elements of chance and uncertainty and make the creative decisions and choices before and during a battle); and *the government* (which must introduce the rational calculus of war in order to protect the interests of the state, provide the goals for war, maximize and preserve the strength of the state relative to other states, and devise the overall strategic direction, including the matching of resources and expenditures to anticipated gains). Clausewitz sought 'to develop a theory that maintains a balance between these three tendencies, like an object suspended between three magnets' (p. 89). We have seen that, although complete for his time, Clausewitz' triad does not account for modern military technology, one of the most principal elements of contemporary warfare.

In fact all three elements of his trinity are non-material in nature. In view of the central importance of military technology to all aspects of contemporary warfare, we can assume that if Clausewitz were alive today, he might well propose a four-variable analytical framework with the material realm as the fourth dimension (see Figure 1).

Trying to reduce his argument to its essence, Clausewitz chose not to emphasize material considerations in the explanation of war. 'It is clear that weapons and equipment are not essential for the concept of fighting, since even wrestling is fighting of a kind' (p. 127). If he were solely interested in explaining the logic of conflict he may have been right, but in reality the philosophical and psychological explanation of war is not enough. Without going so far as to adopt a Marxist interpretation of

FIGURE 1
CLAUSEWITZ' DESCRIPTION OF WAR MODIFIED

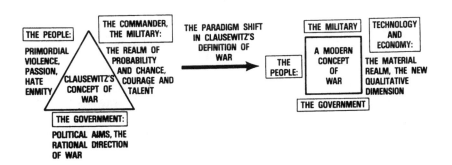

CLAUSEWITZ DESCRIPTION OF WAR MODIFIED

history or politics, we still must realize that the philosophical, political, psychological, social – not to mention the military – aspects of warfare are influenced by material circumstances and developments.

Thus, while the bare essence of war may be explained without resort to the material/technological environment in which wars are fought, any detailed discussion must take that environment into account. Clausewitz himself does, following Book I of *On War*, discuss many issues that cannot be properly understood outside the material context (for example, intelligence, strategic surprise, mobility, military organization, civil–military relations, and the relationship between the offense and defense). Living in an era of slow material progress, Clausewitz naturally viewed the material military environment as relatively static.

It could be argued that had he written *On War* fifty years before, following the wars of Frederick the Great and before the French Revolution, the rise of nationalism and democracy, and the *levée en masse*, he would not have developed his ideas on absolute war. He might not have discussed the differences between absolute war and limited war, for it was the French Revolution which revealed the possibility of a war in reality which approximated the absolute war in theory (p. 593).

Similarly, it can be argued that if Clausewitz had written *On War* fifty or a hundred years later, he could not have ignored the forces released by the industrial/technological revolution. He would probably have adapted his theory to the radically changed material environment, probably dedicating special sections to the economic, technological, and material environment of war.[18]

Theory is meaningful, as Clausewitz has recognized, only in contrast to reality, and is no more important than reality. Clausewitz' most original concepts, such as friction and uncertainty, intervene between theory and reality. *On War* is not merely a philosophical treatise, but a book of practical heuristic value.

To simplistically project contemporary interpretations of certain concepts on the past is anachronistic. For example, we have a different understanding of the concept and role of intelligence in war from that of Clausewitz and his contemporaries (see section V below). We also have a different understanding of technology. Although in its basic purpose technology may have remained the same since the beginning of warfare, it has changed in many of its aspects. From a psychological point of view, technology has become the modern military's panacea, used to solve problems previously solved by non-material means. Modern technology has acquired a momentum, an importance of its own, which explains the changing nature of modern warfare.

Therefore, if Clausewitz' trinity is indeed both unchanged and changeless, technology must be the additional factor required for our understanding of contemporary and future warfare. Without it, we will fail to see the new problems and opportunities that it may present. After all, Clausewitz himself, by developing in Book VIII a historical periodization of warfare, does distinguish between the various environments in which war takes place. Thus, although the essence of war is unchanging, in many ways change is the essence of war.

In the final analysis, the decisive Clausewitzian factor in winning wars and battles was quantitative. True, the 'military genius', the leader who was better able to find a solution to the need 'always to be very strong; first in general and then at the decisive point' (p. 204), appears to be a qualitative element. But the qualitative superiority of a commander was aimed at acquiring a *quantitative* edge on the battlefield. In spite of the attention Clausewitz pays to moral and other qualitative factors directly altering the outcome on the battlefield, he basically believed that battles were won by larger armies. Technology has, however, introduced a new *qualitative* dimension – which is not based on the 'quantity idea', as J. F. C. Fuller called it – but instead concerns an element which could compensate for a disadvantage in numbers, serving as a 'force multiplier'.[19] When Clausewitz devised his theory he could still compare the different European armies of his time and assume that 'all other things could be held equal' and that the 'biggest battalions' led by the military genius would win. In today's world of high technology all things are not equal, and unexpected technological military innovations, technological surprises and breakthroughs may (among other elements) make the size of armies less critical for victory. A smaller but technologically more advanced army has frequently won against a larger army.

Having extended Clausewitz' trinity by adding technology and other economic and material considerations, we must recognize the importance of this fourth element as simply equal to that of the other three elements for the theoretical understanding of war. For under varying circumstances, one or more elements may gain in importance relative to others: for example, in guerrilla warfare the people will play a more critical role than will technology; while in modern conventional warfare weapons may be relatively more important than people. Clausewitz of course recognized this variability:

> These three tendencies are like three different codes of law, deep-rooted in their subject and yet *variable* in their relationship to one another. A theory that ignores any one of them or seeks to fix an arbitrary relationship between them would conflict with reality to such an extent that for this reason alone it would be totally useless. (p. 80, my emphasis)

Yet Clausewitz' caveat concerning the need to maintain a balance among
WSI—C*

all three (or in our case four) groups of variables has not always been heeded. Theorists or creators of military doctrines tend to overemphasize those elements which seem to support their particular biased perspective (for example, overemphasizing the people factor in guerrilla warfare can lead to what Mao has called 'guerrillism' and thus to serious defeats). The temptation is to exaggerate the importance of modern technology in technologically- and materially-oriented societies. Technology may be viewed as a panacea, as it was by the US in Vietnam. The very idea of a trinity or a 'square' is in the search for an equilibrium or a balance between all groups of variables. They exist only in relation to each other – not independently.

Exaggerating the importance of technology is as dangerous as ignoring it. For example, J. F. C. Fuller, author of one of the first and still one of the most interesting books on the role of technology in modern warfare, went too far when he stated that 'tools, or weapons, if only the right ones can be discovered, form 99 percent of victory .... Strategy, command, leadership, courage, discipline, supply, organization and all the moral and physical paraphernalia of war are nothing to a high superiority of weapons – at most they go to form the one percent which makes the whole possible'.[20] According to this logic the United States should never have lost the war in Vietnam, nor would any type of guerrilla warfare ever succeed. Fuller ought to have read Clausewitz more carefully.[21] To be put in its proper context, military technology must be studied in juxtaposition to the other three elements of Clausewitz' theory. Having examined the logic of adding another dimension to Clausewitz' triad, we should consider the impact of military technology and *other* material factors on some of Clausewitz' basic theoretical assumptions.

IV. MOBILITY AND STRATEGIC SURPRISE

Perhaps the greatest revolutionary change in warfare was the tremendous increase in mobility with, first, the introduction of the railway and, later the combustion engine and aviation. Increased mobility compressed time and space, quickened the movement of supplies, altered the relationship between offense and defense on the strategic level, and created a need for much better intelligence and faster mobilization. It did all this by increasing the possibility for strategic surprise. Thus, increased mobility introduced a major destabilizing element into the international system.

Although Clausewitz believed that surprise was a very important element of warfare, he was also convinced that its use was largely confined to the tactical level seldom feasible. For him, therefore, strategic surprise was of greater theoretical interest than practical value:

> While the wish to achieve surprise is common and, indeed, indis-

pensable, and while it is true that it will never be completely ineffective, it is equally true that by its very nature surprise can rarely be
outstandingly successful. It would be a mistake, therefore, to regard
surprise as a key element of success in war. The principle is highly
attractive in theory, but in practice it is often held up by the friction
of the whole machine .... Basically, surprise is a tactical device,
simply because in tactics, time and space are limited in scale. Therefore in strategy surprise becomes more feasible the closer it occurs to
the tactical realm, and more difficult, the more it approaches the
higher levels of policy .... Preparations for war usually take months.
Concentrating troops at their main assembly points generally
requires the installation of supply dumps and depots, as well as
considerable troop movements, whose purpose can be assessed soon
enough.

It is very rare therefore that one state surprises another, either by
an attack or by preparation for war. (pp. 198–9)

Indeed, Clausewitz was certain that strategic surprise lacked the power
to overcome the inherent advantages of the defense.

The immediate object of an attack is victory. Only by means of his
superior strength can the attacker make up for all the advantages
that accrue to the defender by virtue of his position, and possibly by
the modest advantage that this army derives from the knowledge
that it is on the attacking, the advancing side. Usually this latter is
much overrated: it is short-lived and will not stand the test of serious
trouble. Naturally we assume that the defender will act as sensibly
and correctly as the attacker. We say this in order to exclude certain
vague notions about sudden assaults and surprise attacks, which are
commonly thought of as bountiful sources of victory. They will only
be under exceptional circumstances. (p. 545)[22]

Initially, the development of railway networks, particularly in
Germany, seemed to enhance the strategic capabilities of the defense.
Gradually, however, it became evident that a secret or even open concentration of large numbers of troops could, under the guise of conducting maneuvers, employ railway networks and, later on, combustion
engine mobility and air power, to launch a strategic surprise of decisive
impact. Under certain circumstances the aggressor could overwhelm
the defender who would be unable to mobilize his troops in time. As
mobility increased, the warning time available for counter-mobilization
decreased: from months or weeks in the early nineteenth century, to
weeks and days in the railway and combustion engine days, to days and
hours in the age of air power, and finally to hours and minutes in the
nuclear age (see Figure 2).

Modern states and alliance systems had therefore to develop intricate hair-trigger mobilization systems. By 1914 those systems became so complex and difficult to control that mobilization also meant war.[23]

Technological change has thus made a major contribution (not for the last time) to the destabilization of the international system. The possibility of a strategic surprise has become one of the most worrisome problems facing heads of state and general staffs.[24]

Clausewitz could not have anticipated the development of this *reciprocal fear of strategic surprise* into a crucial if not dominant factor in international politics. Now the side which possesses a unilateral advantage is tempted to achieve a quick and decisive victory, while the side with inferior technology could launch a preemptive strike in order to acquire a decisive advantage over its better-armed adversary.[25] For example, when the Japanese attacked the Russians in 1904, they disrupted the construction of the Trans-Siberian railway – the completion of which would have been catastrophic for the Japanese.[26]

Whereas in the past surprise was confined to the tactical and grand tactical levels, and was thus a relatively simple phenomenon, the advent of strategic surprise introduces many complexities: The choice of one's time, place, mode and speed of movement, as well as of the particular weapon or weapons system to be deployed, must be made quickly and simultaneously on several levels. New weapons produce fresh opportunities, new doctrines, as well as new problems for the strategist and military planner.

FIGURE 2
STRATEGIC SURPRISE IN HISTORICAL PERSPECTIVE
– THE DECLINE OF WARNING TIME

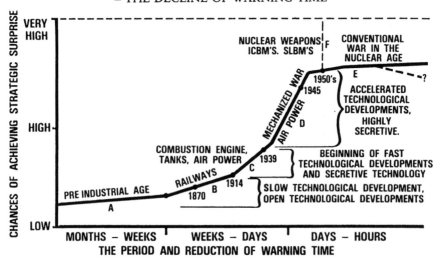

The fact that strategic surprise has now become an integral part of warfare contributes in yet another way to the need to modify Clausewitz' theory. Clausewitz emphasized the superiority of the defense over the offense on both the strategic and tactical levels. He viewed the inherent advantages of the defense as a permanent feature of warfare. One of the few offensive advantages that Clausewitz recognized was on the *strategic* level: the holding of the initiative, that is, the attacker's ability to exploit the element of surprise in the initial phase of the attack to his advantage:[27]

> As regards surprise and initiative, it must be noted that they are infinitely more important and effective in strategy than in tactics. Tactical initiative can rarely be expanded into a major victory, but a strategic one has often brought the whole war to an end at a stroke.

He qualifies this observation by adding that, 'On the other hand, the use of this device [that is, surprise] assumes *major, obvious and exceptional* mistakes on the enemy's part. Consequently it will not do much to tip the scales in favor of attack' (pp. 363–4, his emphasis).[28] He also remarks that:

> ... an aggressor often decides on war before the innocent defender does, and if he contrives to keep his preparations sufficiently secret, he may well take his victim unawares. Yet such surprise has nothing to do with war itself [that is, it is a political decision preceding war], and *should not be possible.* (p. 370, my emphasis)

As we have seen, revolutionary changes in mobility made possible surprise on the strategic level and therefore also contributed to a change in the relationship between the *strategic* defense and offense. The offense gained a unilateral advantage, which has expanded with the concomitant growth in mobility, range, speed, and firepower of modern weaponry. This is especially true in the opening phase of any modern war. The attacker can decide the *time, place, and method* of the attack, concentrate superior forces at the point chosen for the attack, and at least temporarily paralyze and overwhelm the defender. Strategic surprise in the opening phases of war is therefore the most powerful force multiplier in conventional war.

Clausewitz could not have foreseen the unmistakable evidence of modern military history, which affirms that regardless of the defender's excellent intelligence capabilities, it is almost impossible for him to prevent a strategic surprise (that is, to receive a timely warning).[29] If the attacker can learn to exploit fully the initial impact achieved by strategic surprise and to calculate carefully the culminating point of the attack, he can then move over to enjoy the benefits of the defense; thus the attack becomes, on the strategic level, the more powerful form of warfare. (For more regarding the impact of technological change on the relation between the defense and attack, see section VI below.)

V. INTELLIGENCE: FROM FRICTION TO PANACEA

The transformation of strategic surprise from a theoretical possibility to a practical reality necessitated the establishment of better military intelligence organizations. Since military intelligence is a key factor in the discovery of the adversary's mobilization plans and procedures, actual preparations for war, and troop concentrations, its increasing importance – as evidenced by the fact that European general staffs in the last quarter of the nineteenth century began to establish special sections for the collection and analysis of intelligence – was closely linked to the emergence of modern military technology. Thus, the development of military intelligence was related not only to the need to warn against strategic surprise, but also to the need to gather information about the development and production of new weapons systems, their effectiveness and performance, their integration into the military doctrine and so on. The independence of intelligence as a military activity was one aspect of the growing professional specialization and differentiation of military organizations created in response to the technological revolution.

Like surprise, intelligence interested Clausewitz primarily on the tactical and grand tactical levels as a command and control problem. He wrote little that was relevant to intelligence on the strategic level. Nevertheless, although his observations on intelligence must be understood in the tactical context, they can also be seen as part of his general discussion of the problems of warfare, primarily in the context of the key concepts of friction and uncertainty.

Clausewitz had little appreciation of the potential contribution of intelligence for the commander in charge of the conduct of war and to his decisions on the battlefield. Instead of viewing intelligence as we do today – as an element that could potentially reduce the degree of uncertainty, chance, and friction in war – *Clausewitz actually saw intelligence as a source of friction*, and a possible cause of failure:

> By 'intelligence' we mean every sort of information about the enemy and his country – the basis, in short, of our own plans and operations. If we consider the actual basis of this information, how unreliable and transient it is, we soon realize that war is a flimsy structure that can easily collapse and bury us in its ruins. The textbooks agree, of course, that we should only believe reliable intelligence, and should never cease to be suspicious, but what is the use of such feeble maxims? They belong to that wisdom which for

want of anything better scribblers of systems and compendia resort to when they run out of ideas.

Many intelligence reports in war are contradictory; even more are false, and most are uncertain .... One report tallies with another, confirms it, magnifies it, lends it color, till [the officer] has to make a quick decision – which is soon recognized to be mistaken, just as the reports turn out to be lies, exaggerations, errors, and so on. In short, most intelligence is false, and the effect of fear is to multiply lies and inaccuracies (p. 117) .... The general unreliability of all information presents a special problem in war: all action takes place, so to speak, in a kind of twilight, which like fog or moonlight, often tends to make things seem grotesque and larger than they really are.

Whatever is hidden from full view in this feeble light has to be guessed at by talent, or simply left to chance. So once again for lack of objective knowledge one has to trust to talent or to luck (p. 140) .... Consider the unreliable and fragmentary nature of all intelligence in war. Remember that both sides fumble in the dark at all times (p. 462) ....

The unreliability of most intelligence or what he calls 'imperfect knowledge' plays a central role in the Clausewitzian theoretical construction by providing one of the most important explanations for the 'interruption of military activity', or the 'suspension of action' (pp. 81–5). This in turn explains the need to modify the definition of war in theory to that of war in reality.

In general Clausewitz' pessimistic views on the value of intelligence to command and control and on the availability of reliable information and intelligence were correct, reflecting the objective conditions of his own time. Modern technology, however, while far from providing us with any panacea for the problems of uncertainty and imperfect information in war, has nevertheless radically altered our views on intelligence. Despite its flaws, intelligence is viewed today as an indispensable source of support in warfare, providing hope for the reduction of friction and for better control by both political and military leaders over events as they unfold.

The development of the telegraph had an immediate influence on the command and control of troops moving about on the battlefield. (Prussian military field telegraph units were established as early as 1856.) The telephone and radio further improved the transmission of information, and most recently the introduction of electro-optical sensors on mini-RPVs allows the transmission of real-time visual information on the battlefield.[30]

The development of such technological means of communication has in turn led to the establishment of special organizations to deal with them, as well as to the need to monitor the adversary's transmission and reception of this voluminous information. This in turn accelerated the growth of the intelligence bureaucracy, just one aspect of the continuous differentiation of the military bureaucracy.

Undoubtedly, the invention of these varied means of communication revolutionized the ability of commanders to receive information from and on the battlefield, allowing them to dispatch their orders and decisions much more effectively than in Napoleon's time. Clausewitz' (and even more so Tolstoy's) pessimistic view of the commanders' lack of effective control over the course of events on the battlefield is no longer justified – certainly not from the technical point of view.[31] While the difficulties in receiving and transmitting information on the battlefield have not been completely eliminated, they have been considerably reduced. Today almost all failures of command and control and inappropriate uses of intelligence do not stem from a lack of adequate communication instruments or information, as was the case earlier in history, but instead from human error and problems of perception. Similarly, technological developments including radio interception, computer-assisted crypto-analysis, high-altitude photographic aircraft reconnaissance, and satellite intelligence-gathering have all contributed to the tremendous progress in the collection of intelligence. Yet despite these improvements on both the tactical and strategic levels, many of the problems inherent in intelligence procedures as pointed out by Clausewitz have found no satisfactory solution. As he put it, 'We now know more, but this makes us more, not less uncertain' (p. 102). In the final analysis, intelligence problems are human – problems of perception, subjectivity, and wishful thinking – and thus are not likely to disappear no matter how much the technological means of intelligence improve.[32] Therefore the suggestion that war since the time of Napoleon and Clausewitz has lost much of its 'friction' is baseless.[33]

Were Clausewitz to rewrite *On War* today, he might identify different problems. While continuing to emphasize the complexities and uncertainties of the human factor in intelligence, he would probably acknowledge that technological means have changed the nature of friction and the command and control problems on the tactical level. But today's commander may suffer from psychological overdependence on the availability of intelligence, and hesitate to take action without it even when necessary. Modern intelligence may have become an addictive disincentive to the development of the 'military genius' intuition and readiness to accept risks, the qualities of great commanders.

While a lack of intelligence can create indecision and delays in action, the 'overdevelopment' of the technological means of intelligence and its increased availability may cause other serious problems. The modern commander will be so deluged with intelligence that he may become paralyzed trying to sift the relevant data from the trivial information. Such an overabundance of intelligence, like its absence, may cause serious delays in decisions. If a dearth of information was the major cause for friction in the past, the surplus of information in the present has given rise to a new form of friction. Thus while friction and uncertainty continue to exist, their causes and origin have changed with time. Another modern danger is that less-important decisions will be made at higher echelons as political and military leaders attempts to *centralize* the management of war by removing authority from lower-level commanders on the battle-field. Field commanders will thus become agents inspecting the imple-mentation of orders from the rear, rather than military decision-makers grappling with the dangers and uncertainties of war. Technology has changed the nature of intelligence by eliminating some problems while creating others.

VI. THE DYNAMICS OF THE OFFENSE–DEFENSE RELATIONSHIP

For Clausewitz, unlike most military writers of his time, the superiority of the defense over the offense was axiomatic on both the tactical and the strategic levels.[34] This assumption is central to his theory. The inherent asymmetry between the strength of the defense and that of the attack is one of the most important intervening variables between war in theory and war in practice.

Even had Clausewitz been convinced of the perfect equality between the defense and attack, he might still have been tempted to present them as inherently unequal as a 'methodological trick' necessary to make this transition from theoretical to real war. Such a 'methodological trick' was not essential to the development of Clausewitz' argument, however, for he made a very convincing case *for his time* that the defense is stronger:

> It is easier to hold ground than take it. It follows that defense is easier than attack, assuming both sides have equal means. Just what is it that makes preservation and protection so much easier? It is the fact that time which is allowed to pass unused accumulates to the credit of the defender. He reaps where he did not sow. Any omission of attack – accrues to the defender's benefit .... Another benefit, one that arises solely from the nature of war, derives from the advantage of position, which tends to favor the defense. (pp. 357–8)

As mentioned earlier, Clausewitz was also convinced that on the *tacti-cal* level the defender could make better use of the element of surprise.

The attack, unlike the defense, also suffers from its very success, which may contain the seeds of its defeat:

> By initiating the campaign, the attacking army cuts itself off from its own theater of operations, and suffers by having to leave its fortresses and depots behind. The larger the area of operations that it must traverse, the more it is weakened – by the effect of marches and by the detachment of garrisons. The defending army, on the other hand, remains intact. It benefits from its fortresses, nothing depletes its strength, and it is closer to its sources of supply. (p. 365)

In the majority of cases the defense will also benefit from the support of the population. Furthermore, frequently the defender will benefit from the support of friendly states, interested in maintaining the balance of power and the stability of the system. In a paragraph that could easily have been taken from any modern textbook on the systems theory approach to the study of international relations, Clausewitz wrote:

> It may be objected, of course, that history offers examples of single states effecting radical changes that benefit themselves alone, without the slightest effort by the rest to hinder them. There have been cases in which a single state has managed to become so powerful that it could virtually dictate to the rest. We would reply that this does not disprove the tendency on the part of common interests to support the existing order .... We therefore argue that a state of balance tends to keep the existing order intact – always assuming that the original condition was one of calm, of equilibrium. Once there has been a disturbance and tension has developed it is certainly possible that the tendency toward equilibrium will shift direction .... [But] such a change can affect only a few states, never the majority. (p. 374)

Clausewitz concludes that this 'common effort toward maintenance of the status quo' explains 'the fact that Europe, as we know it, has existed for over a thousand years' (p. 374).

Finally, Clausewitz even went so far as to deny the possibility of a change in the relationship between the defense and attack when he argued:

> If the offensive were to invent some major new expedient – which is unlikely in view of the simplicity and inherent necessity that makes everything today – the defensive will also have to change its methods. But it will always be certain of having the benefit of terrain, and this will generally ensure its natural superiority; for today the peculiarities of the topography and the ground have a greater effect on military action than ever. (p. 362)

This static view of the relationship between the defense and offense has been modified in contemporary history. Many contemporary analysts have argued that Clausewitz' emphasis on the superiority of the defense was wrong even for his own day, in light of Napoleon's military successes based primarily on offensive tactics and strategy. Inasmuch as Clausewitz was a great admirer of Napoleon, on this point he may seem inconsistent. This apparent inconsistency resolves itself if we compare his argument for the superior strength of the defense to his concept of the culminating point of victory. The attacker (that is, the offense) can have the best of two worlds. He can enjoy the advantages of the attack (for example, the time, the place, the method, the element of surprise), and at the point where the attack exhausts itself he can move over to the defense and benefit from its inherent advantages. Of course, his success hinges upon his moving over to the defense at the optimum point in time, that is, at the culminating point of victory. On how to identify this point, unfortunately, Clausewitz gives no clues. (But see text, pp. 527, 528, 566–73.) Paradoxically, then, one of the major advantages of the attack lies in its ability to move over to the defense.

It is still true that when all other things are equal, the defense is the stronger form of warfare. In reality, however, things can never be kept equal. Modern military technology, even more so than in the past, causes frequent changes in the relative strength between the defense and offense. The relationship between the two forms of war is cyclical – not static as Clausewitz assumed. Such cyclical changes add to the uncertainty as to which of the two modes of war is stronger, both on the strategic and tactical levels.

Clausewitz cited the influence of imperfect knowledge to explain the frequent suspension of action in war – mentioning especially the human tendency to make worst-case, over-cautious estimates under conditions of uncertainty (p. 117). Yet, even if there was full knowledge as to the relative strengths of both sides, certainty regarding the inherent superiority of the defense was by itself enough to cause inaction. Today inaction may result from another cause: namely, the *uncertainty* of the relationship between the offense and defense.

The cycle of modern weapons development, of weapons and counter-weapons, measures and counter-measures, has shifted the advantage from the defense to the offense, and back, a number of times since the start of the technological revolution. Such changes are not always perceived before the outbreak of war. For example, despite numerous indications from the Boer War and Russo-Japanese War, in which the growing advantage of defensive over offensive weapons was clearly demonstrated, most European armies before the First World War emphasized the development of exclusively offensive doctrines; similarly, the Israeli army before the 1973 war misread the technological trends favoring the defense in anti-tank and anti-aircraft weapons and consequently relied on an exclusively offensive doctrine. Conversely the French, before the Second World War, learned the lessons of the First World War so well that they overestimated the power of defense.

Despite the critical importance of technology in military affairs, very little theoretical work has dealt with this subject. J. F. C. Fuller developed two important analytical concepts that help us to describe and understand the cyclical nature of the relationship between the offense, defense, and technology in modern warfare. The first is the *dominant weapon*, the second the *constant tactical factor*.[35] The first concept suggests there is always a more effective type of weapon (that is, better protected, and/or with greater firepower and/or greater speed, etc.) which dominates (that is, has a greater impact on) the battlefield. Most other weapons as well as the tactical doctrine will therefore have to be organized around that weapon, as will the counter-weapons and counter-doctrine. (The dominant weapon need not be a single weapon excluding all others.) His second concept, that of the *constant tactical factor*, suggests that in the age of rapid technological change (as in earlier times) *no* dominant weapon will remain dominant for too long. This is the concept of change, to a large extent absent from Clausewitz' work. While Fuller's concepts are of great heuristic and analytical value, they usually have little or no predictive value. Thus the importance of uncertainty, an element emphasized by Clausewitz and further complicated by technology, remains unchanged.

VIII. TECHNOLOGY AND DOCTRINE: THE GAP WIDENS

As the rate of technological progress accelerates, resulting in a larger variety of weapons whose synergistic or systemic interaction is unclear, the gap between military technology and strategic/tactical military doctrines is constantly widening. Military organizations adapt even more slowly to change than individuals. Therefore, the gap that has opened up between the birth of a new technology and its proper absorption into military doctrine and practice is likely to be permanent.

Even those armies which are more open to change, frequently as a result of a defeat or a sense of vulnerability, still never completely succeed in matching technology's potential with its actual use on the battlefield. Thus, for instance, Nazi Germany's offensive blitzkrieg represented the culmination of an evolutionary trial-and-error process rather than an inspired flash from the mind of some military genius. The blitzkrieg took a considerable time to perfect in the face of resistance and lack of understanding – a lack clearly demonstrated in the war against Poland and the attack on the West in May 1940.

Another interesting example is the development of naval and air strategy between the two world wars – an excellent case study of the uncertainty involved in the development of new technologies. A comparative analysis of the major navies of the world (those of the US, Great Britain, Germany, Italy and Japan) in the 1920s and 1930s indicates that all committed similar errors in the perception of technology. Although all parties recognized the importance of air power, they had no realistic way of testing aircraft against battleships. The result was that all major powers conservatively chose to invest by 1939 in approximately a 2:1 ratio of battleships to aircraft carriers. The Second World War quickly proved the superiority of air power over traditional sea power, so that by the end of the war the procurement ratio of battleships to carriers had been reversed.

Likewise, although submarines were the only First World War weapon to come close to being decisive, they were neglected between the wars. No major technological improvements occurred in the design of submarines or their main weapons, the torpedoes. Assuming the technological success of British counter-measures, both Germans and British grossly underestimated the full potential of the submarine. The initial German success in U-Boat warfare against Great Britain was not attributable to any new weapons or technology, but rather to new submarine deployment tactics (for example, night attacks on the surface and later wolf pack tactics).

In regard to the blitzkrieg, air power, and the submarine, the strategists of the Great Powers failed to perceive the trends in military technology, developed inappropriate military doctrines, and were, once the Second World War started, slow to modify these doctrines even when they proved inadequate. In many cases, the weapons and the doctrines were mismatched. At times, well-tested weapons such as the submarine or tank could have been better used by the application of more innovative doctrines. Then again, sometimes new weapons rendered older ones obsolete, requiring the invention of completely new doctrines. In any event, weapons and doctrines, technology and its intellectual understanding, were rarely in harmony.

The reason for the gap between technology and doctrine is obvious. It has never been possible in modern times to test the full effectiveness of newly-developed weapons/counterweapons under realistic conditions in peacetime. Frequently the answer as to who is superior, the defense or the attack, is given only on the battlefield when it is too late.

VIII. THE UNITY OF COMMAND IS BROKEN

Although Clausewitz made a clear distinction in his trinity between the political and military direction of war, elsewhere, particularly when he describes his models of 'military genius' (for example, Frederick the Great and Napoleon), he seems to prefer the unity of the two types of leadership in one person:

> A prince or a general can best demonstrate his genius by managing a campaign exactly to suit his objectives and his resources doing neither too much nor too little (p. 177) .... To bring a war, or one of its campaigns, to a successful close requires a thorough grasp of national policy. On that level strategy and policy coalesce: the commander-in-chief is simultaneously a statesman. (p. 111)

Furthermore, he asserted that

> In the highest realms of strategy ... there is little or no difference between strategy, policy and statesmanship (p. 178) .... We argue that a commander-in-chief must also be a statesman, but he must not cease to be a general. On the one hand he is aware of the entire political situation. On the other, he knows exactly how much he can achieve with the means at his disposal. (pp. 111–12)[36]

The growing complexities of modern warfare caused not only by techno-logical but also by political developments, make it increasingly difficult to find a leader who possesses a high degree of both political and military skills. There are two reasons for this difficulty:

First, modern warfare requires a much higher level of professional education (for example, general staff work) and familiarity with military technology than can usually be claimed by any political leader – unless, of course, he had a military career before entering politics. Then, too, the growing demands of military expertise create a universal tendency in all military establishments, to claim a monopoly on military knowledge in order to minimize the participation of civilian leaders in the actual con-duct of war. This tendency runs counter to the most important of all Clausewitz' theoretical assumptions: the primacy of politics in the con-duct of war. In his work on total war, Ludendorff developed an opposing theory emphasizing the primacy of the military leadership over the politi-cal in war:

> All the theories of Clausewitz should be thrown overboard. Both warfare and politics are meant to serve the preservation of the people, but warfare is the highest expression of the national 'will to live', and politics must, therefore, be subservient to the conduct of war.[37]

He continues,

> The World War has already removed any possible doubts as to the necessity of the nation's armed forces to be subordinated to the

> Commander-in-Chief, and his standing above the war minister as the chief of military administration and *above the political chiefs*. In a word, the position of the Commander-in-Chief must be as high and as unlimited in war as was that of King Frederick the Great.[38]

The second reason that political and military leadership are rarely combined is that in the era of modern total war the political leader must direct almost all his energies to the mobilization of political, economic, and popular support for fighting the war. This activity leaves him less time and energy to deal with the conduct of military operations.

Reflecting upon the bygone era of political and military unity of leadership in war, General Sir Archibald Wavell stated:

> The friction between civil and military is, comparatively speaking, a new factor in war, and is a feature of democracy, not of autocracy .... The interchangeability between the statesman and the soldier passed forever, I fear, in the last century. The Germans professionalized the trade of war, and modern inventions, by increasing its technicalities, have specialized it. It is much the same with politics, professionalized by democracy. No longer can one man hope to exercise both callings, though both are branches of the same craft, the governance of men and the ordering of human affairs.[39]

The friction between the political and military professions to which Wavell refers has increased in the age of technology, when many military leaders feel that 'amateur' civilians are not qualified to deal with the growing complexities of modern warfare. Defeat, or simple lack of success, has led military leaders to pin the blame on 'interfering' politicians. Such accusations, ranging from suspicion of 'a stab in the back' to the notion that 'there is no substitute for victory', appear during and following every modern war. This universal problem has prompted other military leaders to express views similar to those of Ludendorff and opposed to those of Clausewitz. For example, after the First World War Lieutenant General Sir Gerald Ellison wrote that Churchill was wrong in asserting, 'At the summit true politics and strategy are one'. 'Ergo, quite obviously', says Ellison, 'the politician is fully qualified to deal with strategy?

> Hence Amateur Strategy?
> Hence Gallipolli!'

He continues, with heavy irony, to explode the popular belief that

> every politician is a heaven-born naval and military strategist, that the man who produces a weapon is necessarily the right man to use

it, that the administrator automatically becomes the commander
…. The politician, unfortunately, either cannot, or will not, recognize limitations in the scope of politics which ordinary common
sense would seem to dictate.[40]

The good general then concludes that '*Politics and strategy are radically
and fundamentally things apart from one another. Strategy begins where
politics end*' (his emphasis).

The record of modern warfare makes one thing very clear: the need to
keep the two types of military leadership separate, *not united*. Many
cases in which the civilian leaders tried either to control or to intervene
excessively in the conduct of military operations (for example, Kaiser
Wilhelm, Hitler, Mussolini, Stalin and at times Churchill) ended in
disaster. Attempts on the part of the military to control the political and
grand strategic goals of wars ended equally badly (for example, the
Schlieffen plan, the decision to launch unrestricted submarine warfare,
and the German high command's literally taking over the political conduct of the First World War).

Clausewitz did not go into detail concerning the problems of co-
ordination between the political and military leadership in war. Given the
frequent unity of the two during his lifetime and the relative simplicity of
both political and military affairs, this is not altogether surprising. Nevertheless, the technological and political complexities of the modern world
have necessitated a degree of 'fine tuning' unthought of by Clausewitz
in order to achieve a workable balance between the civilian and military leadership in modern war. Clausewitz offers few insights into the
problem, beyond his brief comment in Book VIII that

> If war is to be fully consonant with political objectives, and policy
> suited to the means available for war, then unless statesman and
> soldier are combined in one person, the only sound expedient is to
> make the commander-in-chief a member of the cabinet, so that the
> cabinet can share in the major aspects of his activities. But this, in
> turn, is only feasible if the cabinet – that is the government – is near
> the theater of operations, so that decisions can be taken without
> serious loss of time …. What is highly dangerous is to let any soldier
> but the commander-in-chief exert influence in the cabinet. It very
> seldom leads to sound vigorous action. (pp. 608–9)

Although in emphasizing the primacy of politics Clausewitz was ahead
of his time, he could not foresee the complications of civil–military
relations and their impact on the political supremacy necessary to the
conduct of war.

IX. THE DIFFERENTIATION AND BUREAUCRATIZATION OF THE MILITARY

When Clausewitz discussed friction in war he was primarily referring to the uncertainties generated by the collision of two opposing armies on the battlefield. His 'friction' was chiefly the result of the adversary's unexpected actions and their impact on one's own forces and on the outcome of battle. Friction was thus created by *external* causes. He tacitly assumed that one's own army and leader behave as what is called a 'uni-actor', that is, a single unit making decisions *vis-à-vis* other such units. While this may have approximated reality in the days when the king was also the commander-in-chief, it certainly does not describe current reality. In today's military environment it is useful to make a distinction between *external friction*, created as a result of conflict between two opposing sides, and *internal friction*, generated by the growing specialization and compartmentation of the military.

Clausewitz did not think it was important for military leaders to deal with issues of management and organization: 'One would not want to consider the whole business of maintenance and administration as part of the *actual conduct of war*. While it may be in constant interaction with the utilization of troops, the two are essentially very different' (p. 129, his emphasis). The distinction between leading troops to war and administration would appear even more pronounced today. Just as the political leader and military leader are now separate individuals, the military leader may be a manager or even a technocrat, rather than a warrior.

Coordinating many military and civilian organizations requires careful calculation and diplomatic skill, rather than the courage, daring, and acceptance of risks required on the battlefield. In all likelihood the optimal temperament and character required for managing and fighting cannot be found in one military genius, as Clausewitz proposed. The requirements are contradictory. Frederick the Great and Napoleon, the models for Clausewitz' military genius, were very different from Carnot (whom Clausewitz never mentions), Marshall and Eisenhower. Were Clausewitz alive today, he would recognize the need to describe, besides the 'military genius', the 'military-organizational genius'.[41]

Just as there are now several different types of military leader, there are also many different military organizations, set up to maximize the utility of the multiple dimensions of military technology. The military management of technology (for example, organizational decisions concerning the research, design, and choice of weapons; the procurement cycle; the relationship with the scientific and industrial communities; the inspection of production; the testing and maintenance of equipment; the writing of instruction manuals; and training) has created a military bureaucracy of immense proportions that continues to grow with technology.

Furthermore, the basically simple structure of the Napoleonic armies (that is, primarily infantry, cavalry, and artillery) has been greatly complicated, and can no longer be controlled by a single leader.[42] Far more specialized, today's armies are made up of numerous organizations – infantry, artillery, signal, armor, engineers, anti-aircraft, transportation, intelligence, etc. – each having its own weapons, doctrines, school, and unique expertise. Each one of these military organizations enjoys a certain degree of autonomy, and fights to protect its own parochial-professional interests, including its share of the military budget. Thus, although all of these organizations exist in order to contribute to the achievement of the same goal and support each other in the process, they also have many conflicting interests that separate them. The desire to maintain their autonomy and articulate their various perceptions has generated considerable friction within each military organization.

The anonymous, capital-intensive character of modern war led J. F. C. Fuller (with his usual knack for bringing things *ad absurdum*) to reverse Clausewitz' emphasis on the importance of the military genius in war.

> The outstanding lesson of the [Franco-Prussian War of 1870] was that a conflict of masses is a war of conflicts in which genius is out of place. Though the general can still plot and plan, and increasingly must do so, he can no longer lead or command because the masses are too vast to grasp. Command now passes to the General Staff, its foremost problem being the development of firepower.[43]

The truth obviously lies somewhere in between Clausewitz and Fuller. Fuller, like Adam Smith and the Marxists, tends to move the focus to the invisible hand of economic forces or the role of the masses in war. Ultimately, however, much depends upon what Michels has termed 'the Iron Law of the Oligarchy', that is, that a single individual inevitably exists at the top of the decision-making ladder, who, whether a political, military, or managerial-organizational leader, must make the final choice.

Meanwhile, important decisions concerning both peace and war require greater efforts at political compromise and a more intensive search for consensus than they did in Clausewitz' time. Such complications of coordination between different organizational perceptions and interests have offset the advantages gained from great technological advances in command and control. Thus while friction has been reduced in some ways since Clausewitz' time it has increased in others.

X. THE DEMOCRATIZATION OF WAR AND THE NEW PROMINENCE OF DOMESTIC POLICY

Today, both historians and military strategists are concerned about the causes of war and the extent to which war can be waged without popular consent. Clausewitz, however, wrote the greatest book on the logic and conduct of war without devoting much attention to its causes. He does mention two important causes, but fails to develop them in any depth. The first is human nature, or what he refers to as 'hostile feelings and hostile intentions', the 'primordial violence, hatred and enmity, which are to be regarded as a blind natural force ... passions ... inherent in the people' (pp. 76, 89). The second cause of war is the need to restore the 'balance of power', to return the international system to equilibrium (p. 374). The transition from peace to war, international crises, mobilization as a destabilizing factor, preventive and preemptive war, ideological and economic causes of war – all of these did not really concern him. This lack of interest can be explained, but not justified, by two factors. The first is that Clausewitz, as a military man who accepted war as a 'fact of life', focused on the specific task of bringing war, once begun – for whatever reason – to a successful conclusion.[44] The second is that, since his time, the technological revolution and political/ideological changes have made the causes of war inherently more interesting and important. In modern times mobility and the accelerated pace of war have made the specific circumstances under which war breaks out much more relevant to military planning, the preparation of contingency plans, the choice of weapons, and the design of a strategic doctrine.

Nevertheless, even for his own time, the absence of a discussion of the causes of war in a general treatise on war is quite striking. It was, after all, Clausewitz who first emphasized the primacy of political control in war – and the outbreak of war and the decision to go to war are indeed political decisions that bear directly on military planning. Thucydides, for example, devoted considerable space to a discussion of the origins and causes of the Peloponnesian wars.[45] Clausewitz' attitude is all the more puzzling given the unique circumstances that preceded the outbreak of the French Revolution and the Napoleonic Wars.

Clausewitz' attitude to war was amoral. For him, war was an inevitable, legal, and acceptable part of the relationship between states. He felt that 'wars are the willful creation of the state, that wars are made and that they do not "break out"'.[46] He believed in 'the absolute priority of foreign affairs over domestic considerations'.[47] For him, therefore, the decision to go to war was a rational choice made exclusively on the basis of external considerations and was intended to maximize the power and interests of the state *vis-à-vis* all others in the international system. The decision itself, the last resort of kings, was taken by the head of state who knew (presumably) what he wanted and could prepare his army, while largely disregarding domestic considerations.

This simplified *raison d'état* model may have been realistic during the *ancien regime*, but it is less than adequate in an age of democracy and mass mobilization. In fact, it was also Germans like Ludendorff and Eckhart Kehr who emphasized the primacy of domestic politics (*Der Primat der Innern Politik*) over foreign policy.[48] In addition, of course, the Marxists emphasized even earlier the need to examine domestic economic (and political) considerations when seeking the major causes for war.[49]

Thus, starting with Marxist theories, very powerful explanations for the causes of war were shifted from the international system to the domestic environment. This is not the context in which to discuss Lenin's theory of imperialism, Schumpeter's criticism of his theory, the 'military-industrial complex' explanation, or numerous other relevant theories. It is, however, necessary to discuss briefly the contemporary domestic environment in which the decisions concerning the initiation and conduct of war are made. Certainly in a modern democratic society, but in fact in any society, there is a need to explain and justify a war to the people to be mobilized for the supreme effort and the sacrifices it entails. Ludendorff has recognized, for example, that in fighting the modern total war it is essential to mobilize the moral support of the masses:

> It is a mistaken assumption that a war must begin with a declaration of war .... The declarations of war of the Imperial Chancellor Von Bethman-Hollweg on Russia and France in August 1914, are still in everybody's memory. They gave the enemy propaganda a useful start in strengthening the morale of their peoples, and weakened the morale of our people .... The supreme Commander-in-Chief has to see to it that such damage should not be done to the conduct of war and the people alike at the very beginning by war declarations, and also by deficient instruction of the nation, such as the German people and the German Army were destined to suffer in 1914, and in the following years, through the German declarations of war in particular. This is the more necessary as a nation and every individual within it can only help the war leaders with their whole strength when they are firmly convinced that their very existence is at stake.[50]

The task of convincing one's own population of the need to go to war and to continue fighting until the war is won is even more arduous in an era when television brings the images of war and its atrocities into every home. Every military leader must therefore plan his strategy and execution of the war while continuously looking over his shoulder at his own people. Certainly in recent history several wars have been lost through miscalculating the people's willingness to continue fighting a war of attrition. The wars fought by the French in Algeria and Vietnam; by the US in Korea, Vietnam, and Lebanon; by the Israelis in Lebanon; have revealed that the key to winning modern wars may not be on the battle-field but on the home front. The need to maintain a consensus at home demonstrates that, once the domestic scene becomes as important as the external one, many of the assumptions supporting the *raison d'état* model collapse. In modern democracies there is no definitive central source of influence where critical decisions can easily be made, nor is there necessarily an agreement concerning the goals of a war or at what price it should be fought. The fiction of the 'uni-actor' making national decisions collapses very quickly. Thus, the military-cum-political genius cannot make all the decisions by himself as Clausewitz maintains, but must, in order to implement his policies, persevere in his search for an operational consensus.

The dilemma is that the conduct of war by consensus does not necessarily create the best conditions for waging a decisive war. For example, during the war in Vietnam, Presidents Johnson and Nixon had to maintain a delicate and carefully calculated balance between the opposing pressures of doves and hawks – a balance which resulted in a prolonged and indecisive, limited war.[51] The military leader of today is often forced to wage a limited war and to find acceptable substitutes for victory. In this manner, another dimension of internal friction has been added to warfare, for a leader must consider not only the costs and benefits of war but also the need to adjust the burden of war to a level acceptable to his own population.

While Clausewitz in *On War* appears to take domestic support for granted, the modern political leader cannot.[52] Indeed this dimension represents one of the greatest problems in modern warfare for the political leadership (and hence also for the military). Friction, uncertainty, and chance may prevail in the calculation of obtaining domestic public support as much as in gauging the performance and moves of the enemy. Leaders often seem to take the initial domestic consensus to go to war for granted – yet the longer the war, the less decisive and the more costly, the more problematic the domestic support becomes.

XI. IS VICTORY OBSOLETE?

Unlike Sun Tzu who thought that 'to subdue the enemy without fighting is the acme of skill',[53] Clausewitz ridiculed the idea of winning without fighting:

Kind-hearted people might of course think there was some ingenious way to disarm or defeat an enemy without too much bloodshed, and might imagine this is the true goal of the art of war. Pleasant as it sounds, it is a fallacy .... It would be an obvious fallacy to imagine war between civilized peoples as resulting merely from a rational act on the part of their governments and to conceive of war as gradually ridding itself of passion, so that in the end one would never really need to use the physical impact of the fighting forces – comparative figures of their strength would be enough. That would be a kind of war by algebra. (pp. 75–6)

Quite to the contrary, he defined war as 'an act of force to compel our enemy to do our will' (p. 75). Since the aim of war is to disarm the enemy, this must be done by force. In order to 'impose our will on the enemy', we must also win. Achieving a military victory was thus a necessary condition to achieving the political goals of war. The more ambitious the political goals, the more desirable the victory. Conversely, if military victory is unattainable we cannot impose our will on the enemy and hence cannot achieve our political goals.

Clausewitz' repeated emphasis on the necessity of victory on the battlefield is the epitome of Western means/ends rationality, which posits a direct correlation between military and political achievements. Modern wars, in particular guerrilla wars of attrition fought not only against the enemy's army but also against his domestic public opinion front, have demonstrated beyond any doubt that it is possible to lose a war militarily and yet win it politically. In such a war it is enough to play for time. The Algerians in the French War in Algeria, and the Vietnamese against the French and US in Vietnam, are good examples. Perhaps another example was the decision of Egypt's President Sadat to launch a limited war against Israel in 1973. Sadat knew he could not win militarily, but he (correctly) believed that the war would allow Egypt to attain many of its political goals. The Israelis, whose military thinking is typically Western, failed to anticipate the war, despite the many warning signals, because they could not understand why any state would launch a war it could not win. (Here, of course, the Israelis also projected their own attitude, since for them a military defeat would mean political disaster.) Arguably, then, Clausewitz' idea of the primacy of politics has been carried one step farther in the non-Western world, to the point where military victory is no longer a prerequisite for political success.

Nuclear weapons, which also added a revolutionary new dimension to military strategy, are not merely increased firepower, as Curtis LeMay is rumored to have believed, but actually represent a quantum jump in the destructiveness of war. War has undergone a metamorphosis, or, in

Kuhn's term, a paradigm shift. If strategy in Clausewitz' time was the art of using force on the battlefield to achieve political ends, nuclear strategy (that is, deterrence) is precisely the opposite: It is the art not of using force but of avoiding war. In a nuclear war – which resembles Clausewitz' war in the abstract – victory has become a meaningless concept. We would resort to Clausewitz' authority in vain regarding a subject that he could not have anticipated. One should be very cautious about applying Clausewitz to the realm of nuclear strategy.

Nevertheless, the emergence of nuclear weapons has, if anything, even further accentuated Clausewitz' insistence on the primacy of politics in warfare. The awesome destructive power of nuclear weapons and the speed with which a nuclear war can be launched and decided have shifted the center of strategic-operational decision-making from the military to the political leadership.

> Today, therefore, nuclear arms have wrought a drastic transformation by promoting strategy to the policy level, the level of deterrence. No one thinking in terms of deterrence can any longer be satisfied with the military level of thought, but must ascend to the conceptual heights of policymakers.[54]

The swiftness with which nuclear attack can be carried out, its lack of historical precedent, its simplicity compared with conventional warfare, and the need for *absolute* political control, have made the military genius and the whole military establishment redundant in an all-out nuclear war:

> War had aspects of an art in the past. Commanders took pride in their tactical skill, in the degree of imagination and ingenuity required to deploy their forces, in qualities of character, courage and daring, and in the capacity of leadership to implant confidence and enthusiasm in the troops. A man's qualities and character found expression in battle. In all-out nuclear war, the human factor is disappearing and alienation between man and war has been created. This is machine warfare, increasingly transformed into a province of science and technology. All-out nuclear war is a war of covering targets by calculating probabilities of hits, a war of azimuths and computers. War is becoming mathematical, and from many standpoints simpler and more amenable to advance planning ....[55]

Due to the revolutionary change implicit in nuclear warfare, historical experience from previous wars has ceased serving as a guide for such a war. Military experience, therefore, no longer affords an advantage in analyzing the course and results of a future war, and the primacy of the officer corps has ended. Those divining the uncertainties of the next war are all 'arm-chair strategists', without exception, and all are submerged in an area of guess-work and conjecture, whether they are military or civilian. No one possesses experience in the question of how man will behave in the nightmare conditions of nuclear war. Military experience is less helpful in dealing with these questions than some familiarity with scientific problems, an acquaintance with political and psychological reality, and the ability to weigh logical considerations.[56]

Strategic nuclear war has therefore eliminated *the military* from Clausewitz' triad. A Clausewitzian definition of nuclear warfare consists of a new triad: *the people, the government*, and *technology* – perhaps even only the last two elements.

XII. WARFARE AND THE ECONOMIC IMPERATIVE

Thucydides said that 'war is a matter not so much of arms as of money, which makes arms of use'.[57] The Austrian general Montecuculi is quoted by Ludendorff as saying that 'for the conduct of war money, and again money and thirdly and last money is needed'.[58] To be sure the economic dimension of modern warfare includes much more than financial support – it involves industrial capacity, research and development, the availability and distribution of raw materials, and the organization and management of the war economy.

Clausewitz never really discusses the financial and economic aspects of war. He seems to take for granted that all the resources necessary for waging war will be made available by the political to the military leadership.

> The conduct of war has nothing to do with making guns and powder out of coal, sulphur, saltpeter, copper and tin; its given quantities are weapons that are ready for use and their effectiveness. Strategy uses maps without worrying about trigonometric surveys; it does not inquire how a country should be organized and a people trained and ruled in order to produce the best military results. It takes these matters as it finds them in the European community of nations, and calls attention only to unusual circumstances that exert a marked influence on war. (p. 144)

This is certainly a narrow view of war even for the nineteenth century. After all, economic and financial considerations or the cost of war have always been a key element in the decision to launch a war and have played a vital role in the course of war itself. Although Clausewitz frequently followed an economic way of thinking (for example, his numerous references to the need to calculate the means/ends cost/benefit relationship in war) he never directly addressed economic issues. He may have not done so deliberately, as Michael Howard suggests, but by this omission he conveniently ignored a crucial dimension of war that was extremely important even in his own time.[59] Although he studied the Napoleonic campaigns in minute detail, he completely ignored the '... part played in Napoleon's strategy, and perhaps his downfall, by the Continental System – his attempt to use economic as well as military instruments to consolidate and extend his conquests'.[60]

That Clausewitz ignored the economic dimension of warfare is of particular interest for two reasons. The first is that the economic dimension of warfare is closely related to the political dimension, whose primacy he always emphasized. Decisions on the allocation of economic resources for the buildup of the military forces before war, as well as their allocation to different purposes, fronts, and divisions during war itself, are an important link between the political and military authorities. Clausewitz' tacit assumption that all the resources necessary for war will be made available to the commander-in-chief is too simple. Who will decide how much of a nation's resources should be devoted to war and who should decide how and by what priority to allocate such resources to the armed forces are questions which Clausewitz left unanswered.

Clausewitz' omission of the economic dimension of war is interesting for yet another important reason. It seems to be missing from his discussion of the transition from war in the abstract to war in practice. Yet it provides another excellent explanation why absolute war must be modified by reality, for absolute war would require the use of *all* the economic resources of a nation at war. In reality, economic constraints dictate the amount of resources that can be invested in war and related activities, thereby playing a major part in limiting the tendency toward absolute war.

Of course, the industrial/technological revolution has increased the importance of economic considerations. Although many technological developments have forced the consideration of economic calculations on the tactical level, such calculations are of even greater importance on the strategic level. On the strategic level knowledge of economic factors in a prolonged war can considerably reduce the uncertainty of the final results. For the outcome of such modern wars is determined not so much by the inspired military genius as by more subtle factors such as gross national product, industrial and research and development capacities, the organization and management of the wartime economy, and the mobilization of resources. The 'economic' nature of modern warfare has spawned more wars of attrition and fewer of decision. This is perhaps the reason why in the past two World Wars the weapons that came the closest to being decisive, for example, the U-Boat as used against Great Britain in the First and Second World War, and perhaps the Allied blockade on Germany in the First World War, were all directed against the economy of the targeted nation.

In fact, Clausewitz does recognize the need to measure the war potential of nations, which he discusses very briefly in Book VIII, Chapter 9. Here he demonstrates that a simple calculation of the availability of manpower indicates that France cannot be expected to win against a coalition of Austria, Prussia, the rest of Germany, the Netherlands, and England. Nevertheless, this is a very simple measurement of war potential using only one criterion (population) for prediction. Modern warfare requires the use of more variables to evaluate the balance of power and the most likely outcome of war. Such an evaluation could have clearly indicated the disastrous outcome of a German decision to declare war on the US as well as the USSR. In two world wars, German leaders thought that a successful war of annihilation or blitzkrieg could avoid the long-range consequences of economic inferiority – a disastrous illusion. One can only wonder if this neglect of the economic dimensions of war is somehow related to the absence of the same dimension in Clausewitz' study On War.[61]

Our material environment has radically changed since the early nineteenth century. Wars, which simultaneously depend upon material change and promote material change more than any other human activity, have therefore been radically transformed as well. For that reason any book written on war before the industrial/technological revolution must be subject to modification. This, as we have seen, is the case with Clausewitz' work. Much of what he wrote is timeless, but some aspects of his thoughts and theories on war have been overtaken by the march of history. Although Clausewitz is the least dogmatic and the most flexible of all military theorists, in some respects his views of war are inevitably static and difficult to apply to a different material environment.

Military-technological developments permeate every facet of war: its destructiveness, its expansion in space and compression (or acceleration) in time, the relationship between the offense and defense, the role of intelligence and the possibility of achieving strategic surprise, the shifting emphasis from the front to the rear in the conduct of war, and the correlation between economic and military strength. The accelerated development of military technology has increased the complexity of war in innumerable ways since Clausewitz' time. Furthermore, material change is always followed by nonmaterial changes no less important than the material changes themselves. Nonmaterial changes such as the bureaucratization of military organizations, the creation of a permanent gap between technological innovation and the development of a complementary military doctrine, and the new relationship between the military and civilian authorities must be included in our modern calculus. All of these problems could not have been foreseen by Clausewitz and therefore could not be addressed by him.

Theories, like weapons, are replaced in the course of time by other, better ones. As Clausewitz himself suggested: 'Perhaps a greater mind will soon appear to replace these individual nuggets with a single whole, cast in solid metal free from all impurity' (p. 67). It is a tribute to the greatness of Clausewitz that 150 years after his death there has yet appeared no better theory on war.

NOTES

1. Raymond Aron uses this infelicitous neologism – 'transhistorical' – to describe the relevance of Clausewitz theory to any period in history. *Clausewitz: Philosopher of War* (London: Routledge & Kegan Paul, 1983) is an abbreviated translation of *Penser la guerre: Clausewitz* (Paris: Editions Gallimard, 1976). This is a very disappointing book.
2. Quincy Wright, *A Study of War* (Chicago: University of Chicago Press, 1971).
3. See John I. Alger, *The Quest for Victory* (Westport, CT: Greenwood Press, 1982).
4. Unless otherwise stated, all quotations from Clausewitz are from Carl von Clausewitz, *On War*, ed. and trans. Michael Howard and Peter Paret (Princeton, NJ: Princeton University Press, 1976). Page number given in text.
5. Changes on the tactical level do not necessarily occur at a faster rate than those on the strategic level, since the two levels are closely linked. The appearance of the tank, a weapons platform invented to solve a tactical problem, had of course very important implications for strategy in both the First and Second World Wars. Similarly the use of radar or PGMs primarily on the tactical level had critical and cumulative influences on the strategic level. Any important shift in the balance of strength between the offense and defense on the tactical level will have a decisive impact on the strategic level. In this sense strategy and tactics have come much closer than they were in Clausewitz' time.
   It is interesting to note that Ludendorff quoted Moltke as saying, 'Mistakes made in the beginning of war cannot be made good in the later stages of war'. General Erich Ludendorff, *The Nation at War* (London: Hutchinson, 1936), p. 155. Clausewitz, on the other hand, felt that tactical mistakes could always be retrieved on the strategic level (pp. 182, 243, 582). While this remains basically true in today's world, it might be more difficult given the speed of developments on the battlefield and the slowness of the redesign-replacement process for faulty weapons systems. In the age of modern technology, the most important decisions in war are often taken during the period of peace preceding it. The idea that the 'battlefield decision' is to a large extent now made in peacetime would certainly have sounded strange to Clausewitz.
6. The phrase is from Alfred Vagts, *Defense and Diplomacy: The Soldier and the Conduct of Foreign Relations* (New York: Kings Crown Press, 1956), p. 379.
7. This was also the opinion of Hans Delbrück who wrote: 'With the appearance of Clausewitz' works after his death in 1831, the Napoleonic period of history of the art of war comes to a close .... It leads into the new period .... The new period is defined in its content by the new technology, not only of weapons but also of transportation and all the resources of life, from the railroads and telegraph to the foodstuffs, which increased in such unlimited proportions in the course of the nineteenth century.' *History of the Art of War Within the Framework of Political History*, Vol. 4, *The Modern Era* (Westport, CT: Greenwood Press, 1985), pp. 454–5.
   Among the more interesting works covering the accelerated development of military technology since the beginning of the nineteenth century are: J. F. C. Fuller, *Armament and*

History (New York: Scribners, 1945), Chs. 5–7; J.F.C. Fuller, *The Conduct of War 1789–1961* (London: Eyre & Spottiswood, 1972, Ch. 5); Michael Howard, *War in European History* (Oxford: Oxford University Press, 1976), Chs. 5–7; Maurice Pearton, *The Knowledgeable State: Diplomacy, War and Technology Since 1830* (London: Burnett Books, 1982); Hew Strachan, *European Armies and the Conduct of War* (London: George Allen & Unwin, 1983), Ch. 8. For an excellent brief survey of contemporary military technological developments see *The Economist*, 'Marching Forward: A Survey of Defense Technology', 21 May 1983, 5–32.

The surge in the number of inventions in general during the nineteenth century is demonstrated by the following table:

Period	Number of Inventions
1755–1799	680
1800–1824	1,034
1825–1849	1,885
1850–1874	2,468
1875–1879	2,880

(Based on Appendix 17, Table 20, Quincy Wright, *A Study of War*, p. 163.) The military technological revolution had started earlier, at sea, with Robert Fulton's steamship (1803), the first iron steamship (1820), screw propulsion instead of the paddle wheel (between 1843–45), the complete replacement of sail by steam power (1850), and the all-iron warships HMS Warrior (1861) and Whitehead Torpedo (1864).

The military revolution on land was not far behind. Important new 'civilian technologies' relevant for military application, as well as purely military technologies, started to appear by the early nineteenth century and to accelerate in a cycle of invention, adaption, proliferation, mass production, and obsolescence from about the time of the American Civil War onward. Among the major inventions were:

Shrapnel's shell (1803), Appert's canning technique (1810), Forsyth's percussion lock (in place of a flintlock (1807), and in the 1830s the copper cap that made Forsyth's invention of practical military use (the principal attribute of the percussion cap was the certainty of firing in all weathers).

George Stephenson constructed the first practical steam locomotive (1814), and with the advent of the Stockton–Darlington railway line (1815), the Liverpool–Manchester (1830), and the first trains and railway lines in Europe (1832), military technology moved to land warfare.

The breech-loading Dreyse needle gun was invented (1829), ordered by the Prussian government (1840), accepted as regular issue (1851), and finally fully demonstrated at the battle of Koniggratz (1866). This cycle would later be compressed from a whole generation to a few years.

Communication was revolutionized by Morse's telegraph (1832), the opening of the Baltimore–Washington telegraph line (1844), the telephone (1877), Marconi's radio (1895), and the first transatlantic radio call (1901). From here we leap to the teleprinter radar computers, satellite communications, and the microchip.

Colt's automatic revolver (1835) was being mass-produced by 1853. New explosives included nitroglycerine (1846), dynamite (1866), lyddite (1880s), cordite (adopted by the British army in 1890), and melanite (1880s). There was a tremendous increase in firepower with the invention of the Gatling gun (1862) and Maxim's machine gun (1882).

The first oil well was drilled near Titusville, PA, in 1859; Diesel invented the combustion engine (1892); the first cars (Ford and Benz) appeared in 1893; and the first powered flight took place in 1903. From here we advance to rocket propulsion and, finally, nuclear weapons.

Clausewitz certainly should not be expected to have noticed the early signs of the technological-industrial revolution. Although they can be clearly identified in retrospect, they were not demonstrated on the battlefields of Europe during his lifetime. Not long after his death, the gates of technology were opened and the flood of military inventions began, never to cease again.

Michael Howard in his book *Clausewitz* (New York: Oxford University Press, 1983) suggests that Clausewitz ignored technology unconsciously (p. 3). This is incorrect. Clausewitz could not ignore something that did not exist as we know it today.

8. Edwin A. Pratt, *The Rise of Rail Power in War and Conquest, 1833–1914* (Philadelphia: J. B. Lippincott, 1916), p. 2. See also John Westwood, *Railways at War* (London: Osprey, 1980); Dennis Showalter, *Railroads and Rifles: Soldiers, Technology and the Unification of Germany* (Hamden, CT: Archon Books, 1975), Part I; also Pearton, *The Knowledgeable State*; George E. Turner, *Victori Rode the Rails: The Strategic Place of the Railroads in the Civil War* (New York: Bobbs Merrill, 1953).

9. Pearton, *The Knowledgeable State*, pp. 64–9; also Pratt, *The Rise of Rail Power*, pp. 1–14; Showalter, *Railroads and Rifles*, pp. 17–75.

10. Strachan, *European Armies and the Conduct of War*, 115; Showalter, *Railroads and Rifles*, pp. 75–190. In Part 3 of this book Showalter discusses the development of modern cannons. Gordon A. Craig, *The Battle of Koniggratz: Prussia's Victory over Austria, 1866* (Philadelphia: J. B. Lippincott, 1964).

11. Jay Luvaas, *The Military Legacy of the Civil War: The European Inheritance* (Chicago: University of Chicago Press, 1950), p. 226.

12. William James, quoted in Grant T. Hammond, 'Plowshares into Swords: Arms Races in International Politics 1840–1941' (Ph.D. dissertation, Johns Hopkins University, 1975), p. 26.

13. J. F. C. Fuller in *Armament and History*, pp. 115–16, writes: 'The nation which makes the greatest use of peace intervals to advance its mechanical and engineering potentials for war, and which possesses the greatest number of skilled workers as well as trained soldiers, and the most abundant supply of raw materials, as well as of arms, is the nation upon which victory smiles.'

14. For Delbrück's theories, see Hans Delbrück, *Geschichte der Kriegkunst im Rahmen der politischen Geschichte* (Berlin: Georg Stilke, 1900–20). Also, Gordon A. Craig, 'Delbrück the Military Historian' in E. M. Earle (ed.), *Makers of Modern Strategy* (Princton, NJ: Princeton University Press, 1943), pp. 260–87; Richard H. Bauer, 'Hans Delbrück' in Bernadotte Schmitt (ed.), *Some Historians of Modern Europe* (Chicago: University of Chicago Press, 1942).

15. See Arden Bucholz, *Hans Delbrück and the German Military Establishment: War Images in Conflict* (Iowa City: University of Iowa Press, 1985).

16. Aron, *Philosopher of War*, p. xiii, also pp. 92–3.

17. Some scholars may argue that technology and economics are simply part of the environment in which war is carried out. This interpretation – which may be represented by Clausewitz' triangle enclosed by a circle (environment) – minimizes the *qualitative* differences which result from the accumulation of *quantitative* changes.

18. Similarly, the timing and development by Marx and Engels of their theories on communism and dialectical materialism is not a mere historical coincidence. Marx could not have developed his specific form of communist theory before the industrial revolution. That revolution, in fact, made the appearance of a theory like his almost inevitable.

19. J. F. C. Fuller, *Armament and History*, pp. 108, 121.

20. Ibid., p. 18. Although Fuller is far from being a Marxist, it is interesting to note how close he comes to adopting a Marxist analysis of war. It is not surprising, therefore, to find that Fuller's theories on war were favorably commented on and adopted by the British Marxist and military analyst T. H. Wintringham. See, for example, his *Weapons and Tactics* (Harmondsworth, England: Penguin, 1973).

21. Fuller read Clausewitz carelessly, but not as carelessly as Liddell Hart. See J. F. C. Fuller, *The Conduct of War 1789–1861*, Ch. 4, 'The Theories of Clausewitz', pp. 59–77. For Liddell Hart's misperceptions of Clausewitz see Jay Luvaas' essay in this volume.

22. Clausewitz claimed that the successful achievement of surprise (on any level) depends on secrecy and speed. The tremendous changes in mobility (that is, speed) since his time have thus considerably improved the chances of obtaining strategic surprise even by his own criteria. The second variable, secrecy, has not changed in any radical way since his own time but is easier to counter.

23. Pearton, *The Knowledgeable State*, pp. 22–4. For the loss of control, deterioration to war, and mobilization on the eve of World War, see Luigi Albertini, *The Origins of the War of*

1914, Vol. 3 (Oxford: Oxford University Press, 1967); Lawrence Lafore, *The Longest Fuse* (Philadelphia: J.B. Lippincott, 1965); Ludwig Reiners, *The Lamps Went Out in Europe* (Cleveland: World Publishing Co., 1966); Alfred Vagts, *Defense and Diplomacy*, Ch. 10, 'Mobilization and Diplomacy', pp.377–437; Paul M. Kennedy (ed.), *The War Plans of the Great Powers 1880–1919* (Boston: Allen & Unwin, 1985).

24. See Thomas C. Schelling, *The Strategy of Conflict* (Cambridge: Harvard University Press, 1965) and *Arms and Influence* (New Haven: Yale University Press, 1966).

25. Pearton, *The Knowledgeable State*, p.25.

26. Ibid., pp.25–6.

27. 'The enemy force can never assemble and advance so secretly that the defender's first news of it would come from his outposts. If that were to happen, one could only feel very sorry for him.' *On War*, p.454; see also pp.544 and 557.

28. Also pp.200–1. On the tactical level Clausewitz saw the element of surprise as favoring the defender not the attacker:

    > It is self-evident that it is the defender who primarily benefits from the terrain. His superior ability to produce surprise by virtue of the strength and direction of his own attacks stems from the fact that the attack has to approach on roads and paths on which it can be observed; the defender's position, on the other hand, is concealed and virtually invisible to his opponent until the decisive moment arrives. *On War*, p.361.

29. For a summary of the causes of strategic surprise and why it actually comes close to being inevitable, see Michael I. Handel, 'Intelligence and the Problem of Strategic Surprise', *Journal of Strategic Studies*, 7 (Sept. 1984), 229–82. Also Richard K. Betts, 'Analysis of War and Decision: Why Intelligence Failures are Inevitable', *World Politics*, 31 (Oct. 1978), 61–89.

30. There is no comprehensive historical study of the impact on war of the development of modern means of communication, from the telegraph and telephone through the radio and television.

31. Tolstoy's view on the value of intelligence and the ability of military commanders to obtain relevant information in time to control the course of events is even more pessimistic than that of Clausewitz, though influenced no doubt by the same events.

    See in particular Leo Tolstoy, *War and Peace* (New York: Simon & Schuster, 1954); W.B. Gallie, *Philosophies of Peace and War: Kant, Clausewitz, Marx, Engels, and Tolstoy* (Cambridge: Cambridge University Press, 1978).

32. See Handel, 'Intelligence and the Problem of Strategic Surprise', 229–82.

33. As suggested by Peter R. Moody, in 'Clausewitz and the Fading Dialectic of War', *World Politics*, 31 (April 1979), 417–33. The meaning of this statement is as empty as the title of the article (that is, dialectics by definition cannot fade away). The author admits to having read an inadequate 'compilation' of Clausewitz' *On War*.) Even had intelligence been perfect, friction would still exist on the battlefield in other, numerous, and unavoidable ways. The physical world has not lost any of its friction since the days of Newton: nor has the world of war since Napoleon.

34. Strachan, *European Armies and the Conduct of War*, p.96.

35. J.F.C. Fuller, *Armament and History*; T.H. Wintringham, *Weapons and Tactics*.

36. See also Gerhard Ritter's discussion in *The Sword and the Scepter*, Vol. 1, 'The Prussian Tradition 1790–1890' (Coral Gables, FL: University of Miami Press, 1969), p.57. Ch. 3 is on Clausewitz and Napoleon.

37. Ludendorff, *The Nation at War*, p.24.

38. Ibid., p.175.

39. General Sir Archibald Wavell, *Generals and Generalship* (London: Macmillan, 1941), pp.27; 33–4.

40. Sir Gerald Ellison, *The Perils of Amateur Strategy* (London: Longmans, 1926), pp.99–100.

41. Wavell, p.23. Wavell emphasizes the modern general's need for administrative-organizational skills – a dimension neglected by Clausewitz in the study of military leadership. (See section IX below.)

42. During Napoleon's time, the French Army had already become much too large to be effectively commanded by Napoleon himself, who consistently refused to delegate authority

to his subordinates. Given the size of the army, the scope of the problems, and the absence both of adequate technology and of the organizational support a general staff provides – Napoleon's insistence on maintaining centralized control inevitably led to his defeat. For example, until 1812 Napoleon directed the military operations in Spain although he had not been there since 1809. Strachan, *European Armies and the Conduct of War*, p.53.

43. Fuller, *Armament and History*, p.118.

44. As W.B. Gallie points out, Clausewitz' concentration on the conduct of war itself, on its management, prevents him from being seen as a political theorist in the mold of Hobbes, Machiavelli, Locke, Montesquieu, and Rousseau:

> ... A common ground of criticism of Clausewitz ... is that he takes war so entirely for granted ... that he shows no positive interest in the particular kinds of social and political situation that are liable to give rise to or prolong or intensify it; still less does he ask how war might be contained or limited or eventually removed from the scene. In sum, Clausewitz can be criticized, with some cause although not with real justice, for having provided an enlightening anatomy of war – of its action as a whole and of the possible movements of the separate parts – but without adding anything to our understanding of its physiology – the vital forces that call it out and keep it in operation. *Philosophy of Peace and War*, p.62.

While Gallie correctly analyzes Clausewitz' limitations, the reader must recognize that many of Clausewitz' ideas, particularly in Book I, Ch. 1; Book II, and Book VIII, are closely related to major issues of political theory and would merit attention by political theorists, most of whom have unfortunately ignored Clausewitz' work.

45. Donald Kagan, *The Outbreak of the Peloponnesian War* (Ithaca: Cornell University Press, 1969).

46. Jurg Martin Gabriel, 'Clausewitz Revisited' (Ph.D. dissertation, American University, 1971), 233.

47. Ritter, *The Sword and the Scepter*, Vol. 1, p.52.

48. See, for example, in this context Ludendorff, *The Nation at War* (in particular, Ch. 7, 'The Nature of Totalitarian War', pp.12–24); Eckart Kehr, *Economic Interest, Militarism and Foreign Policy* (Berkeley: University of California Press, 1977); Arthur Lloyd Skop, 'The Primacy of Domestic Politics: Eckart Kehr and the Intellectual Development of Charles E. Beard', *History and Theory*, Vol. 13 (Middletown, CT: Wesleyan University Press, 1974), pp.119–32; James J. Sheehan, 'The Primacy of Domestic Politics: Eckart Kehr's Essays on Modern German History', in *Central European History*, 1 (June 1968), 166–75.

49. The Marxists and hence Soviet military analysts seem to have a great deal of respect for Clausewitz – among other reasons, because of his emphasis on the primacy of politics, his dialectical method, the fact that Lenin read and favorably commented on *On War*, and the connection Clausewitz makes in Book VIII, Ch. 36, between different economic and social infrastructures and different military systems. See Donald E. Davis and Walter S.G. Kohn, 'Lenin's Notebook on Clausewitz', in David R. Jones (ed.), *Soviet Arms Forces Review Annual* (Gulf Breeze, FL: Academic International Press, 1977), Vol. 1, pp.188–229.

50. Ludendorff, *Nation at War*, pp.143–4.

51. See, for example, Lesley Gelb and Richard K. Betts, *The Irony of Vietnam* (Washington: The Brookings Institution, 1979).

52. This is at least the tacit and often the explicit assumption that Clausewitz makes in *On War*. Clausewitz did recognize the changed role of the people in warfare since the outbreak of the French Revolution:

> In the eighteenth century, in the days of the Silesian campaigns, war was still an affair for governments alone, and the people's role was simply that of an instrument. At the onset of the nineteenth century, peoples themselves were in the scale on either side. The generals opposing Frederick the Great were acting on instructions – which implied that caution was one of their distinguishing characteristics. But now the opponent of the Austrians and Prussians was – to put it bluntly – the God of War himself.
> Such a transformation of war might have led to new ways of thinking about it. (p.583)
> We will hardly find a more erroneous standard of measurement in history than that

applied in 1792. It was expected that a moderate auxiliary corps would be enough to end a civil war; but the colossal weight of the whole French people, unhinged by political fanaticism, came crashing down on us. (p.518)

Since Bonaparte, then, war, first among the French and subsequently among their enemies, again became the concern of the people as a whole, took on an entirely different character, or rather closely approached its true character, its absolute perfection. There seemed no end to the resources mobilized: all limits disappeared in the vigor and enthusiasm shown by governments and their subjects. (pp.592–3)

While he recognized the new role of the people and *levée en masse* in war he did not address the question of how the mobilization and increased participation and interest of the people in war came about. (At least not in his study *On War*.) This in reality, was one of the major problems the Prussian military reformers had to address after their decisive defeats by Napoleon at Jena and Auerstadt was how to mobilize the support of the German masses. This was by no means a simple task since it involved an extensive political reform of the autocratic Kingdom of Prussia. Peter Paret, *Clausewitz and the State* (Oxford: Clarendon Press, 1976); Peter Paret, *Yorck and the Era of Prussian Reform, 1807–1815* (Princeton: Princeton University Press, 1966); W. Shanahan, *Prussian Military Reforms* (New York: Columbia University Press, 1945); W. Simon, *The Failure of the Prussian Reform Movement, 1807–1819* (Ithaca: Cornell University Press, 1955); Gordon A. Craig, *The Politics of the Prussian Army, 1640–1945* (Oxford: Oxford University Press, 1955); Ritter, *The Sword and the Scepter*, Vol. 1.

53. Sun Tzu, *The Art of War* (Oxford: Oxford University Press, 1982), p.77. For an interesting discussion of the meaning of victory in modern warfare, see Richard Hobbs, *The Myth of Victory: What is Victory in War?* (Boulder, CO: Westview Press, 1979).
54. Harkabi, *Nuclear War and Nuclear Peace* (Jerusalem: Israel Program for Scientific Translations, 1966), p.2.
55. Ibid., p.4.
56. Ibid., pp.5–6.
57. Thucydides, *The History of the Peloponnesian War*, trans. Richard Crawley, Rev. R. Feetham (Chicago: Encyclopedia Britannica, 1971), Bk. I, Ch. 3, p.370.
58. Quoted in Ludendorff, *The Nation at War*, p.67.
59. Michael Howard, *Clausewitz*, p.3.
60. Ibid.; see also Strachan, *European Armies and the Conduct of War*, p.52.
61. See Arden Bucholz, *Hans Delbrück and the German Military Establishment*.

2

Numbers Do Count: The Question of Quality Versus Quantity

'Quality is more important than quantity—but is best in large numbers.'—*Israeli Proverb*

'It has been reported that one of the factors contributing to the present desperate position of the British is the failure to freeze designs. The technical services are never satisfied with anything less than a perfection which is always unobtainable. The best is the enemy of the good. If we are to avoid the catastrophe of "too little and too late", there must be a decision as to production types. Germany has demonstrated that thousands of imperfect tanks on the battlefield are better than scores of perfect tanks on the testing ground.'*

Wars, battles, and campaigns can be won by various types of armed forces, based on different combinations of *quantitative* and *qualitative* components. The choice of a particular force posture is determined by many considerations, among which are found historical traditions, political attitudes, military doctrine, economic, industrial and budgetary constraints, and the availability of manpower.

The quantitative elements are relatively easy to identify and measure (i.e., the number of aircraft, ships, tanks, artillery pieces, divisions, stocks of ammunition, oil). The concept of quality, however, must be divided into two major categories: (1) material aspects and (2) non-material aspects. Material quality stands for the quality and performance of weapons which can be measured by their speed, range, firepower, reliability, and durability. Many of these specifications can be measured, but the trade-offs between them cannot: the amount of emphasis to assign to reliability instead of to state of the art performance, the suitability of a certain weapons system to the quality of manpower available, and its performance in comparison with the enemy's weapons—are all very difficult to estimate, despite claims to the contrary. The second, non-material qualitative dimension includes the qual-

---

* From a letter circulated by the Assistant Secretary of War and based on a report of the US Military Attaché in London, 26 August 1940. Cited in Irving Brinton Holley, Jr. *United States Army in World War II: Material Procurement for the Army Air Forces* (Washington, DC: Office of the Chief of Military History, Department of the Army, 1964), p. 514

ity of manpower, level of training, motivation and morale, the quality of the military doctrine chosen, military organization, staff work, planning, and political leadership; these factors cannot be readily measured. On the whole, therefore, the qualitative dimension, especially the non-material element, is more elusive and difficult to define—let alone to measure precisely.

The total military power available to any given state can schematically be presented as follows:

$$\text{Total Military Power} = \text{Quantity} \times \text{Material Quality} \times \text{Non-Material Quality}$$

Within certain constraints, each country can choose between a number of possible combinations of the quantitative and qualitative elements in constructing its military force posture. Ideally, each country wants to strike the optimum balance between the two elements, thus providing the necessary level of security and the power to meet its goals and needs. Nevertheless, such a choice is far from easy, since the synergistic qualities of various combinations are difficult to evaluate, and new, different weapons, doctrines, and adversaries appear in every war.

The question of whether a war was won primarily because of quantitative superiority or was decided by a qualitative edge is not simple to answer even in retrospect. *History is full of contradictory examples even within the same war.* Only in extreme cases is it relatively easy to point to the decisive impact of one element. For example, given the ratio of forces and the roughly equal material quality available to the British and French allies and their German adversaries, it can be argued that the decisive German victory in the West in 1940 was achieved as a result of the better quality of the invading German Army. Similarly, in light of the overwhelming Arab quantitative superiority and the roughly equal material quality of weapons technology possessed by Israel and its Arab neighbors, it can be argued that the superior quality of the Israeli Army has been the decisive factor in the five Middle Eastern wars fought so far.

On the other hand, Nazi Germany, which was not qualitatively inferior, as we have seen above, finally succumbed to the overwhelming quantitative superiority of the Allies, as did Japan. Likewise, Finland, which was initially successful in defending itself and in proving its qualitative superiority, was quickly crushed by the Soviet Union's quantitative superiority.

There are two lessons that can be drawn from the examples mentioned above.

(a) In the cases in which quality was the decisive factor, it was the non-material elements of quality (i.e., a superior doctrine, superior planning and staff work, high morale and an offensive spirit, and leadership) which proved to be decisive. *No important modern war has been won by the technological superiority of weapons alone.* The United States won the Second World War *primarily* because of its material superiority, while all of its technological excellence could not help it in Vietnam.

(b) Qualitative elements, particularly the non-material ones, appear to be the most decisive in quick and short wars, while quantitative superiority normally yields results only in a prolonged conflict, since not all of the superior quantity of military power available to a state can normally be brought into action from the outset.[1] The outcome of wars is relatively indifferent to material technological quality.[2] Thus, the two most important factors are non-material quality in short wars, and superior quantities in prolonged wars. The United States has neglected both of these vital factors during the last decade.

* * *

From a historical perspective, the possibility of more heavily emphasizing *material* or *technological* weapons in structuring a specific force posture is a fairly new phenomenon. Since the middle of the nineteenth century, warfare has become more and more *capital intensive*.[3] After the First World War, and even more so since the Second World War, war became not only more capital intensive but also more technologically oriented. Until the end of the First World War, military technology, while very important, offered a limited array of weapons. In today's world, revolutionary advances in technology offer many different types of weapons, all of which are designed to accomplish similar military missions; for example, a tank can be knocked out by a variety of hand-held weapons, anti-tank missiles, air-to-ground munitions, other tanks, conventional artillery, guided artillery, and specially-designed mines. Although all of these weapons have the ultimate task of destroying a tank, they vary enormously in cost, reliability, performance characteristics, and operational requirements. Given adequate budgetary support, creative imagination is the most important limit to the choice, design, and production of weapons in the present technological environment. The tremendous increase in the variety of weapons designs has not made purchasing and production decisions any easier.

Nowhere has material quality been emphasized as much as in the United States; technological excellence was and is seen as the panacea for pressing military problems, and technical-engineering solutions seem to offer a 'quick fix'. This not-so-new trend in the American approach to war has reached exaggerated proportions during the last decade and a half, particularly since the end of the war in Vietnam (despite the failure of US superior technology to achieve a victory in that war).

A few reasons for this attitude are:

(a) American society in general depends more heavily on automation and technology than any other society. The attitude that perpetuated the never-ending process of acquiring the latest model cars, television sets, stereos, and home appliances also found its way to weapons acquisition.

(b) Technology is seen as the area in which the United States has a considerable edge, which will compensate for other weaknesses and give the necessary margin of advantage over any adversary. Perceived as the main potential opponents of the United States, the Soviet Union and China had a substantial quantitative advantage over the United States for which the United States could compensate by producing better military equipment. Moreover, since the end of the Vietnam war and with the establishment of its all-volunteer force, the American manpower pool has decreased, touching off a frantic search for superior technology to compensate for the further quantitative decline of the United States Armed Forces.[4]

(c) In the western world, the high value attached to the life of each individual, each soldier, has led to the desire to minimize the loss of human lives in war. Great efforts have been made to obtain the very best weapons for the American soldier. This may paradoxically *reduce* the capacity of American society in general to maintain its strength and increase its total national power vis-à-vis its adversaries. The assumption that the overall power of the United States will increase the most if each soldier or pilot gets the best weapon or aircraft is not true, if too few of these weapons can be purchased. The emphasis on material quantity will only be justified under the following circumstances:

(1) If both adversaries are approximately on a similar quantitative and non-material qualitative level, then improvements in material quality may give one of the states a military advantage. In other words, when all other things are equal, qualitative improvements in material *will* augment a country's total strength. (As we shall see below, however, normally all other things are *not* equal.)

(2) If a country has developed, to the extent of its ability, its quantitative and non-material qualitative elements, then the only way left to increase its power is by developing better weapons.

(3) If and when the development of the qualitative material element *does not* lead to the neglect of the other two dimensions of national power, or to *overreliance* on technical solutions to solve non- or only partly technical problems; in other words, when no imbalance is created between the three elements of power.

* * *

The trend toward greater reliance on material-technological quality in the power equation has led to the development of increasingly sophisticated and complicated weapons systems, which have inevitably emphasized quality over quantity; absolute performance levels over considerations of cost; gadgetry over reliability; 'clean' experimental and laboratory conditions over the 'messy' environment of the battlefield, and in the final analysis, the state of the art technology for its own sake over war-fighting capabilities.

Superior weapons technology is not always more reliable and better suited for combat, and better technology carried to extremes can have some serious disadvantages that may actually *reduce* the total military power of the United States.

(1) Generally, the more sophisticated and technologically advanced weapons systems become, the more they cost in absolute terms, meaning that fewer of these systems and their spare parts can be purchased.

(2) There is always better technology in the near future; and too many weapons systems are produced only in smaller quantities, in anticipation of better things to come. Many weapons systems become conceptually (if not

practically) obsolete before they are produced, but no substitute systems are being prepared to take their places. This develops into a never-ending race in which the best is the ever-present enemy of the good. Thus, large-scale weapons production is constantly deferred to a later date, while experiments and development continue, and sufficient weapons and munitions are not available when they are needed.

(3) An exaggerated emphasis on technology often also leads to the over-reliance on technical performance and firepower instead of on doctrinal and non-material solutions, thereby inhibiting creative military thinking. It results in an emphasis on the material aspects of war and in neglect of critical non-material dimensions such as careful strategic planning; the development of better tactics; improved training; the use of surprise and deception, and other factors related to the human element in war.[5]

(4) Finally, more sophisticated and complex major weapons systems usually require better and more intelligent manpower to operate them. Such higher quality manpower for operation and maintenance is not always available in adequate numbers, particularly not for the all-volunteer US Armed Forces. In such cases, high technology is mismatched with the quality of manpower available.

The cost of modern complex weapons systems, weapons platforms, and all types of guided and unguided ammunition produced in the United States has skyrocketed. 'Even after inflation is removed and the unit costs have been adjusted for the reduced quantities procured, the cost of military equipment has been rising at about 5 per cent per year. Thus, one generation of equipment costs three to five times as much as the prior one, and so significantly lower quantities of military equipment are being procured today. The result is not only reduced military capability, but also low and inefficient production rates.' At the same time, the reliability of many of the weapons produced may have declined. A few examples will demonstrate this trend.[6]

The cost of the latest US Main Battle Tank (MBT), the XM-1, the first newly designed tank to be produced in the United States in more than two decades, is now estimated at $3 million dollars per unit by the mid-1980s. At this price, the United States would be able to purchase a much smaller number of tanks and will have to maintain older models in service for a longer time.

Despite the high cost—and because of the high technology and advanced design—the XM-1 is beset by many problems. To begin with, it suffers from a serious case of excess weight (close to 62 tons!), which means that only a single tank can be transported by the largest US long range military cargo airplane, the C-5A. No other cargo aircraft can carry the XM-1. This is, of course, a serious drawback; in contrast to the Soviet Union, *the United States does not have any modern light tank available in large numbers that can be transported by air.*

The XM-1 is equipped with a modern turbine engine that was used in the past only in helicopters.[7] In tests conducted so far, the engine has proven to be unreliable. Dust—the normal environment of tanks—is apt to interfere with its functioning, rendering it especially unsuitable for desert warfare, one of the most likely areas of operation in the future. In addition, the engine uses 20 per cent *more* fuel than a regular diesel tank engine. This will certainly increase the operational costs of the tank and also increase the need for logistical support in time of war. The XM-1 can operate only 10 instead of 24 hours without refuelling; and although it was designed to have a cruising range of 275 miles, it has demonstrated a range of about 140 miles in field tests. It requires much more maintenance than the older, simpler tanks; it was designed to operate '320 mean miles between failures', but field tests have so far indicated that a breakdown would occur at about half that number. Finally, it has been argued that the turret design of the XM-1 is highly vulnerable to a well-placed shot, and is referred to as a 'perfect shot trap'.

The XM-1 is not without its advantages: it is faster (it can go from zero to 20 mph in 6.1 seconds); it boasts better survivability (despite the vulnerability of the turret); it has better 'first hit' capability, range-finding, and night fighting equipment than its predecessors. Many of its 'bugs' will gradually be ironed out. Still, the new German Leopard and the Soviet T-72 and T-80 tanks now in service will be equipped with better guns for a long while. Altogether, in light of its cost, its excessive weight, engine performance and maintenance problems, and fuel consumption, and in light of the quality of the Soviet tanks and the latest innovations in, and abundance of, anti-tank weapons of all types, the XM-1 appears to be a poor choice.

In all probability, an upgraded version of the M-60A3 or a new, less sophisticated tank would be only marginally inferior in performance to the XM-1—but could be more reliable, simpler, and more economical to operate and maintain, and could be produced in larger numbers. (Between 1977 and 1979, the United States produced on the average 650 M-60A3 tanks per year as compared with over 2,500 in the USSR.) The United States now produces 10 XM-1 tanks per month or 120 per year; but when the production lines of the M-60A3 are closed down in 1982, the production of the XM-1 is expected to rise to 60 per month or 720 per year in two plants. This is a very low rate of production when the Soviet tank production is taken into account, with the high rate of tank attrition expected in any future war, and when we consider that the United States also has to re-equip some of its allies' armies.[8]

The cost increases of high technology, 'gold-plating' practices combined with a considerable decline in reliability and combat readiness, is even more apparent in the American military aircraft industry. The current production costs of three of the four fighter aircraft that constitute the backbone of American air power have escalated to around 20 million dollars per unit. The US Navy F-14 (Tomcat), one of the most sophisticated and expensive fighters, will cost $28.8 million per unit in FY 1981, and $36.4 million per unit in FY 1982. The USAF F-15 (Eagle) now costs approximately $20 million per unit. In the late 1960s and early 1970s, the US Navy and Air Force had decided to compensate for the expected high costs of the F-15 and F-14 by procuring also larger numbers of cheaper aircraft such as the F-16 and F-18. But the Hi-Lo Mix (as it is referred) turned out to be a Hi-Hi Mix.[9]

The F-18 (Hornet), originally designed as a small *light* fighter/bomber *low cost* complement to the expensive F-14, turned out to be neither light nor cheap; its cost is put at $30.2 million for FY 1981, and at a staggering $36.4 million for FY 1982. The original price expected by the Navy for purchasing the F-18 between 1981 and 1986 was around $21 million per unit. In 1979, the F-18 program was 29.3 per cent of the United States Navy's aircraft procurement program; this figure rose to 36.9 per cent in 1980, and will probably be as high as 44.1 per cent by 1982. The total price tag for the complete F-18 program is now calculated to be around $30 billion—larger than the Trident program and not far behind the MX missile program. The F-16, which was supposed to be the mass-produced light fighter of the 1980s at $6 million per unit, now costs at least $15 million.[10]

While there is no doubt that on a one-to-one basis, these technological marvels can outperform all other aircraft presently in use, they are all plagued by serious problems. The state of the art has, on the whole, not resulted in more reliability and battleworthiness. Quite to the contrary, it has led to the procurement of fewer planes, fewer of which are mission-ready.

The latest inventory of US war planes has recently been referred to as 'a giant fleet of elite lemons'. As it turns out, newer and better aircraft are not more mission capable than older aircraft. The US Navy front-line interceptor-fighter, the F-14A, was not ready to perform its missions nearly half of the time, and the Air Force's F-15 was not capable of performing its mission 44 per cent of the time during the fiscal year (1979). The US Air Force had originally tried to attain 70 per cent mission readiness for the F-15s in peacetime. (See Table 1.) (Serious maintenance problems have afflicted not only the US tactical fighter-bomber airfleet but also the giant C-5A cargo planes, only 45 per cent of which are usable at any given time, while the rest are grounded for maintenance or shortage of spare parts.)[11] Because of the growing cost per plane, fewer can be purchased each year, thus generating powerful pressure to invest a larger percentage of the funds available in purchasing as many planes as possible, while relatively reducing the investment in purchasing spare parts and ammunition. As a result, fewer of these more expensive aircraft are airworthy, and in wartime they will have to fly more sorties per aircraft per day; and the pressure to achieve a higher turnaround rate naturally puts a heavier than expected burden on maintenance. This may have created a situation in which the United States does not have sufficient aircraft available to perform the necessary number of missions in a high attrition combat environment.

In some ways, not unlike many underdeveloped countries, the United States has for some time followed a policy which emphasizes purchasing the largest possible number of major costly weapons platforms, but has neglected to pursue an adequate policy of spare parts acquisition and a reliable maintenance level. Experience has shown that a smaller number of better maintained aircraft and better trained pilots can be (depending on the adversary) much more effective than a large number of poorly maintained aircraft, helicopters, or tanks.

FY THE MATERIAL READINESS INDICATORS

	Complexity	Inventory	NMC (%)*	Available Aircraft	Unavailable Aircraft At Any Given Time	MFHBF*	MMH/S*	Cann-WR/100 Sorties*
AIR FORCE								
A-10	LOW	243	32.6	164	79	1.2	18	16.7
A-7D	MEDIUM	376	38.6	231	145	0.9	24	9.3
F-4E	MEDIUM	610	34.1	402	208	0.4	38	13.3
F-15	HIGH	428	44.3	239	189	0.5	34	29.3
F-111F	HIGH	95	36.9	60	35	0.3	75	44.9
F-111D	HIGH	86	65.6	30	56	0.2	98	58.5
		1,838		1,126	712			
NAVY/ MARINE CORPS								
A-4M	LOW	129	27.7	94	35	0.7	28	12.0
AV-8A	LOW	92	39.7	56	36	0.4	44	13.4
A-7E	MEDIUM	386	36.7	245	141	0.4	53	27.1
F-4J	MEDIUM	342	34.2	226	116	0.3	83	22.2
A-6E	HIGH	297	39.3	180	117	0.3	71	39.4
F-14A	HIGH	292	47.1	155	137	0.3	98	69.6
		1,538		956	582			

NOTES TO TABLE

NMC(%) = This factor measures the average percentage of aircraft that were 'Not Mission Capable' during FY 1979, e.g., an F-111D was not capable of performing one of its primary missions. (For that fraction of time it may still have been flyable or capable of flying its missions in a degraded mode.) The NMC data indicates a rough relationship between complexity and NMC . . . as planes get more complex, they tend to break more often, there are more things that can go wrong.

MFHBF = Mean Flying Hours Between Maintenance Events. It is a measure of reliability. The number represents an *average* for a year. (For example, an F-14 may fly for a long time with no maintenance events, then suddenly several can occur.) Again, there is an inverse relationship between complexity and reliability. Simple planes tend to have a greater overall reliability than complex planes.

MMH/S = Maintenance Manhours Per Sortie. This factor represents the total workload required to prepare the airplane for the next flight after it has landed.

Cann-WR/100 Sorties = Cannibalization and War Reserve Withdrawals per 100 Sorties. This factor measures relative shortages of spare parts. If operating stocks are short, maintenance personnel have the option of temporarily obtaining the spare parts from the War Reserve spares kit, or of taking parts off aircraft that are temporarily grounded.

The table and explanations are based on 'Defense Facts of Life' by Franklin C. Spinney, presented to the Subcommittee on Manpower and Personnel of the Senate Armed Services Committee. Also see *The Armed Forces Journal* May 1980, p. 30.

One way in which American designers of modern fighter aircraft (the F-15 in this case) had hoped to reduce the maintenance load was by designing a special computer to test the complex avionics system; yet the diagnostic instrument has no less than 40,000 parts which are subject to frequent failures (it is out of order 50 per cent of the time).[12] Thus, instead of alleviating the maintenance load, a new problem has been created. Another attempted solution was to design modular boxes that could easily be removed from the aircraft, be replaced by similar 'boxes', and be sent to the producing factory for repairs. The US Air Force now depends on factory manpower for a good deal of the maintenance of its ultra-sophisticated equipment. To rely on remote factories for maintenance in wartime is, of course, a somewhat chimerical scheme; the factories themselves often have great difficulties and require a lot of time to repair the equipment. The backlog of repairs and the high cost of these modules do not allow them to stock enough to keep the aircraft operational at all times. Spare parts become too expensive to stock in the quantities needed properly to support the black box concept. (The accumulated shortage of spare parts for the Air Force alone is in the order of close to three billion dollars.) In some cases, the shortage of spare parts for the F-14 and F-15 was so acute that some aircraft had to be cannibalized in order to keep others in operational condition. Current shortages, combined with the fact that the industrial base is unable to produce enough spare parts for both civilian and military aircraft and can only be expanded very slowly, means that the shortage in spare parts for military aircraft will be carried over well into the mid-1980s.

But even without a shortage of spare parts, the newly designed, state-of-the-art aircraft in the US inventory are beset by myriad problems, only a few of which will be mentioned here. Touted as the engine that would open 'a whole new realm of fighter techniques', the F-100 engine, which powers the F-15 and F-16, stalls under certain conditions in midflight, and requires excessive maintenance and spare parts (especially the turbine blades). Over 400 million additional dollars have been invested to improve the performance of this engine, and the end is not in sight. Serious problems have also developed with the Navy's F-14 engines, which must virtually be rebuilt at a cost of 640 million dollars during the next five to six years. Again, there is a good chance that many of these problems will *eventually* be worked out, but in the future, *durability*, not performance, should be the hallmark of power plant design.

The habit of cramming state-of-the-art technology into each aircraft has also resulted in oversized and overweight aircraft. Because the *size* of both the F-14 and F-15 has been considerably increased, these planes are easier to detect at longer ranges by radar, and easier to identify in dogfights. While both types of aircraft could probably outmaneuver any other single aircraft and engage in battle at longer distances (which is often of more theoretical than practical significance under the confused conditions of air battle), smaller aircraft such as the MiG-21 or the F-5E have distinct advantages. The lessons of the air war over North Vietnam taught US fighter pilots that they needed a lighter, faster-turning aircraft.[13] They may have such a plane in the F-16, but the problem with the F-16, quite apart from what has been noted about its engine, is that it is not an all-weather plane suitable, for example, for central Europe.[14] Moreover, extensive air combat exercises conducted by the US Air Force in Nevada in 1977 demonstrated that in one-on-one engagements, the performance of the latest generation aircraft (such as the F-15) was superior to that of the older and simpler F-5E (a plane similar to the Soviet MiG-21). The kill ratio achieved was in the order of 18 to 1 (and not as an earlier Air Force computer model showed—that an F-15 armed with the *unreliable* long range Sparrow air-to-air missile (at $108,000 apiece) would achieve an absurdly high kill ratio of 780 to 1). In the larger and more realistic dogfight configuration (four-on-four or larger), the kill ratio between the superior F-15 and the F-5E 'plummetted' to about 2 to 1. Statistics of air-to-air engagements between the Israelis and Egyptians during the 1973 war show that around 50 per cent of the dogfights involved eight or more aircraft.[15] It can be expected that the Soviet Union in Europe, for example, would be able to send a relatively much larger number of aircraft into battle than the Arabs were able to, and hence the average size air battle involving the USSR would be even larger than those in the Middle East in 1973. Moreover, the latest generation of Soviet fighter aircraft such as the MiG 21 bis, the MiG-23, and the SU-24 are better aircraft than the F-5E; in fact, the latest models of the MiG-21 bis come close in performance to matching the F-16. All of the newer Soviet aircraft are produced in large numbers.[16]

These experiments and experiences indicate that in air-to-air combat, *the number* of aircraft is more important than the sophistication of their design and theoretically superior performance. (Most air battles are conducted well below the maximum speeds and performance limits of modern fighters.)[17] If this is the case, it is of course much wiser to invest in many cheaper, more reliable fighter aircraft armed with proven and improved air-to-air missiles to compensate for any limits in their performance. It appears that less sophisticated, less costly weapons platforms produced in larger numbers and equipped with better precision-guided munitions will be a better investment than a small number of weapons platforms equipped with mediocre missiles.

Two other problems related to the 'quantities' and 'costs' of modern weapons platforms and munitions can be mentioned briefly. Primarily related to weapons platforms (particularly aircraft), the first problem consists of cost/benefit and psychological elements. There is a limit to the amount of national resources that any country can invest in a war without going bankrupt, even if it ultimately wins. The costs of modern high technology aircraft have escalated to the point where endangering them in battle is highly undesirable.[18] Few targets can justify risking a $20 to $30 million aircraft. Aircraft have become progressively more vulnerable to many relatively cheap guided and unguided anti-aircraft weapons systems (an area in which the Soviet Union, as we shall see below, has a relative advantage over the United States and NATO).

Attempts to reduce aircraft attrition resulting from fire from the ground by the use of counter-electronic measures or by the development of stand-off weapons (i.e., weapons that can fire at targets while staying outside their defensive perimeter) all have their limits. In the final analysis, the only solution to the cost/effectiveness dilemma of expensive aircraft is to design and produce larger numbers of cheaper aircraft.

The psychological dimension of this problem is that the *growing* costs of aircraft and their *shrinking* number will undoubtedly make commanders reluctant to commit such aircraft into action. The threshold of committing these aircraft into battle may be raised, and the decisions to send them into combat will have to be made somewhat higher in the hierarchy of command.[19] The time may not be far off when aircraft, like mercenary armies in the eighteenth century, will become too expensive to be risked in war. The conclusion is inevitable: more expensive aircraft in smaller numbers buy *less* security. The same is, of course, true of many other expensive major weapons systems such as tanks, ships, or even precision-guided munitions. (It can easily be seen why a tank commander will be more reluctant to commit XM-1 tanks than M-60s to a battlefield saturated with cheap and effective anti-tank weapons.)

The second point has to do with the escalating costs of modern munitions, particularly the latest types of precision-guided munitions (PGMs). It is very difficult to obtain an accurate estimate of the cost of many of the PGMs purchased by the US government; their prices vary widely in different budget years according to the number ordered, the different makes or models of each weapon, and whether the research and development costs are included.[20] But one thing is clear: their soaring costs allow for purchasing and stocking smaller quantities, while the small production lines lead to increased costs. For example, the McDonnell-Douglas air-to-sea and sea-to-sea Harpoon missile costs from $353,000 to $739,000 depending on the year and source of information used; a Hughes Maverick air-to-ground laser-guided missile costs from $45,000 to $71,000 (future Mavericks guided by a FLIR system will be even more expensive); a Sidewinder air-to-air missile is around $60,000; and a Sparrow radar-guided air-to-air missile is over $100,000; the Navy's long-range air-to-air Phoenix missile (the main armament of the Navy's F-14) has a price tag of one million dollars. The TOW anti-tank missile, the main anti-tank weapon of the US Army, costs around $4,000 per unit. The TOW is a good example of a missile whose large scale production (over 275,000 so far) has actually reduced their cost in real terms.[21]

Such munitions have even become too expensive for practice. Simulators must be used instead of live fire, certainly reducing the effectiveness of the operators, who have had no opportunity to get the 'feel' of the weapons to be used in combat. 'An Air Force pilot often goes through his whole fighter plane career without firing a real missile, while his Navy counterpart fires one every two years.'[22]

The US Air Force and Navy currently suffer from a severe shortage of air-to-air missiles. A number of reports claims that both services have enough air-to-air missiles available for only a day or two (at the most a week) of intense fighting. This would leave the United States in an extremely serious predicament in a prolonged war, since the slow rate of production and the lack of surge capability in the production of such highly complex missiles could not make up for the numbers expended. To expand the production lines would take many months, perhaps even a year.

A cautionary note is in place here. Although the accuracy and kill probability of PGMs is much higher than that of many unguided munitions, it is not as high as predicted by those who are not familiar with their limitations and their performance under actual combat conditions. In laboratory-type simulations and testing, almost all PGMs will achieve a 0.9 (or 90 per cent) probability kill (P_k) (for example, for tests of the TOW, Maverick, etc.). Under battle conditions, against moving targets using active and passive countermeasures, the real probability kill will be much lower. Even according to the often accepted definition of PGMs (i.e., 'A guided munition whose probability of making a direct hit at full range when unopposed . . . is greater than a half'[23]), seven or eight missiles are required to secure a 99 per cent kill. When the probability kill in actual battle is closer to 0.1 (10 per cent), many more missiles will be needed to knock out one target. (Close to 44 will be required to achieve a 99 per cent kill if the P_k is 0.1, and close to 90 if the P_k is 0.05 [5 per cent].) Unlike unguided munitions, which are less accurate but are immune to external interference and countermeasures once they have been fired, sophisticated munitions are *always* vulnerable. Moreover, once a sophisticated adversary has had the time to become familiar with the performance characteristics and weaknesses of the munitions in use, he will develop effective technical and tactical countermeasures. Therefore, it can be expected that in a prolonged war, the effectiveness of some PGMs may sharply decline rather than increase. If American military planners have purchased the *already small* numbers of sophisticated munitions on the basis of their theoretical—not practical—precision, their real number will be in even shorter supply.[24]

The Fallacy of the Passive Enemy

The problem of striking the correct balance between quantity and quality always has another side to it—that of the opponent. No force posture can be planned in a vacuum, independent of an evaluation of the weapons and material available to its major adversary. When it is said that quality compensates for lack of quantity, it is assumed that the 'quality' weapons of one side are clearly superior to the weapons of the adversary who emphasizes quantity. If this assumption is incorrect, i.e., if there is no *meaningful* margin of quality over the weapons systems and manpower of the adversary, then, in the absence of larger quantities of weapons systems, the adversary will obviously have the advantage.

Many Americans take it for granted that the quality of major American weapons systems is superior to that of the USSR, and therefore conclude that the United States can afford to produce fewer weapons systems while still effectively defending its interests against the USSR. But this is an unwarranted assumption.[25]

The following is a typical statement frequently made by Defense Department officials, senior military officers, and other defense experts. 'We have a high technology obsession . . . It's the old question of quantity versus quality. *The Soviets have opted for quantity and we've opted for quality.* But for all we spend, things too often end up overdesigned and just don't work' (my emphasis). The latter part of this statement is indeed often true; the problem lies with the first part of the statement. Does the evidence indicate that the Soviets have opted for quantity and not for quality? The answer appears to be that the Soviet Union has chosen both—and has ended up with a better balanced force posture. While the Russians have modern high technology weapons that are not the final word in the state of the art and that often do not equal *some* of the American major weapons systems on a one-to-one basis, most of their major weapons systems are excellent and fairly reliable. Indeed, if the combination of technology and reliability is taken into account, the major Soviet weapons systems may well be at least as battleworthy as those produced in the United States. The Soviet Union's computer and electronic industries are not as sophisticated as those of the United States, and the Soviets have not yet landed a man on the moon; but by deciding to put most of their industrial and engineering efforts into the weapons industry, they have done very well. (The Soviet Union has *not* landed a man on the moon, but its research and activity in space is currently much more enterprising than that of the United States.) One thing is clear—even if, in some cases, Soviet technology still lags behind that of the United States—the technological gap in weapons design between the two countries has narrowed considerably. Recent American intelligence reports indicate, for example, that the Soviet Union has already closed the quality gap in the production of precision-guided munitions—an area in which the United States was supposed to hold a substantial and important lead.[26]

An examination of certain important weapons systems shows that the USSR is ahead of the United States technologically as well as in the overall quality of these weapons. For example, the T-72 tank produced by the USSR in large quantities is better than the best American tank now in operation, the M-60A3. The T-72 has better protection, a more efficient shape and silhouette, and above all, a better gun than that of the *future* XM-1! (In addition, Soviet tanks are built to operate in a gas warfare environment; the XM-1 is not.) By the time the United States finally unveils its technological marvel, the XM-1 protected by Chobham armor, the USSR will already be producing a better and probably more reliable tank, the T-80.[27] The XM-1 is the first new American tank to be produced in 22 years; the T-80 will be the fourth new Soviet tank produced in 20 years.

In addition to having more tanks, the Soviets also have a much larger number of *much better* armored personnel carriers, particularly of their Infantry Fighting Vehicle (IFV), the BMP.[28] Altogether, the Soviets are estimated to have some 55,000 modern APCs and IFVs; the United States has some 10,000 M-113s, all of them of older design. The Soviets have excellent heavy and medium artillery (some 19,000 pieces), though it is still less mobile than that of the United States. They also have a much better anti-aircraft defense system, which includes the largest variety of anti-aircraft missiles (the SA-3, SA-4, SA-6, SA-8, SA-9, and the new SA-10 and SA-11); in all they have over 150,000 missiles.[29] They also have a large number of mobile anti-aircraft radar-guided guns (the ZSU-23-4), whose great effectiveness was demonstrated in the Middle East war of 1973. Not only does the Soviet Union produce advanced weapons—it also produces them in large quantities, while the American R&D establishment has many problems in moving from research to massive weapons production.

Since the early 1960s, the Soviet Union has made great progress in modernizing and expanding its navy. The United States has lost its long-held naval superiority, and the two navies are now estimated to be at about the same strength.[30] The Soviets have recently put into service a new heavy cruiser, the largest to be built by any country since the end of World War II. The 22,000 ton *Sovremenny* carries, in addition to conventional guns, an array of surface-to-surface missiles (up to 200 SSN-X-19 as well as 12 surface-to-air launchers). The Soviets are now also constructing four large anti-submarine warfare ships and three new missile-cruisers. Recent US intelligence reports indicate that the Soviet Union has already (and surprisingly) launched a new cruise-missile-firing titanium-built submarine of over 13,000 tons which, according to these reports, will make American aircraft carriers ten times more vulnerable (the range of their anti-carrier missiles extends the threat to US carriers from 20 miles to as much as 200 miles).[31]

The different doctrines behind the American and Soviet Navies demonstrate some of the problems involved in comparing the quantity and quality of different weapons designs. Such comparisons may be fairly easy where aircraft or tanks are concerned, but there is no clear way to compare a large surface navy (as the United States had in the 1950s) and a huge submarine fleet (as the Soviets had in the 1950s). Today, the bulk of the United States Navy is concentrated around 13 large aircraft carriers; the Soviet Navy has a powerful submarine fleet and a larger variety of surface vessels, with a considerable anti-carrier missile capability. Which fleet is more powerful to do what against whom is a complicated question. It appears that the United States Navy, with its larger super-carrier fleet, is better equipped for long range intervention and limited war operations (such as in the Persian Gulf), while the Soviet Navy is primarily designed for an all-out war over control of the sea lanes and communications lines of the western world. As long as the United States Navy does not have directly to engage the Soviet Navy, it is more useful as a political and limited war instrument; in an all-out war, however, American super-carriers might prove to be extremely vulnerable to Soviet conventional and nuclear missile attacks. Despite the greater suitability of US carriers for long range intervention, the United States has, over the years, developed a highly unbalanced navy; it has invested too much in the more vulnerable super-carriers, their defense systems and their aircraft, while neglecting the development of other surface vessels, particularly transport and landing capabilities (which are also essential for intervention and limited war) as well as other areas in which the Soviets excel, such as sea-to-sea missiles and conventional submarines.

It is perhaps less well known that the Soviet Air Force underwent an intensive process of modernization. Not only do the Russians now have 8,800 planes of all types as compared with 6,400 for the United States, but they have also introduced better, longer-range tactical aircraft which carry heavier payloads. Most of the aircraft now being added to the Soviet Air Force in large numbers are only half a generation behind the latest American modern aircraft. These planes include the Sukhoi-15, Su-17, Su-20, the Sukhoi-24, and the MiG-23 and -27. The Soviets are now about to introduce three new fighters: an interceptor mission variable-geometry-wing air-superiority fighter (referred to as Model K) similar to the US Navy F-14; a single-seat fighter (Model L) similar to the US F-18; and a small ground attack aircraft (Model J) designed for close air support with an anti-tank gun system similar to the US A-10.[32] It seems as if the Soviets are emulating the United States in trying to produce more sophisticated types of aircraft including the latest avionics such as terrain-avoidance radar, Doppler navigation equipment, Gatling-type guns mounted in pods, side-looking airborne radar (SLAR); real-time electro-optical (television) surveillance for reconnaissance; laser-guided weapons; and new families of anti-air and air-to-surface missiles. They will not be far behind in the development of sophisticated air-to-surface stand-off precision-munitions of all types.[33] In addition, they have made great strides in an area in which the United States held a tremendous advantage a few years ago—that of helicopter gunships. They are now producing large quantities of the Mi-24 'Hind' gunship, considered to be the most advanced of its kind in the world.[34]

Of particular concern to Western observers is the fact that the tremendous qualitative progress made by the Soviet Union during the last two decades was, unlike the American weapons procurement program, accompanied by a considerable increase in the number of major weapons platforms. This may be explained by the larger Soviet military expenditures as well as by the fact that the Soviet Union was not involved in an expensive and prolonged war as the United States was in Vietnam. But the Soviet weapons design philosophy—large production lines and lower production costs—also explains the simultaneous qualitative and quantitative expansion of the Soviet force posture.

A 1976 study comparing the costs of American and Soviet jet engines of similar performance found that Soviet engines were inherently less costly (between one-third and one-half the cost of the comparable American engine); they would have been cheaper even if they had been built by American workers, in American factories, with American materials. The reasons for the far lower cost of the Soviet engines were 'design differences, maintenance philosophy differences, and specification differences'.[35] The Soviets emphasize the development of weapons systems that are *more producible* (although Soviet designs are made to lower standards of tolerances and materials). An example of a very high performance, low-cost system design is the Soviet MiG-25 aircraft:

> It does not require advanced electronics, exotic materials, precise manufacturing techniques, or complex structures. Similarly, it used stainless steel and aluminum as the primary airframe materials, instead of synthetic materials, as used by the US. Rivets were left unground (except in aerodynamically critical areas), and welding was said to be crude, but adequate. Larger engines were used to overcome the drag penalties. The radar, though based on technology that is out of date by American standards, is one of the most powerful ever seen in an aircraft, and therefore less vulnerable to jamming. The overall MiG-25 has been described by American aerospace analysts as 'unsurpassed in the ease of maintenance and servicing', 'a masterpiece of standardization' and 'one of the most cost-effective combat investments in history'.[36]

Similar statements can be made concerning Soviet tanks, anti-aircraft missiles, and radar.

Frequently, the American research and development effort acquires a momentum of its own. Instead of producing large quantities of reliable and battle-proven weapons systems as the Russians do, the American R&D establishment usually prefers to keep developing and improving prototypes. As a result, the United States may have the latest state of the art weapons on paper, but only has limited numbers of not-necessarily-battle-proven weapons for the troops in the field.

The Russians, for example, have been producing night-seeing devices which are cheap and reliable, though by no means as advanced as their American counterparts; but the Russian devices are supplied to the troops in adequate numbers. The US Army, on the other hand:

has done extensive development work on night-seeing devices, but has bought or ordered only 20 per cent of the goggles it needs—30,000 sets at $6,000 each . . . Instead, the Army intends to wait for the next, better generation of the goggles—ones that will permit troops to see by starlight what they now can view only under at least one quarter moon—to fill the order. Those devices will not be ready until 1985.[37]

This is typical of the problems involved in the development of other major weapons systems such as a light air mobile tank or an infantry fighting vehicle.

The explanation for the delay in the large scale production of sophisticated weapons is that the best is the enemy of the good in a never-ending process of improvement.

> Once the facilitating technology is available or can be foreseen, the eventual appearance of new weapon system program ideas is almost inevitable.
>
> As long as major and minor advances in basic physical concepts and specific component performance continue to appear, new ideas for the development of weapon systems and major subsystems will be forthcoming in quantity. Defense firms in particular are prolific sources of evolutionary ideas.[38]

This continuous process can be highly counter-productive; it resembles the frame of mind of the student who constantly improves on his dissertation without ever completing it. This attitude also reflects, no doubt, the different historical experiences as well as the ideologies of both states. For the Soviet Union and for the Marxist ideology, conflict and war are an ever-present and unavoidable reality—and peace is the exception. For the United States, despite its direct participation in more prolonged wars than the Soviet Union since the end of World War II, psychologically, peace is the rule and war is the exception; following every war, the United States temporarily withdraws into isolationism. Due to geopolitical considerations, the Soviet Union cannot afford to withdraw from the affairs of the world, and therefore has a continuous program of massive weapons production and of more incremental changes in its weapons design. The American weapons design and production effort tends to vacillate between the extremes of involvement and resignation. The Soviet Union normally has the edge in the number of troops and weapons available for immediate action; the United States may have the advantage of starting a war with the most advanced weapons. The danger with the American policy is that the expansion of American forces requires *time*. Given the nature of modern war: its speed, growing rates of attrition and the growing complexity of the weapons produced (which require much longer production lead times), it is not clear at all that the United States will have the necessary time available to build up its forces before it is too late in a time of national emergency.

To claim that the USSR is emphasizing quantity over quality in military equipment is to foster a *dangerous misconception*. It may have been true in the 1950s or even the 1960s, but it is certainly not true in the 1970s and the 1980s. When it comes to military equipment, the Russians are second to none. They may have different designs and different types of weapons which do not lend themselves to a simple comparison with Western weapons, but they are certainly *not inferior*. In fact, the Russians appear to have the best of both worlds—they have quantity *and* quality.

Even if the United States had, overall, better weapons systems than the USSR, its qualitative edge would not be so overwhelming as the difference in the quantities of weapons produced by the two countries (i.e., supposing that on the average, the US weapons systems are two to three times better than those of the Soviet Union—which is doubtful—the Soviet Union still produces four to five times as many weapons). In other words, the 'quantity gap' between the US and the USSR is much greater than the 'quality gap' between them. Quality is not, however, limited to weapons systems and technology. The demand for quality must also apply to the soldiers who operate the weapons.

The Quality of Manpower and the State of the Art: Are They Mismatched?

The quality of weapons systems discussed thus far cannot be analysed without considering another qualitative dimension—the manpower available to operate the weapons. Obviously, the higher the quality of manpower—in terms of intelligence, education, training, morale, and motivation—the better they can operate complicated weapons systems in the highly confusing environment of the modern battlefield. In this context, only a limited discussion of this question will be possible.

Contemporary weapons systems can be classified according to their complexity and the number of functions they can fulfill, and according to the battlefield environment for which they are designed. Two 'ideal types' of weapons emerge from such an analysis: on the one hand, we find simple single-purpose weapons operated in a simple environment (i.e., bazookas, rifles, anti-tank missiles), and on the other hand, complex multi-purpose weapons systems operated in a complex environment (i.e., fighters, tanks, electronic warfare systems). Frequently, the more complicated weapons systems become, the more purposes they can serve; that is, a fighter-bomber can be used for interception, bombing missions, air-to-ground support, and reconnaissance. The more operations they have to carry out simultaneously (i.e., fire missiles, monitor radar screen, head-on display, speed, level of fuel, and monitor instruments), the higher the quality of manpower required to operate such a system. Complicated weapons systems tend to break down more frequently in operation; and when they do, they require high quality logistical support, in terms of routine and base maintenance as well as in immediate repairs under battlefield conditions. This puts increased demands on finding higher quality manpower for support operations. The growing demand for higher quality manpower also extends to command and control functions on all levels, especially the lower and middle-range echelons.

A battle between two tanks or between infantry is obviously a simpler affair than a battle involving many fast-moving tanks, assault and anti-tank helicopters, and self-propelled artillery, combined and coordinated with attacks from the air. This takes place in an environment where great attention must be paid to countermeasures of all types or to the possibility of operations in a chemical warfare environment. In the last decade, the complexity of the battlefield and of newly-designed latest generation weapons systems has increased exponentially. (Compare, for example, the World War II M-3 Sherman tank and the Mustang P-51 fighter-bomber with today's XM-1 or the F-14.) There is evidence that during World War II, as well as in the war in Vietnam, some weapons systems had already become too complicated for the average American soldier.[39]

There is little doubt that American weapons systems have become too sophisticated to be efficiently operated in case of malfunction by the caliber

FIGURE 1

MANPOWER QUALITY AND WEAPON SUITABILITY IN RELATION TO FACILITIES OF OPERATION AND DIVERSITY OF WEAPONS SYSTEMS

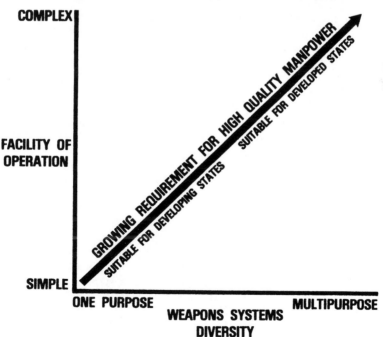

of manpower available to the All-Volunteer Force (AVF). (This situation may be compared to the overall decline in the quality of secondary school education. Now, every child is capable of making much more complicated calculations with the aid of a hand calculator or computer, but he knows less about the mathematical principles and logic behind their operation, and will remain helpless when the batteries run out. Similarly, the XM-1 can do everything faster and better, but if things should go wrong in its fire computer or range finder, its crew will be helpless.)

Currently, the quality of US manpower and its weapons design philosophy seem to work at cross-purposes. In recent years, the salary incentives and a variety of social problems and attitudes have reduced the quality of manpower available to the AVF; since it was established, a larger percentage of new recruits come from the lowest socio-economic and underprivileged groups in the United States than ever before. Some 42 per cent of the Army ranks are now black, and perhaps an additional 10 per cent belong to other minorities, primarily Hispanics. (The Marine Corps is 26 per cent black.) The percentage of blacks and other minorities in *combat units* is even higher—as high as 60 per cent in certain infantry divisions. In addition, given their lower chances of finding satisfactory employment outside the Army, the rate of black re-enlistment is higher than that of whites. The percentage of blacks in the United States Army is over three times higher than their percentage in the overall population.[40] Many of the white enlistees have lower levels of education than the blacks.

This shift in the socio-economic background of enlisted men is of course reflected in their aptitude and intelligence as well as discipline. In 1979, 46 per cent of the Army recruits belonged to what is called 'Category Four'; that is, the lowest intelligence level the Armed Forces are allowed to recruit from. The average percentage of Category Four recruits throughout the armed forces was 30: the Marines have 26 per cent; the Navy has 18 per cent; and the Air Force has 8 per cent. (The lowest IQ level accepted in this classification is 80; these recruits have a fifth grade reading level and are marginally trainable.) As a matter of policy, the percentage of soldiers of this group should never exceed 10. (If the Armed Forces had a choice, they would try not to recruit any soldiers from this group at all.) If we include in this calculation soldiers belonging to 'Category Three', well over 60 per cent of the United States Army belongs to the two lowest intelligence groups that qualify for the service.[41]

The number of high school graduates in the US Armed Forces continues to decline. A full 25 per cent of the non-high school graduates read at the sixth or seventh grade level. Many of the Army's maintenance manuals cannot be understood by the new recruits, and must be rewritten on a simpler level—or as has been suggested, on the 'comic book level'.[42] In a national emergency, the US Armed Forces would have to expand quickly, but the level of NCOs necessary for the training of new soldiers would be very low. Thus, the capacity of the United States to expand its armed forces in time of war is further restricted. This decline in the level of intelligence and education is, in turn, reflected in the level of competence—or rather, incompetence level—of American soldiers. Recent Skill Qualification Test (SQT) scores were unusually low, and very few of those tested managed to pass.[43] According to Senator Sam Nunn, a recent Army Training Study revealed that 21 per cent of American tank gunners serving on NATO duty in Germany did not know how to aim their battle sights.

People in the lowest intelligence categories had great difficulty operating the Army's air defense weapons, including the shoulder-fixed Redeye missile, because they could not remember a complex firing sequence, and could not recall the differences between silhouettes of American and enemy aircraft. They also had trouble reading instruction manuals. Tank crews were found to average 40 to 50 per cent below the skill level required by Army standards for combat readiness. Tank repairmen fared no better. When 666 repairmen were tested, they correctly diagnosed the mechanical problem from 15 to 33 per cent of the time. The chance that they would correctly repair the tank once they found the problem was between 33 and 58 per cent.[44]

Furthermore, the rising cost of fuel and ammunition, difficulties in maintenance, shortages of spare parts, and the decline in available budgets, have all caused a decrease in the amount of training, at a time when it is needed the most. This has been reflected in the lower performance level of American troops in NATO exercises, when compared to the other NATO forces.[45] The AVF also suffers from a manpower shortage; and while the absolute number of soldiers needed is small (about 4 per cent), the major shortages are primarily in the higher quality technical professions (e.g., doctors, engineers, pilots [who prefer the more lucrative civilian market] and many NCOs and petty officers). This results in a further decline of combat readiness of aircraft, tanks, ships, and other major weapons systems which require considerable maintenance work.

Approximately 40 per cent of the enlistees in today's military fail to complete their period of obligation. This high 'turbulence' or turnover rate is an alienating experience that ultimately reduces battlefield effectiveness.[46] Continuity in terms of soldiers working and training together for extended periods of time is crucial for teamwork. Tank crews, maintenance crews, or any other kind of crew, cannot function properly unless their members know each other. Teamwork is essential not only for improving technical efficiency and skills, but also for the creation of an 'esprit de corps'—a sense of comradeship and social cohesion.

The United States, a modern and advanced industrial nation with armed forces possessing the most sophisticated weapons in existence, has gradually been reduced to recruiting soldiers on the level of an underdeveloped society.

The continued existence of the gap between the quality of American weapons systems and the quality of soldiers to operate them will contribute to the further decline of American military power, and may force a war on the United States when it is least ready to defend itself. A credible level of national security comprises an effective conventional military force posture, and requires not only financial, scientific, and technological support, but also a substantial investment in human talent, intelligence, and motivation.

FIGURE 2

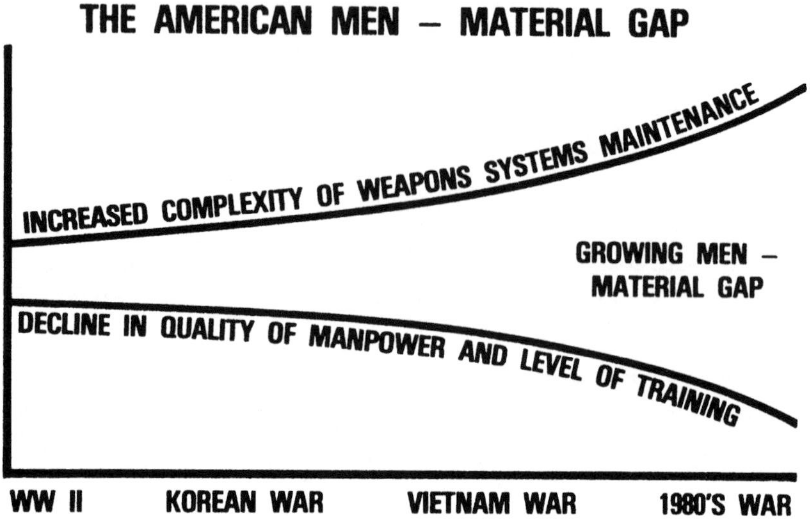

THE AMERICAN MEN — MATERIAL GAP

INCREASED COMPLEXITY OF WEAPONS SYSTEMS MAINTENANCE

**GROWING MEN —
MATERIAL GAP**

DECLINE IN QUALITY OF MANPOWER AND LEVEL OF TRAINING

WW II   KOREAN WAR   VIETNAM WAR   1980'S WAR

One cannot function without the other.

The solution to the current predicament cannot be quick or simple. It will require a new policy simplifying weapons systems procured by the United States together with an all-out effort to increase the recruitment of better qualified manpower. This will necessitate a new recruitment policy—perhaps a return to the niversal draft, or alternatively, an improved set of financial and other incentives.

All of this is not meant to imply that the Soviet Union does not have its own difficulties and weaknesses; it, too, has a serious problem in obtaining the high quality manpower needed for modern warfare. The Soviets, however, find the situation somewhat easier to deal with because of universal conscription as well as a heavier emphasis on the design of simpler weapons systems that require less training to operate.[47]

Conclusions

The current combination of qualitative and quantitative elements in the American force posture is highly imbalanced. It is imbalanced both from within (i.e., the sophistication of its weapons is not ideally suited to the decline in the quality of manpower; spare parts necessary for the maintenance of its major weapons systems are in short supply) and from without, that is, in comparison to the Soviet arsenals.

Most important of all, the American force posture has declined *quantita-*

tively well below the minimum necessary to protect its global interests vis-à-vis the Soviet Union. Overemphasis on technological excellence has actually weakened the United States. Weapons, ammunitions, and spare parts are purchased in considerably lower numbers; they have become less reliable, require more maintenance, and require more sophisticated soldiers to maintain and operate them—all this while the quality of manpower available has been declining for a considerable length of time.

Meanwhile, the Soviet Union has been steadily improving the quality of its weapons and munitions while producing them in increased numbers. Technology is not a panacea; and when carried to the extreme, it creates more problems than it solves. It cannot be decisive against an adversary who has comparable high performance technology in greater amounts.

Achieving a more realistic balance in the United States will require basic changes in the traditional approach to national security, preparations for war, and war itself. It will necessitate major adjustments in weapons design philosophy, self-criticism, and a continuing debate on these issues. It will take time and agonizing decisions, as well as changes in attitude similar to those involved, for example, in the reluctant transition from eight-cylinder gas-guzzlers to small economy cars. But it can be done.

In this context, some of the conditions that will facilitate such changes will be mentioned on a general level.

(a) It must be realized that the US conventional force posture requires as much attention and careful study as the nuclear force posture.

(b) There has been a steady decline, in absolute and relative terms, of the conventional force posture since the war in Vietnam; and the current level of forces and preparedness is inadequate to protect the national goals of the United States.

(c) Conflict is an ever-present reality, not a remote, abstract contingency.

(d) An increased level of preparedness, a more powerful force posture, and the readiness to use force are necessary to back up day-to-day policy-making and to promote American interests. Such a force must *always* be ready and available for use, not only a continually deferred promise for the future.

(e) Improvements and expansion will entail sacrifices for the American people. The constant expansion of Soviet power certainly extracts heavy sacrifices from the Soviet population. For Americans, the sacrifices will include a greater readiness to serve their country in addition to financial support. Greater contributions will also be required of all American allies. Economic realities dictate that European and Japanese allies can no longer expect to get a free ride or spend a smaller percentage of their GNP on defense.

(f) It must be realized that war and national security involve much more than technology, procurement, and material quality, and that wars cannot be won by superior technology. Nevertheless, all of the implied and not-so-implied criticism of US weapons technology is not intended to belittle the importance of advanced technology. Sophisticated technology is crucial in modern war—but it must not become an end in itself. Such technology, however, need not always be more costly, less reliable, or overly complex.

What are some remedies for the current weaknesses of the American force posture?

There must be radical changes in weapons design philosophies. Among other things, more ideas and specifications for the design should emanate from the military itself (e.g., pilots, tank corps, field commands) and less from the R&D people and the industry. Emphasis must be shifted from the state of the art, expensive weapons systems to simpler, more reliable, and more easily maintained weapons systems. The latter type of weapons will be cheaper to produce, and hence can be made in larger numbers. Given the much higher rates of attrition that can be expected in a future war, larger quantities of major weapons systems, spare parts, and ammunition must be produced. Weapons designers must learn to think small, not only in terms of F-15s, XM-1 tanks, or super-carriers, but also concerning smaller A-4 or F-5 types of tactical aircraft, air-mobile tanks, AFV and IFVs, new mortars, cheaper night-sight equipment, trucks, and the like. A greater effort should be invested in the production of precision-guided and other types of munitions. The most sophisticated weapons platforms are only as good as the weapons they carry; less sophisticated platforms with more versatile, accurate munitions will probably be cheaper and more effective.

It is of the greatest importance to introduce changes in the weapons acquisition and procurement procedures in the United States and in other Western countries. It is particularly important to encourage more competition between weapons producing companies with stricter fixed costs and 'design to cost' limits. Under such procedures, one can assume that major weapons platforms and weapons systems would achieve most of the design goals and would be only marginally inferior to weapons designs with no cost limits.

All types of weapons must be better tailored to meet the quality of manpower available, even while the military is trying to attract more highly qualified manpower. Finally, reference must be made to another qualitative point not discussed in this article, which is nevertheless of the greatest importance: more effort must be put into reexamining the US military doctrine, its relevance to modern warfare, and its suitability for different types of war in different regions of the world. Certainly, the heavy use of tactical air support, strategic bombardments, counter-guerrilla tactics, and the incredible emphasis on firepower and technology all failed to yield positive results in the Vietnam war. Furthermore, the above-mentioned suggestions for improvement will be of limited value unless the United States is able to develop a more creative and innovative military doctrine. It may not be what the United States military would like to hear, but in this area is much that requires change and much that can be learned from the experience of other nations.

NOTES

1. See Carl von Clausewitz, *On War*, edited by Michael Howard and Peter Paret (Princeton: Princeton University Press, 1976), chapter 1, section 8. 'War does not consist of a single short blow' (pp. 79-80) '. . . the very nature of war impedes the simultaneous concentration of all forces.' (p. 80.)

2. Concerning the difference in quality between the European colonial states and the colonized nations in the nineteenth century, Michael Howard emphasizes that it was much more than Western material and technological superiority which determined their superiority: 'European artillery, breech-loading rifles, and machine-guns made the outcome of any fighting almost a foregone conclusion.' But as an afterthought, he adds: 'Almost, but not quite . . . as the British survivors of the Zulu victory at Isandhlwana in 1879 and the Italian survivors of the Ethiopian victory at Adowa in 1896 would have been able to testify. Even superior weapons, if deployed without tactical skill and used against forces superior in leadership and courage, did not necessarily guarantee victory. Colonial conquest still owed at least as much to the superior cohesion, organization, and above all self-confidence of the Europeans as it did to their weapons.' See Michael Howard, *War In European History* (London: Oxford University Press, 1979) pp. 121n-122n.

3. 'The tendency of modern fighting is to become increasingly capital-intensive. One measurement of this is the amount of capital expended on killing one enemy; this has been estimated as roughly ten times as much in the Korean War as in the Second World War.' Alan S. Milward, *War, Economy and Society 1939–1945* (Berkeley: University of California, 1977), p. 170.

   In the war in Vietnam, for example, 340 artillery shells were required to achieve one enemy casualty and 1200 shells to effect one kill. See John Marriott, 'Precision-Guided Munitions', *NATO's Fifteen Nations*, Oct./Nov. 1977, Vol. 22, no. 5, p. 115. According to Jack Merrit and Pierre Sprey, 'Combining cost and kills, munitions cost per air-to-air kill has gone up by a factor of 8,000 since the Korean War (to Vietnam)'. 'Quality, Quantity, or Training', *USAF Fighter Weapons Review*, Summer 1979, p. 9. The same trend, although to a lesser extent, has recently also developed in the Soviet Union.

   This development is illustrated for the United States at war since World War II in a very instructive table prepared by William D. White in *US Tactical Air Power: Missions, Forces and Costs* (Washington, D.C.: The Brookings Institution, 1974), p. 6.

THE TREND IN US BATTLE INPUTS, MANPOWER VERSUS FIREPOWER

Item	World War II (1941–1945)	Korea (1950–53)	Southeast Asia (fiscal 1966–71)
Scale of war effort (millions of man years)	31.4	6.0	9.7
Combat exposure (millions of man-years)	6.2	0.4	0.5
Munitions expended (millions of tons)	6.96	3.13	12.92
Surface-delivered	3.94	2.11	6.59
Air-delivered	3.02	1.02	6.33
Rate of munitions expenditure (tons per man-year of war effort)	0.2	0.5	1.3

This trend not only reflects the attitude toward the conduct of warfare by all modern armies in the industrial world, but also in smaller states dependent on them, such as the Arab states, Israel, India, and Pakistan.

4. Perhaps the best example of the attempt to compensate for the quantitative decline in manpower through sophisticated technology is the extensive research effort invested in the development of MIRVED PGMs, e.g., the WAAM program in which one precision-guided missile, bomb, or artillery shell carries many smaller precision-guided warheads, each of which can independently home in on a different target (in this case, armored vehicles). Therefore, one shot by *fewer soldiers* can achieve numerous kills. See, for example, R. D. M. Furlong, 'WAAM The US Air Force's Next Generation of Anti-Armor Weapons', *International Defense Review*, no. 9, 1978, pp. 1378–9; 'Variety, Cost, Key to Munitions Plans', *Aviation Week and Space Technology*, 29 Jan. 1979, pp. 79–94; 'New Weapons System Feasibility Shown', *Aviation Week and Space Technology*, 24 Sept. 1979, pp. 173–81). See also 'The New Defense Posture: Missiles, Missiles and Missiles', *Business Week*, 11 Aug. 1980, pp. 76–81.

5. For example, according to a senior Israeli armaments expert, most of the research teams that the United States sent to Israel after the 1973 War were only interested in weapons performance, and the effectiveness of different types of American and Soviet munitions; almost no one showed interest in tactical problems, doctrinal improvisations under pressure, and the like.

6. See, for example, Jacques S. Gansler, *The Defense Industry* (Cambridge, Mass.: The MIT Press, 1980), p. 57. For the need to produce more reliable weapons, see Robert A. Moore, 'Tactical Warfare Developments Into the 1980s', *National Defense*, Aug. 1980, particularly pages 23 and 25.

7. On the problems of the XM-1 (now referred to as M-1) see for example Phil Patton, 'Battle Over the US Tank', *New York Times Magazine*, 1 June 1980, pp. 28–38, 80–83; 'The XM-1 No-Win Future', *Business Week*, 14 May 1979, pp. 112–3; 'New XM-1 Tank is Just Asking to Have Its Turret Shot Off, Critics Say', *The Christian Science Monitor*, 21 Nov. 1980, p. 11; George Custance, 'Is the XM-1 Tank Obsolete?' *National Defense* (Oct. 1980): 60–2, 88.

8. Small as it is, American tank production comes under further pressure because of the need to supply friendly countries such as Israel and Egypt, which have an insatiable appetite for modern tanks. This has been mentioned as having an adverse impact on the United States' own combat readiness. The United States currently produces, at the most, around 800 tanks per year as compared with the close to 2,700 tanks produced in the Soviet Union. *The Economist* reports that the Soviet Union produced in 1979 no less than 40,000 anti-aircraft missiles; 1,800 combat aircraft (including combat helicopters), 3,000 tanks, and 4,000 armored personnel carriers. *The Economist*, 9 Aug. 1980, p. 36. Similar estimates are also suggested in the 8 Feb. 1978 issue of *Aviation Week and Space Technology* (p. 59). The USSR outproduces the US by a ratio of 5.9:1 in tanks, 3.2:1 in armored personnel carriers, 8:1 in artillery, and 1.9:1 in fighter aircraft. See also *US News and World Report*, 11 Feb. 1980, p. 17; Subrata N. Chakravarty, 'The Great Push-button Delusion', *Forbes*, 15 Sept. 1980, p. 49. The Soviet Union can be said to outproduce the United States in almost all types of major weapons platforms.

9. See John M. Collins, *US-Soviet Military Balance: Concepts and Capabilities 1960–1980* (New York: McGraw-Hill Publications, 1980), p. 229; also Chuck Myers, 'Hi/Lo What?' *Military Science and Technology* 1 (no date): 48–52. Myers contends that the primary motive behind the Hi/Lo mix concept was not so much the wish to produce larger quantities of cheaper aircraft as much as it was to produce less complex and less sophisticated fighters, since the experience of the 1960s demonstrated the 'inverse relationship between sophisticated equipment and a quality combat force' (p. 48). The F-18 can hardly be referred to as an unsophisticated aircraft.

10. The European (West German-British-Italian) Tornado multi-role combat aircraft has also run into very serious cost over-runs, *The Economist*, 21 Feb. 1981, p. 40. During the Second World War, Fighter aircraft were produced in very large series (the P-51 Mustang over 14,000; the P-47 over 15,000; the F-4U over 12,000). During the early 1950s, the F-86 was produced in numbers over 6,000, and by the late 1950s and 1960s, the F-4 Phantom was produced in the lower thousands—over 5,000. The F-5 Freedom Fighter, the most widely deployed in the non-communist world, has also been produced in large numbers.

Over 3,450 have been produced so far at about $4.0 million in current prices. Today's super-sophisticated aircraft are produced in the order of the high-hundreds/lower thousands: 521 of the F-14 were ordered; 729 of the F-15; 1366 of the F-16; and 1377 (1,030) of the F-18. (See William D. White, *US Tactical Air Power* (Washington: The Brookings Institution, 1974), p. 47. This of course means that fewer missions can be flown, that fewer planes can attack fewer targets. See also Seymour J. Deitchman, *New Technology and Military Power: General Purpose Military Forces for the 1980s and Beyond* (Boulder, Colorado: Westview Press, 1979), chapter 3 Tactical Air and Air Defenses, pp. 29-63.

11. It would be interesting to compare the maintenance level of other modern air forces, such as those of Sweden, West Germany, Israel, or even the Soviet Union, with that of the United States. The data for other countries are, however, highly classified and cannot be obtained. It does appear, though, that *other* Western countries maintain higher standards of maintenance.

12. See *Aviation Week and Space Technology*, 16 Feb. 1981, p. 90.

13. See Pierre Sprey, 'Mach 2, Reality or Myth?' *International Defense Review* 8 (1980), 1209–12; also Myers, 'Hi/Low', p. 50.

14. See David R. Griffiths, 'F-16 Questioned in Defense Dept., Congress', *Aviation Week and Space Technology*, 18 Aug. pp. 92–3. 'General Dynamics' F-16 air combat fighter is being viewed within both the Defense Department and Congress as an incomplete system at a time when increased emphasis is being placed on all-weather, beyond-visual range, air-to-air systems. Concurrently, the debate is growing about future procurement rates of the F-16. As a result, there will be increased reliance on the old McDonnell Douglas F-4 and its AIM-7E, beyond-visual-range missile with "Low combat lethality".' (p. 92) Similarly, the US tactical support aircraft, the A-10, is not suitable for all-weather operations required for Europe, while the pilot workload does not enable him to effectively engage his targets. A two-seater version is now planned to improve the operational capabilities of the plane.
     The concepts that gave birth to both the F-16 and the A-10 do not seem to have been carefully thought through and did not fully take into account the European weather and battlefield conditions. These planes are nevertheless still being produced in relatively large quantities.

15. This was the well-known AIMVAL/ACEVAL air-to-air exercise designed to evaluate US air-to-air fighter tactics, as well as the performance of different types of weapons and aircraft. The exercise demonstrated (1) that force ratios are important, (2) that the presence of 'a crowd' severely reduces the effectiveness of sophisticated weapons systems, and (3) that the relative size and signature of the contending aircraft is very significant.
     The importance of force ratios is also as true for other major weapons systems such as in tank battles. This is demonstrated by the two Lanchester Laws. See *Models, Data and War: A Critique of the Foundation for Defense Analyses* (Washington D.C.: The General Accounting Office, 12 March 1980 PAD-80-21), pp. 66–9.

16. According to an article in the authoritative *International Defense Review*, new models of the old mid-1950s MiG-21 will be able to match the new ultra-sophisticated and expensive F-16 in almost all respects. See Georg Danyalev, 'MiG-21 bis and F-16A Air Combat Potential: A Comparison', *International Defense Review*, 11 (1978): 1429–34. Even in its newest versions, the MiG-21 will of course be much cheaper than the comparable F-16.

17. Sprey, 'Mach 2: Myth or Reality?'.

18. In his article (cited above), Myers goes even farther by suggesting that high technology, inexpensive, surface-to-surface missiles can undermine the basis for a separate tactical fighter-bomber air force. Many of the air-to-ground attacks can, in his opinion, be accomplished by surface-to-surface missiles for 20 per cent of the cost and without the loss of valuable pilots. (Myers, 'Hi/Lo', pp. 51–2.) This proposition is highly questionable. Against relatively small and very mobile targets (such as tanks), surface-to-surface missiles cannot be as accurate or effective. Assuming a reasonable rate of attrition (below half a per cent), aircraft can be used again and again, whereas missiles can be used only once.

19. Air Force Colonel John Boyd quoted in Stuart H. Loory, *Defeated: Inside America's Military Machine* (New York: Random House, 1973), pp. 393–9. This is also the conclusion reached by Merrit and Sprey. 'The high cost of new systems inevitably produces a plethora of safety rules which inhibit essential realistic training, for the loss or damage of a unit of equipment is prohibitively expensive.' 'Quality, Quantity or Training', *USAF Fighter Weapons Review*, Summer 1974, p. 14.

20. See for example, Tom Gervasi, *Arsenal of Democracy: American Weapons Available for Export* (New York: Grove Press, 1977).

21. The TOW anti-tank missile is an exception in that its price has been cut by 25 per cent since the first missiles were produced in 1969. There is, however, some doubt that the TOW missile would be able to penetrate the new armor of the T-64, T-72, and T-80. See *International Defense Review* 11 (no. 9, 1978): p.1373; also Drew Middleton, 'Soviets Introducing New Tank in Europe', *New York Times*, 16 March 1980, p. 7.

22. See George C. Wilson, 'Missiles Too Costly for Practice by Pilots', *Washington Post*, 23 June 1980, p. 2. Yet another reason given for this situation is an 'embarrassing shortage' of missiles. (For example, only a third of the necessary Sparrow AIM7 are in stock for the F-15.) The higher costs of air-to-air missiles reduce the number being purchased. The Air Force and Navy have air-to-air missiles sufficient for only a day or two of intense fighting. See Richard Barnard, 'A Short War: Navy, Air Force Face Severe Missile Shortage', *Defense Week*, 19 May, 1980, p. 1.

23. See James Digby, *Precision-Guided Weapons*, Adelphi Papers, no. 118 (London: IISS, 1975), p.1.

24. According to Secretary of Defense Brown, it was assumed before the war in Vietnam that the kill reliability of the Navy AIM-7E would be 0.5. Yet in Vietnam, it demonstrated a kill probability of only 0.11. In his own words, 'If the implied four or fivefold improvement is not realized in the future, the penalty will be much greater because of the difficulty of surging production of such complex weapons.' Cited in 'Secretary of Defense Brown's Memo on Tac Air Readiness', *Armed Forces Journal*, May 1980, p. 34.

25. It is important to recall that the Soviet Union's technological capability has more than once been seriously underestimated by the United States. In the late 1940s, the United States underestimated by a few years the USSR's ability to produce an 'A' bomb and later an 'H' bomb. In both instances, the USSR produced these weapons way ahead of the schedule computed by the Americans. Later, in the mid-1950s, US scientists and engineers refused to believe that the USSR would be able to orbit a satellite before the United States. Despite all preceding Soviet announcements, US political leaders and scientists were completely taken by surprise when the USSR launched its first Sputnik. Yet many Americans still perpetuate the myth of the Soviet Union's technological backwardness and its alleged emphasis on quantity at the expense of quality. Perhaps this is just wishful thinking—or it may be something more dangerous—blind arrogance.

26. According to John Collins, the US technological military superiority (i.e., the American qualitative edge) is tenuous at best. The USSR has the edge in no less than twelve important areas of military technology; the United States has a similar lead in only eleven. Although the US is catching up in four areas of advanced technology, the Soviet Union is closing the gap in eleven. See John M. Collins, *US-Soviet Military Balance: Concepts and Capabilities 1960-1980*, (New York: McGraw-Hill Publications, 1980), pp. 101–4; also Drew Middleton, 'Soviet Arms Technology Has Shown Steady Gains', *New York Times*, 8 December 1980, pp. 1:A10.

27. Middleton, 'Soviet Introducing New Tank in Europe', p. 7. See also John K. Cooley, 'How American Russian Capabilities Match Up', *Christian Science Monitor*, 5 March 1980, p.12; 'The Red Army's New Look', *Newsweek*, 11 Feb. 1980, pp. 46–7; also *International Defense Review* 12 (no. 8, 1979):1279; John K. Cooley, 'Soviet Tanks Carrying West's Secret Armor', *Christian Science Monitor*, 19 Aug. 1980, p. 7.

28. Stuart Aversach, 'Soviet Forces Under Test: Superior Machines, Slow Reaction', *Washington Post*, 12 Aug. 1980, p. 1.

29. Major Tyrus W. Cobb, 'Tactical Air Defense: A Soviet-US Net Assessment', *Air University Review*, 30 (March/April 1979), 18–39.

30. This is the evidence of US Navy leaders. See 'US Has Lost Naval Superiority Over Soviets, Leaders Tell Hill Panel', *Washington Post*, 6 February, 1981, p. 10. A more optimistic view is found in Drew Middleton, 'Amid Shortages Navy Maintains Edge Over Soviets', *New York Times*, 25 Sept. 1980, p.1;16.

31. See Drew Middleton, 'Soviets At Sea: New Ships for Distant Bases', *New York Times*, 25 Jan. 1981, p. 3; George C. Wilson, 'Soviets Launch Huge New Attack Submarine', *Washington Post*, 9 Jan. 1981, p.1, also Stephen Webbe 'Soviet Navy a "Growing Challenge" to West' *Christian Science Monitor*, 3 March 1981, p. 4.

32. 'Soviets to Field Three New Fighters,' *Aviation Week and Space Technology*, 26 March 1979, pp. 14–16.

33. See *Aviation Week and Space Technology*, 15 Dec. 1980, p.13.

34. See Lt. Col. Lynn M. Hansen (USAF), 'Soviet Combat Helicopters', *International Defense Review*, 11 (no. 8, 1978): 1292–1346.

35. Gansler, *The Defense Industry*, p. 83.

36. Ibid., pp. 251–2. Former Under-Secretary of Defense, William J. Perry suggests that Soviet fighter aircraft built in the last decade are in general more complex, and more expensive than comparative US aircraft. (See *Washington Post*, 22 Feb. 1981, p. C1.) This is highly unlikely, although he may use other criteria to measure complexity (he is not clear about the criteria used).

37. Robert C. Toth and Norman Kempster, 'US Pushing Weaponry Technology to the Limit', *Los Angeles Times*, 10 Sept. 1980.

38. Merton J. Peck and Frederick M. Scherer, *The Weapons Acquisition Process: An Economic Analysis* (Boston: Harvard Business School, 1962), p. 236; see also J. Ronald Fox, *Arming America: How the US Buys Weapons* (Boston: Harvard Business School, 1974), p.10.

39. See Alan Milward, *War, Economy and Society 1939–1945*, pp. 192–3. This was also evident in the war in Vietnam, see for example, Stuart H. Loory, *Defeated: Inside America's Military Machine* (New York: Random House, 1973), pp. 341–3, in particular his comments on the maintenance problems of the F-4 Phantom.

40. See James Webb, 'The Draft: Why the Army Needs It', *Atlantic Monthly*, April 1980; Juan Cameron, 'It's Time to Bite the Bullet on the Draft', *Fortune*, 7 April 1980, p. 54; John Fialka, 'Social Upheaval Changes Shape of Enlisted Ranks in the Army', *Washington Star*, 18 Dec. 1980, p.1; also Charles C. Moskos, 'How to Save the All-Volunteer Force', *The Public Interest*, Fall 1980, pp. 74–89.
    Despite their growing proportion in the armed services, blacks make up only 4.7 per cent of the officers in all branches of the armed services. The Navy has the lowest proportion of black officers, 2.3 per cent of its total of 62,127; that is, approximately 1,400 black officers. See Dennis Collins, 'The Navy and Minorities: Two Views', *Washington Post*, 1 Aug. 1980, p. 23.

41. Category Four recruits require one and a half times as much training, both in time and frequency of repetition, as Category Three recruits. The cost of training material, such as ammunition, was 40 per cent more. Performance decay was significantly greater among lower mental groups. See 'Doubts Mounting About All-Volunteer Force', *Science*, 5 Sept. 1980, p. 1095; see also John J. Fialka, '25% of Recruits in Low-Intelligence Category', *Washington Star*, 11 March 1980, p.10; Michael Getler, 'Recruits' Mental Abilities Lower than Reports', *Washington Post*, 1 Aug. 1980, p. 1.

42. 'Doubts Mounting About All-Volunteer Force', *Science*, 5 Sept. 1980, p.1095. A check at Fort Benning in 1976 revealed that 53 per cent of the enlistees had a fifth grade or lower reading ability.

43. See John J. Fialka, 'Army Views Manpower Situation as a Crisis', *Washington Star*, March 1980, p.12; also George C. Wilson, 'Senate Balks at Proposal to Trim Army by 25,000', *Washington Post*, 2 July 1980, p. 2; 'Army, Quantity and Quality', *Washington Star*, 27 June 1980.

These are some of the data for a select number of SQTs.

Number Tested	Percent Passed
—1,547 artillery crewmen	14
—385 nuclear weapons maintenance specialists	10
—371 tank turret and artillery repairmen	2
—1,095 Hawk missile crewmen	18
—2,795 cannon fire direction specialists	19
—1,122 traffic management specialists	26
—3,022 track vehicle mechanics	11
—1,633 computer programmers	23
—8,137 aviation maintenance personnel	19

Among last year's (1979) results in the Skill Qualification Tests 83 per cent of transportation personnel failed; 69 per cent of those working in communications operations could not pass; 75 per cent of food service personnel; 49 per cent of combat engineers failed, as did 49 per cent of field artillery men. For the problems created by the low quality manpower, see also Juri Toomepuu, 'Literacy as a Measure: An Argument for High Quality Military Manpower', *National Defense*, Jan.-Feb. 1979, pp. 47–56.

44. See Fialka, '25% of Recruits in Low-Intelligence Category', *Washington Star*, 11 March 1980, p.10; Webb, 'Why the Army Needs It', *Atlantic Monthly*, April 1980.

45. John Fialka, 'US Posts Dismal Record In NATO Competitions', *Washington Star*, 16 Dec. 1980, p.1.

46. The high turnover and 'personnel turbulence' between military units weakens morale and cohesion of primary groups and considerably reduces combat effectiveness. It has been observed that 'the American Army since World War II has experienced a progressive reduction of primary-group cohesion until the Vietnam War, when it may be argued, it almost ceased to exist. The major thrust of our argument is that the performance of the American Army during the Vietnam War indicates a military system which failed to maintain cohesion under conditions of combat stress. Our data suggest that the Army in the field exhibited a low degree of unit cohesion at initially all levels of command and staff, but principally at the covert squad, platoon and company level . . . It seems evident that to the extent that cohesion is a major factor in maintaining an effective fighting force, the Army in Vietnam had ceased to be effective. Indeed, the Army began to border on an undisciplined, ineffective, almost anomic mass of individuals who collectively had no goals and who, individually, only sought to survive the length of their tours'. See Richard A. Gabriel and Paul L. Savage, *Crisis in Command: Mismanagement in the Army* (New York: Hill and Wang, 1978), pp. 8–9, 13, 31. The Army is trying to improve this situation. See John J. Fialka, 'Army Plans Reforms to Make Fighting Units More Cohesive', *Washington Star*, 6 Sept. 1980, p.1.

47. The Soviets appear to do a little better, although they have their own problems. See 'Soviet Armed Services Showing Weaknesses In Several Key Areas', *New York Times*, 9 Dec. 1980, p.1; A-10.

APPENDIX I

A Graphic Presentation of the Doctrine of Quality Versus Quantity in the Construction of a National Force Posture

Intended to serve as an heuristic device, the following analysis should not be construed as a strictly economic type of argument, nor is it meant to imply that the issues treated here can be analyzed and presented with any measure of precision. My much more limited purpose is to demonstrate some of the considerations and constraints involved in designing a national force posture.

FIGURE 3

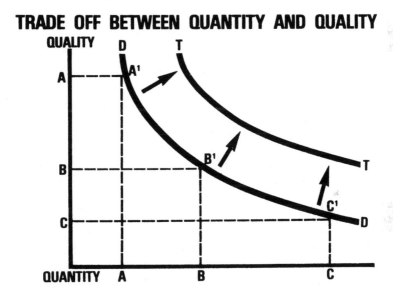

TRADE OFF BETWEEN QUANTITY AND QUALITY

The vertical axis represents the qualitative elements that are necessary in designing a modern military force. The qualitative elements can in turn be divided into two groups: the first, *material quality*, includes advanced technology, reliability of weapons, and performance levels; the second, *nonmaterial quality*, includes the quality of manpower, level of training, leadership, command control and organization, choice of military doctrine, quality of planning, and staff work.[2]

The horizontal axis represents *quantities* of all kinds, that is, the number of soldiers mobilized, the number of combat divisions, the number of fighter aircraft, tanks, stockpiles of ammunition and the like that are available at a given time.

Quantities are relatively easy to measure, but it is methodologically much more difficult to measure the value of material and non-material qualities, which is of course much more subjective.

Curve DD represents the possible combinations of quality and quantity at a given national defense budget; it assumes that a country has adequate and more or less balanced resources (human, financial, technological, industrial) that will allow it to choose between various levels of quantity and quality. The political and military backers of a country might decide to emphasize quality over quantity (AA'A); this could, for example, be the choice made by the United States, Israel,[3] or West Germany.

Another country might opt for combination (BB'B), in which qualitative and quantitative elements receive approximately equal emphasis (e.g., the USSR). A third, less developed nation might prefer quantity over quality due to the lack of sophisticated technology and a large but uneducated population. Because its social and technological infrastructure is less developed, such a country has little choice but to stress quantity in reaching the desired level of military strength (CC'C) (e.g., the People's Republic of China).

Should the Chinese try to improve the quality of their weapons, it can safely be assumed that, given their current level of technological development, such a process would take years if not decades. And if the United States should decide to increase the size of its armed forces, or to shift the emphasis from the material to the non-material elements of quality, this process would also take many years. Thus, once any state has chosen a specific force posture, it will take several years, depending on its resources and earlier investments, to switch to another force posture (i.e., another point on the same curve [DD] emphasizing a different combination of quality and quantity). Moreover, to *increase* its total power by investing more in its armed forces, that is, by moving to a new power curve (TT'), would take even longer.

A state can expand its total military power in one of the following ways:

(a) It can improve the quality of its armed forces without increasing their quantity. This can be accomplished by designing new and better weapons such as PGMs; by increasing firepower and automation and replacing old equipment; by improving the maintenance level of its military equipment; or by intensifying the training of troops. Following the war in Vietnam, the establishment of the AVF, and the reduction of the American force posture from a 2.5 capability to a 1.5 capability, Pentagon experts hoped nevertheless to maintain American military power by developing precision-guided munitions, improving firepower and automation, etc.; in other words, they hoped to compensate for the 'quantitative decline' with high performance weapons systems.[4] This has also been the case with smaller states such as Sweden, Switzerland, and Israel, which do not have the manpower. By increasing the size of its armed forces in the late 1970s, Israel reached the limit for quantitative expansion, and now can augment its power only through an even heavier investment in, and emphasis on, qualitative elements.

(b) Other countries may want to increase their military power, but do not have access to modern technology and/or cannot further improve the quality of manpower by using different recruiting policies or training methods. They cannot improve the qualitative elements of their force posture in the short run, although they can expand their armed forces by adding more of the same—more soldiers, tanks, and fighters.

Countries in a conflict situation will try to increase their military power by investing in *all* dimensions of military power; this means that the 'power curve' will be pushed from DD to TT. The United States may decide to improve the level of training, its military doctrine, command structure, and develop more reliable, better tanks, while at the same time increasing the number of recruits, armored division artillery launch tubes, and other major weapons systems. This is what the United States did when it entered World War II and the Korean War.

The United States has always concentrated on the doctrine of quality primarily in its material manifestations. Since 1970, given the change in missions resulting from the Nixon Doctrine and the American-Chinese rapprochement, the United States reduced the quantitative elements of its armed forces. The total increase in power achieved by the improvement in performance and the 'quality' of its weapons systems appears to have been smaller than the decrease in power resulting from less of the non-material qualitative dimensions (such as the quality of manpower and training) and the lower number of tanks, ships, and divisions, resulting from that choice.

FIGURE 4

CRITICAL QUANTITATIVE MASS AND CRITICAL QUALITATIVE THRESHOLD

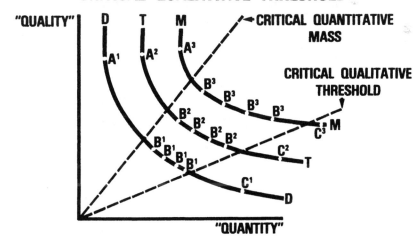

Additional investment in the state of the art technology implies that it will yield increasing returns in terms of overall power for the United States, whereas the point of diminishing returns was passed much earlier.

Moreover, one can take advantage of superior technology only if and when it matches the level of investment and performance in other dimensions, such as higher quality manpower, adequate training, or a high standard of equipment maintenance.

It is also crucial to maintain an adequate balance between the level of quantitative and qualitative expansion. To be able to fight a two front war, the United States will have to expand its investment in conventional power from curve DD to curve TT. To be able to fight on two fronts (e.g., Central Europe and the Persian Gulf), *and simultaneously* maintain a high degree of alertness elsewhere (e.g., Korea or the Far East), the United States would have to increase its investment even further, from curve TT to curve MM.

Not every point chosen on each of these curves (which represents a given combination of quantitative and qualitative elements) would be sufficient. A war on two fronts would, for example, require a certain minimal quantitative level of troops, tanks, fighter-bombers, aircraft carriers, or any other weapons system below which no qualitative edge would compensate for the lack of 'numerical' strength. This level can be referred to as the 'critical mass' (or critical quantitative mass) below which a war cannot be successfully fought on the necessary number of fronts. (See Fig. 2 line of minimum quantitative level.) Points A_1, A_2, A_3 are well below that necessary minimum.

A hypothetical example will clarify this issue. *If* the United States needed four aircraft carriers in the Mediterranean Sea to protect NATO's Southern Flank in time of war, and five in the Indian and Persian Gulf areas to protect the sea routes, but had only five available, it could *not* defend its interests simultaneously on both fronts. It could decide to concentrate the necessary number of carriers on one of the fronts while sacrificing the other. Twenty XM-1 tanks cannot hold their own against 200 Soviet T-72s, no matter how good their crews and material quality are. (Although they might hold out against 200 Iraqi T-72s.) Therefore, the United States cannot afford quantitatively to be on any of the A points on each of the power curves, but in each case any of the B points would be adequate.

Similarly, no amount of quantity can compensate for material quality if it should drop below a certain minimal level (Fig. 2 line of minimum qualitative level). An extreme case would be a country which only has piston-engined World War II-type fighters, having to fight an adversary who possesses many modern jet fighters. (At one point in the early 1950s, Israel actually came close to being in such a situation vis-à-vis its Arab neighboring states.) The Polish cavalry attacks against German tanks in 1939 are a well-known example; and another extreme case was the attacks of Zulu tribesmen or the Mahadi forces in Omdurman against British machine guns. If American infantry had to stop the Soviet T-80 tanks, they would not have a good chance of succeeding if the TOW anti-tank missiles were ineffective against their armor. Any choice of quality at points C_1, C_2, or C_3, below the minimum technological threshold necessary, would therefore not be good enough to combat an enemy who had technological superiority in certain key weapons systems.

*   *   *

Most attempts to evaluate the military balance of power, such as the annual military balance of power publication by the London Institute of Strategic Studies, tend to focus on the measurable quantitative elements while ignoring the no less important but more difficult material and non-material qualitative elements. A more realistic evaluation of the military strength of a nation must consider at least some of these qualitative elements.[6]

FIGURE 5

COMPARATIVE MILITARY BALANCE MEASURED IN TERMS OF QUALITY AND QUANTITY

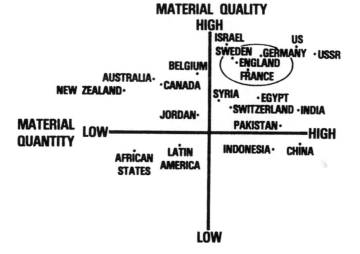

The matrix can help us to classify the military power of states according to the relative part of quality and quantity in the force posture. Ideally, four types of combinations are possible:

1. High Quality and High Quantity (i.e., US, USSR)
2. High Quality and Low Quantity (Canada, Holland, Norway, etc.)
3. Low Quality and High Quantity (China)
4. Low Quality and Low Quantity (Chad, Sri Lanka, etc.)

(A similar matrix can be made with an axis of high-low material quality and high-low manpower quality.)

NOTES – APPENDIX I

1. In reality, a country's ability to change its force posture to meet a new threat is limited in the short to medium run. National security is dynamic subject matter, but its dynamics of adaptation and change have many constraints in the short run. Hence the desirability of designing a force posture that will cover the maximum number of scenarios at a given level of resources.

2. For the sake of simplicity it will be assumed (unless otherwise stated in the text) that I refer primarily to material quality, in particular the quality of major weapons systems. In reality, as stated in the text, qualitative elements also include non-material elements. In fact, there often is a trade-off between the *material* and *non-material* qualitative elements since, for example, a heavy investment in more sophisticated aircraft will reduce the funds available for more training or reduce the budget available for salaries to attract and retain highly qualified soldiers.

3. The US can have a large range of choices between qualitative and quantitative elements in determining or reaching its desired level of military power. Israel, on the other hand, has little choice. Since it is a small country with a limited population base facing an enormous Arab coalition, it must emphasize quality of all types; otherwise, it would simply have no chance of survival.

4. The American decision to focus on material quality to compensate for its overall quantitative decline was *not* matched by an attempt to improve its non-material qualitative elements. For example, qualitative technological improvements were not matched by a corresponding improvement in the quality of training or maintenance. Despite the great increase in the quality of weapons (frequently only a theoretical improvement because of reliability problems), the overall quality of the US military force posture *may have in fact declined.*

5. See also Alan S. Milward, *War, Economy and Society 1939–1945* (Berkeley: University of California Press, 1977), p. 171.

    The trend towards capital-intensiveness in warfare means that in the armaments industry there is often less scope than in other industrial sectors for suiting the nature of the technology to the nature of the economy; once they are engaged in pitched battle, even North Vietnamese soldiers must fight with complex modern machines. There is certainly room for manoeuvre and for marginal adjustments, and it is not necessary to have *all* the best available armaments, technology, but there are many strategic situations where no amount of labour will compensate for certain kinds of technological deficiencies.

6. American military analysts often make this mistake in evaluating the force posture of countries such as Iran during the Shah's regime, Saudi Arabia, or even Iraq and Egypt. Because it had purchased so many modern weapons, Iran under the Shah was considered to be at least a regional power—whereas in fact the Shah had projected an image of power, and the level of maintenance, training and organization of his army was very low. Likewise, F-15s sold to Saudi Arabia may increase its prestige, but do not add much to its real power. The mistaken assumption is that such modern weapons in the hands of Iranians and Saudis will be as efficient as in the hands of Americans.

3

Technological Surprise in War

A hiatus exists between inventors who know what they could invent, if they only knew what was wanted, and the soldiers who know, or ought to know, what they want, and would ask for it if they only knew how much science could do for them. You have never really bridged that gap yet.

Let me point out the need of establishing without delay an Anti-Tank Committee to study the methods by which tanks can be defeated. This body should work in the closest harmony with those concerned in the production and design of tanks, each striving to defeat the other, exchanging information and perfecting their methods. It is not to be supposed that the Germans will not develop tanks in their turn. We have the enormous advantage of being able to experiment on ourselves with them, and to find out the best ways by which they may be defeated. We ought to have a complete anti-tank outfit by the spring.

Don't familiarize the enemy by degrees with these methods of attack. Apply them when all is ready on the largest possible scale, and with the priceless advantage of surprise.[1]

Churchill

STRATEGIC AND TECHNOLOGICAL SURPRISE

The unexpected appearance of new weapons* on the battlefield, from the stirrup[2] to the atomic bomb can have a critical impact on the outcome of war. 'The history of warfare from antiquity to the present records innumerable attempts to secure by some new contrivance an immediate tactical advantage, perhaps a decisive one. In such inventions the essential purpose is to obtain one's end before the adversary can bring counter-measures to bear. It is the time interval that counts.'[3] 'Technology is a means of overcoming strategical and tactical handicaps and inequalities.'[4] Like its strategic counterpart, technological surprise is a powerful force multiplier capable of vastly improving the likelihood of victory. A successful strategic surprise attack facilitates the destruction of a sizeable portion of the enemy's forces at a much lower cost to the attacker by throwing the inherently stronger defense psychologically off

---

* I use the term 'weapons' as an abbreviation for weapon system, weapons platform or equipment depending on the context.

balance and temporarily reducing his resistance. In more general terms, the numerically inferior side seizes the initiative by concentrating superior forces at the time and place of its choosing. Clearly, then, the incentive to resort to strategic surprise and deception is particularly strong for armies that are only too cognizant of their relative vulnerability. Armies perceiving themselves as superior, however, lack the motivation to employ such methods. Although strategic surprise in modern military history has seldom failed in terms of its *initial* impact, surprising the enemy *per se* does not mean that the attacker has exploited the impact of the surprise in the best possible way or that he is assured ultimate victory. The attacker is often so amazed by the effectiveness of his own surprise that he is unprepared to take advantage of the opportunities it presents. The benefits reaped from strategic surprise are maximized to the degree that plans for the attack are flexible and a suitable military doctrine has been developed. Such a doctrine delegates more initiative to field commanders, who are encouraged to improvise and accept risks. Thus, the accomplishment of surprise itself seldom constitutes more than the first phase of planning; the second entails meticulous preparations for the best possible exploitation of the projected surprise attack.[5]

Technological surprise offers similar advantages to *both* the attacker and defender. The achievement (or avoidance) of technological surprise was therefore recognized by R.V. Jones as one of the most important tasks of scientific intelligence. Of the five basic objectives he outlined for scientific intelligence, three directly pertain to this issue:

1. To ascertain the development of new weapons and improvement of existing ones by other countries.
2. To mislead potential or actual enemies about our own weapons.
3. To mislead the enemy about the success of his own weapons.
4. To assist technically in espionage and its counter (including codes and ciphers, where technicians are becoming important at the expense of classical scholars).
5. To co-ordinate scientific and technical intelligence between the services.[6]

Thinking along the same lines, Professor Hinsley noted that

looking back at the end of the war, the intelligence branch of the Air Ministry considered that next only to providing intelligence about the order of battle and the operational intentions of the enemy air forces, its main task had been 'to ensure that the enemy should not spring a surprise through some secret weapons or new type of aircraft or armament'.[7]

There is a common desire on the part of nations at war to employ technological surprise both independently and in support of strategic surprise as a means of gaining an invaluable advantage over their adversaries; this desire has increased tremendously since the Industrial Revolution, most notably during the First and Second World Wars. Progressing at an almost geometric rate, science and technology are today limited *in theory* only by the imagination of the soldier and scientist, and *in practice* by the availability of the necessary resources.

We have now reached the point at which the soldier can order almost any type of weapon tailored to suit his preferred military doctrine and strategic plans or to provide solutions to specific tactical problems. Given this actual and potential technological abundance, one of the most crucial decisions a military organization faces is selection of the best possible combination of new weapons systems – one which will give it the desired edge on the battlefield. As a result of this technological progress and the proliferation of new weapons systems, technological surprise can be expected to become a dominant feature of every future war.

Yet while strategic surprise has been studied extensively as a strategic and intelligence problem, technological surprise has received only scant attention in the open literature. In outlining a tentative theoretical framework for the study of technological surprise, I will discuss the following aspects of the subject: its definition; different types; the conditions necessary for its achievement; the ideal or optimal timing; its net impact on the military balance of power in the short and long run; warning and countermeasures; the similarities and differences between strategic and technological surprise; and its place in future wars.

TECHNOLOGICAL SURPRISE DEFINED

Technological surprise is the unilateral advantage gained by the introduction of a *new* weapon (or by the use of a known weapon in an innovative way) *in war* against an adversary who is either *unaware* of its existence or *not ready* with effective counter-measures, the development of which requires *time*.

This definition requires a brief explanation.

1. *A New Weapon*. True technological surprise involves a new weapon, but in many cases the use of *known* weapons in conjunction with a new doctrine of employment can also cause unpleasant surprises. For example, although submarines were not a new weapon in the Second World War, the innovative way in which the Germans used them during its early phases came as a complete surprise to the British, who had been convinced that the development of ASDIC[8] provided them with a satisfactory anti-submarine countermeasure. As it turned out, ASDIC

was ineffective against the new German submarine attack tactics of attacking ships at *night* and on the *surface*. As in most strategic and technological surprises, adequate and timely warning signals were ignored. In this case, the same tactics had already been tested by the end of the First World War, and in a book published in Berlin (1939), Captain Karl Donitz had openly discussed the possibility of night attacks by surfaced submarines.[9]

Another well-known example is the use of the German 88mm. anti-aircraft (Flak) gun as an anti-tank weapon in North Africa. This adaptation of the 88mm. gun was a powerful shock to the British, although the Germans had previously used it in this capacity during their campaign in the West in 1940.[10] The British continued to underestimate the armor-piercing capabilities of German anti-tank guns until late 1941 because they possessed little information on the subject. Though devastating, British losses to the 88mm. Flak gun during Operation Battleaxe in June 1941 had not even been correctly explained after the battle ended, since Operation Battleaxe produced little new technical intelligence.[11] Correlli Barnett comments on this episode as follows:

> This magnificent German weapon had been designed as an anti-aircraft gun, but the Germans found that it was far superior in hitting tanks to their own new 50mm. anti-tank gun, which was arriving just before *Crusader*, and was itself more powerful than the two pounder. The 88mm. was so dangerous that four of them could stop an armoured brigade. General Messervy considered the surprise of their first appearance in *Battleaxe* was a major cause of the failure of that operation. Yet its possible influence on Crusader does not seem to have been appreciated or countered. The tragedy however lay in that the British also had a magnificent anti-aircraft gun, the 3.7-inch, no more of a conspicuous target than the 88mm., and of even greater penetrative power. In November 1941 there were in North Africa more 3.7's than 88's. But the British never used them in an anti-tank role, either in *Crusader* or in later desert battles. It was a depressing example of a streak of conservatism, rigidity, and departmentalism in the twentieth-century British mind. The 3.7 was an anti-aircraft gun. It was to be used therefore to shoot at aircraft. The two-pounder was supplied to shoot tanks. And that was that.[12]

This German victory was achieved with only 12 88mm. anti-aircraft guns, a small number which almost attained the level of a 'critical mass' (see discussion below).[13]

2. *In War.* I deliberately chose the words *in war* not *on the battlefield*

because some weapons that surprise an adversary do not necessarily have to be deployed on the battlefield itself. This is true for much of the ULTRA weapon as used during the Second World War or the new computer designed to decipher German codes.

3. *Unaware of.*   It is possible to introduce a new weapon which leads to the achievement of surprise without allowing the enemy to discover what caused that surprise or what measures the opponent is using against him. Again the ULTRA system is a good example. The British were able to spring many surprises on the Germans as a result of the development of ULTRA, yet the Germans remained unaware of its existence throughout the war. Although the victim of technological surprise usually becomes aware of the nature of the technology being used against him sooner or later, this need not always be true. Deception can also help to conceal or protect certain technologies from the enemy, as will be shown below.

4. *Not ready.*   The word *ready* is preferable to the word *familiar.* The reason is that technological surprise is often only partial. The victim may know in principle or even in fact that such a weapon can be developed, but either estimates that it will take a much longer time to produce or is simply not yet ready with counter-measures (e.g., German estimates of the time required to develop an A-bomb or centimetric wavelength radars). The Germans were surprised by the use of metallic chaff (Window) against their radars not so much because of the weapon itself, whose principles they already knew, but because of its timing. The key word is *ready*, for although the Germans had tested a weapon similar to Window (*Duppel*). they deliberately chose not to develop counter-measures out of fear that the British might discover their experiments and consequently devise a similar counter-measure from which the Germans stood to lose the most.[14] (This ostrich-like, irrational policy cost the Germans dear in their defensive battle over the Reich. Important weapons that *can* be developed will in fact be developed by more than one side simultaneously, given the universal logic of science. It is therefore more prudent to be a step ahead and assume that the enemy knows as much as oneself rather than to delay research, testing, and production for fear that the system will favor the adversary.) On the other hand, the British, after consciously deciding not to invest their limited resources in the development of flying bombs, were nevertheless ready with excellent counter-measures when the V-1 attack on London began.

5. *Time.*   Time is one of the most critical dimensions of technological surprise. The more time required by the opponent to react and develop effective counter-measures against a new weapon, the greater the impact of technological surprise. This, of course, is also a major consideration in the selection of new weapons. Weapons that can quickly be countered may be a poor investment, whereas those which can continue to operate

over a longer period of time without opposition are generally a better investment.

One way of telescoping the time required for development of counter-measures is to begin research on them while the original weapons themselves are being perfected. This may be difficult or impossible for a number of reasons. Concurrent development of counter-measures tends to focus attention on the original weapon's vulnerability, thereby weakening the incentive for its production. This is the only 'legitimate' reason, according to R.V. Jones, for the resistance shown by Watson-Watt, inventor of radar, to the development of radar counter-measures along with the refinement of radar itself.[15] The vociferous opposition of Watson-Watt (caused by what R.V. Jones referred to as the 'Bridge on the River Kwai syndrome') partially explains why the British introduction of Window was delayed until 1943. Once implemented, Window proved to be an extremely effective counter-measure; it saved the lives of many British bomber crews, and would have saved many more had it been introduced earlier, in accordance with R.V. Jones' proposals to that effect as early as 1937.

Other difficulties causing serious delays in the development of counter-measures stem from organizational and bureaucratic politics, excessive secrecy, and compartmentalization within and among organizations involved in weapons development, scientific intelligence and military pursuits.

DIFFERENT TYPES OF TECHNOLOGICAL SURPRISE AS AN INTELLIGENCE PROBLEM

At this point it is useful to distinguish between different types of technological surprise, each of which poses unique problems for the intelligence community.

Mass-Produced Weapons

The first type of weapon frequently involved in technological surprise is the major weapons system that is mass-produced and distributed to military units for routine use. Among these are aircraft, tanks, anti-aircraft and anti-tank missiles, precision-guided munitions, new types of ammunition, and radar stations. Although every nation tries to keep its weapons systems and their performance specifications a secret as long as possible, their mass production and fielding should not escape the notice of a good intelligence system. Yet despite the relative ease of uncovering the existence of such weapons, military organizations are often caught off guard by their appearance on the battlefield.

When the Germans attacked the Soviet Union in June 1941, they were startled by the appearance of two heavy Soviet tanks that were superior to any in their own possession. These were the new Soviet T-34 and the heavy KV-1 tanks of which 1,475 had already been in service since April 1941. If German intelligence had taken Soviet military capabilities more seriously, it might have gained at least an inkling of the existence of these new tanks. One clue was given to the Germans by the Soviets themselves, as Guderian later recalled:

> In the Spring of 1941 Hitler had specifically ordered that a Russian military commission be shown over our tank schools and factories; in this order he had insisted that nothing be concealed from them. The Russian officers in question firmly refused to believe that the Panzer IV was in fact our heaviest tank. They said repeatedly that we must be hiding our newest models from them, and complained that we were not carrying out Hitler's orders to show them everything. The military commission was so insistent on this point that eventually our manufacturers and Ordnance Office officials concluded: It seems that the Russians must already possess better and heavier tanks than we do. It was at the end of July 1941 that the T-34 tank appeared at the front and the riddle of the new Russian model was solved.[16]

Meanwhile, German troops were not even warned of the existence of heavier Soviet tanks, let alone informed about their performance. According to David Kahn, several hundred T-34s had been used to fight the Japanese in the Manchurian border battles three years before.[17] If this is true, better co-operation with Japanese intelligence should have provided them with an adequate description of the T-34's performance. The KV-1 was exhibited to US photographers at the Stalin tank school near Moscow in May 1941. 'When the heavy KV and original T-34/76A tanks were encountered during the early battles in Eastern Poland and Russia, the Germans were completely unprepared for them. The German High Command had to produce a quick supplement to their Soviet tank recognition manual, which even then confused the heavy KV with the more mobile T-34.'[18] Even after identifying these tanks in one area of the Russian front, German intelligence neglected to warn the troops in other sectors, who had to 'discover' the new Soviet tanks by themselves.[19] (On the eve of Barbarossa, the Germans estimated that the Russians had 10,000 tanks compared with their own 3,500. The Russians in fact possessed no fewer than 24,000 tanks in June 1941.)[20] Perhaps because they felt far superior to their Slavic opponents, the Germans did not worry about Soviet tanks, which they assumed were largely obsolete.

The Germans had no monopoly on such intelligence failures. The appearance of the Japanese Zero over Pearl Harbor and the Far East was a total surprise to the Americans and British. The Japanese Zero was not only superior in performance to the best British and American aircraft available in the Far East at the time, but was also specifically designed to have an extra-long range (more than twice that of the best Allied contemporary fighters.)[21] To a large extent the Japanese gamble in initiating the war in the Far East rested on the outstanding range and performance of the Zero fighter. The story of British and American astonishment at their first encounter with the Zero is a familiar one. Again, there was sufficient information to provide a warning, since the Zero had been a part of Japanese operations in China for 18 months before the attack on the Americans at Pearl Harbor and the British Fleet in the Far East.

> In May 1941 a Japanese Zero fighter was shot down in China. Details of the armament and tankage reached Singapore and were passed to the Air Ministry on 26 July 1941, as well as to Headquarters, Air Command, Far East. Later, the Air Attaché, Chungking, forwarded estimated performance figures which subsequently proved reasonably accurate. On 29 September 1941, the Combined Intelligence Bureau transmitted this data to the same two authorities. Faulty organization at Headquarters, Air Command, whose establishment did not include an intelligence staff, resulted in this invaluable report remaining unsifted from the general mass of intelligence information, and in no action being taken upon it.[22]

In the absence of information on the Zero, British air crews in the Far East were unable to prepare adequate counter-tactics in advance.[23] (Nevertheless, it is doubtful that any change in tactics would have compensated for the superior performance of the Zero and the greater experience of Japanese fighter pilots at that time.)

The causes of this intelligence failure were not only organizational but also psychological. Although we think of them as experts who make objective judgments on the basis of hard facts and observation, even scientists and intelligence analysts are prone to commit errors based on wishful thinking, ethnocentric biases, and subjective concepts. This is another illustration of the limits of rationality in scientific analysis.

> The United States was openly astonished with the quality of Japanese equipment. It had committed the unforgivable sin of underestimating severely the caliber of Japanese designers and men.

> The United States entered the war convinced that nothing could stand up against American fighters. American pilots believed this to be so. That they nurtured this belief is astounding. Long before the air attack against Pearl Harbor the Japanese had flown the Zero in

combat over the Chinese Mainland. Intelligence reports were rushed to the United States.

No one believed them.

Aeronautical experts who studied the reports of performance of the new Japanese 'mystery fighter' snorted in disbelief. When they read the secret reports of speed, maneuverability, firepower and range, they rejected as 'arrant nonsense' the claims that the Japanese had become a grim threat in the air.

Their conclusion was that such a fighter was literally an aerodynamic impossibility. That particular conclusion inevitably led to another, and thus the Americans' obsolete aircraft fell like flies before the agile, swift Zero.[24]

Better British and US exchange of intelligence may have also helped to forestall this type of surprise.

The First World War provides us with two major examples of technological surprise involving radically new weapons. The first is the use of gas by the Germans; the second is the large-scale introduction of tanks by the British. Both are classical, almost ideal cases that demonstrate not only the dramatic and potentially decisive impact of a fully-fledged technological surprise but also the repeated failure of the victim to anticipate it despite numerous warnings, and the neglect of the initiating side to make the most of the benefits flowing from its achievement.

The surprise accomplished by the Germans during the Battle of Ypres on 22 April 1915 and their subsequent failure to take advantage of its impact has been described as follows:

> The Allied troops facing the German attack, which had been achieved with complete strategic and tactical surprise, were totally unprepared and therefore utterly helpless. Having neither the training nor the protective equipment essential to survival in a toxic environment, they retreated in panic and disorder, and by nightfall were facing major disaster. The line of trenches had been ruptured, communications were disrupted, and, most important, the enemy had developed a weapon for which there seemed to be no defense. . . . Yet the Germans did not capitalize on their technological advantage. The Allies reinforced and eventually sealed the breach. . . . Considering the nature of the breakthrough, the Germans could have secured a decisive success in Flanders. It is apparent, however, that they were not prepared to exploit, on other than a limited tactical scale, any success that the use of gas might bring. . . . In short, the Germans demonstrated an astonishing lack of thoroughness in initiating the use of gas. Having accepted gas as

sufficiently promising to justify experimentation on the battlefield, they used it on a scale adequate to alert the Allies to the reality of toxic weapons, but inadequate to ensure success. Their error was threefold. The General Staff apparently had not evaluated either the importance of surprise, or the certainty that the Allies could in time develop defensive measures, or the possibility that the Allies could retaliate in kind. . . . . . [T]he results of the Second Battle of Ypres were indecisive at best and at least represented a significant opportunity lost for the Germans. . . .[25]

The British were unaware of German preparations to use gas for the first time despite numerous warning signals:

The surprise, however, of April 22nd was unjustified, as being due to the neglect of circumstantial warnings. The Western staffs did not, it is true, know that this violation of the conventions of civilized warfare had already been practised against the Russians in January. Possibly the latter did not recognize the experiment, and took it for a protective smoke cloud, as German reports state that the extreme cold made the results of the emission unsatisfactory. More probably, with their habitual unbusinesslike carelessness, the Russians failed to report it to their allies. Still, the accounts given by a prisoner captured by the French on April 14th were most circumstantial: he gave details of the cylinders prepared on the Langemarck front, and, most significant fact of all, actually had a respirator in his possession. This was followed on the 17th by a lying German accusation that the British had employed asphyxiating gases in their shells, the object of which might have been guessed, in conjunction with other evidence – namely, to prepare public opinion for the German action as being merely retaliatory.[26]

This total lack of preparedness cost the British six months: their first gas attack was launched at the Battle of Loos on 5 September 1915.[27]

The period from April 1915 to July 1917 saw the gradual expansion of the use of gas. However, once the Allied and German troops acquired protective equipment, albeit primitive, gas lost its critical role. . . . This situation changed drastically on July 12, 1917, when the Germans achieved their second major technological break-through in chemical warfare. Again, Ypres was the target. This time the Germans achieved complete surprise by introducing mustard gas – a persistent agent that could disable by coming in contact with the skin. It was particularly dangerous because the soldier did not realize that he had been gassed for several hours, by which time he had already received a disabling or lethal dose. Under particularly favorable climatic conditions, mustard gas could retain its disabling properties for several weeks. . . . Mustard gas changed the battlefield environment of World War I. Its use in concentrated doses could make any position untenable. A gas mask was no longer sufficient protection as a soldier could be disabled by vapor or liquid contact anywhere on his body. It would contaminate weapons and rations. Casualty figures reflected the new role of chemical warfare after July 1917: the British had slightly over 20,000 gas casualties from 1915 until the initiation of the use of mustard; from July 1917 to November 1918, they had over 160,000.[28]

This time, it took almost a year (until June 1918) for the Allies to retaliate in kind.

The other well-known example from the First World War is the surprise achieved by the British at Cambrai on 20 November 1917. The degree of surprise experienced by the Germans is even more astounding in light of the fact that British tanks had been used in smaller numbers on the Western front on several occasions, and could not have been easy to conceal, as there were 381 of them poised for action immediately behind the front line. One reason for the British success at Cambrai was that they did not follow their customary procedure of starting the attack with a prolonged period of bombardment, a procedure which the Germans had been conditioned to expect.[29]

An excellent example of a major technological surprise achieved by the Allies during the Second World War was the development of the 'proximity fuse' or VT fuse.[3] A shell incorporating a fuse that could sense the target and detonate close enough to seriously damage or destroy the target without the necessity of obtaining a direct hit could increase the efficiency of anti-aircraft fire by a considerable factor (estimated before the invention to be at least three to 30 times better).[31] This meant a much higher rate of hits on the targets; the saving of a substantial amount of ammunition; and in conjunction with the development of a fire predictor and radar (i.e., a better *local* fire control system) and the ability to engage several targets simultaneously. Known to all military organizations, the relatively simple idea behind the proximity fuse was very difficult to translate into reality.[32] Some of the practical engineering problems to be overcome were formidable: the necessary technological breakthroughs included development of a radio transmitter and receiver that could fit in a space about the size of an ice cream cone; special tiny radio tubes weighing less than an ounce which could withstand an initial acceleration of 20,000g (times the force of gravity) and centrifugal forces of 475 rotations per second; and a special small source of electricity.

After a prolonged period of research and development, a suitable radio proximity fuse was perfected in a collaborative effort of Britain, Canada, and the United States. The project was undertaken with the utmost secrecy. Production of the fuse was compartmented (i.e., most part producers did not know what system they were making parts for) and a special self-destructing mechanism was built into each fuse in case the shell failed to explode. Initially, all shells were authorized for exclusive use by the US Navy and could be deployed only over water to avoid possible retrieval by the enemy. Later their use was permitted over friendly territory (i.e., England), and finally directly against the Germans once it was clear that they no longer had time to manufacture a similar fuse of their own or devise effective counter-measures. The use of anti-aircraft guns firing shells with the VT fuse was authorized in advance as a counter-measure to the V-1 flying bombs. By the winter of 1944, it was also approved for use against Germany as regular artillery. After its initial introduction, General Patton wrote to General Leon Campbell, Chief of Ordnance, that 'the new shell with the funny fuse is devastating. The other night we caught a German battalion, which was trying to get across the Sauer River, with a battalion concentration and killed by actual count 702. I think that when all armies get this shell we will have to devise some new method of warfare. I am glad that you all thought of it first.'[33] At a later stage, the same shells with similar VT fuses were used very effectively by the US Navy against Kamikaze attacks.

The story of the proximity fuse is a noteworthy example of how to achieve technological surprise and maintain a substantial lead until the end of the war through secrecy, perfect timing, and the deployment of adequate quantities. Secrecy was preserved throughout the entire developmental period, and the weapon was introduced incrementally, in order to delay the disclosure of the new technology for as long as possible. Final exposure of the weapon took place only when the enemy was no longer able to produce or counter the new weapon. During each successive phase, the weapon was also introduced in quantities sufficient to bring about effective results. Such exemplary secrecy and perfect timing are rare indeed.

More recently, Israeli troops along the Suez Canal were caught off-guard by Egypt's large-scale introduction of Sagger anti-tank (ATGM) missiles and RPGs that had been transported across the Canal by the Egyptian infantry. Inasmuch as Israeli intelligence had been fully apprised of the existence and performance of these missiles in the hands of the Egyptians and Syrians, how can one then account for the surprise of the Israeli troops in the field? First of all, Israeli intelligence did not distribute much of the available information to lower echelons, and the little information that was distributed received hardly any attention.

Second, the surprise involved not only the weapons themselves, but their use in concert with a new doctrine of deployment. Third, the anti-tank missiles were introduced in very large quantities. To this one might add an explanation previously mentioned in relation to the gross inaccuracy of German intelligence estimates of Russian tank strength on the eastern front and the British–American refusal to believe reports on the Japanese Zero; namely, the Israeli ethnocentric-hubritic view that regardless of the quality of Egyptian or Syrian weapons, they would push ahead with their tanks and win the war as in 1967. The Israelis continued to plan for the last war without realizing that modern technology had provided the Egyptians with valuable counter-measures for the tank. Having invested too heavily, both materially and psychologically, in one weapons system (the tank), they neglected to study the effectiveness of the latest counter-weapons that limited the performance of the tank. One important lesson to be drawn from this is that an overwhelming sense of confidence or superiority is always counter-productive in intelligence work or war. The belief in one's own superiority, whether in terms of equipment or morality, fosters blinding arrogance and in turn erodes one's interest in the opponent's weapons and plans. There is nothing more stimulating for intelligence work than a feeling of weakness and vulnerability, from which comes the impetus to learn as much as possible about the enemy. Those in second place must indeed try harder. In war, as elsewhere, nothing fails like success and nothing succeeds like failure.[34] (This should not be construed as a recommendation that one fail. . . .) A sense of vulnerability is without doubt one of the principal explanations for the alacrity and creativity with which the British strove to perfect their intelligence work and deception operations during the Second World War.

All of the aforementioned illustrations of technological surprise have dealt with mass-produced weapons that were tested and sent to the field in large numbers before being first encountered by the enemy. In each case, sufficient evidence of the weapon's existence, performance parameters, and quantity was available to the surprised party or should have been detected well in advance by its intelligence organization. On many occasions, one side's hope of gaining a strategic advantage was destroyed by the opponent's good intelligence work. Good examples are the timely British discovery of the German radio navigation aids before the Battle of Britain and the subsequent British detection of German plans to introduce the V-1 and V-2 long-range vengeance weapons.

Weapons Systems Produced on a Small Scale

While it is quite possible to detect mass-produced weapons well ahead of their debut on the battlefield and then neutralize much of their potential impact with carefully planned counter-measures, it is much more difficult to discover important weapons systems being produced on a small scale. Examples of this type of weapons research and production are Project Manhattan (the development of the atomic bomb); the British computer and cryptanalysis system assembled to crack German codes during the Second World War; or in more recent times, the secret development of the U-2 (Project Aquatone).[35] Yet even with this kind of weapon, a high-quality intelligence organization should be able to ferret out its telltale signs (e.g., Russian intelligence, unlike that of the Germans and Japanese, *did* learn of the Manhattan Project at a very early stage). It is also very difficult to detect weapons systems developed *ad hoc* to solve unique operational problems; these can perhaps be referred to as 'one-time-use' weapons. Intelligence organizations face a formidable task when they try to uncover the existence of a weapon whose purpose is unique and for which they have no fitting concept[36] (e.g., the Allied artificial harbors (Mulberry, Boysenberry) and the underwater fuel pipeline (Pluto) that were devised to support the invasion of Normandy).[37]

The Allies were confronted with the operational problem of providing large amounts of supplies and reinforcements for the invading troops.[38] Fulfillment of this mission required access to a port, yet all Channel ports were strongly defended by the Germans. Amassing the forces needed to attack a well-defended German port would have unduly delayed the opening of the second front, exposing the Allies to far greater risks and higher costs. Churchill therefore first came up with the idea of equipping the invading force with a portable harbor.[39] The construction of the artificial harbors was consequently the basic assumption upon which the entire Overlord plan for the invasion of Europe was to be undertaken.[40] When General Morgan began planning the cross-Channel attack, Allied engineers had not yet completed experimentation with various break-water devices. It was still necessary to assume the existence of resources that were not at hand and conditions that could hardly be foreseen.[41] (The Japanese had to cope with a similar, although somewhat simpler problem before their surprise attack on Pearl Harbor; they needed a torpedo which could be dropped from the air into shallow water. Though not yet available when they began planning the attack, the torpedo became a reality shortly before it was needed.)[42]

Strategically, the possession of Mulberrry gave the planners the freedom to select a landing area well away from the heavily fortified major ports; psychologically, it gave the Allied High Command a degree of confidence without which the venture, which seemed so hazardous, might never have been attempted.[43] (An additional degree of confidence must have been afforded by Allied deception cover plans.) As they did not have to grapple with similar operational problems, the Germans cannot really be blamed for thinking along more conventional lines; namely, that the Allies would have to attack one of the heavily defended channel ports in order to carry out a full-scale invastion. (The Allied raid on Dieppe inadvertently reinforced such German assumptions.) Even a far better intelligence organization than the Abwehr would have had difficulty uncovering such an unprecedented system in time. Albert Speer commented that 'having by-passed the Atlantic Wall by means of "a single brilliant technical device" the Allies made the German defense system completely irrelevant'.[44]

Unique design was also the hallmark of the 'bouncing mines' (Upkeep) specifically developed by Professor B.N. Wallis to burst the Ruhr dams (the Mohne Eder Sorpe) in Operation Chastise.[45] German intelligence could scarcely have anticipated such an attack, especially since the Luftwaffe possessed no heavy bombers and was therefore not likely to conceive of a similar scheme.[46] The German defense did include anti-torpedo nets and anti-aircraft batteries, but had not anticipated bombs that could jump over the existing defenses. The 'bouncing mines' were secretly manufactured, and specially modified Lancaster bombers were concentrated in a new squadron (617). The operation (17 May 1943) was a success in the sense that two dams (the Mohne and Eder) were breached and seriously damaged, while British morale was boosted at a difficult time.[47]

Two other examples deserve brief mention. First is the surprise carried out by Italian frogmen in the initial use of 'explosive boats' (E-boats) in Suda Bay, Crete, on the night of 25–26 March 1941 when they attacked and sank the cruiser *York* and a number of other ships, and later in the use of the so-called pig boats (Chariots) against Gibraltar and Alexandria. In Alexandria on the night of 18 December, pig boats from the submarine *Scire* badly crippled two British battleships, the *Valiant* and *Queen Elizabeth*, thus seriously altering the naval balance in the Mediterranean at a critical time.[48]

The first operational use of gliders in the Second World War is another illustration of technological surprise on a lower tactical level. Here again, an operational problem called for a technical solution. In the early phases of their attack in the West, the Germans had to occupy quickly the fort of Eben Emael – the key to their advance in Belgium. The location of this 'impregnable' fort was such that it could not be eliminated or bypassed unless surprise were achieved. After much thought and preparation, the Germans decided to use special gliders to land silently on top of the fort, after which they could blow up the fort's armored turrets with newly developed 'hollow charges'. Though certainly not new in principle, the glider solved the problem of achieving surprise through its unprecedented use as a military weapon. The 'hollow charges' solved the second problem of penetrating the fort. Armed with a daring and imaginative plan, 77 German soldiers in 10 gliders with 56 'hollow charge' explosives rapidly defeated the 780 defenders of what had been described as the strongest fort in the world (11 May 1940).[49]

THE CONDITIONS NECESSARY FOR ACHIEVEMENT OF TECHNOLOGICAL SURPRISE

The underpinnings of a successful technological surprise are: (1) secrecy; (2) adequate numbers (or 'critical mass'); (3) a suitable doctrine; (4) optimal timing; and (5) the correct choice of weapon (or expected effectiveness).

1. *Secrecy*

In technological – as in strategic – surprise, an effective cloak of secrecy is necessary for success. It allows introduction of the new weapon under ideal circumstances while preventing the enemy from preparing either material or doctrinal counter-measures. No effort should be spared in trying to conceal the original concept of a weapon, its development and testing, training, and final preparations for operational use. The closer the weapon comes to the later stages of mass production, training and fielding, the greater the probability that its existence will be disclosed. Through measures such as compartmentation and prevention of enemy reconnaissance from the air, it may be possible to preserve secrecy until the new weapon is introduced. As we have seen, even if information indicating the existence of a new weapon is available, the victim's intelligence organization will not always perceive such warnings correctly or take them seriously enough to avoid being surprised. Once, however, the new weapon is actually used, it is almost inevitable that the victim will learn of its existence and adopt a variety of counter-measures. This is why it is so vital that a new weapon be introduced in quantities sufficient to bring about a decisive impact from the start.

There are, however, occasions when it is possible to extend secrecy *beyond* the point at which a new weapon is placed in action, as in the gradual introduction of VT fuse, first over water and friendly territory. In these circumstances, the adversary has no opportunity to inspect the technology being used, and thus cannot ascertain what has caused the dramatic improvement in his opponent's performance. At times, even when the new technology or weapons have been identified, it is difficult to design a proper counter-measure until a sample has been obtained for careful examination. Hence, even after the introduction of a new weapon, every effort should be made to delay its capture and examination by the enemy. This can be accomplished by using the weapon only in areas where it cannot fall into enemy hands or by equipping it with such devices as self-destruct mechanisms. Gaining access to an adversary's new weapon is considered a great coup by every intelligence organization (e.g., the British capture of a German radar in the Bruneval Raid;[50] or an Israeli raid against Egypt in 1970 during the War of Attrition, in which a Soviet radar was captured; attempts to seduce enemy pilots to defect with their aircraft; and the Israeli intelligence coup achieved in the defection of an Iraqi MiG-21 pilot with his aircraft in 1965).

Another way of prolonging secrecy after the actual use of a weapon is through deception; that is, by diverting the enemy's attention from the real weapon and technologies employed. The most outstanding example is the Allied concealment of the ULTRA program from the Germans by pretending that Allied information had been obtained from sources such as visual contact by air or sea reconnaissance. ULTRA was even hidden from the Allied higher command echelons by ascribing its success to agents, captured documents and the like. In much the same way, the effectiveness of counter-measures can also be extended with the aid of deception. (Churchill wanted to convince the Germans that the magnetic mine in which they had placed so much faith was still a very powerful weapon even though the British had already prepared effective counter-measures.)[51]

A principal cause of German technology's failure during the Second World War, despite its excellence,[52] was the inability to conceal major projects from the British. This stemmed from the high quality and good fortune of British scientific intelligence as well as from German mistakes. Seldom surprised by German moves, the British had advance knowledge, for example, of all German radio navigation techniques during the Battle of Britain and of German plans to develop and use the V-1 and V-2. The Oslo Report, received by the British in the early phases of the Second World War, revealed secret programs for weapons development and numerous new technologies the Germans were in the process of developing. This document was of inestimable value to the British because it provided a frame of reference for identification of German weapons at an early point in their research and testing. As a result, the British were often able to prepare adequate counter-measures even before the Germans had put the weapons into operation.[53]

Although necessary, secrecy alone is not always sufficient. Proper exploitation of the surprise achieved hinges on the use of adequate quantities in combination with the development of a suitable doctrine to take advantage of the weapon's full potential.

2. *Adequate Numbers ('Critical Mass')*

> It has often been contended that the Germans threw away an
> unrivalled opportunity of victory through their premature and local
> use of the new weapon. It is true that the military mind always
> moves slowly and tentatively towards novelties (as witness the
> tanks), and the protagonist of gas warfare has related the suspicion,
> scepticism, and dislike of the commanders with whom he had to
> deal. But if its use had been postponed till the next year (for the
> campaign in Russia made any great attack in France impossible in
> 1915), it is most improbable that the secrecy necessary for
> unremedied surprise could have been preserved.[54]

While they achieved a remarkable surprise with their first use of gas on
the western front at Ypres, the Germans were unable to capitalize on it
because of the premature use of the weapon in insufficient quantities and
the absence of a well thought-out plan to exploit their initial success. In
much the same way, during the Battle of the Somme, the first British use
of tanks in small quantities and on unsuitable terrain ended in failure.
Fortunately for the British, another opportunity arose during the Battle
of Cambrai, in which they corrected their previous errors and went on to
achieve one of the few major surprises of the First World War.

Cruttwell and Brown argue that the innate conservatism of the military
with regard to innovative weapons is one of the most important
explanations for the initial use of new weapons in insufficient quantities.
Factors inhibiting technological innovation include suspicion, the
prolonged period of time required for acceptance, and the gradual
introduction of new weapons. Such tendencies practically ensure that
by the time the military has tested the new weapons to its satisfaction,
the enemy will have learned about them as well. This reluctance is
understandable. The senior military commander is asked to base the
success of an important operation on a weapon that has not been tested on
a large scale. While Cruttwell and Brown's explanation is certainly
convincing as applied to the attitude of the military during the First World
War and the early phases of the Second World War, it is much less valid
today. The contemporary military commander accepts change and
innovation as natural and beneficial without hesitating to take advantage
of it. Technology occupies a prominent role – perhaps too much so – in the
mind of the modern soldier. Consequently, the reluctance to use new
weapons systems for the first time in large quantities may not pose as
serious a problem as in the past.

Cruttwell points out yet another substantial obstacle to the introduction of a new weapon in adequate quantities. The demand for a quantity
of weapons large enough to be deployed heightens the risk that their

presence will be detected prematurely. This problem results in more pressure to use the new weapons before sufficient numbers have been concentrated. *On the whole, though, the risks involved in delaying the use of a new weapon are less damaging than the costs incurred and the opportunities missed by the inadequate quantity of weapons used too soon.* Even if the enemy discovers the new weapons before they have been used against him, he may not take the reports seriously; furthermore, his identification of weapons does not mean that he is aware of their exact performance or doctrine of deployment. It may also be *too late* to invent any effective counter-measures.

A third incentive not to introduce new weapons too hastily, thereby gradually preparing the adversary to counter the larger number that will appear later, results from pressure to use whatever small quantities of the weapon that are immediately available as a 'quick fix' or 'stopgap' measure when things go wrong on the battlefield.

An excellent illustration based on the Soviet doctrine of introducing new weapons in quantities large enough to ensure decisive results was the Egyptian (and Syrian) deployment of anti-tank and anti-aircraft missiles during the Yom Kippur War. The 'technological surprise' achieved in this case can be attributed as much to the number of weapons deployed as to their unexpectedly good performance. Their use in conjunction with a suitable doctrine provides the third explanation for this successful technological surprise.

3. *Suitable Doctrine and Planning*

Doctrine and planning furnish the continuing momentum necessary to produce decisive results. Many technological and strategic surprises fall short of a desirable outcome because the initial shock of surprise is not properly exploited. A classical example was the successful British technological surprise at Cambrai, when, despite the effective secrecy and adequate number of tanks used, there were not enough troops and contingency plans to capitalize on the original success achieved.[55] The impact of surprise on a large scale is almost always greater than anticipated by the initiator. 'It remains only to be said of the Battle of Cambrai that the initial success so far exceeded the expectations of the Third Army Staff that no suitable preparations had been made to exploit it.'[56]

Surprise is usually under rather than over-exploited (e.g., the Germans did not move as fast as they could have on the western front in 1940; the Japanese failed to press their attack on Pearl Harbor; the unopposed Allied invasion forces in Anzio and Normandy did not break out of the beachhead as fast as they could have; the Egyptians and Syrians in 1973 did not exploit their initial success and instead unimaginatively adhered to their original plans). It is therefore extremely important to accompany each plan for achieving any type of surprise with proper advance planning and an appropriate doctrine. Adequate reserves must be made ready. From a doctrinal point of view, the more initiative delegated to lower echelons of command (which are in the ideal location – on the battlefield – to make the proper decisions), the better the surprise will work to the maximum advantage of the initiator. This type of doctrine, typical of the German and Israeli armies, explains why the Germans during the attack on Russia in 1941 and the Israelis during the 1967 Six Day War came close to the perfect exploitation of strategic surprise.[57]

4. *Timing*

The most critical decision concerning the choice of an optimal time for the first exposure of a new weapon is closely tied to the element of *secrecy*, an essential condition for the realization of any type of surprise. The development, testing and eventual fielding of a new weapons system in sufficiently large numbers is almost impossible to maintain as a secret for an extended period of time. In wartime, the fear of premature disclosure will generally press the relevant decision-makers into introducing the new weapons system at the earliest possible time consistent with the production and fielding of the *critical mass* of weapons (i.e., the moment when sufficient numbers are available for operation). The need to maintain secrecy may sometimes generate strong pressures to use the new weapons before enough have been produced and fielded; such premature use will at best culminate in indecisive results.

Another type of pressure that could lead to the premature exposure of a new weapon is when the military situation on the battlefield has deteriorated to the point where the new weapons (of which there are an insufficient quantity) represent the only hope of a desperate commander.

The time required by an adversary either to develop counter-measures or to produce the same type of weapons system is another important consideration in the choice of timing. Ideally, the perpetrator of surprise should not give the opponent a chance to accomplish either of these goals. Depending on the degree of surprise that can be achieved and on short- and long-range cost/benefit calculations, however, new weapons will sometimes be introduced even though they are likely to be countered and eventually used with greater effectiveness by the enemy.

The final paragraph of a British report (18 January 1942) on German radars (D.T.) and how to spoof them addresses the question of the best timing for counter-measures.

It is unwise to be squeamish about taking counter-measures against any enemy development because of the *danger of reciprocation.* The enemy is not altogether lacking in ingenuity, and has probably thought of most of the counters. The true reason against undertaking counter-measures is that ultimately the enemy will learn to overcome them, and that it is only during the period of his education that we shall reap the advantage. This period must be made to occur only when we want it, no matter what action the enemy may take against our own system in the meantime. When the correct time arrives there should be no hesitation. Spoofing may require a very considerable degree of effort to be successful, but its cost must be weighed only against the relevant D.T. effort and against the additional damage which we could do with its aid.[58]

Nevertheless, neither the British nor the Germans acted in accordance with the logic of this report in their decisions concerning the introduction of a counter-measure to radar. The story of Window (*Duppel* to the Germans) – the British program to develop metallic chaff to jam German radars – is an excellent example of the problems inherent in the choice of optimal timing. The original idea was proposed by R.V. Jones and others as early as 1937 as a companion project to the development of the radar. By March 1942, the initial technical investigation and testing of the effectiveness of chaff were already complete.[59] The report was immediately approved by the Chief of Air Staff (Sir Charles Portal) who decided on 4 April 1942 that the Bomber Command could begin using Window in support of its operation. Although chaff had already been provided to Bomber Command as early as March 1942, the 4 April decision of the Chief of Air Staff was rescinded under pressure from the Commander-in-Chief of Fighter Command, Sir Sholto Douglas (5 May 1942).[60] This decision called for indefinite postponement of the use of chaff pending the results of trials demanded by Fighter Command concerning the damage that chaff used by the Germans could do to British radars and the effectiveness of British fighter defense against German bombers. Carried out immediately, tests indicated that chaff could severely jam the radars of British night fighters, while other types of radar were not seriously affected. (German radars, in particular Wurzburg, which worked on a half-meter wavelength, were generally more susceptible to jamming than British radars.) Sir Sholto Douglas then asked the Air Ministry to prohibit Bomber Command from using Window until the RAF came up with satisfactory counter-measures in case the Luftwaffe should decide to use the same method. Sir Charles Portal, Chief of the Air Staff, agreed. It must be remembered that by May 1942, the Luftwaffe had only a small number of medium bombers available for the possible attack on England, since most of the bombers were in use at the Russian front. By the spring of 1942, the British strategic bombing campaign against Germany was picking up, while the likelihood of a renewal of the Luftwaffe's bombing raids on England had decreased considerably.

> This surprising decision had allowed the threat of the much inferior and diminishing German bomber force to deny an important tactical advantage to the much greater and increasing striking power of Bomber Command. Moreover, by the time that it was taken, the introduction of the Window had been so imminent that the device had become a subject of common gossip in the Royal Air Force and soon afterwards it had even been the inspiration of a cartoon, which, to the chagrin of the Air Staff, actually appeared in the *Daily Mirror*. Despite the official decision to circulate a rumour to the effect that the trials of Window had shown it to be a complete failure, it was, therefore, hardly likely that the Germans would long remain in the dark as to the truth. Thus, one of the principal reasons for withholding Window, namely the danger of revealing it to the enemy, was seriously undermined from the outset and seemed to have been completely destroyed by the end of October 1942 when an Air Scientific Intelligence report indicated that it was 'certain' that the Germans fully understood the Window principle.[61]

Even though it was clear by the fall of 1942 that the Germans could implement their own version of Window if they so desired, the Commander-in-Chief of Fighter Command still opposed Window's use in support of the strategic bombing offensive over Germany. Another important meeting to debate the Window issue (4 November 1942) ended in victory for those who emphasized its dangers. The introduction of Window was put off once again.

'By the end of March 1943 when the Battle of the Ruhr had begun, the case against Window was, however, probably crumbling. The obvious fact that the German bomber force was an almost negligible factor and that the German fighter force was one of increasingly decisive importance was at last beginning to exact some influence upon the discussions.'[62] About 50 per cent of all the bomber losses could be related to either night fighter or anti-aircraft fire, all of which were controlled by German radar and could be jammed by Window. Bomber Command estimated that the introduction of Window could reduce bomber losses by 35 per cent (or 1.7 per cent of the total Bomber Command sorties being despatched). Another Air Ministry conference to discuss this issue was convened on 22 April 1943. (It was discovered in the meeting that too little chaff had been produced and that the chaff produced was of the wrong size.) The conference concluded with a recommendation to the Chiefs of Staff that Window be introduced on 1 May 1943. The Chiefs of Staff in turn postponed such a move until after the invasion of Sicily (by the middle of June).

It took another meeting on 15 July 1943, attended by Churchill himself, to obtain final approval for the use of Window in spite of continued opposition, this time most vehemently voiced by Herbert Morrison, the Minister of Home Security. The Chiefs of Staff now argued that had Window been implemented on 1 April 1943, some 286 bombers (or 25 per cent of the existing bomber force) and crews could have been saved.[63] The final decision to allow the use of Window was made by Churchill. This is how R.V. Jones describes it:

> At this final Window meeting, Watson-Watt and I were once again in opposition, for Portal let me state most of the Air Staff case for using Window. Watson-Watt again emphasized the damage to our own night defences but Churchill then turned to Leigh Malory, head of Fighter Command, pointing out that he was the man who would have to 'carry the can' if our defences failed, and what did he think? Leigh Malory very decently gave the opinion that even though his defences might be neutralized he was now convinced that the advantage lay with saving the casualties in Bomber Command, and that he would take the responsibility. That concluded the argument, and Churchill said 'Very well, let us open the Window!'[64]

First used in the attack on Hamburg on the night of 24 July 1943, Window was completely unanticipated by the Germans. For some time it reduced bomber losses by half; and despite the subsequent fourfold increase of German fighter planes, British bomber losses never reached the same level that had been suffered before the advent of Window.[65]

Although Churchill himself wrote that 'on the whole it may be claimed that we released it about the right time',[66] his phraseology indicates some doubt as to whether he thought the timing was the best possible. The British official history makes it clear that the decision came far too late. 'The delay of some sixteen months which had been primarily occasioned by the threat of German retaliation was, perhaps, the last, and by no means the least significant, of the achievements of the German bomber force, whose career thus ended, as it had begun, on a note of successful bluff.'[67] The optimal timing would have been any time after October 1942, when it became indisputably evident that the Germans already understood the principles underlying Window[68] and could have used it themselves. The obvious weakness of the German bomber force at that time and the deteriorating situation on the eastern front made delay even less appropriate. This unnecessary and costly foot-dragging was without doubt caused by the conflicting and uncoordinated parochial interests of different organizations. R.V. Jones' discussion of related events reveals just how frequently Window became the focus of an emotional and political debate rather than a rational and pragmatic discussion. 'The use of "Window" was delayed, partly due to a different interpretation of the facts by experts, partly due to the inherent dislike of upsetting the existing order of things.'[69]

British and German decision-makers exhibited somewhat parallel attitudes when considering the possible introduction of chaff as a counter-measure to radar. The Germans carried out their *Duppel* experiments first near Berlin and later over the Baltic during 1942. Like their British counterparts, German scientists concluded that this counter-measure was 'dynamite'.[70] The Luftwaffe's technical office forwarded the test results to General Martini, Chief of the German Air Signals Organization, who passed the findings on to Reichsmarschal Göring. Martini stressed the grave danger involved should the RAF use chaff against German radar defenses. Horrified at this prospect, Göring ordered the immediate destruction of all related documents as well as the cessation of all testing, including the development of counter-measures. He was convinced that only such drastic measures would prevent the British from learning of this effective counter-measure. For over a year, the British and Germans '. . . hesitated to use Window against one another in the fear of losing in the exchange'.[71]

Unlike the British, the Germans had a justifiable reason for not developing *Duppel*; the decline in their bomber strength and the fact that they were on the defensive against British strategic bombing meant that they were also more dependent on radar after 1942 than were the British. The German mistake was, however, their failure to consider the possibility that the British might independently think of the same concept, in accordance with the logic of scientific discovery and technological innovation. For instance, the dreadnoughts were developed almost simultaneously at the turn of the century in England, the United States, and Germany. The radar was invented and perfected at the same time in Great Britain and Germany. By the late 1930s, it was apparent to all aeronautical engineers that the piston-engine monoplane was nearing the end of its technical development for '. . . the only possibility of a radical departure in aircraft technology lay in the discovery of a new source of engine power . . .'[72] The logic of technology led the Germans and the British to begin experimentation with jet engines at about the same time. As a final illustration, the principles behind the potential production of an atomic bomb were known to physicists in England, Germany, the United States, and the Soviet Union by 1938–39.

Knowing that the British 'don't altogether lack ingenuity', the Germans should have continued their development of counter-countermeasures to Window. As it happened their behavior exacerbated the delay in finding an antidote to Window until after the British attack on Hamburg in July 1943. This was a serious blunder, since the Germans should have anticipated the use of a device like Window soon after the British raid on Bruneval (27 February 1942). Shared by members of the scientific community across national borders, common knowledge of the latest technology furnishes the scientific intelligence community with an excellent idea of what to look for in the enemy's military technology. This constitutes a powerful 'objective' perceptual framework that is not available to the strategic or political intelligence analyst.

It must be emphasized that the consideration of when to introduce a new weapons system is very complex. The requirements of maintaining secrecy, producing a 'critical mass', and choosing the optimal time are contradictory. One can envisage a situation in which the existence of a new weapon has been disclosed and yet in order to achieve the greatest possible impact on the battlefield, decision-makers have delayed its introduction (i.e., timing) in order to obtain a 'critical mass'. At other times, secrecy may be so important that the new weapon is used at an earlier stage even if enough weapons have not yet been produced. In this case, the factors of secrecy and hence timing are critical, while questions of quantity are not, for some are effective even when smaller quantities are involved. Much depends on variables such as the speed with which the adversary can implement effective counter-measures or the time he requires to produce the same weapon.

5. The Choice of Weapons

Closely linked to technological surprise, this subject is also of great importance in the study of weapons procurement, R&D, the choice of military doctrine, and the like. In the context of technological surprise it is useful to ask how effective or how decisive the introduction of a new weapon will be; what difference it will make in the outcome of a battle or war; how easily counter-measures can be developed; and finally, in whose favor the weapon will work in the short and long run.

Each new weapons system introduced to the battlefield for the first time may achieve technological surprise, but not all weapons will be equally effective. The primary issue is approximate cost; that is, which weapon will be most effective for a given investment and bring about a decisive impact in the time available for operations. Thus, the German decision to concentrate on the development of the V-1 (and even more so the V-2 rockets) was wrong not only because it was uncovered by the British, who had enough time to prepare excellent counter-measures, but also because Germany could have obtained a far better return on its investment by committing the same resources to a jet fighter program, a ground-to-air anti-aircraft missile, a proximity fuse, or improved radars.

Even if the V-1 and V-2 rockets had not been anticipated by the British, they were developed much too late to bring about any decisive results. Nevertheless, as David Irving suggests, 'Germany preferred the spectacular to the strategic, she preferred rockets to radar; and it was this that cost her the war'.[73] 'The V-2 was an extravagant irrelevance, a product not of military expediency but of German romanticism.'[74]

The second issue is the speed and effectiveness with which counter-measures can be brought to bear against a recently introduced weapon, thereby reducing its utility despite the initial achievement of technological surprise. The magnetic mine and the acoustic torpedo in which the Germans put so much hope are perfect examples of weapons that were costly to produce yet comparatively easy to neutralize within a short period of time. Although completely unanticipated, Germany's use of gas for the first time during the Battle of Ypres (April 1915) was readily countered with gas masks. This is a problem of particular interest today, in view of the heavy reliance on PGMs (Precision Guided Munitions) such as ground-to-air, air-to-air, or air-to-ground missiles that are very expensive to develop but can often be rendered totally useless by relatively inexpensive, simple counter-measures.

An important calculation, therefore, in the choice of new weaponry today should be the estimated period of effectiveness following its initial use. Clearly, weapons having a longer period of immunity to counter-measures are preferable to those which are rapidly neutralized. Moreover, weapons that can maintain some of their effectiveness in a counter-measure environment are preferable to those which appear to be very promising on paper or the testing ground but the antidote to which renders them practically useless (catastrophic behavior).

For contemporary weapons, then, this analysis indicates, first, the increased importance of discovering as early as possible the existence of new weapons, their principles of operation, and vulnerability to defensive measures. Conversely, it reveals the much greater importance of preserving secrecy about those new weapons that are more susceptible to counter-measures. Secondly, it indicates that industrially and technologically sophisticated countries may have an even greater edge over technologically less developed countries, since they can more quickly and independently field effective counter-measures and can be expected to have high-quality technological intelligence organizations.

The third consideration is in whose favor a new weapons system will work in the long run. In the case of Window, the Germans correctly realized that the use of chaff against radar would definitely favor the Allies. This provided them with a sound reason for not introducing the weapon first, even at the cost of forgoing short-range advantages. Similarly, early in the Second World War, the Germans produced a highly secret pressure mine (oyster mine) which, after being planted on the ocean floor, would explode upon any change in water pressure exerted by the hull of an approaching ship. Although the Luftwaffe wanted to use this mine against British and Allied ports, the German Naval Staff barred its production for a long while out of fear that Allied discovery of the 'secret' would lead to its use against Germany in the Baltic.[75] It is interesting to note that the British invented the same type of mine and were equally hesitant to use it for the same reasons.

> The British had recently developed a new type of mine, actuated by the pressure of the displacement of water, when a vessel passed over it. There seemed to be no method of sweeping these 'oyster' mines, and the British were reluctant to use them for fear that one would fall into German hands and that its secrets would then be passed to the Japanese. The effects on the American landing operations in the Pacific might, it was thought, be serious. If, on the other hand, the Germans had also developed a similar type of mine, there was obviously no reason why the British should not use their oyster mines as soon as required. Captain Cowie, Director of the Admiralty's Torpedo and Mining Division, and his deputy, Captain Maitland Dougall, were therefore delighted when, shortly after D-Day, Denning drew their attention to an obscure reference in a routine German signal to the transport to the French coast of a hitherto unknown type of mine, given the prefix 'D'. 'Eureka,' cried Maitland Dougall, 'D for *Druck* – pressure mines! The Germans have them and are going to use them. We can do the same and warn our people what to expect.' It was a small example of the dividends to be won from the careful study of routine administrative messages, and a vindication of Denning's theory that valuable intelligence could only be obtained by first establishing a 'norm' and then looking for any deviation from it. It was also one more contrast with the situation prevailing in Room 40 where for so long messages of no immediate and obvious operational importance had, of necessity, been consigned to the wastepaper basket.[76]

This is one more incident that demonstrates the universal nature of the psychology underlying considerations of introducing a new weapons system. The behavior of those who have to make such decisions is akin to that of Clausewitz' military commander, who, when faced with uncertainty, tends to err on the side of excessive caution.

THE LIMITS OF TECHNOLOGICAL SURPRISE: ITS SHORT- AND
LONG-TERM COSTS

Strange as it may seem, no modern war to date has been decided by the
unexpected appearance of a new weapon or by superior technology
alone.[77] Even a devastating technological surprise will not bring about
any decisive long-term results unless such results immediately follow its
introduction. As the impact of the surprise fades, a variety of
technological and doctrinal counter-measures are introduced in addition
to the interplay of numerous other variables that affect the outcome of a
war. This is an important caveat for those who look upon technological
innovations or technological superiority as a panacea in war.

   Although the short-run benefits arising from the achievement of a
technological surprise are obvious, calculation of the *net* benefits is often
more difficult. We have already seen some of the pitfalls of British and
German hesitation over the development and first use of Window.
Another example is the British decision not to be the first to use gases
during the First World War. The British had been considering the
possible use of noxious gases in combat since early 1915, but they had
decided against it primarily because the British chemical industry was
weaker than that of the Germans. In the long run, the Germans stood to
benefit more than the British from the use of gas.[78] Prediction of who will
benefit most from a new weapon in the long run is not, however, always so
straightforward.

> The unpredictability of the consequences of new developments in
> military technology must also be considered. One of the most ironic
> features in the history of naval inventions is the frequency with
> which new devices proved disadvantageous to those very countries
> which had most energetically furthered their progress. This may be
> due to one or more of three reasons: first, a mistaken interpretation
> of the tactical or strategic consequences bound to eventuate from a
> specific invention; second, failure to predict correctly the technical
> progress of the invention; and third, erroneous conclusions
> respecting the identity of the enemy country in the next war.[79]

   In *Sea Power in the Machine Age*, Bernard Brodie discusses French
naval procurement policy and doctrine as an example of the failure to
estimate correctly the longer-range impact of a new weapon. In the 1840s,
the French were the first to introduce steam warships and iron armor,
and at the turn of the century, they vigorously promoted the submarine as
the weapon *par excellence* to be used against Great Britain. As it turned
out, the British need not have feared French innovation for the British
possessed far superior industrial capabilities as far as the production of
steam engines, iron armor, and new ordnance was concerned.

Meanwhile, the submarine promoted by the French navy almost ruined the British when they became France's chief ally instead of its enemy.[80] by accentuating the role of the submarine in nineteenth century plans for a strategic offensive against Britain, the French may have provided the Germans with their most important strategic weapon and undermined the common interests of Britain and France.

Fear of the unpredictable prompted the British navy in the nineteenth century to adopt a policy of never introducing an innovation that would tend to make existing materiel obsolete. The principle was later used against the Dreadnought policy.[81] Having built the largest navy in the world at considerable expense, the British were reluctant to incorporate major naval innovations, since such a change meant that they would have to relinquish their hard-earned advantage and start from scratch once again. In the case of the Dreadnought, however, as Marder convincingly shows, they had no choice because the universal logic of modern naval technology was such that other nations independently arrived at the stage of developing their own dreadnought type of ship. (The Russians, Germans, and Japanese were considering the design of new battleships in 1904–5, and the US Congress authorized the construction of two dreadnoughts, the *Michigan* and *South Carolina*, in 1905.) The design of the big gun battleship simply became inevitable due to technological, strategic and tactical considerations.[82]

The reciprocal fear that a certain weapon might be produced by the other side creates the dynamics of self-fulfilling prophecy. In the absence of perfect information regarding the other side and in view of the unavoidable uncertainty involved in predicting the impact of new weapons technologies, it is dangerous to expect the enemy to do what is in his own best interest in the long run. First of all, the enemy may miscalculate (or calculate differently) the net benefit to be derived from a new weapon in the long run. He might also prefer to take a high risk, and opt for the certainty of short-run benefits over potential long-run dangers. Furthermore, he may be convinced that the short-run benefits will bring about a decisive victory, thus reducing or eliminating possible long-term risks. Even if he recognizes that the weapons system will ultimately work to his detriment (e.g., England and the submarine; Germany and Window), he may conclude that since the enemy is going to use the new weapon against him anyway, he might as well use it first and derive as much benefit as possible from it in the meantime. The logic here is that although the net gain will go to the adversary, use of the same weapon might reduce the net gain of the enemy whereas non-use will increase it. This is the rationale where the enemy is certain to introduce a weapon independently. The belief that refraining from the use of a certain weapon will cause one's adversary to do the same is nothing more than wishful thinking, assuming that the enemy is clearly aware of the weapon's potential. When defeat or victory are at stake, each country will do its best to introduce any legal or even illegal weapon that improves its chances of survival.

COUNTERING TECHNOLOGICAL SURPRISE

Unlike strategic surprise, which has almost never been successfully prevented or avoided,[83] technological surprise can be averted. British intelligence during the Second World War, especially its scientific branch under Professor R.V. Jones, was quite adept at uncovering the development of new German military technologies and devising counter-measures to neutralize them. (As in the early detection of the German intention to use radio navigation to support bombing operations over England and the timely discovery of the German effort to develop the V-1 and V-2 and the acoustic torpedo.)

Like all types of intelligence work, the prevention of technological surprise is contingent upon many factors. In particular, this type of intelligence work requires a strong scientific community (perhaps it is best if run by civilians who are in fact members of the scientific community 'on loan' to the intelligence community). The work of this department must be appreciated by the military community and seen as equally important to any other type of military activity. Its work must be closely co-ordinated with that of all other intelligence and military departments; and its members must be imaginative enough to put themselves in the enemy's shoes in order to understand his methods, style, organization and operational doctrine. To this must be added a liberal dose of good luck. Perhaps the best understanding of the rationale as well as intuitive-artistic insight required to do well in this type of intelligence work can be gained from the unique memoirs of Professor R.V. Jones. The means chosen to counter a newly designed weapon depend to a large extent upon the stage of development at which its existence, principles of design, and performance characteristics are discovered. According to Jones:

> The adoption of a fundamentally new weapon proceeds through several stages;
> 1. General scientific research of an academic or commercial nature occurs which causes
> 2. Someone in close touch with a Fighting Service, and who is aware of Service requirements, to think of an application of the results of academic research. If this application be considered promising

FIGURE 1: ADOPTION AND USE OF A NEW WEAPON

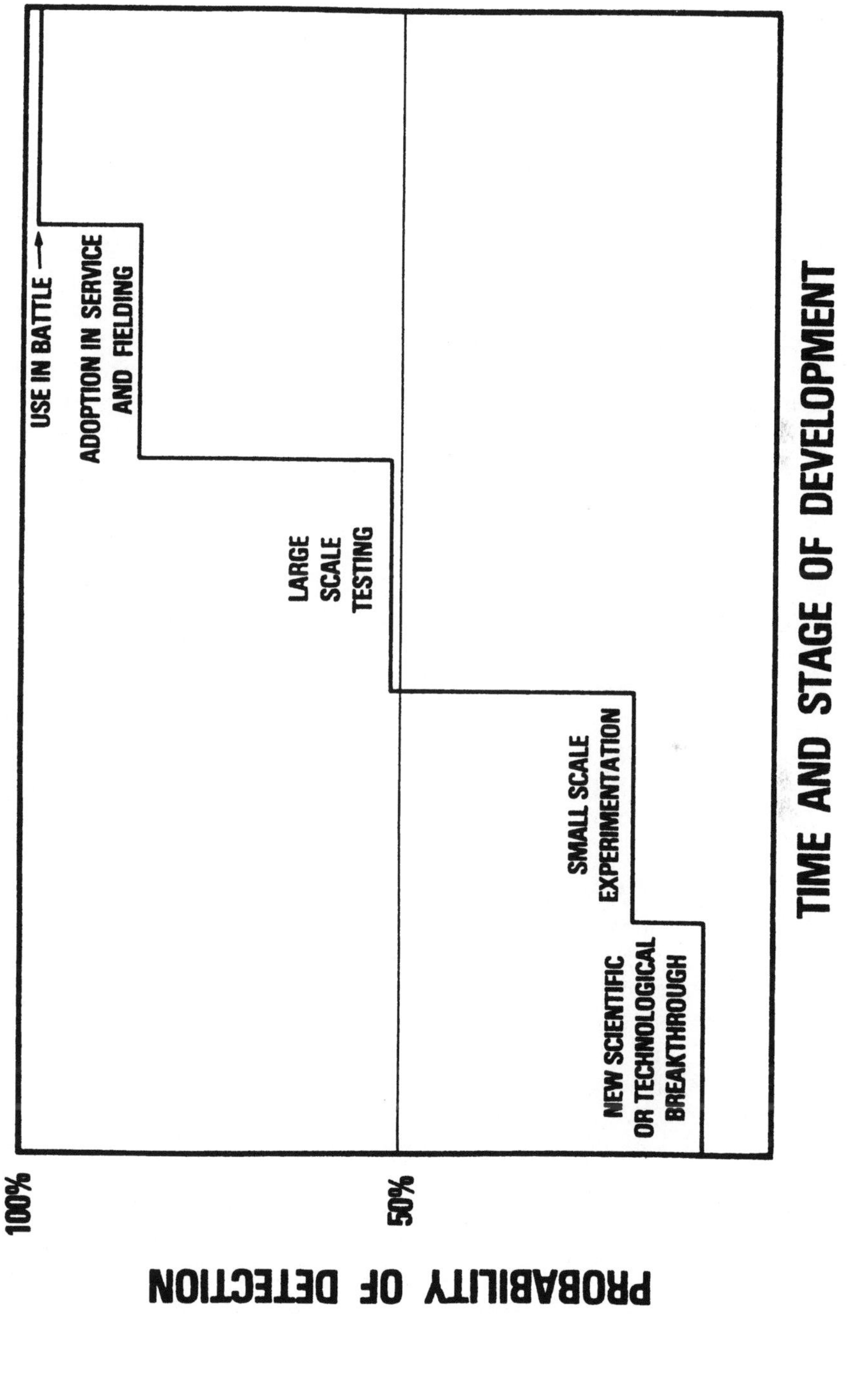

3. Ad hoc research and small-scale trials are performed in a Service laboratory. If these are successful

4. Large-scale Service trials are undertaken, which may lead to

5. Adoption in Service.[84]

To this we can add the sixth stage of use in action (see Figure 1).

The earlier in its development a weapons system is detected, the easier it is to design a variety of counter-measures to neutralize it or at least reduce its effectiveness. While the producer of the new weapons system will do his utmost to conceal its existence for as long as possible, the intelligence organization of his opponent will strive to uncover any tell-tale clues at the earliest possible point. As we have seen in the preceding discussion, British intelligence usually managed to discover the development of German weapons systems in their formative stages, while German intelligence often failed to become aware of the existence of new Allied weapons systems even after their first use in battle.[85]

Once the intelligence community has learned of a new weapon (preferably at an incipient stage) it can then pursue some of the following courses of action:

1. Pre-emptive measures can be taken in order to destroy or cripple the enemy's capacity to either produce or use the weapon.

2. Three main types of counter-measures can be developed:

   (a) New material counter-technologies and counter-measures to neutralize (or reduce the effectiveness of) the new weapons in combination with (whenever possible)

   (b) Deception and

   (c) Doctrinal improvization.

1. *Pre-emptive Measures*

This strategy must be employed against a weapon that promises to be exceptionally difficult to counter once it has been placed in action. The most obvious example is the development of nuclear weapons, which can be delayed or even prevented through pre-emption but cannot be 'countered' once it has been completed. Thus, Great Britain thwarted Germany's capacity to develop an atomic bomb by destroying the German heavy water supply necessary for research at the heavy water plants in Rjukan and Vemork, Norway.[86] This was also the course of action chosen by the Israelis in their 1980 attempt to stop Iraq's research and production of atomic weapons.

Another example is the German decision to produce the V-1 flying bombs and V-2 rocket weapons. Inasmuch as the British could not ascertain the degree to which counter-measures would impair this type of weapon, they had no choice but to assign a very high priority to destruction of the German capacity to manufacture the V-1 and V-2. The British and Americans therefore began attacking German research and testing facilities in Peenemunde. (The first attack took place on the night of 18 August 1943.) At a later stage, the attacks were directed against the 'launching ski sites' (catapults), supply sites of the V-1 rockets, and the logistical infrastructure supporting the production and delivery of the V-1 and V-2.[87] Yet it was very difficult to convince the British and American bomber commands that the German long-range weapons should be made priority targets. These pre-emptive measures alone were not sufficient to halt the project, and in this case a variety of counter-measures, deception operations and new fighter intercepting tactics had to be brought into play.

Pre-emptive strategy had to be more heavily relied upon in the USAAF decision during the summer of 1944 to give the highest priority (with the exception of oil targets) to attacks on jet frame and jet engine factories in Germany. Through deciphering messages to the Japanese Naval Mission in Berlin, the Allies learned that by January 1945 the Germans expected to produce jet fighters at the rate of 1,000 per month. Given the fact that the US Air Force expected to procure its first jet fighters only as late as October 1945, the only feasible strategy was that of pre-emption.[88]

2.(a,b) *Counter-measures and Deception*

Counter-measures are weapons or methods that reduce or eliminate the effectiveness of a new weapon once it becomes operational. Whenever possible, counter-measures should be used in combination with deception.

One of the simplest examples concerns the gas mask. Soon after the Germans' first surprise attack with chlorine gas, the Allies supplied their troops with gas masks which quickly rendered the gas almost completely ineffective. These masks were the ideal antidote until the second German chemical surprise attack, in which they introduced mustard gas on 12 July 1917, again at Ypres.[89] At this point, the existing gas masks became useless. Had British or French intelligence in the First World War been as alert and efficacious as British intelligence was in the Second World War, many lives would have been saved through distribution of gas masks to the front-line troops, for the prolonged German preparations for their first gas attack were impossible to conceal.

Devising counter-measures against the German acoustic torpedo in September 1943 was also relatively simple. Since the U-boat had been defeated by the Allies in 1944, the Germans placed their hope of reviving submarine warfare in new defensive radars and anti-aircraft equipment, and in the offensive use of the new acoustic torpedo. Having developed a similar torpedo, the Allies possessed little specific information on the German acoustic torpedo (T5–ZaunKönig) but were able to prepare an antidote that was later quickly distributed to the Allied escort forces. At first, the Germans achieved the anticipated level of technological surprise, but their high hopes of an outstanding triumph were short-lived. Intercepting and deciphering German U–boat reports on the perform- ance of the new torpedo, the Allies, who now had better information, rapidly improved the so-called 'Foxer', the device (towed astern of the escort vessels) that attracted the acoustic torpedo and caused it to explode harmlessly. Furthermore, the Allies, who followed the exaggerated German reports of success (the Germans estimates that the Zaunkönig achieved 60 per cent hits), wisely decided not to disabuse them of this notion, instead encouraging heavy German reliance on a weapon that was far from an unqualified success.[90]

The British counter-measures brought to bear against the Luftwaffe's navigational radio aids constitute perhaps the best-known example. Working under pressure with a tremendous sense of vulnerability and a good deal of luck, the British profited immensely from the contribution of ULTRA as well as from German errors. British intelligence was often able to anticipate the introduction of successive German navigational aids (i.e., 'Knickebein', X-Gerat, Y-Gerat) and prepare highly effective counter-measures. In this instance, the British resisted the temptation to resort to the most obvious and least expensive counter-measure, jamming, and instead chose to employ the more subtle method of deception. By transmitting their own signals on some of the German navigational beacons (or 'meacons' as these deception beacons were called by the British), they managed to divert the Germans from their original targets so that they dropped their bombs in unpopulated areas. When the Germans resorted to a pathfinder bombing method, 'bending' the beacons was later combined with the use of carefully placed fires to divert German bombers to dummy targets.[91] (The code name of the decoy fires was Starfish.) 'One calculation of the total effect of the counter-measures, despite the delay in bringing them to force, was that no more than one fifth of German bombs fell within the target area.'[92]

The early discovery of the V-1 and V-2 threat enabled the British not only to launch pre-emptive attacks, but in the case of V-1, also to prepare adequate counter-measures. These included stepping up the strength of the anti-aircraft guns around London combined with the timely introduction of the revolutionary proximity fuse and the new anti-aircraft gun-laying radar SCR 584, as well as preparation of the necessary interception fighter air control system. (Again, the timing was crucial.) Had Hitler not delayed research on all new weapons by his halt in the autumn of 1940, when he thought the war all but won, the Germans would have derived more benefit from their long-range weapons.[93] They may have been able to reach a 'critical mass' by 1943 or even earlier, and the British would not have had time to get ready the counter-measures that were being developed in the United States, the SCR 584 radar, and the proximity fuse.[94] As it happened, Hitler was not very enthusiastic about the long-range weapons, whose development had begun as early as 1936, and only decided to lend his full support to the program and assign it high priority in an order dated as late as 25 July 1943.[95]

To reinforce the effect of the counter-measures, the British resorted to the widespread use of deception as their third line of defense. In this they were aided by the complete control they exercised over all 'German' agents reporting from England. In *Double Cross System*, J.C. Masterman describes the British deception plan:

> Early in June the first flying bombs (V-1) arrived and the agents were soon asked to report upon them in detail.
>
> It was soon realized that widely scattered though they were, the majority of the bombs were falling two or three miles short of Trafalgar Square, and the general plan of deception soon took shape. It was, in brief, to attempt to induce the Germans still further to shorten their range by exaggerating the number of those bombs which fell to the north and west of London and keeping silent, when possible, about those in the south and east. The general effect would be that the Germans would suppose that they tended to overshoot and would therefore shorten their range, whereas in fact they already tended to undershoot. The danger was that we could not be sure that the Germans had not a method of themselves accurately locating the fall of bombs, and this compelled caution to our side. . . .
>
> . . . Early in September the rocket attacks (V-2) started, and presented us with similar problems and similar opportunities to those connected with V-1. Consequently our deception was also on similar lines. There was, however, a technical difference. In the flying bomb attacks, location had been the important factor because it was doubtful whether the enemy could tie the times we gave them to particular shots; in the rocket attacks, timings were vital because the enemy could calculate accurately the time of arrival of any shot, and link this up with any information which we gave him. It was therefore decided to give real incidents which would show an M.P.I. in Central London, but to give as the times for these incidents the times of shots falling some five to eight miles short. In this way over a period of some months we contrived to encourage the enemy steadily to diminish his range; thus in the four weeks from 20

January to 17 February 1945 the real M.P.I. moved eastward about two miles a week and ended well outside the boundary of the London region.[96]

Out of the 6,725 V-1 flying bombs that approached England, 1,859 were destroyed by anti-aircraft guns, 1,846 by fighters, and approximately 230 by balloons. The number of V-2 rockets fired successfully was 1,178, out of which 517 reached the London area and 537 fell on other parts of England.[97]

British intelligence was not always so skillful at avoiding technological surprise. In late August 1943, British ships in the Bay of Biscay had been surprised by the first German attacks with the HS 293, a radio-guided missile that was guided to its target by the launching aircraft. (On 25 August, the Germans had a near miss on HMS *Bideford* and on the 27th they damaged HMCS *Athabaskan* and sank HMS *Egret*.) 'Writing after the event, NID12 noted that the new weapons had arrived virtually out of the blue as far as the ships at sea were concerned, although the leads of the appropriate divisions had been kept informed and some ULTRA messages were sent in spite of the scepticism of some authorities. . . . It attributed the oversight to the inefficient handling within the Admiralty of high-grade decrypts containing items of scientific intelligence that might be of interest to the Navy'.[98]

> A few days later the Allies were again surprised, indeed profoundly shocked when, following the announcement of the Italian Armistice the GAF in successful attacks on the Italian Fleet sank the battleship *Roma* (and damaged the *Italia*, September 8, 1943). They were soon to learn from the *Enigma* that the *Roma* had been sunk with the PC 1400 FX high altitude free fall bomb, an armour piercing (AP) weapon whose fall could be corrected by radio beam from the aircraft launching it.[99]

(Of the two weapons the HS 293 was actually the more sophisticated and could hit targets with a 550 kg. warhead up to a distance of 20 km.)[100]

The development of these radio-guided weapons (or 'smart' 'stand off' precision-guided munitions – PGMs as they are called today) need not have come as a shock. It has already been noted that some information on these weapons was available to those in higher echelons, but was never properly distributed to those at lower levels. This may have been caused in part by the skepticism of the intelligence community, which was convinced that the Germans were unlikely to overcome the practical difficulties in perfecting guided weapons. Yet the development of the HS 293 had already been accurately described in the Oslo Report in 1939; moreover, there were occasional references made by POWs and agents in

1941 and 1942 to the fact that the Germans were experimenting with radio-controlled bombs; and finally, similar experiments were taking place in the United States. In fact, the Germans had begun small-scale experimentation with these weapons against Allied shipping off Malta and Sicily in July 1943, but because there were no direct hits, the crews of the ships attacked did not realize that unusual weapons were being used against them.[101]

Had the Germans planned the introduction of these weapons more carefully (instead of using them sporadically), they might have achieved a major technological surprise. They should have waited long enough to stockpile a sufficient quantity of radio-guided weapons ('critical mass') and then introduced them (for the first time) on a massive scale at a more opportune moment such as the invasion of Normandy. The small-scale testing of these weapons against Allied shipping was a serious mistake, since the potential benefits to be reaped were negligible in comparison with the damage that could be done by risking premature disclosure. It is interesting to note that in the spring of 1943 Grand Admiral Dönitz proposed to Hitler to launch a surprise attack on Gibraltar as soon as the Luftwaffe's new radio guided weapons had been stockpiled in sufficient numbers (about the end of June 1943.) Hitler rejected this idea, arguing that it would run the risk of allowing the new weapons to fall into British hands.[102]

As it turned out, the radio-guided weapons were rather easily neutralized by radio-jamming. In 1943, the capture in Italy of German aircraft equipped with radio controls for the guidance of these weapons revealed the radio frequencies used for the HS 293 and FX (which had been similar). Radio counter-measures were then quickly developed. In addition, learning more about these weapons enabled the Allies to come up with more effective evasive maneuvers as well as anti-aircraft tactics against the aircraft controlling the radio-guided weapons. (Aircraft launching the HS 293 and FX were vulnerable to anti-aircraft fire because they had to fly at a reduced speed and in a straight line when launching and guiding the weapons.) Only in the spring of 1944 did the British obtain the detailed specifications for these weapons, when they deciphered the reports of the Japanese Naval Attaché in Berlin.[103]

This last example may indicate the direction of future trends in the development of counter-measures and the avoidance of technological surprise as an intelligence problem. As weapons become more sophisticated and dependent upon highly complex sensors or guidance systems, they also become increasingly susceptible to counter-measures. Unlike ballistically fired shells which are relatively inaccurate but cannot be tampered with once fired, precision-guided munitions are either very accurate or, when successfully countered, very ineffective. The catastrophic nature of PGMs places a greater premium on accurate technical intelligence, which is essential for the design of counter-measures.

2.(c) *Doctrinal Improvisation*

Doctrinal improvisation can be exercised in conjunction with the other options mentioned above. Under certain conditions, however, it will assume a role of pivotal importance such as when: (a) the introduction of a new weapon by the enemy has been discovered so late that there is no time to invent new technological counter-measures; (b) the enemy has successfully achieved technological surprise and the only immediate option available is to counter the new weapon with an improvised fighting doctrine.

In such circumstances, the quickest possible response is the use of existing weapons in an innovative way. When the Israelis were taken unawares by the appearance en masse of 'new' Egyptian anti-tank missiles and RPGs in the opening days of the 1973 Yom Kippur War, the only fast way to respond was through the tactical improvisation of their fighting doctrine. The tanks were moved back while the infantry was moved forward to clear the way for them, a role that had not been considered in the past. Similarly the unexpected effectiveness of the SAM-6 anti-aircraft missile combined with the lethal efficiency of the ZSU-23-4 anti-aircraft gun forced the Israeli Air Force to make tactical improvisations on short notice. In both cases, improvisations improved Israeli performance on the battlefield within four or five days despite the absence of adequate technological counter-measures. While this type of improvisation can be extremely effective, it requires flexible attitudes, doctrines, organization, the delegation of authority to lower levels, and a high level of training. Unfortunately, this is not always possible, as demonstrated by the inability of the French and British high commands to change their doctrines or show any capacity whatsoever to adapt to the new circumstances and prevent numerous disasters on the western front. As mentioned earlier, the British in the Western Desert, unlike the Germans, could not conceive of placing their heavy anti-aircraft guns in anti-tank roles.

Of all the options considered up to this point, deception is by far the most effective way to counter the effects of new weapons in modern technological warfare.[104] A well-planned deception operation causes the enemy to squander his resources and weaken himself more than any other strategy. This is particularly true when he has not discovered or is slow to discover that he has been tricked. Thus the Germans wasted a substantial number of bomber crews and resources on bombarding non-existent targets in England. Simple jamming would have immediately alerted them to the existence of a problem and spurred them on to develop new weapons and tactics. The Germans also wasted valuable resources at a critical time in their commitment to the development of the V-1 and V-2, long-range weapons which were effectively countered or diverted from their intended targets.

A corollary to the observation that deception is the superior choice as a counter-measure is that when a new weapon is introduced, deception should be used to conceal its mode of operation or even existence from the enemy thereby extending the period of time during which it can operate in an environment free of counter-measures. One such example is R.V. Jones' deception plan to conceal the British navigation aid code named Gee. Developed during 1941, Gee was scheduled to be placed in service in March 1942 as the only accurate navigational aid available to Bomber Command when, on 13 August 1941, a bomber carrying an earlier testing version of Gee without the authorization of the air staff was shot down over Germany. (A mistake similar to that committed by the Germans with Knickebein and X-Gerat.) In order to save the system, Jones concocted an intricate deception plan which included substituting a similar code name, 'Jay', for the name Gee (Jay actually described another less useful navigational system); passing information on the 'Jay' system to the Germans through double agents; changing the technical type number of the system from R-3000 to TR 1335 thus causing the Germans to look in other directions, and so on. This deception plan may not only have saved Gee, but also enabled it to avoid being jammed for five months after the start of large-scale operations.[105]

At a later stage, when the British were about to introduce H_2S, a new 10 centimeter radar which was to be used simultaneously by Bomber Command against Jones' advice (he wanted to use it initially only over the ocean where it could not be captured by the Germans), Jones was asked by the Admiralty to develop a cover plan that would stretch the operational use of H_2S as long as possible. The basis of this deception plan was to give the Germans the impression that their submarines were being detected not by H_2S in combination with information obtained from the deciphering of the German Naval Enigma, but by a new infra-red detection device. Duped by a variety of clues provided through the double cross system and other means, the Germans were, for a while, convinced that their U-boats were being detected by infra-red sensors. They were not only slow to recognize that the British were using centimetric radar against them at sea, but also invested great effort in developing (successfully it may be added) an ingenious paint to camouflage their U-boats against infra-red detection.

The new centimetric A.S.V. (Anti-Surface Vessel Radar) set was first used in the Bay of Biscay on 1st March 1943, and it was not until the following September that the U-boats began to dive on its approach, suggesting that they were at least equipped with centimetric receivers to give them advance warning. The six months' uncountered use of centimetre A.S.V. was much longer than we had dared to hope, especially since the Germans must have found virtually the same equipment in our bombers. Writing of this episode in their book, *Methods of Operations Research*, published in 1951, Professor P.M. Morse of the Massachusetts Institute of Technology and Professor G.E. Kimball of Columbia University said, 'How this six months' delay occurred is one of the mysteries of the war (it can perhaps be explained only by a criminal lack of liaison between the German naval and air technical staffs).' An alternative explanation may lie in the infra-red hoax. . . .

. . . When the Germans finally realized that we were using radar after all, they fortunately blamed it for all their U-boat sinkings, Dönitz even going so far as to say that this one invention had changed the balance in the battle of the Atlantic, and our Enigma feat remained secure.[106]

More than any other type of war in the past, modern warfare, based on the continuous development of new weapons systems at an ever-accelerating pace, depends on intelligence. The Battle of Britain was therefore a war of intelligence. Victory or defeat was often decided by the 'battle of intelligence' before combat had even begun. The role played by scientific technological intelligence in war will increase in proportion to the technological advancement of the adversaries and the use they make of state-of-the-art weaponry. Unlike the Second World War, the war of the future will be a fast-paced conflict in which there is little time to learn by trial and error – and the side that makes the best pre-war preparations, especially within the intelligence community, will have a better chance of emerging victorious.

CONCLUSIONS

The intensity of technological surprise and success in its exploitation depend upon the type of new weapons used, the quantities introduced (the 'critical mass' threshold), the timing of their use, and not least upon the development of a suitable military doctrine. This essay has suggested that some of the conditions necessary for the accomplishment of technological surprise are contradictory: in other words, having to wait until a 'critical mass' has been accumulated or the optimal time has arrived might work at cross-purposes with the need for secrecy, by giving an adversary more time to learn of the new weapon system before its initial use. Once a surprise has taken place, every effort must be made to conceal the underlying principles and performance characteristics of the weapon in order to prevent the adversary's development of effective counter-measures. This can be achieved through deception or by operating the weapons only where they cannot fall into enemy hands.

Conversely, the opponent will try to detect the existence of a new weapon at the earliest possible point so that he can be ready with appropriate counter-measures when it comes into use. With the exception of ultra-secret weapons that are tested, manufactured and used in very limited quantities, there is almost always enough information available to provide an adequate warning of the weapon's specifications, quantities and mode of operation, as well as other data concerning the adversary's intentions. In most cases, a good intelligence organization ought to obtain enough information not only to warn of the imminent appearance of a new weapon but also to develop adequate counter-measures and prepare plans to mislead the enemy as to its true effectiveness.

As we have seen, this has not always occurred. The first large-scale use of gas, the tank, the magnetic mine, the 88mm flak gun on the Western Desert, the T-34 and the Japanese Zero, to mention but a few weapons systems, all came as a complete surprise. In almost all of the above-mentioned examples, there was access to more than enough evidence concerning the existence of these new weapons and their previous combat use on different fronts, not to mention their large-scale testing and distribution to the troops, to provide timely warning.

As in the majority of failures to anticipate strategic surprise, the principal technological surprise is not to be found on the collection level or attributed to the absence of information; it is, instead, the outgrowth of problems on the level of analysis (or perception and acceptance on various levels (or 'politics'). In this respect, the causes of strategic and technological surprise are quite similar: they range from perceptual biases, rigid concepts, ethnocentric views, compartmentation, and co-ordination problems between the intelligence community and the military as well as among various intelligence organizations, to bureaucratic politics arising from conflicting priorities and competing interests.

Nevertheless, differences in the nature and degree of complexity of technological and political-strategic intelligence explain one crucial point of divergence between these two types of surprise. While there are virtually no instances in which a strategic surprise has been successfully avoided despite the availability of the necessary information, this article has shown that good intelligence work can prevent a technological surprise. Political–strategic intelligence has the more ambiguous task of estimating both the capabilities and intentions of a potential adversary.

Whereas material capabilities can be identified and evaluated with relative ease, this does not hold true for analysis of the enemy's intentions. Not readily reduced to black and white terms, this dimension must assess national character, the personalities of different leaders, irrational behavior and mutual perceptions, while continuously corroborating intentions and capabilities. In contrast, technological-scientific intelligence is chiefly concerned with the more easily identified dimension of the two—capabilities.

A political leader can take very high risks and make an essentially irrational decision to go to war, but a scientist is highly unlikely to succeed if he behaves in such a manner. Material capabilities can be identified, photographed, their performance estimated and their purpose deduced according to largely objective criteria. Usually having to undergo a slow evolutionary process, the development of a new weapon involves many participants and a long enough period of time to make it more vulnerable to discovery; a political leader, on the other hand, can make decisions alone and change his mind abruptly without giving any prior signals.

TABLE 1

TECHNOLOGICAL AND STRATEGIC SURPRISE COMPARED

Strategic Surprise	Technological Surprise
Very difficult to avoid.	Can be avoided.
Analysis of both intentions and capabilities (heavier emphasis on intentions).	Analysis primarily of capabilities.
Very complex analysis.	Relatively straightforward type of analysis.
No common language or concepts, serious cultural and historical barriers; very different perceptions, assessments, etc.; very rapid changes of course are possible.	The basic options or state of the art technology are usually known to all parties; change is evolutionary in nature and rather slow; many common concepts and perceptions.

Within the scientific and technological intelligence communities, certain fundamental scientific principles and the state of the art technology are well-known in all countries. This pool of information therefore delineates (with occasional exceptions) the range of possible choices or decision that are likely to be made. In other words, all scientific/technological experts talk more or less in the same language, work with similar concepts, and share a common body of knowledge. The political-strategic analyst, though, must grapple with concepts, perceptions, languages and cultures that differ radically from his own. He does not have as much in common with his adversary as the technological-scientific expert has with his counterpart. The logic or art of analysis must be tailored to each adversary and is not universal, nor can it be studied in relatively objective terms. While the technical expert can usually devise counter-measures to diminish the impact of his adversary's weapons, political-strategic experts do not always have access to such readily apparent antidotes.

From the discussion in this essay it becomes apparent that British scientific intelligence managed to sound an early warning of the development of many new and even revolutionary German weapons, while the Germans could seldom respond in kind. The best explanation of British success is that Great Britain was on the defensive. British intelligence harbored no illusions as to the strength and superiority of the German military machine and therefore had to take intelligence more seriously. The Germans experienced no feeling of vulnerability because of their position and respect (or fear) of military superiority. Contemptuous of their 'obviously inferior' adversaries, the Germans had little incentive to improve their intelligence capabilities. In addition, British scientific intelligence (although far from perfect) was much better co-ordinated and more centralized, and also happened to be headed by the right person at the right time. R.V. Jones was young, creative, not committed to any specific organization or interest, and had more than enough common sense and tact. He was willing to wait for the best opportunity in order to make his advice more acceptable, but he knew when to fight for his ideas and insist on the validity of his analysis. It is very unlikely that any individual of his age, self-confidence and open-mindedness could have attained a comparable position in the German authoritarian milieu. (Perhaps the closest case on the German side was that of Albert Speer, who sold his soul to Hitler, only asserting himself after it was too late to be of consequence.) One also cannot discount the element of luck in finding the most suitable man for the right position at such a critical time. R.V. Jones' early success, which again depended on a certain amount of luck, allowed him to establish his authority gradually in a bureaucratic and organizational environment that might have otherwise resented any intruders. The British were also very fortunate to have Churchill as their prime minister. For even though he made many disastrous decisions and often misused intelligence, he recognized more than any other political leader the contribution of modern science to war. Unlike Hitler, who often made major decisions regarding the choice of weapons despite his lack of knowledge on the subject, Churchill was more ready to listen to advice in areas in which he had no expertise.

The much higher quality of British intelligence also stemmed from a superior human intelligence network in Occupied Europe. In contrast, all German agents in Britain were actually controlled by British intelligence. This double-cross system was invaluable in feeding the Germans with false information on British weapons design as well as on the performance of German weapons. Finally, of course, ULTRA played a central role in the success of British scientific intelligence by monitoring the development and operational performance of German weapons in addition to measuring the effectiveness of British counter-measures and deception operations *vis-à-vis* Germany in the war of technology. It is highly improbable that all or even many of the elements contributing to the incredible success of British scientific intelligence will ever again be present within one intelligence organization.

In future wars, the combatants will rely even more heavily on the contributions of science and technology. We can expect the appearance of many more new weapons in each succeeding war. (This becomes evident to anyone who followed, for example, the Israeli-Syrian War in Lebanon in 1982, in which quite a few new weapons technologies were employed by the Israelis.)

Faced with the increased complexity and proliferation of modern weapons, intelligence organizations will be able to function efficiently in the future only by making all the necessary preparations in peace-time. These should include the collection of detailed information on the enemy's weaponry and his doctrines of deployment, the preparation of counter-measures, and the study of what the enemy knows about one's own weapons systems. Deception plans must be prepared in order to conceal the basis of one's own technological success. In order to be a few steps ahead, the intelligence organization should also begin work on new follow-on weapons systems to those that the enemy will be able to counter. Considering the much faster pace of future conventional wars and the increased rate of attrition (as well as the danger of nuclear escalation), it is reasonable to assume that any major conventional wars between Great Powers will be short in duration. The key to victory will thus depend to a large extent on the quality of scientific intelligence, an area in which the Western Democracies may have a considerable advantage if the appropriate preparations are completed.

Most of the case studies and examples cited in this article were taken from the First and Second World Wars. Differing in many ways from short wars, such prolonged wars allow more than enough time for the invention and development of new weapons and counter-measures. Furthermore, the pressure to introduce new weapons prematurely is much stronger in a drawn-out war.

Before the outbreak of what is expected to be a short war, new weapons should be developed and amassed in peace-time in order to lay the ground work for the achievement of technological surprise. This also allows more time for the development and assimilation of a doctrine designed to maximize the impact of the newly developed weapons. At the same time, the greater probability that information will leak out during the relatively long peace-time preparation period considerably reduces the possibility of achieving technological surprise. These and other differences between technological surprise in prolonged and short wars, as well as problems of achieving technological surprise in our own time, and other issues, will have to be saved for discussion in another article.

NOTES

This paper was presented at the U.S Army War College Conference on 'Intelligence and Military Operations' held at Carlisle Barracks, Pennsylvania, 22–25 April 1986. The views expressed in this article are those of the author and do not reflect the official policy or position of the Department of Defense or the U.S. Government. I would like to thank Dr Zeev Bonen whose creative ideas and suggestions first drew my attention to this subject and to my wife Jill for her help in editing this paper.

1. Winston S. Churchill, *The Great War*, Vol. 4 (London: The Home Library edn., n.d.) Appendix 8, War Memorandum, 'Mechanical Power in the Offensive' (9 November 1916). In this original and creative memorandum Churchill explored the potential of the tank as a means of breaking the deadlock in the war of attrition on the Western front. Many of its principles and ideas were later developed in the blitzkrieg era during the Second World War. Churchill's appreciation of the actual and potential contribution of science and technology to modern warfare combined with his fertile imagination are unique among modern leaders and certainly ahead of most military professionals of his time. No other leader has dedicated so much space in his memoirs to the role of science in war.
2. Lynn White, Jr., *Medieval Technology and Social Change*. (New York: Oxford University Press, 1978) Ch.1, pp. 1–39.
3. Bernard Brodie, *Sea Power in the Machine Age*. (Princeton: Princeton University Press, 1941), p. 6.
4. Robin Higham, 'Technology and D-Day,' in *D-Day: The Normandy Invasion in Retrospect*, Eisenhower Foundation (Lawrence: University Press of Kansas, 1971), p. 221.
5. This discussion of strategic surprise as a force multiplier is based on Michael I. Handel, 'Intelligence and the Problem of Strategic Surprise', *The Journal of Strategic Studies*, Vol. 7, No. 3, September 1984, pp. 229–81.
6. R.V. Jones, *Most Secret War: British Scientific Intelligence 1939–1945* (London: Hamish Hamilton, 1978), p. 74.
7. F.H. Hinsley, *et al.*, *British Intelligence in the Second World War*. Vol. 3, Part 1 (London: Her Majesty's Stationery Office, 1984), p. 329.
8. ASDIC is an acronym for the Allied Submarine Detection Investigation Committee of 1917 which was responsible for the development of a new technique to detect a submerged submarine, see J.W. Roskill, *The War at Sea, 1939–1945*, Vol. 1, *The Defensive* (London: HMSO, 1954) p. 34.

9. See Roskill, *The War at Sea*, Vol. 1, pp. 354–7. The book by Dönitz was *Die U-boatswaffe* (Berlin: E.S. Mittler, 1939).

10. For a detailed discussion see F.H. Hinsley, *British Intelligence in the Second World War*, Vol. 2 (Cambridge and New York: Cambridge University Press, 1981). Appendix 14, Technical Intelligence on Tanks and Anti-Tank Weapons in North Africa, p. 707.

11. Hinsley, *ibid.*, pp. 709–710.

12. See Corelli Barnett, *The Desert Generals* (London: George Allen & Unwin, 1983), second edition, p. 109.

13. Hinsley, p. 705.

14. On the German familiarity with the principles of radar counter-measures, on their own tests and on Göring's orders to discontinue all the experiments and the deployment of counter-measures for fear of 'suggesting' the idea by themselves to the British see: Jones, *Most Secret War*, Ch. 33, pp. 287–300, also Alfred Price, *Instruments of Darkness* (New York: Charles Scribner & Sons, 1978), p. 120, and David Irving, *The Rise and Fall of the Luftwaffe* (London: Futura, 1976), pp. 210–12.

15. Jones. *Most Secret War*, pp. 287–300.

16. Heinz Guderian, *Panzer Leader* (New York: E.P. Dutton, 1952), p. 143.

17. David Kahn, *Hitler's Spies: German Military Intelligence In World War II* (New York: Macmillan, 1978), pp. 457–8. The Soviet use of T-34 in their war against Japan in the Far East may be a myth. Japanese sources *do not* mention an encounter with Soviet T-34. Alvin D. Cox in his definitive history of the Japanese Russian War does not mention the appearance of the T-34 in that war: *Nomohon: Japan Against Russia, 1939*, 2 Vols. (Stanford: Stanford University Press, 1985).

18. John Milson, *Russian Tanks, 1900–1970* (New York: Galahad Books, 1970) p. 104.

19. Ibid., p. 104.

20. Data are from Kahn, *Hitler's Spies*, pp. 457–8 and Barry Leach, *German Strategy Against Russsia, 1939–1941* (New York: Oxford University Press, 1973) pp. 201–03.

21. Arthur J. Marder, *Old Friends, New Enemies: The Royal Navy and the Imperial Japanese Navy* (Oxford: Clarendon Press, 1981), p. 306.

22. Quoted from Major General S. Woodburn Kirby, *The War Against Japan*, Vol 1, *The Loss of Singapore* (London: HMSO, 1957), p. 240.

23. Kirby, *The War Against Japan*, p. 240.

24. Quoted from Martin Caidin, *Zero Fighter* (New York: Ballentine Books, 1969), pp. 24–5. See also Masatave Okumya and Jiro Houkoshi with Martin Cardin, *Zero!* (New York: E.P. Dutton, 1956).

25. Frederick J. Brown, *Chemical Warfare: A Study In Restraints* (Princeton, NJ: Princeton University Press, 1968), pp. 3–5.

26. C.R.M.F. Cruttwell, *A History of The Great War, 1914–1918* (Oxford: Clarendon Press, 1964), second edition, pp. 152–53.

27. Brown, *Chemical Weapons*, pp. 10–12.

28. Brown, ibid.

29. Cruttwell, *History of The Great War*, Ch. 18, pp. 467–74.

30. On the development of the proximity fuse see: James Phinney Baxter, *Scientists Against Time* (Cambridge, MA: MIT Press, 1968) Ch. 15, pp. 221–43, also Ralph B. Baldwin, *The Deadly Fuse: The Secret Weapon of World War II* (San Rafael, CA: Presidio Press, 1980), Wilfrid Eggleston, *Scientists at War* (Toronto: Oxford University Press, 1950) Ch. 3, pp. 65–74.

31. Baxter, *Scientists Against Time*, p. 229.

32. Patents to develop proximity fuses were issued in many countries. The Germans worked on the development of no less than 30 different proximity fuses (a typical mistake in their weapon development strategy during the Second World War), and were still working on the development of no fewer than a dozen types of proximity fuses in 1944. Baxter, *Scientists Against Time*, p. 222.

33. Quoted in Baxter, *Scientists Against Time*, p. 236.

34. A serious problem is when a military organization fails in war but invents excuses and builds defense mechanisms to convince itself that it did not fail, or that it failed because

of political interference, a stab in the back, etc. An admission of failure and the encouragement of self-criticism is a necessary condition, the beginning of any serious learning process.

35. On the U-2 see: David Wise and Thomas Ross, *The U-2 Affair* (New York: Random House, 1962) and Francis Gary Powers, *Operation Overflight* (New York: Holt Reinhart and Winston, 1970). For the best discussion of the development of the U-2 see John Ranelagh, *The Agency: The Rise and Decline of the CIA* (New York: Simon and Schuster, 1986). Ch. 10, pp. 310–22. Also Michael R. Beschloss, *May Day: Eisenhower Khruschev and the U-2 Affair* (New York: Harper & Row, 1986).
36. Robert Jervis, 'Hypothesis on Misperception', *World Politics*, Vol. 20, No. 3 (April 1968), pp. 454–79 and pp. 466–7.
37. See Gerald Pawle, *The Secret War, 1939–1945* (New York: William Sloane, 1957) Part III, pp. 191–220; also Guy Hurtcup, *Code Name Mulberry: The Planning Building and Operation of the Normandy Harbours* (London: David and Charles, 1977); Alfred Stanford, *Force Mulberry* (New York: William Morrow, 1951); Robin Higham, 'Technology and D-Day', in *D-Day: The Normandy Invasion in Retrospect* (Lawrence: The University Press of Kansas, 1971). pp. 221–41; Samuel Eliott Morison, *History of United States Naval Operations in World War II*, Vol. 11, *The Invasion of France and Germany, 1944–1945* (Boston: Little Brown, 1957) pp. 24–27; Major L. F. Ellis, *Victory in the West*, Vol. 1, *The Battle of Normandy* (London: HMSO, 1962), pp. 87–90; Gordon A. Harrison, *United States Army in World War II, Cross Channel Attack* (Washington, DC: Office of the Chief of Military History, 1951), pp. 73–5.
38. The requisites for D-Day were to land, supply and reinforce 185,000 men and 20.000 vehicles (Higham, 'Technology and D-Day', p. 222). The average tonnage of supply passed through the artificial harbors was 6,765 tons a day between 20 June to 1 September (Hartcup, p. 141).
39. Winston S. Churchill, *The Second World War*, Vol. 5, Closing the Ring (Cambridge: Houghton Mifflin, 1951), pp. 73–4.
40. Stanford, *Force Mulberry*, p. 33.
41. Harrison, *Cross Channel Attack*, p. 74.
42. For the critical role of the development of a special Japanese torpedo for use in shallow water for the attack on Pearl Harbor, see Gordon W. Prange, *At Dawn We Slept* (New York: McGraw Hill, 1981), Part I, in particular pp. 159–60; 320–33. The special torpedo, without which the attack on Pearl Harbor would not have taken place, was made available less than a month before the attack.
43. Hartcup, *Code Name Mulberry*, p. 141.
44. Albert Speer quoted in Hartcup, *Code Name Mulberry*, p. 141.
45. See John Sweetham, *The Dam Raids: Epic or Myth?* (London: Jane's, 1982); Alan W. Cooper, *The Men Who Breached the Dams* (London: William Kimber, 1982); Charles Webster and Noble Frankland, *The Strategic Air Offensive Against Germany, 1939–1945*, Vol. II (London: HMSO, 1961), pp. 168–89.
46. It is interesting to note that the Germans later experimented with a similar bouncing bomb designed for attacking ships. See Brian Johnson, *The Secret War* (New York: Methuen, 1978), p. 303.
47. For a lively debate on the real value of the attack on the Ruhr dams see: John Terraine, *A Time for Courage, The Royal Air Force in the European War, 1939–1945* (New York: Macmillan, 1984), pp. 538–40, who argues that the damage was minimal and that the really important dam, the Sorpe, which supplied water to the Ruhr industry, could not be breached by the Wallis bomb. (The Mohe and Eder were much less important and were used only for agriculture). A different and more favorable conclusion is reached by John Sweetham, *Operation Chastise*, pp. 179–82. Sweetham's conclusions appear to be more balanced.
48. See J. Valeiro Borghese, *Sea Devils*, (Chicago: Henry Regency Co., 1954). Arrigo Pefacco, *La Battaglie Navali Del Mediterraneo Nella Seconda Guerra Mondiale* (Milan, 1976). The Israelis used Italian explosive boats to spring a surprise on the Egyptian navy in 1948. The Egyptians sent their flagship, *Emir el Farouk*, to bombard Tel Aviv. The

Israelis, who had no comparable vessel, used explosive boats to attack the Egyptian frigate which sank opposite the coast of Tel Aviv. (The Israeli navy frogmen and commanders at that period were trained by the Italians.)

49. For a detailed but unsatisfactory study see Col. James E. Marzek, *The Fall of Eben Emael: Prelude to Dunkerque* (1970). The author does not make clear the connection between Eben Emael and Dunkerque. See also Telford Taylor, *The March of Conquest* (New York: Simon and Schuster, 1958), pp. 210–14.

50. On the Bruneval Raid, see: Jones, *Most Secret War*, Ch. 27, pp. 233, and George Millar, *The Bruneval Raid: Flashpoint of the Radar War*, (Garden City, NY: Doubleday, 1957).

51. See Martin Gilbert, *Winston S. Churchill 1939–1947 – Finest Hour* (London: Heinemann, 1983), p. 97. Churchill's own account, however, shows why such a deception was actually impossible to carry out: see *The Second World War: The Gathering Storm* (Boston: Houghton Mifflin, 1948), pp. 505–07, and Appendix H, pp. 706–11.

52. For some of the achievements of German military technology in the Second World War, see: Rudolf Lusar, *Die deutschen Waffen and Geheimwaffen des 2. Weltkriegs und ihre Weiterentwicklung* (Munich: Lehmans, 1958), 2nd revised edition, and Leslie E. Simon, *Secret Weapons of the Third Reich, German Research in World War II* (Old Greenwich, CT: We Inc, 1971). Among the major explanations for the ultimate failure of German military technology despite its excellence and head start are: (1) Hitler's decision in the autumn of 1940 (and later in force during 1941) having considered the war as good as won to curtail all long-term scientific research; (2) the inferior position of German civilian scientists in relation to the military: in Germany science was the servant of the armed forces – in the West co-equals; (3) the independence and fragmentation of the German industry, leading to the uncoordinated research and development of too many prototypes of weapons; (4) the negative attitude of Hitler to basic scientific research and focusing instead on gadgetry and miracle weapons, which led in turn to the random selection of projects and a heavy investment in the wrong types of weapons; (5) the expulsion of Jewish scientists; (6) lack of co-operation with Allies and other countries (or a narrow scientific base); (7) in the later phases of the war gearing scientific research efforts to counter the Allies' superior technology (i.e., reactive rather than independent research); and (8) a greater tradition of emphasizing theory in German engineering compared with the more empirical tradition in England and the US where workable devices were produced even in advance of theoretical understanding (e.g., the cavity magnetron). See: R.J. Overy, *The Air War, 1939–1945* (New York: Stein and Day, 1981), Ch. 8, pp. 185–202; Jones, *Most Secret War*.

53. See Jones, *Most Secret War*; Alfred Price, *Instruments of Darkness*. For the full text of the Oslo report see Hinsley, *British Intelligence in the Second World War*, Vol. 1, Appendix 5, pp. 508–13.

54. Cruttwell, *History of the Great War*, p. 154.

55. See for example, Liddell Hart, *The Tanks*, Vol. 1, Ch. 7, pp. 128–53 and Cruttwell, *History of the Great War*, Ch. 28, pp. 467–77.

56. Churchill, *Great War*, Vol. III, p. 1068.

57. Handel, 'Intelligence and the Problem of Strategic Surprise', in particular pp. 229–30.

58. Quoted in Jones, *Most Secret War*, p. 289.

59. For the discussion of the development of Window and the delays in its introduction see: Jones, *Most Secret War*, Ch. 33, pp. 287–300. Alfred Price, *Instruments of Darkness: The History of Electronic Warfare* (New York: Charles Scribner's Sons, 1978), in particular pp. 112–20 and Sir Charles Webster and Noble Frankland, *The Strategic Air Offensive Against Germany, 1939–1945* (London: HMSO, 1961), Vol. 1, pp. 400–01, and Vol. 2, pp. 141–67. Martin Streetly, *Confound and Destroy* (London: Macdonald and Jane's 1978).

60. An American representative present in the early discussion on Window (April 1942) expressed fear that this device which favoured the offensive at the expense of the defensive might endanger the Panama Canal. See: Sir Charles Webster and Noble Frankland, *The Strategic Air Offensive Against Germany, 1939–1945*, Vol. 1 (London:

HMSO, 1961), p. 401. This fear appears completely unjustified at that time.
61. Webster and Frankland, *The Strategic Air Offensive*, 1, p. 142. For Jones' comments on the evidence that the Germans must have been aware of the principle of Window in light of intelligence reports by October 1942, see: *Most Secret War*, pp. 293–94. Also Price, *Instruments of Darkness*. Price provides a copy of the cartoon published by the *Daily Mirror* (18 June 1942), pp. 118–19.
62. Webster and Frankland, *The Strategic Air Offensive*, 1, p. 143.
63. Sir Charles Portal estimated that an earlier introduction of Window might have saved 238 bombers and their crews out of 858 lost between 1 April and 14 July 1943. Webster and Frankland, *The Strategic Air Offensive*, 2, pp. 143–4.
64. Jones, *Most Secret War*, p. 297.
65. Churchill, *The Second World War*, Vol. 4, p. 289.
66. Ibid.
67. Webster and Frankland, *The Strategic Air Offensive*, 2, p. 145.
68. See Jones, *Most Secret War*, pp. 293–4.
69. Ronald W. Clark, *The Rise of The Boffins* (London: Phoenix House, 1962), p. 202.
70. Price, *Instruments of Darkness*, p. 120.
71. Jones, *Most Secret War*, p. 299.
72. Ovrey, *The War in the Air*, p. 194.
73. David Irving, *The Mare's Nest* (Boston: Little, Brown & Co 1964), p. 313.
74. Ibid., p. 304. The V-2 was not the most cost-effective mode of delivering 1,620 lb of conventional explosive. The V-1 on the other hand was a very cheap weapon but highly vulnerable to interception and a variety of counter-measures. (The cost of the V-2 was approximately 212,000 RM as compared with the V-1's 2115.) Ibid., p. 304, 314.
75. This weapon was ideal for use against the Allied cross-Channel invasion. By the time of the invasion, Hitler personally authorized the production of this mine, but its actual use was delayed by the Luftwaffe's inefficiency. When it was finally available to be used on the beachhead of Normandy three days after the invasion (7 June, 1944) it was too late. The British were lucky enough to retrieve a sample as early as 20 June, and were able to develop counter-measures within a short time. Morrison, *The Invasion of France and Germany, 1944–1945* (Boston: Little, Brown & Co, 1957), Vol. XI, pp. 46–7.
76. Patrick Beesly, *Very Special Intelligence* (Garden City, New York: Doubleday, 1978), pp. 240–41.
77. See Michael Handel, 'Numbers Do Count: The Question of Quantity Versus Quality', *Journal of Strategic Studies*, Vol. 4, No. 3, September 1981, pp. 225–60, p. 226.
78. Brown, *Chemical Warfare*, pp. 8–9.
79. Bernard Brodie, *Sea Power in the Machine Age* (Princeton, NJ: Princeton University Press, 1941), p. 7.
80. Ibid., p. 444.
81. Ibid., p. 443.
82. See Arthur J. Marder, *'From the Dreadnought to Scapa Flow'*, *The Road to War*, Vol. I (London: Oxford University Press, 1961) pp. 56–60. Also Richard Hough, *Dreadnought: A History of the Modern Battleship* (New York: Macmillan, 1964).
83. On the inevitability of strategic surprise see Handel, 'Intelligence and the Problem of Strategic Surprise', pp. 229–81. Michael I. Handel, 'The Yom Kippur War and the Inevitability of Surprise', *International Studies Quarterly*, September 1977, pp. 461–501. Richard K. Betts, 'Analysis, War and Decision: Why Intelligence Failures are Inevitable', *World Politics*, October 1978, p. 61. Richard K. Betts, *Surprise Attack: Lessons for Defense Planning* (Washington, DC: The Brookings Institution, 1982).
84. Jones, *Most Secret War*, p. 73.
85. Rear Admiral Edwin T. Layton reports that in the summer of 1936 through the analysis of decrypts of Japanese naval radio messages US Naval Intelligence discovered that the sea trials of the refurbished and modernized *Nagato* battleships (built during the First World War) reached speeds exceeding 26 knots. As a result the US decided to change the design of the *North Carolina* class battleships still on the drawing board (originally

designed to reach speeds up to 24 knots) to reach speeds of 27 knots and later classes of battleships to reach speeds of over 28 knots. 'This single piece of radio intelligence gave our new battleships an important tactical wartime advantage'. Rear Admiral Edwin T. Layton, USN, retired with Captain Roger Pineau USNR, retired and John Costello, *And I Was There: Pearl Harbor and Midway, Breaking the Secrets* (New York: William Morrow, 1985), pp. 57–8.

86. Jones, *Most Secret War*, Ch. 35, pp. 306–09. David Irving, *The German Atomic Bomb* (New York: Simon and Schuster, 1967). Samuel A. Goudsmit, *Alsos* (New York: Henry Schumann, 1947). Leo James Mahoney, 'A History of the War Department Scientific Intelligence Mission (Alsos) 1943–1945' (unpublished Ph.D. dissertation, Kent State University, 1981).

87. For the history of the development of the V-1 and V-2 by the Germans, their discovery by the British and the campaign against the long range weapons see: Basil Collier, *The Battle for the V-Weapons 1944–1945* (New York: William Morrow, 1965). Peter G. Cooksley, *Flying Bomb. The Story of Hitler's V-Weapons in World War II* (New York: Charles Scribner's Sons, 1979). David Johnson, *V-1 V-2 Hitler's Vengeance on London* (New York: Stein and Day, 1982). Josef Garlinski, *Hitler's Last Weapons* (New York: Times Books, 1978). Martin Middlebrook, *The Peenemunde Raid* (Indianapolis: Bobbs-Merrill, 1982). Irving, *The Mare's Nest*. Hinsley, *British Intelligence in the Second World War*, Vol. 3, Chs. 39–42, pp. 329–459. Jones, *Most Secret War*, Chs. 38–46, pp. 332–465. Basil Collier, *The Defence of the United Kingdom* (London: HMSO, 1957).

88. Hinsley, *British Intelligence in the Second World War*, Vol. 3, part I, p. 352.

89. Brown, *Chemical Warfare*, Ch. 1, pp. 3–xx.

90. See Beesly, *Very Special Intelligence*, pp. 204–06; 246–7. Johnson, *The Secret War*, p. 232. See also Admiral Karl Donitz, *Memoirs* (Cleveland: World Publishing Co., 1959), pp. 418–20.

91. See Jones, *Most Secret War*, Chs. 11 (pp. 78–92), 15–17 (pp. 120–46), 21 (pp. 172–9), 24 (pp. 203–15); Churchill, *Finest Hour*, pp. 381–91; Hinsley, *British Intelligence in the Second World War*, Ch. 10, pp. 315–30, and Appendix II, pp. 550–65; Price, *Instruments of Darkness*.

92. Churchill, *Finest Hour*, pp. 388–9. Jones, *Most Secret War*, p. 179. Charles Cruikshank, *Deception in World War II* (New York: Oxford University Press, 1980), Ch. 1, pp. 1–19.

93. Hinsley, *British Intelligence in the Second World War*, 1, pp. 326–7.

94. Collier, *The Defence of the United Kingdom*, p. 433.

95. Ibid., p. 339.

96. J.C. Masterman, *The Double Cross System* (New Haven: Yale University Press, 1972), pp. 179–81.

97. Collier, *The Defence of the United Kingdom*, p. 385, and Cooksley, *Flying Bomb*, pp. 174–5.

98. Hinsley, *British Intelligence in the Second World War*, 3, part I, p. 340.

99. Ibid., p. 337.

100. Johnson, *The Secret War*, pp. 298–302. See Lusar, *Die Deutsche Geheimwaffen*, pp. 129–33. (English translation R. Lusar, *German Secret Weapons of the Second World War* (London: Spearman, 1959.)

101. Hinsley, *British Intelligence in the Second World War*, 3, p. 338.

102. Anthony Martienssen, *Hitler and the Admirals* (New York: E.P. Dutton, 1949), p. 176.

103. Hinsley, *British Intelligence in the Second World War*, 3, pp. 338–9, 341.

104. What Churchill called the 'superior alternative'. *Finest Hour*, p. 386.

105. Jones, *Most Secret War*, pp. 217–21.

106. Ibid., pp. 321, 322.

APPENDIX I: CHANCE AND LUCK IN INTELLIGENCE WORK

Second only to Clausewitz' emphasis on the primacy of politics in the direction of war is his repeated reference to the important role played by chance and luck in war. In *On War* he frequently compares war to a game of cards, which is based on rational calculation, strategy and certain rules of the game – but at the same time involves a substantial amount of luck. When rational calculations and chance interact in war, chance may be the dominant factor, at least in the short run.

In principle, chance should influence both sides equally. Yet in the statistical probabilistic sense at least (as distinguished from luck, fate *schicksal*, etc.) chance favors no one. Therefore the military genius whose superior intuition allows him to read the situation more clearly under conditions of uncertainty and ambiguity may better exploit the opportunities presented by unexpected developments. (See Katherine Herbig, 'Chance and Uncertainty in *On War*' in Michael I. Handel, *Clausewitz In Modern Strategy* (London: Frank Cass, 1986).

It has been said that chance works in favor of the well-prepared. To this it may be added that chance also works for those who dare to deviate from dogmatic military doctrines and standard procedures. After reading the history of British scientific intelligence in the Second World War by R.V. Jones, one is indeed impressed by the way in which the British repeatedly managed to exploit chance to their advantage. In the first place the appointment of Dr Jones to head scientific intelligence was remarkably successful. Very rarely in history of warfare is the most suitable person appointed to the right position at the perfect time. Dr Jones was a patriot, an excellent and creative scientist with both feet on the ground, a man of common sense and creative invention-minded – all qualities that were ideal for intelligence and deception work. Those qualities of analysis and judgment were combined with persistence and the readiness to fight for his ideas at the most opportune point in time.

By an unusual and not yet fully explained stroke of luck, the British naval attaché in Oslo received in November 1939 from an unknown German scientist a detailed and highly accurate report of the major scientific, military development programs being conducted in Germany. (R.V. Jones, *Most Secret War*: British Scientific Intelligence 1939–1945 (London: Hamish Hamilton, 1978), Ch. 8, pp. 67–71, and F.H. Hinsley, *British Intelligence in the Second World War*, Vol. 1 (New York: Cambridge University Press, 1979) pp. 99–100, and Appendix 5, pp. 508–512.) In Hinsley's words, 'The very fact that the report dealt with many topics on which no information had been collected led many to disbelieve it, that and the conviction that one man could not possibly know so much and must therefore have passed on planted information.'

(Hinsley, p. 100, also Jones, pp. 69–70.) Fortunately Jones accepted the Oslo report as authentic from the start and used to great advantage throughout the war.

Jones' development of the counter-measures to *knickebein* was one long series of events all based on such good luck. His discovery (12 June, 1940) that the Germans were working on a system of intersecting radio beams to navigate bombs to their targets was not accepted by most of his colleagues, including initially Lindemann, the Prime Minister's scientific adviser. (It was then believed by radio experts that short-wave beams could not be narrowly focused or beamed low enough around the earth surface to be received by bombers.) After listening to the conversation of German prisoners of war flying Heinkel IIIs, Jones was able to determine that the *knickebein* receiver had been cleverly incorporated into the regular German E. Bl. I receiver used for blind landing. The next day Jones was able to convince Lindemann that his analysis was correct, while Lindemann prepared a memorandum for Churchill. Churchill immediately realized the importance of the report and asked the Air Ministry to investigate the matter thoroughly. In a meeting on 15 June it was decided to look for the beams and if necessary prepare suitable jamming equipment. Two days later, Jones briefed Tizard on his findings, but he was not very receptive to the idea of a system such as *knickebein* really existed. Attempts to discover the beams on 18 and 19 June failed. On 21 June a meeting to discuss the subject was held in the Cabinet room at 10 Downing Street; Dr Jones was invited at the last moment and came late and unprepared. (Jones, pp. 100–102; Churchill, *Finest Hour*, pp. 383–5). Despite the skepticism of some of the others present (including Tizard) Jones made a persuasive presentation and obtained Churchill's backing for continuation of his search for the *knickebein* beams. In another meeting on the same day, one of the foremost experts on radio propagation, T.L. Eckersley, argued that a short-wave beam from Cleve could not possibly be received at 20,000 feet in England. The principal Deputy Director of signals, Group Captain O.G.W.G. Lywood, suggested that in view of Eckersley's opinion they should not waste any more time and effort and cancel the flight scheduled for that night to discover the beams. Jones promptly told Lywood that if he cancelled the flights, the Prime Minister would promptly receive a report that his orders had been countermanded. Lywood backed down and the flight took place as planned. That night the *knickebein* beams were discovered and Jones was proved correct. Accordingly, the development of counter-measures was assigned top priority (Jones, pp. 92–105).

This episode demonstrates just how much good (or bad) luck can sometimes dominate intelligence work. Had R.V. Jones been a less secure person who easily bowed to senior scientists' opinions, he might have dropped his search for the *knickebein* beams right from the start. Had he missed the Cabinet meeting (which he almost did) on 21 June or had Churchill not given a junior expert (he was 28 years old) the opportunity to speak, the Germans might have used the *knickebein* navigation beams successfully and the British would not have been able to 'bend' them and foil the attacks. At each step an event or a series of events took place which could have easily led others to disregard Jones' opinion.

Those who opposed him were all honest men, better known experts, and higher in rank and influence. This chain of events appears in retrospect to have evolved with an incredible amount of good fortune. The margin between success and failure was very narrow indeed. What is most surprising is that Jones actually succeeded. The majority of experts were against him and he had no organizational support. The story makes it clear that well-known experts and scientists can approach problems from a closed-mind perspective, relying more on past experience than on new evidence. They frequently assume that problems that they cannot solve cannot be solved by the enemy either. Although we usually think of scientists as open-minded people who base their decisions on empirical evidence, like everyone else they cling stubbornly to old concepts and exhibit powerful defense mechanisms to resist evidence that contradicts their theories.

In addition to his character, Jones' success can be attributed to the great feeling of vulnerability in Britain after the fall of France. This motivated the British to take precautions against all possible disasters and transcend their own interests. The system allowed Jones to express himself as an equal despite his position and age and in the final analysis did not reject his logical proof and evidence. It is doubtful that a German scientist under similar conditions could have succeeded. (Albert Speer was perhaps the only notable exception in Germany, but he was far too long under Hitler's spell to think independently.)

The lesson of course is that intelligence analysis and estimates cannot be decided by a majority vote, and that lower echelon experts who approach subjects from a different perspective must be given the opportunity to express their ideas.

The problem is that situations like this which frequently occur in the world of intelligence have no rational solution. Although of critical importance, luck, creativity and intuition can neither be systematically studied nor taught nor can any rules be developed that would suggest how to take them into account. Like Clausewitz' military genius who can intuitively make the correct decisions on the battlefield, so also the 'intelligence genius' can feel and time the correct analysis of his intuition which cannot always be explained, taught to others or accepted by his colleagues.

WSI—G

PART TWO

Intelligence and Strategy

4

The Politics of Intelligence

The success of all intelligence work depends upon the degree to which three main elements are present. At the most rudimentary level, success hinges upon the availability of sufficient raw data for balanced intelligence estimates, as well as upon the analyst's ability to distinguish between correct and incorrect, relevant and irrelevant information. The second element concerns the extent to which the perceptions of the intelligence analyst and all other participants are accurate, while the third involves the level of political distortion or interference in the intelligence process.

Although these three elements are inextricably linked, they can be studied as discrete 'actors' for analytical expedience. Such *theoretical* isolation has considerably advanced our understanding of the intelligence process, as is evidenced by the ample amounts of systematic attention devoted to the first two elements in the current body of literature. To date, theoretical analysis of the third element – that is, political distortion of the intelligence process – has been somewhat more uneven and less organized. This article therefore attempts to construct a framework for systematic analysis of the various types of political interference or the political pathologies existing within the intelligence process. This is not to say that all political dimensions of the intelligence process are pathological or negative: as in military affairs, the ultimate guidance and control of all intelligence work is political. Policy decisions regarding the use of intelligence estimates, or the benefits of checks and balances between competing intelligence organizations are both examples of 'positive' political influences.

The word politics as used here encompasses at least four different meanings:

1. *Politics as an interest.* In this case, each actor is intent upon maximizing his own strength and protecting or increasing his power in terms of such areas as budgets, manpower, and missions. Given the finite resources available, this of course leads to competition among different individuals and organizations.

2. *Politics as a bargaining process.* This involves the negotiations and co-ordination among different organizations, each of which naturally views the world from a unique perspective. In this situation, the

bargaining skills of each participant may be as important as the power he possesses. Furthermore, the bargaining process is less than ideal from the professional standpoint of the intelligence expert because it reflects a political compromise acceptable to each organization rather than the best possible rational decision. On the other hand, a positive aspect of the bargaining process is that it encourages the comparison of different viewpoints and estimates.

3. *The politicization of the intelligence process.* This includes all types of interference in the intelligence process by leaders and their close aides. Such interference distorts 'purely professional' considerations, estimates, analytical procedures, and the dissemination of the intelligence product in the attempt to bring about a desired outcome or to gain an advantage *vis-à-vis* other interested groups.

4. *The political use of intelligence.* Here, political leaders or organizations do not interfere in the intelligence process as such, but use the estimates or information provided by an intelligence agency to promote their own particular interests rather than those of the state: that is, they employ the intelligence produce selectively, not for its originally intended purpose.

While some political dimensions of the intelligence process are necessary and even helpful, others generate a considerable amount of friction which cannot help but bring about a decline in the quality of the intelligence product and its use. It is primarily the negative political aspects of the intelligence process that are the subject of this article.

THE IDEAL AND REAL WORLDS OF INTELLIGENCE

The nature of intelligence work has frequently been compared with that of meteorology and medicine.[1] Although none of these professions is an exact science, each has some quantifiable dimensions and requires decisions and forecasts to be made under conditions of pressure and uncertainty where failure is immediately reflected in negative results. In each case, failure can lead to severe criticism, even punishment, while success is taken for granted. Yet the intelligence professional suffers from one additional major handicap – namely, political interference: while no one would demand that a meteorologist predict fair weather when rain is indicated or that a doctor change his diagnosis because it is unfavourable, comparable political interference occurs regularly in intelligence work.

Clausewitz's distinction between war in the abstract and war in practice is also applicable to the world of intelligence. War in the abstract is an artificial intellectual concept – an ideal type that cannot exist in reality. In practice it is inevitably modified by uncertainty; 'the fog of war'; psychological factors; the inherent differences between offense and defense; cost/benefit calculations; and political considerations. This does not mean that the analysis of war in the abstract is a frivolous academic exercise. On the contrary, it is a powerful heuristic tool for grasping the logic and dynamic character of war. Moreover, such an ideal type represents a standard against which performance in the real world can be measured.

In much the same way, ideal intelligence work would be objective, autonomous, and free of political pressures. It would function in accordance with '. . . the cardinal rule of separation of policy from intelligence judgments';[2] with the idea that 'intelligence should flourish in its protected sanctuary . . . fortified by its privilege of detachments',[3] and that 'intelligence must be depoliticized'.[4] In the real world, however, this ideal can only rarely be approximated. Not only do ambiguity and uncertainty plague intelligence work, but political concerns permeate every aspect of its higher and, at times, even lower echelons. It is practically impossible to distinguish between policy-making on the one hand and intelligence *input* on the other. Indeed, it has been suggested that 'the unresolveable tension between policymaking and intelligence rests in fact on an unresolveable definitional problem. For no one agrees on what is policy and what is intelligence'.[5]

In modern times, information has become perhaps the most valuable form of capital for political and military decision-makers, who must cope with the ever-increasing complexities of a highly competitive world. The correct or incorrect use of timely information can have a critical impact on every facet of political life. A decision regarding the release of certain information to the public may influence the outcome of an election campaign (e.g., the effect on the 1962 Congressional election of Kennedy's election promises regarding Cuba and the subsequent discovery of Russian missiles there). Releasing intelligence information concerning an adversary's new or increased capabilities may be necessary to convince Congress to maintain or increase defense allocations; hence, it is critical to the survival and well-being of military organizations as well as to the military-industrial complex. The Pentagon frequently produces a glossy report, *Soviet Military Power*, that attempts to justify the government's policies and budget requests by publishing newly declassified material on the alarming growth of Soviet military capabilities.[6] Intelligence can also be used by the Chief Executive or his opponent to evaluate the incumbent's performance. In 1980, for example, the US media were deluged with classified information indicating a widening gap in the US–USSR nuclear and conventional strategic balances, the weak state of US preparedness, and a shortage of spare parts. Publication of this information seriously undermined Jimmy Carter's re-election campaign.

Decisions to release or withhold intelligence selectively can easily sway public opinion. The agency or individual credited with releasing the information gains in popularity or power, in addition to persuading the public to support a particular decision. As First Lord of the Admiralty in 1939 and 1940, Churchill publicized inflated figures of German U-Boat losses to boost British morale (and, no doubt, also to demonstrate the effectiveness of the Royal Navy under his leadership). In BBC broadcasts, the First Lord of the Admiralty claimed that 'the attack of the U-Boats has been controlled and they have paid a heavy toll' (12 November 1939). A few months later, he stated: 'It seems pretty certain that half the U-Boats with which Germany began the war have been sunk, and that their new building has fallen far behind what we expected' (20 January 1940).[7] When the Director of Naval Intelligence's weekly tabular statement of U-Boat losses (based on the conclusions of the Submarine Assessment Committee) contradicted his statements, Churchill ordered 'this information is not to be circulated except to First Sea Lord, Deputy Chief of Naval Staff and First Lord. A monthly statement should be prepared for wider circulation and I will see it before it is issued'.[8] The attempts of Admiral Godfrey [DNI] to correct Churchill's 'methodological biases' in estimating U-boat losses rapidly lost him the favor of the First Lord of the Admiralty.[9] When Churchill subsequently became Prime Minister, however, his public announcements grew more accurate and cautious; in fact, political considerations now dictated the manipulation of information so as to present the public with a more pessimistic view. Accordingly, in October 1940, when the DNI forwarded definitive intelligence estimates to Admiral Pound (and obviously also to the Prime Minister) making it clear that German plans to invade England had been called off, the good news was not passed on to the public.[10] 'The War Office was telling the Admiralty in the same month that "they thought the time would never come, except on account of weather conditions, when it would be safe to say invasion was off".'[11]

There were, however, sound political reasons for this decision. The British public's continued belief in the threat of invasion was, after all, 'the greatest stimulus to effort [i.e., increased production] the nation ever had'.[12] Furthermore, Churchill was then doing everything in his power to heighten anxiety in the United States about the fate of Britain, including the possibility that its fleet could fall into Hitler's hands. In December 1940, Harry Hopkins reported to President Roosevelt from London that 'most of the Cabinet and all military leaders here believe that the invasion is imminent . . . I therefore cannot urge too strongly that any action you may take to meet the immediate needs here must be based on the assumption that invasion will come before May 1, 1941'.[13] Politically, Churchill's 'management' of information undoubtedly paid off. By 1942, though, the specter of a German invasion that continued to haunt the British led the Army to retain in Britain substantial forces that could have been used to better advantage elsewhere. Thus, Churchill's less than judicious use of intelligence for short-range political advantage may have caused a longer-range military problem.[14]

Although all types of regimes and organizations have misused intelligence to augment their own political power, the temptation to exploit intelligence for political purposes is the greatest in democratic societies. Both a government and its opposition will scramble to take advantage of intelligence information when appealing to public opinion, to the legislature and to the mass media. In non-democratic countries, where often there is little or no need to appeal to public opinion and where the mass media are completely under governmental control, such pressures to involve the intelligence community and/or classified information in the political process are weaker. In fact, democratic societies often make the very performance of the intelligence community into a political issue, as evidenced by the Pearl Harbor Hearings, Congressional investigations, the Rockefeller White House Commission, the Church-Pike Committees on intelligence and policy-making, the Gaither report, the Team A versus Team B experiment, the Franks' report in England, and the Agranat Commission in Israel.[15]

As early as 1929, Churchill, while in opposition to Chamberlain, made extensive use of highly classified information to warn the British public of the dangers of German rearmament. Though Churchill acquired some of the information with the government's blessing,[16] most of it was privately supplied to him by government officials. Churchill was far more receptive to alarming intelligence (among other reasons because of his interest in proving that government policies were all wrong) than were the various governments and prime ministers who were preoccupied with their day-to-day responsibilities and wanted to prove the success of their own policies.

Churchill himself might have been less responsive to the same information had he come across it earlier, when he was Chancellor of the Exchequer. While serving in that capacity, he did not hesitate to attack the Service estimates, and later invented the self-perpetuating Ten Year Rule in 1928. Subsequently, his access to classified information lent a great deal of force to his attacks on the government in Parliament; successive prime ministers were often embarrassed by the more accurate data on which he based his repeated warnings and incessant criticism. He was able to have his cake and eat it too – that is, have access to highly classified information without the responsibility of acting upon it. To the aforementioned officials who leaked information for use against the government, Churchill was an excellent channel through which to communicate their growing frustration with the government's policies. In Vansittart's words, 'He suited me much better outside, for information on German trends would at least be voiced'.[17]

Although the British prime ministers Churchill so vociferously criticized were irritated by his attacks, they took no action to sever his private intelligence connection. By the time Churchill became a Cabinet member and, later, Prime Minister, his own experience had convinced him of the wisdom of imposing tighter controls on the use and dissemination of classified information. In the 1930s, however, Churchill was clearly in a unique position and could probably get away with more than any other politician outside the government.

Such intimate connections between government, intelligence officials, and a powerful political opponent would be far too sensitive to be conceivable in today's world. Private initiatives involving the dissemination of closely guarded information would probably lead to an immediate investigation as well as to some sort of censure and punishment. Daniel Ellsberg's release of the so-called Pentagon Papers is another example of how classified reports and estimates can be leaked to the public in order to furnish the opposition with the information necessary to fight government policies – in this case, US policies in Vietnam.[18] In both instances (those of Churchill and Ellsberg), the unauthorized use of information may have served a worthy political cause that was later seen to be justified. Nevertheless, can any democracy in today's world afford to permit the unauthorized disclosure of classified information based on the judgement of *one* individual even for a just cause? And who will determine which causes are just?

In the shrinking modern world of accelerated military technological development and intense ideological competition, the formerly unmistakable boundaries between foreign and domestic affairs have become blurred. This intertwining of domestic and foreign affairs has progressively intensified political pressure on the intelligence community, causing its information to assume even greater significance in domestic politics. Each intelligence community continuously studies, measures and analyses the behavior and policies of other states in order to provide its government with the informational basis for its national security and foreign policies. The process continues when the intelligence community follows up the reactions of other countries to its own government's policies. As a result, the intelligence community is in fact making a comment on its government's own policies, once again blurring the distinction between intelligence and policy. Thus, intelligence provides not only the government, but also its domestic opponents and public opinion, with a standard by which to judge its relative performance. Governments have a powerful incentive to regulate the flow of information in a way that vindicates their policies; yet this situation also provides an equally strong incentive for the opposition to try to prove the opposite case.[19]

For any democratic government, the cost of ignoring or misusing intelligence – even in times of peace – has increased tremendously[20] even as the political rewards to be gained have become more tempting. In as much as the actual and potential stakes now affect all of the major participants in the political system, intelligence has become, in many of its manifestations, part and parcel of politics.

As the preceding discussion implies, two approaches to the problem of the politicization of intelligence can be found in the current literature. The first can be referred to as 'the professional approach', the second as 'the realistic approach'. Almost all advocates of the first are professional intelligence experts (e.g., McLachlan, Cline, Howells, Kirkpatrick). Fully aware that political pressures are inevitable, they nevertheless, consider such pressures to be a dangerous and unethical type of interference in intelligence work that must be minimized. While they realize that the objective, neutral and professionally-oriented intelligence community must remain an ideal, they still aspire to approximating it even at a relatively high cost. These experts put truth in reporting above all else, even if this means undermining the influence of the intelligence community in the policy-making process. For them intelligence in the abstract is not just an ivory-tower concept, it is a standard of performance. They are not ready to compromise the truth to please policy-makers, but they are prepared to make some cosmetic concessions in terms of better packaging of the product for the political customer and improved salesmanship and public relations;[21] some are even prepared to avoid squabbles over procedural and professional issues of secondary importance by adopting a more 'positive' attitude in their dealings with policy-makers. These professionals hold that the only hope for improving the quality and reliability of the intelligence community in the long run lies in distancing it from the political arena.

Proponents of 'the realistic approach' also recognize the inevitability of political pressures – but they reach the opposite conclusion. Rather than pursuing the utopian dream of an independent, objective intelligence community, they recommend 'flowing with the tide' while trying to turn the situation to one's advantage. According to them, politicization of the intelligence process may be a blessing in disguise from which the truth will emerge as a result of the competitive relationship between intelligence organizations representing various political–organizational interests as well as different perspectives; that is, a system of checks and balances. Most importantly, the intelligence community must be made more relevant to the world of the policy-maker. Greater emphasis must be placed on the particular interests and idiosyncrasies of the policy-maker in order to supply him with the best and most useful information on topics that interest him.

> Success depends on maintaining a delicate balance between discrediting analysts as a result of their total absorption into policy debate or isolating them and keeping them pure but unhelpful to decision makers. How well this can be done depends very much on the personalities involved, and especially on the adeptness at bureaucratic politics of the intelligence managers who can act as brokers or salesmen for their subordinates' products and buffers against political pressure. This kind of management of intelligence – policy interaction – is more a matter of art than science. It cannot succeed unless policy makers as well as managers agree on a need for the delicate balance, and agree that for an analyst who produces really useful assessments, political promiscuity is destructive but political virginity is impossible. *Most of all, success depends on the attitudes of the consumers.*[22]

> Rather than try to solve the problem by completely getting rid of the biases from the intelligence process, however, it may be just as reasonable to accept some sort of bias – in the sense of assumptions on about how the world works and about what political questions or values are most relevant – some sort of bias is inevitable in any treatment of a subject that happens to be crucial, complex and controversial, in short, any of the most difficult of our intelligence problems.

> If so, then improvement of intelligence management might better focus on clarifying and structuring the competition of different biases within the process, getting a grip on what may be inevitable and making use of it in a conscious way rather than either pretending that the problem is not there or doing without intelligence assessment where the problem is unavoidable.[23]

> We should seek a way to artfully manage and make use of contending biases rather than try to get rid of the political contamination of intelligence altogether.[24]

Each approach has its strong and weak points. The potential drawbacks of the 'idealistic approach' are obvious – that intelligence will maintain its professional integrity at the cost of political sterility and aloofness.

On the other hand the realistic approach is over-sensitive to the attitudes of 'consumers'. Statesmen have their own political interests uppermost in their minds and cannot therefore be expected to change their priorities. Indeed, many major intelligence failures have occurred on the consumer level of acceptance. Moreover, the unequal distribution of power among the different intelligence agencies belies the hope that the artful management of competing intelligence organizations would produce less distorted, more reliable intelligence. Truth is monopolized by the most powerful rather than by the most qualified. In fact, the management of checks and balances may further politicize the intelligence process by giving rise to permanent or *ad hoc* coalitions among different intelligence agencies (this is one of the greatest dangers of maintaining too many intelligence agencies). Finally, managing political competition among different intelligence organizations might politicize the quest for better bargaining positions and also favor the honing of the intelligence professional's political skills over the development of his analytical qualifications.

As Betts emphasizes, the difficulty lies in trying to strike the correct balance between the idealistic and realistic aspects of the intelligence process. Although there are no perfect solutions to such problems, perhaps it makes sense in the abstract to suggest that all intelligence organizations continue working toward the standards set by the ideal model of intelligence work while minimizing their involvement in politics on all levels. From the vantage point of the intelligence community, it is imperative that intelligence professionals accept the standards of the ideal system in order to develop a 'professional superego' that may, in the long run, be the best check on the excesses of political interference.

As for the policy-maker, much depends upon his personal traits, as well as upon the political culture and socialization process of his country. An important guarantee of a policy-maker's detachment from the intelligence process is the knowledge that he will pay for interference with his own career. In this sense, democratic procedures furnish the best weapon against excessive politicization of the intelligence community. Herein lies the paradox – for on the one hand, it is democracy and the struggle for influence over public opinion that increases politicization of intelligence, but on the other hand it is democratic pressure that contains and limits that politicization. Logically, politicization results from the elementary fact that intelligence is essential to the promotion of almost all political interests (including those of the intelligence community). Other explanations of the politicization process are unnecessary. Even if intelligence 'facts', reports, estimates, or predictions were unambiguous – that is, understood or perceived in the same way by all observers – there are still those who would distort, ignore or misuse the information for purely political reasons.

'Indeed, were decisions based only on intelligence data, decisions and policy would simply "follow" from it and there would be no need for policy makers.'[25] The very fact that a leader is elected to implement a specific policy gives him the right and duty to make political decisions contrary to the evidence or advice provided by the intelligence community.The 'primacy of politics' or political control in the strict sense of *hierarchy of importance* must be recognized. '*Intelligence must be the servant and not the master of operational policy.*'[26] Yet political primacy should be clearly distinguished from political interference, a task which is not always easy.

There is a thin line between the right and duty to formulate a policy based on subjective political values, and the conscious or unconscious temptation to abuse or ignore the intelligence process. It is one thing for a statesman to listen carefully to his intelligence advisers, then make a decision counter to their best judgement; and another for him to wield his political strength and authority in the interest of receiving only that information which conforms to his preconceived ideas and political biases. The danger is, in Hughes' words,that 'policy makers quickly learn that intelligence can be used the way a drunk uses a lamp post – for support rather than illumination'.[27]

The ambiguous and uncertain nature of intelligence is a major reason for its distortion – whether political or otherwise.[28] The sole reason for the existence of the intelligence community exists for the purpose of reducing uncertainty on political and military issues. Only very rarely can ambiguity and uncertainty be eradicated. When a scientist speaks of 'facts' the meaning is clear to his colleagues (e.g., one gram is one cubic centimeter of water at four degrees centigrade). Such facts leave little room for subjective interpretation, since they can be independently verified according to widely accepted rules. In the world of intelligence, even technical data concerning performance or number of weapons, let alone less quantifiable issues such as intentions, military doctrine, and morale, cannot be objectively assessed – which means that clear agreement on their 'meaning' cannot be reached. It is often mistakenly assumed that the quality of objective comprehension improves to the degree that a subject is technical and narrowly defined. Thus, although it is a relatively straightforward task to outline the performance parameters of an F-16 or MiG-23 as well as the numbers of each kind of aircraft available in a given country, it is far more troublesome to reach agreement on their turn-around ratio, problems of maintenance, availability of spare parts, the relative quality and training of pilots, the doctrine governing their deployment, and hence on the net balance of air power between any two states. It is of course even harder to ascertain if, when, and how foreign leaders intend to use their weapons. In intelligence, facts do not speak for themselves.

R. V. Jones cites an excellent example of the way in which ambiguity and uncertainty can be used to distort even scientific intelligence. In 1942, Jones strongly recommended the use of Window (metallic chaff) as a counter-measure to German defense radars. Watson-Watt, the inventor of radar, opposed this suggestion because he did not want to undermine the position of his invention (what R.V. Jones calls 'the Bridge over the River Kwai' syndrome). British fighter command also resisted the introduction of chaff, fearing that it could be used by the Germans against British radar defenses (although by the end of 1942, the Germans could no longer seriously threaten Britain due to the diminished number of bombers at their disposal). It was therefore decided that each of the parties should provide data estimating the amount of chaff that British bombers would need to carry over Germany in order to be effective. Fighter command concluded that at least 84 tons should be carried on each raid (i.e., British bombers would be forced to carry far fewer bombs per raid). Watson-Watt thought this estimate far too low, whereas R.V. Jones calculated that no more than 12 tons would be needed. As it turned out, R.V. Jones was right, and Window became a very effective weapon (R.V. Jones, *Most Secret War*, pp.295–6). Faced with conditions of uncertainty, each organization and interested party had skewed the analysis to support its case.

The degree of ambiguity is heightened by different organizations' varying approaches to the same subject. In the mid-1930s, for example, confusion reigned over the projection of trends in the Anglo-German balance of air power; the Cabinet under Baldwin compared the absolute numerical sizes of the Luftwaffe and the RAF, while the air staff had argued since 1934 that the potential threat to Great Britain was best measured by comparing the number of bombers. Meanwhile, the Foreign Office 'regarded numerical parity as the wrong test'. The real standard, they believed, should be a comparison of the capacity to manufacture machines and train pilots.[29]

It is this inherent ambiguity, the lack of objective criteria for analysis, and absence of common analytical standards, that render the intelligence process so susceptible to political interference. Ambiguity 'legitimizes' different interpretations, allowing politically-motivated parties to select the one they prefer. The absence of clarity may also strengthen the tendency of some statesmen to become their own intelligence officers.

During the war in Vietnam, 'Presidents and their principal advisers were never clearly deluded about prospects in [the war]. But there were times when the combination of desperation, ambiguity or uncertainty in information, and the hope that optimistic reports reinforced that additional force might bring decisive results helped tilt the balance of choice and impel the leaders to gamble on another step in escalation'.[30] 'Under conditions of uncertainty, officers have reason to overstate threats in order to hedge against failure but also to overstate results in order to prove their own competence. Military staffs and intelligence agencies are caught in the middle of these divergent impulses.'[31]

In 1967, although data concerning the order of battle of the North Vietnamese and Viet Cong forces in South Vietnam were rather ambiguous, military intelligence consistently underestimated the size of the anti-government forces. In trying to demonstrate the efficiency of the United States armed forces operations, they provided proof of the decline in enemy capabilities, which created an optimistic atmosphere that the President welcomed as vindication of his Vietnam policy. 'President Johnson preferred the optimistic estimates of the Joint Chiefs and resented what he saw as carping by the CIA that upset the delicate process of consensus-building.'[32] Although the evidence concerning the war in Vietnam had grown more pessimistic by 1967, there were always enough ambiguous reports from Vietnam which the President's 'intelligence waiter'[33] – his National Security adviser Walt Rostow – could use to present Johnson with his favorite sugar-coated dish of good news.[34] In much the same way, the US Air Force in Vietnam, Korea and the Second World War – as well as every other air force – consistently over-rated the effectiveness of strategic bombing in the light of ambiguous evidence.[35]

By overestimating both the conventional and nuclear strength of the Soviet Union, US military intelligence organizations created the much-touted bomber and missile gaps which became the focus of intense public debate. As it turned out in both cases, if any gaps existed, they favored the United States. In each instance, the vacuum created by a lack of hard evidence was filled in a way consistent with the political interests of the estimating services.[36] Meanwhile, conservative observers have continually accused the CIA of underestimating Soviet capabilities.[37]

In each of the cases mentioned above, the biases and distortions were ubiquitous and consistent. Whether committed by political leaders or organizations, these cannot be considered honest or random mistakes – they reflect political interests. 'It is the law of bureaucratic behavior that agencies with operating responsibilities produce intelligence, analyses and advice that support their own policies or programs. The cause is not dishonesty – indeed, the process may be barely conscious – but the tendency is universal.'[38]

In even more general terms:

> The more politicized an issue, that is, the greater the organizational and electoral stakes in its resolution and the greater the divisions between the contending parties, the more likely it is that those involved will act as political animals marking out and defending positions with guile and determination. Any attempt to provide objective or independent advice will be doomed to failure. Those making such an attempt will be sucked into the struggle.[39]

THE ORGANIZATIONAL AND BUREAUCRATIC POLITICS OF INTELLIGENCE; POLITICS AS A BARGAINING PROCESS

Thus far we have discussed the politics of intelligence primarily in terms of individuals and/or organizations seeking to maximize their power. Clearly each intelligence agency would like to achieve monopolistic control over all intelligence concerns, but the growing complexities of intelligence work, combined with bureaucratic politics, have steadily added to the number of organizations participating in the production of intelligence. Once the minimal goals of survival and maintenance of the status quo have been accomplished, each organization works to broaden its influence on the decision-making process, its budgets, personnel and missions. Because of the limited resources available, the competition between organizations acquires a zero-sum-game character – that is, the gain of one organization is the loss of another in either relative or absolute terms. Hence, it is only natural to find at least some degree of distortion in an intelligence unit representing a specialized professional point of view. In general, therefore, military intelligence organizations emphasize the military over the civilian point of view (e.g., focus more on researching and studying military capabilities than on discovering other nations' intentions).[40] In peacetime they exaggerate the threat posed by an adversary in order to obtain more resources and influence and to play it safe (worst case analysis), then proceed to underestimate his performance after the action has taken place; in wartime they tend to overestimate the effectiveness of the branch they represent while playing down the contribution of other friendly forces.[41]

It would be unusual indeed for an intelligence agency of the army, air force or navy to produce an estimate undermining the influence of its own branch. The air force cannot be expected to conclude that because the enemy's ICBMs are so accurate it makes no sense to maintain land-based ICBMs; and that therefore all missiles should be positioned at sea, leaving control of the US strategic missile forces in the hands of the navy. Nor is the air force likely to conclude that the manned strategic bomber is obsolete, or the navy that fleet carriers are vulnerable to any number of land and sea-based threats and that its battleships are ineffective in providing accurate cost/effective fire support to troops ashore. The navy, of course, would be more open-minded about the manned strategic bomber, while the army and air force might assert that the battleship no longer serves a logical military purpose in modern warfare. It is not surprising to discover that 'every rival group within the system – the bomber pilots, the fighter jockeys, the missile-men and the carrier admirals – produces its own interpretation of Soviet behavior to justify its claim for more money'.[42] Nevertheless, organizations usually find it more advantageous to avoid mutual criticism and may even form mutual-support coalitions if the competition is intense. During the Vietnam War, Secretary of State Dean Rusk requested that the State Department's INR refrain from writing pessimistic reports about the course of the war without first consulting the Pentagon.[43] Richard Helms, as Director of Central Intelligence (DCI), was reluctant to quarrel with the Pentagon (supported by Walt Rostow in the White House) over the CIA's finding concerning the Order of Battle (OB) of the anti-government troops in Vietnam, so he signed a report (14 March 1967) containing the old deflated military figures.[44]

These examples surely illustrate the imbalance of power within the US intelligence community during the war in Vietnam – a factor which handicapped the ability of those in strategic intelligence to influence the course of the war.

For related reasons, military intelligence officers are not likely to produce estimates and analyses contradictory to their superiors' interests and beliefs. The tradition of obeying orders, remaining loyal to the service and friends, and furthering their careers may influence them consciously. On a less conscious level, their work may reflect a narrowly professional experience and education that prevent the development of a broader outlook.

Truth, therefore, for reasons of experience, but also as a result of more subtle professional and socialization factors, is relative and mirrors parochial organizational biases. Another closely related type of political bias emerges from the *political process* of intelligence co-ordination among different intelligence organizations. This is a complicated and important subject that can be discussed only briefly in this context. Biases are generated in the process of integrating the collection, research and estimative efforts of multiple intelligence organizations, and because this involves forming a consensus as well as co-ordination and common reporting, it is, in a sense, a search for a common denominator in which the final 'truth' is not necessarily the best possible product but rather the most generally acceptable one. The co-ordination process therefore introduces another type of political bias that transcends the particular interests of any single organization.

The *political process* of co-ordination among intelligence agencies, while crucial, introduces a number of inevitable biases into the final intelligence product. Much depends on the number of organizations participating in the process, their character, and relative strength. For example, according to Allison and Szanton, 80 per cent of the US intelligence community is military and the 'national intelligence estimates are a composite of judgments of the CIA, the DIA, the INR and the service intelligence agencies. Compromises among these perspectives often lead to estimates that project an exaggerated military oriented view of the threat'.[45]

The search for consensus may also reduce the objective quality of estimates in the sense that truth becomes a vector of the relative power and influence of each of the participating organizations – rather than the result of the best and most professional judgement. Reaching a consensus may even become a goal itself, often leading intelligence estimates to smother different judgements with bland compromise.[46] Hughes has, however, suggested that:

> Unfortunately the drive for . . . consistency has become a felt necessity . . . Estimators now give it more than its due. In part the problem is a function of over-institutionalization in the intelligence community . . . The more coordination, probably, the more consistency.
>
> But inconsistency is a virtue which should by no means be avoided at all costs. Consistency, after all, is not a goal of intelligence. There is little virtue in self-consciously adhering to a particular line of interpretation simply because a prior estimate on the subject took that line. Just because it was said last time is no reason to say it again. The intelligence community is not the Supreme Court. It need not strain over the precedents or labor to extend the meaning of sanctified words. On the contrary, intelligence is supposed to provide current unimpeded judgments. As a vehicle for ventilating a variety of viewpoints, the intelligence process should be highly suspicious of consensus . . . The freedom to be inconsistent is a major argument bolstering the independence of the intelligence community.[47]

R.V. Jones also has some sharp comments on the consensus-seeking approach:

> ... The implementation of the J.I.C. proposals is now taking place, and is one of the main reasons for my resignation ...
>
> A single head in Intelligence is far better than a committee, however excellent the individual members of the committee may be. A committee wastes too much time in arguing, and every action it undertakes merely goes as far as common agreement and compromise will allow. Common agreement and compromise, as every commander knows, generally do not go far enough. The head of an intelligence organization is really in the position of a commander planning a perpetual attack on the security of foreign powers, and he must be allowed all the privileges of a commander.[48]

By-products of the consensus-seeking process include not only the introduction of additional biases and the slowness of the process, but also the lack of clarity as a basis for action. 'Though some national intelligence estimates series are of high quality, most deliver compromise judgments in an *ex cathedra* fashion that makes it next to impossible for policymakers to uncover the analytic basis for the judgments offered or educate themselves about the grounds for disagreement.'[49] 'The bedrock of CIA metaphysics was not "either/or" but "maybe/if" and it drove decision-makers from Truman to Nixon half-crazy.'[50] McLachlan suggests that had there been no need to reconcile the views of five intelligence departments, the forecasts and reports of enemy strategy and intentions would have been worded in a 'firmer' way.[51]

Despite these problems and imperfections in the co-ordination process, it must be borne in mind that co-ordination is absolutely essential for the production of high-quality strategic intelligence estimates. For those countries in which co-ordination among the different intelligence organizations was at times weak (such as the US before Pearl Harbor)[52] or never successfully achieved (such as in Nazi Germany), the results were disastrous for the production of strategic intelligence.

This political process of co-ordination and consensus also occurs in microcosm *within* each organization; and the higher the number of participating organizations, the greater the degree of co-ordination and corroboration required for the numerous sets of opinions emanating from agencies with a wide range of perspectives. Furthermore, the larger the number of participating organizations, the longer the amount of time required for the process to take place. Under conditions of crisis or war, in which time and quick reactions are critical, the process of co-ordinating a large number of participants can become sluggish and insufficiently responsive to the needs of decision-makers.

Experts generally agree that a group of competing, equally powerful intelligence organizations would serve the civilian and military leadership better than a single monopolistic one. It is assumed that by virtue of having undergone the rigors of an adversarial process, the final intelligence product will be of superior quality. 'In a multitude of counselors there is safety'; but there is no agreement on and little discussion of what would constitute the optimal number of organiztions under various conditions. The system which errs on the side of allowing too many organizations to participate is costly and unwieldy, and can easily become too politicized.

There is of course a difference between 'alternative analysis' and the 'analysis of alternatives'.[53] A serious problem can arise when the search for alternative analysis becomes an end in itself.

> Since each department of the executive branch of government with foreign interests has its own intelligence section, it follows from the bureaucratic role-playing facts of life that the combined intelligence community will take into account all worst and best cases from all points of view, and that these representatives in collegium will systemize a set of conclusions – even if abetted by individual alternate views. All realistically conceivable alternatives must be analyzed and in my own modest experience with this process. I have never been in a group of interagency representatives that did not – in time – do just that.
>
> This means that the net result of 'alternative analysis' cannot be an analysis of alternatives but of extraneous impulses ranging from, at best, over-use of anomaly to whimsy or even, at worst, sheer malice. Whatever the motive, if the analyst does not analyze from the perspective of policy or action responsibilities of his parent agency, it follows that his analysis will be irresponsible. Why then, should we commission an additional alternate view with no purpose other than to be alternate even to all the other possible and pertinent alternate views? What does this mean to the decision-maker? How many alternatives does it take to make you feel secure?[54]

The existence of a number of competing organizations may be a necessary but not a sufficient condition for improvement of the intelligence process. Much depends on the character of the leaders and policy-makers interacting with the intelligence community. Accordingly, access to still more intelligence estimates does not prevent a

leader from choosing the estimate that will confirm his own preconceived ideas, or from pursuing (as Hitler did) a divisive policy to the
point where little or no co-operation among them is possible.[55]

When Secretary of Defense Robert McNamara needed estimates to
justify expansion of the military budget or stepping up involvement in
Vietnam, he found it useful to listen to the Defense Intelligence
Agency (DIA); yet once the war in Vietnam fell short of the success he
had hoped for, an increasingly doveish McNamara relied more on
reports from the CIA.[56] When McNamara, in the summer of 1966,
asked the CIA for a current study of the effectiveness of the bombing in
North Vietnam, the Pentagon and DIA were infuriated.[57] Likewise,
during the war in Vietnam, both President Nixon and Secretary of State
Kissinger dismissed the CIA as too doveish and preferred to deal with
the military intelligence organizations; once they shifted their attention to the Strategic Arms Limitation Talks, however, they preferred
the estimates of the CIA.[58]

There is certainly no positive correlation between the number of
intelligence organizations within the intelligence community and the
quality of its overall contribution. If anything, a larger number of major
intelligence organizations whose efforts require co-ordination can be
identified with inefficiency, wasted resources and increased pressures
for the politicization of the intelligence process. On the other hand, it
must be emphasized that simply limiting the number of intelligence
organizations does not guarantee success.

Inter-organizational biases increase further if the same intelligence
organization not only collects and analyses information but also con-
ducts extensive covert operations. One cause of the US intelligence
community's failure to predict the revolution in Iran is that Iran was
one of its major listening posts for monitoring Soviet missile testing and
military activities in general. Reluctant to anger the Shah and risk
losing this crucial 'window' on the Soviet Union, the CIA avoided
establishing contacts with the Iranian opposition. Nevertheless, such
contacts were essential for remaining attuned to the internal political
situation in Iran. Deepening the intelligence community's dilemma,
political leaders who had already invested heavily in the Shah's regime
were averse to receiving pessimistic forecasts regarding his future.[59]

In Vietnam, the DCI was frequently caught '. . . between his intelligence division's quite pessimistic judgments and his operation arm's
optimism not only about its own programs but also about prospects for
general success in the war'.[60]

Although little is known about the Israeli *Mossad*, it appears to have
been caught in a similar bind in Lebanon, where its agents became
deeply involved and to a certain extent identified with the Christian

Phalangists in Beirut. From their perspective, increased Israeli involvement in the Lebanese Civil War promised great success. In contrast, both the analytical units of the Mossad and military intelligence units advised great caution. Because the Israeli government, for its own reasons, was bent upon increasing its interference in the Lebanese Civil War, the senior officers of the Mossad probably felt it best to go along with this policy in order to demonstrate the effectiveness of their agency's contribution.[61]

During the Vietnam War, DIA analysts '. . . were torn between the office of the Secretary of Defense and the Joint Chiefs of Staff. For the latter they felt pressed to present statistics that would support requests for more troops in Vietnam; for the former they were supposed to provide assessments of the strength of the South Vietnamese Army, enemy body counts and bombing results that could block such requests'.[62] This inevitably led to inconsistent and self-contradictory reporting: 'Enemy infiltration continued at a rate higher than last month. However, the cumulative effect of U.S. bombing has seriously degraded his ability to mount a large scale offensive'.[63] Squaring a circle can cause organizational schizophrenia and seriously reduce the quality of intelligence work.

The most effective antidote for politicization of the intelligence community is the integrity, character and personal and professional ethics of each member of the community. This leads us to an examination of the individual in the intelligence process, a subject which can be viewed from two standpoints. The first considers the individual as a member of an organization pursuing his professional career. The second examines him in terms of general character, suitability for honest and open-minded research, and capacity to listen and work with a team.

THE INDIVIDUAL IN THE ORGANIZATION

Each individual within an organization simultaneously seeks to promote the goals of his agency and to advance his own interests. At times these two objectives clash. Personal factors such as the desire for economic stability and promotion as well as the psychological need to be appreciated do much to erode the ideal qualities of independent judgement and objectivity in the search for 'truth'. Few individuals are ready to disclose their opinions if this might cause them to be dismissed or reduce their chances for promotion or pensions after many years of service. We are all familiar with the unfortunate fate of those few honest but naive Don Quixotes who have dared to insist on the truth although it was in opposition to the policy of their organization or that of senior decision-makers: certainly the treatment meted out to these individuals does not encourage others to do likewise. The few individuals who resign rather than compromise their integrity are often independently wealthy. Wealth, or at least the guarantee of a stable income or the standing offer of another job, is one of the best assurances of integrity. For most members of an organization 'resignation is not the answer – it usually is forgotten in a fortnight anyway'.[64] It is much less troublesome to hold on to one's income and hope to live to fight another day from within the system.

Since most intelligence organizations are part of the military system, many of their employees are career military officers. Historically the majority of military organizations regarded intelligence with a great deal of suspicion. 'Intelligence is rather despised by the services . . .', wrote R.V. Jones in his letter of resignation to Chief of the Air Staff Lord Tedder.[65] In drawing his conclusions from the lessons of naval intelligence during the Second World War, Donald McLachlan stressed: 'Let this, then, be the first axiom; *fighting commanders, technical experts and politicians are liable to ignore, despise or undernote intelligence*'. (His emphasis.)[66] This is not entirely unexpected. Military education has traditionally emphasized obedience, bravery, loyalty and performance in combat – not the dedicated intellectual pursuit of truth. Wisdom is often assumed to be the exclusive province of those with rank and seniority rather than of those with more knowledge or experience. McLachlan also concludes that '*intelligence should so far as possible be directed by civilians*'.[67] 'The case for civilian predominance in this work is based not only on the services' low regard for it. It has to do also with the war-time lesson that it is the lawyer, the scholar, the traveler, the banker, even the journalist who shows the ability to resist where the career men tend to bend.'[68] '. . . The civilian also commends himself by a reasonable independence of service loyalties, even though he will temporarily share them enthusiastically.'[69]

This points up yet another intelligence paradox; namely, that the best professionals are the amateurs. They serve their country for the duration of the war, bringing with them their analytical skills and scientific discipline. Since they do not seek military promotion, they are in a much better position to insist upon the truth as they see it, secure in the knowledge that when it is over they can return to their old positions.

In almost all military establishments during the Second World War – British, American, German, Japanese – military intelligence was not part of the preferred career pattern for an ambitious officer. In the United States (until recently) 'intelligence assignments have little promotion value in service careers, and are generally avoided by promising officers. Intelligence assignments outside one's own service in particular are viewed as dead ends'.[70] When an officer is assigned to temporary intelligence duty, it is often viewed as a nuisance to be endured until a better position becomes available.

> Imagine, if you will, what the prospect of a tour with DIA looks like to a military officer. He knows or soon learns that he will be thrust into a position in which, on occasion, his professional judgment will vary markedly from that of his parent service. He will be expected to defend a position that could enrage his chief of staff – but officers who do so more than once get known fast and are awarded an appropriate 'reward' at a later date in terms of promotion and assignment. Consider also that a tour at DIA – normally two to three years – is very short when compared to a 20-to-30 year military career. And so most officers assigned to DIA go through a predictable pattern. They come aboard as 'hard chargers,' ready to set the world on fire. They stick to their principles through one or two scrapes. Then they become a little more circumspect, letting individual issues slide by and rationalizing that it wasn't a crunch question anyway. Finally, they resign themselves to 'sweating out' their tour and playing every situation by ear. They avoid committing themselves or making decisions. They refuse to tackle the agency's long term organizational ills, because doing so would make too many waves.[71]

The process by which an individual career intelligence officer is persuaded, for the sake of his own future, to deviate from his best judgements is very subtle; it does not involve any direct orders or conspiracies to rewrite conclusions or omit bits of information. Career officers do not usually need such incentives in order to discern where their interests lie. They 'decode messages that have never been sent. Indeed there is a whole range of tacit influence (and indeed tacit power) that falls into the category of anticipated reactions. An actor tacitly subjects himself to influence or power by *asking himself* questions about the likely outcome of his actions'.[72]

'Often hidden messages lurk behind or within apparently innocuous communications. Understanding the hidden meaning in a conversation (meta talk) requires that we constantly decode messages, verbal and not verbal, to figure out what they "really mean" and how we should respond to them.'[73]

At times the pressure is more overt. Cited by McGarvey, the

following passage is an oft-quoted example of the pressure tactics directed at analysis during the Vietnam War:

> For one thing, there is something called the 'eyes only' cable that is sent 'back channel' and is severely restricted in dissemination. Usually no more than five people see it. (Which makes the process less visible and difficult to counter.) I have seen 'eyes only' cables come in from the US Commanders in Honolulu and Saigon to the Director of the DIA requesting that he give more than a passing consideration to the command viewpoint about this or that. The language is always moving. Such a cable is likely to start off complimenting the recipient for the fine job he is doing and then work in high-sounding phrases which evoke motherhood, apple pie, the American flag and, of course, the uniform., It then implies that the sender would like to see a particular judgment of set figures changed to conform to the command view. It rarely offers any evidence to support this request. It is sure to close with a veiled threat that the recipient's career is in jeopardy if he does not play the game and get on the team. Many estimates have been changed or reworded because of an 'Eyes Only' cable from a field commander. In one instance the Air Force Chief of intelligence called my boss at DIA about a nearly completed estimate on U.S. bombing in Laos. He told him that he was sending a team down to change the wording of the estimate and that my boss had better remember what color his uniform was. Of course it was the same as the General's: blue. The team arrived, and over the protests of the DIA analyst, a compromise was reached.[74]

It is not difficult to conclude that during the war in Vietnam, for example, the 'dynamics of careerism compromised the objectivity and quality of military reports and analysis'.[75] As long as the military intelligence analyst remains a second-class citizen in the military service the situation is not likely to improve. While the situation has improved considerably within the United States, the politics of survival will always exert serious pressures for compromise on the professional intelligence analyst.

PERSONALITY, POLICY-MAKING AND INTELLIGENCE

Schematically speaking, intelligence work can be divided into three related levels of analysis: Acquisition, Analysis, and Acceptance (AAA). The history of modern intelligence, in particular some of the major failures to anticipate strategic surprise, indicates that the political level of acceptance often proves to be the weakest link in the intelligence process. As R.V. Jones comments, 'The test of good intelligence service is not merely that you were right, it is that you persuaded your operational or research staff to take the correct measures'.[76] 'It is no good having good intelligence and clear thinking unless it can be brought to the notice of the operational command in a way that they like and they will take notice and believe in. The objective of the intelligence officer must be that he should send out to the fleet or to the command or to the force the shortest possible message and be at once believed without hesitation. That is the ideal.'[77] This is even more true of the relationship between the political leader and his senior intelligence advisers. For if, despite all the political difficulties – not to mention the methodological problems omitted from this article[78] – an intelligence organization has managed to produce what proves to be in retrospect a perfectly correct estimate, the major hurdle of accceptance has yet to be overcome. Correct analysis is therefore a necessary but not a sufficient condition for success. The question of acceptance will be dealt with in this context from two major vantage points. The first discusses the personalities of leaders and their place in the intelligence process; the second addresses the interaction between the leader and the director of the intelligence community or of any other intelligence organization. In both cases, the political background (i.e., whether decisions are made in a democratic or authoritarian environment and how they are arrived at) plays a crucial role in the entire process.

Personality and Leadership Style

No leader is expected to accept intelligence estimates without first considering their relevance to his preferred policy or strategy. When we consider intelligence organizations' capacity to co-operate with a leader, two extreme types of leaders present themselves. On the one hand, leaders such as Hitler or Stalin cannot tolerate information that contradicts their own beliefs or policies. Hitler told Ribbentrop that 'when he had to make great decisions, he considered himself the instrument of the providence which the Almighty has determined. He once told [Ribbentrop] that before big decisions, he always had a feeling of absolute certainty'.[82] Having developed no habits of co-operation and orderly staff work, Hitler insisted on imposing his ideas on others. Early successes in the face of the opposition of senior military commanders and foreign policy experts convinced him that his intuition was infallible and spurred him on to even more hubristic behavior. Hitler had no use for intelligence whatsoever – unless it confirmed his own preconceived ideas or supported his plans. When subjected to such strictures, strategic intelligence is of very little use.

At the other extreme, a leader accepts all intelligence estimates as gospel. This can happen when the leader has no policy regarding, or knowledge of, the subject at hand; thus, he has complete faith in his intelligence advisers and little confidence in his own judgement. For example, although Prime Minister Golda Meir's intuition told her that the evacuation of Soviet families from Egypt and Syria in early October 1973 signalled an impending Arab attack, she deferred to the opposite conclusion advanced by trusted intelligence experts. Such faith in intelligence estimates is rare indeed; in reality, the approach of most leaders, depending on personality and working habits, falls somewhere between these two extremes.

Leaders in democratic political systems are generally more inclined to consider a wide variety of opinions than those rooted in authoritarian regimes. In authoritarian countries, where the climb to the top is an unrelenting and brutal struggle for power, habits of co-operation and openness are usually less developed. The rigidity of prevailing doctrines – whether religious or ideological – precludes criticism or contradictory ideas. Leaders in totalitarian countries expect ideas to follow the 'party line', because anything else threatens their legitimacy and the accepted ideology. This rigidity, among other reasons, explains why the Axis countries' strategic intelligence systems were out-performed by those of the Western democracies during the Second World War.[79]

What has been said so far does not imply that relatively open-minded leaders who are capable of co-operation cannot assume power within totalitarian systems or conversely, that narrow-minded, authoritarian leaders cannot emerge in democracies. Ultimately, much depends upon the idiosyncrasies and personality of each leader. But, since the struggle to reach the top within any type of system is not easy, political leaders must have some traits in common regardless of the environment in which they operate.

By definition, those who seek power are more inclined to give orders than to follow, to reshape their surroundings rather than to accept them passively, to suggest rather than to listen. The champion of a certain policy often reacts to intelligence estimates and implied or explicit advice with a 'Don't tread on me', and 'Don't fence me in'.[80]

> He sees intelligence arming his opposition – and no wonder, for it can't keep its analysis from being used against him by his opponents. All this is particularly annoying to the policy-maker with a purpose – to the man who wants to create and change. Naturally a policy-maker wedded to a project – the competent man with a viewpoint – is more put off by a discouraging assess-

ment bearing on his favorite project than is his project-less, viewpoint-less colleague. Unless he is exceptionally broad-minded he may take the bad news personally ... The policy-maker may find that intelligence can crowd him and his self-esteem, frustrate his efforts to take off on a policy, alarm him with its negativism about policies under way and in extreme cases, lead on from persecution to martyrdom.[81]

These tendencies are reinforced in every political system by a coterie of sycophants. Such an environment discourages open-mindedness and diversity, quickly making even a leader who is initially open-minded less tolerant of criticism and diversity.

Although a modicum of inter-organizational competition can be beneficial, Hitler's divide-and-rule policy was counter-productive in its politicization of German intelligence. An intelligence organization seeking attention from the Führer had to furnish him with the information that he wanted to hear. The dynamics of this competition brought about a rapid deterioration in the quality of German intelligence, fostering mistrust between the various agencies. It is not surprising that some of the earliest and most active opposition to Hitler began in the German military intelligence agency (the *Abwehr*), whose senior officers were perhaps most aware of the dangers courted by Hitler's irrational decision-making style. This opposition probably further weakened Hitler's incentive to consult intelligence reports.

An examination of the leaders and military assistants closest to Hitler – men such as Jodl and Keitel in the OKW and Ribbentrop, Himmler, Goering and Goebbels – reveals that almost all were syco-phants. Ribbentrop and Goering, for example, carefully saw to it that Hitler received only the reports that confirmed his own beliefs and images. Even after the most serious defeats, Hitler never encouraged any other type of reporting. Good intelligence existed but was circum-spectly filtered. 'In light of Hitler's preconceptions and distorted images, one must question the usefulness of foreign reporting even if it had been one hundred percent correct.'[83]

That Hitler cultivated and encouraged the emergence of an en-tourage of 'yes-men' was inevitable given his character and the unique nature of the Nazi political system. Yet as we can see from the fact that leaders have many traits in common, those in democratic countries also promote sycophancy among their close aides. The process, may be somewhat more subtle, but it frequently leads to similar results:

Senior participants are reluctant to come to the President with what they know is unwelcome advice and risk an argument or quarrel with him. They recognize that any President will tune out

senior participants who frequently come to him with counsel that
he finds uncongenial, and therefore they will save such attempts
for issues on which they feel very strongly.[84]

Indeed if one examines the attitudes of Rostow or Kissinger towards
Presidents Johnson and Nixon it becomes clear that they survived so
long because they seldom risked being 'uncongenial'. Senior White
House advisers or Secretaries of State or Defense have rarely resigned
over a matter of principle – but rather because some other adviser with
more acceptable views gained the confidence of the President. [See
also discussion in the next section.] Nor did Churchill during the
Second World War promote any senior military men or advisers whose
opinions or actions challenged his own. The Darwinian logic of survival
around most leaders is universal – and leads to similar results: the
gradual establishment of a Greek chorus of admiration and support.

Hitler made most of his important decisions alone. Many of
his moves, particularly the diplomatic surprises in the 1930s which
required no telltale military preparations, were unanticipated by his
close associates and 'victims' alike. Leaders of democracies have
launched similar surprises. President Nixon did not inform the US
intelligence community of his decision to initiate the rapprochement with China, nor did he apprise the CIA of his plans to invade
Cambodia. (Nixon and his closest advisers suspected that CIA analysts
would disapprove of this operation.)[85] President Sadat never consulted
anyone before making his most important decisions, including the 1972
decision to expel the Russians from Egypt and his later visit to Jerusalem on his peace offensive. Prime Minister Begin did not inform
Israeli military intelligence or his cabinet ministers – with the exception
of Dayan – that direct negotiations with Egyptian emissaries were
taking place in Morocco.[86] The withholding of information by leaders
from their own intelligence organizations is a dangerous and highly
demoralizing practice.[87]

A 'lone-wolf' style of leadership is intensified by dogmatic adherence
to an ideology (especially if the ideology itself is irrational). Hitler
dismissed intelligence reports on American or Soviet behavior as an
over-estimation of Jewish, Bolshevik-Slav, or plutocratic groups that
were racially or politically inferior and therefore could not be as
motivated or efficient as German Aryans. In much the same way,
Stalin's adherence to Communist ideology, which viewed the world in
zero-sum-game terms, led him to believe that any intelligence from
British or Western sources could not possibly be genuine (that concerning, for instance, the German plan to attack in 1941); Stalin refused to
believe that the delays in opening the second front in Europe stemmed

from genuine difficulties and not from foot-dragging caused by anti-Soviet sentiments.[88]

In contrast, the relative openness of Roosevelt, Churchill or Truman to intelligence reports seems to have yielded better results. From his early days at the Admiralty in the First World War to his daily use of Ultra intercepts during the Second, Churchill certainly paid close attention to intelligence reports. His work habits have been described in this somewhat idealized way:

> We see Churchill following up daily on the performance of his subordinates. We see him emphasizing the importance of science and technology in the development of new weapons. We note his skill in using information acquired through the interception and decoding of German communications, and his success in keeping the knowledge of that decoding a secret. We note how effective was Churchill's insistence on transmitting instructions in writing, on keeping orderly track of every decision and on tracing the progress of decision to action. Such habits make for efficient administration.[89]

While far more flexible than Hitler, Churchill did not exemplify the co-operative leader either.

'When Churchill was certain that he was right *ruat coelum*, nothing could shake or distract him: an inflexibility which marred his war leadership as it did that of Hitler.'[90] And once he made up his mind he had extraordinary powers of argument; 'to get his own way he used every device and brought the *whole* battery of his ingenious, tireless and highly political mind to bear on the point of issue. His battery of weapons included persuasion, real or simulated anger, mockery, vituperation, tantrums, ridicule, derision, abuse and tears, which he would aim at anyone who opposed him or expressed a view contrary to the one he had already formed, sometimes on quite trivial questions'.[91]

> Yet unlike Hitler, he displayed constant interest in the latest information about the enemy . . . He made it a matter of principle that he should be supplied with such intelligence 'raw' – that is, not in the doctored pieces of a staff assessment but as it had come to hand. Thus he felt, often with good reason, that in his central position he was exceptionally equipped for keeping himself 'in the know'. All that was romantic in him, moreover, thrilled with excitement of intercepted signals, Delphic reports from the agents, the broken codes, the sense of participation. This knowledge is essential if one is to understand his decisions, and at the lower level his impatience with his commanders.[92]

In the words of Major Sir Desmond Morton, Churchill '. . . was a *politician* who wanted to be a soldier'.[93] And while he interfered too much in military operations, he never committed Hitler's error of assuming direct command of an army in action. Although Churchill did not always feel comfortable among colleagues with superior intellects, 'his chiefs of staff – unlike Hitler's – were professionals of exceptional calibre. None were puny or pusillanimous . . . Pound . . . Dill . . . Alanbrooke, Portal, and Cunningham . . . They were a different team from Hitler's entourage – the subservient lackeys, Keitel, Halder, Jodl, Zeitzler and the transient subordinates, their opinons disregarded, uncertain of their tenure, their very lives dependent on a master's whim'.[94]

When critical issues were at stake, Churchill's military advisers did not hesitate to argue with him. In such cases, if they were sufficiently persuasive and persistent, their opinions prevailed (e.g. Dowding's resistance to Churchill's judgement in a Cabinet meeting on 15 May 1940 that no more Hurricane fighters be sent to France).[95]

'Churchill's disqualifications as a warlord were manifold – disqualifications both intellectual and temperamental. . . . He succeeded in spite of them. Hitler's defects of character were of fundamental significance: Churchill's peripheral.'[96]

As an intelligence consumer Churchill stands somewhere on the continuum between the co-operative and non-cooperative leader. On the one hand he appreciated the importance of intelligence work more than any other leader during the Second World War and made an immense contribution to its development; on the other, he did not hesitate to ignore it when it did not suit his strategy and too often tended to become his own intelligence officer – a dangerous role which no head of state should take upon himself.[97]

Though authoritarian in his attitudes toward his subordinates and advisers, Churchill nevertheless assembled an outstanding group of professional advisers whose counsel he continuously sought during the war. Despite the many mistakes Churchill could have avoided by heeding his intelligence advisers more closely, his overall record as an intelligence consumer was impressive. For him more than for any other leader in modern times, strategic intelligence was the key to victory.

Beyond the problem of a leader's psychological profile, there are other more general political behavioral patterns that can affect his attitude toward intelligence. For example, once a leader has invested time and energy in promoting a particular policy direction – especially when his prestige is on the line or he has acted against the advice of his aides – he will be that much more reluctant to admit defeat even when faced with contradictory data. This, for example, was the case with

President Johnson's increasing reluctance to listen to any evidence that contradicted his Vietnam policy. In 1964, President Johnson asked the intelligence community to consider the validity of the so-called Domino Theory. Controlled by the CIA, the Board of National Estimates essentially rejected its validity. 'President Johnson never again asked for the CIA's opinion.'[98] The greatest danger is present when the leader supplants serious deliberation with wishful thinking, as, for example, when Chamberlain and the advocates of appeasement resisted the overwhelming evidence that such policies actually whetted Hitler's appetite. Equally blinded by wishful thinking, Stalin rejected all evidence that Hitler intended to break the German–Soviet Non-Aggression Pact of 23 August 1939. Having invested so much in this project, Stalin simply abandoned any sense of political realism. He desperately needed the non-aggression pact to gain time to resurrect the Red Army, which lay in a weakened condition in the aftermath of the purges and the war against Finland. Similarly, successive US administrations, which based their policies in the Persian Gulf on the survival of the Shah of Iran, ignored and discouraged the collection of information indicating that his regime was not as stable as their policies implied. Leaders in democratic systems are particularly susceptible to such wishful thinking before elections. This partially explains French paralysis on the eve of the Rhineland crisis, Kennedy's behavior before and during the Cuban missile crisis, and the Israeli government's actions before the Yom Kippur War. In the Israeli case, elections had been scheduled for November 1973, and the incumbent government party was claiming that it had brought peace and stability to Israel. Obviously, the government was in no state of mind to recognize that war was imminent.

Faced with persistent contradictory estimates, a truly great statesman (as opposed to a political leader) will realize sooner rather than later that he was wrong. Too many leaders fail this time test. It is ironic that leaders in democratic societies, who feel they must justify their policies to the public, may be as reluctant as, or even more reluctant than, their authoritarian counterparts to accept unfavorable evidence. But in behaving as Chamberlain, Johnson or Begin did, they in fact damage their chances of staying in power; for instead of courageously preparing public opinion for the possible failure of current policies, they increase expectations of success, to the point where, if failure occurs, they have to resign. Although Chamberlain, Johnson and Begin all eventually admitted the failure of their policies by resigning from office or declining to stand again, they rejected the contradictory intelligence evidence until the very last moment.

WSI—H

The Leader and his Intelligence Adviser

In the preceding section, we discussed the critical impact of the individual leader on the intelligence process. Leaders, however, are always influenced by their close advisers, whose interaction with them is decisive. The effectiveness of this relationship will therefore also be influenced by the character of the heads of the intelligence community. Is there a positive or negative chemistry between them? Do they complement or contradict each other in temperament, character, or ambition? Can they co-operate with and respect each other? Do they share a common ideology and a common social or professional experience?

To answer these questions we must also know something about the intelligence estimator – the DCI, DNI, or whoever he may be. Is he a man of absolute integrity to whom ambition is secondary to service? Does he put his objectivity and professional judgement above all else or is he primarily interested in maintaining the confidence and friendship of the leader as a means to gaining influence? Did he become a leader in the intelligence community because of his political connections and views, or because of his professional achievements and experience? Is he prepared to resign if his professional views are consistently rejected?

The number of possible relationships between the leader and his intelligence or national security advisers is very large indeed. Some of the better-known examples have already been mentioned: Presidents Johnson and Nixon with Helms; Churchill with Godfrey; Hitler with his advisers. Another important example is Kennedy's problematic relationship with McCone, whose correct prediction of Soviet behavior in Cuba (of which he did not hesitate to remind the President) was a blow to Kennedy's ego; nor was McCone able to establish a more workable relationship with President Johnson.

Though Churchill probably found Godfrey stubborn and argumentative, his relationship with Menzies, head of the SIS, was excellent. Menzies, who assumed control of the SIS at a low point in its influence when its very survival was in question, made every effort to cultivate the Prime Minister: Churchill was provided with daily Ultra intercepts which always included some spicy tidbits to be used as ammunition in his arguments or conversations with other senior advisers. In this way, Menzies was gradually able to inspire the Prime Minister's confidence in SIS. Furthermore, Menzies also demonstrated his political astuteness in defusing the opposition of the military and Foreign Office intelligence organizations by inviting the DNI, DMI and DAI to recommend candidates to fill three co-ordination positions for Deputy Directors of the SIS.[99] Whether or not Menzies was capable as the professional manager of an intelligence organization is debatable – but no one would deny his political talents.[100]

A less well-known twosome was that of Israeli Defense Minister Moshe Dayan and the head of the Israeli Military Intelligence, Eli Zeira. In this case, it has been argued that since both of them had been combat commanders and were 'heroic types', they suffered from similar perceptual defects; the fact that they reinforced each other's views may have been a major cause of their failure to heed the numerous warnings preceding the surprise attack of the Yom Kippur War.[101]

The relationship between a leader and his intelligence adviser, even if it starts on a personal and friendly basis, is essentially political, and as such is seldom very happy given their unequal positions. As with all human relationships, the desired level of rapport is not always possible. Many of the ups and downs in the policy-making process have been a function of the potential for co-operation between the President and his DCI. Interestingly enough, even the best relationships between the President and the DCI will eventually begin to deteriorate. Given the unusual concentration of power in the hands of US presidents ('a King and prime minister rolled into one'), this can be expected. For no Chief Executive will long tolerate estimates and reports that contradict his policies; and because any President will at some point have to commit himself to a policy that is not necessarily supported by the intelligence community's assessment, the DCI and President are bound to quarrel. Even the most agreeable DCI will have to defend his opinion or else risk demoralizing his own organization and losing integrity. 'Almost all the DCI's . . . lost the confidence of their Presidents and were fired or replaced: Hillenkoetter by Truman, Bedell Smith by Eisenhower, Dulles by Kennedy, McCone and Raborn by Johnson, Helms by Nixon, Colby by Ford, and George Bush by Carter. Presidents have a lot more influence on what the CIA does and says than the other way around.'[102]

Instead of discussing each leader/intelligence adviser pair in detail or adding any further examples, I will outline a few general observations.

1. A high degree of rapport between the leader of the state and his intelligence advisers is very important, for without a good relationship, the effectiveness of the intelligence community will diminish considerably, regardless of how good its work is.
2. Political finesse, tact, salesmanship, and other related qualities are essential for the leaders of the intelligence community. Unfortunately, however, the professional analyst educated to prefer truth to tact, objectivity to political influence, may lack the requisite qualities.

Rarely is a head of intelligence both a first-rate intelligence expert and an intuitive politician. In fact, some of the qualities required of a highly qualified intelligence expert conflict with those required to achieve political influence. Political finesse is therefore a necessary if not a sufficient condition for an intelligence adviser. In addition to his political skills, he should have some professional intelligence experience.

> In 'the real world, one does not need an exceptional memory to recall that success as a director of intelligence has been as elusive as success in 'fine-tuning' the economy has been in recent decades. Allen Dulles, John McCone, William F. Raborn, Jr., and Richard Helms were forced to resign. George Bush was not reappointed, and both William E. Colby and Stansfield Turner were under bitter criticism as they ended their terms in office. Similarly, the careers of many senior U.S. intelligence officials have ended on an unhappy note.[103]

Similar tensions between the Prime Minister and the Chief of Military Intelligence can also be found in Israel from the 'Lavon Affair' in the mid-1950s to Ben Gurion's tense relations with Iser Harrel, the head of the Mossad, over the German engineers and development of missiles in Egypt down to Begin and Sagui over the war in Lebanon. In each instance, the deterioration of personal relations between the Prime Minister and the head of intelligence forced the head of intelligence to relinquish his position.

3. Experience has shown that leaders tend to select Directors of Intelligence whose political views and character traits are consonant with their own (e.g., Carter–Turner, Reagan–Casey, Dayan–Zeira). Hence, the intelligence adviser is less likely to challenge the views of the leader or to come up with a fresh, alternative way of viewing a situation, so that better co-operation is achieved at the expense of the quality of intelligence estimates.

4. While there is no doubt that better intelligence estimates with a wider spectrum of views will emerge if the political leader and his intelligence adviser have different or even contradictory views, such an antagonistic relationship is bound to deteriorate sooner or later. The leader will eventually ignore the intelligence estimates of an adviser he cannot co-operate with, and the product of the adviser's intelligence organization will be wasted. For his part, the intelligence adviser will become aware that he is being ignored and is contributing little, if anything, to the decision-making process.

This tension between the necessity for co-operation between

political leaders and their intelligence advisers on the one hand, and the need to present objective if objectionable estimates on the other, has no simple solution in the real world. The ideal, of course, would be to have a secure and open-minded leader seeking the advice of an intelligence expert with political finesse, who knows his leader's wishes and policies but who has enough courage and skill to give him the most realistic estimates possible. In actuality, a more likely occurrence is the combination of a dogmatic, stubborn leader who prefers to indulge in wishful thinking and an 'intelligence waiter' prepared to serve up the most expedient intelligence palliative.

CONCLUSIONS

All social and human affairs that touch upon the allocation of scarce resources and individual struggles for power, whether occurring at the group, national or international level, cannot be politically neutral. Intelligence is in fact essential to the maintenance and expansion of political (and military) power. Thus, the goal of operating an intelligence community that is scientifically objective and politically neutral remains unattainable.

Yet many scholars and intelligence experts continue to propose reforms intended to bring about greater if not absolute political neutrality and hence heightened effectiveness. Such recommendations range from the utopian to the practical but hard to implement. Of the many intelligence reforms so widely introduced after each intelligence failure, few would effect a radical improvement. Each reform involves inevitable trade-offs. For example, reducing the co-ordination between intelligence organizations can waste resources and cause failures, while increasing it may reduce the clarity of analysis and further politicize the intelligence process. A highly sensitive intelligence alert-and-warning system may reduce the chances of strategic surprise but it increases the likelihood of false alarms and inadvertent confrontations, and is also very costly: a less sensitive warning system, though conducive to stability and lower costs, might fail to sound the tocsin at the right moment. Encouraging senior intelligence advisers to be objective, independent and politically disinterested is of course very commendable, but may weaken influence on the policy-making process. Having a small number of independent organizations might be less costly and easier to co-ordinate, but could result in less analytical diversity. Multiple organisations, on the other hand, might lead to greater analytical variety, but would be expensive, unwieldy and conducive to mindless acceptance of politically popular or acceptable positions. Moreover, the mere existence of more competing intelligence organizations does not guarantee that the political leader will give equal consideration to all or that he will not select the estimate that fits his preconceived ideas anyway.

No administrative panacea will help in making the optimal choice between excessive and insufficient co-ordination, professional objectivity and political influence, more or fewer intelligence organizations. Improving the effectiveness of the intelligence process might therefore be best left to a process of organic evolution and growth rather than to abrupt and ambitious reforms. The success of radical reform is apt to be marginal at best. Even if the intelligence community could somehow become more independent, objective and politically neutral, the quality of the intelligence process might be unchanged because of inherent methodological problems and paradoxes basic to intelligence work (e.g., the problems of signals *vs* noise, deception, problems of perception, ethnocentric biases, ambiguity).

While intelligence work will always remain vulnerable to political interference, the idealistic approach to intelligence does serve a practical purpose: it can moderate and to a certain extent counterbalance some of the worst consequences of the politics of intelligence. Ultimately, the performance of the intelligence community in a democratic system will rest primarily on the responsibility and dedication of all participants (the leaders in particular) to a cause which transcends their own immediate political or material interests. The world of intelligence, like that of war, is dominated by ambiguity and uncertainty, which will never be eliminated, and while the quest for certainty, clarity and foresight is a powerful motivating factor in human behavior it is destined by the nature of men to remain forever unfulfilled.

NOTES

The views expressed in this article are those of the author and do not reflect the official policy or position of the Department of Defense or the US Government.

I would like to thank my wife Jill Handel for her editorial assistance in preparing this article. I would also like to thank my friend Richard K. Betts for his suggestions and criticism.

1. See Walter Laqueur, 'The Question of Judgment: Intelligence and Medicine', *Journal of Contemporary History*, 18 (October 1983, special issue on Military History, ed. Martin van Creveld), 533–43.
2. Quoted from an excellent article by W.D. Howells, 'Intelligence in Crises' in Gregory R. Copley (ed.), *Defense '83* (Washington D.C.: D and FA Conferences Inc. 1983), pp. 349–66, esp. 362.
3. Thomas L. Hughes, *The Fate of Facts in a World of Men – Foreign Policy and Intelligence Making* (New York: Foreign Policy Association, December 1976, No. 233), p.5. This is one of the best essays on the interaction between the

intelligence community and political decision-makers.

4. Quoted from the Congressional testimony of Ray S. Cline, 'The Role of Intelligence in the Foreign Policy Process', *Hearings before the Subcommittee on International Security and Scientific Affairs of the Committee on Foreign Affairs House of Representatives*, 96th Congress (Washington, D.C., 1980), pp.7–8.

5. Hughes, *The Fate of Facts*, 16.

6. *Soviet Military Power 1987* (Washington, D.C.: GPO, 1987). This is the sixth edition of this publication.

7. Donald McLachlan, *Room 39: A Study in Naval Intelligence* (New York: Atheneum 1968), pp.127, 129. On this episode see also: Patrick Beesly, *Very Special Intelligence: The Story of the Admiralty's Operational Intelligence Center* (Garden City, NY: Doubleday 1978), pp.37–8, and Arthur J. Marder, *From the Dardanelles to Oran* (London: Oxford University Press, 1974) Ch. 4, pp.122–5. Also Stephen Roskill, *Churchill and the Admirals* (New York: William Morrow, 1978) p.94. He describes the incident in this way:

> Another Director of a Staff Division who brought about his dismissal by 'arguing the toss' with Churchill was Captain A.G. Talbot, the Director of Anti-Submarine Warfare. The staff had assessed that by 10 March 1940 only nineteen U-boats had been sunk and forty-three were fit for service. The actual figure was we now know fifteen sunk; but Churchill had publicly made far more optimistic claims and, doubtless advised by Lindemann, strongly challenged the staff's figures. His estimate that only a dozen U-boats remained effective (Pound admitted it might be twenty-two) was in fact fantastic; and the minute whereby he demanded, and obtained, Talbot's dismissal was an act of cruel injustice.

8. Ibid., pp.128–9.

9. Ibid., see Ch. 6, 'Godfrey and Churchill', pp.124–43. Actually a more suitable title for this chapter would be 'Churchill versus Godfrey'. See also Patrick Beesly, *Very Special Admiral: The Life of J.H. Godfrey C. 13* (London: Hamish Hamilton, 1980), pp.126–31, and *Very Special Intelligence*, p.37. Numerous other such examples of political pressures exerted on the reports of the intelligence community during the Second World War can be cited. A well-known case was 'the extraordinary pressures that were applied to photographic interpreters on occasions' by the highest echelons in Bomber Command to demonstrate the success of attacking specific targets – even if there was none to report. In the words of one such interpreter: 'We were constantly being pressurized by the Station Commander to publish glowing reports of glorious successes. If the interpreters found no trace of damage or craters, they were accused of minimizing the results, and our unfortunate officer in charge received hell – no one believed in our reports and our reputation was nil . . .'. Great firmness and self-reliance were required to withstand such pressures from above; see Ursula Powys-Lybbe, *The Eye of Intelligence* (London, 1983), pp.25–7.

10. Roskill, *Churchill and the Admirals*, p.347. The report was based on concrete facts: photographic reconnaissance of barge movements and military concentrations across the Channel; special knowledge obtained from Ultra; captured German agents ordered Berlin to lie low for six months; and the failure of the Luftwaffe to win the Battle of Britain.

11. Ibid., p.347.

12. Ibid., p.255. See also John Colville, *The Fringes of Power* (New York: Norton, 1986). 'He [Churchill] emphasised that the great invasion scare (which we only ceased to deride six weeks ago) is serving a most useful purpose: it is well on the way to providing us with the finest offensive army we have ever possessed and it is keeping every man and woman tuned to a high pitch of readiness. He does not wish the scare to abate therefore, and although personally he doubts whether invasion is a serious menace he intends to give that impression, and to talk about long and dangerous vigils, etc., when he broadcasts on Sunday' (p.19).

13. Roskill, *Churchill and the Admirals*, p.348.

14. Ibid.
15. As much as intelligence may be used to manipulate or influence public opinion it is even more frequently used to achieve similar results in the debates within the political elite. After all, for policy-makers, succeeding in bureaucratic politics is often even more crucial than influencing public opinion. In non-democratic societies the political manipulation of intelligence occurs primarily on this level.
16. Martin Gilbert, *Winston S. Churchill: The Prophet of Truth 1922–1939*, Vol. 5 (Boston: Houghton Mifflin, 1977), p.555n.
17. On the art and uses of leaking see Morton H. Halperin, 'Why Information is Leaked', *Bureaucratic Politics and Foreign Policy* (with the assistance of Priscilla Clap and Arnold Kanter, Washington, D.C.: Brookings Institution, 1974), pp.176–89. Classified information is leaked 'by those who are dissatisfied with the decisions being taken within the executive branch and who have reason to believe that public attitudes are likely to be more favorable to their position . . . Leaks may be designed to simply alert participants outside the executive branch in order to bring influence to bear, or they may be designed to affect the information which the public and the Congress has and which will lead them to make up their minds in a particular way on a particular issue' (pp.181–2). The following are the types of results that leaking is meant to achieve: To get the message through; to undermine rivals; to attract the attention of the President; to build support; to insure implementation; to alert foreign governments; to alert outside supporters; to affect public information or to announce a policy. The quote in the text is from Gilbert, *The Prophet of Truth*, p.625.
18. See Leonard B. Boudin, 'The Ellsberg Case: Citizen Disclosure' in Thomas M. Franck and Edward Weisband (eds.), *Secrecy and Foreign Policy* (New York: Oxford University Press, 1974), pp.291–311.
19. 'The intelligence service should enter the policy-making process twice: first, by providing data and assessments of the situation, which will contribute to shaping of policy; and secondly after the policy has been formulated, intelligence should also evaluate the likely reactions of adversaries and third parties to that policy and its success or failure. However, it often happens that statesmen refrain from seeking the intelligence services on this for basic reasons. For by making such a request of the intelligence they elevate it to the position of judging their policy. Thus a tangle is created whereby the intelligence arm which is a subordinate body, becomes an arbiter, a kind of supervisor over its master.' Yehoshafat Harkabi, 'The Intelligence-Policymaker Tangle'. *The Jerusalem Quarterly*, No. 30, Winter 1984, 125–31.
20. There may be an inverse correlation between the degree of risk involved and the readiness to compromise the intelligence process politically. Thus in times of peace and when the immediate political costs of ignoring intelligence warnings are low, such warnings can be ignored or tampered with politically according to the interests of the executive or military. In the early and mid-1930s British governments could, in the short run, ignore or underestimate warnings of German rearmament and aggressive intentions. The order of priorities of most British governments at that time did not include wide-scale rearmament. But attempting to secure short-run political advantages by ignoring or distorting estimates may lead to very high costs in the long run. Certainly, subsequent British governments had to pay the price of earlier policies that ignored politically inconvenient intelligence reports. As the danger increases, the tendency to tamper with and politicize intelligence work will be reduced. After Munich, the British government had to take intelligence reports more seriously and do something about them. Since the cost of manipulating intelligence in wartime is immediate and much higher, conscious attempts to influence intelligence procedures politically do decline. Normally, under war conditions, the intelligence community can hope to approximate more closely the professional ('theoretical' or 'ideal') conditions of work. But when there is neither full-scale war nor normal peace, the risks fall somewhere between the two conditions. In circumstances such as the US

war in Vietnam the political incentive to interfere in the 'professional' intelligence process may increase. That war never posed a critical danger to the survival of the US – yet it did present considerable domestic political dangers to the President. In this sort of situation, the real issue the political leadership or organizations have to face is their short-run survival: as in this case, they encouraged and accepted more optimistic and self-serving reports from the battlefield in Vietnam to serve political ends: 'The accuracy of any early intelligence reports and evaluations from the field was discouraged organizationally because pessimism became politically counter-productive. The administration had to justify its policy. As involvement grew, the bureaucracy became less responsible for reporting the truth than for making the war effort successful. As high policymakers became more committed, they developed a vested interest in optimistic readings of events, and the high officials' minions became increasingly susceptible to pressures to provide such interpretations where ambiguity allowed'. By the time President Johnson and his advisers became ready to listen to more pessimistic estimates the damage was done, and President Johnson had to pay the full price for discouraging honest intelligence reporting: he decided not to run for office again. Wishful thinking could substitute for the facts only in the short run. Richard K. Betts, *Soldiers, Statesmen and Cold War Crises* (Cambridge: Harvard University Press, 1977), pp.183–208, esp. 188. See also: *US Intelligence Agencies and Activities: The Performance of the Intelligence Community. Hearings Before the Select Committee on Intelligence*, Congress, First Session, Part 2, pp.683–719; Sam Adams, 'Vietnam Cover-Up: Playing War with Numbers', *Harpers Magazine*, May 1975, 41–4 and 62–73. Thomas Powers, *The Man Who Kept Secrets: Richard Helms and the CIA* (New York: Alfred A. Knopf, 1979), in particular Ch. 10–12. John Ranelagh, *The Agency: The Rise and Decline of the CIA* (New York: Simon Schuster, 1986), Ch. 13, pp.427–78. I do not discuss in this article the Westmoreland vs. CBS trial which is directly relevant to the topic. Given the complexity and importance of the trial for the study of the 'politicization' of the intelligence process, the trial deserves to be treated separately, and an article by T.L. Cubbage, 'Westmoreland vs. CBS: Was Intelligence Corrupted by Policy Demands?' will appear in a future issue of this journal. Among the books already published on the subject are Renata Adler, *Reckless Disregard: Westmoreland vs. CBS et al.; Sharon vs. Time* (New York: Alfred A. Knopf, 1986) – reviewed in this issue – and Bob Brewin and Sydney Shaw, *Vietnam on Trial: Westmoreland vs. CBS* (New York: Atheneum, 1987).

Similar pressures for political distortion can be expected in other non-critical, protracted wars such as the Israelis in Lebanon and the Soviets in Afghanistan (although the Soviet élite is not under public scrutiny). The cold war and the nuclear arms race have increased the risks that may result from inaccurate intelligence analysis and misestimates of the nuclear strategic balance. Being more critical in peacetime, intelligence concerning the nuclear balance has therefore probably been taken more seriously and less consciously tampered with by the political élite.

21. On the importance of learning how to 'package and sell' intelligence, see McLachlan, *Room 39*, p.357, and Donald McLachlan, 'Naval Intelligence in the Second World War', *RUSI*, Vol. CXII (August 1967), No. 647, 221–8; 221–2. 'They [Intelligence Analysts] must be able to present their findings with a positive degree of showmanship and credibility, and not allow themselves to be deflected simply because their views do not suit senior military leaders and politicians.' James Rusbridger, 'Winds of Warning: Mythology and Fact About Enigma and Pearl Harbor', *Encounter*, January 1986, 6–13; 13.

22. Betts quoted from: *'The Role of Intelligence in the Foreign Policy Process'*, Hearings Subcommittee on International Security and Scientific Affairs, 96th Congress, p.22. (Also in 'Intelligence for Policy Making' in *Washington Quarterly*, 1980).

23. Hearings, ibid., p.19.

WSI—H*

24. Hearings, ibid., p.20.
25. Quoted from Harkabi, 'The Intelligence-Policymaker Tangle', 128.
26. McLachlan, *Room 39*, p.353. Also, Chester L. Cooper, 'The CIA and Decision Making', *Foreign Affairs*, (Jan. 1972) 50, 223–37, makes a distinction between a leader's decision to *disregard* and *override* intelligence, 234–5.
27. Hughes, *The Fate of Facts in the World of Men*, p.24.
28. For the problem of ambiguity in intelligence work and policy making see: Betts, *Soldiers, Statesmen and Cold War Crises*, pp.199–208 in Ch. 10; also, Richard K. Betts, 'Intelligence for Policymaking', *The Washington Quarterly*, 3 (Summer 1980), 118–29; and Hughes, *The Fate of Facts in the World of Men*, pp.3–14.
29. See Wesley K. Wark, 'British Intelligence on the German Air Force and Aircraft Industry, 1933–1939', *The Historical Journal*, 25 (1982), 627–48; 634. See also Wesley K. Wark, *The Ultimate Enemy* (Ithaca: Cornell University Press, 1985).
30. Betts, *Soldiers, Statesmen and Cold War Crises*, p.184.
31. Ibid., p.193. This was also the case of the British Army: '. . . the perennial sin of the soldier . . . seemed to be to inflate the number of German divisions: There must have been some psychological need for the British Army to reinsure in this way after the traumas of Dunkirk and Crete.' McLachlan, *Room 39*, p.257.
32. Betts, *Soldiers, Statesmen and Cold War Crises*, p.195.
33. This apt term is taken from Harkabi, 'The Intelligence-Policymaker Tangle', 129. The intelligence restaurant includes other participants as well. Hughes, in his monograph, *The Fate of Facts in the World of Men*, adds the following classification of intelligence officers: 'The Butcher' is the eager-to-please supplier of last minute sexy raw intelligence who caters to those who have developed a 'succulent taste for the hot poop' (36–41). (McLachlan also suggests that 'career officers and politicians have a strong interest in cooking raw intelligence to make their masters' favorite dishes'.) 'The Baker' is the more responsible, politically uncommitted, and cautious-to-overcautious analyst who says, 'chances are just better than ever', 'highly likely', 'we doubt', 'tomorrow's weather will be fine, if it does not rain or snow'. He represents the indecision of the 'may or may not' formula (42–52). Then there is the *'Intelligence Maker'*, the senior intelligence official who provides the link between the intelligence community and the statesman. 'Market analyst and salesmen, middleman and promoter, quality controller and balance wheel, . . . he will . . . render off-the cuff judgments in fast-moving situations and affect, if not set priorities' (53–60). To extend the restaurant analogy a little further, one can introduce tips for good performance, health inspectors, culinary reporters and their columns, and food poisoning (i.e. major failurs in analysis such as the failure to anticipate strategic surprise).
34. Rostow's role as head waiter is described in David Halberstam, *The Best and the Brightest* (New York: Random House, 1972), pp.635–9. Rostow was well aware of the ideal type of intelligence in theory. He has written that 'any man who tried to distort the flow of information to President Johnson would not have lasted two weeks in his job . . . A president is extremely sensitive to the biases of his subordinates and to conscious or unconscious efforts to improve them. . . . My objective was not to determine the President's view but to make sure he had available the widest flow of information possible – a kind of intelligence ticker, if you like.' Quoted in Herbert Y. Schandler, *Lyndon Johnson and Vietnam: The Unmaking of a President* (Princeton, NJ: Princeton University Press, 1977), p.257. Halberstam describes Rostow's behavior in very different terms: '. . . he eventually served the purpose of shielding the Presidents from criticism and from reality. He deflected others' pessimism and rewarded those who were optimistic'. 'If any of the incoming reports indicated any kind of progress, Rostow immediately authorized a leak . . . He could always see the bright side of any situation and in that sense he became a legend. In the thousands of items flooding from Saigon as part of the information glut he could find the few positive ones, pounce on them and bring them to his boss. . . . Within the bureaucracy the word went out among those who briefed him (Rostow) that if they wanted to get his

attention they had to bait their news with sugar, get positive information in first, and then before he could turn off, quickly slip in the darker evidence.' Halberstam, *Best and Brightest*, pp.636–7.

35. On the USAF optimistic estimates of the effect of strategic bombing, see Betts, *Soldiers, Statesmen and Cold War Crises*, pp.199–208. In *Room 39*, McLachlan reports that the RAF overrated the effectiveness of its bombing in general; pp.258, 361. See also Morris J. Blachman, 'The Stupidity of Intelligence' in Morton H. Halperin and Arnold Kauter (eds.), *Readings in American Foreign Policy: A Bureaucratic Perspective* (Boston: Little Brown, 1972), pp.326–34.

36. See: Lawrence Freedman, *U.S. Intelligence and the Soviet Strategic Threat* (Boulder, CO: Westview Press, 1977), Ch. 4. John Prados, *The Soviet Estimates: U.S. Intelligence Analysis and Russian Military Strength* (New York: Dial Press, 1982), Chs. 38–51 and pp.7–8; 96–127 comments. See also Herbert S. Dinerstein, *The Making of a Missile Crisis October 1962* (Baltimore: John Hopkins University Press, 1976), p.75, and Arthur M. Schlesinger, *A Thousand Days* (Boston: Houghton Mifflin, 1965), p.499.

37. See for example, Albert Wohlstetter, 'Is There a Strategic Arms Race?' *Foreign Policy*, No. 15, Summer 12974, 3–20. 'Rivals But No Race', *Foreign Policy*, No. 16, Fall 1979, 48–81. Albert Wohlstetter, 'Optimal Ways to Confuse Ourselves', *Foreign Policy*, No. 20, Fall 1975, 170–98.

38. Peter Szanton and Graham Allison, 'Intelligence: Seizing the Opportunity', *Foreign Policy*, No. 22, Spring 1976, 183–215; 190.

39. Freedman, *U.S. Intelligence and the Soviet Strategic Threat*, p.183.

40. Betts, *Soldiers, Statesmen and Cold War Crisis*, p.95. Also Les Aspin, 'Misleading Intelligence', *Foreign Policy*, No. 43, Summer 1981, 166–72.

41. Betts, ibid., Ch. 10; McLachlan, *Room 39*, Ch. 11.

42. Aspin, 'Misleading Intelligence', 168; Harry Truman, *Memoirs*, 2, p.58.

43. Betts, *Soldiers, Statesmen and Cold War Crisis*, pp.110, 192; and David Halberstam, *The Best and the Brightest*, pp.255–9.

44. Thomas Powers, *The Man Who Kept Secrets*, pp.187–8.

45. Szanton and Allison, 'Intelligence: Seizing the Opportunity', 191.

46. See Irving Janis, *Victims of Groupthink* (Boston: Houghton Mifflin, 1972).

47. Hughes, *The Fate of Facts in the World of Men*, pp.49–50.

48. R.V. Jones, *Most Secret War* (London: Hamish Hamilton, 1978), p.517.

49. Szanton and Allison, 'Intelligence: Seizing the Opportunity', 192.

50. Powers, *The Man Who Kept Secrets*, p.205.

51. McLachlan, *Room 39*, p.298, Ch. 11, 'Three Heads are Better . . . 'Includes an excellent discussion of British Intelligence co-ordination at the highest level during the Second World War. Also McLachlan, 'Naval Intelligence in World War II', 222. See also F.H. Hinsley, *et al.*, *British Intelligence in the Second World War*, 1 (London: Her Majesty's Stationery Office, 1979), Ch. 9, 'Reorganizations and Reassessment During the Winter of 1940–1941', pp.267–314, in particular, 291–314. Also, Vol. 2, (New York: Cambridge University Press, 1981), Ch. 15, 'Development and Organization of Intelligence', pp.3–41.

52. Rear Admiral E.T. Layton with R. Pinneau and J. Costello, *And I Was There. Pearl Harbor and Midway* (New York: William Morrow, 1985).

53. Howells, 'Intelligence in Crises', pp.366–7.

54. Ibid.

55. See David Kahn, *Hitler's Spies: German Military Intelligence in World War II* (New York: Macmillan, 1978); Peter R. Black, Ernst Kaltenbrunner, *Ideological Soldier of the Third Reich* (Princeton, NJ: Princeton University Press, 1984), Ch. 6, 'Struggle with Rival Chieftains, 1943–1945', pp.176–217; Paul W. Blackstock, *The Strategy of Subversion*, (Chicago: Quadrangle, 1969), Ch. 4, 'Divided Policymaking and Operational Responsibilities', pp.95–120.

56. Halberstam, *The Best and the Brightest*, p.256.

57. Powers, *The Man Who Kept Secrets*, p.173.

58. Lawrence Freeman, *U.S. Intelligence and the Soviet Strategic Threat* (Boulder,

CO.: Westview Press, 1977), pp.194–5.

59. See Abdul Kasim Mansur, 'The Crisis in Iran: Why the U.S. Ignored A Quarter Century of Warning', *Armed Forces Journal International*, January 1979, 26–33. *Iran: Evaluation of US Intelligence Performance Prior to November 1978*. Staff Report Subvcommittee on Evaluation Permanent Select Committee on Intelligence. US House of Representatives, January 1979; and Robert F. Ellsworth and Kenneth L. Adelman, 'Foolish Intelligence', *Foreign Policy*, No. 36, Fall 1979, 147–59.

60. Szanton and Allison, 'Intelligence Seizing the Opportunity', 191. McLachlan in 'Naval Intelligence in the Second World War' emphasizes that '. . . intelligence should be rigorously separated from skulduggery, by which I mean, subversive operations, para military organizations, James Bond activities', 222.

61. See Zeev Schiff and Ehud Ya'ari, *Milchemet Sholal* (Hebrew) (*Misleading War*) (Tel Aviv: Yediot Acharonot, 1984).

62. Betts, *Soldiers, Statesmen and Cold War Crisis*, 193.

63. See Patrick McGarvey, 'DIA: Intelligence to Please' in Morton H. Halperin and Arnold Kanter (eds.), *Readings in American Foreign Policy: A Bureaucratic Perspective* (Boston: Little Brown, 1972), pp.318–28; 320, 321.

64. Admiral Forbes quoted in Stephen Roskill, *Churchill and the Admirals* (New York: William Morrow, 1978), p.276.

65. R.V. Jones, *Most Secret War*, p.517. See also Sherman Kent, *Strategic Intelligence for American World Policy* (Princeton NJ: Princeton University Press, 1949), p.97.

66. McLachlan, *Room 39*, p.342.

67. Ibid., p.342.

68. Ibid., p.343.

69. Ibid., p.345.

70. Szanton and Allison, 'Intelligence: Seizing the Opportunity', 188. Betts, *Soldiers, Statesmen and the Cold War Crisis*, p.196.

71. McGarvey, 'DIA: Intelligence to Please', 325.

72. David J. Bell, *Power, Influence and Authority: An Essay in Political Linguistics* (New York: Oxford University Press, 1975), pp.33–4.

73. Ibid., p.32.

74. McGarvey, 'DIA: Intelligence to Please', quoted also in Betts, *Soldiers, Statesmen and Cold War Crises*, pp.189–90; and Halperin, *Bureaucratic Politics and Foreign Policy*, pp.85–9; 164.

75. Betts, ibid., 199.

76. Quoted in Harold Lowell Ashman, 'Intelligence and Foreign Policy: A Functional Analysis' (Ph.D. diss., University of Utah, 1973), p.50.

77. McLachlan, 'Naval Intelligence in the Second World War', 221–2.

78. For the methodological problems and paradoxes of intelligence work, see for example: Roberta Wohlsletter, *Pearl Harbor: Warning and Decision* (Stanford: Stanford University Press, 1962), Richard K. Betts, *Surprise Attack: Lessons for Defense Planning* (Washington, D.C.: Brookings Institution, 1982) and Betts, 'Analysis Warning and Decision: Why Intelligence Failures are Inevitable', *World Politics*, 31 October 1978, 61–89; Michael I. Handel, 'The Yom Kippur War and the Inevitability of Surprise', *International Studies Quarterly*, 21 September 1977, 461–501, and Michael I. Handel, *Perception, Deception and Surprise: The Case of the Yom Kippur War* (Jerusalem: The Leonard Davis Institute, 1976) and 'Intelligence and the Problem of Strategic Surprise', *Journal of Strategic Studies*, September 1984, Vol. 7, No. 3, 229–81.

79. Michael I. Handel, *The Diplomacy of Surprise* (Cambridge, MA: Harvard Center for International Affairs, 1981), pp.1–31; 241–53.

80. Hughes, *The Fate of Facts in the World of Men*, p.20.

81. Ibid., pp.20–22; also p.44.

82. Ashman, *Intelligence and Foreign Policy*, 53.

83. Ibid., On Hitler's ignoring of intelligence in crisis when information was

'unpleasant' or contradicted his assumptions, see Geoffrey Jukes. Churchill said this on the distortion of intelligence by the dictators: the men at the top would be fed only with the facts 'which are palatable to them'. Scandals and shortcomings, instead of being exposed, 'continue to fester behind the pompous frontage of the State'. These men at the top 'may be very fierce and powerful, but their ears are deaf, their fingers are numb; they cannot feel their feet as they move forward in the fog and darkness of the immeasurable and the unknown'. Quoted in Martin Gilbert, *Winston Churchill: Finest Hour*, Vol. 6. (Boston: Houghton Mifflin, 1981) pp.142, 61.

84. Halperin, *Bureaucratic Politics and Foreign Policy*, 121.
85. Powers, *The Man Who Kept Secrets*, 201-2.
86. Handel, *The Diplomacy of Surprise*, Chaps. 5–6.
87. Hughes, *The Fate of Facts in The World of Men*, pp.28–30.
88. See John Erikson, *The Road to Stalingrad* (New York: Harper & Row, 1975) and Seweryn Bialer (ed.), *Stalin and His Generals* (New York: Pegasus, 1969). Also Jukes.
89. Gaddis Smith, 'How the British Held the Fort', *The New York Times Book Review*, 25 December 1983, 1–2. (This is a review of Martin Gilbert, *Winston S. Churchill: Finest Hour*, Vol. 6.)
90. Ronald Lewin, *Churchill As A Warlord* (New York: Stein and Day, 1982), p.5. More critical studies of Churchill as a military leader are: R.W. Thompson, *Generalissimo Churchill* (New York: Charles Scribner's Sons, 1973) and A.J.P. Taylor, *et al.*, *Churchill Revisited: A Critical Assessment* (New York: Dial Press, 1962).
91. Admiral J.H. Godfrey, the DNI quoted by Arthur J. Marder, *From the Dardanelles to Oran* (London: Oxford University Press, 1974) Ch. 4, 'Winston is Back: Churchill at the Admiralty 1939-1949'), p.109.
92. Lewin, *Churchill as a Warlord*, p.75. Churchill has this to say in his memoirs: 'I had not been content with this form of collective wisdom, and preferred to see the originals myself. I had arranged, therefore, as far back as the Summer of 1940, for Major Desmond Morton to make a daily selection of titbits, which I always read, thus forming my own opinion, sometimes at much earlier dates'. He sent the following note on 5 August 1940 to General Ismay. 'I do not wish such reports as are received to be sifted and digested by the various Intelligence authorities. For the present Major Morton will inspect them for me and submit what he considers of major importance. He is to be shown everything, and submit authentic documents to me in their original form.' Winston Churchill, *The Second World War*, Vol. 3, *The Grand Alliance*, (Cambridge, MA: Houghton Mifflin 1951) p.356.
93. Major Sir Desmond Morton, quoted in R.W. Thompson, *Churchill and Morton* (London: Hodder & Stoughton, 1976), p.45.
94. Lewin, *Churchill As A Warlord*, p.21.
95. Ibid., pp.30–31. See also Roskill, *Churchill and the Admirals*, pp.276–7, for a similar comment.
96. Ibid., p.20.
97. McLachlan, *Room 39*, p.359. Many leaders cannot resist the temptation to become their own intelligence officers. This practice is dangerous for the following reasons:
(a) Leaders have only a limited amount of time to devote to the in-depth analysis of almost any subject.
(b) Most often they are not experts or have only limited knowledge of the problems they intend to analyse.
(c) Above all they will be unable to be objective on exactly those subjects that interest them the most.
(d) They tend to focus on pressing issues but may ignore other important issues. This danger is best demonstrated by the statement attributed to Kissinger, 'I don't know what kind of intelligence I want, but I know it when I get it'.

98. Leslie Gelb and Richard K. Betts, *The Irony of Vietnam* (Washington: Brookings Institution, 1979), pp.229–30.
99. See Nigel West, *MI5: British Secret Intelligence Service Operations 1909-1945* (London: Weidenfeld & Nicolson, 1983), pp.137–9.
100. See Dennis Wheatley, 'Deception in World War II', *RUSI*, 121 (Sept. 1976), 87–8.
101. Alouph Hareven, 'Disturbed Hierarchy: Israeli Intelligence in 1954 and 1973'. *The Jerusalem Quarterly*, Nov. 1978, 3–19, and Janice Gross Stein, 'The 1973 Intelligence Failure: A Reconsideration', *The Jerusalem Quarterly*, No. 24, Summer 1982, 41–54.
102. Powers, *The Man Who Kept Secrets*, p.347.
103. Walter Laqueur, *A World of Secrets: The Uses and Limits of Intelligence* (New York: Basic Books, 1985), p.7.

5

Intelligence and the Problem of Strategic Surprise

... The textbooks agree, of course, that we should only believe reliable intelligence, and should never cease to be suspicious, but what is the use of such feeble maxims? They belong to that wisdom which for want of anything better scribblers of systems and compendia resort to when they run out of ideas. (Clausewitz, *On War,* Book One, Ch. 6)

... the general unreliability of all information presents a special problem in war: all action takes place, so to speak, in a kind of twilight, which, like fog or moonlight, often tends to make things seem grotesque and larger than they really are.

Whatever is hidden from full view in this feeble light has to be guessed at by talent, or simply left to chance. So once again for lack of objective knowledge one has to trust to talent or to luck.

(Clausewitz, *On War,* Book Two, Ch. 2)

The study of strategic surprise can be rather disappointing for those who have always assumed that a better *theoretical* understanding of the subject at hand would logically lead to the discovery of more effective *practical* means to anticipate strategic surprise and alleviate its impact. Thus far in its application to the real world, improved insight into the causes and pattern of strategic surprise has made only a negligible contribution to the search for ways to warn of a sudden attack in an accurate and timely fashion. If anything, the scrutiny of this phenomenon in recent years has chiefly served to explain why surprise is almost always unavoidable – and will continue to be so in the foreseeable future – despite all efforts to the contrary.

Strategic Surprise as a Force Multiplier

From a military point of view, the advantages to be derived from achieving strategic surprise are invaluable. A successful unanticipated attack will facilitate the destruction of a sizable portion of the enemy's forces at a lower cost to the attacker by throwing the inherently stronger defense psychologically off balance, and hence temporarily reducing his resistance. In compensating for the weaker position of the attacker, it will act as a force multiplier that may drastically reverse the ratio of forces in the attacker's favor. Stated in more general terms, the numerically inferior side is able to take the initiative by concentrating superior forces at the time and place of its choosing, thereby vastly improving the likelihood of achieving a decisive victory. Clearly, then, the incentive to resort to strategic surprise (as well as to deception) is particularly strong for countries that are only too cognizant of their relative vulnerability. Stronger armies, however, lack the 'natural incentive' to employ such methods, and must therefore make a conscious effort to exploit the full potential of strategic surprise if they are to maintain a superior position and achieve more decisive results at a minimal cost.[1]

Although strategic surprise in modern military history has seldom failed in terms of its initial impact, surprising the enemy *per se* does not necessarily mean that the attacker has reaped the fullest possible benefits or will be assured ultimate victory. (There is, in fact, no positive correlation between the initial success of a strategic surprise and the outcome of a war.[2]) One reason for this is that the attacker is often so amazed by the effectiveness of his own attack that he is caught unprepared to exploit fully the opportunities it presents. For example, the Japanese did not follow up their success at Pearl Harbor with repeated attacks on US oil depots and other naval and air installations in Hawaii, nor did the Allies take advantage of the opportunities produced by their surprise landing in Anzio. The same holds true for the Egyptian and Syrian armies in their 1973 attack on Israel: rigidly adhering to the original plan of attack, they prematurely halted their advance following the first phase of the attack, when they could have continued to make considerable progress at little cost to themselves.

The benefits accruing from a strategic surprise will be maximized to the degree that plans for the attack are flexible, and more initiative is delegated to field commanders, who are also encouraged to improvise and accept risks. (The Germans very successfully exploited the surprise gained in the opening of their attack on Norway and the west in 1940, and in the earlier stages of their attack on the Soviet Union in 1941, although they failed in this respect during the Ardennes offensive in 1944. In another instance, the Israelis came close to fully exhausting the potential of their unanticipated attack on Egypt in the opening phase of the 1967 war.) Thus, accomplishment of the surprise itself is only the *first* phase of planning; the *second* must consist of detailed preparations for the best possible exploitation of the projected surprise attack; frequently, this objective can be produced through a maxi–max (high risk–high gain) strategy as practiced by the Germans in Norway, the Japanese in Singapore, MacArthur in Inchon, and the Israelis in 1967. While the first phase, as we shall see below, rarely fails, the second one poses serious, sometimes insurmountable problems. Yet the whole *raison d'être* of launching a strategic surprise will collapse if the first stage cannot be followed up by the second.

*   *   *

Surprise in Historical Perspective

Although surprise has always been possible on the *tactical* level, its feasibility on the *strategic* level is a relatively new historical phenomenon of the twentieth century. Before the technological-industrial revolution, the rapid movement of large troop formations over long distances in a short period of time was virtually impossible. The slow pace of mobilization, not to mention that of troop concentration and movement, provided ample clues as to an adversary's offensive intent. Furthermore, such evidence could be gathered in time to countermobilize and make all preparations necessary to intercept the expected attack. This was recognized by Clausewitz, who believed that strategic surprise was of greater theoretical interest than practical value.

> Basically, surprise is a tactical device, simply because in tactics, *time and space* are limited in scale. Therefore in strategy, surprise becomes more feasible the closer it occurs to the tactical realm, and more difficult, the more it approaches the higher levels of policy .... While the wish to achieve surprise is common and, indeed, indispensable, and while it is true that it will never be completely ineffective, it is equally true that by its very nature surprise can rarely be outstandingly successful. *It would be a mistake, therefore, to regard surprise as a key element of success in war. The principle is highly attractive in theory, but in practice it is often held up by the friction of the whole machine ....* Preparations for war usually take months. Concentrating troops at their main assembly points generally requires the installation of supply dumps and depots, as well as considerable troop movements, whose purpose can be assessed soon enough. It is very rare therefore that one state surprises another, either by an attack or by preparations for war.[3]

Indeed, Clausewitz was convinced that, *in his time,* strategic surprise was not powerful enough to overcome the inherent advantages of the defense.

> The immediate object of an attack is victory. Only by means of his superior strength can the attacker make up for all the advantages that accrue to the defender by virtue of his position, and possibly by the modest advantage that this army derives from the knowledge that it is on the attacking, the advancing side. Usually this latter is much overrated: it is short-lived and will not stand the test of serious trouble. Naturally we assume that the defender will act as sensibly and correctly as the attacker. We say this in order to exclude certain vague notions about sudden assaults and surprise attacks, which are commonly thought of as bountiful sources of victory. They will only be that under exceptional circumstances.[4]

In the past, surprise was thus confined to the tactical and grand tactical levels. With the advent of technology came the ability to achieve strategic surprise, as well as a change in the modes and aims of surprise, which, in its strategic form, is a much more complex phenomenon. Surprise could now be achieved simultaneously on several levels: in *timing,* the *place* of attack, *rapidity* of movement, the use of *new technologies delivery* and *weapons systems*, the frequent appearance of new doctrines and innovative tactics to match the new technologies, as well as in the choice of the political-military goals for war itself.[5]

The beginning of the railroad era, shortly after Clausewitz's death, touched off the revolution in mobility in warfare. Half a century later, the combustion engine further expanded the flexibility of movement and maneuver while obviating the necessity of dependence on railroad tracks for rapid mobility. The introduction of tracked vehicles and tanks by the end of the First World War improved the possibility of movement over difficult terrain, thus bringing the revolution of movement on land to its logical conclusion. Such trends conducive to strategic surprise were even further boosted by the development of air power, which added a third dimension of movement across all natural barriers, in all directions, and in very short periods of time. Air power brought to near perfection the possibility of success in the use of strategic surprise. Readying air power for the initial strike did not require an unusual concentration of forces, since it was based on the use of forces in being. Furthermore, the transition from peace to war was instantaneous, while the firepower that could be concentrated and unleashed was tremendous. Air power was particularly suitable for the attack of targets such as headquarters, communications centers, airfields, fuel depots, bridges, roads and other choke points vital for a counter-mobilization and the effective management of the defense against surprise attack. Moreover, it surpassed all other types of power in the ability to effect deep penetration bombardments and airborne attacks and/or provide support for deep penetration operations in land warfare.

In general, the existence of a variety of means of transportation made possible an accelerated pace in the initial mobilization and concentration of troops for the attack. This, in turn, improved the likelihood of achieving a breakthrough to be followed up by deep penetration into the adversary's territory. In addition, supplies could now be transported to the attacking forces more rapidly and over longer distances, thereby widening the range of options for maneuvering on the battlefield. When employed in conjunction with the enormously increased capacity of conventional firepower, the efficient, rapid means of transportation multiplied the power with which one could attack at a selected point and catch one's adversary completely off guard. Time and space, to use Clausewitz's apt phrase, had now been compressed.

In the twentieth century, technological surprise has become one of the most formidable forms of surprise in war. The unexpected appearance of new weapons in massive quantities, and/or their use in an innovative way, can be of decisive importance. Among some of the better known technological surprises, the first massive use of gases and tanks in the First World War and the appearance of and, even more so, the methods of use of the radar and radar counter-measures in the Second World War, are outstanding. The use of gliders by the Germans during their attack in the west in 1940 on the Belgian fort of Eban-Emael, the performance of the Japanese Zero and the Russian T-34, the British code-breaking effort and the strategic and tactical use of Ultra and the American atomic bomb are also among the best known surprises of wartime.

Technological surprises can be divided into two categories. The first involves the secret development of 'one' large system which is not deployed on the battlefield itself, such as Ultra and the atomic bomb. This type of technological surprise is extremely difficult to discover or anticipate. The second category involves the massive battlefield deployment of a new weapon system, such as the Zero or the T-34, which takes considerable time and is difficult to conceal. Yet very much like all other types of strategic surprise and for the very same reasons discussed below, technological surprise never fails. Given the rate of technological change since the end of the Second World War and evidence from recent wars, there is little doubt that technological surprise and deception will play a much more critical role in future wars.

As technological developments made unprecedented contributions to the feasibility of strategic surprise, the warning time available to the intended victim decreased dramatically. During the opening phases of the war at the very least, it significantly enhanced the power of the offense over the defense. The possibility that an unanticipated attack could quickly determine the outcome of an entire war thus became a very serious threat to the survival of states, especially in an ideologically competitive political environment.

In this manner, then, advanced military technology unintentionally opened up a highly destabilizing pandora's box. The fact that any country could clandestinely mobilize its armed forces and/or gain a tremendous advantage by simply starting to mobilize its forces first, created a situation in which *the reciprocal fear of surprise attack*[6] could, under crisis conditions, trigger automatic mobilization responses, loss of control, and preemptive attacks (i.e., become a self-fulfilling prophecy). Having produced optimal conditions for strategic surprise, technology emerged as one of the principal destabilizing factors in the international system of the twentieth century.

This trend reached its acme with the invention of modern nuclear weapons and ICBMs, whose staggering concentrated firepower, capable of being activated in minutes, meant that a strategic surprise could be both the beginning and the end of a war. That which Clausewitz considered to be a strictly *theoretical* possibility – the idea that a war might be decided by 'a single short blow'[7] – has become part of reality. Technological progress in the last hundred years or so has reduced the time required for concentrating troops or launching weapons for a strategic surprise from months to weeks, to days, and ultimately to hours or even minutes (see Figure 1).

A significant by-product of the military-technological revolution was the tremendous increase in the importance and number of functions assigned to military intelligence. The connection between the rise of technology and that of military intelligence is a subject that has received very little attention from military historians.

In times of little technological progress or change, intelligence and up-to-

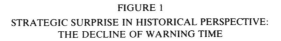

FIGURE 1
STRATEGIC SURPRISE IN HISTORICAL PERSPECTIVE:
THE DECLINE OF WARNING TIME

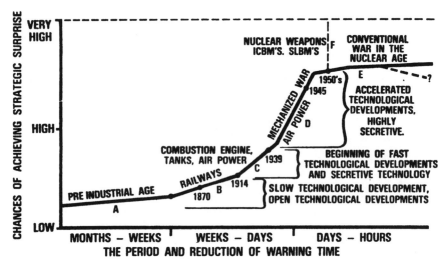

Notes:

A. Pre-industrial age. Slow mobility, limited fire power. Chances of a successful strategic surprise very low.(1870)
B. Railway age. Increased mobility, mobilization. Slow increases in fire power. Chances of a successful strategic surprise low but possible. (1870-1916)
C. Combustion engines, tracked vehicles and tanks, rise of air power and fire power. Mechanized warfare blitzkrieg. Chances of strategic surprise high. (1916-1939)
D. Further improvement in mobility and fire power. Chances of strategic surprise high – but also improvements to intelligence. (1939 to present)
E. Development of nuclear weapons and later ICBM's and SLBM's par excellence the weapons of strategic surprise. War can be decided – theoretically and practically – in minutes. (1945 to present)
F. Improvements in conventional mobility and fire power. Increased importance of air power. High chances of success for strategic surprise – but slowed increase given the technical developments of reconnaissance (air photography, satellites, electronic intelligence). Potential for surprise is somewhat leveled off by reconnaissance and familiarity with tactics of blitzkrieg. Yet, despite all the technological improvements that may help the defense, the basic problems of anticipating an attack are perceptual and psychological and remain without a satisfactory solution.

date information were not of paramount importance, because the behavior and strength of one's adversary did not change very frequently. The shape of each war differed only marginally from that of earlier wars. This is *not* the case in a world of rapid technological change, where each new weapon and the continuously changing rates of military industrial production may give the innovator a critical unilateral advantage almost overnight. For the first time in history, intelligence itself has become a major defensive weapon. Furthermore, most of the technological innovations and preparations for war continue in peacetime, indicating that intelligence work has become as important in peacetime as it is in war.

Although military technology has revolutionized almost every conceivable aspect of military performance, the one area in which it has, ironically enough, made little progress is that of anticipating surprise attack. The warning gap between the attacker and defender has remained as wide as in the past and still favors the offense over the defense. This will continue to be so, mainly because intelligence work, despite its access to electronic monitoring equipment, high-powered computers, and satellites, to name a few, is still based upon the human factor. As it is labor-intensive, intelligence work must reflect human nature, not technological excellence. The quality of results achieved in the world of intelligence and strategic warning in particular depends upon finding solutions to human problems which sometimes defy technological (or for that matter, any other) solutions. Among these are problems of: human psychology and politics; wishful thinking; ethnocentric biases; perception and misperception of reality; conflicting interests; political competition over scarce resources; organizational biases. As long as men interact with machines in the decision-making process, the quality of the decisions made will be most heavily influenced by the human factor, the complexities of which can be explained but not done away with.

In the past, it has often (either explicitly or implicitly) been assumed that intelligence work can be pursued by professional, detached experts working within an objective environment, and that they will be able to present the truth, as best they can determine it, to the policymakers. The policymakers in this scenario will of course recognize the quality and relevance of the data provided them, and will use this information in the best interest of their country (as they identify it). This 'purely rational decision-making model' and belief in the viability of a 'strictly professional intelligence process' is nothing but an idealized normative fiction. And yet many scholars and even some experienced intelligence experts continue to believe in the possibility of creating – through the 'right' reform – the perfect intelligence community.

Like Clausewitz's war in practice, the real world of intelligence is rife with political friction and contradictions, an environment in which uncertainty is the only certain thing.

*   *   *

Intelligence work can be divided into three distinct levels: *acquisition* (the collection of information); *analysis* (its evaluation); and *acceptance* (the readiness of politicians to make use of intelligence in the formulation of their policies).[8] As suggested earlier, past failures in avoiding surprise cannot be blamed on a dearth of information and warning signals. Consequently, one must look to the levels of analysis and acceptance for an answer.

The major problems stemming from these two levels can be discussed under three principal categories, two of which are primarily related to the analytical process. These are, first, the methodological dilemmas inherent in intelligence work and problems of perception and second, explanations corresponding mainly to the level of acceptance. The third category includes organizational and bureaucratic problems.

A. Methodological Dilemmas and Problems of Perception

1. SIGNALS AND NOISE

Basically, information collected by the various intelligence acquisition modes can be divided into two types: correct and incorrect, or as they are called in intelligence jargon, signals and noises.[9] Although this dichotomous method of classification is of great theoretical value, in reality it is usually impossible to distinguish between signals and noises. Instead of falling neatly into one of the two categories, much of the information is a combination of both elements and therefore cannot be considered either completely reliable or totally unreliable. In attempting to determine the reliability of any single piece of information, analysts need to corroborate it with many other bits of data. The analysis and evaluation process is further hampered by the often contradictory nature of the information, which defies simple quantitative analysis. (This statement is not meant to suggest that a sophisticated quantitative analysis has a better substitute.) Much of the important data acquired do not lend themselves to a quantitative presentation because the criteria used to determine their selection, categorization and corroboration are ultimately determined by human beings, who cannot detach themselves from their ethnocentric biases, preconceived ideas and concepts, and wishful thinking. Much of the criticism directed at the use of quantitative methods in the social sciences, particularly in international relations, is even more applicable to intelligence work. In many facets of intelligence work, there is often no substitute for the experience and intuition of the expert. Intelligence must, as a result, generally be described as an art despite the many scientific disciplines that make critical contributions to its success.

It has been observed that 'if surprise is the most important "key to victory", then stratagem is the key to surprise.' The ever present possibility of deception further complicates the already difficult task of the intelligence analyst.[10] Deception can be defined as the deliberate and subtle dissemination of misleading information to an intelligence service by its adversaries.

Since the deceiver intends to present noise as highly trustworthy information, most successful uses of stratagem are based on the supply of largely accurate and verifiable data to the adversary. Having worked hard to obtain this information, the adversary is psychologically predisposed to believe it. In view of the aforementioned danger, the intelligence analyst regards most information as suspicious until proven otherwise. This is especially true under two circumstances: (a) when the intended victim of deception frequently makes use of it himself, as he will be more sensitive to its possible use by an adversary; (b) any intelligence organization that has been duped once tends to become overcautious. The latter situation can be summarized by this paradox: *The more alert one is to deception, the more likely one is to become its victim.*[11] And the better the information appears to be – the more readily it fits into a neat pattern – the greater must be the caution of the analyst. For example, Belgian intelligence obtained German plans for the invasion of the west when a German aircraft carrying two staff officers made a forced landing in Belgium on 10 January 1940. Upon receiving the information, the British and French would exclude the possibility that it had been planted for their benefit.[12] The danger here is that the better the information is, particularly when based on one source, the less credible it may seem to be.

Deception, and uncertainty in general, create an environment in which almost all information, at least in the short run, is accompanied by a question mark. This gives rise to yet another paradox.

'As a result of the great difficulties involved in differentiating between "signals" and noise in strategic warning, both valid and invalid information must be treated on a similar basis. In effect, all that exists is noise, not signals.'[13] Attempts to separate the noise from the signals are aggravated by the fact that *the collection of additional information also contributes more noise to the system, and the higher the amount of data collected, the more difficult it becomes to filter, organize and process them in time to be of use.*[14]

The collection of information is of course only a necessary but not a sufficient condition for the success of an intelligence organization. A balance must be struck between the collection effort and the analytical process. If an intelligence organization operates an excellent acquisition and collection mechanism but lacks enough qualified experts to process the information *in time*, its excellence in collection may come to naught insofar as warning of a strategic surprise attack is concerned. The emphasis on acquisition in the United States and the USSR has resulted in American overreliance on technological intelligence and, in the case of both countries, led to the collection of so much data that their analytical capacities have no doubt been seriously taxed.

2. UNCERTAINTY AND THE TIME FACTOR

From the preceeding discussion, it is clear that the analytical process of distinguishing between signals and noises requires *time*. Normally, a certain amount of time elapses (A–B on Figure 2) before the intelligence organization of the 'victim' gains some inkling of the attacker's plans. The lead time of the would-be attacker (A–B) shrinks in direct proportion to the degree of excellence of the prospective victim's intelligence service. By the time the defender seriously begins to consider the possibility of an attack (at point B), the attacker is well ahead of him in his preparations for war. (Point BB represents the attacker's lead time.) But even then, the defender-to-be is not yet convinced that he will be attacked; therefore, despite the initial warning, he does not fully mobilize (point C). While the attacker continues his preparations, which become increasingly difficult to conceal from the defender's intelligence, the 'victim' may gradually become persuaded of the gravity of the threat and begin to mobilize his own forces (point D). Meanwhile, the attacker has already completed his preparations and launches his

FIGURE 2

THE NORMAL WARNING AND PREPARATION GAP BETWEEN THE ATTACKER AND
DEFENDER (THIS CHART EMPIRICALLY REFLECTS *MOST* CASES OF STRATEGIC
SURPRISE ATTACKS)

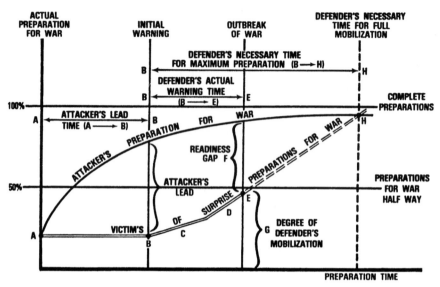

Notes:

A. Attacker starts preparations for war.

B. Defender issues initial warning, but is uncertain of the real probability of war.

C. Due to uncertainty the initial phase of preparation proceeds relatively slowly.

D. As the probability of war increases and becomes more certain the defender accelerates preparations.

E. War breaks out (e.g. surprise attack). Defender's preparations incomplete and lag behind the attacker.

F. The readiness gap favoring the attacker.

G. The degree of mobilization completed by the defenders at the time of attack (E).

H. At this point the defender may have reached his highest level of preparations. Line A⟷B represents the *attacker's lead time;* line B⟷E represents the *defender's actual warning time;* line B⟷H represents the time the defender needs to complete his preparations. The greater is B⟷H minus B⟷E the more intense is the impact of the surprise attack.

attack (point E). Represented by gap F, the time lag between the preparations of the two adversaries depends upon the warning received by the defender and his speed of mobilization. While the defender's actual warning time was B–E, he might require more time (B–H) to complete his mobilization. (G represents the forces the defender managed to mobilize before the attack took place.) This sequence of events is typical of a strategic surprise that is not 'out of the blue'. It offers some explanation as to why surprise is not absolute, since the defender normally manages to mobilize at least some of his troops. In many instances, the defender's preparations have been underway for a matter of hours (B–E), while the time required for full mobilization (B–H) can be measured in days or even weeks. The ratio of the defender's actual mobilization (G) to the readiness gap F (or the attacker's degree of preparation for war) is a good conceptual indicator of the intensity and effectiveness of the ensuing surprise attack.

Two possible exceptions to this otherwise typical sequence of events should be mentioned. In the first situation, the defender, having acquired definitive, fully credible information concerning an imminent attack, may therefore decide to launch a preemptive attack even before his own forces have been fully mobilized. He may thus seize the opportunity to begin the war on his terms by immediately using the most flexible and readily available forces at his disposal (e.g., the most suitable would normally be the air force) to attack although his own actual preparations are less than 50 per cent completed. This, for example, would have been the case in the Yom Kippur War of 1973, when the Israelis acquired incontrovertible information warning of an impending Egyptian-Syrian attack. Immediately placed on alert, the Israeli Air Force was instructed to make preparations for a preemptive strike on Arab troop concentrations. The attack was cancelled at the last moment, however, because of political considerations. Under such circumstances, the defender calculates that making the first move will allow him to cancel out, if not surpass, the attacker's advantage.

The second exception occurs in prolonged crisis situations when one side is the first to mobilize fully but then decides to delay his attack. The opponent may then catch up and perhaps reach the point where he can launch his attack first. This type of scenario occurred before the outbreak of the First World War, and again when Egypt mobilized first in May 1967 but allowed the Israelis eventually to exceed Egypt's own preparations and launch a preemptive surprise attack of their own.[15]

3. INTENTIONS AND CAPABILITIES

All information gathered by intelligence concerns either the adversary's *intentions* or his *capabilities*.[16] Although this sounds simple enough, the actual sorting, evaluation, and corroboration of the information is an extremely intricate and time-consuming process which involves many interrelated steps. An error of judgment in one phase may set off a chain reaction of other mistakes, causing potentially serious analytical distortions.

Perhaps the most fundamental problem concerns the difference in the collection and analysis of the two types of information. Needless to say, it is far simpler to obtain information about capabilities than about intentions. *Capabilities* can be material or non-material. Material capabilities, that is, weapons, their performance specifications, and quantities are not easy to conceal. Non-material capabilities such as the quality of organization, morale, and military doctrine are more difficult to evaluate in a precise way, although considerable knowledge about them can be obtained. A pitfall to be avoided at all costs is concentrating on the measurable and quantifiable while neglecting the less precise, non-material ones.

Political and military *intentions,* on the other hand, are much simpler to conceal; only a handful of leaders, and at times a single leader (e.g., Hitler,

FIGURE 3

THE COMPLEXITY OF THE ESTIMATIVE PROCESS

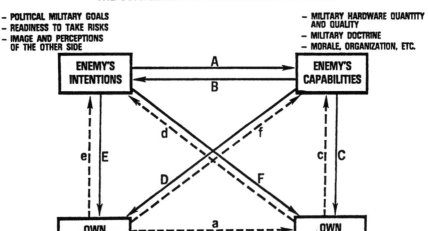

Stalin, Sadat), will shape the strategy of a state. Intentions can be changed at the last minute, and defy evaluation in the absence of direct access to the adversary's political-military elite. Yet even the most secretive leaders can provide intelligence analysts with clues to their intentions in their earlier memoirs, speeches, briefings in closed or open circles, and the like. In addition, a better understanding of the adversary's intentions can be developed through the careful corroboration of all evidence with his capabilities (see Figure 3). In the long run, if a leader harbors offensive intentions, he will have to invest in and expand his nation's capabilities (arrow A). This would range from heavy investments in military hardware to a preference for long range offensive weapons over short-range defensive weapons. Limited capabilities may, however, force leaders to choose a defensive strategy in the short run. For example, Hitler needed to build up Germany's military strength before actively pursuing a policy of breaking away from the Versailles Treaty, reoccupying the Rhineland, or annexing Austria or the Sudetenland. In the absence of such strength, Hitler had to conceal his intentions behind the rhetoric of his peace offensives.[17] The process is further complicated by the fact that the adversary may claim that he merely needs to have capabilities comparable to one's own (arrow C). Thus, Hitler demanded equality with, or disarmament for, everyone else, even as he was announcing German plans for conscription and rearmament. At other times, the adversary may augment his capabilities in response to his perception of the hostile intentions of other nations (arrow D). Such actions and reactions are intrinsic to every arms race. Furthermore, an adversary may assert that he is gearing his intentions to one's own (arrow E). And actual or perceived changes in one's own capabilities as evaluated by the adversary may trigger a change in his intentions out of fear and suspicion (arrow F). This can heighten antagonism and, in extreme cases, ignite a preemptive war. The description of the evaluation process thus far indicates that one must not only have a thorough grasp of the opponent's intentions and capabilities as such, but also an understanding of how he reacts to and perceives the observer's own intentions and capabilities. A similar mirror image process occurs on the observer's side (arrows a,b,c,d,e,f,). To complicate matters, there is no direct correlation between capabilities and intentions; that is, a country with weaker capabilities may nevertheless decide to go to war. There may be a gap or time lag between the two (e.g., a leader might have aggressive intentions without adequate capabilities, or vice-versa). Finally, the evaluation process as outlined above requires exacting coordination and a lengthy period of time for the analysis.

Although capabilities and intentions should undoubtedly be subject to equally careful collection and analytical efforts, it seems more prudent to emphasize the study of intentions for the following reasons.

(A) An adversary can still decide to attack even though his capabilities are relatively weak (1) if he miscalculates the strength of the intended victim (as did the Germans in their attack on the Soviet Union in 1941, or the Arabs in their underestimation of Israeli capabilities in 1967); (2) if he is more interested in applying political pressure or making political gains even at the cost of a military defeat; (3) if he gambles that his surprise attack will have a force multiplier effect sufficient to compensate for his inferior capabilities.

(B) War and surprise attack are determined not by the existence of capabilities *per se,* but by the political intention to use them. The mere possession of superior, equal, or inferior strength is therefore less important. A corollary of this is that, while the adversary's intentions can be influenced at any point (i.e., he can be deterred from taking action), it is impossible to have comparable impact on capabilities immediately before the outbreak of war.[18] Since it is, of course, much easier to obtain information on capabilities than intentions, the temptation to concentrate on that which is simpler to identify or measure must be consciously resisted.

4. THE TRICKY BUSINESS OF ESTIMATING RISKS

> Boldness in war ... has its own prerogatives. It must be granted a certain power over and above successful calculations involving space, time, and magnitude of forces, for wherever it is superior, it will take advantage of its opponent's weakness. In other words, it is a genuinely creative force.[19]

Procedural, analytical, and methodological difficulties constitute only a small fraction of the problems involved in the intelligence estimation process. Other, no less complex problems must also be discussed briefly. The first of these concerns the element of risk assessment in the planning of military operations.[20] The contradictory nature of risks in military operations adds another dimension of uncertainty to all intelligence estimates. Assuming rational behavior on the part of his opponent, the intelligence analyst can supposedly predict that a very risky operation, which may entail very high costs and uncertain benefits, will not be implemented. Conversely, he might assume that an operation involving low risks and high benefits will be selected. Although correct in theory, this premise is unreliable in practice. In the first place, that which is considered a high risk in one culture may be acceptable in another. The danger, therefore, is that the analyst's cultural values will be projected upon the adversary. In the summer of 1962, after US intelligence had received numerous reports that the Soviet Union was installing offensive missiles in Cuba, the National Security Council requested a National Intelligence Estimate (NIE) on the subject. 'In early fall 1962, the NIE was completed. The estimate stated that it was highly unlikely that the Soviet Union would pursue a policy of such high risk as the placement of offensive missiles in Cuba. The estimate was made on the assumption that such a course of action would be irrational (at least from the American intelligence community's frame of reference).' Second, what sometimes appears to be great risk for an adversary may actually be less hazardous as a result of developments unknown to the intelligence analyst.[21] Before the Yom Kippur War, Israeli intelligence overestimated the risks the Egyptians would face from the superior Israeli air force. (So, by the way, did the Egyptian planners. They anticipated some 10,000 casualties in the initial crossing of the Suez Canal. Actually, they suffered about 200 casualties. Overestimating the risks caused them to adopt, perhaps wisely, a very cautious strategic plan.) Certainly no rational Israeli planner would go to war against an enemy who maintained control of the skies. The Israelis were unaware that the Egyptians had reduced much of this threat from the air by building an extremely powerful anti-aircraft defense system consisting of anti-aircraft guns and surface-to-air missiles.[22] The intelligence analyst may also underrate the readiness of the enemy to take risks by assuming that his adversary knows as much as he does about his own strength. In 1941, the Russians may have felt confident that the Germans would not attack because of the extent of Russian strength. But they did not know that German intelligence had, in light of the Red Army's performance in Finland, grossly underestimated Russian strength by as much as 100 divisions on the eve of Barbarossa.[23] In this manner, excessive secrecy can undermine deterrence and lead to negatively reinforcing fallacious estimates. On such occasions, the attacker-to-be underestimates his victim's strength, while the victim, sure of his own position, is more likely to be taken by surprise.

The assessment of a specific risk is further complicated by the estimated impact of the strategic surprise itself. Although the Germans in 1941, the Japanese in 1941, and the Israelis in 1967 knew that their respective adversaries possessed greater capabilities, they calculated that a successful strategic surprise would be the force multiplier needed to redress this imbalance. This expectation thus lowered the anticipated risks for the attacker. In contrast, the defender frequently underestimates the impact that a surprise attack could have, and is, instead, confident that his retalia-tory strength and capacity to respond would not be diminished by such an occurrence (e.g., the USSR in 1941, Israel in 1973).

In many instances, the stronger defender, who is interested in perpetuat-ing a status quo that works in his favor, does not fully comprehend the potential attacker's desperate frame of mind. On the eve of Pearl Harbor, the United States was unaware of the degree to which Japanese military and political leaders felt cornered. These leaders were cognizant of the United States' superior war potential and knew that unless the United States was ready to accept Japanese terms after the initial campaign, Japan could not win in the long run. Nevertheless, the Japanese felt they had no choice but to attack. For similar reasons, in 1967 President Nasser of Egypt did not realize how desperate the Israelis felt, while in 1973, the Israelis failed to under-stand how the lack of progress on the diplomatic front since 1967 caused mounting frustration in the Arab world, culminating in the decision to resort to war regardless of the *military* consequences.

Estimating risks requires an intimate grasp of the adversary's culture and capabilities, his political and psychological frame of mind, and above all, what he knows and feels about the defender. Such detailed knowledge of one's opponent is rarely available, and even if obtained, it is easily distorted by many perceptual biases.

Finally, the paradoxical nature of the calculus of risk should be consi-dered. Superficially, it is rational to assume that very high risk strategies, whose apparent chances of success are low, are normally unacceptable whereas lower risks would be readily taken. In reality, such assumptions may be less than rational: an attacker can calculate that because attacking at a certain place or time would involve high costs, his adversary would rationally conclude that the probability of his choosing this strategy is extremely low. Paradoxically then, opting for a high-risk strategy might be less foolhardy than is first assumed. This was intuitively understood by many of the great captains of war and is associated with some of the most decisive strategic and tactical victories throughout history. The invading Allies' choice of Normandy as their landing beach despite its lack of harbors and greater distance from their starting point than other possible landing sites (Pas de Calais); MacArthur's 5000-to-1 gamble at Inchon; and Israel's attack on Egypt in 1967 and rescue operation in Entebbe in 1976 are but a few examples of maxi–max strategies that actually reduced the risks involved.

There is no *rational connection* between the degree of risk on the one hand and the choice of strategy on the other. The temptation to choose a high risk–high gain strategy is always present. Perhaps the only logical observa-tion that can be made regarding this strategy, on the basis of historical evidence, is that, while it can prevail in the short run, it is bound to fail in the long run. Napoleon and Hitler are the best known practitioners of this approach.

In war ... 'The idea that something "cannot be done" is one of the main aids to surprise .... Experts tend to forget that most military problems are soluble provided one is willing to pay the price.'[24] But once someone is prepared to pay a high price, it may be added, his price is actually reduced. This leads to the following paradox: '*The greater the risk, the less likely it seems to be, and the less risky it actually becomes. Thus, the greater the risk, the smaller it becomes.*'[25]

5. WHY MOBILIZATION CAN BE SELF-DEFEATING

The uncertain, politically sensitive nature of intelligence work is accentuated (perhaps more than in any other type of politico-military decision) by deliberations concerning whether or not to declare an alert or mobilization. This is the most critical policy recommendation an intelligence organization will ever have to make. If correct and timely, it may save many lives and significantly increase the chances of a vulnerable state's survival; if ill-timed, it can set off an uncontrollable chain of events, and possibly lead to war through miscalculation. In the long term, such a grave mistake can also have harmful repercussions upon the ability to make correct decisions in the future.

Every mobilization involves heavy political, material and psychological costs in addition to greatly increasing the danger of war. A status-quo-oriented country (such as the US and NATO, Israel in 1967 and 1973), which does not intend to go to war by its own initiative, will therefore try to avoid mobilizing except in the most extreme circumstances; at times, such a nation can bring even more harm upon itself by taking precautionary mobilization measures which eventually do not end in war. A single alert, let alone a series of alerts or a prolonged period of high alert which is not followed by war will have a decisively *negative* impact on future decisions. A series of false alarms will undermine the credibility of the intelligence organization (the so-called cry wolf syndrome); and by the time subsequent decisions on similar matters have to be made, prolonged periods of mobilization and the routinization of alerts will have brought about 'alert fatigue'[26] (i.e., condition the high command and troops to a state of alert and therefore progressively erode their readiness for action). A continual or 'permanent' state of alert can therefore be self-defeating.

The predicament of intelligence organizations is that many alarms which are deemed false in retrospect may have actually been justified. Although the cause for alarm is usually known, the defender's intelligence may find it much more difficult to produce a *timely* explanation (before the next crisis occurs) as to why the predicted attack failed to materialize. Three basic reasons for this can be set forth.

One. The enemy did not plan to attack in the first place. This is the outcome of an intelligence failure stemming from faulty information, an incorrect analysis, and/or a low threshold for mobilization (see ensuing discussion on worst case analysis). In view of the normal reluctance to declare alerts or to mobilize, this type of faulty estimate is actually not very common. Of much greater interest and complexity are the remaining two explanations.

Two. The enemy had decided to attack, but canceled or delayed the D-Day at the last minute for reasons such as bad weather, unsuitable political conditions, dissatisfaction with the plan of attack or the military doctrine, or a high level of alert on the defender's side. The best known example of this sequence of a planned attack, followed by a countermobilization and then the deferring of the attack, is Hitler's series of decisions to launch an offensive in the west: attacks were planned and then cancelled in November 1939 and January 1940, while the attack was finally carried out in May 1940. Before each of the planned offensives, a number of timely and, in retrospect, reliable warnings were received by British and French intelligence. Yet the Allies lost their confidence in some reliable sources of information (such as Colonel Oster of the Abwehr) because the predicted attacks did not take place. By 10 May, the day the Germans at last launched their offensive in the west, the Allies were completely surprised despite the multitude of warnings they had received but brushed aside.[27]

A failure in prediction does not necessarily mean that something is amiss with an intelligence service or the information it has gathered. On the contrary, a *correct* prediction can be based on faulty information or a flawed analysis. For example, on 25 September 1962, the US intelligence community agreed 'on balance' that the Soviet Union would *not* install missiles in Cuba which were capable of reaching the United States. 'The reason the intelligence community gave for its "on balance" conclusion that the Soviets would not place "offensive" missiles in Cuba was that according to its analytical framework, the Soviets were not prepared for this kind of confrontation .... In the event the Soviets got their confrontation and found a way to withdraw the missiles .... The intelligence community was wrong but for the right reasons: Khrushchev had miscalculated.' Referring to this, an American former senior intelligence officer said, '... While it is most blessed to be right, it is more blessed in our business to be wrong for the right reasons that it is to be right for the wrong reasons.'[28] In other words, a very small number of even significant intelligence failures may not constitute proof that something is intrinsically wrong with an intelligence organization; only a higher incidence of repeated failures indicates that reform or reorganization might be required.

The rush to investigate the performance of intelligence organizations after each 'failure' may not only be unjustified, but also counterproductive. The absence of a direct correlation between the quality of intelligence and its actual results may be further illustrated by the fact that the more nearly 'perfect' the operation of an intelligence system, the greater the reliability which decision makers attribute to the information received. Therefore, an 'imperfect' intelligence system is the safest, since decision makers are more wary of the data distributed to them.[29] The saying that 'there is no failure like success' comes to mind. The continual success of an intelligence organization reduces the incentive for improvement, and thus aids in the concealment of less salient weaknesses. Failure or defeat, on the other hand, are catalysts for improvement. The unquestioned reputation of British intelligence during the First World War diminished British competitiveness between the two world wars, causing a decline which went unnoticed for some time. Accordingly, it can be suggested that *the greater the credibility of an intelligence agency over time, the less its conclusions are questioned, and the more serious the risk in the long run of overrelying on its findings.*[30]

Three. Even more difficult to cope with is a situation in which the enemy prepares for an attack, and the defender reacts by mobilizing upon receiving a timely warning. The would-be attacker may then be deterred after realizing that he can no longer reap the benefits of surprise. The prospective attacker might also fear that his secrets have been betrayed, giving the adversary precise knowledge of his plans. But even after such events have occurred, the defender's intelligence can be hard pressed to determine whether the predicted attack was deterred by his counter-mobilization (which would justify similar measures in the future), or whether there was no attack planned in the first place. This, for instance, was the dilemma faced by Israeli intelligence in the wake of a mobilization in May 1973 that was not followed by an attack. This is summarized by the paradox of the self-negating prophecy: *Information on a forthcoming enemy attack triggers a counter-mobilization, which, in turn, prompts the enemy to delay or cancel his plans. It is therefore extremely difficult – even in retrospect – to know whether or not the counter-mobilization was warranted.*[31]

*   *   *

The methodological problems discussed thus far have no perfect solutions. The intelligence expert is constantly searching for a better way to overcome the difficulties he faces. Other than acquiring more and better information in real time, this search involves three basic strategies. The first is to 'purge' the intelligence process (as much as possible) of human biases and perceptions, the second is a more costly approach in which the analyst takes all threats seriously and implements the necessary precautionary measures; and the third strategy, to be discussed later, calls for certain organizational reforms designed to improve the objectivity of the intelligence decision-making process by either reducing negative political influences or increasing the variety of participants and input involved in the process.

INDICATORS AND WARNINGS

The most familiar methodological device neutralizing the effect of the human element on the analytical intelligence process is the development of a detailed list of Indicators and Warnings (I & W). In theory, this is a simple and elegant solution. 'Essentially, the purpose of the method [is] to help the warning analyst pick and choose the significant from the massive amounts of ambiguous and possibly conflicting data that would be abundantly available in crisis situations. To do this, the analyst need only ask three simple questions: is it *necessary* (i.e., mandatory rather than optional to *prepare* for an attack); is it *unambiguous* (i.e., a move one takes only to prepare for war rather than for other purposes as well); and can we *monitor* it (i.e., can we observe the indicator we seek).'[32] Warning indicators might include, for example, the cancellation of all leaves; large-scale simultaneous maneuvers by several bordering countries; the intensification of, or unusual reduction in, wireless communication; the departure of foreign military advisors; distribution of live ammunition among units; mobilization of reserve units; the opening of civilian and other shelters; the clearing of minefields and certain roads; and emptying large refineries of highly flammable materials.

Naturally, even a detailed set of warning indicators does not always speak for itself. If the changes occur slowly over a long period of time (acclimatization),[33] they may be overlooked. Experience has shown that political leaders and analysts, if their concepts exclude the possibility of an imminent war, will go out of their way to dismiss as harmless all of the warning signals (e.g., the adversary is mobilizing defensively because he fears an attack; or he is preparing for extensive maneuvers; there are *other*, contradictory signals; it's a game of nerves and bluffs intended to shore up his bargaining position). 'Even the best I & W scheme can only tell you whether and to what extent a government is prepared or preparing to act. It cannot tell you why or what its intentions are ....'[34] Moreover, if the adversary knows which indicators a given observer considers to be warning signals, he can deliberately manipulate such indicators in order to deceive the observer.[35] Of all methodological devices intended to aid in the avoidance of strategic surprise, paying close attention to indicators and warnings appears to be the most promising.

In addition to simpler types of warning indicators, a number of other kinds of developments merit close observation. These include situations in which the adversary and/or the observer are frozen in a hopeless and unacceptable political deadlock which may encourage the resort to war (Japan in 1941; the Arabs in 1973; Argentina over the Falkland Islands in 1982). The conclusion of a military treaty between former enemies (e.g., the Ribbentrop–Molotov agreement in 1939; Egypt and Jordan in May 1967), as well as the appearance of new leaders, unusual domestic pressures, and unexplicable anomalies in a adversary's pattern of behavior are also developments that should not escape scrutiny.

WORST-CASE ANALYSIS

A less elegant and more costly strategy essentially involves lowering the threshold for taking precautionary measures in response to emerging threats. This method may prove to be more attractive to the intelligence community. As a result of continuously monitoring the actual and potential threats posed by the enemy, and because of their professional socialization, intelligence (in particular senior) analysts are a cautious and pessimistic lot. The degree of pessimism and extreme caution is exacerbated by a major intelligence failure such as the inability to anticipate a strategic surprise. This is likely to result in the adoption of a 'worst case' approach, which can be described as the attitude that it is most prudent to base one's assumptions and analysis on the worst that the other nation could do; to assume, when presented with ambiguous evidence, that a threat will be carried out, even if the weight of indicators to the contrary appears to be greater.[36] According to Ken Booth,

> the worst case is more easily definable than the probable case, and so provides a firmer basis for a policy prescription. Worst case forecasting also frees individual analysts from blame if things go wrong. This is another reason why the tendency is always to think the worst. To base a policy on a less than worst-case forecast will turn out costly if the prediction is wrong. To underplay what turns out to be a real threat may bring defeat: but to overestimate, and perhaps provoke, a potential threat into an actual one, might only increase tension. In the past, when war was a less serious business, it nearly always made sense to defer to the alarmist. In the context of a nuclear confrontation, the balance of the argument should logically change. Risks should be taken for peace rather than war .... [37]

The psychology behind the worst-case analysis is obvious, as is the play-it-safe, bureaucratic attitude, and at times the political desire for increased defense budgets or fear of failure. But the worst-case approach in its crude form may exact a heavy price.

(1) It can be extremely expensive in terms of the cost of frequent mobiliza ion and higher military expenditure.
(2) It may bring antagonistic feelings to the boiling point, and prove to be a major destabilizing factor when both opponents adopt a worst-case approach. Under such conditions, one party might mobilize prematurely, which could prompt an identical move by the other, and then result in preemption and a war that no one wanted. (Reciprocal fear of surprise attack played an important role in the loss of control over mobilization and counter-mobilization before the First World War; the almost simultaneous German and British invasions of Norway; and the 1967 Six Day War.)[38]
(3) In the event that this approach does not contribute to the loss of control or escalation, it may touch off many mobilizations and alerts that do not culminate in conflict, thus encouraging susceptibility to the 'cry wolf' syndrome and ultimately defeating its own purpose.
(4) Frequent and facile resort to worst-case analysis can become an easy escape from analytical responsibility and reduce the quality of threat analysis.

Yet in spite of the social, material, and political costs of mobilization, it is advisable for more vulnerable states – those which are considerably weaker than their adversaries, lack strategic depth, or maintain only small armies – to lower somewhat their threshold for mobilization. The danger and costs entailed could be minimized by introducing a flexible, modular, multi-stage alert and mobilization system. If alerts and mobilizations occur repeatedly, care must be taken not to relax one's vigil. When survival is at stake, fewer risks should be taken. The high cost of false alarms is still lower than that of being caught unprepared.

*   *   *

PRECONCEPTIONS, ETHNOCENTRISM, AND MISPERCEPTION

> I'll believe it when I see it.
> I'll see it when I believe it.[39]

Given the urgent nature of much of intelligence work as well as the general process by which human learning takes place, all analysis must inevitably be based on preexisting concepts concerning, for example, the adversary's intentions or his capabilities and military doctrines. The concepts, belief systems, theories and images comprising the framework for the assimilation of new information can be old or new, detailed or sketchy, rigid or flexible, static or dynamic.[40] If a long-held concept has served well as a basis for interpretation and prediction and is rooted to the fundamental belief systems of a country, it is likely to be less open to adaptation stemming from new evidence. Therefore, the more successful a concept has proven to be as a tool for explanation and prediction, the less its fundamental premises will be questioned. But since few areas of human or political activity remain unchanged in antagonistic situations, its very success is eventually bound to be self-negating. If, however, a concept is not founded on any deep-rooted beliefs, and if it has had limited success as a basis for explanation and prediction, then it will be easier to change.

Each of these ideal types has its strong and weak points. A rigid concept provides continuity and a solid foundation from which to take action. The danger is that its adherents tend to ignore contradictory evidence; furthermore, the concept may become obsolete, thus endangering policies and stategies which are detached from reality. Commonly-held concepts that have resulted in the failure to avoid strategic surprise range from the belief in one's own power as an effective deterrent posture, and the idea that a war will be preceded, as in the past, by a crisis or ultimatum, to the conviction that without air or sea superiority certain actions are highly unlikely. Other concepts have held that Nazis and Communists would never have enough common interests to reach an agreement (believed by the British and French before the Ribbentrop–Molotov agreement); that no Arab leader would publicly negotiate an agreement, not to mention a peace treaty, with the Israelis (a concept accepted by all intelligence services);[41] and that the Soviet bloc was a monolithic state-system controlled from Moscow (a western belief during the 1950s and early 1960s).

In contrast, open-ended ideas do not provide enough basis for action or longer planning, as continuous change can bring about confusion and paralysis. For this reason, the majority of erroneous concepts tend to emanate more from the rigid than from the flexible end of the scale.[42]

Generally speaking, perceptual errors are the result of either projecting one's own culture, ideological beliefs, military doctrine, and expectations on the adversary (i.e., seeing him as a mirror image of oneself) or of wishful thinking, that is, molding the facts to conform to one's hopes.

Psychological, cultural, and anthropological studies of perceptual errors have arrived at similar conclusions: human perceptions are ethnocentric. They see the external world inside out, which typically involves the projection of one's own belief systems, and by definition causes the underestimation, if not denigration, of the opponent's culture; motivations; intentions; material and technological achievements; and capacity to identify with others. According to Kenneth Booth, ethnocentric biases are, to a certain extent, unavoidable because they also serve a positive function as a defense mechanism in conflictual situations; if a group were to understand its adversary's motives and problems as well as its own, it might become demoralized.[43] Arising between different racial, religious, linguistic, economic and political groups, ethnocentric biases furnish powerful explanations for most strategic surprises. The Americans by and large believed that the Japanese (and the Vietnamese) were technologically inferior and lacking in determination in comparison to themselves; the Germans believed that the Russians or Slavs were racially inferior and from this extrapolated that they were also organizationally, technologically and motivationally inferior. In 1947–1948 and 1967, the Arabs viewed Israel as weak and demoralized only to discover the opposite; while, by 1973, the Israelis had begun to believe in their own superiority as a result of past victories. In each of these cases, subjective oversimplifications of reality led to the underestimation of the adversary's will to resist, which in turn was responsible either for a hasty decision to open or to become involved in a war, or for a war that could have been avoided had the costs and consequences been more realistically calculated.

Correction of ethnocentric biases is the obvious answer to this problem, but the various measures that can be taken to this end are complex and should not be regarded as pat solutions.[44] The most general suggestion is 'know thine enemy'. This stresses the need to intensify one's knowledge of the adversary's language, culture, political culture, ideology, and so on. Of course, this is always easier said than done, since even in the largest, most ethnically diverse society there are few who are intimately familiar (in the Weberian sense of *'Verstehen')*with other cultures; moreover, such experts are not necessarily available for intelligence work. As it is self-evident, this point need not be elaborated upon here.

More original is the suggestion calling for intelligence organizations to spend more time studying their *own* culture and society in depth in order better to comprehend (a) how the adversary reacts to or perceives the observer; and (b) how one's own environment can bias the perception of another society. The need to know 'thyself', according to this approach, is as essential as knowing the enemy. In view of this country's experiences, it is not surprising that this proposal should come from an Israeli former senior intelligence analyst, Zvi Lanir.[45] After the Yom Kippur surprise attack in

1973, many Israeli intelligence analysts concluded that one of the principal causes of their misperception was the unconscious projection of Israeli society and its contentment with the status quo on their Arab neighbors.[46] This was largely based on an inflated sense of self-confidence coupled with a lack of self-criticism, all of which culminated in delusions of grandeur and wishful thinking. According to Lanir, 'the subject matter of the basic national intelligence research – as a necessary condition for its success – will include not only the study of the adversary, but also the study of oneself as related to the adversary. The recommendation is *not* to study primarily the daily tactical moves – but for a deeper understanding of [one's own country's] trends in policy and principles shaping the policy.[47]

Although original and interesting, this proposal is, however, highly impractical for the following reasons. (a) Intelligence organizations often lack the resources necessary properly to analyze the adversary's intentions and capabilities, let alone to study their own society. (b) Whether intentional or not, the examination of one's own society and its politics will inevitably involve subjective political views and values, and thus contribute to the politicization of the intelligence community. Such studies are likely to alienate leaders (unless the observations made are very flattering) and therefore will become totally unacceptable from a political point of view. (c) It is unclear why it can be assumed that the perceptual distortions which lead to the misperception of other societies will suddenly disappear during the examination of one's own society. There is no reason to suppose that greater objectivity can be attained by those who study their own country.

Perceptual analytical distortions can be formed by either individuals or organizations. The perceptual errors of an individual can at times be critical, but the mistake of a low-ranking individual is more likely to be counterbalanced and corrected by others working on the same problem at various levels within the hierarchy. On the other hand, an individual at the top of the political or military hierarchy is not subject to such corrective procedures, which means that his errors in judgment are much less likely to be rectified. Therefore, individual decisions taken in the lower echelons can be examined most profitably in a bureaucratic, organizational context, while top-echelon decisions can be understood best in a psychological setting.

B. The Politics of Intelligence

In his seminal work, *The Soldier and the State,*[48] Professor Samuel P. Huntington develops two ideal types of interaction between the civilian government on the one hand, and the military professionals on the other. He refers to the first type of interaction, which is more normative and idealized, as 'objective control'. 'The essence of objective civilian control is the recognition of autonomous military professionalism.'[49] In this relationship the military stands ready to carry out the wishes of any civilian group, while the civilians allow the military to perform its duties or advise the government according to its best professional judgment. Here, a sharp distinction is made between the professional world of the military and the civilian world of politics. The two groups therefore are able to interact to their mutual benefit, and the military recognizes its duty to obey the government, yet each group preserves its functional independence, thereby permitting achievement of the highest possible level of national security. The pattern of objective civilian control is, however, virtually nonexistent in the real world of politics and competition.

The actual relationship between the military and the civilian government is more accurately described by Huntington's model of 'subjective control', which involves the maximization of civilian power in relation to the military; reduces the professional autonomy of the military; leads to civilian interference in professional military affairs; and politicizes the armed forces by employing the services of the military for narrow partisan interests. In the long run, a pattern of subjective control may reduce the likelihood of having the best possible national security.

We can consider the intelligence community either as part of the military establishment or as a discrete professional group whose relationship to the civilian could be considered close to one of Huntington's ideal types.

The relationship between the intelligence community and the civilian authority also requires a continuous search for a careful balance between the professional independence of the former and the authority of the latter. For the civilians in authority, the temptation to exploit the intelligence community's control over information for the furtherance of political interests may be even greater than any desire to control the military.[50]

Violation of the intelligence community's professional autonomy occurs not only for the sake of gaining access to critical information possessed by the intelligence community, but because it is an important stepping stone in facilitating subjective control of the military in general. Furthermore, the position of the intelligence community is rendered even more sensitive to outside interference by the desire of the *military* professionals to influence and control it in order to promote their special interests *vis-à-vis* those of the civilian authorities. The professional autonomy of the intelligence may thus be compromised, and is constantly challenged, from these two directions.

INTELLIGENCE–LEADERSHIP RELATIONS

> Intelligence is the voice of conscience to a staff. Wishful thinking is the original sin of men of power.[51]

> The unresolvable tension between policy-making and intelligence rests in part on an unresolvable definitional problem. For no one agrees on what is policy and what is intelligence.[52]

The correct and timely analysis of the information acquired by intelligence organizations is only a necessary, but not sufficient, condition to guarantee the success of the intelligence community. One of the most critical phases in the entire cycle of intelligence work lies in convincing the military and political leadership to make the best use of the information and analysis supplied to them.

Much depends on whether leaders are open-minded and encourage criticism and accurate, though unpleasant, information. Leaders in a democratic
system are generally more inclined to consider a wider variety of opinions
than those who have always functioned within authoritarian or totalitarian
political systems. In authoritarian countries, where the climb to the top is an
unrelenting struggle for power, habits of cooperation and openness are
usually less developed. The prevalence of a rigid influential doctrine, religious dogma, or ideology naturally restricts openness to variety, criticism,
and the consideration of contradictory ideas. Leaders in totalitarian countries ordinarily have little tolerance for ideas that deviate from the 'party
line', since they are seen as personal criticism – a dangerous element undermining the existing ideology. Among other reasons, this explains why the
intelligence systems of the democracies, on the whole, performed better
than those of the totalitarian nations during the Second World War.[53]

What has been said up to this point does not imply that relatively open-
minded people who are capable of cooperation cannot rise to the top in
totalitarian systems or that authoritarian-style, narrow-minded leaders cannot emerge in democracies. Ultimately, the idiosyncrasies and personality
of each leader play a decisive role. From the vantage point of intelligence
organizations and their capacity to cooperate with a leader, two ideal types
of leaders can be considered.

Leaders such as Hitler or Stalin could not tolerate information which
contradicted their own beliefs or policies. When such structures are
imposed, however, strategic intelligence is of very limited use. Hitler once
told Ribbentrop that 'when he had to make great decisions, he considered
himself the instrument of the providence which the Almighty had determined. He ... [added] that before big decisions, he always had a feeling of
absolute certainty.'[54] Having no habits of cooperation and orderly staff
work, to put it mildly, Hitler insisted on imposing his ideas on others. Early
success in the face of the opposition of senior military commanders and
foreign policy experts had convinced him that his intuition was infallible. A
look at the leaders and military assistants closest to Hitler – men such as Jodl
and Keitel in the OKW, and Ribbentrop, Göring, and Goebbels – reveals
that almost all of those with whom he had any contact were sycophants.
Ribbentrop and Göring (as well as others in Hitler's coterie) carefully
ensured that he received only the reports that confirmed his beliefs and
images. At no point, even after the most serious defeats, did Hitler encourage another type of reporting. Good intelligence existed but was circums-
pectly filtered. 'In light of Hitler's preconceptions and distorted images, one
must question the usefulness of foreign reporting even if it had been one
hundred percent correct.'[55] Although Hitler and possibly Stalin are extreme
examples, the danger involved in distorting information to suit a leader's
policies exists in every type of government and between all leaders and their
lieutenants. In Donald McLachlan's words, 'wishful thinking [is] that ever-
lurking temptation for politicians dealing with military affairs – and for
serving officers involved in politics ....'[56]

Hitler made most of his important decisions without consulting anyone.

(This was also true of Egypt's President Sadat.)[57] The members of his entourage often were as surprised as the victims of his moves were, particularly during the period of diplomatic surprises in the 1930s which, unlike his subsequent military surprises, required no material preparations. Such decisions, generally made on the spur of the moment, are very difficult to anticipate. Intelligence agencies are oftentimes called upon to issue warnings *before* the adversary's leader has made up his own mind. The psychoanalytical study of leaders is beset by uncertainty and speculation. '... If our own predictions are based on a "rational" move it is because we know that irrationality can lead to deviant behavior in *any direction* and is inherently unpredictable and that irrational behavior is, in the end, the admission of failure equally for he who commits and he who predicts.'[58] This observation is an exaggeration: irrational or deviant behavior is not random, and in fact normally follows a regular pattern (e.g., Hitler, DeGaulle, Sadat and their frequent use of surprise or their indentification with the state and tendency to take high risks; Begin's legalistic mind; Chamberlain's 'rationality' and aversion to taking any risks). It can be difficult to make day-to-day predictions of an irrational leader's behavior, but in time a general pattern of behavior will gradually emerge, thereby helping the observer to gauge some of the leader's reactions and readiness to take risks, if not to make more precise forecasts.[59]

An 'atomistic' style of leadership reaches more severe proportions when accompanied by dogmatic adherence to an ideology (especially if the ideology is irrational). Hitler dismissed intelligence reports on American or Soviet behavior as an overestimation of Jewish, Bolshevik-Slav, or plutocratic groups that were racially or politically inferior and therefore could not be as motivated or efficient as German Aryans.[60] Similarly, Stalin's adherence to Communist ideology, which viewed the world in zero-sum-game terms, led him to believe that any British or western intelligence supplied to him could not be genuine (reports concerning, for instance, a German plan to attack in 1941); Stalin refused to believe that delays in opening the second front in Europe stemmed from *real* difficulties and not from anti-Soviet sentiments.[61]

Although encouraging a modicum of inter-organizational competition can be beneficial, Hitler's proclivity for pursuing a divide-and-rule policy was counterproductive in its politicization of German intelligence. An intelligence organization desiring recognition from the Führer had to furnish him with the information that he wanted to hear. The dynamics of this competition encouraged a rapid deterioration in the quality of German intelligence and fostered mistrust between the various agencies.

In contrast, the *relative* openness of Roosevelt, Churchill, or Truman to intelligence reports seems to have yielded better results. From his early days at the Admiralty in the First World War, to his daily use of Enigma intercepts during the Second World War, Churchill certainly paid careful attention to intelligence reports.[62] His work habits have been described in this somewhat idealized way:

We see Churchill following up daily on the performance of his subordinates. We see him emphasizing the importance of science and technology in the development of new weapons. We note his skills in using information acquired through the interception and decoding of German communications, and his success in keeping the knowledge of that decoding a secret. We note how effective was Churchill's insistence on transmitting instructions in writing, on keeping orderly track of every decision and on tracing the progress of decision to action. Such habits make for efficient administration . . . .[63]

Yet, unlike Hitler, '. . . he displayed constant interest in the latest information about the enemy . . . . He made it a matter of principle that he should be supplied with such intelligence "raw" – that is not in the doctored pieces of staff assessment but as it had come to hand. Thus he felt, often with good reason, that in his central position he was exceptionally equipped for keeping himself "in the know". All that was romantic in him, moreover, thrilled with excitement of intercepted signals, Delphic reports from the agents, the broken codes, the sense of participation. This knowledge is essential if one is to understand his decisions, and at the lower level his impatience with his commanders.'[64] His insatiable appetite for raw intelligence tempted Churchill too often to become his own intelligence officer – a dangerous practice which no head of state should take upon himself.[65]

On the negative side, Churchill did not hesitate to interfere in the direction of military operations against the better professional opinion of his military advisers.

In the words of Major Sir Desmond Morton, Churchill '. . .was a *politician* who wanted to be a soldier'.[66] And, while he interfered too much in military operations, he never committed Hitler's error of assuming direct command of an army in action. Although Churchill did not always feel comfortable among colleagues with superior intellects, unlike Hitler 'his chiefs of staff were professionals of exceptional calibre. None were puny or pusillanimous . . . Pound . . . Dill . . . Alanbrooke, Portal and Cunningham . . . They were a different team from Hitler's entourage – the subservient lackeys, Keitel, Halder, Jodl, Zeitzler and the transient subordinates, their opinions disregarded, uncertain of their tenure, their very lives dependent on a master's whim.'[67]

When critical issues were at stake, Churchill's military advisors did not hesitate to argue with him. In such cases, if they were persuasive and persistent enough, their opinions prevailed[68] (e.g., Dowding's insistence against Churchill's judgment that no more Hurricane fighters should be sent to France in a Cabinet meeting on 15 May 1940). 'Churchill's disqualifications as a warlord were manifold – disqualifications both intellectual and temperamental . . . he succeeded in spite of them. Hitler's defects of character were of fundamental significance: Churchill's peripheral.'[69]

In reality, Churchill's handling of intelligence was far more complicated than is commonly realized. As an intelligence consumer Churchill stands somewhere in between the cooperative and non-cooperative type of leader.

On the one hand, he appreciated the importance of intelligence work more than any other leader during the Second World War and made an immense contribution to its development; on the other, he did not hesitate to ignore it when it did not suit his strategy and too often tended to become his own intelligence officer. Though authoritarian in his attitudes toward his subordinates and advisers, he nevertheless assembled an outstanding group of professional advisers whose counsel he continuously sought during the war. Despite the many mistakes he committed which could have been avoided by more closely heeding his intelligence advisers, his overall record as an intelligence consumer was impressive. For him, more than for any other leader in modern times, strategic intelligence was the key to victory.

Beyond the problem of a leader's psychological profile, there are other, more general political behavioral patterns that can influence his attitude toward intelligence. For example, once a leader has invested substantial energy in promoting a particular policy direction – especially when his prestige is on the line or he has acted against the advice of his aides – he will be that much more reluctant to admit defeat even when presented with contradictory evidence. Under such circumstances, the most attractive course of action may be to ignore contradictory data and insist that subordinates supply him with the 'right' information.[70] The greatest danger is present at the stage in which the leader supplants serious deliberation with wishful thinking. Chamberlain and the advocates of appeasement policies long resisted the overwhelming evidence that their policies actually encouraged Hitler's aggressiveness and appetite. Leaders in democratic systems are particularly vulnerable to such wishful thinking before elections.

There is no perfect remedy for the problems discussed in this section. Whether operating within an authoritarian or democratic political system, the intelligence community normally can do very little to encourage the leader to develop a more cooperative and receptive attitude toward intelligence work. Two suggestions can be made in this context: one is that more time be devoted to the 'education' of leaders on this subject before they rise to power. Obviously, this would not be easy, and it is often too much to expect to change the working habits of leaders. The second suggestion is directed primarily at the intelligence community. It concerns making the operation of this organization more effective by gearing its presentation, arguments, and showmanship to the specific character of the leader.[71] Learning how to work with a leader may be a lengthy task that raises some ethical questions and cannot always achieve the desired results.

INTELLIGENCE ADVISERS AND LEADERS

So far we have discussed the critical impact of the individual leader on the intelligence process. Each leader, however, is always influenced by his close advisers, whose interaction with him is of decisive importance. The effectiveness of this relationship will therefore also be influenced by the character of the head (or heads) of the intelligence community. Is there a positive or negative chemistry between them? Do they complement or contradict each other in temperament, character or ambition? Can they cooperate with and respect each other? Do they share a common ideology and/or a common social or professional experience?

To answer those questions we must also know something about the intelligence adviser. Is he a man of absolute integrity to whom ambition is secondary to service? Does he put his objectivity and professional judgment above all else or is he primarily interested in maintaining the confidence or friendship of the leader as a means of gaining influence? Did he become a leader in the intelligence community because of his political connections and views, or because of his professional achievements and experience? Is he prepared to resign if his professional views are either ignored or consistently not accepted?

The number of possible combinations between the character of the leader and that of his intelligence adviser(s) is very large indeed. Some of the better-known examples include: President Kennedy and McCone; President Johnson and Rostow; Presidents Johnson and Nixon, and Helms; Churchill and Godfrey; Hitler and his advisers. Though Churchill probably found Godfrey stubborn and argumentative, his relationship with Menzies, head of the SIS, was excellent. Menzies, who assumed control of the SIS at a low point in its influence when its very survival was in question, made every effort to cultivate the best possible working relations with the Prime Minister; Churchill was provided with daily Ultra intercepts which always included some spicy titbits to be used as 'ammunition' in his arguments or conversations with other senior advisers. In this manner, Menzies was gradually able to inspire the Prime Minister's confidence in SIS and consolidate its position.[72]

Another perhaps less well-known twosome was that of Defense Minister Dayan and head of Israeli Military Intelligence, Eli Zeira. In this case, it has been argued that since both of them had been combat commanders and were 'heroic types' they suffered from similar perceptual defects; the fact that they reinforced each other's views may have been a major cause of the failure to take seriously the numerous warnings preceding the surprise attack of the Yom Kippur War.[73]

The above discussion leads to a number of observations.

First of all, a high degree of rapport between the leader of a state and his intelligence advisers is of the greatest importance – for without a good relationship, the effectiveness of the intelligence community will diminish considerably, regardless of how good the quality of its work is.

Second, having political finesse, tact, salesmanship and other related qualities is of critical importance for the leaders of the intelligence community. Unfortunately, however, the professional analyst, educated to prefer truth to tact and objectivity to political influence, may often lack the necessary qualities. It would therefore be difficult to find a head of intelligence who is both a first-rate intelligence expert and an intuitive politician. In fact, the qualities which a highly qualified intelligence expert must possess stand in contradistinction to those required to achieve political influence. Political qualifications, in the above-mentioned sense, are therefore a necessary if not a sufficient condition for an intelligence adviser. In addition to his political skills, he should preferably have the professional experience necessary to understand the problems and intricacies of the intelligence profession.

Third. Experience has shown that leaders tend to choose Directors of Intelligence who share their political views, if not other common traits of character (e.g. Carter–Sorenson, Carter–Turner, Reagan–Casey, Dayan–Zeira). The danger of this natural tendency is that the intelligence adviser is less likely to challenge the views of the leader or come up with a fresh, alternative way of viewing a situation. In the end, better cooperation is achieved at the expense of the quality of intelligence estimates.

Fourth. While there is no doubt that better intelligence estimates with a wider spectrum of views will be considered if the political leader and his intelligence adviser have different or even contradictory views, it is also clear that their relationship is bound to deteriorate sooner or later. The result is that the leader will tend to ignore the intelligence estimates presented by an adviser he does not or cannot cooperate with, and the product of the specific intelligence organization he represents will be lost. Usually, the intelligence adviser will notice that he is being ignored and is making increasingly smaller (if any) contributions to the decision-making process.

This tension between the capacity for cooperation between political leaders and their intelligence advisers on the one hand – and the need to present objective if objectional estimates on the other – has no simple solution in the real world of the politics of intelligence. The ideal, of course, would be to have a secure and open-minded leader seeking the advice of an intelligence expert with political finesse, who knows his leader's wishes and policies but who has enough courage and skill to give him the most realistic estimates possible. In the real world, the combination of a dogmatic, stubborn leader who prefers to indulge in wishful thinking and an 'intelligence waiter' prepared to serve up the most expedient intelligence palliative is probably more likely to occur.

Political and other biases can also be introduced into the professional intelligence community from below, as will be explained in the ensuing discussion of the organizational and bureaucratic elements underlying strategic surprise.

*   *   *

C. Organizational and Bureaucratic Explanations

Complex systems are simply not responsive to warnings of unimaginable or highly unlikely accidents. Because they are complex, organizational routines must be carefully followed and off-standard events reinterpreted in routine frameworks.[74]

Much of an intelligence organization's professional integrity depends upon the degree to which freedom of expression and criticism are encouraged, whether the system of military and civil administration is based on merit, whether corruption and favoritism are common, the quality of the educational system, and the history of military involvement in political matters. Of course, the control of information and the possibility of manipulating it ('massaging information') to promote the intelligence community's political influence or beliefs is an ever present danger which gives rise to some serious ethical questions. (Were British intelligence analysts during the late 1930s justified in privately supplying Churchill with information he could use against the Government's appeasement policies? Was Colonel Oster of the German Abwehr morally correct when he notified Allied intelligence of Hitler's plans to attack Norway and the west? Should the CIA have leaked to the public some of the conclusions reached during the Vietnam War regarding its futility?) Despite the powerful temptation, intelligence analysts ought to resist direct involvement in policymaking when, for example, after a briefing, they are asked by senior politicians, 'OK, that's your analysis. What would you do about it?' The temptation can be overpowering for the intelligence officer, but his reply should be 'Sorry, sir, that's your business,' even though he might have a pretty clear idea of what to do.[75] This is the point at which many a good intelligence officer has committed himself actively to one policy or another, with the result that his objectivity and judgment were severely impaired.

The purely 'rational' or 'professional' behavior of any organization is modified by many factors such as parochial views, organizational interests and survival, the need for cohesion, and *esprit de corps*.[76] The neutral intelligence process, unencumbered by such complications, is a theoretical ideal which cannot be found in practice.

MILITARY PATTERNS OF THOUGHT AND INTELLIGENCE ANALYSIS

Most intelligence organizations are either part of a larger military organization or include many members with military backgrounds. This unavoidably imbues intelligence organizations with a perspective that emphasizes such elements as military motives, capabilities, hierarchy, discipline and worst-case analysis. These traits are not always the most suitable for intelligence work, which deals as much with political as with military affairs, and in which 'freedom' of research and expression may be more important than rank and position.

The primacy of politics in strategic affairs can, as a result of the military perspective, be ignored in a more subtle way. Clausewitz's dictum that war must serve a political purpose is by now a cliché. Yet the extent of this logic merits further thought. Rational western political and military leaders naturally assumed that war could be a political instrument *only* if, as Clausewitz said, we can compel our adversary to do our will, that is, defeat him on the battlefield. In western tradition, it is usually (and often correctly) assumed that if it were impossible to win a war, starting one would be counterproductive and irrational. For the Chinese, the Vietnamese and the Arabs, for example, the Clausewitzian primacy of politics has been taken one step farther; in other words, it makes sense to resort to war even if victory is impossible, as long as one can win *politically*. This crucial point was repeatedly missed by western analysts and policymakers in their experiences in Indochina, Algeria, and the Middle East. In 1973, Israeli intelligence, believing from its own experience that a military defeat was also, by definition, a political defeat and a direct threat to survival, did not understand that Egypt and Syria would even contemplate initiating a war with the full knowledge that they could not win militarily, but that they could triumph politically. Western rationality, national experience, and a military view of strategy caused Israeli intelligence to underestimate a weaker adversary's intention to resort to war. (This is another demonstration of the methodological difficulties hindering the rational assessment of risk across different cultures.)

It is therefore crucial to devote more attention to the corroboration and integration of military and political intelligence, especially at the highest levels of analysis. Focusing primarily on one or the other may give rise to serious analytical distortions, as evaluation of military situations cannot be made in a political vacuum, and vice versa. It is not desirable, then, that a preponderance of intelligence activity be controlled by the military, as was the case in Israel before 1973. This conclusion, though seemingly straightforward, has not been borne in mind by those who stand to profit from it the most. The majority of cases of strategic surprise evince a prior lack of coordination between political-diplomatic and military activities on the part of the victim, and grave errors in judgment are clearly shown to be biased in one direction. Observed military warning signals are completely dismissed or underestimated because of the absence of corresponding political-diplomatic activity. The attacker takes care to maintain a facade of routine diplomacy, lulling diplomats of the intended victim into suppressing the military warning signals through optimistic political interpretations. States planning an attack no longer present their victims with ultimatums or declarations of war, nor do they initiate hostile diplomatic campaigns. Contemporary conflicts are often begun against a quiet diplomatic-political backdrop. This leads to the paradox of *the sounds of silence. A quiescent international environment can act as background noise which, by conditioning observers to a peaceful routine, actually covers preparations for war.*[77] All meaningful changes in military warning signals should trigger an intensified probe into an apparently calm diplomatic-political environment. The reverse situation can be equally volatile; this occurs when an intensive diplomatic dialogue is deadlocked or abruptly terminated, yet is *not* accompanied by the observation of unusual military activity (e.g., the United States before Pearl Harbor, Egypt prior to the Suez and Sinai Campaigns).

Another example of the damage that can result from the treatment of an intelligence problem as a purely military one concerns the head of Israeli military intelligence in 1973 – Eli Zeira – who felt that as a military officer, he should give the government an unequivocal yes or no reply regarding the likelihood of an Arab attack. Although the probability of war may have been 45 per cent 'yes' and 55 per cent 'no', he decided to take the responsibility and give the government a definite 'no' as his answer. A commander on the battlefield may indeed have no choice but to take clearcut action: an intelligence officer, however, must make his doubts known and let political and military leaders draw their own conclusions.[78]

ORGANIZATIONAL PAROCHIALISM, COMPARTMENTALIZATION AND EXCESSIVE SECRECY

The analytical quality and objectivity of intelligence is also distorted by parochial views arising out of the specialized functions of an organization. Of course, a naval or air force intelligence agency will have a narrower focus of attention than one that covers a broader area, such as the CIA. But even less specialized intelligence agencies often find it necessary to set an order of priorities. Specialization can produce a better analysis of specific problems, but this may also hamper the formulation of a more general outlook and increases the difficulty of coordination within and between intelligence organizations. Such tradeoffs are, however, inevitable.

Before the Second World War, British naval intelligence focused on assessing German naval preparations for war. Far weaker than that of the British, the German navy was unprepared for war in 1939. From the vantage point of British naval intelligence, therefore, Germany was unlikely to launch a war because of the high risk involved. Considering Hitler's political intentions and the fact that Germany was a primarily continental power, Nazi intentions to go to war should not have been gauged by a naval estimate. '... The Admiralty remained untroubled by German activity in every other sphere – foreign policy, internal policy, the economy, the air force, and the army. Naval intelligence drew from too narrow a field of information conclusions which were too broad, if eminently rational.'[79]

It is worthwhile quoting at some length Basil Collier's analysis of the failure of British intelligence to warn of the German attack in Norway, as it was brought about by similar departmental biases or preconceptions.

> Each of the departments concerned had its own opinions about these questions, and inevitably these opinions coloured their attitudes to reports and predictions received from the intelligence agencies and from diplomatic sources. The Foreign Office was anxious that Britain should not imperil her relations with a friendly neutral power by putting troops ashore in Norway without at least the tacit consent of the Norwegian government. At the same time, it was not in a position to rebut the argument that Allied intervention was strategically desirable and that consequently any German move which gave the Allies good reason to intervene would be beneficial to the Allied cause. It tended, therefore, to view forecasts of imminent German intervention in Norway with scepticism because they seemed too good to be true. The War Office admitted that reports that the Germans were preparing for a seaborne expedition might have some substance, but it could trace only six divisions – about the normal peacetime strength – in the area in which troops were said to be assembling. This was the number

of divisions eventually used by the Germans in Norway, but it was less than a quarter of the number the War Office thought they would need to tackle the Norwegians and the Swedes. Moreover, Military Intelligence could not exclude the possibility that the troops were intended not for an invasion of Norway but for some other purpose, such as a series of seaborne raids on the United Kingdom. The Admiralty was troubled by the fear that German surface raiders might break into the Atlantic, as had happened at the beginning of the war. It was determined, therefore, not to commit the Home Fleet to a wild goose chase on the strength of rumours. It was all the more disposed to assign reports about German intentions towards Norway to that category because the First Lord, Winston Churchill, believed that invasion of Norway was beyond Germany's powers. The Air Ministry was in some respects less sceptical about such reports than the other service departments. Even so, it tended to interpret them in the light of its preoccupations with the danger of a major air offensive against the United Kingdom.

Examination of the evidence by a body of experts not wedded to the preconceptions of any particular department could scarcely have failed to lead to the conclusion that the second and third interpretations were too far-fetched to be accepted . . . . But the evidence was not examined by independent experts. The Joint Intelligence Committee was not yet an effective body. It provided intermittent contact between Directors of Intelligence or their deputies, and between them and the Foreign Office; there was little or no contact between departments at the level at which reports were scrutinized by specialists. Inevitably, interpretations put upon reports by naval, army, or air intelligence officers were influenced to some extent by opinions current in the higher echelons of the departments they served. Also, there was a good deal of fragmentation within departments. Military intelligence officers concerned with Scandinavian affairs did not receive reports about events in Germany. In the Admiralty, the section of Naval Intelligence Division concerned with Scandinavian affairs did receive such reports, but some reports from MI6 or diplomatic sources were withheld from the Operational Intelligence Centre, which dealt with movements of German shipping and other day-to-day events. In both cases, provision was made for contributions from different sections to be co-ordinated at a higher level or by a section to which the task was delegated. But these arrangements did not work very well, because the co-ordinators lacked the detailed background knowledge needed to grasp the connections between two or more apparently unrelated sets of facts.[80]

Although the coordination between different intelligence organizations is crucial, it introduces a number of inevitable biases into the final intelligence product. Much depends on the number of organizations participating in the process, their character and above all their relative strength. The search for consensus may reduce the objective quality to truth of estimates in the sense that truth becomes a vector of the relative power and influence of each of the participating organizations – rather than the best and most professional judgment. Even the process of reaching a consensus may turn into a goal itself, often leaving intelligence estimates to smother different judgments with bland compromise. Hughes has, however, suggested that:

> Unfortunately the drive for . . . consistency has become a felt necessity . . . . Estimators now give it more than its due. In part the problem is a function of over-institutionalization in the intelligence community . . . the more coordination, probably, the more consistency.

> But inconsistency is a virtue which should by no means be avoided at all costs. Consistency, after all, is not a goal of intelligence. There is little virtue in self-consciously adhering to a particular line of inter-pretation simply because a prior estimate on the subject took that line. Just because it was said last time is no reason to say it again. The intelligence community is not the Supreme Court. It need not strain over precedents or labor to extend the meaning of sanctified words. On the contrary, intelligence is supposed to provide current unim-peded judgments. As a vehicle for ventilating a variety of viewpoints, the intelligence process should be highly suspicious of consensus . . . . The freedom to be inconsistent is a major argument bolstering the independence of the intelligence community.[81]

R.V. Jones has also some sharp comments on the consensus-seeking approach to intelligence work:

> A single head in Intelligence is far better than a committee, however excellent the individual members of the committee may be. A commit-tee wastes too much time in arguing, and every action it undertakes merely goes as far as common agreement and compromise will allow. Common agreement and compromise, as every commander knows, generally do not go far enough. The head of an intelligence organiza-tion is really in the position of a commander planning a perpetual attack on the security of foreign powers, and he must be allowed all the privileges of a commander.[82]

A byproduct of the consensus-seeking process is not only the introduction of additional biases and the slowness of the process, but also its lack of clarity as a basis for action. McLachlan suggests that had there been no need to reconcile the views of five intelligence departments, the forecasts and reports of enemy strategy and intentions would have been worded in a 'firmer' way.[83]

Despite the aforementioned problems and imperfections of the coordina-tion process, it must be kept in mind that coordination is absolutely essential for the production of high-quality intelligence estimates. In those countries in which the coordination between the different intelligence organizations was at times weak (such as in the US before Pearl Harbor) or never successfully achieved (such as in Germany or in Italy), the results were disastrous for the production of strategic intelligence.

Better coordination might correct somewhat the parochial biases of different intelligence organizations, but there is no perfect solution to the problem. Complicated and time-consuming, the coordination process itself can spur on competition for influence as well as a search for an acceptable compromise.[84]

Although each organization aspires to monopolistic control over its area of responsibility, *some* inter-organizational competition can be constructive. There are certainly considerable dangers in relegating all intelligence work to one agency. The need for diversity in intelligence estimates in order to provide leaders with a wider choice of interpretations is obvious, but there is also a price to be paid for competition. More organizations demand more resources, they duplicate efforts, and require coordination; like all other types of organizations, those in intelligence will fight for greater influence and larger budgets. Furthermore, the larger the number of organizations participating in the process, the longer the amount of *time* required for the process to take place. Under conditions of crisis or war, in which time and quick reactions are critical, the process of coordination will become sluggish and insufficiently responsive to the needs of decision makers in direct proportion to the number of participants.

The drawback of such competition is that it can encourage the politicization of the working process if the protection and expansion of parochial interests is enhanced by supplying the executive leader with the 'right' intelligence. These distortions are amplified if the executive or military leadership practices a policy of divide and rule. Since intelligence organizations do not function in a political vacuum, the biases occasioned by inter-agency competition are unavoidable; nevertheless, they should be minimized. The degree of objectivity achieved therefore depends largely upon the character of the leaders in the political, executive and military arenas, as well as upon the integrity of those responsible for the intelligence community. It is the political culture in the wider sense (e.g., freedom of expression, tolerance of different opinions, respect for professional skills, respect for the law), which makes the difference.

Finally, the need for coordination and the development of a political modus operandi *between* organizations also exists *within* each of them. It has been observed that individuals within groups feel compelled to develop a consensus, the maintenance of which may become a goal in its own right. 'Groupthink', like most of the aforementioned pathologies in organizational (and intelligence) work, can also fulfill positive functions. Individuals working together often share a similar educational and career background and common interests that need to be defended *vis-à-vis* other organizations. Moreover, any group that must achieve a common goal and implement a policy must also be able to arrive at an operational consensus that permits its members to work on a routine basis. No group can ever hope to implement the ideas of each of its members at the same time. Any collective action hence necessitates a political-social search for consensus.

The key question is, however, how was the group consensus arrived at? Was it reached through an open discussion based on the presentation of opposing opinions; was it enforced by a single person who discouraged debate; or was it brought about by submission to group pressure to conform? Agreement for its own sake will only prematurely stifle the expression of diverse, potentially valuable, opinions. The pitfalls of groupthink as demonstrated by Janis of course exist in the intelligence evaluation process, in particular when under the strain of crisis conditions. Groupthink may have been one cause for the adoption of unrealistic images and concepts by US intelligence before Pearl Harbor and the Bay of Pigs fiasco, and during the war in Vietnam.[85]

Excessive secrecy in the handling of information poses a related problem. Perhaps the most obvious symptom of this approach is the exaggerated compartmentalization that exists within and among intelligence organizations as well as between the intelligence community and other military or civilian agencies. Consequently, one organization often is not privy to the information held by another, an arrangement which may bring about failure to act, the duplication of efforts, or the inadvertent interference of one agency in the operations of another. Recent examples of such costly miscalculations are the Bay of Pigs operation and the ill-fated attempt to rescue the American hostages in Iran.

The overall vice of excessive secrecy may leave actors unaware of the pressing need to coordinate actions, or even of *which* new issues require coordination. Furthermore, valuable information may not be used to the fullest possible extent. Particularly in times of crisis, information should be passed more readily to lower and parallel echelons, for in all failures to anticipate sudden attacks, much data were misinterpreted or improperly corroborated with other information. In addition, information and the exchange of opinions should flow both upward and downward in the intelligence hierarchy and between it and its political counterpart, while better coordination between tactical intelligence and its headquarters must be ensured.[86]

Donald McLachlan had observed that 'Intelligence is indivisible. In its wartime practice, the divisions imposed by separate services and departments broke down.'[87] The process of breaking down these artificial barriers may, however, take a prolonged time in the natural course of events, and should therefore be deliberately practiced to a greater extent in peacetime.

Some degree of tension will always exist between the desire to protect intelligence sources and the need to make the best and most profitable use of information. There is no formula by which to calculate the potential costs and benefits or missed opportunities in such circumstances. Almost miraculously, the Allies managed to protect the secret of 'Ultra' from the Germans, and in fact from the world, until the early 1970s. Yet, the decision to attribute 'Ultra' information to spies or special operations in many cases discredited the information in the eyes of some senior field commanders, who were not informed of the *actual* source. A wider distribution of Ultra may have improved performance on the battlefield, reducing the number of opportunities missed. Nevertheless, Ultra and the double-cross system are unique events in the history of intelligence and may confuse the issues involved. It seems that in general, though, intelligence organizations tend to err in the direction of excessive caution and under-utilization of information. This may be an innate professional bias – yet information that is not used is ineffective and has repercussions beyond the mere wasting of the collection effort.[88]

THE (ELUSIVE) QUEST FOR EFFECTIVE ORGANIZATIONAL REFORMS

Every major intelligence failure, especially if a traumatic error involving strategic surprise, is followed by a reexamination of the organizational structure of the intelligence community (or agency), including a detailed review of the decision-making process of each organization and its relationship to others. A serious and earnest attempt is made to introduce reforms that will once and for all improve the performance of the intelligence/policy-making communities and provide better warning of the approach of the next crisis. These structural reforms are chiefly directed at developing inter- and intra-organizational mechanisms to improve the analytical objectivity of the intelligence process, as well as to reduce the negative consequences of inter-organizational politics and competition, or the negative political interference of either the political elite or that of senior military and intelligence professionals. In the final analysis, all of the newly introduced mechanisms are designed to encourage greater objectivity by increasing the variety of inputs (i.e., different and competing opinions of diverse individuals and organizations into the intelligence process).

The simplest way to attempt to achieve this goal is by increasing the number of participating organizations. As mentioned earlier, this creates new difficulties in coordination and cooperation and steps up political competition over scarce resources and for influence between the various agencies.[89] Another approach to improvement of the decision-making process starts *within* each organization. The two types of reform will usually be carried out simultaneously, and generally complement each other. In each case, an attempt is made to neutralize inter- and intra-organizational political competition, 'equalize' the roles and influence of the participants by providing each the opportunity to express his views without fear of suffering any negative consequences.

Since no two (or more) organizations are ever equal – in their functions, performance, *esprit de corps,* or leadership – they are never equal in influence. Furthermore, the creation of new organizations does not always achieve the desired outcome, since they often lack the vital support of a power base. (After the Yom Kippur War, the Agranat Commission in Israel recommended the establishment, in fact re-introduction, of the Israeli Foreign Ministry's intelligence unit. Unable to compete with the far more powerful position and resources of the Israeli military intelligence and the Mossad, this organization remains unimportant in the intelligence process in Israel.) On the positive side, new organizations can be provided with an extra amount of resources and powerful leadership in order to secure their productive survival.

While some of the reforms eventually succeed (e.g., the reform of the US intelligence community after the Second World War), many are difficult to put into practice and, while implemented *de jure,* cannot always take hold in a *de facto* sense. In any event, as has been observed by Richard Betts, most of these reforms involve some kind of trade-off, so none can be expected to solve completely the problem of avoiding strategic surprise.

Having warned the reader against putting too much hope in any reforms, we will proceed to discuss mechanisms designed to improve the objectivity and variety of input into the intelligence process. The first, multiple advocacy, is *primarily* intended to ensure each organization an equal opportunity to influence the intelligence decision-making process. The second, the Devil's Advocate, is supposed to guarantee diversity within each agency.

Multiple Advocacy[90]

Multiple advocacy entails the deliberate establishment of several independent intelligence agencies in order to foster increased competition and greater analytical variety, thereby affording policymakers access to a wider spectrum of views. Ideally, 'red·undancy inhibits consensus, impedes the herd instinct in the decision process, and thus reduces the likelihood of failure due to unchallenged premises or cognitive errors'.[91] Yet multiple advocacy is more than the encouragement of free market competition. It requires strong, alert management if the competition is to have constructive direction and centralized coordination. For this system to function properly, three major conditions must be fulfilled. *One,* there should be an equal distribution of all types of intellectual, bureaucratic, and other assets (e.g., experts, adequate information, analytical support, equal political influence with the top executive, and equal bargaining skills). Alexander George emphasizes the need for a balanced distribution of assets and influence among the participants. 'The mere existence within the policymaking system of actors holding different points of view will not guarantee adequate multi-sided examination of a policy issue.'[92] *Two,* it requires the active participation of the top executive in monitoring and regulating the process. *Three,* time is required for adequate debate and give-and-take. Other requirements include the establishment of a special custodian-manager assistant to the top executive, if his own participation in the process is limited. The assistant would be expected to balance actor resources; introduce new advisors to argue for unpopular views; search for new channels of information or avoid dependence on a single channel of information; arrange for the independent evaluation of decisional premises when necessary; monitor the process and introduce appropriate corrective action. The process can be further strengthened by introducing 'adversary proceedings'; that is, a requirement that intelligence reports or policy recommendations 'run the gauntlet' of critical scrutiny by analysts other than those who produced them (or even by competing organizations).[93]

While the absence of competition and variety in intelligence is a recipe for failure, the institution of a multiple advocacy system does not guarantee success. To begin with, not every leader will possess the qualities needed for direct participation in the management of this type of system. 'Some executives find it extremely distasteful, disorienting, and enervating to be exposed directly in a face-to-face setting to the clash of opinion among their advisors .... Such executives prefer a depersonalized presentation of the arguments.'[94] In other cases, the leader may lack a sense of balance or judgment, and can transform controlled competition into cut throat competition. Or, if the chief executive does not have time to manage the multiple advocacy process, his advisor may lack sufficient prestige or leverage to maintain the desired level of competition.

The competition may also be corrupted from below, as it will always be beseiged by parochial, bureaucratic interests. Actors ... 'may decline to raise unpromising options even if they believe in them, for fear of ending up on the "losing side" too often, thereby losing "influence" or tarnishing their reputation or expending limited bargaining resources on fruitless or costly endeavors.'[95] In addition, ' competition within the advisory circle may occasionally get out of hand, strain the policy-making group's cohesion, and impose heavy human costs .... Officials may be quicker to go outside the executive branch in search of allies for their internal policy disputes. This may encourage "leaks" and create difficulties for the executive.'[96]

Multiple advocacy at its best can lead to the presentation of a wide variety of opinions, but it cannot contribute to identification of the better choice; '... it may simply highlight ambiguity rather than resolve it.'[97] Variety does not prevent a leader from choosing the option or policy that he would have preferred anyway; it may merely serve as an objective facade for a subjective choice.[98] Another possible incorrect choice by the chief executive can stem from the temptation to ' ... accept the middle-of-the-road view, a compromise between advocates of opposing ideas, which may be indecisive ... 'Thus, the fundamental biases of neither the intelligence community nor the political executive are resolved by this system, while variety does not necessarily produce 'high quality policymaking. The content and quality of policy decisions is determined by many other variables – ... the ideological values and cognitive beliefs of policymakers and others.'[99]

Multiple advocacy requires time for the give-and-take process among advocates, which may occasionally impose undue delays on decisionmaking. This prerequisite can seriously restrict its utility in times of crisis and war.

Despite its many imperfections, multiple advocacy makes sense. In reality, all other things are never held equal – neither resources nor the influence of different organizations or actors. Naturally, in a politically competitive environment some organizations (or one) will come to prevail over the others. Then in the aftermath of a major intelligence failure, multiple reforms will again provide corrective relief until one agency manages to build up its relative power to the point where the same cycle begins once more.

Other, and at times simpler, organizational mechanisms have been proposed as antidotes to the dangers of groupthink and conformity. In demonstrating his willingness to accept criticism, the executive (or other relevant leader) should encourage each member of a group to raise his objections and doubts. The executive leader 'should be impartial instead of stating preferences and expectations at the outset .... [He should] limit his briefings to unbiased statements about the scope of the problem and the limitations of available resources without advocating specific proposals he would like to see adopted.' This allows the conferees the opportunity to develop an atmosphere of open inquiry and to explore impartially a wide range of policy alternatives:[100] to encourage multiple advocacy, to divide groups into new subgroups under new chairmen and then to come back together to discuss their differences again; whenever possible, individual group members should discuss the group's deliberations with trusted outside friends; to invite outside members to group discussions; after searching a preliminary consensus the group should hold a second chance meeting at which every member can express his residual doubts and rethink the entire issue before making a definitive choice.[101] Some of these suggestions are theoretically easy to implement and involve relatively little cost, while others, such as an initial neutral attitude on the part of the leader, would be much more challenging to bring about.

As stated earlier, organizational reforms cannot be expected to completely overcome the fundamental problems of inaccurate perception and insulate the intelligence policymaking process from political influences. Ultimately, the effectiveness of these mechanisms depends upon the general quality of the political culture and the character of the leaders who must make the final decisions. Yet even though the expected returns from organizational reforms can only be limited, all changes that increase diversity, criticism and free discussion must be advocated.

The Devil's Advocate[102]

The institution of the devil's advocate is well known. The idea is to encourage an individual to freely express unpopular, dissenting opinions, which allows decision-makers to consider alternative views while protecting those who present them. The role can be assigned on an *ad hoc* basis to individuals in a given discussion, or be institutionalized down to the smallest detail and assigned on a continuing basis to an individual or group. The problem with this mechanism is that it is an artificial method of introducing unpopular concepts. If the role is assigned to a typical member of an intelligence organization, for example, he cannot be expected to express the conviction and in-depth understanding of someone who genuinely believes in that position. In general, a true advocate of opposing views on an important issue would not be employed in an intelligence organization in the first place, unless he were to conceal his actual opinions in order to survive. If the dissenter is not expressing his personal viewpoint, he will end up playing the *role* of the opposition as perceived by the group to which he belongs. (This is akin to playing chess against oneself.) More misleading than helpful, such an arrangement would perpetuate the accepted image of the adversary instead of penetrating to the core of his (very different) perceptions. On the other hand, if the devil's advocate is presenting his real opinions, he will be singled out as hostile to the group's interest and will not be taken into its confidence. A genuine devil's advocate should come from outside the organizational system, but in practice he is usually part of it. In fact, the very obstacles that make it impossible to perceive the adversary correctly would also apply to him. Furthermore, the role of devil's advocate would soon become so routinized that no one would take it seriously.[103] An environment which can tolerate dissent would be far more constructive than the artificial tolerance of opposition.

Clearly, the majority of failures to anticipate strategic surprise can be correlated with conceptual rigidity and a high incidence of perceptual continuity. Therefore, analysts (and to a lesser extent, political or military leaders) should be encouraged to consider alternative interpretations of data and new evidence, and continuously to reevaluate their concept while avoiding dogmatic adherence to given concepts. The search for ways to promote more open-minded attitudes is basic to almost all proposals for the improvement of intelligence work; to this end, analysts must be encouraged to present their views openly, to be critical, to fight for their opinions if necessary, and to resist group and political pressures. This is perhaps the most rudimentary condition necessary for the upgrading of intelligence work – yet it is also an ideal demand that can never be fully attained within a human environment.

Inasmuch as the independent judgment of individual analysts at all levels can not be guaranteed *within* each organization, the fostering of *inter*-organizational competition may enhance the diversity and freedom of the intelligence process in general.

*   *   *

Far-reaching advances in the technical means of gathering intelligence information, and the greater awareness of political, perceptual mechanisms undermining the intelligence process, have not yielded corresponding progress in the ability to anticipate strategic surprise.[104] On this account, understanding but not being able to avoid this phenomenon has led to a certain sense of futility. Napoleon once said, ' ... Uncertainty is the essence of war, surprise its rule.' If anything, history provides us with the consoling observation that there is no direct correlation between achieving the highest degree of surprise at the outbreak of a war and ultimately emerging victorious. The next best thing to avoiding the surprise, therefore, is to be able to cope with it once it has occurred, and this requires the judicious build-up of military strength in peacetime.

Post Surprise Measures (PSM)[105]

In light of the preceding observations, it is of the utmost importance to prepare an array of methods to deal with a sudden attack once it has taken place. Only a few of such measures will be mentioned in this context.

(a) Upgrade military plans and preparations for operations in the event of a surprise attack. This must include detailed contingency plans, staff exercises, and military field exercises.

(b) Special emphasis must be placed on the preparation and protection of headquarters, communications centers, military airfields,[106] mobilization centers, weapons, ammunition, and fuel depots, major bridges, tunnels, and other "choke points". All key bases and communication centers must be able to withstand a conventional first strike in order to provide a conventional second strike capability, and communication networks should be designed with positive redundancy sufficient for post-attack survival.

(c) Special plans must be drawn up to carry out effectively and even accelerate mobilization procedures under attack conditions. Furthermore, they should be maintained and checked by exercises and updating at regular intervals.

(d) A variety of defensive counter-surprises, both technical and operational, should be prepared.[107]

(1) On the technological side, the defender can ready more effective anti-aircraft and/or anti-tank missiles to be operated in layered concentrations. New technologies can include dynamic mining, or the preparation of minefields that will channel the attacker into specific killing zones; electronic and other counter-measures to disrupt the attacker's communications (C^3I facilities); and neutralization of his major weapons systems.

(2) The initiation of counter-operations, and if possible interceptive attacks, against the attacker. A select number of units should always be available for counter-operations against the enemy's rear echelons, airfields, and communication and supply lines, to name a few. The defender's goal should be to throw the attacker off balance by resorting to aggressive, unexpected moves that concentrate on vulnerable points in the attacker's 'armor'. Most suitable for such operations is air power, the flexibility and nature of which allows for a short reaction time and the ability to attack all echelons of the enemy forces. (For this reason, it is of great importance to develop the conventional second-strike capabilities of the Air Force, which includes protecting the aircraft, runways, ammunition and fuel depots from the enemy's first strike.) In addition to the air force, special operations units such as rangers, paratroopers, and SAS can react quickly and effectively to a sudden attack.

APPENDIX

Complex Man–Machine Accidents[108]

It is of great heuristic interest to compare accidents arising from the complex interaction of man and machine to the problems involved in trying to anticipate or prevent a strategic surprise. Complex man–machine accidents (such as the Three Mile Island nuclear reactor mishap) are in some ways simpler than a human conflict type of situation. Complex machines, unlike enemies, don't *deliberately* try to conceal aggresive intentions, nor do they resort to deception operations or tailor their strategies to 'attack' different operators. Furthermore, although the number of potential causes for an accident is very large, it is still finite and the possible structure or consequences of an accident *may* be better analyzed before it occurs (i.e., if a valve fails at point X, then the flow of water will be reduced by Y per cent which will increase the temperature in the reactor by a certain percentage, and so on). For this reason, it can also be expected that, in the future, the decision-making process in complex man–machine crisis situations could be left to computers, which would 'automatically' make better and faster decisions than any human being. Nevertheless, it has proven to be impossible either to predict or to avoid accidents (or man–machine 'surprises'). It is of course the human element in this situation which is the weakest, least predictable link.

Three types of accidents are recognized in complex man–machine disasters: they are unique accidents, discrete accidents, and calculated risk accidents. To the first type of accident belongs, for example, the collapse of a dam in a powerful earthquake; or the simultaneous heart attack of a pilot and co-pilot in an airliner. 'No reasonable protection is possible against freak accidents or Acts of God.' Discrete accidents can involve equipment failure, a condition that can be corrected so that it will not happen again. Such mishaps frequently occur in all human–machine interactions and result from a limited design error, an operator's mistake, and the like. In a discrete accident, the system responds to that source of error without any significant synergistic developments, and backup systems and isolation devices come into play. The system as such is not abandoned, as it can be made 'safer' through modification.

Calculated risk type of accidents are of a statistical nature (i.e., the probability of their occurrence could conceivably be calculated, and preventive or corrective measures can or will be taken according to a cost/benefit analysis and the probability involved). In reality, though, highly complex systems are susceptible to many unknown risks and, therefore, the actual risk of an accident occurring cannot be calculated.

These three types of accidents can also be relevant to the analysis of strategic surprise. In many respects, particularly for each different country, strategic surprise in its magnitude has the characteristics of a unique accident. This is especially true of large-scale, out-of-the-blue surprise attacks. (The unprecedented launching of a nuclear surprise attack could fall under this category.)

Military and intelligence tend to treat strategic surprise as if it were a discrete accident which can be 'fixed'. History teaches us that no such fail-safe corrective measures exist, and moreover, that strategic surprise *will* take place regardless of the improvements or modifications that have been made. Mistaking strategic surprise for a discrete accident can, in fact, be very misleading, for it creates illusions of safety leading to even more intense surprise in the future.

The calculated risk explanation for accidents is pertinent to strategic surprise in those situations where politicians or intelligence analysts assume that they know or can estimate the calculus of risk for an enemy attack with reasonable accuracy, whereas such calculations are rarely possible or reliable.

The student of strategic surprise is struck by the similarities between complex man–machine accidents and the latter phenomenon.

A. Complexity and inevitability. 'The accident at TMI was not a preventable one ...., 'They cannot be prevented. They are unanticipated. It is not feasible to train, design, or build in such a way as to anticipate all eventualities in complex systems where the parts are tightly coupled ... the complexity of systems outruns all controls.' ' ... Normal accidents, whose origins lie fallow and simmer in the very complexity of the interactive system, waiting upon some failure of equipment, design, or operator action to give then brief, fierce life, cannot be eliminated. Indeed, they grow with the complexity of the system, *including the complexity added by the safety features.*'

B. Warning: signals and noise. The normal accident is characterized by 'signals which provide warnings *only* in retrospect, making prevention difficult'.

> Complex human-machine systems abound in warnings – signs in red letters, flashing lights, horns, sounding, italicized passages in training manuals and operating instructions, decals on equipment, analyses of faults in technical reports, and a light snowfall of circulars and alerts .... Warnings work; but not all the time. We should not be surprised; the very volume of warning devices testifies to this likelihood. If warnings were heeded, we would need only a few modest and tasteful ones rather than a steady drill of admonitions punctuated by alarms and lights.

> ... Why are warnings not always heeded? There are many reasons, and when we consider the overpopulation of complex, high-risk systems that someone has decided we cannot live without, they are disturbing.

> Consider three categories of warnings. First, there are deviations, steady-state conditions that do not activate significant alarms. There was a rather long list of these at Three Mile Island .... Each one individually is considered trivial or interpreted in a routine framework. Only hindsight discloses the meaning of these deviations. Second, there are alarms, such as flashing lights or circuit breaker trips or dials reading in the red zone. But operators are accustomed to interpreting these alarms as insignificant when they have a conception of the problem which triggered them. Or if the operators have no conception of the problem, the alarm may be attributed to faulty alarm equipment .... Alarms, like deviations, always outnumber actual accidents: warnings are in greater supply than actual malfunctions.

> Past accidents, mute predictors of future ones, form the third category of warnings. But history is no guide for highly infrequent events. They are not expected to occur again; generally they don't.

> Following an accident, reforms, improvements, better procedures will be implemented .... Operators will be flooded with new warnings. But it is normal for the systems to have accidents; warnings cannot affect the normal accident. Tight coupling encourages normal accidents, with their highly interdependent synergistic aspects, but loose coupling muffles warnings.

> Whether systems are loosely or tightly coupled, they all face another problem with warnings – the signal-to-noise ratio. Only after the event, when we

construct imaginative (and frequently dubious) explanations of what went wrong, does some of the noise reveal itself as a signal. The operators at TMI had literally to turn off alarms; so many of them were sounding and blinking that signals passed into noise.

The student of strategic surprise will be able to identify many additional similarities such as: problems of coordination and failures of communication when warnings are not made available to the proper people; the political dimensions in which top decision-makers have other priorities and/or refuse to listen to warnings because they are reluctant to pay the *costs* of improvement and precautionary measures; problems of human perceptions where the possibility of unfamilar types of accidents and malfunctions is not taken seriously. ' ... The normal accident is unforeseeable; its "warnings" are *socially constructed.*'

There is still much more the strategic analysts can learn from man–machine accidents and disaster theory.

NOTES

1. On the inverse correlation between strength and the incentive to resort to surprise, stratagem and deception, see Michael I. Handel, 'Intelligence and Deception', *The Journal of Strategic Studies* 5 (March 1982), 122–54, 145.
2. This is perhaps the reason that in early Soviet military doctrine, surprise was seen as a 'transitory' but not a decisive factor. Primarily identified with Stalin's contribution to military science, these early views were still paid lip service after the German attack on the Soviet Union and even as late as the early 1950s and the nuclear age. The appearance of nuclear weapons rendered earlier Marxist–Leninist observations on the transitory (temporary) and permanent elements of war obsolete. Despite theoretical lip service to the secondary importance of strategic surprise, in practice the Soviet military doctrine assigns it a great deal of importance in conventional as much as in nuclear war. See Raymond L. Garthoff, *The Soviet Image of Future War* (Washington DC: Public Affairs Press, 1959), Ch.3: 'The Role of Surprise and Blitzkrieg'.

   By the 1970s, Colonel Savkin, a leading Soviet strategist, went one step further and referred to the principle of surprise as ' ... a most important principle of military art since olden times'. Col. V. Ye.Savkin, 'Surprise', *Military Review* (April 1974), 84–91; Col. Dr. L. Kuleszynski, 'Some Problems of Surprise in Warfare', and Maj. Mgr. Z. Poleski, 'Psychological Aspects of Surprise', both in Joseph D. Douglass and Amoretta M. Hoeber (eds), *Selected Readings From Military Thought 1963–1973* (Washington DC: GPO, 1983), Vol.5,Part II, US Air Force; and John M. Caravelli, 'The Role of Surprise and Preemption in Soviet Military Strategy', *International Security Review* 6 (Summer 1981), 209–36. See also Amnon Sella, 'Barbarossa: Surprise Attack and Communication', *The Journal of Contemporary History* 13 (July 1978), 555–83; John Francis O'Neil, 'German Counter-C³ and its Effects on Soviet Command Communications During Operation Barbarossa' (MA dissertation, Naval Post-graduate School, Monterey, CA, 1980); John Erickson, 'The Soviet Response to Surprise Attack: Three Directives, 22 June 1941', *Soviet Studies* 23 (April 1972), 519–59; Reuben Ainsytein, 'Stalin and June 22, 1941', *International Affairs* 42 (October 1966), 662–73; Vladimir Petrov, *'June 22, 1941' Soviet Historians and the German Invasion* (Columbia, SC: University of South Carolina Press, 1968).
3. All three quotations are from: Carl von Clausewitz, *On War*, eds. Michael Howard and Peter Paret (Princeton, NJ: Princeton University Press, 1967), pp.198–9.
4. Ibid., p.545.
5. For the impact of modern technology on warfare see: Michael Howard, *War in European History* (New York: Oxford University Press, 1979), in particular Chs. 5–7; J.F.C. Fuller, *The Foundations of the Science of War* (London: Hutchinson, 1926), pp.278–9; J.F.C.

Fuller, *Armaments and History* (New York: Charles Scribner's Sons, 1945); J.F.C. Fuller, 'The Mechanization of War', in *What Would Be the Character of a New War,* The Inter-Parliamentary Union, Geneva (New York: Harrison Smith and Robert Haas, 1933), pp.49–75; J.F.C. Fuller, *The Conduct of War 1789–1961: A Study of the Impact of the French, Industrial and Russian Revolutions on War and Its Conduct* (London: Eyre Methuen, 1972); Tom Wintringham, *Weapons and Tactics* (Harmondsworth: Penguin Books, 1973); Edwin A. Pratt, *The Rise of Rail-Power in War and Conquest 1833–1914* (Philadelphia: Lippincott, 1916); Brian Ranft (ed.) *Technological Change and British Naval Policy 1860–1839* (New York: Holmes & Meier, 1977).

6. This apt phrase was suggested by Thomas C. Schelling in *The Strategy of Conflict* (Cambridge, MA: Harvard University Press,1960), pp.207–30, and in *Arms and Influence* (New Haven: Yale University Press, 1966), p.221. These two books have been neglected by the students of strategic surprise.

7. Clausewitz, p.79. On strategic surprise in the nuclear age, see, for example, Richard K. Betts, *Surprise Attack: Lessons for Defense Planning* (Washington DC: The Brookings Institution, 1982), pp.228–54; see also Paul Bracken, *The Command and Control of Nuclear Forces* (New Haven: Yale University Press, 1983), pp.5–74.

8. Michael I. Handel, 'The Study of Intelligence', *Orbis* 26 (Winter 1978), 817–21.

9. These terms were first applied to the study of strategic surprise and intelligence analysis by Roberta Wohlstetter in *Pearl Harbor: Warning and Decision* (Stanford: Stanford University Press, 1962), pp.336–8. On the inevitability of surprise, see Michael I. Handel, 'The Yom Kippur War and the Inevitability of Surprise', *International Studies Quarterly* 21 (September 1977), 461–501. An expanded version is Michael I. Handel, *Perception, Deception and Surprise: The Case of the Yom Kippur War* (Jerusalem: The Leonard Davis Institute, 1976); and Richard K. Betts, 'Analysis, War and Decision: Why Intelligence Failures are Inevitable', *World Politics* 31 (October 1978), 61–89. Other interesting theoretical works on strategic surprise include (in addition to Roberta Wohlstetter's *Warning and Decision* and Richard Bett's *Surprise Attack):* Klaus Knorr and Patrick Morgan (eds.), *Strategic Military Surprise* (New Brunswick, NJ: Transaction Books, 1983), pp.147–71; Barton Whaley, *Stratagem, Deception and Surprise in War* (Cambridge, MA: MIT Center for International Studies, 1969, mimeo) (by now dated, this was unfortunately never published as a book); Alexander L. George and Richard Smoke, *Deterrence in American Foreign Policy: Theory and Practice* (New York: Columbia University Press, 1979), pp.567–87; Ephraim Kam, *Failure to Anticipate War: The Why of Surprise Attack* (Ph.D. dissertation, Harvard University, 1983). Robert Jervis, 'Hypothesis on Misperception', *World Politics* 20 (April 1968) 454–79, is a pioneering study on the perceptual-psychological dimension of intelligence and decision-making in foreign affairs; earlier studies are Klaus Knorr, 'Failures in National Intelligence Estimates: The Case of the Cuban Missiles', *World Politics* 16 (April 1964), 455–67; Benno Wasserman, 'The Failure of Intelligence Prediction', *Political Studies* 8 (June 1960), 156–69; Abraham Ben-Zvi, 'Hindsight and Foresight: A Conceptual Framework for the Analysis of Surprise Attacks', *World Politics* 28 (April 1976), 381–95; Janice Gross Stein, "Intelligence" and "Stupidity" Reconsidered: Estimation and Decision in Israel, 1973', *Journal of Strategic Studies* 3 (September 1980), 147–78; Avi Shlaim, 'Failures in National Security Estimates: The Case of the Yom Kippur War', *World Politics* 28 (April 1976), 348–80.

10. On deception, see for example: Barton Whaley, *Codeword Barbarossa* (Cambridge, MA: MIT Press, 1973); Whaley, *Stratagem;* Barton Whaley, 'Covert Rearmament in Germany 1919–1939: Deception and Misperception', *The Journal of Strategic Studies* 5 (March 1982), 3–39; Donald Daniel and Katherine Herbig (eds.), *Strategic Military Deception* (New York: Pergamon, 1982).

Among the more interesting Second World War memoirs dealing with deception are: Ewen Montague, *Beyond Top Secret Ultra* (London: Corgi, 1979); R.V. Jones, *Most Secret War: British Scientific Intelligence in World War II 1939–1945* (London: Hamish Hamilton, 1978); R.V. Jones, 'Intelligence and Deception', in Robert Pfaltzgraff (ed.), *Intelligence Policy and National Security* (London: Macmillan, 1981), pp.3–23; David Mure, *Practice to Deceive* (London: William Kimber, 1977); David Mure, *Master of Deception: Tangled Webs in London and the Middle East* (London: William Kimber,

1980); Charles Cruickshank, *Deception in World War II* (Oxford: Oxford University Press, 1979); J.C. Masterman, *The Double Cross System* (New Haven: Yale University Press, 1972); Richard J. Heuer, Jr., 'Strategic Deception: A Psychological Perspective', *International Studies Quarterly* 25 (June 1981), 294–327; *Thoughts on the Cost-Effectiveness of Deception and Related Tactics in the Air War 1939–1945* (Deception Research Program, Mathtech Inc., Princeton, NJ, and ORD/CIA Analytic, March 1979); *Covert Rearmament in Germany 1919–1939: Deception and Misperception* (Deception Research Program, Mathtech, Inc., Princeton, NJ, and ORD/CIA Analytic, March 1979).

11. See also Michael I. Handel, 'Intelligence and Deception', pp.122–54.
12. For background and numerous alerts preceeding the German attack in the west in May 1940, see Telford Taylor, *The March of Conquest* (New York: Simon & Schuster, 1958); Erich von Manstein, *Lost Victories* (London: Methuen, 1958); Hans Adolf Jacobsen, *Fall Gelb: Der Kampf uber Den Deutschen Operationplan in Westoffensive 1940* (Wiesbaden: Franz Steiner, 1957); Major L.F. Ellis, *The War in France and Flanders 1939–1940* (London: HMSO,1953); Basil Collier, *Hidden Weapons: Allied Secret or Undercover Services in World War II* (London: Hamish Hamilton, 1982),pp.78–96; Betts, *Surprise Attack*, pp.28–34; André Beaufre, *1940: The Fall of France* (London: Cassell, 1965); William L. Shirer, *The Collapse of the Third Republic* (New York: Simon & Schuster, 1969).
13. Handel, *Perception, Deception and Surprise*, p.15.
14. Handel, 'Intelligence and Deception', p.154n.
15. See Michael I. Handel, 'Crisis and Surprise in Three Arab-Israeli Wars', in Knorr and Morgan (eds.), pp.111–46.
16. Handel, *Perception, Deception and Surprise*, pp.18–28.
17. For the difficulties involved in estimating Hitler's intentions and in predicting his style of operation, see Michael I. Handel, *The Diplomacy of Surprise* (Cambridge, MA: Harvard Center for International Affairs, 1981), Ch.2, pp.31–96. Underestimating the capabilities of an adversary may lead to erroneous conclusions concerning his short-term intentions. Given the fact that capabilities are normally easier to assess than intentions, a competent intelligence organization is less likely to commit this type of error. Japanese intelligence in 1945 vastly underrated Soviet capabilities in Manchuria and therefore miscalculated Soviet intentions to launch a large-scale offensive in August 1945. For an interesting and detailed analysis, see Edward J. Drea, 'Missing Intentions: Japanese Intelligence and the Soviet Invasion of Manchuria, 1945', *Military Affairs* (April 1984), 66–73.
18. Handel, *Perception, Deception and Surprise*, p.62.
19. Clausewitz, p.190.
20. Handel, *Perception, Deception and Surprise*, pp.15–16.
21. See Kam, p.182. For the assessment of risks primarily on the tactical level, see Elias Carter Townsend, *Risks: The Key to Combat Intelligence* (Harrisburg, PA: Military Service Publishing Company, 1955).
22. Handel, *Perception, Deception and Surprise*, pp.46ff.
23. Barry Leach, *German Strategy Against Russia 1939–1941* (Oxford: Oxford University Press, 1973), pp.91–4 and Appendix 4, p.270; Albert Seaton, *The Russo-German War 1941–1945* (London: Praeger Publishers, 1971); *German Military Intelligence* (Fredrick, MD: University Publications of America, 1984).
24. Waldemar Erfurth, *Surprise* (Harrisburg, PA: Military Service Publishing Company, 1943), pp.6–7.
25. Handel, *Perception, Deception and Surprise*, p.16.
26. The term is Schelling's. See *The Strategy of Conflict*, pp.244–5.
27. For literature on this case, see note 12 above.
28. Both quotations are from: W.D. Howells, 'Intelligence in Crises', in Gregory R. Copley (ed.), *Defense '83* (Washington DC: D and F Conferences, Inc.. 1983), pp.351,350.
29. Handel, *Perception, Deception and Surprise*, pp.52–4; Betts, *Surprise Attack*, pp.122–3.
30. Handel, *Perception, Deception and Surprise*, p.54.
31. Ibid.
32. Howells, pp.359–61; Betts, *Surprise Attack*, pp.190–2; Kam, pp.127–39.

33. For an interesting case, see Jones, *Most Secret War,* pp.233–5.
34. Howells, 'Intelligence in Crises', p.361.
35. Robert Jervis, *The Logic of Images in International Relations* (Princeton, NJ: Princeton University Press, 1970).
36. Betts, 'Analysis, War and Decision', pp.73–5; Kam, pp.461–2.
37. Ken Booth, *Strategy and Ethnocentrism* (New York: Holmes & Meier, 1979), pp.123–4.
38. Luigi Albertini, *The Origins of the War of 1914,* Vols. 2,3 (Oxford: Oxford University Press, 1952); Ludwig Reiners, *The Lamps Went Out in Europe* (Cleveland, OH: World Publishing Co., 1966), pp.134–9; Lawrence Lafore, *The Long Fuse* (Philadelphia: Lippincott, 1965), pp.269–75; L.F.C. Turner, *The Origins of the First World War* (New York: W.W.Norton, 1970), p.91–112; Gerhard Ritter, *The Schlieffen Plan* (London: Oswald Wolf, 1958).
39. Paraphrased from an article by Charles Perrow, 'Normal Accident at Three Mile Island', *Transaction (Social Sciences and Modern Society)* 18 (July/August 1981), 17–26,21.
40. See Jervis, 'Hypothesis on Misperception'; Robert Jervis, *The Logic of Images in International Relations;* and Robert Jervis, *Perception and Misperception in International Politics* (Princeton, NJ: Princeton University Press, 1976); Joseph de Rivera, *The Psychological Dimension of Foreign Policy* (Columbus, OH: Charles Merrill Pub., 1968); Jack S. Levy, 'Misperception and the Causes of War: Theoretical Linkages and Analytical Problems', *World Politics* 36 (October 1983), 76–100; Arthur S. Stein, 'When Misperception Matters', *World Politics* 34 (July 1982), 502–26; Herbert Goldhamer, *Reality and Belief in Military Affairs* (Santa Monica, CA: The Rand Corporation, Feb. 1979 R–2448–NA); *Misperception Literature Survey* (Mathtech Inc., Princeton, NJ and ORD/CIA Analytic, March 1979).
41. Handel, *The Diplomacy of Surprise,* pp.97–176, 241–354.
42. For a detailed discussion, see Jervis, 'Hypothesis on Misperception'.
43. Booth. He refers to this phenomenon as the 'Hamlet syndrome'.
44. On problems of ethnocentrism, national character, and the difficulties of understanding other cultures, see the following sample: Washington Platt, *National Character in Action: Intelligence Factors in Foreign Relations* (New Brunswick, NJ: Rutgers University Press, 1961); Booth; A.J. Marder, *Old Friends, New Enemies: The Royal Navy and the Imperial Japanese Navy,* Vol.1: *Strategic Illusions 1936–1941* (Oxford: Oxford University Press, 1981). The classic study of national character is still Salvador de Madariaga, *Englishmen, Frenchmen, Spaniards* (Oxford: Oxford University Press, 1927).
    On the importance of familiarity with languages, see for example: Lev Navrozov, 'What the CIA Knows About Russia', *Commentary* 66 (September 1971), 51–9.
45. Zvi Lanir, *Fundamental Surprise: The National Intelligence Crisis* (In Hebrew) (Tel Aviv: HaKibbutz HaMeuchad, 1983).
46. Handel, *Perception, Deception and Surprise,* pp.40–42.
47. Lanir. By basic or fundamental surprise, Lanir means the lack of 'correct' understanding by a given society of its *own* problems, situation, capabilities, direction of development, the gap between its goals and means, the absence of understanding how its neighbors perceive it and the like. This new concept does not add any constructive dimension to the study of intelligence for reasons mentioned in the preceeding text, and may be methodologically more confusing than helpful.
48. Samuel P. Huntington, *The Soldier and the State* (New York: Vintage Books, 1964).
49. Ibid., p.49.
50. For an excellent discussion of this point, see Richard K. Betts, *Soldiers, Statesmen, and Cold War Crisis* (Cambridge, MA: Harvard University Press, 1977), Ch.10, pp.183–209.
51. Donald McLachlan, *Room 39: A Study in Naval Intelligence* (New York: Atheneum, 1968), p.365.
52. See Thomas L. Hughes, *The Fate of Facts in the World of Men: Foreign Poilcy and Intelligence Making* (New York: Headline Series, Foreign Policy Association, December 1976, no.233), p.15. This is one of the best essays on the use and misuse of intelligence by political leaders, and on the problems of cooperation between the intelligence community and political decision-makers.
    Despite its importance, little has been witten on politics and intelligence, or the politics

of intelligence. Most of the existing observations are scattered throughout memoirs, histories of specific intelligence operations, and the like. An excellent chapter on this subject can be found in McLachlan, Ch.15, pp.338–66, as well as in the rest of the book. Some material concerning the bureaucratic politics of intelligence can be found in Mark M. Lowenthal, *U.S. Intelligence: Evolution and Anatomy*, The Washington Papers, 105, Vol.12 (1984).

An interesting case study in the politics of intelligence concerns the process used to estimate the North Vietnamese-Vietcong order of battle. See Sam Adams, 'Vietnam Cover-Up: Playing War with Numbers', *Harpers Magazine* (May 1975), pp.41–4, 62–73; also Patrick J. McGarvey, *CIA: The Myth and the Madness* (Baltimore: Penguin Books, 1974), Ch.7, 'Intelligence to Please', pp.148–60. A brief discussion can also be found in Richard K. Betts, *Soldiers, Statesmen and Cold War Crises*, Ch.10, 'Careerism, Intelligence and Misperception', pp.183–208.

Similar to those of Howells, are the observations of Yehoshafat Harkabi in 'The Intelligence Policymaker Tangle', *Jerusalem Quarterly* 30 (Winter 1984), 125–31. For a different angle on intelligence and policymaking, focusing on the influence of intelligence estimates on US–USSR relations, see Raymond L. Garthoff, *Intelligence Assessment and Policymaking: A Decision Point in the Kennedy Administration* (Washington DC: The Brookings Institution, 1984).

53. Handel, *The Diplomacy of Surprise*, pp.1–31, 241–53; or Michael I. Handel, 'Surprise and Change in International Politics', *International Security* 4 (Spring 1980), 57–85. On the failure of Japanese intelligence, see Ashman, *Intelligence and Foreign Policy: A Functional Analysis* (Ph.D. dissertation, University of Utah, 1973), pp.99–119. See also Christopher Andrew and David Dilks (eds.), *The Missing Dimension: Governments and Intelligence Communities in the 20th Century* (Urbana, IL: University of Illinois Press, 1985).

54. Ashman, p.53.

55. Ibid., p.61. On Hitler as a decision-maker, see Walter Warlimont, *Inside Hitler's Headquarters* (London: Weidenfeld & Nicolson, 1964); Percy Ernst Schramm, *Hitler: The Man and the Military Leader* (Chicago: Quadrangle Books, 1971); Franz Halder, *Hitler as a Warlord* (London: Putnam, 1950); Andreas Hillgruber, *Hitler's Strategie: Politik und Kriegsfubrung 1940–1941* (Munich: Bernard Greife, 1982).

On Ribbentrop's attitude, see D.C. Watt's introduction in David Irving, *Breach of Security* (London: William Kimber, 1968) in particular pp.39–40. Also David Irving, *The War Path* (New York: Viking Press, 1978), pp.243–4.

56. McLachlan, *Room 39*, p.135.

57. Handel, *The Diplomacy of Surprise*, pp.241–355.

58. Howells, p.352 (my emphasis).

59. A well-known example is Walter Langer's psychoanalytical study of Hitler for the OSS during the Second World War. Walter Langer, *The Mind of Adolf Hitler* (New York: Basic Books, 1972); also James David Barber, *The Presidential Character: Predicting Performance in the White House*, 2nd ed. (Englewood Cliffs, NJ: Prentice Hall, 1977).

60. Gerhard L. Weinberg, 'Hitler's Image of the United States', *American Historical Review* 69 (July 1964), 1004–21.

61. See John Erickson, *The Road to Stalingrad: Stalin's War with Germany* Vol.1 (New York: Harper & Row, 1975); John Erickson, *The Soviet High Command* (London: Macmillan, 1962). See also Seweryn Bialer (ed.), *Stalin and His Generals* (New York: Pegasus, 1969).

62. Ronald Lewin, *Churchill as a Warlord* (New York: Stein & Day, 1982). For a different viewpoint, see A.J.P. Taylor *et al.*, *Churchill Revisited: A Critical Assessment* (New York: Dial Press, 1969). More sympathetic is Martin Gilbert's *Winston S. Churchill*, Vol.5, *The Prophet of Truth* (Boston: Houghton Mifflin, 1977) and Vol.6, *Finest Hour 1939–1941* (Boston: Houghton Mifflin, 1983). R.W. Thompson, *Generalissimo Churchill* (New York: Charles Scribner's Sons, 1973).

63. Gaddis Smith, 'How the British Held the Fort', *The New York Times Book Review* (25 December 1983), pp.1–2. This is a review of Martin Gilbert's *Winston S. Churchill*, Vol.6, *Finest Hour*.

64. Lewin, p.75.

65. See McLachlan, *Room 39*, Ch.6, pp.124–43, and Ch.15, pp.338–67. Many leaders cannot resist the temptation to become their own intelligence officers. This practice is dangerous for the following reasons: (a) Leaders have only a limited amount of time to devote to the in-depth analysis of almost any subject. (b) Most often they are not experts or have only limited knowledge of the problems they intend to analyze. (c) Above all, they will be unable to be objective on exactly those subjects that interest them the most. (d) They tend to focus on pressing issues but ignore other important issues. This danger is best demonstrated by the statement attributed to Kissinger, 'I don't know what kind of intelligence I want, what I know is when I get it.'

66. Major Sir Desmond Morton, quoted in R.W. Thompson, *Churchill and Morton* (London: Hodder & Stoughton, 1976), p.45.

67. Lewin, p.21.

68. Ibid., pp.30–31.

69. Ibid., p.20.

70. Howells, p.364. On supplying US Presidents with the 'right information' or the information they like to hear, see, among others: Thomas Powers, *The Man Who Kept Secrets: Richard Helms and the CIA* (New York: Alfred A. Knopf, 1979), in particular Chs.10–12; David Halberstam, *The Best and the Brightest* (New York, Random House); and Morton H. Halperin, *Bureaucratic Politics and Foreign Policy* (Wasington, DC: The Brookings Institution, 1974).

71. McLachlan, *Room 39*, p.366.

72. See Nigel West, *MI6: British Secret Intelligence Service Operations 1909–1945* (London: Weidefeld & Nicolson, 1983), pp.137–9.

73. Alouph Hareven, 'Disturbed Hierarchy: Israeli Intelligence in 1954 and in 1973', *The Jerusalem Quarterly* 9 (Fall 1978), 3–19; and Janice Gross Stein, 'The 1973 Intelligence Failure: A Reconsideration', *The Jerusalem Quarterly* 24 (Summer 1982), pp.41–54.

74. Perrow, p.21.

75. Howells, p.362.

76. A recently published article by a former senior Israeli intelligence officer (apparently the former head of collection of Israeli military intelligence) tries to demonstrate that the 'purely rational' decision-making process in intelligence analysis as well as in intelligence relations with policymakers can exist. The author recommends that the collected facts be allowed to speak for themselves. In light of his experience, this is a startlingly naive recommendation (yet a persistent one) because (a) the intelligence process cannot be totally isolated from the effect of politics; and (b) facts *don't* and cannot speak for themselves. See Brigadier General (ret.) Yoel Ben-Porat, 'The role of the Political Level in Estimates', *Haaretz* (in Hebrew) (20 March 1984), p.3; see also Yoel Ben-Porat, 'Estimates – Why They Collapse', in *Ma'arachot*, (in Hebrew) (October 1983), pp.29–39.

77. Handel, *Perception, Deception and Surprise*, p.17.

78. On the military personality and intelligence see: Aluf Hareven, 'Disturbed Hierarchy: Israeli Intelligence and 1954 and 1973', *Jerusalem Quarterly* 9 (Fall 1978), 5–19.
    For the reasons outlined in the preceeding text – and primarily, for the low interest in, and regard for, intelligence work by military people (according to McLachlan), McLachlan suggests that this work is better performed by civilians. See McLachlan, *Room 39*, Ch.15. In his conclusion he recommends that ' ... intelligence for the fighting services should be directed as far as possible by civilians'. pp.365, 342–5. He makes a powerful case, but seems to carry it a bit too far. See also Handel, 'Intelligence and Deception', p.140.

79. Quoted from Wesley K. Wark, 'Baltic Submarine Bogeys: British Naval Intelligence and Nazi Germany 1933–1939', *The Journal of Strategic Studies* 6 (March 1983), 60–81, 78.

80. Quoted from Collier, pp.64–5, 70.For the problems of, and measures taken to improve, the coordination of British intelligence operations during the Second World War, see:McLachlan, *Room 39*, p.298, Ch.11, 'Three Heads are Better ... '. Includes an excellent discussion of British intelligence coordination at the highest level during the Second World War. See also McLachlan, 'Naval Intelligence in World War II', p.222. See also F.H. Hinsley *et al.*, *British Intelligence in the Second World War*, Vol.1 (London: HMSO, 1979), Ch.9: 'Reorganizations and Reassessment During the Winter of

1940–1941', pp.267–314, in particular pp.291–314; and Vol.2 (New York: Cambridge University Press, 1981), Ch.15, 'Development and Organization of Intelligence', pp.3–41.
81. Hughes, pp.49–50.
82. R.V. Jones, *Most Secret War* (London: Hamish Hamilton, 1978), p.157.
83. McLachlan, *Room 39*, Ch.11, 'Three Heads are Better ... ', p.298.
84. Graham T. Allison, *Essence of Decision* (Boston: Little Brown, 1971); Morton Halpern, *Bureaucratic Politics and Foreign Policy* (Washington DC: Brookings Institution, 1974); and Patrick McGarvey, 'CIA: Intelligence to Please', in Morton Halpern and Arnold Kanter (eds.), *Readings in American Foreign Policy: A Bureaucratic Perspective* (Boston: Little Brown, 1973), pp.318–28.
85. Irving Janis, *Victims of Groupthink* (Boston: Houghton Mifflin, 1972).
86. Michael I. Handel, 'Avoiding Political and Technological Surprise in the 1980s', in Roy Godson (ed.), *Intelligence Requirements for the 1980s: Analysis and Estimates* (New Brunswick, NJ: Transaction Books, 1980), pp.85–112, 105.
87. On the problems of parochialism, over-secrecy, compartmentalization, coordination, and the 'indivisible nature' of intelligence work, see also McLachlan, *Room 39*, pp.360, 362–3; also Lowenthal.
88. McLachlan, *Room 39*, p.366.
89. See Lowenthal.
90. Alexander L. George, *Presidential Decision Making in Foreign Policy: The Effective Use of Information and Advice* (Boulder, CO: Westview Press, 1980), in particular, pp.145–169; and Alexander L. George, 'The Case for Multiple Advocacy in Making Foreign Policy', *American Political Science Review* (September 1972), 751–95.
91. Betts, 'Analysis, War and Decision', pp.77–8.
92. George, *Presidential Decision Making*.
93. Ibid., pp.195–6, 207.
94. Ibid., p.203.
95. Ibid., p.204.
96. Ibid. Betts, 'Analysis, War and Decision', p.77.
97. Betts, 'Analysis, War and Decision', p.76.
98. Ibid.
99. George, *Presidential Decision Making*, p.204.
100. Janis, pp.210–11.
101. Ibid., pp.207–24.
102. See George, *Presidential Decision Making*, pp.169–74; Jervis, *Perception and Misperception in International Politics*, pp.415–18; Betts, 'Analysis, War and Decision', pp.80–81; Janis, pp.215–16.
103. Betts, 'Analysis, War and Decision', p.80.
104. In the acquisition of information, a balance must also be struck between technological and human intelligence. The trend during the last two decades has been to invest more heavily in the technical collection of information and relatively to weaken the human effort. This is not an unexpected development in view of the fantastic progress in technology in recent years, yet it will inevitably result in a search for 'the coin not where it fell but under the lamp'. The emphasis on technical collection through such methods as satellite reconnaissance and electronic monitoring will naturally focus on the military and not the political-diplomatic dimension, and on military capabilities rather than on intentions. Nevertheless, there is no substitute for the human collection effort when it comes to the political dimension. Normally, only the agent on the spot may be able to give timely warning of a plan for a coup d'etat in Saudi Arabia. No satellite could report a last-minute decision by Galtieri and the Argentinian military junta to launch an attack on the Falkland Islands half a year ahead of earlier plans, nor could it warn against a car bomb or terrorist attack by a radical Iranian group in Lebanon. See also Patrick J. McGarvey, *CIA: The Myth and the Madness* (Baltimore: Penguin 1972), Ch.5, 'Technology: The Tail Wagging the Dog?', pp.93–116.
105. See Handel, *Perception, Deception and Surprise*; Betts, *Surprise Attack*, pp.285–312.

106. On protecting air fields against surprise attacks, see P. Korobkov, 'Dispersed Basing of Aviation Under Conditions of Waging a Modern War', in Douglass and Hoeber (eds.), pp.216–25.

107. One weapons system that was considered to have great potential to halt a surprise attack (with the central front in Europe being the particular consideration) was the neutron bomb – a low-yield intense radiation nuclear bomb which presumably could be used instantaneously with less fear of the conflict deteriorating into nuclear escalation. See Col. Daniel Gans, 'Neutron Weapons: Solution to a Surprise Attack?', *Military Review* (January 1982), 19–37 (Part I) and (February 1982), 55–72 (Part II).

108. This discussion is primarily based on Perrow; all quotations are from this excellent article. See also Daniel F. Ford, *Three Mile Island: Thirty Minutes to Meltdown* (Harmondsworth: Penguin Books, 1982), and Barry A. Turner, 'The Organizational and Interorganizational Development of Disasters', *Administrative Science Quarterly* 21 (Sep. 1976), 378–96.

6

Diplomatic Surprise

Surprise is an inherent part of human affairs – it occurs in politics, economics, technology, psychology, literature, and music as well as in war; yet research on the subject has thus far been confined to its military use alone. Problems such as the causes of frequent intelligence failures; the methods and paradoxes involved in predicting surprise attacks; the role of deception; and the optimal timing of a surprise attack have all been thoroughly explored.[1] Since research on the theory of military surprise seems to have reached the point of diminishing returns, it is necessary to expand in new directions. Although the development of a general theory of surprise may be possible in due course, studies of the non-military manifestations of surprise must come first. This article examines one such non-military area – that is, the role of surprise in foreign policy.

In order to narrow the scope of the article, it is assumed that there is little difference between military and diplomatic surprise as far as the difficulty in avoiding a surprise is concerned. Although developed in the study of military surprise, the following theories serve as valid explanations in the diplomatic realm: signal to noise ratio; deception; rigid concepts projected upon the enemy; pathologies in communication and organization; uncertainties and contradictions inherent in intelligence work; and alert fatigue, or the so-called 'cry wolf syndrome'.

NORMAL AND SURPRISE DIPLOMACY

In *The Structure of Scientific Revolutions*, Thomas S. Kuhn makes a distinction between normal science and revolutionary science.[2] Normal science consists of the routine, day-to-day research with which the majority of scientists are concerned. Revolutionary science, which arises in response to scientific anomalies and crises in research, advances new concepts that involve a paradigm shift. A similar distinction can also be made in the world of diplomacy. Normal or routine diplomacy[3] characterizes most diplomatic activity – and revolutionary or surprise diplomacy[4] involves radical changes in well-established policies. The following spectrum schematically illustrates these poles of diplomatic activity and the gradations of conduct that can occur between them.

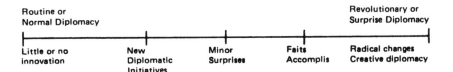

Most foreign policy is based on a high degree of continuity, inertia, and incremental decision-making that is rarely questioned by those who participate in the implementation process. Nevertheless, it is often claimed that 'the uncertain nature of international affairs creates a demand for flexibility as a safety valve'.[5] In reality, the shapers of foreign policy seldom avail themselves of this safety valve. Instead of exploring new, imaginative courses of action in order to cope with uncertainty, political leaders usually cling to the 'security' of well-known policies. Such behavior is typical of must bureaucracies, not only those responsible for the implementation of foreign policies. As a result, most of the actions taken by states in foreign affairs are readily predictable. Moreover, the adherence to obsolete policies on major issues often prevents the improvement of relations between states and diverts attention from more basic problems.

The normal solution to a stubborn foreign policy problem is the *new policy initiative*, which is a new but not unexpected move in a familiar direction. A new initiative is usually intended to avoid stagnation or crisis rather than to facilitate a change in policy. Slightly more than an incremental change, the policy initiative is a variation on a theme; in this category, we can include for example the numerous American mediation efforts between Israel and its Arab neighbors prior to the Sadat peace initiative in 1977, and new American or Soviet proposals in the SALT talks. As will be shown in Table 1, in a basic typology of surprise in international politics, we can distinguish between surprises according to the *impact* they have on the international system (either major or minor), and according to the *number* of states participating in launching the surprise (that is, whether the surprise is unilateral, requiring no collaboration, or a bilateral surprise, requiring the collaboration of two or more states).

When a new initiative is not sufficient to bring about the desired change in the international environment, a statesman may resort to the

Table 1.

	Minor Surprises	Major Surprises—Faits Accomplis
Bilateral Surprises	—Joint American-Soviet Middle East declaration, October 1977	—Rapallo agreement, 1922 —Nazi-Soviet Non-Agression Pact, 1939 —American-Chinese rapprochement, 1971 —Arab oil embargo, 1973
Unilateral Surprises	—Soviet recognition of Israel, 1948 —Sadat's first peace initiative, February 1971 —Sadat's declaration of his intention to open the Suez Canal, 1975	—Sadat's Peace Initiative, November 1977 —Mendes-France's decision to terminate French involvement in Indo-China, 1954 —Hitler's *faits accomplis*: German rearmament, 1935 Remilitarization of the Rhineland, 1936

use of a *minor surprise* or a *fait accompli*. A minor surprise can be defined as an unexpected move which is intended to change the trend in relations between two or more states although it *does not* have a radical impact on the balance of power in the international system and may be reversible. Sadat's first peace initiative on 4 February 1971, or his decision to open the Suez Canal ahead of time in 1975 are examples of unilateral minor surprise. However, minor surprise can also be bilateral, as is demonstrated by the joint American-Soviet statement on the Middle East which was issued on 1 October 1977.

Furthermore, there are situations in which old policies can only be changed through a major diplomatic surprise or *fait accompli*. A shift in policy that could otherwise take decades to accomplish (if at all), may, as a result of a daring diplomatic maneuver, be compressed into a considerably shorter period of time. Sadat's decision to embark on a peace initiative in 1977 is the most obvious example. By going to Jerusalem, he circumvented the prolonged negotiations, cut short the formalities, and accelerated the chance of achieving peace in the Middle East – goals which would have taken years to accomplish at the scheduled Geneva Peace Conference.

Surprise diplomacy can be used to transcend old policies through two interrelated elements, namely, secrecy and shock. Secrecy provides a safe atmosphere in which the two (or more) sides in a bilateral or collaborative surprise can negotiate and make the necessary preparations for fundamental policy changes. In this kind of situation, surprise is not necessarily a goal in its own right – it is merely the by-product of the secrecy which is needed to protect the embryonic relationship from the interference of other states. Secrecy is always important, but in some cases, the element of shock is the goal of the diplomatic surprise.

Shock is intended to throw the adversary off balance and force him to change an earlier policy in a more positive direction. The purpose is to facilitate a breakthrough in routine and stagnant situations; and while the adversary is still paralyzed from the effect of the shock, quick action must be taken to prevent a return to the routine. Surprise in this case is almost always unilateral as in President Sadat's expulsion of the Soviet military experts in 1972, or his peace initiative in 1977. By throwing the Soviet military experts out of Egypt, Sadat compelled the USSR to supply his country with massive weapons shipments that it had previously refused to send.[6] By coming to Jerusalem to negotiate directly with Israel, Sadat forced Israel to bypass the Geneva conference and make greater concessions.[7]

A *fait accompli* is usually defined as any *unilateral act* (which can involve either a major or minor surprise) taken by one state against the interests of another. In this context, the term *fait accompli* will be more specifically defined in order to distinguish it from a major diplomatic surprise, with which it can have common elements. On the above spectrum, a *fait accompli* should appear between a major and minor surprise.

Like a major diplomatic surprise, a *fait accompli* can have a decisive effect on the balance of power in the international system (e.g. Hitler's declaration in March 1935 of Germany's intention to rearm and the remilitarization of the Rhineland in March 1936). The difference between the two, however, is that while having a strong impact, a *fait accompli* is only a surprise in terms of *timing*. Thus, Hitler's decision to remilitarize the Rhineland surprised most observers in the choice of *time*, but not by his choice of object. The Western democracies were fully aware of Hitler's intention to rearm Germany and his long-range plan to remilitarize the Rhineland. From Taiwan's point of view, the American decision in January 1979 to establish full diplomatic relations with the People's Republic of China and to simultaneously sever relations with Taiwan, must have come only as a surprise in timing. Similarly, should the United States decide to negotiate with or recognize the Palestinian Liberation Organization, it could surprise Israel only by its timing. A major diplomatic surprise, on the other hand, is unexpected in terms of timing and object. In addition, a *fait accompli* is always a unilateral act, while a major surprise can be a unilateral act *or* the outcome of collaboration between two or more states. Therefore, a *fait accompli* is an important surprise whose impact is tempered by the fact that its substance was known in advance.

A major diplomatic surprise is an unexpected move which has considerable impact on the real or expected balance of power in the international system or a major subsystem. Such a surprise involves the great powers either directly or indirectly and has implications that transcend the regional system. An unanticipated agreement between Libya and Chad, Morocco and Algeria, or Uganda and Tanzania for instance, does not seriously affect the global balance of power.

The astonishing Rapallo agreement in 1922 between the Soviet Union and the German Weimar Republic was exaggeratedly *perceived* by the Western democracies as a major shift in the European balance of power.[8] A rapprochement between the same two countries in August 1939 not only affected the fate of Poland and the European balance of power, but also, for example, soured Japanese–German relations.[9] The American–Chinese rapprochement of 1971 also had global repercussions: it improved Japanese–Chinese relations and caused tensions in American–Japanese relations. The Soviet Union may have been induced to seek accommodation with the United States through the SALT talks or with NATO in order to counterbalance the American tilt toward China. Alternatively, the new US–PRC relationship could force the Soviet Union to invest more in its national security. The Russians, as a matter of fact, seemed to do *both* things. Immediately following Nixon's announcement of his planned trip to Peking, the Russians hastily unfroze negotiations which had deadlocked for months on Berlin and on the problem of guarding against accidental nuclear war (see Kissinger's *White House Years*, pages 766–7). At the same time, they continued to increase their nuclear and conventional arsenals. In total, the agreement could gradually transform the loose bipolar international system into a world with three power centers. It is effects such as these that characterize the major diplomatic surprise.

Finally, Sadat's peace initiative transformed the regional balance of power in the Middle East by at least temporarily eliminating Egypt from the military coalition of Arab confrontation states; and it also led to the exclusion of the Soviet Union from the Middle East peace process while the United States was able to intensify its involvement. Indirectly, it might also have important implications for the oil export policies of Saudi Arabia and the Persian Gulf states.

It is important to distinguish between bilateral and unilateral major diplomatic surprises. The bilateral surprise requires a coordinated change of policy by two or more states. The often prolonged and public signalling process that takes place between the two states before they arrive at an agreement, makes it easier (in theory but not in practice) for intelligence organizations to gain some inkling of an impending rapprochement. A major unilateral surprise, as well as a *fait accompli*, is initiated by one state, often at the decision of a single leader. When a single leader springs a surprise without even consulting his close advisors, then that type of surprise is undoubtedly very difficult to anticipate because of the limited, perhaps non-existent, warning signals. Table 1 categorizes examples of surprise according to the above analysis.

Another important factor in the initiation of major shifts in foreign policy is a function of commitments to allies and the degree of dependence on other countries. If allies agree to modify existing relations, the new foreign policy will be easily implemented. However, a state that is planning to reorient its policies cannot usually afford to consult its allies for two main reasons: (1) Allies would never agree to a move that jeopardizes their own interests; and (2) Secrecy would be compromised. Naturally, the United States could not consult Taiwan (or even Japan) on its decision to approach the People's Republic of China because Taiwan could never be expected to agree to a move which was diametrically opposed to its interests. Furthermore, any state resenting such a move would automatically breach the secrecy in an attempt to foil the rapprochement. In the extreme case of the Middle East, it is obvious that Sadat would never have gotten anywhere if he had consulted with Arab allies on his decision to negotiate directly with Israel. (Sadat shrewdly consulted his Arab allies *after* he had already committed himself to go to Jerusalem.)

In the Middle East, certain American commitments to Israel have hampered the ability of the United States to redirect its policy with regard to the Palestinian Liberation Organization. Earlier American promises to Israel not to negotiate with the PLO as long as the PLO refused to amend its national covenant and recognize United Nations Security Council Resolution 242, meant that the slightest deviation from this promise would evoke loud cries of protest from those who had been betrayed. Usually, the government initiating a diplomatic surprise has decided that it will sacrifice the interests of its allies; very often however, this choice is not made or is made too late because of moral or practical commitments to close allies.

THE PATTERN OF BILATERAL DIPLOMATIC SURPRISE

The most interesting cases of major bilateral diplomatic surprise fit a common pattern which can be divided into three main stages. During the first stage, both sides re-evaluate their basic interests and conclude that a reorientation in their foreign policies is necessary. In the second stage, they establish a dialogue to determine whether or not an agreement can be reached. The third stage follows once an agreement has been reached and made public.

Stage I

Both sides begin to realize, at first independently of each other, that their foreign policies must be revised. Oftentimes, these policies are no longer logical in view of changing circumstances and goals. For example, the American embargo on the People's Republic of China, as well as the ban on American visits to China, had lost much of their original purpose by the 1970s. Likewise, Chinese anti-American policy gradually weakened when faced with the mounting Soviet threat in the late 1960s.

It must be emphasized that a bilateral surprise (and sometimes even a unilateral one)[10] cannot occur unless *both sides* have more or less simultaneously concluded that earlier policies should be discontinued. A potential diplomatic maneuver by Israel and the PLO has not been possible because the two sides have been unable to even open a dialogue. In 1968, then-Israeli Defense Minister Dayan tried to arrange a meeting with the PLO's Yasir Arafat through an Arab intermediary (Fadua Tokan of Nablus), but he was ignored; in 1970, Israel again signalled the PLO by actually offering refuge to PLO members who were fleeing from Jordan after King Hussein opened an all-out war against them. Again, the signals received no reply, and constructive change was effectively blocked. Dayan may have been ahead of time in the same way that Sadat was when he announced his Peace Initiative in 1977; yet while Sadat was also ahead of Israel, the Israelis fortunately responded positively to his signals.

A reorientation of basic policies is facilitated by a change in leadership. A new and uncommitted leader may, at first, appear to wholeheartedly support established policies because it is dangerous to provoke opposition during a period of transition. Nevertheless, this same leader will find it easier to change the order of national priorities at a later stage. In Israel, for example, Begin was not committed to the same goals as the Labor Party which had been in power from 1948–1977. He was therefore in a better position to respond to Sadat's signals. For his part, Sadat did not have Nasser's commitment to either collaboration with the Soviet Union or to war against Israel. After claiming victory in 1973, he could afford to change the policy of confrontation with Israel, thereby giving his 'Egypt first' policy top priority.

It is relatively easy for leaders to maintain secrecy during the first stage, since few people participate in the formation of high level policy. (Authoritarian systems are for the same reason conducive to the preservation of secrecy.) It is, of course, vital that a similar revision of policies occur on both sides, but each step in the re-evaluation process need not be synchronized – one side may be in a greater hurry, as in the

Ribbentrop–Molotov case. Germany and the Soviet Union began to recognize the need for a policy change at about the same time; however, Hitler was under pressure to reach an agreement by 1 September 1939, which was the latest date he had set for his attack on Poland. The severe time constraints during the summer of 1939 forced Hitler to make many concessions to the Russians. Although not in a hurry, the Russians could ill-afford to refuse German offers and the corresponding pressure for speed.

During the first stage, both sides frequently make use of foreign mediators who are not necessarily told the exact meaning of the messages they convey. The Israelis and Egyptians used the good offices of Rumania and Morocco; and the United States employed the good offices of the French, Rumanians, and Pakistanis in order to signal its policy changes to the People's Republic of China. When the preliminary feelers have proven successful, the parties establish direct contact. Symmetrical interests are not necessary, but the existence of a common, viable interest is essential.

Stage II

At this juncture, each party must determine to its own satisfaction that the other side is serious in its intentions. Secrecy is crucial so that each side has the option of withdrawing without losing face or undermining existing relationships with other states should the move fail. During the negotiations between Nazi Germany and the Soviet Union in 1939, most exchanges were oral, and the few documents which did exist were not written on official paper. In general, care is taken to keep direct contacts behind a veil of secrecy. Kissinger's trip to China prior to the American–Chinese rapprochment was covered by an elaborate deception plan, as was the meeting between Israeli Foreign Minister Dayan and Egyptian Deputy Prime Minister Hassan el Tohamy in Morocco in 1977. Successful preservation of secrecy allows the two sides to build confidence in each other. Should a leak occur, both parties would be quick to deny any contact, and subsequent renewal of such contacts would be difficult.

In the first and second stages, *some* signals are transmitted publicly, but secret information may also be passed to third parties by participants who object to the new policies. In fact, it can be argued that some of the signalling must be made in public in order to convince the other side of serious intentions. In most cases however, the open signals are perceived only by the two sides directly involved in the process. As more and more people, however, take part in the preparations for negotiations and cover-up plans, the likelihood of a breach of secrecy increases. In the case of the Ribbentrop–Molotov agreement, for example, Germans who opposed Hitler's plans warned the British intelligence and Foreign Office several times that Germany was making offers to the Soviet Union. Although preconceptions, excessive noise, and deliberate deception make a clear analysis difficult in such instances, alert observers may detect significant changes at this stage.

The intricate process of action and reaction continues until the intentions of each side are unmistakable; then the negotiations are usually accelerated and culminate in the surprise agreement. Henry Kissinger has described the U.S.–China signalling process preceding the announcement of President Nixon's intended visit to China in the following terms:

> Behind the climax were thirty months of patient and deliberate preparation as each side felt its way, gingerly, always testing the ground so that a rebuff would not appear humiliating, graduating its steps so that exposure would not demoralize nervous allies or give a new strategic opportunity to those who did not wish them well.[11]

According to some analysts, President Nixon sent signals to the People's Republic of China in his *Foreign Affairs* article of October 1967[12] – this means that the American–Chinese exchange of feelers took place over a period of approximately three years. Nazi Germany and the Soviet Union exchanged signals (stages 1 and 2) for at least half a year before concluding the non-aggression pact in late August 1939.

After basic decisions have been made at the highest level during the first stage, lower level officials can continue the talks. The negotiations do not always directly concern political issues; sometimes, the two sides begin with the less binding subjects of economic and cultural relations. The preliminary United States–China exchange of signals concerned cultural and economic matters (e.g. the ping-pong team invitation). Finally, the parties progress to direct talks on political issues that were only obliquely mentioned in previous meetings.

The re-evaluation of fundamental policies continues well into the second stage, since the first two stages are overlapping phases in which the evolution of basic interests and policies occurs first, but does not come to an abrupt end as the second stage begins. By definition, no one is certain of the final course of action until the last moment, so both sides keep their options open. The continuation of earlier policies while negotiations are in progress, as well as the conflicting trends within the political elite of each state, add to the noise to signal ratio. The predicament of the political intelligence analyst was aptly described by a bewildered British intelligence officer after the failure to anticipate the Ribbentrop–Molotov agreement.

In general, we feel ourselves, when attempting to assess the value of these secret reports, somewhat in the position of the captain of the Forty Thieves when, having put a chalk mark on Ali Baba's door, he found that Morgiana had put similar marks on all other doors in the street and had no indication to show which mark was the true one. In this case there were passages in many of our reports which told against the probability of a German–Soviet rapprochement. We had no indications that these statements were in general any less reliable than those in a contrary sense.[13]

Stage III

The new course of action is made public soon after an understanding is reached. All that remains is to establish the final details of the agreement and to devise strategies to counter the objections of third parties. Diplomatic surprise is theoretically simpler to forecast, but in practice the record of timely warnings is no better than that of military surprise. Most often, third parties are totally surprised despite the available indicators. President Nixon's announcement that he was going to visit China evoked the following reaction from some observers. 'The moment the president completed his surprise announcement, the cameras switched to the studio commentators for a reaction. They were all flabbergasted, and one anchorman was literally speechless as he looked out into the living rooms of America. The country was stunned and so was the world.'[14]

DIPLOMACY OF SURPRISE IN DIFFERENT INTERNATIONAL SYSTEMS

Surprise diplomacy can take place in any type of international system where there is a need to break away from old policies. Historical evidence would suggest a connection between the type of international system and the frequency with which major surprise can be expected to occur. The key factor is the ideological character of the system in question. Diplomatic surprises occur more frequently in the classical balance of power system than in a tight bipolar system or a multipolar system; and more in a loose bipolar system than in a tight bipolar one. The impact and intensity of such a diplomatic maneuver stands in inverse relation to the probability of its occurrence.

In the classical balance of power system the actors, who share a common ideology and common values, are allowed (and required) to make rapid shifts in alliances in order to enhance their own power and maintain systemic equilibrium.[15] Surprise diplomacy therefore serves as the regulator of the system;[16] the fact that such maneuvers occur often does not mean that they are any less surprising. The absence of conflicting political beliefs smooths the way for rapid transitions from one alliance to another because there are no ideological barriers to impede communication. In this system, the higher the number of principal actors or centers of power, the higher the probability of surprise.

The theory of international systems makes a distinction between homogeneous and heterogeneous (or revolutionary) systems. The homogeneity of the classical balance of power system means that diplomatic surprises are more frequent, and consequently are of lower intensity and impact than those that occur in a heterogeneous, ideologically split bipolar or multipolar system.

In a revolutionary international structure, incompatible ideologies exacerbate tensions and impede communication between states. All states, in particular the weaker ones, find it more difficult to maneuver.[17] Major diplomatic surprises are much less likely to take place in this rigid environment – but once they do occur, they have a correspondingly stronger effect on the division of power. Ideological competition tends to repress creative diplomacy – and promote a routine and unimaginative diplomacy in which states interpret the behavior of other states according to rigid concepts. While it is more difficult for leaders in such circumstances to embark on new policies, dramatic surprise eventually becomes the only way to shake off the restrictions of old patterns of behavior.

The European multipolar system between the two world wars is a good example of a heterogeneous system;[18] it was divided among democratic, fascist, and communist ideologies which made it increasingly difficult to maneuver and maintain the European equilibrium. Given the venomous ideological conflict between Nazi Germany and Communist Russia in 1939, a treaty uniting them behind a common cause seemed to be an extremely unlikely event. When such a treaty was actually signed, it had a powerful effect on the European balance of power. Prior to the completion of the treaty, the British had been repeatedly warned that the two states might reach some agreement, but they misinterpreted the signals. Dismissing warnings with the attitude that the treaty was impossible, 'the British counted confidently on ideological estrangement between Fascism and Communism ...'.[19]

At the height of the Cold War, intense ideological competition meant that the great powers made extensive efforts to prevent the defection of small allies. The defection of even a relatively unimportant state (e.g. the Russian–Egyptian arms deal of 1955, or the 'defection'

of Cuba to the Eastern bloc) was perceived as having global repercussions.

A more recent example of unforeseen agreements between the
adherents of competing ideologies is the American–Chinese rapprochement of 1970–1971. Experienced observers of the more than twenty-
year-long propaganda war between the capitalist and communist
systems assumed that they would be unable to even hold constructive
talks, let alone agree to establish diplomatic relations or collaborate in
the international system. Similarly, analysts of Middle Eastern politics
felt that after five wars and thirty years of bitter propaganda warfare,
Egypt and Israel were unlikely to enter into direct and constructive
negotiations. In the above hetereogeneous systems, long-standing
ideological rivalries and preconceptions made it difficult for observers
to anticipate changes in allegiance.

All of these moves across ideological barriers have one element
in common. *In the final analysis, the states involved preferred their
national interests to their ideological commitments*. Stalin opted for an
agreement with Nazi Germany – the anathema to communism – in
order to preserve the security and interests of the Soviet Union; Nixon
preferred a rapprochement with the People's Republic of China to
American commitments to Taiwan; and Sadat chose to focus Egypt's
energy inward rather than continue an endless Arab–Israeli conflict.
The political intelligence analyst can derive an important lesson from
these examples: that is, he should concentrate on power calculations
rather than on ideological rhetoric.

The problem of anticipating a major diplomatic surprise is directly
related to the more familiar problem of forecasting and prediction in
international politics.[20] This problem has received much attention,
either directly or implicitly, in the theories of *realpolitik* and 'interests'
as developed by Thucydides (common interests are the best agreement
between states); Machiavelli (the ideas of *necessitas* and *raison d'état*);
and more recently, Hans Morgenthau (the concept of interest defined
in terms of power). *According to these theories, the most important
foreign policies of states can be predicted and identified because they
operate on a logic of their own, and do not depend on a particular leader.*
Therefore, an observer will be aided in his prediction of a state's actions
once he understands its basic interests. Thus, if China feels threatened
by the Soviet Union and is not strong enough to defend itself against the
threat, it must seek help from another country. The only nation with
strength sufficient to counter the Soviet menace is the United States, so
China has no choice but to turn to the United States. Likewise, if any
German government (regardless of the form of government) between
the two world wars had wanted to occupy Poland (as was the goal of

many German politicians during the Weimar Republic when Germany was too weak to act), then sooner or later Germany would have had to seek an agreement, even if a temporary one, with the Soviet Union.

Reality is, however, much more complicated than is implied by the theory of *realpolitik*. Although it helps the analyst to explain the inevitable logic of a major diplomatic surprise or *fait accompli* from hindsight, the theory does not enable him to make forecasts with a high degree of accuracy. Even if *raison d'état* could demonstrate that a particular event would have to take place in the long run, it could never predict *when* the event would occur. This is true because such theories do not adequately consider the *human or psychological factors* in foreign policy: different leaders of the same country *do not* have to behave according to the same logic; and countries with different political systems deal with similar circumstances in various ways.

Above all, it is the human element which makes the anticipation of surprises so difficult in international politics. There are few innovative leaders who will run the risk of replacing ossified political concepts; most tend to follow the foreign policies of their predecessors, making few, if any, incremental changes.

It is interesting to note that most of the major diplomatic surprises have been initiated at the senior policymaking level – and not by professional diplomats. Professional diplomats rarely approach foreign policy with innovative ideas despite their greater familiarity with many issues. This is partially explained by the fact that diplomats, as members of a bureaucracy, usually work to secure and consolidate existing ties rather than explore alternative courses of action.

The frequency with which surprise is used in foreign policy depends on the combination of two variables: leadership style and the type of political system. Diplomatic surprise can theoretically be carried out in four different situations.

An authoritarian leader in a non-democratic system. This combination is most conducive to the use of surprise tactics because it offers maximum control and secrecy to the leader, who is inclined to act independently and can afford to disregard legal or parliamentary opposition to his decision. Leaders such as Hitler, Stalin, and Sadat had to be cunning and brutal in the prolonged climb to the top; and since surprise and shock tactics were their most valuable tools in the consolidation of domestic power, it was logical that they would continue to employ the same tools in the practice of foreign policy.

An authoritarian style leader in a democratic system. Because of their powerful style, leaders such as de Gaulle and to a lesser extent

President Nixon or Prime Minister Begin, were able to channel the foreign policies of their respective nations in radically new directions. Nevertheless, many features of democratic politics reinforce incrementalism and inhibit the use of 'surprise' strategies; the 'slower reaction' of a democratic system often poses problems in competition between democratic and non-democratic regimes.[21] Strong leadership is the key element that enables surprise to occur in this system.

A democratic leader in a democratic system. In this situation, the leader is usually limited to the implementation of incremental changes in major foreign policy issues since he works by consensus and is open to cross-pressures. A rare example of surprise involving this combination was, perhaps, the decision of French Prime Minister Pierre Mendes-France to quickly withdraw from Indo-China in 1954.

Collective leadership in a non-democratic system. Surprise would seldom take place in this combination because it also works by consensus-building and compromise. Khrushchev's shock diplomacy in Berlin and the Cuban missile crisis may be regarded as rare instances of surprise generated by collective leadership in a non-democratic system.

The most important factor in the launching of a diplomatic surprise is the presence of an authoritarian style *leader*; the nature of the political system itself is secondary. Nevertheless, the presence of an authoritarian leader is only a necessary but not a sufficient condition – he must also be creative and inclined to take high risks. Despite the fact that *raison d'état* may dictate changes in entrenched policies, such changes do not occur very frequently because the right type of leader is not in charge. A change in American policies toward China may have been justified perhaps as early as 1961 (and certainly from the mid-1960s onward) but without President Nixon's initiative, the normalization of relations with China still might not be accomplished today.

MILITARY AND DIPLOMATIC SURPRISE COMPARED

A military surprise attack is an antagonistic act that is intended to obtain immediate short range objectives (such as decisive military victory), and it enables the attacker to dictate the direction and pace of developments. A diplomatic surprise, which can be either positive (i.e. improve relations between states) or belligerent, also has an immediate dramatic impact, but its most important results often materialize long after the original effect of the shock has worn off.

Table 2.
Favorable or Unfavorable Conditions For Radical Political Changes

	Favorable Conditions	Unfavorable Conditions
Type of Leadership	—Strong, authoritarian style —Little consulting with aides —Creative, open-minded, secure —Inclined to take risks	—Democratic, consensus-building style —Tends to consult excessively with aides —Uncreative, conservative, insecure —Low tendency to take risks
Type of Political System	—Authoritarian —Secretive —Government-controlled media	—Democratic, open society —Many conflicting and influential interest groups —Diplomacy conducted in a visible and open manner (high degree of mass media involvement)
Expectations From Old Policies	—Old policies conflict with national interests —Continuation of old policies will create dangerous situations; the state's position will be weakened —New national goals are identified	—Continuation of old policies is not perceived as conflicting with national interests —No new national goals are identified—no changes in national priorities
Allies and External Factors	—Weak or few conflicting commitments to allies —Little dependence or perception of dependence on other states that would be opposed to a change in policy —A non-ideological international system—homogeneous	—Strong commitments to allies who would object to policy change —Credibility of commitments to other nations may be weakened —Heavy dependence on states that would oppose a change —Highly ideological, heterogeneous global system

Perhaps the most critical difference is that in military affairs, surprise is an ever-present factor that must be taken for granted; military men are educated to consider the use of surprise on every level of action (though this does not necessarily make it easier to predict). In diplomacy, on the other hand, stability, and continuity are the accepted norms.[22] Surprise in foreign policy therefore requires an unconventional approach, since it is not an integral part of the education of diplomats and decision-makers. While the military analyst is always trying to avoid a possible surprise, the political analyst is less attuned to abrupt change, concentrating instead on existing trends.

Military surprise also differs from diplomatic surprise in its much greater complexity, for it can occur on many levels and involve any combination of the following elements: area or areas chosen for the attack; strategy and tactics employed; use of new military doctrines; technological surprise in the use of new weapons systems; surprise in terms of timing, and so on. *In theory*, the task of predicting a diplomatic surprise should be simpler because the number of possible major shifts in the foreign policy of a given state is limited. But in practice, political intelligence analysts commit the same perceptual errors as their military colleagues. A few examples will clarify this point.

Early in 1921, both Germany and the Soviet Union were faced with only two viable choices: they could (1) improve diplomatic relations with the Western democracies, or (2) turn to each other. Choice of the latter option would mean the improvement of relations despite all earlier animosity and conflicting interests. At first, the two countries preferred the first choice, although they never wholly relinquished the second; and in order to keep both options open, they negotiated simultaneously with the Western democracies and with each other. After coming up against the obstinate and short-sighted bitterness of England and France in the wake of the First World War, they had no alternative but to turn to each other. For this reason alone, the Western powers should not have been so surprised by the ensuing German–Soviet accord.

In 1939, history repeated itself. Once Hitler resolved to dismember Poland, he faced two choices in the accomplishment of his goal. Given his earlier moves in Austria and Czechoslovakia, he could attempt to obtain (1) British and French consent, or (2) Russian consent. When Hitler failed to receive the open or tacit approval of the West for such a move, he could only turn to the Soviet Union. As for the Russians – they desired security through a reliable defense agreement with Great Britain and France or, alternatively, through an understanding with Germany itself. As in 1921, each side initially attempted to reach an agreement with the reluctant French and British governments while paralleling discussions in the West with direct negotiations with each other. Moreover, the USSR and Germany gradually developed an interest in preventing each other from reaching a separate understanding with the Western democracies. Britain and France should have foreseen the 'bombshell' of the Ribbentrop–Molotov non-aggression pact which was as much the outcome of their own policies as it was the result of German and Soviet perfidy. The British subsequently tried to counter the Russian–German surprise with a bombshell of their own: the ratification of the Anglo-Polish treaty on August 25 did indeed surprise Hitler, but it came too late to change the course of events.

As far as the Chinese–American relationship was concerned, a dramatic maneuver could only be in one direction. After the Chinese communists gained power in 1949, the American–Chinese relationship steadily deteriorated into the direct military conflict of the Korean War, and remained hostile until the late 1960s. The only form which a major diplomatic surprise could take would be the normalization of U.S.–Chinese relations.

Sadat's unprecedented visit to Jerusalem is analogous to the American–Chinese rapprochement. For the second time, Sadat shattered the conceptions of Israeli policymakers and the intelligence community, catching all sides unawares. This time, though, he destroyed political instead of military conceptions. It was a political 'Ramadan'. Before Sadat's peace initiative in November 1977, the Israelis had continuously tried to organize a meeting between Israeli and Egyptian leaders through the good offices of Rumanian President Ceauşescu and the Shah of Iran; and despite Foreign Minister Dayan's secret meeting with Egyptian Vice-Premier Tohamy in Morocco, Israelis did not put much hope in this kind of meeting which had been taking place since 1948. At best, the Israelis hoped for a ministerial-level meeting on neutral ground. In the words of former Israeli head of military intelligence, Major-General Shlomo Gazit,

> we encountered a methodological problem but we had no established procedures telling us how to seek out and examine signals indicating a movement toward peace. We had had much experience involving war – we knew what signals to search for. But what indicated peace? We had seen a form of Arab expression that was different in both form and content. But could we ignore the possibility that such talk might be Arab propaganda intended to dull our senses and deceive us?[23]

President Sadat had secretly revolutionized his own concepts of the Arab–Israeli conflict and left the rest of the world behind. A similar change had also to precede the U.S.–Chinese rapprochement. According to Kissinger, this change occurred when 'the leaders in the two countries had begun for the first time in a generation to regard each other in geopolitical rather than ideological terms'.[24]

Diplomatic surprise may appear to be less complicated than military surprise in terms of possible combinations, but it is in fact no easier to anticipate, especially since it does not require many participants: a radical diplomatic move can often be planned and initiated by a single leader with the knowledge of few, if any, of his advisers. Because the number of people taking part in the preparation and execution can be kept to a minimum, the emission of signals can be tightly controlled. In the analysis of diplomatic surprise, heavy emphasis must be placed on the psychological makeup, motives, and perceptions of one political leader.

Almost all military surprises not only require a large number of participants, but also necessitate the movement of troops and supplies, periods of intensified communications, extensive planning efforts, training, and finally, the concentration of the formations to be used in the attack. The emission of signals is thus practically unavoidable. All of Sadat's political surprises were so successful as surprises because he did not even inform anyone of his decisions until just before they were made public (e.g. the ouster of the Soviet military advisors in July 1972 or the declaration of his readiness to visit Jerusalem in November 1977). Paradoxically, the only one of his surprises which was preceded by quite a few signals (that were ignored!) was his decision to launch the 1973 war against Israel. Here, military activities provided many signals that were never available in his diplomatic surprises. Obviously, in a unilateral diplomatic surprise or in a *fait accompli*, the preservation of secrecy is even easier because they do not require collaboration with another state.

Military intentions can almost always be corroborated by examination of material evidence and capabilities. The intelligence analyst can at least compare declared intentions of peaceful coexistence with the development of military hardware. If he observes that a state is building a substantial offensive military capability, he will doubt its intentions, and continuously re-evaluate them in light of these developments. The political intelligence analyst, on the other hand, cannot adjust his conclusions on the basis of any 'objective' material evidence, but he *can* carefully watch for changes in his adversaries' attitude through media reports and the speeches of various leaders. His analysis nevertheless lacks an important dimension which is available to the military analyst, as changes in attitude of the mass media can be controlled and manipulated by the government (unlike material military developments).

It is virtually impossible to maintain complete secrecy in bilateral diplomatic surprises because of the interaction between the states planning the political maneuver. For example, Hitler and Stalin exchanged many public signals before commencing negotiations in 1939. In his anniversary speech to the Reichstag on 30 January 1939, Hitler omitted his customary diatribe on communism and the Soviet Union. On March 10, Stalin signaled back by declaring that the Soviet Union would not let itself be drawn into a senseless conflict with Germany on behalf of the weak Western democracies. This reply was not lost on the Germans.[25] An additional public signal was sent on May 5 when the Russians announced that Maxim Litvinov, the commissar for foreign affairs, 'had resigned'. Litvinov had been a well-known advocate of closer collaboration with the Western democracies. Then, beginning in May 1939, the German newspapers restrained their attacks on the Soviet Union.

In the case of the American–Chinese accord, public signals took the form of positive moves toward China by President Nixon and National Security Advisor Kissinger in 1969. The United States allowed the automatic validation of passports for scholars, journalists, and Congressmen who wished to visit China, and permitted American tourists to purchase Chinese goods up to a maximum of $100 (July 1969). The $100 limit was lifted in December 1969. In 1970, Nixon's special report to Congress on American foreign policy included many positive references to the Chinese. Another positive sign was the fact that on October 1, 1970, during China's National Day celebration, Edgar Snow, an old American friend of China, was seen standing next to Chairman Mao. On the same occasion, Mao expressed his growing dissatisfaction with the Soviet Union while making what Mr. Snow construed as sympathetic remarks directed at the United States. On October 26, Nixon became the first American president to refer to mainland China as the 'People's Republic of China' – the use of China's official name was an important symbolic move. On 6 April 1971, relations between the two countries had thawed to the point where a cultural exchange could take place; when the American ping-pong team was invited to visit China, it eagerly accepted, and the Americans were able to meet with Chou En-lai in Peking only eight days later. Nixon's 15 July 1971 announcement of his plans to visit China caused complete surprise because all of these public signals had not been perceived as leading to a change in policy.

Military and diplomatic surprise also differ in the emphasis that is placed on assessing the participants' *intentions* and *capabilities*. In the study of military surprise, analysts must devote equal attention to these two factors and their interaction, whereas the study of diplomatic surprise requires that attention be skewed in favor of intentions. Obviously, the launching of a military surprise means that the potential attacker must possess a certain minimum level of capabilities; and the greater the capabilities, the more attention military analysts should give to the way in which capabilities influence intentions.

This is not usually a primary consideration for the political analyst because he does not deal with actions that necessitate the immediate use of capabilities. In fact, the opposite is true – he should becorr e more alert when a state's power is weak relative to its most important goals, since diplomatic activity is often intended to compensate for the lack of capabilities. Though weakness can provide incentive to resort to diplomatic surprise, it is not a sufficient condition. Although Israel is a weak and isolated nation, its leaders (with the possible exception of former Foreign Minister Dayan) were not creative enough to come up with the kind of new ideas that Sadat did. Other examples illustrate the importance of weakness in unexpected political maneuvers. The Rapallo agreement in 1921 allied two exhausted states whose capabilities had been seriously drained during the First World War. In the case of the Ribbentrop–Molotov treaty in 1939, the Soviet Union signed a non-aggression pact with Germany because it realized that war with Germany would be disastrous as long as the Western democracies remained remote and impotent. Even if Stalin realized that the Soviet Union would eventually have to fight Germany, this agreement still gave him valuable time to prepare for war. Hitler needed the treaty with the USSR primarily because Germany was not strong enough to fight a war on two fronts.

The People's Republic of China desired better relations with the United States in order to counterbalance the powerful Soviet threat; and to a lesser extent, the same was true of the United States. Finally, Sadat did not come to Jerusalem as a result of some lifelong devotion to peace – he came because Egypt had not been able to accomplish its goals (i.e. regaining the Sinai) through the use of military force. For its part, Israel was aware that its military capabilities might not hold out indefinitely in a protracted war against all Arab states.

THE COSTS AND BENEFITS OF MILITARY AND DIPLOMATIC SURPRISE

The act of surprise offers only advantages to the initiating side in war, while in diplomacy it involves a trade-off. Surprise is the multiplier of any military force. As a fundamental part of military planning, it dictates the course of war on the attacker's terms, reduces his casualties, and improves his chance of achieving victory.[26] However, diplomatic surprise entails both costs and benefits.

When Rathenau decided to sign the treaty with Russia at Rapallo, he knew that it would undermine Germany's relations with the Western democracies. Similarly, Hitler's decision to sign a non-aggression agreement with Soviet Union without consulting his allies, Italy and Japan, may have cost him dearly in the later stages of the war. When Mussolini later took his 'revenge' and attacked Greece without consulting Hitler, he embroiled the Germans in a Balkan war at a strategically difficult time. The Japanese on the other hand turned south against the United States instead of north against the Soviet Union, remaining neutral on the Russian front in part as a result of the humiliating way that the Germans had treated them. As for the Russians, the agreement with Nazi Germany damaged their political standing with the communist parties of Europe, perhaps convincing the Europeans that Russian interests took precedence over communist ideology. From a historical perspective, this might have been one incentive for the development of Euro-communism and diverse communist ideologies.

In his visit to Jerusalem, Sadat also had to pay a substantial price. He alienated almost all of the Arab states, thus losing much of his prestige and some economic support in the Arab world. Sadat did gain the Sinai Peninsula and American economic and military support for Egypt, but he sacrificed at least in the short run, Egypt's bid for leadership of the Arab world.

There is also a price to be paid on the domestic scene. The reversal of a policy to which the state, and many interest groups have long been committed engenders sharp criticism. The leaders responsible for the change in policy must therefore be sure that they have adequate support with which to implement the desired new policy – or in non-democratic systems, they must be sure that they possess sufficient power to crush any resistance by force.

It is easier to undertake a major diplomatic revolution in an authoritarian system than in a democratic one: government-controlled media can ease the people's acceptance of new ideas. This does not guarantee that internal opposition to such moves is nonexistent. Of course, when Stalin and Hitler were at the peak of their power and in full control of their political systems, they faced no real opposition. But in Egypt, Sadat is in a more precarious position. He must contend with opposition from the army, religious groups, and political parties from the left (those who follow the Soviet line) and the right (nationalistic and Pan-Arab groups).

The leader of a democratic country faces stiffer opposition. President Carter's decision to establish full diplomatic relations with the People's Republic of China and to unilaterally sever relations with Taiwan brought him under attack in Congress. Carter was simply paying the price for bringing President Nixon's China policy to its logical conclusion.

In Israel, Prime Minister Begin encountered strong criticism of the negotiations with Egypt from both his own party and the opposition. Since he could secure the delivery of certain goods by himself, Sadat found it difficult to understand why Begin had to undergo the lengthier, more arduous process of obtaining Knesset approval. Soon, Sadat realized the advantages this system held for him, and he learned to manipulate the Israeli opposition forces. The difficulties involved in

calculating the costs and benefits of a decision to implement a controversial new policy can offer some explanation for the infrequency of
major diplomatic surprises.

Table 3.

Military Surprise	Diplomatic Surprise
—An inherent part of military planning. It does not require a shift in military concepts and thinking.	—Not accepted as part of normal procedures. It requires that a leader make a creative shift in his political concepts.
—Forecasting or warning against military surprise is very difficult because of the large variety of possibilities for surprise in terms of time, place, methods, doctrine, and weapons technology. The emission of signals prior to a large-scale military operation is unavoidable.*	—Forecasting is difficult as a result of the small number of participants and the problem of anticipating the changing concepts and perceptions of a single leader. Secrecy is relatively easy to preserve, especially in unilateral surprise. There are always signals preceding a bilateral surprise. A unilateral surprise or *fait accompli* may sometimes have no signals at all.
—Has immediate impact. The price paid by the surprised side is heavy.	—The impact can be immediate or delayed. Surprised parties are seldom subject to immediate danger.
—Offers *only* advantages to the attacking side from the military point of view—but can otherwise increase the desire for revenge on the part of the attacked side or evoke a strong political reaction from non-involved states.	—Always involves a trade-off for the initiating side (a trade-off between conflicting interests, goals, and political allies).
—Is always an antagonistic, "negative" act.	—Can either be a bilateral, cooperative effort—or a unilateral act or *fait accompli*. Can be positive or negative.
—Equal importance must be attached to the complex interaction between the enemy's *intentions* and *capabilities*.	—Attention must primarily though not exclusively be paid to intentions (especially those of individual leaders). Capabilities are not a limiting factor in non-coercive diplomacy and cannot on the whole be meaningfully corroborated with intentions.

* Without going into detail, it must be mentioned that the signals inevitably emitted can be
shrouded by noise through deliberate deception. In other words, the observer can be deliberately misled as to the true goals of the activities that cannot be hidden from public view
(e.g. the Soviet and Warsaw Pact exercises prior to the invasion of Czechoslakia, or the
Egyptian and Syrian maneuvers before the 1973 war with Israel). Infrequently, an attack can
be launched from an almost static position through the use of forces in being. (This last
situation also depends on the risks an attacker is willing to take.)

CONCLUSION

There is still much to learn about the positive and negative aspects of
surprise and abrupt change in diplomacy. The failure to anticipate a
surprise and prepare countermoves can have serious implications, as a

Table 4.

	Type of Surprise	Type of International System	Availability of Warning Signals
Hitler's remilitariza-tion of the Rhine-land March 1936	Unilateral *Fait accompli*	Multipolar Heterogeneous Ideological ten-sions	Many warning signals avail-able Surprised in terms of timing only
The Ribbentrop-Molotov Agree-ment August 1939	Bilateral Major diplomatic surprise	Multipolar Heterogeneous Powerful ideologi-cal competition	Considerable number of sig-nals available Major block to prediction of this surprise was the be-lief that ideological com-petition precludes political agreements.
American-Chinese Rapprochement 1971	Bilateral Major diplomatic surprise	Loose bipolar Heterogeneous Ideological ten-sions	Many public signals ex-changed Deception on the tactical level to maintain secrecy
Sadat's Expulsion of the Soviet Mili-tary Advisors From Egypt July 1972	Unilateral *Fait accompli*	Loose bipolar Heterogeneous Ideological compe-tition	Very few, if any signals Not expected because of the belief that Egypt was too dependent on the Soviet Union
Sadat's Peace Initi-ative November 1977	Unilateral Major diplomatic surprise	*Global system:* Loose bipolar Heterogeneous Ideological tension *Local system:* High tensions Zero-sum-game characteristics	No signals

Major States Surprised	Mediation by Other States	Type of Leader and Domestic Political System	Short and Long Range Impact
France Great Britain France's eastern allies		Authoritarian leader in an authoritarian system Very few German decision-makers apprised of the decision in advance	Drastic shift in the European balance of power France's East European system collapsed German power grew
Opponents France Great Britain Poland *Allies* Japan Italy Communist parties	Italy for Germany Bulgaria for the Soviet Union Both played a minor role	Authoritarian leaders in authoritarian systems	Immediate result was the division and partition of Poland, and WWII USSR & German collaboration
Opponents USSR *Allies* Japan S. Vietnam Taiwan	The good offices of Rumania, Pakistan, and France were used	China: Authoritarian leadership in authoritarian system USA: Strong leadership in a democratic system	Eased American way out of Vietnam Caused friction in American Japanese relations PRC joined the UN Counterbalanced power of the USSR Enhanced Nixon's popularity before the US elections
USSR USA Israel		Authoritarian leader in authoritarian system No one knew of Sadat's plan until the last moment	Blackmailed the USSR into supplying Egypt with weapons Enabled Egypt to prepare for the 1973 war Showed possibility of a shift to pro US policy
Opponents Israel USSR *Allies* Other Arab states PLO USA	The good offices of Morocco, Rumania were used	Authoritarian leader in authoritarian system Announcement is total surprise to everyone, including Egyptian foreign minister	Bypassed the Geneva Peace Conference, Accelerated negotiations; Excluded the USSR from talks; Drove a wedge between Israel and the US, Major change in Middle Eastern balance of power

look at historical examples clearly demonstrates. Had the British and French been more alert to the signals indicating a possible Soviet–German agreement in the summer of 1939, they could have taken diplomatic or military steps to block or hinder such an agreement. They might have taken one, or a combination of the following steps: (1) pressured the Polish government to allow the presence of Soviet troops on their soil in the event of a German attack; (2) outbid the Germans by recognizing the Soviet Union's right to an extended sphere of influence along the Baltic; (3) shown more interest in their military negotiations in Moscow by sending a higher level delegation to attend the conference; (4) made strong statements or taken military moves to convince the Germans of British and French readiness to come to Poland's rescue. The British government did in fact make such a statement but only after the signing of the Ribbentrop–Molotov agreement when it was already too late.

If fully aware of the contacts between the United States and the People's Republic of China from 1969 to 1971, the Soviet Union might have tried to 'blow up' the process of rapprochement by starting an intense propaganda campaign or by reducing troop concentrations and tensions on the Soviet–Chinese border.

The 'Arab Oil Embargo' that was imposed during the Yom Kippur War caught Western Europe and the United States by surprise although there had been ample signals that the Arabs would use the oil weapon as part of their war against Israel.[27] A thoughtful evaluation of these signals might have stimulated the planning of countermeasures (e.g. a new policy for storing oil, earlier attention to the problem of developing alternative energy sources, and better political co-ordination between Western nations). Such countermeasures would have at least eased the psychological pressure – that is, the sense of helplessness and frustration felt by the Western nations in the wake of the surprise move.

All available evidence (not discussed in this article) indicates that despite the narrower scope of diplomatic surprise, it is nevertheless difficult to avoid. Particular attention must be given to the role of individual leaders, who indisputably play a central role in the initiation of a diplomatic surprise. On the positive side, more must be learned about surprise as a means to introduce constructive changes in foreign policy. Study of this topic may also help us to discover more about the conditions for *change* in foreign policy in general, and the circumstances which are more conducive to the emergence of diplomatic surprises. As recent events have proven, surprises confined to the political arena can be very unpleasant, but can also present new, positive opportunities.

NOTES

1. On this point see Michael Handel, *Perception, Deception and Surprise: The Case of the Yom Kippur War* (Jerusalem: The Leonard Davis Institute for International Relations, the Hebrew University, 1966, Occasional paper no. 19), pp.1–2; or Michael Handel, 'The Yom Kippur War and the Inevitability of Surprise', *International Studies Quarterly* Vol. 21, No. 3, Sept. 1977, pp.461–501. This is also the point made by Richard K. Betts, 'Analysis, War and Decision: Why Intelligence Failures are Inevitable', *World Politics* Vol. 31, No. 1, Oct. 1978, pp.61–89.
2. Thomas S. Kuhn, *The Structure of Scientific Revolutions* (Chicago: University of Chicago Press, 1973) Second edition enlarged. For criticism on his theory see Imré Lakatos and Alan Musgrave, *Criticism and the Growth of Knowledge* (Cambridge: Cambridge University Press, 1970); For the application of his theory to the social sciences and history see David A. Hollinger, 'T.S. Kuhn's Theory of Science and Its Implication for History', *American Historical Review* Vol. 78, No. 2, April 1973, pp.370–93.
3. George Liska, *Beyond Kissinger: Ways of Conservative Statecraft* (Baltimore: The Johns Hopkins University Press, 1975). Liska has described routine diplomacy as follows:

    Routine diplomacy smooths and implements established relations with the aid of only marginal adjustments [i.e. it is the opposite of surprise]. Its most constructive performance is in evolving formulas of mutually acceptable compromise which permit the existing configuration to endure and avoid thus the risks of convulsions of radical change. (p.25)

4. Liska defines creative diplomacy or the diplomacy as the means to reach a higher or new level of normal diplomacy.

    Creative diplomacy rearranges the setting within which negotiations for compromise occur ... the supreme expression of creative diplomacy is the 'diplomatic revolution' [i.e. a major diplomatic surprise]: a fundamental recasting or reversal of existing alignments which automatically marks a major stage (and a rare turning point) in the evolution of the international system. Revolutionizing diplomacy is not, therefore, to be confused with revolutionary diplomacy ... Creative diplomacy can be either offensive or defensive in strategic purpose; and the transformation sought may be for repose as well as for major or continuing change. (pp.25–6)

5. Charles Lockhart, 'Flexibility and Commitment in International Conflict', *International Studies Quarterly* Vol. 22, No. 4 December 1978, p.550. This article discusses the question of flexibility versus commitment in the specific context of direct conflict and bargaining in crisis situations.
6. See Anwar el Sadat, *In Search of Identity: An Autobiography* (New York: Harper Books, 1978), pp.228–31; Mohamed Heikal, *The Sphinx and The Commissar* (New York: Harper and Row, 1979), Chapter 15, pp.242–56; and Alvin Z. Rubinstein, *Red Star On the Nile* (Princeton: Princeton University Press, 1977), pp.188–212.
7. *Ibid.* Chapter 15, pp.188–212. Sadat's calculations in his decision to launch the peace initiative in 1977 (and all other examples used in this article) are discussed in detail in my book, *The Diplomacy of Surprise* (Cambridge: Harvard Center for International Affairs, 1981).
8. Walter Laqueur, *Russia and Germany: A Century of Conflict* (London: Weidenfeld and Nicolson, 1960), pp.128–131.
9. The German chargé d'affaires in Washington summarized the impact of the German announcement of Ribbentrop's forthcoming visit to Moscow in the following way:

    That the impending conclusion of the German–Soviet non-aggression pact has caught all the other Powers entirely unawares, and has decisively altered the balance of power, not only in Europe but throughout the world, in favour of the

Axis Powers with all that that implies, is the first reaction of the American press, which was itself completely taken by surprise. (Documents on German Foreign Policy, Series D, Vol. 6, 1939, p.180).

10. Sadat's peace initiative was a unilateral surprise; but through earlier contacts with Israel, Sadat knew in advance that Israel would respond positively to his move.

11. Henry Kissinger, *White House Years* (Boston: Little, Brown and Company, 1979), p.163. See also pp.187, 685.

12. Richard M. Nixon, 'Asia After Viet Nam', *Foreign Affairs*, Vol. 46, No. 1, Oct. 1967, pp.111–25.

13. Quoted in Sidney Aster, *1939: The Making of the Second World War* (New York: Simon and Schuster, 1973), p.318.

14. Marvin Kalb and Bernard Kalb, *Kissinger* (Boston: Little, Brown, 1974), pp.251–2.

15. For the characteristics of the balance of power system see Edward Vose Gulick, *Europe's Classical Balance of Power* (New York: W.W. Norton, 1967); Morton A. Kaplan, *System and Process in International Politics* (New York: Wiley and Sons, 1967), part 1; Butterfield, 'The Balance of Power' in Herbert Butterfield and Martin Wright, eds., *Diplomatic Investigations* (Cambridge, Mass: Harvard University Press, 1968), pp.132–48, 149–75; Hans J. Morgenthau, *Politics Among Nations*, 5th ed. (New York: Alfred A. Knopf, 1973), pp.167–224; Ernst B. Haas, 'The Balance of Power – Prescription, Concept, or Propaganda', *World Politics* Vol. 5, July 1963, pp.442–77; Stanley Hoffmann, 'Balance of Power', *The Encyclopedia of the Social Sciences* (old) Vol. II, pp.395–9; Kyung-Won Kim, *Revolution and International System* (New York: New York University Press, 1970).

16. For the development of this concept see Richard N. Rosencrance, *Action and Reaction in International Politics* (Boston: Little, Brown, 1963).

17. For a detailed discussion on the bargaining position of weak states in different international systems see Michael I. Handel, *Weak States in the International System* (London: Frank Cass, 1979) Chapter 4, pp.169–216.

18. For the multipolar system, see Raymond Aron, *Peace and War* (Garden City, N.Y.: Doubleday, 1966), pp.94–149; and Stanley Hoffmann, *Gulliver's Troubles* (New York: McGraw-Hill, 1968), pp.3–52. (The term multipolar is actually inexact since there can only be two poles by definition.)

19. A.J.P. Taylor, *The Origins of the Second World War* (New York: Atheneum, 1968), p.229.

20. See for example Saul Friedländer, 'Forecasting in International Relations', *Futuribiles* (Geneva: Librarie Droz, 1965); Klaus Knorr and Oskar Morgenstein, *Political Conjecture in Military Planning* (Princeton, N.J.: Princeton Center of International Studies, Nov. 1968), Policy Memorandum No. 35.

21. Yehezkel Dror, 'How to Spring Surprises on History' (Mimeo), A paper presented at the Leonard Davis Institute for International Relations – International Conference, 'When Patterns Change: Turning Points in International Politics', 1979, p.3. Even if leaders in democratic societies decide to reverse earlier policies either by their own initiative or by public pressure, the process of change will be slowed down and implemented more gradually.

22. I am grateful to Major-General Shlomo Gazit, former head of Israeli Military Intelligence for suggesting this point to me.

23. Quoted from Major-General Shlomo Gazit, *Notes: The Arab-Israeli Conflict After the Camp David Agreements* (Mimeo), p.6.

24. Henry Kissinger, *White House Years* (Boston: Little, Brown and Company, 1979), p.685.

25. For a detailed discussion of the background to the Ribbentrop–Molotov Agreement, the Nixon rapprochement with the People's Republic of China, and Sadat's shock diplomacy, see my book, *The Diplomacy of Surprise: Hitler, Nixon, Sadat (Op. Cit.)*.

26. A common fallacy concerning military surprise attacks is that a true surprise has only taken place if the whole war (of which the surprise is only one battle) ends in

victory. The side that initiates a very successful attack may ultimately lose the war (e.g. the Nazi attack on Russia in 1941, the German offensive in the Ardennes in 1944, the Japanese attack on Pearl Harbor in 1941, the Arab attack on Israel in 1973). The major decision is whether or not to go to war. Once one side decides that it will go to war, it is naturally interested in maximizing its gains in the opening move by destroying the highest possible proportion of the enemy's forces. Whether the initiating side ultimately wins or loses, it still profited from the surprise attack. A surprise attack always strengthens the surprising side. Every state wants to avoid being the object of surprise, because even if it has the strength to recuperate from the initial shock, the price it pays will be high. Generally, the attacking side plans to emerge victorious (the Japanese attack on Pearl Harbor and the Arab attack on Israel in 1973 are unusual in the sense that the attacking sides did not necessarily expect to win – but rather planned on making temporary gains that would improve their political bargaining positions).

27. See Raymond Vernon (Ed.), *The Oil Crisis* (New York: W.W. Norton, 1976) pp.11–12; 61–2; 80–1. Typically, despite the many explicit warning signals, the radical increase in oil prices by OPEC, and the OAPEC embargo came as a total surprise and caught the Western world off guard.

7

Military Deception in Peace and War

*The ultimate goal of stratagem is to make the enemy quite
certain, very decisive, and wrong.*[1]

*If surprise is indeed the most important 'Key to Victory', then
stratagem is the key to surprise.*[2]

*Ming: Lay on many deceptive operations. Be seen in the west
and march out of the east; lure him in the north and strike him
in the south. Drive him crazy and bewilder him so that he
disperses his forces in confusion.*[3]

THE TAKING OF AI[4] (Fig. 1)

Deception can be defined as a purposeful attempt by the deceiver to
manipulate the perceptions of the target's decision makers in order to
gain a competitive advantage. Whenever and wherever a situation
exists – be it in the conduct of business, economic life, politics, or love –
through which cheating might provide the needed advantage, there are
always individuals or groups prepared to resort to it. Although cheating, deception and fraud are commonly punishable by law or discouraged by informal sanctions when they occur in civilian affairs, this
is obviously not the case in war or, to a lesser extent, in international
politics, which are subject to their own norms of behavior and morality
(i.e., *raison d'état*). Deception in international politics (not to be
discussed here) and more frequently in war is rewarded by greater
achievements and success; yet while it is potentially very helpful in the
conduct of war, deception has often failed, or failed to achieve the
intended objectives, and on occasion has even proved to be counter-
productive. Despite this note of caution, deception must be seen as an
accepted and integral part of every military commander's repertoire.
In the words of Sun Tzu, 'All warfare is based on deception'.[5]

Deception in war should be considered a *rational*, necessary activity
because it acts as a force multiplier, that is, it magnifies the strength or
power of the successful deceiver.[6] Forgoing the use of deception in war
is tantamount to undermining one's own strength. Therefore, when all

Figure 1

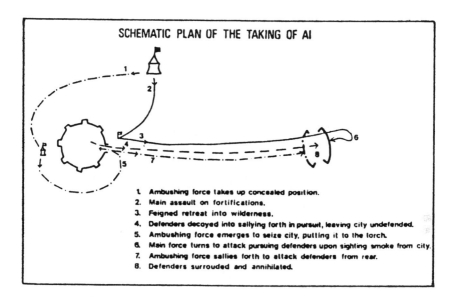

SCHEMATIC PLAN OF THE TAKING OF AI

1. Ambushing force takes up concealed position.
2. Main assault on fortifications.
3. Feigned retreat into wilderness.
4. Defenders decoyed into sallying forth in pursuit, leaving city undefended.
5. Ambushing force emerges to seize city, putting it to the torch.
6. Main force turns to attack pursuing defenders upon sighting smoke from city.
7. Ambushing force sallies forth to attack defenders from rear.
8. Defenders surrounded and annihilated.

other elements of strength in war are approximately equal, deception will further amplify the available strength of a state – or allow it to use its force more economically by achieving victory at a lower cost and with fewer casualties. If opponents are unequally matched, deception (and surprise) can enable the weaker side to compensate for its numerical or other inadequacies. For this reason, the side that is at a disadvantage often has a more powerful incentive to resort to deceptive strategy and tactics. This was recognized by Clausewitz, who did not otherwise stress the importance of deception in war.

> The weaker the forces that are at the disposal of the supreme commander, the more appealing the use of cunning becomes. In a state of weakness and insignificance, when prudence, judgment, and ability no longer suffice, cunning may well appear the only hope. The bleaker the situation, with everything concentrating on a single desperate attempt, the more readily cunning is joined to daring. Released from all future considerations, and liberated from thoughts of later retribution, boldness and cunning will be free to augment each other to the point of concentrating a faint glimmer of hope into a single beam of light which may yet kindle a flame.[7]

This implies the existence of an inverse relationship between strength and the incentive to employ deception – a relationship which is readily borne out by a look at military history. During the Second World War, the British had a stronger incentive to use strategic deception than the Germans did; and as long as the Israelis perceived themselves as being weaker than their Arab opponents (in 1948, 1956, 1967), they often made use of stratagem and deception, while the Arabs, who believed themselves to be superior, did not. In 1973, however, the reversal of these perceptions saw a concomitant change in the incentive to resort to deception: the Israelis relied more on material strength while the Arabs resorted to 'cunning'.

Having enjoyed overwhelming material superiority in the Vietnam War or even during the Second World War, when deception was left primarily in the hands of the British, the United States rarely used deception, with the exception of a few instances that took place on the tactical level.[8] In the early stages of the Korean War (i.e., MacArthur's landing at Inchon) when the Americans were weak, they did, as mentioned by Clausewitz, exhibit a readiness to take very high risks (a maximax strategy) and make use of deception and surprise. But as the United States increased its strength in the later stages of the Korean War, it failed to employ such elements. The landing at Inchon may, however, be linked more to General MacArthur's character and style than to a substantive change in the US high command's approach to war.

Although the tendency of more powerful states to rely on 'brute force' can be understood, it certainly cannot be justified; the strong and powerful need not waste their strength or increase their own costs simply because they are confident of victory. Strength unaccompanied by stratagem will become sterile and lead to a general decline. Perhaps for that very reason, the more powerful military establishments *must make a conscious effort* to incorporate deception into their military thinking.

*   *   *

The rational use of deception can assume a number of forms. One type of deception attempts to misdirect the enemy's attention, causing him to concentrate his forces in the wrong place. In doing this, the deceiver tries to make his adversary violate the principle of *concentration of forces* in space.[9] Well-known examples of this are the Allied plans that duped the Germans into believing that Norway and/or Pas de Calais (and not the beaches of Normandy) were possible landing sites for an Allied invasion.[10] Similarly, in 1940, the Germans helped the Allies to deceive themselves by causing them to concentrate their troops in northern France on the Belgian border rather than opposite the Ardennes.[11]

A second and related type of deception attempts to make the adversary violate the so-called principle of the *economy of force*.[12] The objective here is to make the opponent squander his resources (e.g., time, ammunition, weapons, manpower, fuel) on non-existent targets and in unimportant directions. A simple example would be to cause an adversary to fire many scarce and expensive anti-aircraft missiles at a cheap RPV decoy or an artificially created radar signature instead of at real attacking aircraft; during the Battle of Britain, the British succeeded in having the Germans attack non-existent airfields and factories by setting up phony targets and interfering with German electronic navigational aids. Other, much more complex strategic or technological ploys directed at making the enemy waste his resources can also be devised. One can 'leak' information that a revolutionary technological breakthrough (such as the development of 'death rays' or 'particle beam weapons')[13] has been achieved; this will induce the enemy to invest prodigious amounts of money, scientific man-hours and time in the wrong direction, whereas the deceiver knows that it will lead to a dead end or be too costly to be practical. An interesting example of such a 'technological' deception plan is mentioned by Montagu. The idea was to allow the Germans and Japanese to uncover Allied plans for a new design of ship that combined half the armament of a battle cruiser with the ability to carry as many as half of the aircraft of a fleet of aircraft carriers. The British, who had seriously considered constructing such battle-carriers, concluded that the ship design was technologically unfeasible, and that even if such vessels were to be built, they would be inefficient in either role. 'It had been decided that the same effort and resources as would produce and man an efficient battle cruiser and an efficient aircraft carrier would be needed to produce and man two inefficient battle-carriers with the same total armament and aircraft.'[14] The end of the war prevented this scheme from being implemented.

A third type of deception, which is also related to the two mentioned above, is intended *to surprise* the opponent – to create a situation that will subsequently cause him to be caught off guard and unprepared for action. In this case, the variety of deceptive methods most frequently employed is supposed to dull his senses and create the impression that no offensive plans are being entertained by the deceiver. This can be accomplished through the maintenance, and in fact cultivation, of normal political and economic relations up to the moment of attack, as was Hitler's policy toward Russia until the eve of Barbarossa in June 1941.[15]

When two or more states are already at war it is much more difficult to launch a surprise attack out of the blue. On such occasions, the deceiver may attempt to create an impression of routine activity by very gradually conditioning the adversary to a particular repetitive pattern of behavior. Such a ruse was used by the Germans during the Second World War when they jammed British radar stations in order to enable the German battle-cruisers *Scharnhorst* and *Gneisenau* and the cruiser *Prinz Eugen* to break out of the English Channel undetected on the night of 11 February 1942. 'The German radar officers, headed by General Wolfgang Martini, had subtly increased the intensity of their jamming over a period so that we could get acclimatized to it, without realizing that it was now so intense that our radar was almost useless.'[16]

Another way of moving large concentrations of troops towards an attack without alerting the adversary is to disguise those preparations as military maneuvers. Secrecy is further enhanced in such cases when not even the participating troops are informed that they are about to go into action. A favorite of the Soviet Union, the latter type of strategem was used on the eve of the Soviet attack on Manchuria in 1945 and the invasion of Czechoslovakia in 1968. A similar deception cover was carried out by the Syrians and Egyptians just before their attack on Israel in October 1973.

In the final analysis, all types of deception operations can be said to be directed at misleading, misinforming, or confusing an opponent on only two basic categories of information. The first is to deceive him concerning one's own *intentions*; the second is to deceive him concerning one's own *capabilities*.[17] (See figure 2.) A successful deception operation can focus primarily on one of these categories, although it often deals with both simultaneously. After all, intentions and capabilities are closely related to one another in the conduct of war.[18] Thus, convincing an adversary that one lacks certain capabilities may also convince him that because of the absence of such capabilities, the deceiving party also has no intention of carrying out a given type of operation. For example, on the eve of the Yom Kippur War, the Egyptians spread rumors that their anti-aircraft missile systems had been short of certain spare parts (capabilities) since the expulsion of the Soviet advisors in June 1972, and that therefore they obviously were not yet ready to initiate war (intentions).[19]

Deception concerning intentions will in most cases try to conceal the actual goals and plans of the deceiver. This can be brought about through secrecy (a *passive* mode of deception) or through a more deliberate, *active* plot that diverts the opponent's attention from the actual set of intentions to another. In fact, the more active type of deception must always be based on the successful concealment of one's

Figure 2

TYPOLOGY OF DECEPTION

ANALYTICALLY IN PEACETIME OR WAR DECEPTION CAN BE DIRECTED
TO CONCEAL AND/OR MISLEAD BY "REVEALING" AN ADVERSARY
CONCERNING THE DECEIVER'S INTENTIONS AND/OR CAPABILITIES. ALL
TYPES OF DECEPTION MAY BE PURSUED SIMULTANEOUSLY (THEY CAN
BE COMPLIMENTARY AND ARE NOT MUTUALLY EXCLUSIVE) AGAINST
DIFFERENT ADVERSARIES, SUBJECTS, FRONTS, ETC.

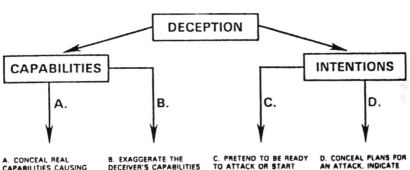

A. CONCEAL REAL
CAPABILITIES CAUSING
ADVERSARY TO UNDER-
ESTIMATE THE
DECEIVER'S REAL
STRENGTH.

AIM: TO SURPRISE
ADVERSARY ONCE THE
WAR STARTS OR LURE
HIM TO ATTACK AND
BEAT HIM.

DANGERS: CAN LEAD TO
FAILURE OF DETERRENCE,
BE DESTABILIZING, INVITE
AGGRESSION, ETC.

EXAMPLES: GERMANY
DURING WEIMAR
REPUBLIC; USSR BEFORE
1941, ISRAEL BEFORE 1967
WAR.

B. EXAGGERATE THE
DECEIVER'S CAPABILITIES
BY BLUFF, SELECTIVE
REVELATIONS OF
EQUIPMENT, WEAPONS,
ETC.

AIM, APPEAR STRONGER
THAN IN REALITY DETER
ENEMY, GAIN PRESTIGE,
INFLUENCE

DANGERS: CAN LEAD TO
AN ARMS RACE, ADVER-
SARY MAY INCREASE HIS
OWN EFFORTS OR BLUFF
MAY BE EXPOSED.

EXAMPLES: HITLER
DURING THE 1930's
MOUSSOLINI DURING THE
SAME PERIOD, "USSR'S
BOMBER" AND "MISSILE
GAPS"

C. PRETEND TO BE READY
TO ATTACK OR START
WAR EVEN WHEN NOT.

AIM; BLACKMAIL;
CONCESSIONS FROM
ADVERSARY.

DANGERS: CAN LEAD TO
AN UNDESIRED WAR,
LEAD ENEMY TO
INCREASE HIS OWN
MILITARY STRENGTH;
CHANGE HIS INTENTIONS
TO BECOME MORE
AGGRESSIVE.

EXAMPLES: HITLER IN
RHINELAND CRISIS, FIRST
AND SECOND MUNICH
CRISIS, BERLIN CRISIS,
FORMOSA STRAITS
CRISIS, ETC.

D. CONCEAL PLANS FOR
AN ATTACK, INDICATE
DESIRE TO MAINTAIN
STATUS QUO WHILE
PREPARING FOR WAR.

AIM: ACHIEVE STRATEGIC
SURPRISE.

DANGERS; WAR.

EXAMPLES. MOST
STRATEGIC SURPRISES,
BARBAROSSA, 1941;
PEARL HARBOR, 1973
WAR, ETC

actual intentions in combination with convincing the enemy of the
validity of the 'decoy' intentions. Any breach of security concerning
one's actual intentions will of course lead to failure and probably to self-
deception, and may even become an instrument for the adversary's
own purposes, in that the enemy can pretend to be deceived while he is
in fact anticipating the deceiver's move and planning to spring his own
trap.

In complex deception operations, it is therefore extremely important to have a special unit that will attempt to ascertain whether the
adversary has really swallowed the bait or is only pretending to have

been deceived.[20] Penetration of the enemy's intelligence and/or his command echelons is essential. Through the use of Ultra, the British in the Second World War were unusually successful in following up and monitoring complex plans for deception. The detailed deciphering of German codes enabled the British to check and recheck the degree of success of their deception plans and then to modify them accordingly in order to render them even more effective.[21]

Returning to the question of deception intended to conceal one's actual intentions, we find a number of examples. Before launching their first offensive against the Italian 10th Army in the Western Desert in December 1940, the British under Wavell had convinced the Italians that their intentions were purely defensive. Here is how the official British historical account summarizes this operation:

> The fact is that in war, it is usually possible to produce some sort of evidence in support of almost every course of action open to the enemy; the art lies in knowing what to make of it all. In this case, the Italian Air Force ... had observed and reported movements and dispositions with fair accuracy – indeed, it was often intended by the British that they should. The important point is that these reports were consistent with what the 10th Army were convinced was happening. They themselves were very much occupied with their own preparations for renewing the advance, and were only too ready to interpret the air reports as indicating that the British were actively improving their defensive arrange-ments. The British attempt at strategic deception was therefore successful.[22]

In this context, it is interesting to note that General Wavell was perhaps the first high-ranking British officer in the Second World War to make extensive use of strategic deception. During the summer of 1940, he established a special organization dedicated exclusively to deception operations; under the leadership of Lieutenant Colonel 'Galveston' (better known later as Brigadier Dudley W. Clarke and also as Colonel Craft Constable), this organization was located in Cairo under the cover title of Advanced Headquarters 'A' Force. As the first of its kind to initiate and control many deception operations, this organization's contribution to the overall war effort transcended the Middle East and made additional contributions to the war in Italy and the Far East, as well as in the invasion of Normandy. In fact, its operations were so successful that they later inspired the much more widely-publicized deception plans which originated in London and were coordinated by the so-called London Controlling Section.[23]

Wavell's interest in deception operations, atypical as it was, can be explained by two factors. The first and most immediate was the desperate military weakness of the British in the Middle East in general and in the Western Desert in particular. As David Mure suggests, 'Deception was really Wavell's only chance'. He *had* to inflate the Italian perception of British capabilities in the area in order to discourage, or at least slow down, the continuation of the Italian offensive towards the Suez Canal. (The Italians concentrated about 250,000 soldiers in the Western Desert while approximately 50,000 were available to the British.)

This capability-inflating type of deception was quite successfully carried out by Galveston's Advanced Headquarters 'A' Force unit in Cairo, which artfully built up a notional (i.e., non-existent) army on the southern flank of the Italian forces by placing rubber inflated tanks and 25-pounder field guns in the area, as well as a complete fake military infrastructure. The existence and location of this 'massive concentration' of British troops was then 'verified' in the reports of both German and Italian real and notional agents in Cairo, most of whom were controlled by Galveston's organization. To lend further credence to this plan, the British, among other measures, assembled almost all of their available anti-aircraft guns around the notional concentration of troops. This served the twofold purpose of convincing the Italian Air Intelligence that this terrific volume of firepower 'was part of a lavishly equipped army and moreover kept the planes well up so that they could never take a close look nor photograph too accurately'.[24] As a result, the Italians concentrated a major part of their forces on the southern flank while the real British assault led by O'Connor came from the northwestern flank. Completely caught off guard, the Italians conducted a confused battle against a force that never really materialized; in Mure's words, 'whilst [the battle was] virtually imaginary to our troops, it was terribly real to Italians'.[25] General O'Connor had exploited the situation brought about by the deception plan, and won a significant victory against a far superior Italian force.[26]

This important deception cover plan is only hinted at in the official British historical account, and is not discussed in any detail in the vast literature on the war in the Western Desert. A battle that has been accurately presented as a triumph of quality over quantity, however, should emphasize the contribution of British intelligence to the 'quality'.[27] Official British history offers only one sentence in reference to this imaginative use of artifice: it somewhat cryptically remarks that 'the keynote [of the operation] was to be surprise, achieved by secrecy and deception'.[28]

Mure's description of the seminal role played by strategem (if it is accurate) throws new light on Wavell's contribution to the offensive as compared to that of O'Connor, and explains (but does not excuse) at least some of the reasons for the dismal performance of the Italians on the battlefield. Equally elaborate and successful deception operations also preceded the two other British offensives in the Western Desert. The first laid the groundwork for 'Crusader', launched under General Auchinleck in November 1941, and the second set the stage for Montgomery's El Alamein offensive in October 1942.[29]

The second explanation for Wavell's interest in strategic and tactical deception is related to the fact that he was also the biographer of Field-Marshal Allenby, perhaps the only field commander of World War I to make extensive and systematic use of deception during his military campaign in Palestine.[30] Field-Marshal Allenby's successful resort to deception must have had a major impact on Wavell's military thinking in its formative stages.

Turning to additional examples of this type of stratagem, we see that although the British and Americans did not, and could not, conceal their intention to invade somewhere in Southern Europe, they led the Germans to believe that the invasion would take place in Sardinia, southern France, and Greece instead of in Sicily, which was the more obvious target. Similarly, Operation Fortitude, the code name of the deception preparations for Operation Overlord (the invasion of Normandy), did not try to hide Allied intentions to invade Europe or even more specifically to cross the Channel, but focused German attention on Pas de Calais.[31] So convincing was this stratagem that the Germans, anticipating a major attack in Pas de Calais, still had most of their forces in that area a few days after the invasion of Normandy was well under way. There is, by the way, very little doubt that the greatest deception efforts ever invested in a military operation were those laying the groundwork for the invasion of Normandy in 1944. Over- lord was covered by numerous complementary deception operations (some of which are probably unknown even to this day) which required careful and elaborate coordination and a meticulous follow- up operation in order to estimate the extent to which the Germans had been deceived. This tremendous and ultimately successful investment in deception plans for D-Day is not surprising. Landing operations are notoriously tricky and involve unusually high risks. The sheer number of participants in Operation Overlord (the largest landing operation in history) made it even more essential to use intricate ruses to conceal the preparations and areas selected for attack. The success of the Allied deception plans is amazing even today, and no doubt was achieved through meticulous preparation, good luck, and the poor quality of

German intelligence. The degree of surprise achieved in Operation Overlord was total – one of the few cases of a 'surprise out of the blue' with no real warning time, or any lead warning time or alert.[32]

In planning their attack on Egypt in collaboration with the British and French in 1956, the Israelis deliberately created the impression that they intended to attack Jordan by concentrating their troops closer to the Jordanian border and by escalating reprisal raids against Jordan.[33] (Secrecy was so well guarded that the British ambassador was sent to the Foreign Ministry to protest Israeli reprisals and warn against an attack on Jordan, while the British Government knew that the real object of the forthcoming attack would be Egypt.)

In another instance, President Nasser of Egypt decided to send his troops into the Sinai in mid-May 1967, thereby initiating the crisis which continued to escalate throughout the month. By the end of May, Israel and Egypt were fully mobilized and ready for war. By 2 June it became clear to the Israeli Government that war was unavoidable. The problem was how to launch a successful surprise attack when *both* sides were in a state of full alert. As part of a deception plan to conceal Israel's intention to go to war, Dayan told a British journalist on 2 June that it was both too early and too late for Israel to enter into a war. He repeated this statement during a news conference on 3 June:

> It is too late for a spontaneous military reaction to Egypt's blockade of the Tiran Straits ... and still too early to learn any conclusions of the possible outcome of diplomatic action. The Government ... embarked on diplomacy and we must give it a chance.[34]

Furthermore, a number of reservists were released for the weekend in order to create the impression that the level of preparation and alert had been reduced. It is also possible that other plans which never became known were implemented at that time. In this case, the deception was simple and successful, and Israel achieved total surprise on the morning of 5 June despite the atmosphere of crisis and the intensified intelligence alert.[35]

It is perhaps not widely known that Israeli preparations for the raid on Entebbe in July 1976 also included a plan that was intended to mislead primarily the Americans, who were apparently watching by satellite. The Israelis indicated (mainly through spreading rumors to the press) that they planned to launch a large-scale attack on PLO targets in Lebanon in order to capture hostages who could be exchanged for the hijacked airline passengers in Entebbe. As far as is known, this deception plan did indeed direct attention away from the possibility of a direct raid on Entebbe itself, and the attack was a total surprise for everyone.

During peacetime or before the initiation of hostilities, it is possible, as can be observed in the extensive literature on surprise attack, to succeed in concealing one's intention to attack; but once a state of war and conflict already exists, the intention to attack in one place or another is already taken for granted. In the latter situation, deception assumes a much more important role because it must foster in the enemy the wrong expectations concerning one's inevitable and known intention to take action. The fewer the possible avenues of attack, the more crucial a deception cover becomes. Since it was practically taken for granted that the Allies would have to attack across the Channel, the probability of success had to be increased by the use of stratagem.[36]

*   *   *

Deception can also be employed to mislead an opponent concerning the would-be perpetrator's military, primarily material, *capabilities*. The discussion of deception in this particular context presents a convenient opportunity to point out some of the potential dangers and possible damage that can result from miscalculations and the incorrect application of this art. It is important to emphasize that deception is by no means a panacea for weakness, nor is it always as successful as most of the enthusiastic literature about it seems to indicate.

Capability-oriented deception can be divided into two types. The first is intended to cause the exaggerated evaluation of capabilities in terms of both quality and quantity; the second attempts to conceal existing capabilities. The former type of bluff is normally practiced by a weaker state in an effort to deter a more powerful adversary, to translate its imaginary military superiority into political gains, or to gain enough time to close a dangerous capability gap. The second type of deception minimizes the extent of a state's real capabilities primarily in order to create the impression that is is incapable of executing certain offensive plans (i.e., to conceal its offensive intentions). The two types of deception need not be contradictory or mutually exclusive, particularly in wartime. A state may find it desirable to simultaneously conceal certain capabilities and inflate others (e.g., in terms of absolute quantities or relative quantities at different places, rates of production, qualitative achievements).

Pretending to have larger than existing capabilities is a well-known ruse in times of peace and war alike. As mentioned above, the intention behind this exaggeration is normally to deter a *stronger* adversary. This was the trick played by the Germans from 1936 onwards on the French in particular and less successfully on the British and other nations concerning the actual strength of the nascent Luftwaffe. The Germans did their utmost to impress foreign visitors such as Charles Lindbergh; Italian Air Marshal Italo Balbo; RAF Air Vice Marshal Christopher Courtney; and, later, the chief of the French Air Force, General Joseph Vuillemin. The Germans staged exciting air shows, flew in most of their latest aircraft to those airfields the guests were visiting, casually reported high production rates for advanced aircraft that in fact never went beyond the experimental stage, and gave tours of aircraft factories:

> In general, perceptions in the West of the Luftwaffe's strength were exaggerated precisely as Hitler and Göring intended. Aerial blackmailing of Germany's neighbors became an important ingredient in Hitler's diplomatic negotiations which led to his brilliant series of triumphs; the policy of appeasement was founded partially on the fear of the Luftwaffe.[37]

The inflated strength attributed to the Luftwaffe combined with the fear of British and French political leaders that 'the bomber will always get through' helped the Nazis to extract considerable political concessions from the West.[38] As Telford Taylor has noted, this was in fact the only strategic victory ever won by the Luftwaffe.[39]

Perhaps the best and also the most extreme instance of an attempt by a country to overstate its military capabilities was that of Fascist Italy in the 1930s. Signor Mussolini tried to impress upon all foreign observers the great power of the Italian armed forces – although in this case he probably fooled no one but himself.

> By another confusing piece of legerdemain, in 1938 the composition of [Italian] army divisions had been reduced from three regiments to two. This appealed to Mussolini because it enabled him to say that fascism had sixty divisions instead of barely half as many, but the change caused enormous disorganization just when the war was about to begin; and because he forgot what he had done, several years later he tragically miscalculated the true strength of his forces.[40]

Like Hitler, Mussolini tried – with little success – to demonstrate to all the superior quantitative and qualitative strength of the Italian Air Force.

> By 1935 Italy claimed most of the international records for flying, and this was a great achievement. The chief of the air staff informed parliament *that they had been won with ordinary machines*. It was his further boast that Italy no longer needed the help of foreign technology in this field, and indeed that Italian

planes were not only 'the best in the world' but in wartime would be able to control the whole Mediterranean. Such statements were, as they were intended to be, greeted with enormous enthusiasm, and the authorities proceeded to draw the conclusion that the Italian air force was second to none, and that Italy must be impregnable.[41]

Italy did its best to exaggerate the figures on the number of aircraft.

When the Second World War broke out, figures were given to show that Italy had 8,530 planes, but the air ministry privately admitted in April 1939 that there were only 3,000 front line aircraft, and the naval information service reduced this to under a thousand. On further investigation the figure turned out to be 454 bombers and 129 fighters, nearly all of which were inferior in speed and equipment to contemporary British planes ... [Mussolini] can hardly have been intending to bluff foreign observers, because they had their own means of knowing that the official figures of the air ministry were nonsense, and indeed the British were quite sure that the efficiency of the Italian air force was growing less, not greater; the intention was to bluff Italians, and unfortunately it succeeded.[42]

The Italian navy was not in much better shape. Although its battleships and battle cruisers looked elegant and impressive, they were poorly designed. They were built for high speed and therefore were thinly armored; they had no radars or any effective anti-submarine detection capability. In 1939 their submarine fleet was the largest in the world, but had no firing computers. It was ill-organized and its doctrine, training, and tactics were obsolete. It was suitable for displays but not for war.

Mussolini successfully deceived not only himself but also Hitler from May 1938 onwards.

The Italian military services performed much better during Hitler's visit in May 1938. An excellent one-battalion exercise combined with a superficially competent show by the navy (which included a simultaneous submerging and surfacing by eighty-six Italian submarines) to give Hitler the impression that Mussolini had revitalized Italy's military forces.[43]

This misperception on Hitler's part cost Germany and Italy dearly later on. Hitler's professional military advisors on the other hand were not nearly as impressed as he was by the Italian military's public relations campaign. They reported that the Italian army was poorly equipped and badly trained, and unlike Hitler, they viewed Italy as a military burden which they would prefer to see neutral rather than fighting on Germany's side.[44]

During the early 1950s, US intelligence had very little information concerning the weapons procurement programs of the USSR. A major problem facing US intelligence soon after the Soviet Union developed its nuclear weapons arsenal was to try to evaluate the buildup of Soviet nuclear weapons delivery capability, which at that time was primarily confined to long-range heavy bombers. Initially, US intelligence estimated that because Soviet bomber design technology was lagging considerably behind that of the United States, the number of Soviet bombers capable of delivering nuclear weapons would not even approach the number held by the US Strategic Air Command at least until the late 1950s.

On 13 July 1955, during their Air Force Day, the Soviets performed some sleight of hand for the benefit of Western observers. They brought together all of their available M-4 Bison long-range heavy bombers for a flyover: the first formation included 10 bombers, which, when out of sight turned around and returned twice at regular intervals in formations of 9 bombers each. This bit of deception convinced at least some observers in the US intelligence community SAC that the Soviets had almost four times the number of comparable aircraft (B-52 bombers) possessed by the United States. Their conclusion was that the 'bomber gap' created by the Soviet Union had relegated the United States to a decidedly inferior position. This 'trick', as Lawrence Freedman suggests, reinforced a trend that had begun to emerge in US estimates. Furthermore, the US Air Force's doctrinal emphasis on the procurement of heavy bombers may have been projected in a mirror-type image on the Soviet Air Force. In any event it was certainly not incompatible with the interests of the US Air Force to emphasize if not exaggerate the amount of Soviet heavy bomber production in order to justify the expansion of its own bomber procurement. Indeed, the Soviet strategem thus backfired when Congress substantially increased the budget of the US Air Force. When it eventually became clear that the 'bomber gap' had never existed, the US Air Force was already in a much stronger position than it would have been without the 'boost' from the Soviet Union.[45] The Soviets did not, however, learn their lesson from this episode.

Another example of the deliberate overstatement of capabilities was Premier Nikita Khruschev's boast (following the launching of the first Soviet sputnik satellite) that the USSR had obtained tremendous superiority over the United States in the design, testing, and production of Intercontinental Ballistic Missiles (ICBMs). Initially the

Soviet Union exaggerated the stage of development that it had pur-
portedly reached, later it lied about the extent of their production
(supposedly massive), and finally it misrepresented their capabilities
and accuracy by a wide margin. The Russians were indeed ahead of the
United States in launching satellites and in the space program, but
there was no *direct* connection between the success of their space
program and the military deployment of ICBMs. Western intelligence,
however, could not obtain much information on Soviet military ICBM
strength, and the Russians used the opportunity to deceive the world
(especially the Americans) concerning the advanced deployment of
the ICBMs. The following statements by Khruschev were common
throughout 1957 and 1958: 'We *now have* all the rockets we need: long-
range rockets, intermediate rockets, and short-range rockets.' 'I think
it is no secret that *there now exists* a range of missiles with the aid of
which it is possible to fulfill any assignment of operational and strategic
importance.' 'The fact that the Soviet Union was the first to launch an
artificial earth satellite, which within a month was followed by another,
says a lot. If necessary, tomorrow we can launch 10–20 satellites. All
that is required for this is to replace the warhead of an intercontinental
ballistic rocket with the necessary instruments. There is a satellite for
you.'[46] In fact, the Soviet military ICBM program lagged far behind its
space program, but this was not so, of course, in the minds of Western
political and military leaders, who had little reliable information and
were at first impressed by the Soviet space program.

Initially believing Khrischev's statements, the Americans redoubled
their efforts to overtake the Soviet Union and close the dangerous
'missile gap'. Within four years of the missile gap hoax, the United
States had not only closed the fictitious missile gap but had achieved a
significant lead over the USSR in the military deployment of ICBMs.
This translated into concrete political gains for the United States and a
loss of face for the Soviet Union during the missile crisis in Cuba.
(One common explanation for the Russian placing of Medium Range
Ballistic Missiles (MRBMs) in Cuba was that the USSR was trying to
close an ICBM missile gap favoring the United States.) Ultimately,
Khruschev paid for his hoax with his own career.[47]

Thus, successful capability-inflating deception operations can be too
much of a good thing. Unwarranted fear of German air superiority led
the British (and French) to make excessive political concessions in the
short run in order to gain time to catch up with the Germans and
increase their own investment in air power and anti-aircraft defenses
(radar in particular). By the time war broke out, the British were in
much better shape to meet the German challenge, perhaps defeating
Hitler's purpose in the long run.

The second danger of an effective capability-inflating deception is that the deceiver may eventually fall for his own bluff even as he ignores the corrective measures that have been taken by his adversary in the meantime. That is, the deceiver may view a temporary advantage as reflecting a permanent position of superiority which in fact does not exist. What may have been true in 1937 or 1938 was not accurate in 1939 or 1940 for the relative air strength of the British and Germans. What was true for the United States and the USSR in 1957 had changed by 1962. The deceiver may, therefore, fall into his own trap when he decides to take action which is based on a past real or imagined balance of capabilities. Such a situation may have caused Hitler to attack Great Britain (or even open the Second World War), believing as he did in the superiority of the Luftwaffe; it led Mussolini to embark on his adventures in Ethiopia, Albania, and Greece, and may have convinced Khrushchev that the Soviet Union was strong enough to challenge the United States in its own backyard in Cuba (although the United States probably will never again have such an advantage in capabilities over the Soviet Union).

Consequently, successful capability-inflating deception operations can backfire in three ways. The first danger is that the 'target' state will redouble its efforts to improve its capabilities in reaction to the imagined threat and therefore will gain the upper hand even if that was not the original intention; second, the deceiver's bluff might be called and his weakness revealed; thirdly, there is the pitfall of self-deception, i.e., accepting one's own bluff as reality and acting upon that premise.

The other variety of capability-related deception is exactly the opposite; that is, it tries to hide and minimize the deceiver's *real* strength so that he will be able to surprise the opponent on the battlefield with capabilities that may make the difference between victory and defeat. While attempts to exaggerate one's capabilities can often be identified with ambitious and aggressive leaders (e.g., Hitler, Mussolini, Khruschev, Nasser), attempts to conceal one's real strength are more frequently characteristic of military leaders and organizations whose standard operating procedures require secrecy and discretion.

Between 1956 and 1967, for example, the Israel Defense Forces (IDF) carefully veiled its real numerical strength and qualitative improvements. Success in camouflaging its strength is certainly one of the explanations for the astounding blitzkrieg-type victory that Israel achieved over its Arab neighbors in June 1967. Arab intelligence services completely failed to get an accurate picture of Israel's actual military power, a fact which contributed to Nasser's decision to initiate the May crisis in 1967. But again, success in concealing one's real strength can also be a double-edged sword. The weakness Israel projected in 1967 was not the intended goal but rather the unplanned byproduct of secrecy. It diminished Israel's deterrence, tempting the Arabs to attack. Had Israel's real strength been known, deterrence might have forestalled war. It can therefore be argued that strategic deception, in view of this dangerous aspect, must be used judiciously.[48]

A similar example is the secrecy maintained by the Soviet Union until 1941 concerning its military capabilities. Given the earlier external threats to the Soviet Union, the long-held tradition of conspiracy, the closed nature of the Soviet political system, and Stalin's own paranoia, the emphasis on total secrecy in the Soviet Union is not surprising. For that reason, the Germans had very poor intelligence concerning the real strength of the USSR. On the eve of Barbarossa, German intelligence may have underestimated Soviet strength by as much as 120 divisions (at that time German intelligence had identified 247 Soviet divisions and soon after the war broke out, as many as 360). If the Germans had been aware of the actual strength of the Soviet Union, they might have decided against attacking at all, as Hitler later told the Italian Foreign Minister, Count Ciano. Excessive Soviet secrecy was therefore instrumental in the collapse of Soviet deterrence and led to a war the Soviet Union did not want.[49] The continued closed nature of Soviet society today will exact its price too. The United States may overreact to exaggerated perceptions of Soviet strength by investing huge sums in its own military machine – more than it perhaps might have if current Soviet *real* capabilities and intentions were known.

Capabilities can normally be concealed best in closed and/or homogeneous societies which are difficult to penetrate – e.g., the Soviet Union, Japan, Israel (particularly until 1967) – if the opponent's intelligence is weak. In today's world of spy satellites, electronic intelligence, and high-altitude air photography it is, of course, much more difficult to conceal material military capabilities (although one can assume that in the age of satellite intelligence, new types of deception and camouflage have been developed).

Another interesting variant of capability-reducing deception (on either a quantitative or qualitative level) assumes the form of policies designed to evade and break arms control agreements. A well-known case was the German navy's handing of falsified information to the British concerning the real tonnage of German battleship construction. Although the Germans were technically not allowed to build battlecruisers over 35,000 tons standard displacement, both the *Bismarck* and the *Tirpitz* were closer to 45,000 tons, a gross violation of the Washington and London Naval Agreement. Yet despite ample evidence, the British Naval Intelligence did not report such a violation, nor did British politicians register any protests with the Germans. This

seemingly myopic behavior was primarily based on political considerations, the desire to maintain the London agreements, the good faith of
Germany (more specifically that of Admiral Rader), confidence in
Britain's own deterrent power, and above all, wishful thinking and self-
deception. A convenient supporting belief for this policy was that the
German navy was oriented towards fighting a war in the Baltic against
the Soviet Union and not against Great Britain.[50] Similar types of
deception have often occurred in the breaching of arms control agreements and have had similar results, namely that the party more
interested in the status quo and which places more faith in arms control
agreements has, to its own detriment, ignored the evidence and thereby assisted the deceiver's effort to gain a unilateral advantage.

At this point, it is useful to make a distinction between *passive* and
active deception. Passive deception is largely dependent upon secrecy
and camouflage,[51] on hiding one's intentions and/or capabilities from
the adversary. Some experts view passive deception as inferior and not
likely to succeed against any competent intelligence organization. As
we have seen in the preceding text, this is not necessarily true. While
measures of secrecy do not have the same aura of romance and
intellectual excitement as that associated with active deception, they
can frequently be as effective as other more elaborate operations.
*Moreover, active types of deception are dependent upon the efficacy
of the passive operation.* Even more crucial, passive deception can
tremendously complicate, and therefore increase the costs of, intelligence work – in terms of time, money, and the like. A recent example
appeared in Jack Anderson's column in the *Washington Post*. The US
DIA was interested in determining the caliber of the cannon mounted
on the new Soviet T-64 and T-72 tanks. It spent over 18 million dollars
on the project (including computer time, satellite photographs and
their development, electronic eavesdropping) and could not find the
answer. The DIA finally discovered that the British and French had
obtained the same information for next to nothing.[52] In view of the
freedom and lack of discretion of the American press, the Soviet
Union can normally acquire similar information with little effort and
expense (or to be more exact, at the cost of subscribing to major
US publications). The number of very successful passive concealment deception operations concerning capabilities is very impressive
indeed, for instance the development of the proximity fuze by the
United States (and Britain) during the Second World War, and the
development of the 'window' radar jamming chaff by the British for the
bomber offensive over Germany.[53] These two examples illustrate not
only the decisive importance of passive deception but also the critical
nature of timing, that is, when exactly to introduce a new weapon in

order to obtain the best possible results.[54] This problem is related to the study of technological surprise, a subject which has received scant attention in the open literature on intelligence.[55] Finally, of course, there are the atypical examples of Ultra and the development of the atomic bomb.

In contrast to its passive counterpart, active deception usually involves a calculated policy of disclosing half-truths supported by 'proof' (verifiable information) and other material evidence. This information must be picked up by the intelligence network of the intended victim. The deceived party must 'discover' the evidence himself, and he should have to work hard for it to be more convinced of its authenticity and value. Frequently, information that is easily obtained seems to be less credible and of doubtful value.[56] Psychologically speaking, the 'consumer' tends to equate a better product with higher cost.[57] David Mure suggests that the motto of Galveston (the head of Force 'A', the British deception organization in the Mediterranean in the Second World War) was that 'the lie – the cover plan – was so precious that it should be flanked with an escort of truths'.[58] 'Truths should make up at least 90% of the information fed to the enemy.'[59] '[There must be] ... an insistence on the prime necessity for truth whenever truth is possible. A lie when it is needed will only be believed if it rests on a firm foundation of previous truth.'[60]

The insistence on providing the enemy's intelligence with correct and verifiable information at every possible opportunity is one of the major explanations for the reluctance of traditional-conventional officers and military organizations to cooperate in deception operations.

Feeding the enemy's intelligence with such information should be guided by the following rules: (1) whenever possible, supply the adversary with correct but low grade information, bits of gossip, and 'chicken-feed'; (2) feed him correct information that *he is known* to have already obtained *independently*; (3) pass on correct, important information that will arrive *too late* to be of any real use to him and will not have actual operational value; (4) finally, supply him with information that is actually important if the sacrifice will allow one to reap much greater future benefits *which could not otherwise* be obtained.

In each case, deception operations must be tailored to the target's unique character and conditions. To ensure that his adversary will indeed pick up the threads of evidence, the deceiver must prepare the bait by taking into account the quality of the target's intelligence, his methods of working and his agents, his perceptual frame of mind, his cultural framework, and other factors.

Deception should not be a mere exercise in intellectual gratification.

A strategem that is too sophisticated may be intellectually satisfying to those who devise it, but may not be picked up by the intended victim. Israel, for instance, often found that very polished and seemingly simple deception plans were not picked up by Arab intelligence organizations because they were not able to identify the bait offered. There is an obvious danger that 'the message developed by the deception planners is *understood by them* in the context of the endless meetings in which alternatives were weighed and details worked out. They are so familiar with their own thinking that they risk overlooking the degree to which the message is clear to them only because *they know what to look for*'[61] (emphasis added). Ewen Montagu in *Beyond Top Secret U* (one of the best studies of deception) repeatedly emphasizes the need to match the bait to the character and level of sophistication of the intended victim.

> It occupied a great deal of time and energy but it was fascinating work. In a way it was like a mixture of constructing a crossword puzzle and sawing a jigsaw puzzle and then waiting to see whether the recipient could and would solve the clues and place the bits together successfully, except that it was we who would get the prize if the recipient succeeded. We had no illusions about the efficiency of the German Abwehr, so we had to make sure that the puzzle was not too difficult for them to solve.[62]

Paradoxically, therefore, when complicated intelligence puzzles seem to fall into place a little too easily with few remaining question marks (especially when the puzzle seems to confirm preexisting notions or desired developments) extra caution should be exercised against the possibility of deception.

Part of the art of deception is learning to think like the adversary.[63] The bait must be designed on the basis of reliable intelligence on how he thinks and what information is available to him; this in turn requires penetration of the adversary's most guarded secrets.

It is worthwhile to quote Montagu at some length on this matter. In *Beyond Top Secret U*, he discusses a proposal for a detailed deception plan intended to ease the pressure on the Russians by creating an imaginary threat for the Germans in the Bay of Biscay area. The additional advantage of this ploy was that it would force the Germans to thin out their defenses in the Channel area. Montagu proposed this plan on the basis of information received through Ultra (the deciphering of top secret German codes), which indicated that the Abwehr, German army, and the Luftwaffe were particularly afraid of such a development. (Montagu, for example, suggested that they try to

reinforce existing German fears.) Nevertheless, his plan did not win the
approval of the Chiefs of Staff.

> They [the Chiefs of Staff] turned it down flat on the grounds that
> an attack on the Biscay coast was so impossible that the deception
> would be incredible. With great respect, that last point usurped
> our function – we were the experts on deception, they were wholly
> ignorant about this art. If they thought, as they apparently did,
> that the deception would be useful, it was for us to decide whether
> we could put it over.
>
> Their reason was that they knew that the Biscay coast was
> outside the range of our fighter aircraft, so the necessary cover
> could not be given for a prolonged invasion, and they knew that
> we hadn't got enough aircraft carriers to spare to give fighter
> cover even for an 'in and out' operation of real magnitude – all of
> which was of course quite correct. But they couldn't make them-
> selves think as Germans. The Germans did not know what our
> Chiefs of Staff did and, on their information, they did think that
> we had enough forces and materiel for us to risk at least a major in
> and out operation under Russian pressure.
>
> It was so important to deception work to be able to put oneself
> completely in the mind of the enemy, to think as they would think
> on their information and decide what they would do – ignoring
> what you knew yourself and what you could do ... We had given
> the Chiefs of Staff the facts about the Bay of Biscay Operation and
> they ought to have done better. But perhaps I am being unfair to
> them. Service training is not the same as that of a barrister. We
> have to learn throughout our career to put ourselves in our
> opponent's place and try to anticipate what he will think and what
> he will do on his information.[64]

Unfortunately, deception is a creative art and not an exact science or
even a craft. For that reason, it is difficult to teach someone how to
deceive unless he has an instinct for it. This explains why, despite the
numerous wartime memoirs and detailed military histories which
discuss deception, little has been written on the theory of deception or
how to practice it.[65] It is normally assumed that some military or
political leaders are 'deception-minded' while others are not. There is
probably no systematic, structured way to teach the art of deception,
just as it is impossible to teach someone to become an original painter.
Perhaps the only way to learn this art is through one's own experience.

What are some of the conditions which facilitate the development of
the art of active deception? In the first place, active deception requires
that an individual or organization (preferably a small one) be able

to see things from the enemy's vantage point. This should include, as mentioned above, a thorough grasp of his culture, language, mode of operation, and procedures, to name a few. In formulating the deception ploy, the deceiver must be both practical and imaginative, and not allow himself to be too sophisticated or enjoy deception for its own sake. He (almost every important deception operation originates and is developed in its early stages as the brainchild of one individual) must have a flexible combinatorial mind – a mind which works by breaking down ideas, concepts, or 'words' into their basic components, and then recombining them in a variety of ways. (One example of this type of thinking may be found in the game of Scrabble.) He must be able to transcend the routine thinking or procedures normally imposed by large organizations and bureaucracies. Barton Whaley has tried but failed to find 'some general personality type with the ability to understand and use surprise and deception and to associate its reverse type with the failure to do so'.[66] But perhaps one general pattern of personality emerges for the greatest past users of deception. They are highly individualistic and competitive: they would not easily fit into a large organization or into any type of routine work and tend to work alone. They are usually convinced of the superiority of their own opinions. In some ways, they fit the supposed character of the lonely, eccentric bohemian artist, only the art they practice is different. This is apparently the only common denominator for great practitioners of deception such as Churchill, MacArthur, Hitler, Dayan, and T.E. Lawrence. Conversely, individuals who feel comfortable in larger groups, who prefer the democratic consensus type of agreements, and who can easily become involved in routine work will make poor candidates.

From an organizational point of view, the art of deception can be practiced only by organizations that are willing to delegate much authority to, and have confidence in, a small group of people.[67] In short, there must be tolerance for the existence of 'artists' among 'bureaucrats' and enough confidence and patience not to insist on immediate results. Such an organization (normally an intelligence organization of course) must be able to maintain the highest degree of secrecy. Above all, it has to be able to obtain the best possible information on the adversary and to penetrate his ranks with spies, decipher his codes, etc., in order to know what he knows, what he *wants* to know, and how he obtains his information. Conversely, the more successful an organization is in avoiding the penetration of its own ranks, the more it will be able to carry out its own deception operations. (In his extensive research on deception, Barton Whaley claims that he found no case of a deception operation that failed or was intercepted by an adversary.)[68]

Finally, for the success of any type of deception operation, it is imperative to coordinate the policies of all other organizations that might inadvertently disclose or undermine the plan.

Historically speaking, military organizations have always held the role of the combat officer and soldier to be paramount. To advance in rank and gain influence in military councils, it was considered most important to have had combat experience. With the growth in complexity of warfare, supportive roles in logistics, communications, and staff work gained increased recognition – if not full equality. Until the Second World War (and during the war itself), intelligence work was not considered an important military profession and certainly was not the route to promotions, and thus was never the choice of those interested in a shining military career. This provides (as mentioned earlier) an explanation for the failures of military intelligence, particularly those of the Germans and Japanese during the Second World War. The patent reluctance of conventional military organizations to recognize the key role of intelligence was even more entrenched as far as deception was concerned. (We have already noted Clausewitz's lack of interest in deception.) This may be explained in a number of ways:

1. The conservative, gentlemanly education of officers in almost all military organizations before the Second World War epitomized by US Secretary of State Stimson's comment that 'Gentlemen do not read other people's mail.' Whether conscious or not, such attitudes also spilled over into military planning and operations.
2. The results achieved by an effective stratagem are very difficult to measure and are often intangible.
3. Deception requires cooperation at the highest operational, command, and political levels. Senior officers and politicians seldom have the time to invest in such operations, particularly when they are not convinced of their utility. Furthermore, the extreme delicacy and level of secrecy involved contributed to the reluctance of senior commanders to delegate authority on these matters to lower ranking officers.
4. Finally, the fact that most deception operations involve supplying the adversary with correct information is viewed with great suspicion, as some believe that this is too risky.

It is therefore not surprising that prior to the Second World War, the majority of deception operations were ad hoc initiatives on the tactical level implemented by local commanders. 'Organized deception was an entirely new development in World War II.'[69]

                        *   *   *

It is much more difficult to advise a potential victim how to avoid or uncover ruses directed at him before any damage has been done. In this respect, the problems involved in avoiding deception are very similar to the difficulties inherent in anticipating a surprise attack. Military history shows that surprises are in fact inevitable. Whaley has therefore concluded that not only do the most sophisticated deceivers fall prey to deception, but that 'exhortations to *avoid* being deceived are ... as uselessly homiletic as those to use it'.[70]

Nevertheless, some evident, though not necessarily effective, precautions can be taken. Intelligence services must continuously ask themselves what are the most likely directions from which an adversary might attack, even if the available evidence contradicts these contingencies. This can probably best be accomplished by asking how one would do the same thing oneself. Such estimates can be prepared by analysts who are not familiar with the available information, and who work only by trying to think as the enemy might. Only in the second stage must such an analysis be corroborated with the intelligence information.

Another, and again not very helpful, method of avoiding deception is to be wary of information which falls too neatly into a single pattern that seems to exclude other, no less reasonable possible courses of action. R.V. Jones has added the following advice:

> Both for deception and unmasking, one of the personal qualities required is being able to imagine yourself in the position of your adversary and to look at reality from his point of view; this includes not only being able to sense the world through his eyes and ears, and their modern analogues such as photographic and electronic reconnaissance, but also to absorb the background of his experience and hopes, for it is against these that he will interpret the clues collected by his intelligence system. Thus it was not too difficult to convince the Germans that the 'Jay' system was going to depend on beams because they would naturally be gratified by our copying their techniques. To guard against this weakness when one is danger of being deceived, I can only recommend Crow's Law, formulated by my late friend John Crow: 'Do not think what you want to think until you know what you ought to know.' And if a good guide to successful intelligence is Occam's razor – hypotheses are not to be multiplied without necessity – then an equally relevant guide to avoid being deceived is to multiply your channels of observation as far as possible.[71]

Although this last bit of advice may sound reasonable, it can also generate its own problems. Instead of bringing in more reliable information, more channels may only serve to add 'noise' or render one susceptible to other deception operations. R. V. Jones probably meant that one should obtain a variety (rather than simply quantity) of opinions, which may contradict his suggestion not to multiply hypotheses. Alternatively, it can be said that what is important is reliable information – but of course that is precisely the basic and unsolvable problem of all intelligence work.

Another piece of advice, not unlike that of R. V. Jones but based on psychological tests, is not to put too much confidence in conclusions drawn from a very small body of consistent data, since tests have shown that they are highly unreliable because people tend to be overly sensitive to consistency.[72] Heuer's final recommendation is as follows:

> As a general rule, we are more often on the side of being too wedded to our established views and thus too quick to reject information that does not fit these views, than on the side of being too quick to reverse our beliefs. Thus, most of us would do well to be more open to evidence and ideas that are at variance with our preconceptions.[73]

Alas, one is tempted to say, on the basis of historical evidence, that 'to be closed-minded is human'.

                    *   *   *

Totalitarian regimes, such as those of Nazi Germany, Fascist Italy, Japan of the 1930s, or the Soviet Union under Stalin and his successors (until this very day),[74] seem to have fewer scruples about using deception and fraud as an accepted, perhaps even common, means in the conduct of their foreign policy in times of peace.[75] This may be because they view the peaceful 'interim' merely as a cease-fire in a continual war over resources and ideology. In a perpetual state of war and zero-sum game competition for survival, all means and methods can be justified. Hitler's foreign policy is, in fact, nothing but a history of deception and fraud. In times of peace, this appears to give the totalitarian states a considerable advantage over the 'naive' Western democracies; yet this very advantage may be their undoing in the long run both in peace and war. Some of the reasons behind this backlash are self-evident while others are more subtle.

To begin with, those who frequently make use of strategem rapidly lose their credibility; what they may get away with one, two, or three times in succession they cannot hope to succeed with indefinitely. Although they may continue to believe in the efficacy of deception, their peaceful adversaries will have already learned their lesson. As a result, the deceiving nation may find itself in a position in which no state will voluntarily seek any agreement with it: instead, it will have given peaceful nations the impetus to be more alert, to have better intelligence, and eventually to resort to similar means.

Paradoxically, the 'naive' states may turn out to be much better at the game of deception. One explanation for this is simple. Someone who is known to be honest and naive can rely on his reputation (at least for a while) to lend his occasional use of strategem an aura of credibility. Not expecting him to play by their rules, his adversaries may be caught off guard.

This situation can be summarized in a 'paradox': *The more one has a reputation for honesty – the easier it is to lie convincingly.* Even more concisely: *Honest people/states can deceive the best.*

This may be why the Germans so easily fell for British deception. They probably could not bring themselves to believe that the same nation which had allowed itself to be hoodwinked time and again in peacetime would develop the art of deception to new heights in times of war. While this explanation holds true for the Germans, it might not describe the attitude of the Soviet Union, whose communist ideology assumes that the capitalists will always try to deceive and that they should never be trusted in the first place.[76] Stalin may have deceived himself by imagining that trickery lurked behind too many of the moves of other states. Thus when Churchill and the British warned him of the impending German attack in 1941 based on knowledge acquired through Ultra, he refused to believe them and viewed this information as bait to drag the Soviet Union into war against Germany in order to ease the pressure in the West. Given Stalin's communist background and his paranoia, such an attitude is not altogether surprising.[77]

A second, more interesting explanation which will require further research to substantiate it, is that those who practice deception continuously during peacetime, as did the Germans and the Russians, usually have to establish special agencies for that purpose (normally as part of their intelligence organizations). The operation of deception by professional military men or government officials will tend to routinize the planning and execution of operations; over an extended period of time, this will, in turn, undermine their creativity and flair for the art of deception. By the time they have reached the point where they view deception as a regular rather than a special operation, their level of effectiveness will already have dropped. (This phenomenon can also be detected in the routinized deception operations of the CIA during the 1960s and early 1970s, before such practices were brought to a halt in the United States.)[78]

On the other hand, the Western democracies, and the British in particular, benefited considerably from their late entry into this area of

intelligence. In both the First and Second World Wars, the British and
Americans started to reorganize their intelligence organizations either
immediately before the war broke out or soon thereafter. Therefore, unlike the German and Soviet intelligence organizations, which
were composed primarily of 'professionals', those of the British and
Americans were staffed largely with amateurs recruited from all walks
of civilian (but mainly from academic) life.[79]

Amateurs typically bring with them new enthusiasm, a creative
imagination, informality, perhaps some academic openness, and a
somewhat better ability to conduct a more detached and objective
search for *veritas* – all of which are intellectual qualities well-suited to
intelligence work, and more specifically, deception work.[80] Being able
to make a fresh start enabled the British and American amateurs to
reexamine old problems from a new point of view; they did not feel
obligated, as did the pre-war professional intelligence bureaucrats, to
commit themselves to earlier, not always fully rational, traditions or
long-standing politics. Donald MacLachlan, an astute and experienced
observer of this phenomenon, states that 'it is the lawyer, the scholar,
the traveller, the banker, even the journalist, who shows the ability
to resist where the career men tend to bend. Career officers and
politicians have a strong interest in cooking raw intelligence to make
their masters' favorite dishes.'[81] Indeed, one of MacLachlan's principal
recommendations, stemming from the conclusion that professional
officers have a low regard for intelligence work,[82] is that '*intelligence
should as far as possible be directed by civilians*'[83] (italics in original).
Pre-war professionals certainly resented the massive penetration of
their organizations by the 'professional-type' amateurs.[84]

> The Western democracies, unlike the Germans ... drafted
> civilians as intelligence officers even of army groups (i.e., military
> field position) with great success. First class minds became expert
> on the enemy; *with no worries about career*, they could both be
> kept in a post for the duration of the war and express their
> opinions more forcefully.[85] (italics in original)

The more conservative German officer corps strongly resisted the
integration of intelligence officers into the *Wehrmacht* and all other
branches of the armed forces. Their penchant for tradition and
aversion to civilian intellectuals prevented them from tapping the
enormous intelligence potential of the civilian amateurs. While this
kind of resistance to civilians was also manifested by British intelligence professionals, it was easily quashed. It was perhaps easier for the
British, since their civilian amateurs had performed very competently
during the First World War.

The mobilization of British intelligence for the two World Wars provides at least a partial vindication for the now unfashionable virtues of British amateurism. To a remarkable degree the British intelligence system during the First World War was the result of the brilliant last-minute improvisation by enthusiastic volunteers. That the volunteers failed to achieve more – for example, at Jutland and Cambrai – was due chiefly to the short-sightedness of the professionals. The renaissance of the British intelligence community at the beginning of the Second World War after two decades of considerable neglect, was, once again, largely the work of brilliant amateurs, able in some cases to build on the achievements of their predecessors. And the man chiefly responsible for the coordination of the British intelligence effort for the first time in its modern history was a much criticised amateur strategist, Winston Churchill.[86]

For a field such as deception, which leaves so much to imagination and creativity, the amateurs proved to be ideal practitioners who, in the final analysis, outsmarted the professionals.

This provides one of the best explanations for the curious and dismal failures of German strategic intelligence and its almost total neglect of deception during the Second World War. David Kahn thus reaches the conclusion that 'Germany lost the intelligence war. At every one of the strategic turning points of the Second World War, her intelligence failed. It underestimated Russia, blacked out before the North African invasion, awaited the Sicily landing in the Balkans, and fell for thinking Normandy landing a "feint".'[87] These mistakes were caused not only by the inherent structural weakness of German intelligence, but also by the effectiveness of Allied deception operations. Some of the basic reasons for German intelligence failures as enumerated by Kahn are:[88]

(1) 'Unjustified arrogance, which caused Germany to lose touch with reality.' Early and easily attained military successes caused the Germans to feel vastly superior to their adversaries, to believe that they were immortal. This, in combination with their traditional nationalism, assumed racial superiority, and ethnocentric view of the world, reduced their incentive to learn about others. Such arrogance also encouraged the Arabs in 1948 and 1967 to wage war against Israel with almost no intelligence and knowledge about the object of their attack. To a lesser extent, arrogance also blinded the Israelis in 1973, and the Americans vis-à-vis the Japanese on the eve of Pearl Harbor. As already mentioned, deception operations in particular require an intimate knowledge and understanding of the adversary, and perhaps even a certain degree of compassion and respect.

(2) 'Aggression, which led to the neglect of intelligence.' This is a more subtle point based on an understanding of military strategy, in particular on the writings of Clausewitz. Clausewitz viewed defense as the stronger mode of warfare and also as passive and reactive in nature (neither of which is necessarily true).

> 'What is the concept of defense?' asked Clausewitz. The parrying of a blow. What is its characteristic feature? Awaiting the blow. Now an army can await a blow only if it believes that a blow is planned, and such a belief can only be created by information about the enemy. Defense requires intelligence. There can be, in other words, no defense without intelligence.[89]

The offense, on the other hand, is 'complete in itself'. It can decide when, how, and where to attack. It can concentrate a superior force at the point of its choice and can frequently dictate the early moves on the battlefield as it has planned. For this reason, the offense is less dependent upon the availability of intelligence than the defense is. 'The information about enemy intentions, while helpful and to a certain degree always present (for the offensive), is not essential to an offensive victory ... *In other words, while intelligence is integral to the defense, it is only contingent to the offense. As a result – and this is a crucial point – emphasizing the offensive tends toward a neglect of intelligence'*[90] (emphasis added).

Although this explanation is elegant and does seem to accurately describe existing psychological attitudes, it is not necessarily true from the military point of view. (It is not true because a successful offensive may require as much or perhaps even more detailed information than the defensive. Indeed, inadequate German intelligence concerning the Soviet Union in 1941 proved to be disastrous.) Kahn's point on the negative incentive of an offensive-minded military organization to invest in intelligence work may thus be true from a psychological standpoint, and can certainly be regarded as an important explanation for German military behavior. It may, however, be somewhat less persuasive as a general explanation. In any event, Nazi Germany's offensive military doctrine of blitzkrieg did not stress the central contribution of intelligence to warfare. By the time the Germans were on the defensive, it was too late for them to begin building the infrastructure necessary for intelligence work. The Allies, especially the British, who were strategically on the defensive when the war broke out, greatly appreciated the value of intelligence work and wasted no time in investing heavily in it; and when they were able to go over to the offensive, they enjoyed the advantage of a superior intelligence organization.

(3) *'The authority structure of the Nazi State, which gravely impaired its intelligence.'* Governments based on the 'Führer principle', the cult of personality, or any other dogma which makes the leader infallible, create at the highest strategic decision-making level of the state an environment which is far from conducive to 'objective' and 'rational' intelligence work. The leader who always knows best, who intimidates his advisors and cannot be criticized in the least, will render even the finest intelligence useless. Thus, Stalin refused to listen to any reports indicating the possibility of a German surprise attack. Hitler often ignored the intelligence information supplied to him and refused to listen to information that contradicted his views. Later on his subordinates, on their own initiative, ceased to supply him with 'depressing intelligence' about failures, possible dangers, or the superiority of the enemy. The fact that throughout the 1930s until the outbreak of war, and actually until the Battle of Britain and the invasion of Russia, Hitler's intuition was often more successful than the rational advice of the military professionals certainly made things worse. Dictators (who always know best) and heads of state who do not encourage their aides to express a wider spectrum of opinions obviously make bad intelligence consumers. Eventually they receive only the information they want to hear, which gradually causes them to lose touch with reality and ultimately fall victim to self-deception and defeat.[91] Successful use of deception by totalitarian regimes during times of peace may therefore not be a reassuring indicator of similar success in times of war.[92]

Deception is cheap, for it is neither labor- nor capital-intensive. Among the least expensive types of modern intelligence work, it yields a high return for a relatively small investment. Even if deception were more costly than the material and other investments in the military operation it was designed to cover, it would still be worthwhile if it led to a quick, decisive victory. Even the most complex, elaborate deception operation normally involves only a relatively small number of men. Barton Whaley has estimated that the total number of participants in the deception operations for the Allied invasion of Europe in 1944 – the largest operation of its kind in history – was 'in all perhaps 2,000 soldiers, sailors, and airmen; but none of whom were regular first line combat troops'.[93] Smaller, less intricate operations involve no more than a few dozen to a few hundred men.

The material investment is, in most cases, also negligible. Making use of inexpensive, relatively easily available resources, the deception operation will often require radio and other electronic gear to simulate or create intensified radio traffic in one direction or another, some wood and canvas, and film experts to build dummy aircraft, tanks, or other installations. It can necessitate the movement of already existing military equipment in and out of an observed area during the course of the day. More often than not, it is even cheaper than this, since deception operations involved, above all, 'non-material' activities such as spreading rumors, organizing campaigns to manipulate the publication of certain information in the press, planting agents, passing misleading information to the enemy, and following up the planted information. The top-secret nature of deception requires limiting the number of participants to the bare minimum necessary.[94]

If the costs of deception are relatively small, the benefits can be considerable if not decisive. Deception will facilitate surprise, which in turn 'multiplies the chances for quick and decisive military success, whether measured in terms of sought goals, ground taken, or casualty ratios'.[95] The effective use of stratagem will cause the adversary to waste his resources, spread his forces too thin, vacate or reduce the strength of his forces at the decisive point of attack, commit considerable forces to the wrong place at the worst time; it will divert his attention from critical to trivial areas of interest, numb his alertness and reduce his certainty. In short, *reducing the cost for the deceiver implies increasing the cost for the deceived.*[96]

Implicit in every intelligence operation, the possibility of deception will cause a degree of doubt to exist in any important intelligence work. This ever-present threat always introduces 'noise' into the collection and analysis of intelligence; consequently, there is no reason to forfeit the use of artifice or ignore its potential contribution to every facet of planning for action in war. That would seem as irrational as someone refusing to receive interest for money deposited in the bank. In war as a rational activity, there is never a reason to make life easier for the adversary or more difficult for oneself. Therefore even if stratagem is not always used as part of a military plan or strategy (which would be a mistake), the adversary must *always* be given the impression that he is the object of a deception operation. Like surprise, deception must be seen as inevitable in conflict, as an inherent factor in intelligence work and war that should never be discounted.[97]

Since no effective measures to counter or detect deception have yet been devised, the unavoidable conclusion is that deception – even if it fails to achieve its original goals – almost never fails (see below) and will therefore always favor the deceiver, the initiating party. 'Perceptual and cognitive biases strongly favor the deceiver as long as the goal of deception is to reinforce a target's preconceptions or simply create ambiguity and doubt about the deceiver's intention.'[98] Rationality dictates that a move which involves little cost and a negligible risk of failure should never be left out of one's repertoire.

Deception as a dilemma of intelligence work has been described as follows:

> Alertness to the possibility of deception can influence the degree of one's openness to new information, but not necessarily in a desirable direction. The impetus for changing one's estimate of the situation can only come from the recognition of an incompatibility between a present estimate and some new evidence. If people can explain new evidence to their own satisfaction with little change in their existing beliefs, they will rarely feel the need for drastic revision of these beliefs. Deception provides a readily 'available' explanation for discrepant evidence: if the evidence does not fit one's preconceptions, it may be dismissed as deception. Further, the more alert or suspicious one is of deception, the more readily available is this explanation. Alertness to deception presumably prompts a more careful and systematic review of the evidence. But anticipation of deception also leads the analyst to be more skeptical of all the evidence, and to the extent that evidence is deemed unreliable, the analyst's preconceptions must play a greater role in determining which evidence to believe. This leads to a paradox: The more alert we are to deception, the more likely we are to be deceived.[99]

One more paradox may, with caution, be mentioned. Under certain circumstances, *the more perfectly an intelligence puzzle fits together, the greater the danger of a possible deception ploy.* This is particularly true when information – the solution to an important and complex intelligence puzzle – is received in the absence of much noise or contradictory evidence, and when the resulting conclusions conform neatly to one's hopes and expectations.

Experience and conditioning can work in two opposing ways to impair one's ability to detect deception. The first is that once victimized by deception, one finds it difficult to accept *any* information as reliable. The other is that once a source of information is thought to be trustworthy, it is difficult to discredit it.

Excessive alertness to the possibility of deception can have its price too. After the success of the Allied deception operation that covered the landing in Sicily (Operation Mincemeat), the Germans became overly sensitive to the possibility of a 'repeat performance'. When the detailed plans of the impending landing in Normandy fell into their hands via the British embassy in Ankara (Cicero), they were convinced that this was yet another instance of Allied trickery; consequently, they refused to accept the detailed plan as authentic. Conversely, a double agent who supplied the Germans with useless information on a regular basis was employed by the Allies to furnish them with the *correct* date of the operation in order to discredit it. Once he was proven to be correct on this vital piece of information, however, the Germans thenceforth accepted his information as correct even if it was useless. In other words, the intended victim's extreme sensitivity to the possibility of being duped can be very deftly used against him.

In the final analysis, whether the enemy plants a deception plan to fit our preconceptions or we perceive the use of stratagem where in fact it does not exist, it can be said that from a strictly logical and perceptual point of view, 'We are never deceived, we deceive ourselves' (Goethe).[100]

Yet deception is not a panacea which can replace the other military factors required for success in war. Believing otherwise courts military disaster. The most ingenious ploy is useless if not backed by military power or properly exploited.

Occasionally, deception operations – whether simple or complex – fail to achieve their intended goals or are even counterproductive. This can happen, as we have seen, in three possible ways:

1. The enemy simply fails to take the bait dangled before him. This can occur when the quality of his intelligence work is low or when the bait has not been carefully matched to his perceptions.
2. The short- and long-term impacts of deception work at cross-purposes. In other words, deception which is very effective and credible in the short run, can be counterproductive in the long run; that is, be too successful. This problem will arise when a plan is designed to intimidate the adversary and convince him of his relative weakness. Feelings of insecurity will usually hasten a corrective change in the adversary's policies, eventually transforming his 'weakness' into an advantage. In addition, this type of problem can often be correlated with self-deception: flushed with success, the deceiver will convince himself that his *temporary* advantage is a permanent one. As a result, he will underestimate his adversary and overestimate his own capabilities.
3. The adversary has learned of the deception plan and uses it against the deceiver. This is one very good reason that deception plans require excellent intelligence and continuous feedback from the target about what the enemy knows or does not know.

Any perpetrator of deception will be in a much more vulnerable position if he assumes that his plan is working, whereas in reality his opponent is manipulating it to his own advantage. I know of no such double or even infinite regression-types of deception, but they cannot be discounted in theory or in practice, although the likelihood of their occurrence is very small.[101]

To deceive successfully may become more difficult, certainly much more complicated, in the future. In a world of high-altitude reconnaissance aircraft, intelligence satellites with high resolution photographic equipment and a variety of other sensors, as well as AWACS aircraft that can trace any movements on air, sea, or land at distances of up to more than 350 miles, the use of stratagem has already become far more complex. To these factors we can add the contribution of high-powered computers to cryptoanalysis and the fact that everyone monitors his opponent's telephone, radio, and cable communications. If, in the Second World War, deception seemed primarily to be the game of academics from a variety of disciplines, future deceptions will primarily require the work of electronic and computer experts. Inevitably, deception will become less of an art and more of a science; this will be true chiefly in the execution of the deception plan and perhaps less so on the initiation level. Modern deception will, accordingly, exact much greater skill from its participants in highly technical areas, as well as in detailed and systematic preparations (such as a large number of exercises, or laboratory war games).

Unlike many of the large-scale strategic deceptions of the Second World War, technological deception is a short-lived game with built-in obsolescence. Under normal conditions, technological deception can be employed for only a relatively short period of time before it is uncovered by the adversary. For this reason, two important considerations must be taken into account. The first of these is that extra care should be exercised in pinpointing the optimal time in which to introduce a certain type of technological deception. For example, the principle underlying the use of metallic chaff (window) for jamming radar transmissions was recognized by both sides even before the outbreak of the Second World War. More advanced in their development of this weapon, the British nevertheless decided to reserve their jamming capabilities for use at the most critical moment – that is, in 1943 – when it was calculated to have the greatest destructive impact on German defenses while the Germans were no longer likely to be in a position to use it against British defenses.[102] A more recent interesting example was the Israeli use of sophisticated deceptive technologies to defeat the Syrian SAM-6 batteries in the Bekaa valley in Lebanon in June 1982. This deception operation, as well the disclosure, for the first time, of numerous new technologies proved to be very successful. But was it really worthwhile exposing so many valuable technological secrets for the sake of a less than critical military operation?[103]

The second consideration is that whenever technological deception is being used, the deceiver, aware of the limited survival time of each successive technology, must always be one step ahead in relation to the adversary's defensive or counter-technologies. (The British, for instance, convinced the Germans that each of the generations of British naval radars was at least one model behind that which they actually possessed.)[104]

Greater efforts for the preparation of deception plans will have to be made in peace-time so that they will be available if war should break out. Thus it appears that deception will be left less and less in the hands of amateurs and again more in the hands of professionals, intelligence bureaucrats, and 'engineers'. Inexorable though it may be, this trend is also likely to limit the scope of deception operations primarily to super-sophisticated electronic warfare, neglecting the more traditional classical *ruses de guerre*. This should be avoided at all costs, so that the advancement of the modern science of deception does not exclude the ancient art of deception.

Finally, to paraphrase David Dilks: It would be an exaggeration to say that successful deception by itself enables wars to be won. But it is precisely when the resources are stretched and the tasks many, when the forces are evenly matched and the issue trembles in the balance, that successful deception matters most.[105]

NOTES

1. Barton Whaley, *Stratagem: Deception and Surprise in War* (Cambridge, Mass.: MIT Center for International Studies, 1969), p.135.
2. Ibid., p.263. This was also recognised by Clausewitz: 'each surprise action is rooted in at least some degree of cunning.' Carl von Clausewitz, *On War*, ed. and trans. Michael Howard and Peter Paret (Princeton, NJ: Princeton University Press, 1976), p.202.
3. Sun Tzu, *The Art of War*, trans. Samuel B. Griffith (New York: Oxford University Press, 1973), p.133.
4. This is the schematic presentation of the plan of deception employed by the Israelites in the battle of the Ai against the Canaanites (following an earlier defeat after a direct assault of the same citadel). This scheme was used as an epigraph because it is one of the most simple and primitive types of deception – yet it always seems to succeed.

   So Joshua arose, and all the people of war, to go up to Ai; and Joshua chose out thirty thousand men, the mighty men of valour, and sent them forth by night. And he commanded them, saying: Behold, ye shall lie in ambush against the city, behind the city; go not very far from the city, but be ye all ready. And I, and all the people that are with me, will approach unto the city; and it shall come to pass, when they come out against us, as at the first, that we will flee before them. And they will come out after us, till we have drawn them away from the city; for they will say: They flee before us, as at the first; so we will flee before them. And ye shall rise up from the ambush, and take possession of the city; for the Lord your God will deliver it into your hand. (Joshua 8: 3–7)

The scheme is reproduced by permission from Abraham Malamat, 'Conquest of Canaan: Israelite Conduct of War According to Biblical Tradition', *Revue Internationale d'Histoire Militaire*, no. 42, pp.25–52. Sun Tzu expressed the same idea: 'Offer the enemy a bait to lure him; feign disorder and strike him. ... Pretend inferiority and encourage his arrogance.' Sun Tzu, *The Art of War*, pp.66–7.

A more recent version of this 'oldest of diversionary ruses' was devised by the North Vietnamese during the Vietnam war. They attacked the Khe Sanh area in January 1968 in order to draw the American forces away from the populous coastal plains. Despite a warning from two DIA analysts that this was a feint representing General Giap's most recent methods, General Westmoreland swallowed the bait. The real attack – the Tet offensive – materialized in March 1968 and occurred largely on the coastal plain after the North Vietnamese ended the siege of Khe Sanh without ever assaulting it. See Patrick J. McGarvey, 'DIA: Intelligence to Please', in *Readings in American Foreign Policy: A Bureaucratic Perspective*, eds. Morton A. Halperin and Arnold Kanter (Boston: Little Brown, 1973), pp.318–28.

5. Sun Tzu, *The Art of War*, p.66.
6. 'Deception in war is the act of misleading the enemy into doing something, so that his strategic or tactical position will be weakened.' Charles Cruickshank, *Deception in World War II* (Oxford: Oxford University Press, 1979), p.1.
7. Clausewitz, *On War*, p.203. Clausewitz did not view deception as an important element in war and often thought that it was not worth the bother:

> To prepare a sham action with efficient thoroughness to impress an enemy requires a considerable expenditure of time and effort, and the costs increase with scale of the deception. Normally they call for more than can be spared, and consequently so-called strategic feints rarely have the desired effect. It is dangerous, in fact, to use substantial forces over any length of time merely to create an illusion; there is always the risk that nothing will be gained and that the groups deployed will not be available when they are really needed (Ibid., p.203).

> But words, being cheap, are the most common means of creating false impressions. ... Plans and orders issued for appearances only, false reports designed to confuse the enemy etc. – have as a rule so little strategic value that they are used only if a ready-made opportunity presents itself. They should not be considered as a significant independent field of action at the disposal of the commander (Ibid., pp.202–3).

> ... feints ... by their very nature do not lead to a decision ... (Ibid., p.240). See also chap. 20, 'Diversions', pp.562–4.

Clausewitz viewed deception in a much narrower context than is customary today. Placing emphasis on *diversions* and *feints* at the tactical level, he related deception to maneuvers intended to disperse and reduce the concentration of the opponent's forces on the battlefield; he paid little attention to deception on the strategic level – that is, as a *means* to increase one's economy of force while reducing that of the adversary.

This is, in part, understandable. In Clausewitz's time, before the technological revolution and the revolution in speed and mobility, it was far more difficult to either conceal a deception plan from the adversary or to carry it out. I have discussed Clausewitz's lack of interest in *strategic* deception and surprise in greater detail elsewhere.

Interestingly enough, Frederick the Great, who did not share Clausewitz's preoccupation with the 'Vernichtungschlacht' or decisive battle and concentration, considered both intelligence and deception to be very useful. The weakness of Prussia relative to its adversaries was also an important incentive. See Jay Luvaas, ed., *Frederic the Great On the Art of War* (New York: Free Press, 1966, pp.122–4; 323–7).

The Prussian attitude expressed by Clausewitz may have been accepted by the

Germans, but certainly not by the British or ancient Chinese. In any case, the only criterion by which to judge deception is not how much it costs, but how effective it is. Will it reduce costs in terms of casualties? Will it lead to a major surprise and therefore to decisive results? As far as deception is concerned, Sun Tzu is more modern and rational than Clausewitz.

8. According to Montagu, 'Eisenhower, with his great talent for inter-Allied co-operation and the avoidance of those inter-Allied jealousies which caused so much harm in the 1914–1918 war, recognized that the British had far more experience in deception than did the Americans and wisely decided to leave it to us, merely appointing a few officers to liaise with L.C.S.' [London Controlling Section – the British organization responsible for the coordination of all pre-invasion deception plans.] Ewen Montagu, *Beyond Top Secret Ultra* (New York: Coward, McCann and Geoghegan, 1978), pp.151–2.
9. Ibid., p.204.
10. For this deception plan see, for example, Ewen Montagu, *Beyond Top Secret U* (London: Corgi Books, 1979); Charles Cruickshank, *Deception in World War II*; J.C. Masterman, *The Double-Cross System* (New Haven: Yale University Press, 1972), chap. 2, pp.145–63.

   Operation 'Fortitude North', the deception plan intended to convince the Germans of a possible invasion of Norway, succeeded in two important ways. First, the Germans were led to believe that the invasion across the Channel would come only *following* the invasion of Norway, which was notionally set for July. This helped to convince German intelligence that the invasion across the Channel would start later than it actually did. Second, Fortitude North caused the Germans to tie up no less than 18 divisions (12 in Norway and 6 in Denmark) which could otherwise have been used in the defence of the beaches of Normandy or the Eastern Front. For details, see Cruickshank, *Deception in World War II*, pp.99–113.

   During the same period of time preceding the invasion of Normandy, British deception operations in the Middle East also persuaded the Germans to tie down an additional 19 divisions in the Balkan 'soft belly' to counter a possible (fabricated) threat. See David Mure, *Practise to Deceive* (London: William Kimber, 1977), p.107.

   All in all, the complex deception cover operations for 'Overlord', conducted on numerous fronts requiring careful coordination and meticulous planning, may have, in a conserative estimate, diverted, tied down, or kept out of action perhaps as many as 25–35 German divisions that would have otherwise been available for the defense of Fortress Europe.
11. For the German plan of attack in the West in 1940 see Hans-Adolf Jacobsen, *Dokumente zur Vorgeschichte des Westfeldzuges 1939–1940* (Berlin: Muster-schmidt, July, 1956); Hans-Adolf Jacobsen, *Fall Gelb: Der Kampf um Den Deutschen Operationplan zur Westoffensive 1940* (Wiesbaden: Franz Steiner, 1957); Ulrich Liss, *Westfront 1939/1940* (Neckargemund: Kurt Vorwinkel, 1959); Major L.F. Ellis, *The War in France and Flanders 1939–1940* (London: HMSO, 1953); Telford Taylor, *The March of Conquest: The German Victories in Western Europe – 1940* (New York: Simon and Schuster, 1958).
12. Clausewitz, *On War*, p.213.
13. On the 'deathray', see R.V. Jones, *Most Secret War: British Scientific Intelligence 1939–1945* (London: Hamish Hamilton, 1978), p.63. Mussolini never lost his faith in the death ray! 'In the last month of his life, Mussolini, searching for an alibi, traced the beginning of decline in his fortunes to the fact that Marconi before his death in 1937, had refused to impart the secret of the death ray which he had brought to perfection.' Denis Mack Smith, *Mussolini's Roman Empire* (New York: Penguin Books, 1977), p.189.
14. Montagu, *Beyond Top Secret Ultra*, pp.169–71.
15. See Barton Whaley, *Codeword Barbarossa* (Cambridge, Mass.: MIT Press, 1973); John Erickson, *The Road to Stalingrad: Stalin's War With Germany*, Vol. 1

(New York: Harper and Row, 1975), chaps. 2–3; Gerhard L. Weinberg, *Germany and the Soviet Union 1939–1941* (Leiden: E.J. Brill, 1954); Vladimir Petrov, *"June 22, 1941": Soviet Historians and the German Invasion* (Columbia, South Carolina: University of South Carolina Press, 1968). Stalin told Harry Hopkins 'that the Russian army had been confronted with a surprise attack; he himself believed that Hitler would not strike ... *Hitler made no demands on Russia*' (emphasis added). Quoted in Nathan Leites, *A Study of Bolshevism* (Glencoe, Illinois: The Free Press, 1953), p.497.

16. See Jones, *Most Secret War*, pp.233–5. The British kept an eye on the German warships for a long time. There were a few indications of a possible German attempt to break out of Brest between 10 and 15 February. But the continued routine watch by the British dulled their attention. Jones brings the following quote from Francis Bacon's essay *Of Delayes* in this context: 'Nay, it were better to meet some Dangers halfe way, though they come nothing neare, than to keepe too long a watch, upon their Approaches: For if a Man watch too long, it is odds he will fall asleepe' (Ibid., p.235).

On this episode, see also Peter Kemp, *The Escape of the Scharnhorst and Gneisenau* (Annapolis: Naval Institute Press, 1975); John Dean Potter, *Fiasco* (London: Heinemann, 1970); Terence Robertson, *Channel Dash* (London: Evans Bros. 1958); and Wing Comdr. J.D. Warne, 'The Escape of the Scharnhorst, Gneisenau and Prinz Eugen.' RUSI 97 (May 1952), 201–5.

17. R.V. Jones, 'Intelligence, Deception and Surprise' (essay presented at the 8th Annual Conference of the Fletcher School of Law and Diplomacy, Tufts University International Security Studies Program, April 1979). He has summarized the *negative* and *positive* objectives of all deception operations as follows. Most of the goals on his list can be classified under one of the two basic deception types I have suggested: (1) deception concerning intentions or (2) deception concerning capabilities.

NEGATIVE OBJECTIVES	POSITIVE OBJECTIVES
Prevent the enemy from deducing at least one of the following:	Persuade the enemy to deduce:
i. *Where* you are.	i. You are *somewhere else.*
ii. *What weapons and forces* you have at your disposal. (cap.)	ii. Your *weapons and forces are different* from what they are. (cap.)
iii. *What* you intend to do. (int.)	iii. You intend to *do something else.* (int.)
iv. *Where* you intend to do it. (int.)	iv. You intend to do it *elsewhere.* (int.)
v. *When* you intend to do it. (int.)	v. You intend to do it *at a different time* (int.)
vi. *How* you intend to do it. (int.)	vi. You intend to do it *in a different manner.* (int.)
vii. Your knowledge of the enemy's intentions and techniques. (cap.)	vii. Your knowledge of the enemy is either greater or less than it actually is. (cap.)
viii. How successful his operations are.	viii. His operations are either more or less successful than they actually are.

int. = intention   cap. = capability

This table is based on his essay which can also be found in Raanan, Platzgraff, and Kemp, *Intelligence Policy and National Security* (London: Macmillan, 1981). Similarly: 'Therefore, when capable, feign incapacity; when active, inactivity. When near, make it appear that you are far away: when far away, that you are near.' Sun Tzu, *The Art of War*, p.66. Herbig and Daniel in their essay 'Propositions On Military Deception' classify all military deceptions in two categories: one group is termed 'ambiguity-increasing' deception, which seeks to compound uncertainties on the deceived side, and the second is the misleading type, which is designed to *reduce ambiguity* by building up the attractiveness of one wrong alternative. Donald Daniel and Katherine C. Berbig, eds. *Strategic Military Deception* (New York: Pergamon Press, 1982), pp.3–30.

18. For a detailed analysis of this problem, see Michael I. Handel, *Perception, Deception and Surprise: The Case of the Yom Kippur War*, Jerusalem Papers on Peace Problems, no. 19 (Jerusalem: The Leonard Davis Institute, The Hebrew University, 1976); or Michael I. Handel, 'The Yom Kippur War and the Inevitability of Surprise', *International Studies Quarterly* 21 (19 Sept. 1977), 461–502.

19. Handel, *Perception, Deception and Surprise*.

20. On the importance of intelligence feedback from the target, see Daniel and Herbig's paper 'Propositions On Military Deception'.

21. The literature on Ultra's contribution to British Intelligence operations and to the war effort in general is growing very rapidly. For a sample, see Ralph Bennet, *Ultra In the West: The Normandy Campaign of 1944–1945* (New York: Scribner's, 1980); Patrick Beesly, *Very Special Intelligence: The Story of the Admiralty's Operational Intelligence Centre 1939–1945* (Garden City, N.Y.: Doubleday, 1978); Ronald Lewin, *Ultra Goes to War* (New York: McGraw Hill, 1978); P.J. Calvocoressi, 'The Secrets of Enigma', *The Listener* 97 (Jan. and Feb. 1977), 70–1, 112–14, 135–7; Harold C. Deutsch, 'The Historical Impact of Revealing the Ultra Secret', *Parameters* 7, no. 3 (1977), 16–32, and Harold C. Deutsch, 'The Influence of Ultra on World War II', *Parameters* 8, no. 4 (1978), 2–15. See also Patrick Beesly, 'The British View', Jürgen Rohwer, 'The German View'; Kenneth Knowles, 'The American View'; and Harold C. Deutsch, 'The Historical Impact of Revealing the Ultra Secret' in *Cryptologic Spectrum* 8, no. 1 (1978), 5–29. Peter Calvocoressi, *Top Secret Ultra* (London: Cassell, 1980); David Kahn, 'Codebreaking in World Wars I and II: The Major Successes and Failures. Their Causes and Their Effects', *The Historical Journal* 23, no. 3 (1980), 618–39; Jürgen Rohwer, 'Der Einfluss Der Alliierten Funkaufklärung Auf Den Verlauf Des Zweiten Weltkrieges', *Vierteljahrsheft für Zeitgeschichte* 23 (July 1979), 525–70; Jürgen Rohwer and Eberhard Jackel, eds. *Die Funkaufklärung und ihre Rolle im Zweiten Weltkrieg* (Stuttgart: Motorbuch Verlag, 1979). On the Polish contribution see: Richard A. Woytak, *On the Border of War and Peace: Polish Intelligence and Diplomacy in 1937–1939 and the Origins of the Ultra Secret* (New York: Columbia University Press, 1979). Ultra was of course an invaluable follow-up instrument extremely useful for the elaborate British deception operations in World War II. On the technical aspects of Enigma see Gordon Welchman, *The Hut Six Story: Breaking the Enigma Codes* (New York: McGraw-Hill, 1982), and Jozef Garlinski, *The Enigma War* (New York: Charles Scribner, 1980).

22. Major-General I.S.O. Playfair, *The Mediterranean and Middle East: The Early Successes Against Italy*. Vol. 1, *History of the Second World War* (London: HMSO, 1954), p.274.

23. See Mure, *Practise to Deceive*; David Mure, *Master of Deception: Tangled Webs in London and the Middle East* (London: William Kimber, 1980); and Dennis Wheatley, *The Deception Planners: My Secret War* (London: Hutchinson, 1980). See also Cruickshank, *Deception in World War II*, chap. 2, pp.19–33.

24. Mure, *Practise to Deceive*, p.23.

25. Mure, *Practise to Deceive*, p.24n.

26. See Correlli Barnett, *The Desert Generals* New enl. ed. (Bloomington: Indiana University Press, 1982), pt. 1; John Strawson, *The Battle for North Africa* (New York: Charles Scribner's Sons, 1969), chap. 3; and Playfair, *The Mediterranean and Middle East*, chaps. 14–15.

27. Playfair, *The Mediterranean and Middle East*, p.260.

28. Ibid., p.260.

29. Cruickshank, *Deception in World War II*, chap. 2, pp.19–34.

30. See Sir Archibald Wavell, *Allenby: A Study in Greatness* (New York: Oxford University Press, 1941); and A.P. Wavell, *The Palestine Campaign*, 3rd ed. (London: Constable, 1936). On Allenby's use of deception in his Palestine Cam-

paigns see also Captain Cyril Calls, *Military Operations in Egypt and Palestine*, 3 vols. (London: HMSO, 1930). For Wavell's interest in intelligence see also Ronald Lewin, *Ultra Goes to War* (New York: McGraw Hill, 1979), p.159.

31. For the success of Overlord see, among others, Anthony Cave Brown, *Bodyguard of Lies* (New York: Harper and Row, 1975); Gilles Perrault, *The Secret of D-Day* (Boston: Little Brown, 1965); Cornelius Ryan, *The Longest Day* (London: Gollancz, 1959). All are competent journalistic accounts. Hans Speidel, *We Defended Normandy* (London: Herbert Jenkins, 1951); G.A. Harrison, *Cross Channel Attack* (Washington D.C.: The U.S. Army in World War II, European Theater of Operations, 1951); L.F. Ellis, *Victory in the West*, (London: HMSO, 1962), vol. 1. The latest literature on D-Day includes Carlos D'Este, *Decision in Normandy* (New York: E.P. Dutton, 1983) and Max Hastings, *Overlord: D-Day and the Battle for Normandy* (New York: Simon and Schuster, 1984).

An interesting thesis written on the subject in 1969 (and thus without advantage of the disclosure of Ultra) is: T.L. Cubbage, 'Anticipating Overlord: Intelligence and Deception – German Estimates of Allied Intentions to Land Invasion Forces in Western Europe' (Washington, D.C.: Defense Intelligence School, 1969). This book provides an excellent example of the possibility of producing a thought-provoking and stimulating analysis without resorting to classified information. The definitive history of Overlord in light of Ultra has still to be written.

On the deception plans to cover Operation 'Husky', the invasion of Sicily, see Mure, *Practise to Deceive*, pp.93–105. This deception plan was so successful that by the time the invasion took place, the British had managed to draw seven German and seven Italian divisions to Greece, compared with the two German and four Italian divisions remaining in Sicily. Equally impressive was the fact that on the day of the invasion, Rommel arrived in Athens to take command of the German anti-invasion armies in Greece. Mure, *Practise to Deceive*, p.103; also Cruickshank, *Deception in World War II*, pp.50–60.

32. Surprise is relative and only rarely complete or total. In most cases of sudden attack, the surprised side normally had enough information and warning signals to indicate the possibility of a forthcoming attack – its timing, place, direction, and the like. Attacks out of the blue, i.e., achieving total surprise without *any* warning are almost non-existent. Surprise attacks preceded by a very small number of warning signals are also very rare. The Allied attack across the Channel was, from the German point of view, preceded by only very few signals indicating the existence of an immediate danger, and therefore comes as close as possible to an attack out of the blue. The various degrees of surprise that can be achieved and the relativity of surprise to warning or alert are presented in figure 3.

FIGURE 3

THE RELATIVITY OF SURPRISE

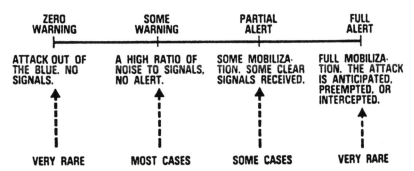

350 WAR, STRATEGY AND INTELLIGENCE

33. See Michael Handel, 'Crisis and Surprise in Three Arab–Israeli Wars', in *Strategic Military Surprise*, eds. Klaus Knorr and Patrick Morgan (New Brunswick, N.J.: Transaction Books, 1983).

34. Quoted in Whaley, *Stratagem, Deception and Surprise*, p.575.

35. For a detailed analysis, see Handel, 'Crisis and Surprise in Three Arab–Israeli Wars'.

36. On this episode, see Donald McLachlan, *Room 39: A Study in Naval Intelligence* (New York: Atheneum, 1968), pp.56, 129.

37. Quoted from Edward L. Homze, *Arming the Luftwaffe: The Reich Air Ministry and the German Aircraft Industry 1919–1939* (Lincoln: University of Nebraska Press, 1976), p.169. See also Walter Bernhardt, *Die Deutsche Aufrüstung, 1934–1939* (Frankfurt: Bernard and Grofe, 1962); Williamson Murray, 'The Change in the European Balance of Power 1938–1939' (Ph.D. dissertation, Yale University, 1975), chap. 3, pp.58–90. A revised version is Williamson Murray, *The Change in the European Balance of Power 1938–1939: The Path to Ruin* (New Jersey: Princeton University Press, 1984). John Edwin Wood, 'The Luftwaffe as a Factor in British Policy 1935–1939' (Ph.D. dissertation, Tulane University, 1954); Michael Mihalka, *German Strategic Deception in the 1930s* (Santa Monica, California: The Rand Corp., July 1980, N-1557–NA); Mathtech, *Covert Rearmament in Germany 1919–1939: Deception and Misperception*, Part of CIA Deception Research Program (Princeton, N.J.: Mathtech, March 1979); Wesley K. Wark, 'British Intelligence on the German Air Force and Aircraft Industry, 1933–1939', *The Historical Journal* 25 (March 1982), 627–48. In his article 'Appeasement and Intelligence', David Dilks claims there is evidence that part of the deception campaign concerning the strength of the *Luftwaffe* and the possibility of a German 'knock out' air bombardment on Britain and Holland was planted by the German anti-Hitler elements in order to force Great Britain to accelerate its rearmament and pledge itself to a continental commitment. David Dilks, ed., *Retreat from Power: Studies in Britain's Foreign Policy of the Twentieth Century 1906–1939* (London: Macmillan, 1981), p.158.

38. Exaggerated strength was attributed to the *Luftwaffe* more by British civilian leaders than by British intelligence estimates. But psychology and fear proved to be more powerful than the cold intelligence calculations. See Murray, 'The Change in the European Balance of Power', pp.71–2; also H. Montgomery Hyde, *British Air Policy Between the Wars 1918–1939* (London: Heinemann, 1976); Gerhard L. Weinberg, *The Foreign Policy of Hitler's Germany: Starting World War II, 1937–1939* (Chicago: Chicago University Press, 1980), for example pp.22–3; 164–5; also Gordon Scott Smith, 'RAF War Plans and British Foreign Policy 1935–1940' (Ph.D. dissertation, MIT, June 1966), in particular chap. 3, pp.71–99. The problem was that not only did the British exaggerate German capabilities, they also overestimated the devastation of strategic air bombardments. The CID (Committee of Imperial Defence) estimated in 1937 that 60 days of strategic bombing in England would result in 600,000 dead and 1,200,000 injuries (Smith, 'RAF War Plans', p.186).

    Certainly appeasement was a consequence of a serious misunderstanding of Hitler's intentions and capabilities. This misunderstanding, however, was reinforced by the fear of the "knock-out blow." Had the fear of the "knock-out blow" not been so great it might have been easier for the appeasers to see their folly in trying to meet Hitler's demands. Fear of the "knock-out blow" made the appeasers even more prepared to accept German demands than they might otherwise have been. The consequences of war were visualized as so awful that almost any cost was worth paying if war could be avoided. From the Air Ministry poured forth the facts and figures that made war seem impossible, the true opiate of the appeasers (Smith, 'RAF War Plans', pp.167–8).

39. Telford Taylor, *Munich: The Price of Peace* (Garden City, N.Y.: Doubleday, 1979), p.xv.

40. Quoted from Mack Smith, *Mussolini's Roman Empire*, p.170; also pp.174–75.
41. Ibid., p.174. During the Second World War itself, the Italians and Japanese never developed new or advanced weapons. 'Their equipment was for the most part imitative and as the war continued, inferior in design.' Alan S. Milward, *War, Economy and Society 1939–1940* (Berkeley: University of California Press, 1977), p.175.
42. Mack Smith, *Mussolini's Roman Empire*, pp.174, 177–8.
43. Murray, 'The Change in the European Balance of Power', p.213.
44. After the war, the *Luftwaffe*'s General Plochner claimed that he had warned Hitler about the low quality of the Italian armed forces. The words he used to describe his Italian allies were unkind indeed:

> I reminded him [Hitler] that a King of Naples had once said the following about them [the Italians]: "You can take as much trouble with the Italians as you want, you can give them the very best weapons, a mountain of ammunition to practice with, you can dress them in red, blue or green uniforms, but you will never succeed in transforming them into a useful military instrument. There are two principles to which they will always remain true. The first is: when the enemy comes in view, the best thing that you can do is to run the other way; and the second: better to be a coward for five minutes than dead all your life." I told Hitler the only thing that had changed in Italy was Mussolini's big mouth, which was trying to convince the Italians that they had been the real victors of Vittorio Veneto. (Quoted in Murray, 'The Change in the European Balance of Power', p.217.)

While the Italian philosophy of life might have seemed strange and contemptible to a Prussian, there are certainly a few good things that could be said for it.
45. For details on the 'bomber gap', see Lawrence Freedman, *U.S. Intelligence and the Soviet Strategic Threat* (Boulder, Co.: Westview Press, 1977), pp.64–7; and John Pardos, *The Soviet Estimate: U.S. Intelligence Analysis and Russian Military Strength* (New York: The Dial Press, 1982), Chapter 4, pp.38–50.
'Capability-enhancing' deception is a long-standing practice. Military parades have often been used to deceive observers by having the same troops repeatedly pass by the reviewing stand with minor changes to make them seem like additional troops. See for example: Heinz Werner Schmidt, *With Rommel in the Desert* (London: George Harrap, 1951), chap. 2, pp.16–21.
Under Nasser, the Egyptians used a parade to demonstrate their development of medium-range ballistic missiles that were actually made out of cardboard. However, this display backfired because it gave the Israelis the impetus to increase their efforts to expel from Egypt the German scientist participating in the project and perhaps even to step up their *own* efforts in missile design.
46. For the missile gap story, Khrushchev's policy, and the American reaction, see Edgar Bottome, *The Missile Gap: A Study of the Formulation of Military and Political Policy* (Rutherford, N.J.: Fairleigh Dickinson University Press, 1971); Arnold L. Horelick and Myron Rush, *Strategic Power and Soviet Foreign Policy* (Chicago: Chicago University Press, 1966) (from which the quotes were taken, pp.45–6); Freedman, *U.S. Intelligence* 4, 'The Missile Gap', pp.62–80; Pardos, *The Soviet Estimate*, pp.80–95; 111–26.
Another, different capability-oriented deception must be mentioned in this context. Even if US intelligence was aware of the fact that no *real* missile gap existed between the US and the USSR, or soon learned that it was a hoax, it was in the interest of the US Air Force or Army to maintain this myth in order to justify a greater investment in their own capabilities. It is not unusual for rumors of the real and imagined new strength of the Red Army to become rife before the Pentagon budget is decided. Whether conscious or not, this deception can be expected of almost any military organization.
47. For other wartime deception operations that backfired or got out of control, see Jones, 'Intelligence and Deception', pp.8–11.

48. The Israelis did not plan or want to go to war in 1967. The May crisis caught them
    completely off guard. The veil of secrecy concerning their real strength did involve
    conscious deception planning, yet what was not realized at the time was that *too
    much secrecy* regarding capabilities will project an image of weakness, which in
    turn could lead to a war that no one desired. See Handel, 'Crisis and Surprise in
    Three Arab–Israeli Wars'.
49. On the German underestimation of Soviet capabilities, see, among others,
    Lyman Kirkpatrick, *Captains Without Eyes: Intelligence Failures in World War II*
    (London: Macmillan, 1969), pp.15, 51, 268; Barry A. Leach, *German Strategy
    Against Russia 1939–1941* (Oxford: Oxford University Press, 1973), pp.91–94 and
    Appendix 4, p.270; Albert Seaton, *The Russo-German War 1941–1945* (New
    York: Praeger, 1972), chap. 3, 'A Little Knowledge', pp.43–50; Seweryn Bialer,
    ed., *Stalin and His Generals* (New York: Pegasus, 1969); Robert Cecil, *Hitler's
    Decision to Invade Russia 1941* (London: Davis-Poynter, 1975); David Kahn,
    Hitler's Spies: German Military Intelligence in World War II (New York: Mac-
    millan, 1978), pp.457–61, John Francis O'Neil, 'German Counter – C³ Activity
    and its Effects on Soviet Command, Control and Communications During
    Operation Barbarossa' (thesis, Naval Postgraduate School, Monterey, Cali-
    fornia, March 1980). Bryan I. Fugate, *Operation Barbarossa* (Novato, CA:
    Presidio Press, 1984). Herbert Goldhamer suggests that Soviet secrecy brought
    about the collapse of Soviet deterrence and led to a war the Soviet Union had
    wanted to avoid:

    > Soviet deterrence policy, even though combined with massive forces, failed in the
    > end to deter the Nazis. Perhaps a continuation of past Soviet overt hospitality
    > would have served the Soviet Union better than did the Nazi-Soviet pact.
    > Perhaps, too, Soviet military secrecy – also a form of manipulation of perceptions
    > – may have had an anti-deterrent effect since it led Nazi intelligence to estimate at
    > only one half of its true value the number of Soviet divisions that would be
    > available after the onset of war.

    Herbert Goldhamer, *Reality and Belief in Military Affairs* (Santa Monica, Ca.:
    The Rand Corp., February 1979, R-2448–NA), pp.39, 111.
    By April 1941 the Russians had apparently become aware of the fact that their
    excessive secrecy might be seriously undermining their deterrence posture, for
    they invited a group of German military experts to visit a number of aircraft and
    other defense plants in the Soviet Union.

    > The visiting group of specialists, headed by Col. Heinrich Aschenbrenner, Air
    > Attache in Moscow, soon discovered that the myth of Soviet deficiencies in the
    > area of workmanship was completely false. They also found out that Soviet
    > industry had achieved a great degree of independence. Even in individual plants
    > considerable self-sufficiency had been effected, and instalations were widely
    > dispersed. *The German contingent was probably invited specifically to receive a
    > warning from the Soviet Union, a message which, according to Colonel Aschen-
    > brenner, was unmistakable in intent*:

    > After the inspection of Fighter Aircraft Factory No. 1 at Moscow's Central
    > Airport, an unequivocal warning was imparted to us by none other than the
    > brother of the People's Commissar for Economics, Mikoyan, who was busy as
    > chief engineer in Factory No. 1. and after whom the famed Russian MIG fighters
    > are named. There is not the slightest doubt that this occurred at the order of the
    > highest [Soviet] authority. Mikoyan explained to me literally: "We have now
    > shown you everything that we have and what we can do; and whoever attacks us,
    > we destroy!" I passed this statement on, word for word, with corresponding
    > commentaries to all duty stations concerned, without, however, so much as
    > finding the slightest response.

    This warning came too late. Hitler had already made up his mind.

Hitler reacted to the report of the armament commission with the following words: *"Well, there you see how far these people are already. We must begin immediately."* That our report would have a reaction of that kind, we had of course not expected, let alone wanted (emphasis added).

Ironically enough, this report had the unexpected effect of increasing Hitler's determination to attack the USSR without any further delays. Source: General-lieutenant Herman Plocher, *The German Air Force Versus Russia, 1941* USAF Historical Studies, no. 153 (New York: Arno Press, July 1965), pp.17–18.

50. On Germany's deception concerning the construction of its battlefleet and the failure of British naval intelligence and the political leadership to acknowledge and protest this breach of faith, see Wesley K. Wark, 'Baltic Myths and Submarine Bogeys: British Naval Intelligence and Nazi Germany, 1933–1939', *The Journal of Strategic Studies* 6 (March 1983), 60–81; Roberta Wohlstetter, 'The Pleasures of Self-Deception', *The Washington Quarterly* 2 (Autumn 1979), 54–64; and McLachlan, *Room 39*, pp.135–142. McLachlan has made the following relevant observations as to some of the causes of this episode.

(1) The unwillingness of authority to believe information that has awkward political implications. (2) The tendency of naval officers and others who have taken part in negotiations to become advocates of the persons with whom they secured the agreement and to lose the scepticism which is part of vigilance. (3) Our technicians may not be the best judges of enemy intentions and achievement. They find it hard sometimes to believe that what they cannot do or have not thought of doing has been done by the other side. (Ibid., p.142.)

51. For 'passive deception' see Seymour Reit, *Masquerade: The Amazing Camouflage Deceptions of World War II* (New York: Hawthorn, 1978); G. Barkas, *The Camouflage Story* (London: Cassell, 1952).

It is important not to confuse *initiative* and *passivity* (or non-use) in the employment of deception, with the *offensive* and *defensive* uses of it. In his discussion of German deception in *Deception in World War II*, Cruickshank seems to commit such an error when he suggests, 'Deception may help the side holding the initiative, but is not much use to the side on the defensive' (p.206). It may be true that it is *easier* to design and implement deception on the offensive – but it is no less important on the defensive. This contradicts Cruickshank's own example of the successful deceptive measures taken during the Battle of Britain (chap. 1). The defender should by no means relinquish the advantages afforded by deception (primarily the technological and scientific types). This can be done by causing the attacker to waste his energy on phony targets or on heavily defended targets, by pretending to have more capabilities at weaker points of defense and fewer capabilities at the stronger points; by interfering with the enemy's nagivation aids; and by pretending to launch counterattacks at the enemy's rear or to outflank him (which would force him to spread his forces). Perhaps the best example of the use of deception for defensive purposes is the way that British intelligence used German double agents to divert the V-1 flying bombs away from London to an area further to the south, where the damage caused was much less severe. A carefully coordinated deception campaign by the British controlled double agents convinced the Germans (despite the contradictory evidence available to them) that the V-1 bombs 'tended to overshoot and would therefore shorten their range, whereas in fact they already tended to undershoot' (Masterman, *The Double Cross System*, p.179). This delicate operation required that a balance be struck between the passing of correct, independently verifiable information to the Germans and the passing of deceptive information. For the details of this fascinating operation, see: Masterman, *The Double Cross System*, pp.178ff; Montagu, *Beyond Top Secret Ultra*, pp.157–61; and Jones, *Most Secret War*, pp.420ff.

52. Jack Anderson, 'Old Fashioned Spying Methods Often the Best', *Washington*

Post, 24 Nov. 1981, p.D-15. See also Andrew Cockburn, *The Threat: Inside the Soviet Military Machine* (New York: Random House, 1983), pp.19–20.

53. See Jones, *Most Secret War*; Alfred Price, *Instruments of Darkness: The History of Electronic Warfare* (New York: Scribner, 1978); Alfred Price, *Battle Over the Reich* (New York: Charles Scribner, 1973); Brian Johnson, *The Secret War* (London: Methuen, 1978).

54. A detailed case study of this problem can be found in Ralph Baldwin, *The Deadly Fuze: Secret Weapons of World War II* (San Rafael, Ca.: Presidio Press, 1980). 'Window' was also a classical case of the problem of timing in the introduction of new weapons.

55. On this see Michael Handel, 'Surprise and Change in Diplomacy', *International Security* 4 (Spring 1980), 57–80; and Michael I. Handel, 'Avoiding Political and Technological Surprise in the 1980s' in *Intelligence Requirements for the 1980s: Analysis and Estimates*, ed., Roy Godson (New Brunswick, N.J.: Transaction Books, 1980), pp.85–111.

56. 'The perfect deception plan is like a jigsaw puzzle. Pieces of information are allowed to reach the enemy in such a way as to convince him that he has discovered them by accident. If he puts them together *himself* he is far more likely to believe that the intended picture is a true one' (Cruickshank, *Deception in World War II*, p.1).

57. A case in mind is that of 'Cicero', who, while operating in the British Embassy in Ankara, supplied the Germans with a great deal of correct and important information, some of which indicated the preparations for Operation Overlord. Much of the correct information was rejected by the Germans, in this instance for the wrong reasons, as being too good to be true. See L.C. Mayzisch, *Operation Cicero* (London: Fitzgibbon, 1950); and Franz von Papen, *Memoirs* (New York: E.P. Dutton, 1953), chap. 28, 'Operation Cicero', pp.506–29.

In fact, the Cicero affair was much more complex than has been realized until recently. Whether or not Cicero was employed by the British from the beginning (which appears to be likely), or whether or not he was a double agent, is less important than the fact that he was apparently used by the British intelligence-deception section in the Middle East (the so-called 'A' Force) as a vital channel for passing credible but deceptive information to the Germans intended to cover Operation Overlord. The deception was primarily intended to exaggerate the threat of a combined Allied and Turkish force in the Balkans. This operation, by the way, would have been impossible without the aid of Ultra in following the Germans' attitude toward the documents supplied by Cicero. For this see: Mure, *Practise to Deceive*, pp.107–15; also Anthony Cave-Brown, *Bodyguard of Lies* (New York: Harper and Row, 1975), pp.391–409.

For the best use of double agents as a major channel for passing decep-tive information, see Masterman, *The Double Cross System*; Mure, *Practise to Deceive*; and Mure, *Master of Deception*. The conclusions of these two experts on how to best employ double agents differ greatly and often contradict each other. This may be explained by the different operating conditions and problems in the Middle East and London.

Unlike the Germans, who were so naively deceived by Cicero, the Allies had the advantage of Ultra, which allowed them to *objectively verify* the validity of information they received, for example, in Switzerland from the so-called 'Schwartze Kapelle' and which appeared too good to be true. See Cave-Brown, *Bodyguard of Lies*, pp.300–17.

For the inter-bureaucratic power struggle between the German intelligence services (i.e., the military Abwehr headed by Canaris and the Gestapo's RSHA headed by Kaltenbrunner) and the Cicero case, see Peter R. Black, *Ernst Kaltenbrunner: Ideological Soldier of the Third Reich* (Princeton, NJ.: Princeton University Press, 1984), chap. 6, 'Struggle with the Rival Chieftains, 1943–1945', pp.176–217.

58. Mure, *Practise to Deceive*, p.14. This paraphrases Churchill's famous remark that

'in wartime truth is so precious that she should always be attended by a bodyguard of lies'.

59. Ibid., p.14.

60. Masterman, *The Double Cross System*, p.20.

61. Quoted from Richard J. Heuer, Jr., 'Strategic Deception: A Psychological Perspective' (paper presented at the 21st Annual Convention of the International Studies Association, Los Angeles, California, March 1980), pp.17–18. An abbreviated and less exciting version of this excellent paper also appeared in *International Studies Quarterly* 25 (June 1981), 294–327, under the title 'Strategic Deception and Counter-deception'.

62. Montagu, *Beyond Top Secret U*, p.60.

63. For an original, if somewhat exaggerated, discussion of the need to try to see things also from the adversary's point of view, see Ken Booth, *Strategy and Ethnocentrism* (London: Croom Helm, 1979).

64. Montagu, *Beyond Top Secret U*, pp.138–9.

65. The only systematic discussion of deception work is found in Whaley, *Stratagem: Deception and Surprise in War*; Whaley, *Codeword Barbarossa*; Daniel and Herbig, *Strategic Military Deception: Perspectives on its Study and Use*. Of the published memoirs, the best by far are those of Montagu, Jones, and Masterman.

66. Whaley, *Stratagem: Deception and Surprise in War*, pp.6–12.

67. Montagu claims he had more difficulties in convincing his superiors of the utility of deception than in executing the deception plans themselves. 'To deceive the German High Command was nothing like as difficult as it was to persuade their British opposite numbers that we could do that.' *The Man Who Never Was* (New York: Avon Publications, 1953), p.37.

68. Jones brings one example of a German deception plan to cover the number of V-3 launching sites – which actually helped Allied intelligence to deduce the correct number and rate of fire. 'Intelligence and Deception', p.22.

69. Dennis Wheatley, 'Deception in World War II', *RUSI* 121 (September 1976), 87. This of course should not be understood to mean that the systematic resort to deception operations did not exist prior to World War II. There is, however, a meaningful and important difference between deception initiated privately by individuals such as Allenby or Admiral 'Blinker' Hall on the one hand, and deceptions as a formal organizational activity.

70. Whaley, *Stratagem: Deception and Surprise in War*, p.147. Although there is no foolproof way to avoid deception, a number of possible rules for caution may be suggested:

(a) Avoid overreliance on one source of information. 'Reliance on one source is dangerous, the more reliable and comprehensive the source, the greater the dangers.' McLachlan, *Room 39*, p.366.

(b) Never rely on agents who have never been seen or directly interviewed. (This is primarily to avoid what, according to Mure, are the most successful sources of deception – notional agents, see *Practise to Deceive*.) Furthermore, real agents who cannot be directly interviewed can also be controlled by the adversary as was the case with the German spying system in England. (See Masterman, *The Double Cross System in the War of 1939 to 1945*.) This rule should be even more strictly observed if the information obtained from agents who may be notional seems to dovetail nicely with one's own preferences, needs, or wishes.

(c) Check and double check all cases in which agents' reports that appeared right turned out to be wrong on an important issue and yet seem to have a good explanation. For example, despite the fact that British-controlled double agents informed the Germans of the Allied intention to land in the Balkans after which the Allies landed in Sicily; or that the Germans were passed information indicating that the planned invasion of Europe would begin with an Allied landing in Pas de Calais after which the Allies landed in Normandy – the Germans *continued* to trust the same agents, a mistake which led to additional intelligence disasters. In both cases, the agents' failures were explained by last minute improvisations (e.g., the

Americans changed their plans on the spur of the moment and opted for Sicily instead; and in Normandy, after the Germans failed to counter-attack (which was, of course, the whole idea behind the deception plan), the Allies decided to improvise and land the forces originally intended for Pas de Calais in Normandy instead – which was what German intelligence wanted to believe). The continued faith of the German Abwehr in its agents despite these major failures led Mure to the somewhat speculative conclusion that this agency, being in opposition to Hitler, deliberately cooperated with British Intelligence by accepting what was known to be deceptive information in order to defeat Hitler. He concludes that British deception was so successful precisely because of the 'active connivance of the chief of the Abwehr, Admiral Canaris, and his colleagues of the Schwarze Kappelle' (Mure, *Practise to Deceive*, p.12).

Although some top officers of the Abwehr undoubtedly passed information and otherwise helped British Intelligence, it remains to be proven that *this* was the major reason for the success of British deception operations. According to Mure, this was also the suspicion of Galveston. This thesis is developed in Mure, *Practise to Deceive* and further elaborated upon in his book, *Master of Deception*.

71. Jones, 'Intelligence and Deception', p.23.
72. Heuer, 'Strategic Deception: A Psychological Perspective', p.28. Like Jones, he suggests:

> The bias favoring a small amount of consistent information over a large body of less consistent data supports the common maxim in deception that the deceiver should *control* as many information channels as possible in order to reduce the amount of discrepant information available to the target. Deception can be effective even with a small amount of information as long as the target does not receive contradictory data. Not only should the notional picture be consistent, but the deceiver should actively discredit the real picture as well. To achieve maximum consistency, it is necessary to discredit the true as well as to build up the false (Heuer, ibid., pp.33–4).

73. Heuer, ibid., p.45.
74. On recent Soviet deception and disinformation practices, see Joseph D. Douglass, Jr., 'Soviet Disinformation', *Strategic Review* (Winter 1981), 16–25; 'State Department Documents Soviet Disinformation and Forgeries' in *American Bar Association Standing Committee Law and National Security Intelligence Report* vol. 3, no. 11 and vol. 3, no. 12 (November and December 1981); also Ladislav Bittman, *The Deception Game: Czechoslovak Intelligence in Soviet Political Warfare* (Syracuse: Syracuse University Research Corporation, 1972); Roger Beaumont, *Maskirovka: Soviet Camouflage, Concealment and Deception* (College Station Texas: Texas A and M University, Stratech Studies SS82–1, November 1982); Jennie A. Stevens and Henry S. Marsh, 'Surprise and Deception in Soviet Military Thought', pt. 1, *Military Review* 6 (June 1982), 2–11 and pt. 2, *Military Review* 7 (July 1982), 24–35; and a letter by Richard W. Bloom, 'Surprise and Deception', *Military Review* 11 (Nov. 1982), 73–74; Roy Godson and Richard E. Schultz, *Desinformazia: Active Measures in Soviet Strategy* (New York: Pergamon, 1984).
75. See Goldhamer, *Reality and Belief in Military Affairs*; Mihalka, *German Strategic Deception in the 1930s*; and Michael I. Handel, *The Diplomacy of Surprise: Hitler, Nixon, Sadat* (Cambridge, Mass.: Harvard Center for International Affairs, 1981).
76. For a detailed analysis of Communist and Soviet attitudes to deception, see Nathan Leites, *A Study of Bolshevism*, chap. 13, 'Deception', pp.324–40.
77. Stalin's belief that every act of diplomacy (let alone war) involved deception is characterized by his statement that:

> When bourgeois diplomats prepare war, they begin with increased stress to talk about "peace" and about "friendly relations." If some Minister of Foreign Affairs

begins to advocate a "peace conference" you can infer that his government has already ordered new dreadnoughts and planes. With a diplomat, words *must* diverge from acts – what kind of diplomat would he otherwise be? Words are one thing and acts something different. Good words are masks for bad deeds. A sincere diplomat would equal dry water, wooden iron. (*Sotsial Demokrat* 25 (12 January 1913), quoted in Leites, *A Study of Bolshevism*, p. 325.)

For commentary on the inevitability of at least some deception in diplomacy, see Thomas A. Bailey, *The Art of Diplomacy: The American Experience* (New York: Appelton-Century-Crafts, 1968), pp. 165–66. Also Paul W. Blackstock, *The Strategy of Subversion* (Chicago: Quadrangle, 1964); Paul W. Blackstock, *Agents of Deceit: Frauds, Forgeries and Political Intrigue Among Nations* (Chicago: Quadrangle Books, 1966).

78. For an interesting analysis of this phenomenon see: Patrick J. McGarvey, *CIA: The Myth and the Madness* (Baltimore: Penguin, 1974).

79. See Christopher M. Andrew, *The Mobilization of British Intelligence for the World Wars* (Washington, D.C.: *International Security Studies*, no. 12, The Woodrow Wilson Center, no date, 1981?).

   On the recruiting of amateurs, university scholars, intellectuals, and the 'old boy' system, see also: Donald McLachlan, *Room 39*; Dennis Wheatley, *The Deception Planners* (London: Hutchinson, 1980). For the same practice during the First World War, see Patrick Beesly, *Room 40: British Naval Intelligence 1914–1918* (New York: Harcourt Brace Jovanovich, 1982), chap. 2.

80. McLachlan, *Room 39*, p. 354. He emphasizes the special contribution of civilians to deception.

   In his memoirs, Fieldmarshal Montgomery reached a similar conclusion:

   In the Second World War, the best officers in the Intelligence branch of the staff were civilians; they seemed to have the best brain for that type of work, trained in the "rules of evidence," fertile and with great imagination. ... (*The Memoirs of Field-Marshal The Viscount Montgomery of Alamein* (Cleveland: World Publishing Co., 1958), p. 151; also in Alun Chalfont, *Montgomery of Alamein* (New York: Atheneum, 1976), pp. 177–178).

81. McLachlan, *Room 39*, p. 343.

82. Ibid., p. 342.

83. Ibid., p. 343.

84. This attitude is also expressed by Mure, who formed a very negative and clearly biased view of the suitability of civilians for military intelligence work, in particular for deception operations. His argument is twofold. In the first place he argues (correctly) that operational military experience, a solid understanding of military affairs, and good habits of staff work are absolutely essential, and that the absence of such qualities among civilians led to bad staff work, poor coordination, and failure to fully exploit successful deception. His best example of this type of failure is the incident in which the 'Tricycle' (Ivan Popov) questionnaire concerning Pearl Harbor was passed to J. Edgar Hoover of the FBI, who failed to see its importance, instead of to the Office of Coordinator of Information – the American predecessor of the OSS. (Mure, *Master of Deception*, pp. 169–185.)

   His second argument is that the indiscriminate recruitment of civilians into the British intelligence community through 'old boy' networks resulted in serious breaches of security during the Second World War and to Soviet penetration of British intelligence by moles such as Philby. According to Mure this penetration had very serious consequences when Philby, who was in charge of MI6's Iberian desk Section 5, rejected overtures from Canaris and the Abwehr to negotiate a separate peace with the Allies (Mure, *Master of Deception*, chap. 11).

   While there is a grain of truth in the first accusation, the second is not really relevant. Bad staff work, problems of coordination, and the lack of understanding for military operations can be found among military men as much as among civilians; no doubt British Intelligence would not have been nearly as effective as it was in the absence of civilians. Furthermore, his Tricycle example fails to prove the point in question (see Montagu's answer, Mure, *Master of Deception*, pp.183–5).

One very important implication of his criticism which cannot be discussed in this context is that at least some part of the deception operations must be handled by the 'Operations' Branch of the staff, and *not* that of 'Intelligence' (Brigadier Dudley Clarke's first observation on the practice of deception in Mure, *Master of Deception*, Appendix, p.273).

Insofar as his second criticism is concerned, his point is factually correct but irrelevant first of all because, in the final analysis, the choice of civilians was in the hands of the military, which either failed to insist on the clearance procedures necessary for the recruited civilians or delegated the authority to civilians themselves. Given the circumstances of war, in which hundreds of civilians had to be rapidly recruited and integrated into the intelligence system, the routine procedures were probably too slow to be adhered to. Finally, breaches of security by civilians of course do not *as such* implicate all civilians. The only correct and logical conclusion is that security must be improved.

Both Mure books are of interest for the student of deception. Yet his tendency to prefer so-called Devil's (and speculative) theories and his heavy reliance upon circumstantial evidence to demonstrate the validity of his theories are unfortunately not the best qualities in a first-rate intelligence officer.

85. Kahn, *Hitler's Spies*, p.533.
86. Andrew, *The Mobilization of British Intelligence*, p.28. The advantage of British amateurism was also evident in the war in the Western Desert, in which British desert navigation amateurs from before the war were much better than the Germans in long-range navigation raids and commando-type operations carried out behind German lines. See Ronald Lewin, *The Life and Death of the Afrika Corps* (London: Corgi, 1979), in particular pp.12–13; also W.B. Kennedy Shaw, *Long Range Desert Group* (London: Collins, 1945); Virginia Cowles, *The Phantom Major* (London: Collins, 1958); Vladimir Peniakiff (Popski), *Private Army* (London: Jonathan Cape, 1950). German professionalism under Rommel clearly had its advantages too.
87. Kahn, *Hitler's Spies*, p.523. German intelligence on the lower tactical levels was much better than on the strategic level. For a more technical description of German intelligence see *German Military Intelligence 1939–1945* (Military Intelligence Division, U.S. Army War Department, April 1946), now declassified and published (Frederick, Maryland: University Publications of America, 1984).
88. Ibid., pp.524–43. Japanese intelligence suffered from many of the weaknesses of its German counterpart and performed even worse. See Harold Lowell Ashman, 'Intelligence and Foreign Policy: A Functional Analysis' (Ph.D. dissertation, University of Utah, 1973), chap. 3, Intelligence Failure in Militarist Japan, pp.91–118. For Japanese attitudes toward intelligence work, see also Marder, *Former Friends New Enemies* (Oxford: Oxford University Press, 1981), p.334.
89. Kahn, *Hitler's Spies*, p.528.
90. Ibid., p.528. The same dilemmas were later faced by the Germans themselves when moving on the strategic level from the offense to the defense. The predicament of the side on the strategic defense was summarized by Grossadmiral Karl Dönitz in his memoirs:

A maritime power which intends to undertake an invasion always retains the strategic and tactical advantage since the choice of landing points remains in its hands. For a continental power which is called upon to defend its coastline it is therefore always difficult to decide which are the right places upon which to concentrate the main weight of the defense; for to be equally strong along a coast line of any great length, as Europe, is impossible. The continental power, too, has to wait, before it can take its operational decisions, until the maritime power has made its choice of landing points.

Karl Dönitz, *Memoirs, Ten Years and Twenty Days* (Cleveland: The World

Publishing Company, 1959), p.392.

91. For a detailed analysis, see Handel, *The Diplomacy of Surprise*.

92. Kahn mentions two other reasons for the failure of German intelligence during the Second World War which are of less interest in this context: (1) German anti-Semitism, which caused the flight of knowledge and brains from Germany and simultaneously added to the Allies' pool of knowledge; and (2) the poor organization and large number of competing German intelligence agencies, which caused considerable waste of resources, lack of coordination, fragmentation, and hostility between the various organizations.

93. Whaley, *Stratagem, Deception and Surprise in War*, p.233. According to Wheatley, only seven officers were privy to the 'whole truth' or the extent of the *entire* British deception effort during the Second World War. See Dennis Wheatley, 'Deception in World War II', *RUSI* 121, no. 3 (Sept. 1976), 87–8.

   According to Mure in *Practise to Deceive*, the total number of British Intelligence personnel involved in the highly successful deceptions in the Mediterranean area of 'A' Force was not more than fifty (p.128).

   In *Deception in World War II*, Cruickshank reports that the total number of British soldiers involved in the extensive deception plans in the Mediterranean–Middle East area was 41 officers and 76 NCOs (p.19). The total number of participants in the deception cover-up for Operation Fortitude North was 28 officers and 334 other ranks (p.112).

94. The exception is expensive and complicated cryptoanalysis and decoding operations such as Ultra, which require a large number of participants. These of course relate to intelligence operations in general, not only to deception work. In retrospect, one of the amazing things about Ultra was the length of time it remained an undisclosed secret.

95. Whaley, *Stratagem, Deception and Surprise in War*, p.234.

96. For an attempt at devising a methodology for estimating the cost-effectiveness of deception see: *Thoughts on the Cost-Effectiveness of Deception and Related Tactics in the Air War 1939 to 1945*, Deception Research Program (Princeton, N.J.: Mathtech, and ORD/CIA Analytic Methodology Research Division, March 1979).

97. See Handel, *Perception, Deception and Surprise: The Case of the Yom Kippur War*. Also in Michael I. Handel, 'The Yom Kippur War and the Inevitability of Surprise', *International Studies Quarterly* 21 (Sept. 1977), 461–502; and Richard K. Betts, 'Analysis, War and Decision: Why Intelligence Failures are Inevitable', *World Politics* 31 (October 1978), 61–80. The inevitability of surprise (and deception) therefore makes the suggestion that the very 'knowledge that cover and deception is being deployed *must* be denied to the enemy' seem rather useless. In war and conflict situations, it must always be assumed that the adversary will employ some sort of deception in any rational and intelligent military planning. See Herbig and Daniel, 'Propositions On Military Intelligence', p.21.

98. Heuer, 'Strategic Deception: A Psychological Perspective', p.43.

99. Ibid., p.47. Elsewhere I have suggested the other following paradoxes (or inherent contradictions) of intelligence work:

   As a result of the great difficulty in differentiating between 'signals' and 'noise' in strategic warning, both valid and invalid information must be treated on a similar basis. In effect, all that exists is noise, not signals.

   The greater the risk, the less likely it seems to be, and the less risky it actually becomes. Thus, the greater the risk, the smaller it becomes.

   The sounds of silence. A quiet international environment can act as background noise which, by conditioning observers to a peaceful routine, actually covers preparations for war.

   The greater the credibility of an intelligence agency over time, the less its reports and conclusions are questioned; therefore, the greater the risk of overrelying on its findings in the long run.

Self-negating prophecy. Information on a forthcoming enemy attack leads to counter-mobilization which, in turn, prompts the enemy to postpone or cancel his plans. It is thus impossible – even in retrospect – to know whether counter-mobilization is justified or not.

The more information is collected, the more difficult it becomes to filter, organize, and process the data in time to be of (relevant) use.

The more information is collected, the more noise will be added.

The more alerts are sounded, the less meaningful they become (alert fatigue).

Making working systems more sensitive reduces the risk of surprise but increases the number of false alarms.

100. Quoted in Handel, *Perception, Deception and Surprise*, p.9.
101. This is very common in detective stories, films (such as *The Sting, Sleuth,* etc.), and drama (such as works by the Swiss playwright Friedrich Dürrenmatt) or Spy vs. Spy in *Mad Magazine*.
102. See Jones, *Most Secret War*, chap. 22 'Window', pp.287–300; Brian Johnson, *The Secret War* (London: BBC, 1978), chap. 2, in particular pp.116ff; Williamson Murray, *Strategy For Defeat: The Luftwaffe 1933–1945* (Maxwell Air Force Base, Alabama: Air University Press, 1983), pp.167, 179, 212–14.
103. Other than disclosing technologies related to the destruction of the SAM-6 batteries, the Israelis exposed for the first time a vast array of modern weapons from the Merkava tank through mini-RPVs, 'live' protective armor for tanks, new anti-tank shells and missiles, and numerous other tactics and technologies.
104. Montagu, *Beyond Top Secret U*, pp.60–61.
105. David Dilks, 'Appeasement and Intelligence', in David Dilks (ed.), *Retreat From Power*, p.169.

8

Strategic and Operational Deception

... each surprise action is rooted in at least some degree of cunning.

The use of a trick or stratagem permits the intended victim to make his own mistakes, which, combined in a single result, suddenly change the nature of the situation before his very eyes.

But words, being cheap, are the most common means of creating false impressions.[1]

The invaluable ruse [Meinerzhagen's 'haversack ruse'] which has been described would not have worked the other way. The Turks could be confirmed in their belief that Gaza was the objective; they could not have been dissuaded from this belief by any faked plan of attack on Beersheba.[2]

What is or is not possible matters less than what the enemy believes possible.[3]

Deception has long been recognized as one of the most important elements inherent in warfare. In a nutshell, deception may be defined as: The process of influencing the enemy to make decisions disadvantageous to himself by supplying or denying information.[4] Sun Tzu concluded that 'All warfare is based on deception',[5] while Clausewitz, who did not assign a role of key importance to deception in his theory of war, nevertheless observed:

... it seems not unjust that the term 'strategy' should be derived from 'cunning' and that, for all the real and apparent changes that war has undergone since the days of ancient Greece, this term still indicates its essential nature. ...

No human characteristic appears so suited to the task of directing and inspiring strategy as the gift of cunning.[6]

Yet despite their recognition of deception as a very important – perhaps even decisive – dimension in waging war, strategists have never accepted it as one of the 'basic principles' of the art of war.[7] A special principle of deception has been omitted because deception *per se* has no value; it assumes significance only when used as a *means* of achieving surprise. In comparison, surprise is a decisive factor on all levels of warfare that has been duly acknowledged as an autonomous principle by all compendia of the maxims of war. Thus, deception is a valuable tool at the disposal of military commanders seeking to achieve strategic, operational and tactical surprise which may, in turn, provide them with one of the keys to victory.

DECEPTION IN HISTORICAL PERSPECTIVE

In classical antiquity, the use of stratagem in warfare was not only accepted – it was expected. Many accounts of war and battles in ancient epics, the Bible, the *Iliad* and the *Odyssey*, or Greek, Roman and Chinese histories abound with examples. The reason is obvious. During a time when almost all other factors were held as equal (there being minimal differences between the weapons available to adversaries), battles were primarily decided by either superior numbers or superior military leadership. Inasmuch as material changes evolved slowly, the 'cutting edge' of the battlefield was to be found in inspired ruses of war. Deception was consequently one of the few 'force multipliers' available that could lead to a decisive victory.

In medieval Europe, however, the inter-related influences of Christianity and chivalry caused the resort to deception to be considered a dishonorable and unfashionable course of action. Exerting an influence that endured at least until the First World War, the altruistic credo of the chivalrous knights was exemplified by their solemn vow 'to speak the truth, to succor the helpless and oppressed and never to turn back from an enemy.'[8]

> Christianity had a part in fashioning medieval warfare in both theory and practice. The central idea of a just Christian war for the sake of punishing evildoers was perhaps of little real significance for practice. But the same cannot be said of the military guild of knighthood with its strong individualistic moral code of chivalry shaped by a common Christian outlook. Widespread belief in the chivalrous virtues and in the Christian faith, the idea of common membership in the Republica Christiana, may have helped to prevent warfare from becoming the very bloody and total kind of activity that it had been among the ancients. Between medieval foes there was the bond of Christian conduct and gentlemanly behavior that tended to mitigate the nature of the punitive action resorted to by the victor. *This may account for the fact that medieval commanders did not make full use of the stratagems that had been a common part of the classical military leader's repertoire. Conversely, the medieval commander seemed particularly suscep-*

tible to the employment of deception and trickery by a ruthless and unchivalrous opponent.[9] [my emphasis]

The ethic of chivalry stressed a reverence for order that was regulated by commonly understood, formalized rules for combat. Preservation of honor and the demonstration of bravery were more important than victory in this type of warfare cum social ritual.[10]

Today the code of chivalry still forms part of the education of officers and gentlemen in some Western and Latin American countries; in fact, it may put them at a subtle disadvantage in confrontations with officers from either communist or Third World nations who do not feel bound by Western norms (examples include the US and Japan in the Pacific; the Germans and Russians on the Eastern Front; and the US in Korea and Vietnam).[11]

Even while chivalry was at its zenith, not all Christian states played according to the rules of the game. The Byzantine emperors were only too willing to take advantage of the attitude of the Franks, as illustrated by Emperor Leo's advice to his generals:

> The Frank believes that a retreat under any circumstances must be dishonorable; hence he will fight whenever you choose to offer him battle. This you must not do until you have secured all possible advantages for yourself, as his cavalry, with their long lances and large shields, charge with a tremendous impetus. You should deal with him by protracting the campaign, and if possible lead him into the hills, where his cavalry are less efficient than in the plain. After a few weeks without a great battle, his troops, who are very susceptible to fatigue and weariness, will grow tired of the war, and ride home in great numbers. . . . You will find him utterly careless as to outposts and reconnaissances, so that you can easily cut off outlying parties of his men, and attack his camp at advantage. As his forces have no bonds of discipline, but only those of kindred or oath, they fall into confusion after delivering their charge; you can therefore simulate flight, and then turn on them, when you will find them in utter disarray. On the whole, however, it is easier and less costly to wear out a Frankish army by skirmishes and protracted operations rather than to attempt to destroy it at a single blow.[12]

Charles Oman has commented on Byzantine strategy as follows:

> Of chivalry there is not a spark in the Byzantine, though professional pride is abundantly shown. Courage is regarded as one of the requisites necessary for obtaining success, not as the sole and paramount virtue of the warrior. Leo considers a cam-

paign successfully concluded without a great battle as the cheapest and most satisfactory consummation in war. . . . He shows a strong predilection for stratagems, ambushes and simulated retreats. . . . The Art of War as understood at Constantinople in the tenth century, was the only scheme of true scientific merit existing in the world, and was unrivaled till the sixteenth century.[13]

In stark contrast to the ethic of chivalry, the principles of Sun Tzu and Emperor Leo emphasized that the greatest skill a commander could demonstrate would be to subdue the enemy without fighting.[14] It is clear that strategists who prefer victory at the lowest possible cost or even without bloodshed also show much more interest in deception than those who see the acme of a commander's skill as being demonstrated in battle itself and are therefore continually searching for the decisive engagement.

The transition from the age of chivalry to the limited wars of the *ancien régime*, wherein the divine right of kings superseded Christianity as the highest moral guidance for the conduct of war, produced little incentive to resort to deception. When the stakes are relatively limited, adversaries who share common values and have a common interest in maintaining a general framework for order (in other words, the balance of power) are not as concerned by the search for a decisive victory nor do they fear total defeat. In such circumstances, the rules of the balance of power reduce military interest in deception by limiting the objectives and consequences of war. (There were, of course, always some individual leaders or states during each of these periods who relied extensively on deception thereby taking advantage of those who played by the rules.) Thus, to the influence of the *Republica Christiana* and the ethic of chivalry was now added the moderating effect of universal adherence to the rules dictated by the balance of power.

The French Revolution, however, gave rise to a revolutionary international system of total war in which no common rules were accepted by the opponents.[15] At first glance, it might seem as though wars between ideologically divergent groups whose pursuit of immoderate goals is fed by mass mobilization and backed by the whole of their industrial might would provide fertile ground for the use of deception. Yet this did not prove to be true from the outbreak of the French Revolution up to the end of the First World War. How can this be explained?

The experience of the Napoleonic wars seemed to bear out the effectiveness of the search for the decisive battle. Although Napoleonic warfare was largely based on maneuver, the purpose of maneuver was not so much deception, or even surprise, as the concentration of a larger number of soldiers ahead of the enemy on the battlefield. As Clausewitz and Jomini emphasized, superiority in numbers was the real key to victory. 'The best in strategy is always to *be very strong* first in general, and then at the decisive point. . . . There is no higher and simpler law of strategy than that of *keeping one's forces concentrated.*'[16] [Emphasis in the original.] 'An impartial student of modern war must admit that superior numbers are becoming more decisive with each passing day. The principle of bringing the maximum possible strength to the decisive engagement must therefore rank higher than it did in the past.'[17]

It is not surprising, therefore, that Clausewitz considered diversions a waste of strength since they reduced the number of troops available to the commander at the decisive point.

> To prepare a sham action with sufficient thoroughness to impress an enemy requires a considerable expenditure of time and effort, and the costs increase with scale of the deception. Normally they call for more than can be spared, and consequently so-called strategic feints rarely have the desired effect. It is dangerous, in fact, to use substantial forces over any length of time merely to create an illusion: there is always the risk that nothing will be gained and that the troops deployed will not be available when they are really needed.[18]

In circumstances in which victory was sought through firepower and attrition in the decisive battle and in which the ability to achieve surprise was limited – deception had no role to play.[19] The mobility and speed necessary to achieve strategic or operational surprise on a larger scale only became feasible during the First World War. Hence, the approach to strategic and operational success during the nineteenth century and the 1914–18 war emphasized the concentration of a larger number of soldiers at the decisive point on the battlefield – and ultimately, therefore, the superior concentration of firepower. Reinforced by the industrial–technological revolution, which supplied the weapons and ammunition required for superior firepower, this trend reached its most extreme manifestation during the First World War. It must again be emphasized that this describes a general trend not without some notable exceptions.

Paradoxically, deception and surprise appear to have reached their lowest ebb during the First World War even as the groundwork was being laid for their vital contribution during the Second World War. In the first place, new technologies such as the radio, the increase in speed and mobility, and air power created new opportunities for deception. Second, the lack of decisiveness combined with incredible losses led many to realize that more effective methods of waging war must be found. Third and on a different level, the experience gained from some of the deception operations in the Great War, in particular by Admiral Blinker Hall in the Admiralty and even more so by Wavell in Allenby's Palestine Campaign, proved to be of great importance in initiating deception operations during the Second World War.

Almost all the elements that made strategic and operational deception on a large scale possible in the Second World War already existed in the First. This is perhaps best demonstrated by Allenby's deception cover plans for the Third Battle of Gaza (November 1917) and the Battle of Megiddo (September 1918). Following two costly abortive attacks on Gaza in March and April 1917, the British government decided to send General Sir Edmund Allenby to command the Egyptian Expeditionary Force (EEF) in Palestine. It was hoped that a successful offensive in Palestine would not only ease the pressure of a possible Turkish offensive in Mesopotamia against Baghdad, but above all convince the Turks to abandon the war on the German side once Jaffa and Jerusalem were under British occupation.[20]

Soon after his arrival in late June 1917, General Allenby approved plans (August to October 1917) for a major offensive in Palestine. He decided to change the *Schwerpunkt* of the attack from Gaza to Beersheba (the Turkish left flank) in order to roll up the defenses of Gaza and defeat the Turks in central Palestine. Given the marginal superiority of the British (10 better-equipped British versus eight Turkish divisions), the difficult terrain, the obstacles to be overcome in providing logistical support, and the fact that the forthcoming attack could not be concealed from the Turks, the success of the offensive hinged mainly on the possibility of misleading the Turks as to the exact timing and place of the attack.

The overall deception plan was divided into two levels: strategic and operational. The strategic plan (much as the Palestine Campaign itself) was to pin down four to five Turkish divisions in Northern Syria in order to prevent them from serving as reinforcements in Palestine or taking part in Operation 'Yelderim' ('Thunderbolt'), the Turkish plan to reoccupy Baghdad. With this goal in mind, Allenby approved a scheme to convince the Turks that a large landing operation was going to take place in Northern Syria. Most of the deception activities supporting this notional threat of invasion focused on Cyprus, where new camp sites were set up and the small garrison force tried to give the impression of increased activity. The British also made extensive use of bogus wireless traffic in, to and from Cyprus, openly loaded equipment, soldiers and horses in the port of Cyprus; and entered into negotiations for the purchase of large quantities of food and other supplies. After being alerted to the possibility of suspicious activity, the Turks sent a special reconnaissance mission over Cyprus which apparently determined that there was no threat of invasion from that direction after all.

Much like Operation Starkey (the subject of Campbell's article that follows), this deception operation failed primarily because there was not enough *time* for careful preparation of the necessary cover plan, and there were not enough real troops and other resources available to create a convincing notional order of battle.[21] Without the benefit of a pre-existing Turkish concept that such an invasion was quite possible, the time and resources at Allenby's disposal were simply not sufficient to convince the Turks that the threat was genuine.

The deception plan on the operational level, however, was very successful and made a major contribution to the success of Allenby's offensive. In many ways, this plan was the prototype for operational deception in the Second World War, for it incorporated elements later found in the deception plans preceding the battles of Alam Halfa and El Alamein, the invasion of Sicily, and the invasion of Normandy.

The scheme called for a *double bluff*, in which the forthcoming attack on Beersheba was presented as a diversion intended to draw attention away from the 'main objective' of Gaza. The great advantage of this type of deception is that even when the main attack has begun in earnest, the opponent still believes it is merely secondary. Expecting the 'real' blow to fall elsewhere, the opponent is usually reluctant to reinforce the attacked area and instead uses most of his troops to protect what he mistakenly perceives to be the true target. This often prolongs the effect of the deception plan even after the real attack has opened. During the Second World War, the Allies carried out a double bluff on a much larger scale when they presented Normandy as the planned site of a diversionary attack and the Pas de Calais as the main objective. This completely notional threat to the Pas de Calais was so convincing that the Germans believed in its veracity throughout the war. (See Cubbage's article.) Similarly, Operation Mincemeat presented the real invasion of Sicily as a diversion to cover the 'attack' on Sardinia and the Peloponnese. Since Turkish and German commanders had already surmised that Gaza was the most logical target for the British attack, it was relatively easy to reinforce their beliefs. A variety of active and passive deception means were used to achieve this.

The best known and most successful of these activities was the 'haversack ruse' of Major Richard Meinerzhagen, Allenby's intelligence officer. The ruse was so successful that in the Second World War it became the inspiration for similar operations such as the 'going map ruse' that preceded the battle of Alam Halfa and the more complex Operation Mincemeat ('The Man Who Never Was') that preceded the invasion of Sicily.[22]

After a number of unsuccessful attempts, Meinerzhagen finally managed to 'lose' a haversack containing carefully prepared documents in a staged encounter with a Turkish patrol. Among the documents were staff papers ostensibly prepared for discussion at Allenby's headquarters. From these it was possible to infer that the main operation would take place against Gaza supported by a landing from the sea, while the attack on Beersheba would be a diversion. Also included was an officer's notebook which discussed transport difficulties and the shortage of water and supplies necessary to support a large force in the Beersheba region as well as the fact that no solution to all these problems had been found. 'Private' letters from officers stationed near Beersheba implied that it was a mistake to choose Gaza as the main focus of the coming offensive. The orders of the day instructed officers and soldiers to complete the study of a detailed model of Gaza's defenses by mid-November; this, of course, suggested a later date for the attack, which was actually scheduled for 31 October. A central accomplishment of all major strategic/operational deception plans in the Second World War – from Sidi Barrani to El Alamein, Husky, Diadem and Normandy – was their convincing indication to the enemy that the attack would take place later than was actually planned. According to other accounts, the haversack also contained £20 in small notes and a cipher book which enabled the Turks to decipher British wireless traffic from Egypt. To lend credence to this *ruse de guerre*, an urgent signal was sent to GHQ ordering an immediate search for the lost haversack, while a second complained of Meinerzhagen's carelessness. A third signal ordered him to report to GHQ for a court inquiry and warned him to return in time for the attack on 19 November 1917.[23]

In the meantime, additional deceptive measures were set in motion. Misleading 'information', transmitted both in cipher and *en clair*, suggested that no offensive would take place before 19 November, for General Allenby had gone to Egypt on leave and would not be returning before 7 November. Moreover, most of the British formations were concentrated in front of Gaza in accordance with the rule that whenever possible all order-of-battle deception operations should be based on real formations. Just ten days before D-Day, the British gradually started to move the troops toward Beersheba under cover of darkness; at the same time, they made every attempt to maintain a façade of normal routine activity 24 hours a day in the now-empty Gaza camps. In other complementary deception activities, landing boats and troops were concentrated in the Deer el Balah area (south of Gaza); warships were sent to patrol the coast near Gaza, where they pretended to measure the depth of the water for a landing operation; and alarming rumors were spread concerning a landing in the rear of Gaza.

From August onwards, the British began an elaborate *acclimatization* program for the benefit of the Turkish forces in Beersheba.

> About once a fortnight throughout the summer a reconnaissance was pushed close up to the defences of Beersheba by the cavalry division in the line. These reconnaissances served a double purpose. Their constant repetition suggested to the enemy that our efforts in this direction would be confined to demonstrations; it was hoped that the real attack on Beersheba would gain the advantage of surprise by being mistaken at first for another reconnaissance, an impression to which our Intelligence Service adroitly insinuated at the right moment by certain cipher wireless messages which were meant to be read by the Turk. *Secondly*, these periodical advances towards Beersheba provided a screen under cover of which commanders and staff became acquainted with the somewhat intricate ground towards Beersheba and worked out their arrangements for the approach to and assault on the Turkish works.[24]

The logistical infrastructure necessary to support the troop concentrations opposite Beersheba was prepared in great secrecy. The extension of the railway and water pipelines across the Wadi Ghuzze into no-man's land was postponed to a late stage of the program, while the stockpiling of stores was compressed into as little time and space as possible. All work was conducted at night after which the new sections of the railway and pipeline were carefully camouflaged. (This aspect of the plan closely resembles the cover and deception operations preceding the Battles of Sidi Barrani and El Alamein.)[25]

A week before the main attack on Beersheba was to take place, a large-scale artillery bombardment of Gaza from both the land and sea began. A day before D-Day, hundreds of Egyptian workers accompanying the EEF were marched in military formation during the day, embarked on landing ships, then disembarked during the night. To prolong the effectiveness of the deception and divert Turkish attention away from Beersheba even after the offensive had begun, the XXI Corps directly assaulted a portion of the Gaza defenses on D-Day.

In General Wavell's view, the achievement of air superiority in order to prevent the possibility of Turkish and German air reconnaissance missions was a key factor in the success of the whole deception operation.

> All these devices to mislead the enemy would have been of much less avail had not the new squadrons and more modern machines received from home enabled our Air Force in the late

autumn to wrest from the enemy the command of the air which he had enjoyed for so long in the theatre. After a few trials of strength had convinced the German aviators of the superior speed and performance of the Bristol Fighters, they came over only at a very respectful height, and by the beginning of the operations had been almost driven out of the skies.[26]

All the vacated camps behind Gaza had been left standing, and were lighted up at night. By day all troops were carefully hidden. To the enemy airmen, forced by the superior speed of the British 'planes and the antiaircraft artillery to observe at a great height, no change in the dispositions of the army was apparent. It is known from an order subsequently captured that on so late a date as October 29th the enemy believed *that six divisions* were still opposite Gaza, and that a movement by one division and one mounted division only need be apprehended against Beersheba.[27]

This was also his explanation for the success of the cover plan preceding the decisive battle of Megiddo.

But it was above all the dominance secured by our Air Force that enabled the concentration to be concealed. So complete was the mastery it had obtained in the air by hard fighting that by September a hostile aeroplane rarely crossed our lines at all.[28]

This operational deception plan was as complex and meticulously prepared as any of the major deception plans of the Second World War. How effective was it?

Turkish intelligence estimates – documents and maps captured during the operation – clearly show that three days before D-Day the Turks had identified the changes in the British order of battle, discovered that many of the British camps opposite Gaza were in fact empty, and identified the general direction of movement of the British troops (towards Beersheba) with their true dispositions. It is also evident that the Turks were not misled by the bogus threat of landing in the rear of Gaza.

Nevertheless, these last-minute discoveries had little impact on the decisions of the Turkish-German high command. The reasons for this are not entirely clear, but may be, among others, an overestimation of the size of the British real order of battle; the existence of a powerful and rather rigid concept that the British would direct their major effort toward Gaza, and perhaps the inability of the German-Turkish High Command to digest the latest information in such a short time.[29]

General Kress von Kressentein had a fleeting suspicion concerning the genuineness of the haversack documents (much like Hitler's rhetorical question as to whether the documents provided to the Germans in Operation Mincemeat were not deceptive). (See Müller's article.)

> The success of the ruse to deceive the Turks as to the point of attack has been mentioned. It appears that the documents were examined with great care by Kress, and that, while not overlooking the possibility that they were faked, he inclined strongly to believe in their authenticity. At any rate, even after the attack on Beersheba had begun, he refused to believe the reports of the commander of the III Corps as to the British strength, ordered Beersheba to be held, and sent no reinforcements.[30]

Yet, in both cases, the documents fitted conveniently into the pre-existing concepts of the deceived, who were psychologically predisposed to accept them.

Even before the battle had begun, the British could observe that the Turks had reduced preparations on their left flank in Beersheba and significantly increased their work on the fortifications of Gaza. According to both the official history and Wavell's report, the Turks were completely surprised at Beersheba, not by the fact that an attack took place, but by its unexpected weight and direction.[31]

Even if the British somewhat exaggerated the success of their ruse, there is still no doubt that it succeeded with regard to the overall goal of achieving surprise, which in turn confused the Turkish–German defense and slowed down its reactions. As long as it is clear that the deception plan accomplished its principal objectives, one need not be over-concerned with the degree to which the success of the Third Battle of Gaza can be attributed to subterfuge as opposed to other factors such as the marginal British superiority or conflicts within the Turkish–German High Command. Suffice it to say that without deception, the Third Battle of Gaza might very well have ended in disaster like its two predecessors (and almost all other attacks on the Western Front).

A year later, Allenby once again relied on a major operational deception plan to conceal preparations for the battles of Megiddo (September 1918). Since the experience of the Turkish–German High Command in the Third Battle of Gaza had conditioned it to expect an inland attack, Allenby now reversed his deception cover to indicate that the next major British offensive would take place inland along the river Jordan and in Transjordan in conjunction with a 'diversionary attack' along the shore and in the Sharon valley. (A similar type of reversed conditioning deception took place in the Italian campaign during the Second World War. To begin with, the Germans were completely surprised by the Allied landing in Anzio (January 1944), for

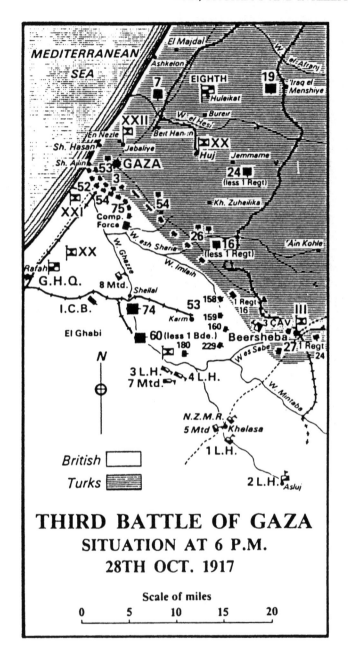

THIRD BATTLE OF GAZA
SITUATION AT 6 P.M.
28TH OCT. 1917

Scale of miles

MAPS 1 & 2: THE THIRD BATTLE OF GAZA. Note the concealed shift of

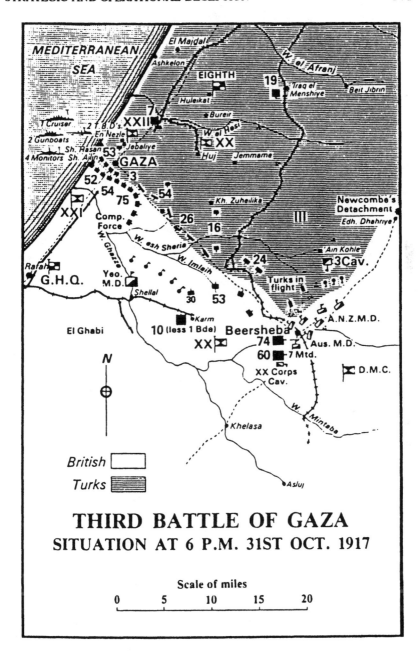

MEDITERRANEAN SEA

El Majdal

Ashkelon

W. el Afranj

EIGHTH

19

'Iraq el Menshiye

Beit Jibrin

Huleikat

Bureir

1 Cruiser

7

XXII

2 T.B.'s

En Nezle

W. el Hesi

2 Gunboats

Sh. Hasan

Jebaliye

XX

4 Monitors

Sh. Ailin

53

Huj

Jemmame

GAZA

52

3

54

54

Kh. Zuheilika

XXI

75

Newcombe's Detachment

Comp. Force

26

III

Edh. Dhahriye

16

Rafah

W. Ghazze

W. esh Sheria

'Ain Kohle

G.H.Q.

Yeo. M.D.

W. Imleih

24

3 Cav.

Shellal

Turks in flight

30

53

El Ghabi

Karm

A.N.Z.M.D.

10 (less 1 Bde)

Beersheba

74

Aus. M.D.

XX

60

7 Mtd.

XX Corps Cav.

D.M.C.

N

Khelasa

W. Mintaba

British

Turks

Asluj

THIRD BATTLE OF GAZA
SITUATION AT 6 P.M. 31ST OCT. 1917

Scale of miles

0   5   10   15   20

British troop concentrations from Gaza on left to Beersheba on the right.

various Allied ruses had led them to anticipate an attack from the interior along the established front line. In the next phase of the attack on the Gustav line (Operation Diadem (May 1944)), the Allies tricked the Germans (Operation Nunton) into expecting another landing at Civitavecchia, whereas the main attack actually occurred on land and was directed against the Gustav line.)[32] There is no doubt that the susceptibility to conditioning is one of the most fundamental human proclivities to be exploited by deception operations.

As a result of thorough British preparations, the Turks and Germans were once again caught unawares when the 'major British offensive' turned out to be a diversion, and the supposed diversion along the shore quickly became a full-scale attack. Again Allenby employed a wide variety of complementary deception covers: bogus headquarters were established in a Jerusalem hotel for everyone to see; the main forces chosen for the offensive were secretly concentrated on the plain around Jaffa, while many empty camps were set up in the vicinity of Jericho; and T.E. Lawrence was sent to execute large-scale diversionary raids in Transjordan along the Deraa-Aman line. These detailed preparations, as can be seen from a captured German intelligence order-of-battle map, were completely successful. (Compare Map 3 showing the real British troop concentration, with Map 4, a captured German intelligence order of battle (OB) map.) As Wavell commented, 'the battle was practically won before a shot was fired'.[33]

For Allenby, unlike almost all other generals of the Great War, elaborate deception plans were a key element of every operational plan. As T.E. Lawrence remarked, 'Deceptions, which for the ordinary general were just witty *hors d'oeuvres* before battle, had become for Allenby a main point in strategy.'[34] The phenomenal success of Allenby's stratagems can be ascribed in large part to the use of many different imaginative complementary deception methods: meticulous planning of all details, the extensive use of real military formations whenever possible, adequate material support and secrecy. Three of the most critical factors were the achievement of air superiority in order to deny the opponent any possibility of air reconnaissance, adequate time for the execution of the plan, and a good intelligence system that could monitor the enemy's reaction to the deception baits. The need to know whether the enemy had 'swallowed the bait' which became even more crucial during the Second World War, was even more effectively satisfied by ULTRA and the double-cross (XX) system.

In their intricate preparations and exploitation of the opportunities provided by modern technology (in particular wireless deception and air superiority), Allenby's deception operations closely resemble the more complex schemes devised during the Second World War. Thus, Allenby's skillful use of stratagem represents a transition from earlier periods of either non-existent or *ad hoc* deception to deception at its zenith during the Second World War.

While the potential contribution of deception was generally ignored during the First World War, it eventually came to be appreciated as an essential part of strategic and operational planning in the Second. The principles of deception may not have changed in the interim but there is no doubt that its scope, means, organization and methods had.

It is interesting to note that there was a direct link between Allenby's imaginative use of stratagem in the Palestine Campaigns and the subsequent recognition of deception as an important source of support for all military operations during the Second World War. This link was provided by General Sir Archibald Wavell, the British Commander-in-Chief in the Middle East (1939–41), who had served in Allenby's headquarters and was personally acquainted with his deception operations. In his *A History of the Palestine Campaigns*, published in the late 1920s, Wavell strongly emphasized the contribution of deception operations to Allenby's achievement of victory. Having so closely observed the successful use of deception in military operations, Wavell was prepared to make extensive use of it when he became Commander-in-Chief of the Middle East. He once commented: '. . . I have always believed in doing everything possible in war to mystify and mislead one's opponent. . . '.[35]

In the fall of 1940, Marshal Graziani advanced into Egypt with close to a quarter of a million men under his command, while the Duke of Aosta in Eritrea and Abysinnia had another 100,000. In contrast, Wavell could field no more than 50,000 British and Commonwealth soldiers. Under such conditions, deception was really Wavell's only hope. Wavell therefore directly encouraged the extensive resort to deception in the Middle East. The first large-scale deception operation led to a brilliant British victory at Sidi Barrani by General O'Connor in Operation Compass. Two British divisions ultimately defeated ten Italian divisions by achieving complete surprise at the opening phase of the attack. In 10 weeks, two divisions under General O'Connor advanced over some 500 miles of difficult terrain and destroyed 10 Italian divisions at a loss of 500 killed, 1,373 wounded and 55 missing. The spoils of victory were 130,000 prisoners, numerous tanks, guns and other equipment.[36]

Although the British official history indicates that deception played a key role in achieving surprise, it gives no detailed account of how this was done. When the official histories first began to appear in the mid-1950s, the topic of deception was still too sensitive to be discussed

WSI—M

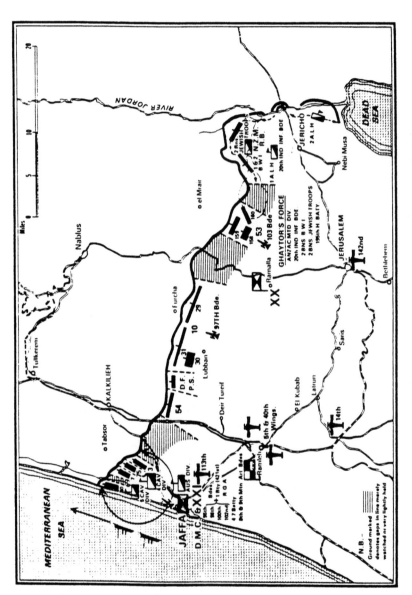

MAP 3   MEGIDDO, 1918. SITUATION AT 18 SEPTEMBER 1918

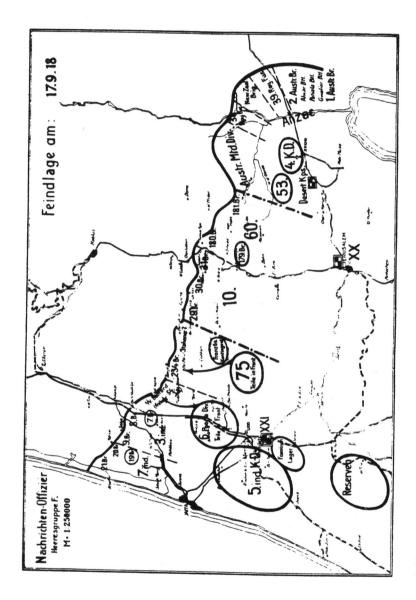

MAP 4   BRITISH DISPOSITIONS AS SHOWN BY ENEMY INTELLIGENCE SERVICE

in depth. Personal memoirs and partial accounts in other historical studies published in the 1970s only fragmentarily disclosed some of the stratagems and methods used in the Middle East in the second half of 1940. A comprehensive study of the evolution and history of deception in the Middle East and Mediterranean has yet to be written, though it is expected that much light will be shed on the subject after the release of the long-awaited official history of deception by Sir Michael Howard.

The circumstances under which Wavell established a special organization to develop deception plans in the summer of 1940 are still largely obscure. What is clear is that the cover plans before the Battle of Sidi Barrani called for the creation of a phantom army to threaten the flanks of Graziani's invasion force as well as for the extensive use of camouflage and other concealment techniques. In addition, Wavell's special deception outfit started to co-operate with SIME (Security Intelligence Middle East) in constructing a double-cross system to communicate deceptive information to the Germans and Italians.[37]

Despite their strenuous efforts to ascertain the truth through general intelligence gathering and air reconnaissance, the Italians were ultimately confounded by the British sleight of hand.

> Primed by alarming intelligence messages provided by the star network of his senior ally [i.e., German agents] Graziani sent his aircraft to photograph the area of the reported concentrations, where the British, in pursuit of their cover plan, had assembled about all the anti-aircraft guns they possessed. The Italian planes were greeted with a terrific volume of fire which in itself gave the impression of a lavishly equipped army and, moreover, kept the planes well up so that they could never take a close look nor photograph too accurately.
>
> The impact on . . . Graziani and his commanders was overwhelming. Here was confirmation of the alarming reports that he had reviewed. The British didn't just have reinforcements, they had an entirely new army encamped on his flank and ready to destroy him. In desperation he ordered his forces to create fortified positions along the Alexandria road in which they would prepare to defend themselves against the enemy on their flank. In these isolated positions they would be attacked and destroyed piecemeal. While the notional army was advancing, the factual contingent was concentrating for their attack.[38]

These are the oblique words in which the official history describes the deception cover for Compass:

> The fact is that in war, it is usually possible to produce some sort

of evidence in support of almost every course of action open to the enemy; the art lies in knowing what to make of it all. In this case the Italian Air Force had observed and reported movements and dispositions with fair accuracy – indeed, it was often intended by the British that they should. The important point was that these reports were consistent with what the 10th Army were convinced was happening. They themselves were very much occupied with their own preparations for renewing the advance, and were only too ready to interpret the air reports as indicating that the British were actively improving their defensive arrangements. The British attempt at strategic deception was therefore successful.[39]

The pattern of deception employed here was later refined and expanded in means, methods and scope for use in concealing preparations for the battles of Alam Halfa and even more so El Alamein. The outstanding results achieved in this deception operation led to the establishment of a special permanent organization under the Middle Eastern Command (Cairo) on 18 December 1940, while Operation Compass was still in progress. Referred to as 'A' Force, this special organization was to be headed by Brigadier Dudley Clarke, who had been hand-picked for the job by Wavell.

Following the campaign, Wavell probably personally briefed the military authorities in London on the methods and success of the deception plans in the Middle East. Dudley Clarke was sent by Wavell to report to the Chief of Staff in October of 1941.[40] 'A' Force soon became the inspiration for deception operations initiated in London on a much wider scale later in the war. Furthermore, it was Dudley Clarke's suggestion at that time which led to the appointment of a special controlling officer responsible for the co-ordination of all deception operations, a position that later developed into the London Controlling Section (LCS). In January 1944, Noel Wild, Dudley Clarke's deputy in 'A' Force, was sent to head Ops. (B) – the operational section in charge of all deception cover plans for the invasion of France (Fortitude).[41] Thus, the seed planted by Wavell in the Middle East bore decisive fruit in the victory over the Axis and the liberation of Europe.

The details of various other deception operations, their successes and their failures, are the subject of the essays assembled in this volume. At this point, it is useful to summarize some of the reasons for the success of strategic and operational deception in the Second World War, and how it differed from the type of deception practiced in earlier periods. These differences and unique characteristics can be grouped under two broad inter-related categories: (a) Means and Methods, and (b) Attitudes and the Environment.

The term 'means and methods' includes all mechanisms such as 'organizations' and 'special means' that were used to communicate the false information to the enemy. The further refinement of the radio in the First World War was a decisive factor in the renaissance of deception during the Second World War, for it provided the perfect means of listening in on an enemy's innermost plans, broadcasting 'valuable' information to an unsuspecting eavesdropper, and verifying the extent to which the proffered bait had been swallowed.

Environmental factors are primarily the general political and psychological attitudes which freed political and military leaders from any previous inhibitions they may have had concerning the large-scale resort to deception on all levels.

MEANS AND METHODS

1. *Organization.* Until the close of the First World War, deception was always left to the initiative and creativity of individual military commanders, who usually improvised *ad hoc* on the lower tactical and operational levels – that is, on the battlefield. Improvisation on the strategic level was rare indeed. Since deception was not a systematically continued activity, it required little or no co-ordination. All this changed during the Second World War, when deception became the focus of formally organized staff work. Dennis Wheatley noted that: 'organized deception was an entirely new development in World War II. From time immemorial ruses to mislead an enemy have been employed. But until the 1940s, force commanders had always given the job of making a cover plan to an individual'.[42] J.C. Masterman commented: 'Double-cross agents have been used since time immemorial but usually for short-time purposes and never, I believe, on the scale to which we developed the plan during the war'.[43] Special permanent organizations were required to manage this unprecedented deception effort which involved the complex co-ordination of activities among different commands and regions, as well as among different intelligence and military organizations; the control of double agents; and the use of ULTRA to monitor the impact of deception on the enemy.

On the regional level, or preceding each battle, a deception operation had to be co-ordinated among those who planned the operations and those who implemented them. Troop movements had to be carefully orchestrated and camouflaged while dummy forces had to be positioned. Co-ordination on the local level at each front had become a full-time occupation. Moreover, the complexity of strategic deception increased to such an extent that it required a high degree of co-ordination among different commands and regions.[44] In the words of the *Hesketh Report*: '. . . the control of a deceptive operation must be decided upon the self-evident principle that no people can safely tell the same lie to the same person except by closely concerted action'.[45]

For example, 'A' Force's creation of a notional threat to the Greek Islands and the Balkans in 1943–44 required the circumspect co-ordination of every move with other deception plans taking place simultaneously in Northwest Europe, the Western and Central Mediterranean, and India. For this complicated scheme, both real and notional Indian divisions stationed in Palestine, Syria and Iraq were used to build up the illusion of a threat directed towards Greece and the Balkans, though some of the troops were gradually transferred to fight against the Japanese. If the Allies had not exercised extreme care, collaboration between German and Japanese intelligence might have resulted in simultaneous identification of the same divisions (real or bogus) in two different areas and thus disclosure of the whole deception operation.[46] Acting in support of Operation Fortitude, 'A' Force later attempted to divert German troops and attention from the threat to the English Channel by creating large-scale notional threats in the Aegean and Balkans ('Zeppelin' and 'Royal Flush'). The implementation of this ruse again necessitated close co-ordination of details between the deceivers in London and the Middle East.[47] Fabrication of a threat to the Balkans as part of the cover plan for Normandy even led to unsuccessful attempts to co-ordinate deception with the Russians. The extensive co-ordination required by all this intricate strategic deception activity was considered so crucial that it was handled by the London Controlling Section (LCS) – a special organization created exclusively for that purpose. Flawed co-ordination risked exposure of the entire deception effort, and perhaps even jeopardized the whole intelligence system on which it was based (i.e., the double-cross systems and Ultra). As it turned out, efficient co-ordination combined with good fortune and the overall weakness of German strategic intelligence enabled the Allies to convince Germany that it faced substantial threats in Northwestern Europe and the Mediterranean. This, in part, prompted the German dispersal of troops to protect fortress Europe against non-existent forces. It appears that from 1943 to the end of the war, Germany consistently overestimated the size of Allied forces by about 100 per cent.

Although permanent because of security considerations, limited resources and the nature of the work, the specialized deception organizations were all quite small. (At its peak, 'A' Force, according to Cruickshank, included only 41 officers, 76 NCOs, and three units of company strength specially trained in the operation of visual deception devices.)[48] Given the organizational affiliation of Ops. (B) with SHAEF, it is more difficult to estimate the number of those participating in deception activities within England. If we consider those who played a more supportive role in the double-cross system and the XX Committee, the London Controlling Section (LCS), and B.1.A (the subsection of MI5 controlling the double agents) as well as the few who were *directly* involved in Ops. (B) activities – the number would be substantially larger than that of 'A' Force.

2. *Ultra.* In conjunction with the double-cross system which depended on it, Ultra was the single most important means of facilitating deception available to the Allies. Indeed, this revolutionary source of information provided the deceivers with *real time* access to the most closely-guarded plans, perceptions, wishes and fears of their enemy. It was the ideal tool for determining how to design a deception cover plan that would best reinforce existing German perceptions of the Allied threat. After implementing a particular ruse, the deceivers could rely on Ultra to monitor the degree to which it had been accepted by the Germans, then follow this up by fine-tuning continuing deception cover plans with the other means at their disposal. Ultra was therefore essential for the protection and growth of the double-cross system because it provided the corrective mechanism to cover up mistakes and carry on with this most reliable communications link to the enemy from one success to another.

Without doubt, Ultra gave the Allies an excellent picture of German strategy and the strategic decision-making process. The Allies were constantly a step ahead of the Germans not only because they were almost fully aware of German plans and strategy but also because they played a direct role in shaping them. Reading Masterman's *The Double-Cross System* and the *Hesketh Report* gives one the impression that the Allies were playing chess against themselves.

Yet the enormous strategic and operational advantages of Ultra and the double-cross system did not guarantee an easy victory at each stage. This is a tribute to the quality and tenacity of the German Army. It illustrates that no matter how good intelligence and deception may be, they can never replace combat and material strength. All they can do is reduce the cost and make the fighting somewhat easier.

3. *The Double-Cross System.* Developed in the Middle East by 'A' Force in co-ordination with SIME as well as in England by MI5's section B.1.A., the double-cross system eventually became the best means of communicating false information to the Germans,[49] although the original reason for turning around German agents was more to

prevent the Germans from learning what was going on (and so improve security) than to create channels for deception. Only gradually did the British realize that their control of German agents represented an excellent opportunity for deception. This could be achieved only when it was finally recognized that no *bona fide* independent German agents remained in England.[50]

The double-cross system was based on German agents who had been turned around after being intercepted by the British early in the war. The idea of using captured agents to pass deceptive information to the enemy is as old as spying itself, and was used quite extensively by Admiral Blinker Hall during the First World War.[51] While in the past the manipulation of captured agents took place on an individual *ad hoc* basis, through exploitation of opportunities that occasionally presented themselves, the use of double agents by the British during the Second World War was systematically organized on a large scale by a permanent organization that carefully co-ordinated its activities through the Twenty Committee (XX) in London and even earlier through 'A' Force in the Middle East. The success of the double-cross system was based not only on the existence of Ultra unit but also on the judicious management of the double agents. The guiding principle of the controllers was to supply their German counterparts with the greatest possible amount of accurate information in order to protect the deception plot with a bodyguard of truth.[52] Such information could be either correct but trivial ('chickenfeed' or 'foodstuff' in the controller's jargon) or correct and important but received too late to be of any use. For example, a few hours before the invasion of Normandy was to begin, Garbo sent his German controller an urgent warning. This seemingly important tip-off enhanced Garbo's credibility but was received too late to be of any practical use to the Germans.

Each double agent in turn mobilized quite a few sub and sub-sub operatives who funneled additional information through the original double agents who had been recruited directly by the Germans. In this way, British counter-intelligence was gradually able to develop and control a vast network of real and imaginary agents who virtually monopolized the German espionage effort. By 1943 the British could be reasonably sure (chiefly as a result of information supplied by ULTRA) that no important actual agents were independently providing the Germans with information either in the Middle East or in England. The double-cross agents' further expansion of their own notional network and the credibility they had established with their controllers in German intelligence apparently reduced the German incentive to create additional networks for corroborative purposes. Armed with the knowledge of German perceptions and fears provided

WSI—M*

FIGURE 1

THE GARBO (ARABEL) NOTIONAL NETWORK*

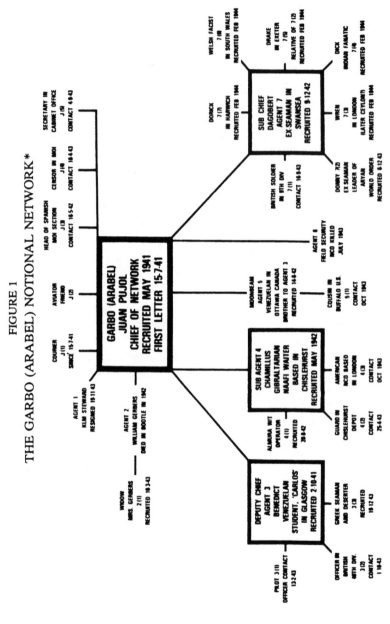

Based on the Hesketh Report and Pujol *Garbo*. In all the network employed 27 'agents' at different times. There is a descrepancy between Hesketh's and Pujol's accounts. According to Pujol agents J(1) and J(2) are one.

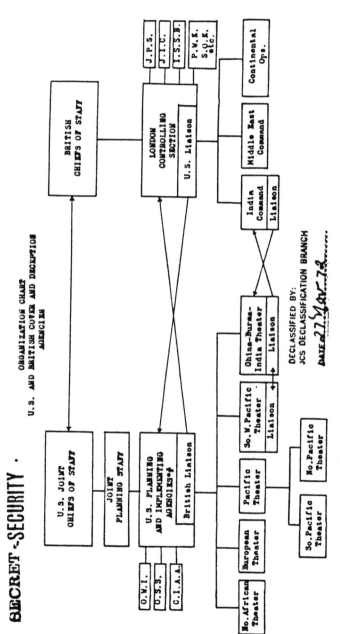

SECRET -SECURITY .

ORGANIZATION CHART

U.S. AND BRITISH COVER AND DECEPTION
AGENCIES

BRITISH
CHIEFS OF STAFF

LONDON
CONTROLLING
SECTION

U.S. Liaison

J.P.S.
J.I.C.
I.S.S.B.
P.W.E.
S.O.E.
etc.

Continental
Ops.

Middle East
Command

India
Command
Liaison

China-Burma-
India Theater
Liaison

So.W.Pacific
Theater
Liaison

U.S. JOINT
CHIEFS OF STAFF

JOINT
PLANNING STAFF

U.S. PLANNING
AND IMPLEMENTING
AGENCIES*†

British Liaison

O.W.I.
O.S.S.
C.I.A.A.

No.African
Theater

European
Theater

Pacific
Theater

So.Pacific
Theater

No.Pacific
Theater

DECLASSIFIED BY:
JCS DECLASSIFICATION BRANCH
DATE 27 Mar 72

Notes: 1. This chart based on utilization of present U.S. Deception Agencies, as set up by U.S. Joint Chiefs of Staff.
        2. U.S. Deception Staffs in Pacific to be established by Theater Commanders.

* Composed of one planner from each of the Army, Navy and Air Forces and a representative of Joint Security Control.
† No actual group under this name exists. Deception planning is accomplished by a sub-committee of the Joint Staff
  Planners; implementation by Joint Security Control.

by Ultra, these double agents continued to channel misleading
information to the Germans until the end of the war. Some of them such
as Garbo (Juan Pujol)[53] were even decorated by the Germans for their
achievements. Descriptions of the double-cross system make it clear
how complex this operation was and how much it depended on co-
ordination between Bletchley Park (Ultra), counter-intelligence MI5-
B.1.A, the deceivers in 'A' Force or Ops (B), and others. The co-
ordination effort alone was a noteworthy achievement in its own right.

Most of the deceptive information passed to the Germans had to do
with Allied intentions, primarily regarding the *time* and *place* of their
planned offensives. This was accomplished by continuously supplying
the Germans with carefully doctored information about the Allied
order of battle in the Middle East and Europe. Through this system the
Allies succeeded in doubling German estimates of the number of
Allied troops available in Europe and the Middle East.

The uniqueness of the double-cross systems lay in their capacity
to prepare convincing cover stories before, during and after each
operation, thereby ensuring success on a continuous and uninterrupted
basis until the end of the war. The outstanding accomplishments of
the double-cross systems have prompted some to speculate that the
German *Abwehr* collaborated with British intelligence (*Schwarze
Kapelle*). Although there is no doubt that individual *Abwehr* officers
did help the Allies, this devil theory cannot be proven. The truth is
probably much less dramatic. The overall analytical weakness of
German strategic analysis is one likely explanation, while another may
be that the German controllers could not bring themselves to question
seriously the loyalty of their agents. The controllers were too committed to the protection of their investment in the spying networks to
admit failure as long as the British continued to supply them with
information they wanted to accept as true. Relying on Ultra, the British
operators carefully crafted their messages to suit the German mind-set.
Finally, the Germans did not (and later could not) corroborate the
information they received with the type of material evidence that could
have been obtained from air reconnaissance.

If a single element is to be identified as the key to the extraordinary
record of the Allied deception operations, it is the means provided by
the double-cross/Ultra combination. From convincing Rommel to
attack at Alam Halfa (much to his detriment), through the creation of a
notional threat to the Peloponnese and Aegean in preparation for the
invasion of Sicily, to achieving surprise at Normandy, the double-cross
systems were decisive. Indeed, the Hesketh Report makes it clear that
the work of double agents not only laid the groundwork for the Allied
invasion of Normandy, but also prevented the Germans from mount-

ing a major counterattack against the invading forces; a message from Garbo received precisely when the Germans were considering reinforcement of their troops at Normandy convinced them that Normandy was a mere diversion and that the real attack had yet to occur at the Pas de Calais. (See Figure 3, a facsimile of this document.) The double agents' influence on the direction of the war was usually much less dramatic; it consisted of an extended effort to supply the Germans with bits and pieces of misleading information. Each deceptive bit of information alone was almost trivial – yet when pieced together with the other tidbits it formed a beguilingly coherent though incorrect estimate of Allied capabilities and intentions. This painstaking process of course required time.

4. *Time*. Time is an essential ingredient in the preparation of complex deception cover plans. As mentioned earlier, such schemes depend upon the completion of a wide variety of time-consuming activities including co-ordination on many levels; the transmission of bogus wireless messages; the establishment of the necessary units; and the positioning of dummy aircraft, tanks, landing craft and depots. Rarely (such as in Garbo's message on 9 June 1944 to the *Abwehr* mentioned above) can a deceptive message be allowed to appear dramatic. The essence of deception is that it lets the enemy convince himself that the misleading picture presented is valid. Deception operations attempting to convey false information to the enemy over a short period of time without adequate material support were doomed to fail – not necessarily because the deception plan was exposed by the adversary but because there was not enough time at hand to make him convince himself. (See Campbell's discussion of Operation Cockade/Starkey.)

As Hesketh notes in his conclusions:

> Although there may be occasions when its [i.e., deception] services can be usefully enlisted to give immediate aid, it is generally more correct to regard it as a method which achieves its results by a slow and gradual process rather than by lightning strikes. Like the fly-wheel of an engine, it requires time to gain momentum and time again to lose it.[54]

During the shorter wars of the future, deceivers may not have the time to implement intricate deception operations; instead, cover plans will have to be prepared *before the outbreak of the war in order to be used in its initial stages and may be much more difficult to apply at later stages.*

5. *Allied air superiority*. When the Allies achieved virtual air superiority in both the Mediterranean and North-west Europe, their

FIGURE 3
FACSIMILE REPRODUCTION OF GARBO'S MESSAGE OF
9 JUNE 1944, AS RECEIVED BY THE OKW

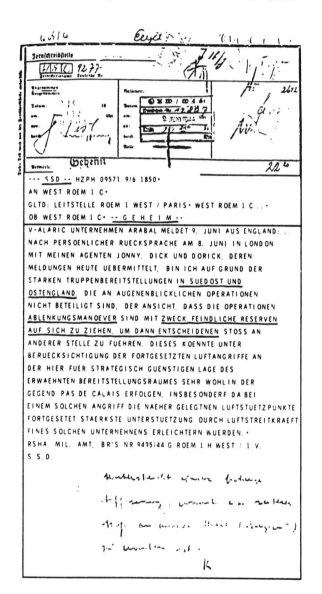

TRANSLATION

Garbo's message of 9th June, 1944, as received by teleprinter at O.K.W. and seen by Krummacher, Jodl and Hitler

---

Message received at 2230 hours on 9th June, 1944, sent by Garbo.

"V-man Alaric network Arabal reports on 9th June from England:—

After personal consultation on 8th June in London with my agents Jonny,* Dick and Dorick, whose reports were sent to-day, I am of the opinion, in view of the strong troop concentrations in South-East and Eastern England which are not taking part in the present operations, that these operations are a diversionary manoeuvre designed to draw off enemy reserves in order then to make a decisive attack in another place. In view of the continued air attacks on the concentration area mentioned, which is a strategically favourable position for this, it may very probably take place in the Pas de Calais area, particularly since in such an attack the proximity of the air bases will facilitate the operation by providing continued strong air support."

Krummacher underlined in red the words "diversionary manoeuvre designed to draw off enemy reserves in order then to make a decisive attack at another place," and added at the end—

"confirms the view already held by us that a further attack is to be expected in another place (Belgium?)."

This message was seen by Jodl, who underlined the words "in South-East and Eastern England." His initial in green may be seen at the top of the message. The green hieroglyph in the upper left-hand square indicates that Jodl considered it of sufficient importance to show to the Fuehrer, while the letters "erl" (erledigt) which appear in pencil immediately to the right indicate that it was seen by Hitler.

* Misprint for Donny.

Source: Reproduced from Roger Hesketh's unpublished 'Fortitude: A History of Deception in North Western Europe, April 1943 to May 1945'.

deception operations enjoyed a concomitant increase in effectiveness. From 1943 onwards, the Germans shifted most of their activity in the air to the Russian Front and to the defense of the Reich; air reconnaissance over the Mediterranean dropped to a level of sporadic rather than extensive and systematic activity. This neglect of air reconnaissance thus reflects the lack of co-operation between the Luftwaffe and the *Abwehr*, inter-service rivalries, a faulty order of priorities, and the reluctance to allocate equipment for air reconnaissance. Perhaps the Germans considered air reconnaissance to be of much greater use when on the offensive and less so on the defensive or perhaps the elaborate spy system in England and the Mediterranean was perceived as sufficient. Certainly, the Allied air superiority made it much more difficult to penetrate their air space (unless it was a case in which the Allies *wanted* the Germans to photograph certain areas).

This, of course, was a major stumbling block for German strategic and operational intelligence. If the Germans had chosen to allocate adequate resources to the matter, Allied deception might have faced some serious challenges. Air reconnaissance, or in today's world satellite reconnaissance, is one of the principal means of countering strategic and operational deception, while denial of air reconnaissance to the enemy (illustrated in Allenby's Palestine campaigns) is essential to the success of deception.

6. *The overall performance of German intelligence.* The consensus among experts is that the generally poor quality of German strategic intelligence contributed significantly to the success of Allied deception operations. As the Achilles' heel of the German war effort, this fatally flawed system reflected a variety of deep-rooted problems which deserve brief mention in this context. At the most fundamental level were German racism and a hubristic assumption that the German army would emerge triumphant regardless of the quality of German intelligence. True to his embodiment of this outlook, Hitler ignored intelligence estimates that he did not like and surrounded himself with an entourage of senior officers who furnished nothing but reassuring news; this, in turn, must have demoralized the German intelligence community.[55] Furthermore, career and recruiting patterns did little to encourage the most successful and ambitious officers to join the intelligence services, while the German educational system's emphasis specialization compared unfavorably with the more eclectic approach of the British. Nor was all well with inter-agency relationships. The high command lacked confidence in the *Abwehr*, while ruthless competition between the *Abwehr* and SS intelligence made co-ordination very difficult and wasted dwindling resources.[56] Finally, Germany's initial concentration on the offensive may have conditioned it to rely more on holding the initiative than on intelligence. In the end, as Hesketh remarked in a hand-written addendum to his report, the German High Command acted solely on the basis of evidence supplied by the controlled agents.

A more critical examination of the information and less wishful thinking might have changed the course of the war. Ironically, the very elements that brought about the initial success of Germany's political-military system – the Führer's leadership and the blind devotion of the German military – also precluded the establishment of an effective intelligence organization. The ideal function of intelligence is to ferret out the truth, yet the truth more often than not cannot be accepted by a totalitarian regime. Consequently, the short-run success of German might on one level contained the seeds of defeat on another.

ATTITUDES AND THE ENVIRONMENT

1. *Weakness and vulnerability.* History clearly demonstrates that an inverse correlation exists between strength and the resort to deception.

When states assume that they will win easily regardless of what the enemy does, they feel little need to resort to stratagem and deception; instead, they opt for the most direct way to attack and defeat the enemy. Such attacks often end in disaster. (The Soviet Union's attack on Finland in the winter war, Germany's attack on Russia, and the Arab attack on Israel in 1948 – which was announced in advance on the radio – are all cases in point.) On the other hand, the side which *a priori* recognizes its own numerical and material inferiority is therefore anxious to avail itself of all possible courses of action. Thus, even before the Second World War, the British were fully aware of their overall numerical and material weakness *vis-à-vis* Germany. Their early defeat in 1940 and the threat of invasion left the British no choice – they had to resort to deception. This argument may also explain why the British so rarely resorted to deception in the First World War. Then, the British Empire was at its zenith, the Royal Navy ruled the oceans, and the threat of air power to the British Isles was still small.

A similar observation can be made concerning the Israelis. While they perceived themselves as vulnerable and weak in 1948, 1956, 1967, they frequently and successfully resorted to the use of deception. By 1973 and 1982, they neglected stratagem in the hope of prevailing on the battlefield through superior firepower and technology. Only in those areas in which they felt weak or faced a threat such as the Syrian anti-aircraft missile and gun systems (1982) were they ready to resort to deception (though it was almost exclusively technological deception). Conversely, having been defeated three times by the Israelis, the Arabs in 1973 had a much stronger incentive to employ deception and indeed did so with success in the opening phase of the Yom Kippur War.

2. *The ideological environment.* When one is faced with an enemy who is completely ruthless and fanatically motivated by extreme ideology, religious fervor or racist doctrine, war acquires a zero-sum-game character. There is no room for compromise. In such conditions, both sides, particularly the more threatened one, will not recognize any constraints when the very survival of a state, religion or race is at stake. In a way, this is closely related to the preceding section, for war against a fanatical opponent creates a sense of vulnerability.

Hitler's Nazi Germany certainly posed such a threat to British survival. By 1939–40, German fanaticism and Hitler's complete lack of moderation had removed the scales from the eyes of the world. The British, however, did not threaten Germany in kind, so Germany did not contemplate the possibility of total defeat until late in the war. The British needed the best possible intelligence right from the start; the

Germans did not. By the time the tide had turned and Germany's existence was threatened, it was too late to build a high quality intelligence system or make extensive use of deception.

A homogeneous international system, a moderate environment and limited goals would not create the conditions for the wide scale resort to deception, while a revolutionary heterogeneous system, limitless goals and fanaticism would.

3. *Attitudes of leaders*. A sense of weakness and a threat to his survival would convince almost any leader to adopt those measures necessary to guarantee the survival of the state. Nevertheless, not all leaders are equally ready to engage in the widespread use of deception.

The British were fortunate to have such a leader as Churchill, who had always been interested in intelligence work and was fascinated by cloak-and-dagger stories. He was not only interested in deception – he was one of its sources of inspiration. His positive experience and familiarity with intelligence operations in the Admiralty during the First World War came in handy in the 1939–45 war, for the active interest and at times direct participation of leaders in deception operations was of critical importance. When England's fate hung in the balance, Churchill was ready and eager to open other gentlemen's mail.[57]

By virtue of a happy coincidence for the British, Wavell was Commander-in-Chief in the Middle East at a most critical time. Wavell's experience under Allenby during the First World War had left him with a deep appreciation of the decisive role deception could play in support of military operations. His readiness to resort to deception was unusual, if not unique, among military commanders. The early success achieved against the Italians in North Africa and Abyssinia (which may not have been achieved *even with* deception against a similar-sized German force) convinced Wavell that deception could work and ought to be regarded as an important force multiplier. Nothing, of course, as the saying goes, 'succeeds like success'. Had Wavell's early experiment with deception failed, it may have been viewed later on as an idle waste of time never to be repeated. The unique combination of an open-minded commander, a desperate situation, a weak enemy, and early success gave deception in the Middle East a good reputation, which helped in selling it to other commanders and to those in London.

In contrast, Hitler engaged in non-stop lying and deception only during the period following his rise to power, when Germany was still weak.[58] But after the Wehrmacht's spectacular early victories, deception became redundant. There was no time for reflection or carefully prepared deception operations – the blitzkrieg-style attack was the surest and quickest guarantee of victory. Unlike Churchill, Hitler had no need for intelligence – his intuition and will-power were enough. Those who take action for the sake of action do not need accurate intelligence reports, for sooner or later it will tell them that continued action will lead to inevitable defeat. At that point, intelligence becomes an obstacle to their policies and egos.

The combination of a leader interested in deception and intelligence and restrained from hyperactivity by his military staff, and a leader who often ignored intelligence and was restrained by no one, proved ideal for the Allies in the long run. While the British could direct all of their deception at a single man whose strategy they were well acquainted with, the Germans had to deal with intelligence organizations and military staffs, not ultimately with Churchill alone.

The following table puts deception in a historical perspective by comparing deception operations as they evolved in the Second World War with those of earlier periods.

DECEPTION PAST AND PRESENT

PAST	PRESENT
SIMPLE	COMPLEX
Initiated by individual leaders	Initiated by specialized organizations
Improvised, ad hoc, does not require long preparations	Requires extensive preparations, extensive coordination, material support, long lead time
Short ranged, 'one time shot'	Long range, continuous 'on going', not terminated by one operation
Primarily tactical operational less so strategic	On all levels
Did not depend on feedback from target; independent action	Requires continuous feedback and monitoring of enemy

THE FUTURE OF DECEPTION

'It is always unsafe to apply too literally the experiences of one war to the changed circumstances of another.'[59]

This is the opening sentence of the conclusions to the Hesketh Report. Stratagem will always remain part of the essence of war. The

basic principles and objectives of reinforcing the desires and perceptions of the deceived will not change, since human nature and the
psychological mechanism of human perception are ever the same. In
terms of its forms and the means employed, deception will, like war
itself, change as new weapons and technologies appear.

It is unlikely that strategic deception in future wars will resemble that
of the Second World War. The technological environment has radically
changed, and the unique conditions that facilitated the success of
strategic deception in that war are not likely to recur.

This can be explained in a number of ways. In the first place, the
lessons learned from the Second World War, the existence of Ultra,
and the double-cross systems, the influence of which on the course of
the war is widely recognized, might make it difficult to play the same
trick twice. (This very thought might encourage deception along
similar lines because deceivers like to manipulate the expectation that
something cannot happen again.) As I have stated elsewhere, the fact
that something is unlikely to happen greatly increases the probability
that it *will* happen.[60] Finally, the publication of the histories of intelligence and deception in the Second World War reveals a cautionary
tale.

Ultra was the most critical element in the success of the Allied
deception operations. It is not clear whether the deciphering of codes
leading to a similar large-scale penetration of the enemy's innermost
secrets on such a continuous basis will be possible again. Awareness of
the possibility ought to make all military organizations much more
careful. Moreover, the deciphering effort and development of a proper
distribution system require a great deal of time to perfect. Such time
may not be available in the future, although attempts to protect and
break codes will continue.

That this is still a real possibility was recently made clear by the
Walker spy trial, in which the defendant was convicted of supplying the
Soviets with the key to the US naval codes during the war in Vietnam
over a period of many years. It is quite possible that the information
gained from US message traffic was used by both the Soviets and the
North Vietnamese to deceive the US.

The double-cross systems managed by the British in the Middle East
and in London appear to have been unique. It would be extremely
difficult to replicate such an arrangement. The double-cross systems
themselves depended on Ultra which, as I have argued, may not always
be available. Yet again, the Soviet Union has more than once demonstrated its skill in penetrating the intelligence networks of the West
(including the one created by those who developed the double-cross
system).

Finally, the circumstances which allowed the Allies to gain control in the air and prevented the Germans from effective air reconnaissance may not recur. In the age of satellites, U-2s, SR-71s, infra-red sensors, radars, improved radio location equipment and a variety of other sensors, camouflage, concealment of troop concentrations, or the building of dummy weapon concentration will prove to be more difficult, though not impossible.

Deception, however, will continue to be as important as ever in all forms of warfare. It will require more attention, greater sophistication, and may become increasingly technological. Larger organizations will be required both to detect and implement it. In the end, even if in a different form, deception will always remain an integral part of all military activity.

CAN DECEPTION BE AVOIDED?

The evidence seems to indicate that even those who are well acquainted with the art of deception can be deceived as easily as anyone else. In theory, the deceiver's own use of stratagem should give him a heightened awareness of its existence and possible use aginst him. Yet, this very familiarity with deception can be used by an opponent to deceive the deceiver. This paradox has been described in the following way by Richard Heuer:

> Alertness to the possibility of deception can influence the degree of one's openness to new information, but not necessarily in a desirable direction. The impetus for changing one's estimate of the situation can only come from the recognition of an incompatibility between a present estimate and some new evidence. If people can explain new evidence to their own satisfaction with little change in their existing beliefs, they will rarely feel the need for drastic revision of these beliefs. Deception provides a readily 'available' explanation for discrepant evidence: if the evidence does not fit one's preconceptions, it may be dismissed as deception. Further, the more alert or suspicious one is of deception, the more readily available is this explanation. Alertness to deception also leads the analyst to be more skeptical of all the evidence, and to the extent that evidence is deemed unreliable, the analyst's preconceptions must play a greater role in determining which evidence to believe. This leads to a paradox: The more alert we are to deception, the more likely we are to be deceived.[61]

While deception often fails to attain its objectives, it rarely fails because the adversary has identified it as deception.

What counter-measures can be taken in order to reduce the possibility of being deceived? Some can be suggested, although their effectiveness cannot be guaranteed.

1. Avoid over-reliance on one source of information. 'Reliance on one source is dangerous, the more reliable and comprehensive the source, the greater the dangers.'[62] This statement by Donald McLachlan is based on the lessons learned from Germany's almost exclusive reliance on spy networks in England and the Middle East that were actually controlled by the Allies. (Perhaps it was also a warning not to depend on Ultra or similar systems in the future as the panacea for intelligence problems.) The Biblical words of wisdom, 'In multiple advisers you shall find safety' are as valid as ever.

The corroboration of any potentially valuable information by other independently verifiable sources such as air reconnaissance, radio and radars, and different sensors is imperative. In retrospect, Germany's readiness to rely so heavily on one (or few) sources is astounding.

2. A corollary of the last remark is that intelligence organizations should never rely exclusively on non-material evidence. As Clausewitz remarked, 'Words, being cheap, are the most common means of creating false impressions'. All information from sources such as agents' messages or radio traffic must be checked against material reality and positively verified.

3. Never rely on agents who have not been seen or directly interviewed. This simple advice is the only safe way to avoid reliance on notional spy networks that have been recruited indirectly.[63] Furthermore, even agents who were recruited directly in the past must be interviewed periodically in order that their continued reliability not be taken for granted. Controllers must be warned not to fall into the trap of identifying too closely with their agents: this might cause them to overprotect questionable agents whose activities should be examined with a critical eye. This rule should be even more strictly observed if the information obtained from possibly notional agents dovetails nicely with one's own preferences or needs, or when it fits without contradictions into the reports of other possibly notional agents.

4. Check and double-check all instances in which agents' reports that initially appeared correct turned out to be wrong on an important issue and yet always seemed to offer a good explanation for the discrepancy. Even more so, a special investigation should be made of any agents who supply first-rate information of the greatest importance *only when it is too late to be of any use* – even if it arrives before the action it warns against has taken place. As Hesketh, Masterman and Mure noted, this

was the most common device used by the British to build up the credibility of their agents in the eyes of the German controllers.

5. Controllers of agents should also be encouraged to heed more closely the opinions of lower-level intelligence analysts. To put it in a somewhat different way, deception (or a potential surprise) has a better chance of being detected by lower-level intelligence analysts, who are less wedded to any specific strategy or operations; wishful thinking is not as likely to sway their judgement. Less biased by political interests, the analysts' viewpoint is based more on narrower technological and professional considerations. As Dudley Clarke pointed out in a memorandum written for US military intelligence after the war, many deception operations are designed to appeal to the top intelligence and political leaders (see Appendix 1). It would therefore be easier to identify deception at lower levels, where the experts have different and narrower concerns and are therefore less likely to fall for specific deception baits.

Indeed, a lower-echelon German intelligence analyst who questioned the trustworthiness of an independent agent, Josephine, was simply ignored.[64] Had senior German intelligence analysts paid more attention to his analysis, it is quite possible that the entire double-cross system might have come under critical scrutiny in Germany.

As mentioned earlier, lower-echelon Turkish intelligence did manage to uncover some of the British deceptive measures before the Third Battle of Gaza. In much the same way, a junior Israeli intelligence analyst who warned of an impending Egyptian attack in a September 1973 memorandum was not taken seriously.

Following every realization that one has been surprised or deceived, the *post mortem* inquiry always reveals that there were those whose efforts to sound a warning were ignored. What makes sense in retrospect cannot necessarily be established as true before the event. Yet time after time, it appears that the 'negative' or unpleasant conclusions reached by those in the lower echelons have been given short shrift. It is therefore important to find a more formalized way of dealing with dissenting observations on lower levels and to encourage rather than ignore them whenever possible.

6. It is as necessary to know the enemy's limitations as his capabilities. With the 'aid' of deceptive information, German intelligence consistently overestimated the number of divisions available to the Allies, as well as their capacity to move troops, their number of landing craft, and the like. The Germans' most common perceptual mistake was to project not only their own preferences and fears on the enemy, but also their own military doctrine. As a result, they failed to understand that

air cover was in fact a necessary condition for each of the Allied landing operations. For the Allies, landing in Sardinia, the Bay of Biscay or the Peloponnese was out of the question because air cover could not be secured. Looking only through the lens of their own military doctrine, the Germans saw Sardinia – not Sicily – as the key to Italy; for them, the Balkans were the key source of raw materials, and the Pas de Calais was the most obvious direction of attack. Yet in each case, the Allies had totally different considerations: for them Sicily was the key to Allied communication in the Mediterranean while Sardinia was out of their fighter cover range; moreover, the Balkans were not viewed as an important source of raw materials. In fact, the Balkans were considered a dead end, a strategist's nightmare.

Most fundamentally, the Germans failed to understand the political dimensions of higher strategy because their attitudes and intelligence estimates incorporated too much of their own narrow military views. The principal motivation behind the Allied strategy was more often political than military. What makes sense politically often does not make sense militarily and *vice versa*.

Each year, the Allied political leaders were under pressure to show that they were making progress through decisive action. This political, not exclusively military, logic dictated the direction of operations and the implementation of deception cover plans. From a purely logical military point of view, the Germans were often right; in reality they were often wrong. The enemy's intentions must be estimated in accordance with *his* political and military needs – not one's own. This requires intimate knowledge of the enemy and a true interest in his problems. Since Germans saw their enemies as military objects, not as equals worthy of study and understanding, their capacity to expose Allied deception plans was severely undermined. High quality intelligence can be developed only when there is curiosity about and respect for the enemy, not an ethnocentric view of the enemy as a military object.

DECEPTION AND MILITARY OPERATIONS; OR DECEPTION AS A
FORCE MULTIPLIER

Sun Tzu's ideal victory, that is, victory achieved without the need to resort to force, is not a very common phenomenon in war. Clausewitz' view of the essence of war as a duel in which, through the physical use of force, the enemy is compelled to do one's will is more realistic. Yet the fact that war is as much an intellectual activity on its higher levels, as it is a material activity, cannot be denied (as Clausewitz would surely agree). While manpower, the number and quality of weapons, ammunition and other supplies are essential to wage wars – qualitative or non-material elements such as the quality of planning, organization, suitable military doctrines, morale, and intelligence are no less important.[65] Otherwise, the victory of larger armies over smaller ones would be a foregone conclusion. In war, however, there is no direct correlation between the size of armies and victory. As often as not, wars have been won by the numerically inferior side. The fact that bigger armies often fail to win may imply that the qualitative, non-quantifiable elements in war are usually more decisive.

Superiority in the qualitative dimension allows for a more efficient, more economic use of the material resources available. The non-material dimensions of war can thus be seen as force multipliers. (A material force multiplier, for example, would be the technological superiority of weapons.) One of the most important force multipliers available to the military commander is deception, which as stated earlier is primarily a means of achieving surprise on the battlefield.

Deception can provide the strategist and commander with effective answers to problems that are otherwise difficult to solve, or that could otherwise be solved only through material superiority. This indeed is the prime reason that real or perceived material superiority weakens the incentive to resort to deception. If a commander must launch an attack in an area where concealment of preparations would be difficult, passive deception (such as camouflage, and the use of decoys and dummies as was the case before the Third Battle of Gaza, Sidi Barrani or El Alamein) might be the best solution. The artful use of stratagem can also permit a numerically inferior army to concentrate superior forces at the decisive point through the device of notional threats. The enemy's perception of such threats as only too real will induce him to disperse his own troops, thus breaking the principle of the concentration of force and giving the weaker side an opportunity to achieve superiority at his point of choice. Furthermore, benefits flowing from the fabrication of illusory threats need not be limited to the weaker party. Even for the numerically superior side, the use of such a ruse facilitates the achievement of decisive results at a lower cost by reducing the opponent's resistance at the key point. (Good examples are the Third Battle of Gaza, El Alamein, the invasion of Sicily, Anzio, the Allied spring offensive in Italy (1944) and Diadem/Nunton or Normandy.)

Deception in such instances offers a solution primarily to armies on the offensive. In addition to facilitating the achievement of surprise in terms of place and strength, deception can also help the attacker to surprise his adversary in terms of timing: to launch an attack earlier than expected. This is borne out by the many cases in which the enemy commander was away when his forces were attacked. This was true of Rommel at El Alamein and Normandy, as well as General Vietinghoff, commander of the 10th German Army in Italy, who chose 11 May (D-Day for Operation Diadem/Nunton) to go on leave, while his own chain of command was in the midst of a complicated reorganization effort.[66]

Deception also provides operational opportunities for those on the defensive. It is always a rare but major achievement to lure the enemy into attacking at a point where one has a superior defensive position and is ready to meet the attacker. This is the best way to weaken the enemy at the lowest possible cost. In a classical example of this technique, the British succeeded in inducing Rommel to pursue his attack into Egypt long after he had passed the culminating point of victory and was running out of supplies, while the British, fully informed by Ultra, were dug in and waiting for his attack. Rommel's attack on Alam Halfa, which was the real turning point of the war in the Western Desert, might not have taken place without the aid of a carefully devised ruse.

Technological warfare is another area in which defensive operational deception has great application. In a brilliant, very successful scheme to divert the Luftwaffe bombers from their targets during their offensive against England, the British bent German navigational beams and induced them to bomb false targets. Another example was the use of the double-cross system to direct the German V1 and V-2 bombing attacks away from London.[67] This type of technological deception promises to become more important in the future.

While operational deception on a strategic or higher level requires time and elaborate preparations, feints and diversion on a lower level provide the commander with a simple though effective means of deception that can be improvised on relatively short notice. Clausewitz was mistaken in his assertion that feints and diversions were dangerous because they reduced the number of troops available for the decisive blow. A well-thought-out diversion will allow the deceiver to *increase* rather than decrease the number of troops at the decisive point. Again, the more that one learns about the enemy's expectations and fears from one's own intelligence, the more effectively real and notional diversionary threats can be designed.

Deception in war should be considered a *rational* and necessary activity because it acts as a force multiplier, that is, it magnifies the strength or power of the successful deceiver. Forgoing the use of deception in war is tantamount to deliberately undermining one's own strength. Therefore, when all other elements of strength in war are approximately equal, deception will amplify the available strength of a state – or allow it to use its force more economically by achieving victory at a lower cost and with fewer casualties. If opponents are unequally matched, deception (and surprise) can enable the weaker side to compensate for its numerical and other inadequacies. For this reason, the side that is at a disadvantage usually has the more powerful incentive to resort to deceptive strategy and tactics.

Although the tendency of powerful states to rely on 'brute force' can be understood, it certainly cannot be justified: the strong and powerful need not waste their strength or pay a higher cost simply because they are confident of victory. Strength unaccompanied by stratagem will become sterile and lead to eventual defeat. For that very reason, the more powerful military establishments must make a conscious effort to incorporate deception into their military thinking.

Unfortunately, while officers must be continuously reminded of deception's potential contribution to military operations, there is no systematic way in which deception can be taught. On its higher levels, deception by its very nature cannot be reduced to a simple set of principles set forth in an instruction manual. By definition, a manual deals with routine and standardized operations while deception can succeed only through deviation from the routine. Accordingly, the teaching of deception by manual would inevitably become so routinized and predictable that it would be self-defeating.

The art of deception can only be cultivated and learned through history, the experience of one's contemporaries, the encouragement of creativity and imagination in the military, constant emphasis on the need to reduce the cost and casualties of war, and an understanding of the enemy's own fears. Though deception is one of the more creative tools available to the commander in developing his grasp of the operational art of war, it is bound to remain an art. The recognition, in Clausewitz's words, that '. . . talent and genius operate outside the rules . . .'[68] is essential for developing the use and understanding of this tool.

THE CONTROL OF DECEPTION OPERATIONS

It is often asked whether deception operations should be controlled by the intelligence branch or operations branch. Operations provide the reason and rationale for deception while the intelligence experts supply the means. Should deception organizations have direct control over troops (as with 'A' Force), or should they operate through forces made available to them by regular army formations? There is no one answer to such questions, for there are certainly more than one or two legitimate, effective ways to organize and place units whose special task

WAR, STRATEGY AND INTELLIGENCE

is to *develop, implement,* and *follow up* deception operations. (Despite their great differences, both 'A' Force and Ops. (B) were eminently successful.) Therefore, instead of searching in vain for a single perfect solution applicable to all situations, I will explore some of the conditions necessary for the formation of an effective deception organization.

'Broadly speaking, deception has three phases. First, the preparation of the deception plan; secondly, the execution of the plan in terms of movements of men, ships, etc.; and thirdly, measures to ensure that the movements become known for the enemy. . . .'[69] To these, a fourth stage can be added: following up the enemy's reaction to the deception and determining to what extent it has been accepted as reflecting reality. Success during each stage necessitates the closest co-operation and co-ordination among all concerned; those in the operations branch on the one hand and intelligence on the other must understand each other's needs, priorities, capabilities and limitations, and professional frame of mind. This is no easy task in view of the fact that operations and intelligence in many ways represent two very different cultures – two different mind-sets.

Deception is never an end in itself. It exists solely to support military operations by facilitating the achievement of surprise. In this sense, Brigadier Dudley Clarke was right in stating that, 'Deception is essentially a matter of the "Operations" Branch of the staff, and *not* the "Intelligence".'[70] This does not mean, however, that those directly in charge of leading deception organizations cannot or should not be primarily intelligence experts. There are a number of reasons for this.

Officers who are experts in operations are rarely as well-grounded in intelligence (and *vice versa*). Their training and experience are predominantly geared to battle and the planning of operations; indeed, most officers show relatively less interest in intelligence work and are not closely familiar with its potential and limitations. The consensus among those who have practiced and studied deception is that convincing most military commanders of its value on all levels has traditionally been a slow, uphill process. Had it not been for the early successes of 'A' Force under Wavell, it might have been impossible to convince the average commander of the importance of deception; those responsible for planning and executing military operations tend to view it as a last resort. G-3 officers are otherwise preoccupied with the minutiae of planning an operation, training the troops, and obtaining the necessary material support (ranging from soldiers and weapons to ammunition and food). The use of troops for purely deceptive operations strikes them as a waste of scarce resources. 'The reliance in deception operations on real troop movements . . . must inevitably interfere with normal training and movement.'[71] Other objections are raised by the fact that deception always entails the disclosure of some relatively important correct information. Those unfamiliar with deception often believe that the danger of selectively supplying accurate information to the enemy outweighs the potential benefits of misleading him, since exposure may result in betrayal of one's own real intentions and plans. Finally, the effectiveness of a particular stratagem is not always easy to assess or prove.

Being less familiar with the enemy, commanders with little intelligence-related experience may fall victim to the belief that what they know about their own problems and limitations is also known to the enemy. In *Beyond Top Secret Ultra*, Ewen Montagu explains why the Chiefs of Staff rejected the suggestion that the Allies create a notional threat to the Bay of Biscay. Even as Ultra, according to Montagu, indicated that the Germans feared such a development, the Chiefs knew that mounting this type of invasion was impossible since the Bay of Biscay was not within range of the Allied fighter cover. While the deceivers were interested in reinforcing German perceptions and fears, the Chiefs of Staff acted on the basis of reality *as it was known to them*. But what was known to them was not known to the enemy.[72] Therefore, it is the responsibility of intelligence officers to provide those in charge of operations with insights on enemy perceptions.

Once deception has proved itself, most commanders will quickly come to accept it as an indispensable part of all operational planning: the most common danger at this point is that the opposite problem of over-reliance may occur. 'There is a tendency on the part of those who are constantly at grips with compelling realities to regard deception as a swift panacea to be invoked when other remedies have failed.'[73]

Intelligence specialists are subject to a somewhat different set of problems. Having little experience in the planning of military operations, they may not know what is reasonable and what cannot convince the enemy. If unfamiliar with the details of the plans for which they must provide support, they may fail to perfectly synchronize the use of stratagem with the real plans. Such lack of familiarity with operational details may also inadvertently result in a deception plan that too closely resembles the actual one.[74] As Hesketh remarked,

> It may be mentioned in passing that the information most often required [by the deceivers] was about our own side and not about the enemy, a kind of inverted intelligence, for we were after all, posing as part of the enemy's Intelligence Service. That meant that our links with the Intelligence Division were slender as compared with those built up with Staff Duties, Training, Move-

ment and Transportation and other branches of the operational and administrative staffs.[75]

A thorough understanding of the operational commander's plans and problems is absolutely essential for the would-be deceiver, whose ultimate objective should be to make the enemy react in a specific way. Otherwise, a deception plan could easily backfire when the enemy, though persuaded by the false information, nevertheless takes action detrimental to the deceiver. Having learned this lesson the hard way, Brigadier Dudley Clarke recalled that 'it became a creed in 'A' Force to ask a General "What do you want the enemy to *do*?" and never "What do you want him to *think*?"'[76]

Major General de Guingand, General Montgomery's Chief of Staff, asked the right question when he gave the deception cover plan for Normandy its final twist in proposing that the Pas de Calais be presented as the real objective of the Allies. On 25 January 1944, General de Guingand raised the post-assault phase to a level of importance which it had not hitherto enjoyed. He said:

> I do not agree with the object which has been given for the attack on the Pas de Calais. If we induce the enemy to believe the story, he will not react in the way we want. I feel we must, from D-Day onwards, endeavour to persuade him that our *main* attack is going to develop later in the Pas de Calais area, and it is hoped that NEPTUNE will draw away reserves from that area.[77]

After this change was accepted, the final draft of Fortitude expanded the post-assault story to present Normandy as a mere diversion to the Pas de Calais. As a result, the Germans were persuaded that 'the operation in the NEPTUNE area is designed to draw German reserves away from the Pas de Calais and Belgium. . . . When the German reserves have been committed to the Neptune area, the main Allied attack will be made between the Somme and Ostend. . . .'[78] De Guingand's familiarity with Allied operational problems in planning the post-assault advance on Normandy forced him to search for a way to pin down the Germans in the Pas de Calais. At that time, no intelligence specialist was even in a position to recognize the need for such a solution.

In theory, those who head deception organizations ought to be equally familiar with the ins and outs of operational planning and intelligence. This is a demanding requirement which few officers can fulfill. Organizations must be kept relatively small in order to guarantee secrecy, and whether independent (like 'A' Force) or part of an operational staff (like Ops. (B) at SHAEF) they must be very close to the commander-in-chief and his planning staff. Such organizations do not necessarily need to control their own independent means, although a core of specialists in such areas as wireless simulation and camouflage would be useful. A better acquaintance with their own order of battle and resources makes it easier for those who prepare the operational plans to design a false order of battle. This arrangement may also make access to the requisite resources more direct.

A close relationship with operations is essential. It eliminates the need to differentiate between the real and deception operations or to depart from normal staff channels.[79] It allows the deceivers to remain in the operations picture and be in constant touch with the commander's thoughts. At the same time, the commander is able to be as well informed about his shadow armies as he is about his real ones.[80]

At the same time, a deception organization should try to develop the best possible rapport with all the necessary elements of the intelligence community. The deceivers must be thoroughly acquainted with all the capabilities of the intelligence community, which is the source of continuous, real-time insights into the enemy's reaction to their planned deception. In the final analysis, the ability to co-ordinate effectively the activities of several organizations is much more important than organizational independence, location and direct or indirect control over resources. Varying circumstances in different states and different wars will dictate unique solutions to the operation and control of intelligence. The order of battle deceptions so prominent in the Second World War may be less feasible for smaller states, whose war potential is well-known, than it is for great powers. Modern war may require more technological deception and less camouflage, while short wars will pose completely different problems and opportunities from long wars. In each case, the organization and location of deception planners within the bureaucracy may change to fit the circumstances.

John Campbell's article on Operation Starkey (1943) draws on extensive evidence from the German side to analyse an Allied deception operation that failed completely.[81] Operation Starkey was actually part of a general deception operation code-named Cockade, which was intended to pin down as many German troops as possible in north-west Europe (France and Norway) to prevent them from being sent to either the Eastern front or Italy. Cockade consisted of three operations: Starkey, which was supposed to create a notional threat against the north-west coast of France (targeted for 8 September, later postponed to the 9th), to be followed by other bogus threats; Wadham, which was designed to convince the Germans that an American landing in Brittany was imminent; and Tindall, which was intended to tie down

German troops in Norway by creating a limited landing and airborne threat to Stavanger.Only Starkey called for the movement of some real troops, landing craft and air bombardments while Tindall and Wadham were basically notional. Operation Starkey also had a secondary goal of trying to draw German interceptors into the invasion area in order to defeat them in an all-out air battle, similar to the one that occurred during the Battle of Dieppe.

This elaborate but immature deception plan was an unmitigated disaster. The Germans were not alarmed, no extra formations were tied down (in fact, von Rundstedt, commander-in-chief West, gave up seven of his divisions and two Corps HQs for deployment in the Mediterranean area), and the air battle never materialized. 'In the end,' according to Campbell, 'nothing made the slightest difference. . . . Hitler and the staff at *Oberkommando der Wehrmacht* (OKW) concentrated on events in the Mediterranean, so that Starkey was buried by Avalanche' (the landing in Salerno that occurred on the same day as Starkey.) Tindall 'completely failed to interest' the Germans,[82] while 'Wadham was so weak as to be laughable'.[83] In these three operations, the deceivers may have deluded themselves about the prospects for success; or perhaps they had no illusions at all but persisted through sheer inertia and a reluctance to admit failure. As Campbell puts it, '. . . there was an element of inevitability about Cockade, of deception for the sake of deception'. At this point it is useful to summarize some of the reasons for Cockade's failure and the lessons that can be learned from it. The causes of failure discussed here are not listed in order of priority.

1. The Germans had no preconception of a cross-channel attack as early as 1943. As mentioned earlier, it is always much easier to reinforce an existing concept than to create a new one.

2. At that time the Allies did not possess sufficient resources to construct truly convincing notional threats; nor were the Allied Commanders, particularly those in the Royal Navy and Bomber Command, ready to allocate their scarce resources to deception plans that *did not cover any real operation*. The navy refused to risk battleships for shelling German shore batteries at close range, while both British and American Bomber Commands saw their priority in bombing Germany – not unimportant targets in France. 'Of the 42 aerial operations planned, 14 were abandoned and only 15 were carried out in full'.[84] (For example, the original deception plans called for 3,000-day sorties of American bombers, although General Eaker agreed to only 300.)[85] In addition, there were not enough wireless operators to simulate the appearance of new formations, and there were not enough real

formations available to create a more credible notional order of battle. Finally, another important resource was missing: that is, ample *time* to allow for development of the deception plan and its gradual absorption by the Germans.

3. The plans were poorly co-ordinated with other agencies not directly taking part in the deception operations such as the BBC and newspapers or the *Political Warfare Executive* (PWE). A number of uncoordinated leaks on the BBC and other channels contradicted the scenario designed to be conveyed to the Germans. While it is not clear how it affected the Germans, it certainly did not help.

4. Lack of realism in the deception cover plans. As a prerequisite, any deception plan must in general make operational sense, that is, be feasible to the enemy. As Campbell quotes Colonel William Harris, 'Fortitude South succeeded because it was in scale with the facts, whereas Wadham was wildly out of scale'. The same can be said for Tindall.

The signals directed at the Germans were too obvious, too crude. As Campbell shows, because the Allies were trying to draw the Germans into an all-out air battle, they did not attack the German radars which would normally have been a target in a real invasion. In a powerful critique referring to the uncoordinated leaks mentioned above, David Mure stated:

> ... If you are factually going to invade something, you do not announce it in the press and on the wireless, therefore, notional plans should not be announced either. . . . Plan Cockade and its constituents . . . broke every rule that had been laboriously formulated in the Mediterranean over a period of three years.[86]

The use of the press, or what we now call the mass media, for deception would be more productive not in telling the enemy one's intentions (positive deception) but rather for cover or negative deception.

5. The weakness of German intelligence was not properly exploited. While the Fortitude cover plans depended on the German failure (particularly of their air reconnaissance) to penetrate British secrecy, Operation Cockade was based on the opposite, *incorrect* assumption that the German Air Force would be able to detect the dummy concentrations of landing craft and aircraft prepared for them to 'discover' as part of the deception scenario. Apparently not up to the task, German intelligence never detected the intended bait. Thus, successful deception must always be carefully tailored to match the quality of the enemy's intelligence. As noted in the preceding para-

graph, it is dangerous to design a bait that is too obvious or crude; conversely, it is useless to devise a bait that is too subtle. Of the two types of failure, the former is more risky. A ruse that has not been picked up by the enemy, especially if this is known to the deceiver, is not too dangerous. In contrast, exposure of an attempt to deceive is extremely risky because it can lead to betrayal of the deceiver's means and methods as well as of his real intentions; worst of all, it can be turned against him.

The failure of Cockade gave rise to several dangers that were very narrowly averted. In view of the fact that the British conveyed so much information to the German *Abwehr* through their double agents, in particular Garbo (who later provided the decisive link for transmission of misleading information to the Germans in Fortitude) the entire network was placed in jeopardy. Had the Germans begun to suspect the authenticity of their agents in England, the most important means in the hands of the British deceivers would have been lost. Fortunately for the British, as Campbell proves, the Germans harboured no such suspicions, although they were aware that Starkey was possibly part of a deception plan.

Secondly, the failure of Cockade could certainly have discredited the potential contribution of deception in the eyes of many Allied commanders. Luckily, the arrival of Eisenhower and Montgomery and their staffs from the Middle East, where deception by 'A' Force had proved a great success, had already confirmed their belief in its value as a force multiplier. Moreover, the tremendous problems and risks involved in planning Overlord made it clear that there was really no substitute for deception. One danger that Campbell mentions seems to be fallacious. 'What,' he asks, 'if a twin threat to the Pas de Calais and Brittany persuaded them [the Germans] of the advantages of deploying their reserves in a central position, namely, Normandy?' This is a historical anachronism. For in such a case, the Allies may have decided to invade the Pas de Calais instead of Normandy and divert the Germans to Brittany. . . .

Ironically, the worst possible outcome for Cockade would have been success! Since no military operation followed the deception, the Germans would have been forced to recognize that they had been duped. Unlike the deception operation that had already been carried out by 'A' Force in the Mediterranean, Cockade was a sort of 'one-time', self-terminating ploy that neglected to supply the Germans with a proper explanation to conceal its existence. As David Mure observed:

> The most the cover plan, when it is aimed simply at containing enemy forces away from your chosen battle area, can do, is to

preserve a continual ever growing, changing and developing threat. It must never come to a climax and this should not be difficult to avoid as, in the case of a real operation, all security precautions exist for the specific purpose of concealing (1) that there is going to be a climax and (b) if there is, when is it likely to be. The same should apply in the case of a cover plan. The only way in which even a whisper of a climax should be hinted at is by finding a way by which over-elaborate attempts to cover up the possibility of one are leaked to the enemy. If the Archbishop of Canterbury called on the nation to pray for those 'about to invade the continent of Europe' as he did in the course of Plan Cockade, this means that no one was going to cross the channel.[87]

Whereas the failure of Cockade nearly exposed the double-cross system, its success would have almost certainly motivated the Germans to re-evaluate their intelligence sources and as a result discover British methods of deception. One possible lesson here is that deception operations not in support of real action may be counter-productive in that they could easily betray the whole deception system needed for the support of real operations.

In perspective, the failure of Cockade was a blessing in disguise. It probably convinced the Germans (certainly Rundstedt) that future Allied attempts to deceive would be equally inept and therefore relatively easy to detect. In the second place, the failure of Cockade impelled the Allied deceivers to refine their techniques and bring in new experts (such as Noel Wild, deputy of 'A' Force). By the time they began working on Fortitude many of these lessons had been learned. While Cockade is the paramount example of stratagem gone awry, Fortitude represents strategic and operational deception at its best.

A final lesson, simple but important, is that it is far better to relinquish a half-baked ruse with a high probability of failure than to carry it out to the bitter end and risk exposing the inner workings of one's entire deception organization.

Two articles in this volume explore the hitherto neglected subjects of strategic and operational deception during the Second World War as practiced by the United States in the Pacific and by the Soviet Union on the Eastern Front. Inasmuch as the use of deception on these fronts is barely mentioned in the existing body of literature, these chapters make an original and significant contribution to the historiography of the era and also serve as a starting point for further research. While it appears that the revelations concerning deception on the Pacific Front will not substantially change our observations on the course of the war in that arena, this is not the case with the war on the Eastern Front between Nazi Germany and the Soviet Union. David Glantz's detailed reconstruction of Soviet strategic and operational deception indicates that the scope of deception employed by the Soviet Union on the Eastern Front dwarfed even the largest Allied deception operations in Europe and the Mediterranean. His article may therefore prompt a complete re-evaluation of the war on the Eastern Front, especially since one critical dimension – *maskirovka* – has been omitted from all studies in the field.

First let us turn to a brief discussion of Katherine Herbig's chapter. According to Dr Herbig, the scope of deception as employed by the United States in the Pacific always remained small in comparison with that of similar undertakings in Western Europe and the Mediterranean, and on the Eastern Front. While they fared better than Starkey (i.e., did not fail), Operations Wedlock, Husband, Bambino, Valentine and Bluebird ultimately had no decisive impact on the course of events.

Unlike its European counterpart which had proved effective in the earlier phases of the war, deception in the Pacific never gained complete acceptance as a crucial dimension in the planning of military operations. 'To some extent,' Dr Herbig points out, 'deception remained suspect in American military circles throughout the war. . . .' Only with great reluctance did the US Navy begin to overcome its distaste for deception. 'No one, it seemed, had time in the fall of 1943 to develop strategic deception plans. . . . It was still considered an offbeat technique for many. . . . The American high command never granted its deception agency [i.e., the JSC] the access to top level commanders and the sweeping authority enjoyed by the London Controlling Section, a fact bitterly resented by US deception planners.' This can, at least in part, be explained by the fact that the British perceived themselves as extremely vulnerable and locked in a fight for their very survival, while the Americans were more inclined to believe that their victory was never in doubt but was merely a question of cost and time. As argued earlier, the essential point is that the incentive to resort to deception increases in direct proportion to the perceived gravity of the threat.

Even if fully successful, US strategic deception managed to pin down no more than 80,000 Japanese troops in the Kurile Islands. While this was a modest achievement, it was not critical relative to the scale of the Pacific war: the US would have won with or without it.

Moreover, it is not entirely clear whether the Japanese decision to station 70,000 to 80,000 troops in the Kurile Islands was a reaction to American strategic deception. The Japanese began to reinforce the Kurile Islands even *before* the US deception operation (i.e., it was an autonomous decision); the first Japanese reinforcement arrived in

March while the US wireless deception started in mid-April. Furthermore, as Dr Herbig shows, the Japanese always considered the Kuriles as a secondary problem. Regardless of the picture that American strategic deception tried to present, the Japanese gave top priority to the southern threat to their oil and other minerals.

The Japanese also failed to change their behavior or call for a special alert before the US deceivers' notional day of invasion for Wedlock (15 June 1944). At best, it can be argued that the Japanese tied down more troops than were really necessary in the Kurile Islands and did not see through the American deception. It is worth noting that the US deceivers do not appear to have exaggerated their claims for success in this (and later) operations.

What were some of the major weaknesses of the US deception operations? As Dr Herbig shows, the American deception planners were far less familiar with Japanese perceptions than their British colleagues were with the German mind-set. This made it all the more difficult to design appropriate baits. To make matters worse, faulty co-ordination both among US military commands and with the British in the Far East (India in particular) generated even more friction for deception plans. US commanders and military branches (Army, Navy, Army Air Force) were much more jealous than the British in protecting their turf. Some of this may be attributed to the different organization of the US command structure and the greater independence of each branch of the armed forces compared with that of the British unified command system.

As in the failure of Starkey, much can be explained by the shortage of resources. 'Criticism of Wedlock later would note that there was probably not enough activity, especially not enough reconnaissance and bombing of the area to support the threat being portrayed by other means. Accordingly, actual operations were called "the weakest link" in the operation.' Other weaknesses discussed by Dr Herbig concern the lack of detailed attention given to wireless deception. Had the Japanese been more thorough in their traffic analysis, they might have detected serious anomalies between the patterns of real traffic and the simulated wireless traffic.

A major difference between deception in the European theater of war and that in the Pacific involved the means used to transmit false information to the enemy. In Europe the most critical link was the double-cross system. It was direct, fast and had a powerful impact on the Germans. In the Pacific, the double-cross system played only a marginal role and was used, in Dr Herbig's words, to pass 'tidbits' to the Japanese. The American deceivers were thus deprived of their most effective link. Other special operations (such as Mincemeat) which could have provided highly convincing evidence were apparently not carried out.

From an organizational point of view, it is interesting to note that the American deception planners were *never directly* incorporated in the planning of military operations. Although the Joint Security Control (JSC) was originally modeled on the British London Controlling Section (LCS), it actually acquired a very different character. The LCS was exclusively a clearing house, a co-ordinating body which did not plan deception operations; instead, it co-ordinated the deception operations of Ops. (B) or 'A' Force, organizations which were very close to or a direct part of operational planning. On the other hand, the US Joint Chiefs of Staff not only designated the JSC to co-ordinate all deception-related developments, but also agreed to a proposal that the JSC write deception annexes for all war plans. Approval of this proposal gave '. . . Joint Security Control its first official role in deception planning'. This alienated the JSC from various operational commands which probably resented an independent, remote deception agency. Consequently, the distance created between the deceivers and the operations people did much to undermine the potentially influential role of deception in the Far East. Dudley Clarke's insistence that 'Deception is essentially a matter for the "Operations" Branch of the staff and not intelligence' was apparently very wise and practical advice.

A final note must consider the quality of Japanese intelligence. Like that of the Germans, Japanese strategic intelligence was not very effective nor was it held in great esteem by the Japanese Armed Forces.[88] The inefficiency of Japanese intelligence, which depended primarily upon a single channel of information as discussed by Dr Herbig, made it quite vulnerable to deception, yet also less likely to pick up the baits dangled before it by US deceivers, for whom success was very uncertain in this respect. The fact that the Americans were forced to rely almost completely on wireless deception considerably limited their access to Japanese intelligence-gathering channels. In comparison, the British double-cross system guaranteed that all the messages which were supposed to reach German intelligence actually did so. In the Pacific many of the deceptive signals were probably never picked up and were simply ignored or lost. At times, the Japanese High Command seemed to plan its strategy and troop dispositions on the basis of its own autonomous judgement, evincing a disregard for intelligence which ironically rendered it immune to deception.

Paradoxically, it is as difficult to deceive an excellent intelligence organization as it is an inferior one. When the enemy's intelligence organization is extremely efficient and thorough, the danger is that a deception operation may be exposed and even turned against the deceiver (although I know of no such case). With a weak intelligence organization, the deception planners take the risk that their 'bait' will not even be noticed. This seems to have occurred with the Japanese, which may explain the rather limited impact of US strategic deception operations. Hence, it appears that mediocre or competent intelligence organizations are the most likely to be deceived.

David Glantz provides the first systematic survey of deception on the Eastern Front – the Unknown War, to use Churchill's phrase. While the average reader is probably familiar with deception operations in the north-west European and Mediterranean theaters of war, even the expert knows little about Soviet deception operations during the Second World War. After completing this article, Colonel Glantz continued his intensive research and concluded that his earlier work represents only a very small fraction of Soviet activities related to *maskirovka*. He is now preparing a full-length book on the subject.

Land warfare on the Eastern Front was, by a quantum leap, larger than all land operations in all the other theaters of war. This is also true of the scale on which the Soviets used deception. Colonel Glantz contrasts the success of Soviet deception operations with the enormity of the German failure to deal with the problem. In fact, despite one success after another, the Germans could never effectively pierce Soviet cover and deception operations. Glantz bases his pioneering essay on a careful study of Soviet and, to a lesser extent, German sources, including the comparison and corroboration of Soviet and captured German Order of Battle maps.

The weakness and desperation of the Soviets in 1941 left them with no hesitation whatsoever in resorting to deception on all possible levels – political, strategic, operational, and tactical. Through four fascinating case studies – the Battle of Moscow 1941, Stalingrad 1942, Belorussia 1944, and Manchuria 1945 – Colonel Glantz traces the evolution of Soviet skill in this art. Whereas Soviet deception was relatively crude before the Battle of Moscow 1941, it had improved considerably by the Battle of Stalingrad, was even more mature in the fighting in Belorussia, and had been perfected by the time the USSR invaded Manchuria. By 1943, as he shows, the Soviets were incorporating deception in every strategic and operational plan.

The magnitude of deception operations on the Eastern Front is staggering. Before the Battle of Moscow, the Soviets concealed no fewer than three complete armies from German intelligence; by the Battle of Stalingrad, using very sophisticated camouflage techniques, the Soviets managed to conceal the forward deployment of 160,000 men, 430 tanks, 600 guns, 14,000 vehicles, and 7,000 tons of ammunition across the Don. Before their offensive in Belorussia, German intelligence had identified 140 Soviet division equivalents and three tank corps facing Army Group Center. In fact the Soviets managed to concentrate in the same region no less than 168 division equivalents, eight tank or mechanized corps, and two cavalry corps (with significant armored strength). The Germans estimated Soviet tank strength to be somewhere between 400 and 1,100 tanks, when it was actually more than 5,000 tanks at the same front! The difference between the number of Soviet forces the Germans were able to identify and those the Soviets were able to conceal was as large as the whole invasion force that landed at Normandy. In Manchuria, the Japanese underestimated the strength of the Soviet forces confronting them by no less than 30 to 50 per cent.

In their major offensive in Belorussia, the Soviets capitalized on a German obsession with the south-eastern flank (the Balkans) when they 'helped' the Germans to convince themselves that the next attack would indeed come from the south and north. As Earl Ziemke suggested in a quote selected by Glantz, 'To a Soviet deception, the German commands added an almost self-induced delusion: "the main offensive would come against Army Group North Ukraine because that was where they were ready to meet it".' Following their attack against the Germans on the central front, the Russians proceeded to attack the Germans on both the northern and southern fronts in what I described earlier as reverse conditioning deception.

The means employed by the Soviets to conceal their troop concentrations, as Glantz points out, were simple and labor-intensive but effective. Measures such as strict secrecy, heavy use of camouflage, movement at night and in bad weather, as well as pretending to prepare for defensive rather than offensive operations, served them well. Colonel Glantz also mentions the extensive, though not always successful, use of bogus wireless traffic to mislead the Germans and the occasional use of disinformation and rumors.

This picture is undoubtedly incomplete, for Soviet deception is portrayed as relying mainly on passive means. While this may be true for the most part, no mention at all is made of Soviet decoding operations, agents, double agents and the like. Only the Soviet archives, which remain closed, may reveal some of the other means of deception used by the Soviet Union. Indeed, Glantz remarks at one point that 'One of the deadliest weaknesses of deception planning was lack of knowledge about what the enemy knew concerning one's own *maskirovka* techniques'. Perhaps so, but on the other hand, the Russians may have known much more than they have thus far been ready to disclose. It is possible that, like the British and Americans, they had their own Ultra system with which to keep track of German reactions. In fact, it would be surprising if they had not acquired such a capability in one form or another. Given their traditional skill in the development of spy networks, it may also turn out that the Soviet Union had its own version of the so-called special means. At present, though, these are only speculations which cannot be verified.

A comparison with other chapters in this book also shows that the overall weakness of German and Japanese intelligence was pivotal to the success of Allied deception operations. The difference in this case is, however, that while the Germans and Japanese consistently *over-estimated* the Allied Order of Battle before each new landing campaign by as much as 80 to 100 per cent, they consistently *underestimated* the Soviet Order of Battle by 30 to 50 per cent. This accurately reflects the divergent aims of the deceivers on different fronts. Since the Soviets' main advantage was quantitative, they had the most to gain from concealment of their real capabilities. This they did with great success. Colonel Glantz's latest research (not reflected in his chapter in this book) indicates that while the Germans *overestimated* the size of the Red Army in the strategic sense, they *underestimated* the Soviet order of battle at each front before the Soviets launched a new offensive. On the other hand, the Western Allies, who did not enjoy a marked quantitative edge over the Germans, had to exaggerate their real strength in order to disperse German troops.

Glantz makes another interesting observation which was also true of the Allied experience in Western Europe and the Mediterranean. He argues that lower level German intelligence units were much more sensitive to deception and managed to detect developing threats much earlier than those at the highest OKH levels. 'There was a dichotomy between intelligence assessments at lower levels and high level head-quarters, with lower level headquarters taking a more realistic view of the situation.'

Being closer to the front, Army Group intelligence is in a better position to observe material developments and troop concentrations; it is more alert because the threat is direct – not abstract and remote. Unlike those in the highest echelons, a lower level analyst may be less committed to certain strategies and therefore less prone to wishful thinking and self-delusion. In attempting to counter deception, then, greater attention should be devoted (in a prolonged large-scale war) to any discrepancies between the upper- and lower-level echelons of intelligence as well as to lower echelon intelligence reports. Most of the Allied deception efforts in north-west Europe and the Mediterranean were indeed directed at the upper echelons. Luckily for the deceivers,

German regional commands always accepted the OKW views, even when such views seemed to be contradicted by locally obtained evidence. Under the Nazi system, all critical decisions related to strategic intelligence were ultimately made by the Führer himself.

Colonel Glantz concludes his article with a look at lessons the Soviets learned from their extensive use of deception. Their spectacular success in using *maskirovka* against the Germans certainly convinced them to take deception seriously in the future. There is probably no other military organization in the world today whose military doctrine *on all levels* emphasizes the use of stratagem to such an extent. Yet contemporary Soviet deception experts face a task which has grown increasingly complex given the more sophisticated reconnaissance and sensor technology of today, the improved traffic analysis, the quality of Western intelligence organizations and the greater general awareness of the possibility that one's adversary might be using deception. From its own experience in the Second World War, the Soviet Union learned the importance of using deception to achieve surprise in the opening phase of every offensive. Having come full circle since the days of Stalin, who once claimed that in modern warfare objective economic factors – not strategic surprise – determined the outcome of war, the Soviet Union employed strategic and operational deception in its invasion of Czechoslovakia in 1968, which caught NATO intelligence off guard, and probably also in its invasion of Afghanistan. Its allies, Egypt and Syria, achieved a major strategic surprise in their October 1973 attack on Israel by basing their cover and deception plans on Soviet strategic and operational doctrine. Dealing with the Soviet *maskirovka* on all levels will always remain a major problem for the Western Allies and all other Soviet adversaries, even those within its own bloc.

This makes the Soviet Union an exception to the rule that weakness is the main incentive for the use of deception. Perhaps, in some ways, the Soviet Union still feels inferior, unable and unwilling to ignore a historical experience of vulnerability despite its current control of a formidable arsenal of nuclear weapons. Such tendencies may be re-inforced by Marxist ideology, which depicts a continuous struggle between capitalism and communism requiring eternal vigilance and guile. Finally, as noted above, *maskirovka* proved to be an immense success in the Soviet military experience. While the United States may consider deception to be an exclusively wartime activity, for the Soviet Union it exists both in peace and war.

Tom Cubbage contributes two inter-related articles to this volume: the first synthesizes a number of theories explaining intelligence failures in general and applies them to Germany's inability to anticipate the invasion of Normandy, while the second reviews Roger Fleetwood Hesketh's definitive account of Fortitude – the largest-scale Allied deception cover plan of the Second World War. Cubbage's first article includes a survey of much of the recent literature on the causes of intelligence failure. The bulk of this literature has focused on possible explanations for the better-known strategic surprises that launched a new war or opened a new front (e.g., 'Barbarossa,' Pearl Harbor, the invasion of Korea in 1950, and the Yom Kippur War). Less has been written on the differences between the type of strategic surprise that marks the onset of a new war compared with that which occurs during a war, where an attack is already expected although its specific time, location, or intensity are not known. Cubbage applies many of these theoretical observations in explaining how strategic surprise can be achieved even though the enemy is anticipating an attack. In a systematic analysis of intelligence problems that are largely psychological, he examines the nature of human biases and the impossibility of accurately perceiving reality. Distortions arise from factors such as preconceived ideas, wishful thinking, drawing conclusions from an unrepresentative sample of evidence, the human need for order, the need for consistency, and commitment to earlier analysis.[89] Cubbage also explains how the usual biases in combination with certain psychological, structural and organizational biases unique to German intelligence further aggravated the problems they faced in estimating Allied intentions.

As Cubbage has shown, the clever deceiver intuitively understands that he must take advantage of the enemy analyst's instinctive desire to reduce ambiguity and impose order on an uncertain environment. He must help the enemy to be quite certain, decisive and wrong. The deliberate introduction of deception by an enemy further complicates the intelligence analyst's work. The very fact that deception is an ever present possibility adds a question mark to every bit of information. Cubbage concludes that good intelligence can reduce, but never completely eliminate, the fog of war. To refrain from subterfuge is tantamount to simplifying the enemy's problems, though he will always deceive himself to some degree in any event. Deception simply convinces him to deceive himself in a way more conducive to one's plans.

Cubbage's second contribution is a review essay of Roger Fleetwood Hesketh's after-action report on Fortitude. While Masterman's *The Double Cross System* makes much easier reading, the Hesketh Report is a far more thorough and detailed account and thus of greater interest to the professional reader. Through close attention to minute details, Hesketh constructs a much more realistic view of how deception work

is actually carried out and guides the reader through the development
of a major deception plan, from its time-consuming inception and
implementation to its adjustment according to information received
from the enemy, including a follow-up of how it was absorbed at each
stage by the enemy's intelligence and command systems. Cubbage's
excellent introduction to this unusual document serves only to whet the
appetite of those interested in this hitherto closely guarded information. Publication of the Hesketh Report, of Dudley Clarke's final
report on the history of 'A' Force, and of Sir Michael Howard's official
history of deception will be extremely helpful in putting the history of
deception in the Second World War, and of course the history of the
war itself, in a more accurate and complete perspective.

EVALUATING THE EFFECTIVENESS OF DECEPTION

> But in war, as in life generally, all parts of a whole are inter-
> connected and thus the effects produced, however small their
> cause, must influence all subsequent military operations and
> modify their final outcome to some degree, however slight. In the
> same way, every means must influence even the ultimate
> purpose.[90]
>
> It would however be disastrous to try to develop our under-
> standing of strategy by analyzing these factors in isolation, since
> they are usually inter-connected in each military action in mani-
> fold and intricate ways. A dreary analytical labyrinth would
> result, a nightmare in which one tried in vain to bridge the gulf
> between this abstract basis and the facts of life. Heaven protect
> the theorist from such an undertaking.[91]

An important but difficult question to answer is: How can we evaluate
the effectiveness of a deception operation on any given level? In an
after-action report, it is very difficult to isolate or separate a single
variable from the extremely complex interaction of numerous
variables. Attempting to determine the influence of each element may
be convenient for analytical purposes, but it is still an artificial process.
Recognizing this, Clausewitz warned against the danger of studying the
various components of any type of military action in isolation. In *The
Poverty of Historicism*, Karl K. Popper referred to this problem as '. . .
a complexity arising out of the impossibility of artificial isolation. . .,'[92]
while in his stimulating book, *Historians' Fallacies*, David Hackett
Fisher analyses the issue as follows:

> The reductive fallacy reduces complexity to simplicity, or
> diversity to uniformity, in causal explanations. It exists in several

common forms, none of which can be entirely avoided in any historical interpretation. As long as historians tell selected truths, their causal models must be reductive in some degree. But some causal models are more reductive than others. When a causal model is reductive in such a degree, or in such a way, that the resultant distortion is dysfunctional to the resolution of the causal problem at hand, then the reductive fallacy is committed.[93]

In contemporary work on military strategy and technology, this problem is referred to as *synergy*, which is defined by the *Oxford English Dictionary* as increased effectiveness, achievement, etc., produced as a result of a combined action or co-operation. Even more relevant to our discussion is the definition of *synergism*: the combined activity of two drugs or other substances when greater than the sum of the effects of each present alone. *Webster's Dictionary* defines synergism as 'the co-operative action of discrete agencies . . . such that the total effect is greater than the sum of the two or more effects taken independently'. In certain actions, therefore, it is almost impossible to study each component separately and determine the relative contribution of each to the final process.

Similarly, while it is difficult to measure with any degree of precision the impact of deception on the outcome of a war, campaign or battle, we *can* assume that in its absence the final outcome would be very different.

One can evaluate the effectiveness of deception in two ways: either before and during a military operation (or implementation), or after the operation has taken place. Before a military operation has taken place and while the deception is being implemented, the only way to attempt to evaluate its success is by following its impact on the enemy's behavior. Has he changed his order of battle and dispositions as desired by the deceivers? Are his commanders aware of the time and place an operation will take place? The impact of deception can be assessed through such means as air reconnaissance, wireless interception, breaking the enemy's codes, and noting the extent to which surprise has been achieved at the location of the attack. For example, before the invasion of Normandy, the Allies knew through Ultra intercepts, special means, air reconnaissance and local agents, that the Germans had reacted as the deceivers wanted them to by concentrating their troops around the Pas de Calais without reinforcing the Normandy area. How much of this can be attributed to deception alone and how much to existing concepts of Hitler and the German High Command is difficult and unnecessary to determine because the two reinforced each other. Nevertheless, in this case the Allies knew in *advance* that their deception was working, or at least that the Germans had done nothing to negate it.

Before the Battle of El Alamein, British deception and camouflage operations obscured their concentration of forces from the Germans in order to conceal the *Schwerpunkt* of their attack. On the basis of information on German troop dispositions obtained through Ultra and air reconnaissance, the British could determine that the Germans had *not* anticipated where the main attack would fall. When the attack came earlier than expected, Rommel was away (as he was when the invasion of Normandy began).

By monitoring their deception measures before Anzio, the Allies knew that the Germans had not concentrated their troops at the landing area. As a result, the Allies subsequently achieved complete surprise and met no resistance at the landing area. This type of continuous assessment can give the deceivers a reasonable idea of how effective their deception is, though they can never afford to become complacent and assume – on the basis of such feedback – that their ruse will be completely effective.

The second way to gauge a particular plan's success is to interrogate the enemy commanders and examine captured documents after the battle is over. Only after the war did the Allies determine that Garbo's message of 9 June had been transmitted all the way up to the OKW and Hitler. In a post-war interrogation of Jodl, it became apparent that this message had a decisive impact on the German decision not to send reinforcements to Normandy. In this case, both documented evidence as well as German action (or lack of it) match perfectly, indicating beyond doubt that the deception worked. An examination of the diary of OKH *Lagebericht West* (OKH intelligence in north-west Europe) showed that out of 208 messages received and recorded in the *Üerblick des Britischen Reiches,* no fewer than 188 messages came from British-controlled agents.[94] Many more facts could be cited to make the point that Allied deception was highly effective. It is, however, not always so easy to prove the effectiveness of deception, as illustrated in the case of the 'going maps' ruse that preceded the battle of Alam Halfa.

As a prisoner of war, General Thoma in a conversation in Cairo admitted that Rommel had relied on a carefully doctored British 'going map' to plan and execute his offensive. Although the Germans never realized that the maps had been planted by the British (that is, they did not expose the deception), it is impossible to prove that this ruse had a direct impact on Rommel's planning and conduct of the offensive. Most authorities agree that he changed his plan during the battle as a result of a petrol shortage, and then may or may not have been misguided by the false 'going maps'. Basically, there are three schools of thought regarding the impact of this ruse on Rommel's division at Alam Halfa. Major General Sir Francis de Guingand, Sir David Hunt, Field Marshal Alexander (who participated in the deception) and Winston Churchill concluded that the 'going map' ruse was probably very effective and achieved its goal; whereas Liddell Hart was more skeptical, and more recently Hinsley, Carver and Barnett did not credit the ruse with any impact whatsoever. The original version of the story was recounted by Major General Francis de Guingand in *Operation Victory*.

> I will break off here to describe a ruse which we afterwards learnt had helped to defeat Rommel. We always produced 'going' maps which were layered in colours to show the type of desert in so far as it affected movement. We knew the enemy had captured many of our maps and was making use of them. At the time of the retreat to Alamein no 'going' maps existed of the area to the rear of our positions. These we produced after we had settled in. I, therefore, decided to have made a false 'going' map which would link up quite correctly with the maps already in enemy hands, and then to falsify a particular area to suit our plans. The area I selected, in consultation with our Intelligence staff, was one south of Alam Halfa. Due south of the highest point was an area of very soft sand. As we appreciated the enemy would make for this ridge I thought that by showing this bad area as good going, the enemy might be tempted to send his tanks around that way. It would also give him a shock if he were making for El Hamman, for instead of a 'good gallop', he would find himself wallowing in deep sand. We had this map secretly printed in very quick time by the energy of an old associate of mine in the M I Directorate in Cairo – Stuart-Menteith. Then we plotted with 13th Corps to have it 'captured' by the enemy. In the south, light forces were continually patrolling around the enemy's minefields, and so it was arranged that a scout car should get blown up on a mine, and that the crew would be taken off in another truck. Left in the scout car were soldier's kits and the usual junk, whilst stuffed away in a haversack was an old and dirty 'going map' (the fake) covered in tea stains, but quite readable. The car had been ransacked by the next morning, and the map had disappeared.
>
> The enemy certainly got badly 'bogged down' in this particular area, but how much the map was to blame I don't quite know. From interrogation of prisoners, however, we did obtain confirmation that a falsified map led the enemy to send their tanks into this sandy terrain, which trebled their fuel consumption. We

MAPS 5 & 6
THE EL ALAMEIN 'GOING MAPS' RUSE

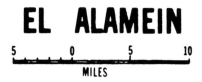

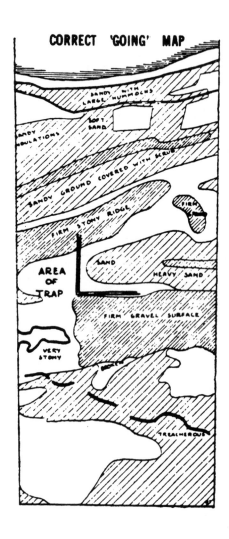

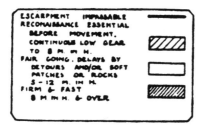

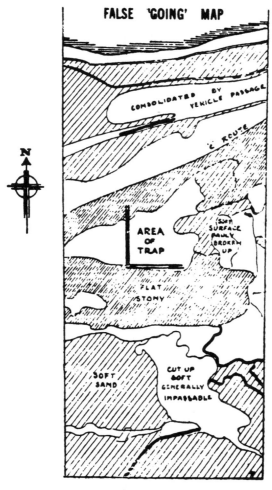

Source: Major-General Sir Francis de Guingaud, *Operation Victory*
(London, 1947), maps 16 and 17.

also knew that Rommel put down the failure of his offensive to petrol shortage. So it looks as if it probably helped.[95]

What is seen as highly probable by General de Guingand is accepted as a fact by Churchill.

Montgomery hoped that they would not take the latter course. He preferred to fight on his chosen battleground, the ridge. A map which showed easy going for tanks in that direction, and bad going farther east, had been planted upon Rommel. General von Thoma, captured two months later, stated that this false information had its intended effect. Certainly the battle now took the precise form that Montgomery desired.[96]

A middle position is taken by Liddell Hart:

Here one must pause for a moment to refer to a striking story that has gained wide currency. It was first told authoritatively, soon after the war, in *Operation Victory*, written by Major-General Sir Francis de Guingand, Montgomery's chief-of-staff. He there described how he planned 'a ruse which helped to defeat Rommel' by luring the enemy forces into 'an area of very soft sand' just south of the Alam Halfa Ridge. He devised a map of the 'going' which showed this area fairly firm, and in conjunction with Horrocks, the commander of the 13th Corps, planted it on the enemy by leaving it in a scout car that purposely ran on to a mine. The story was repeated in a footnote to Alexander's Despatch, written in 1947, which stated that it had been subsequently learned from the captured General von Thoma that 'the enemy had intended to outflank the ridge to the north-east but had altered his plan on the basis of this false information'. But Thoma was in Russia when this battle took place, and it is clear from the records that Rommel had intended the Afrika Korps to drive eastward, on a line far south of this treacherous area, and only altered his plan because of the time lost in the passage of the initial mined belt. The most that can truly be claimed for de Guingand's clever ruse is that it may have led Rommel to imagine, when he changed course, that the Alam Halfa Ridge was more easily accessible than it proved. The soft sand area cramped the scope for local manoeuvre there.[97]

Professor Hinsley reached the following conclusions:

Deprived of the advantage of surprise, Rommel's thrust failed to make the quick penetration he had hoped for. In the afternoon of 31 August, Rommel, having been forced to abandon his original intention of trying to outflank the position to the south, turned north in an attempt to capture the Alam el Halfa ridge, consuming abnormally large amounts of fuel in this manoeuvre. . . . A deception plan had been prepared by the intelligence and survey branches responsible for the production of 'going' maps. This was designed to lead Rommel up to the ridge by the route he eventually adopted. But the fact that this original plan would have sent the DAK overground marked on this map as bad 'going' suggests that he was not influenced by the deception.[98]

Correlli Barnett, in *The Desert Generals*, wrote:

Now Rommel was seen to turn sharply north, a move forced on him not by a planted 'false-going' map, but by the delays in the mine-fields and by shortage of petrol.[99]

And finally, a similar conclusion was reached by General Michael Carver in his book *Al Alamein*:

At the same time efforts were made to mislead the enemy. First of all he was to be led into deferring his attack altogether by an impression of great strength in the south. Two dummy tank battalions were moved into the area east of Himeimat, a dummy infantry brigade position was dug at Samaket Gaballa and dummy minefields were also laid. All this was completed by August 25th. If in spite of this Rommel were to break through, he was to be misled as to the nature of the 'going' by a false 'going' map deliberately lost on patrol in the forward area. There was in fact an area of very soft sand south of Alam el Halfa: this was shown as good hard 'going', and the good 'going' shown as bad in the hope of luring Rommel into that area. Unfortunately for those who planned to deceive, there is no sign that any of these measures had any effect on Rommel's plans or even came to his notice, certainly not the first.[100]

It seems as though the impact of the 'going map ruse' has been questioned more and more with the passage of time. Perhaps this trend confirms Cruickshank's observation: 'As a rule, the success of deceptive activities was overestimated, especially by those directly responsible for them'.[101] Sir David Hunt suggests that Professor Hinsley may not be right: 'In fact the map was planted between the making of the original plan and the adoption of the final plan. I don't contest [writes Sir David] the possibility that the change of the *Stoss-linie* was dictated by shortage of fuel and not by the deception; but that remains to be proved'.[102] In the end, this question will have to remain unresolved. What is important, however, is that the 'going map ruse' was only one of many other evidently more successful deception plans preceding the Battle of Alam Halfa. These included laying dummy (and real) minefields, creating a bogus threat on the southern flank of the German advance, and inducing the Germans to take action, despite their shortage of petrol, by the use of special means.[103] Although it may be difficult to try to assess the effect of one factor such as the 'going map ruse' in isolation from the much wider plan of deception, and further-more, to separate the impact of deception from that of other factors, one can nevertheless safely conclude that operational deception played a key role in the Battle of Alam Halfa one way or the other.

The methodological difficulties inherent in determining the effectiveness of deception are exacerbated by the fact that even if deception fails to achieve its intended objectives, it almost always fools the enemy – he is unable to identify the information he receives as false. While the impact of the 'going map ruse' will always be debatable, no one has ever argued that the Germans doubted its authenticity.

In 'A German Perspective on Allied Deception Operations in the Second World War', Professor Klaus-Jürgen Müller challenges the widely accepted idea that Allied deception operations were generally successful in influencing the decisions of the German High Command. He claims that much of what has been written on this subject – particularly by former practitioners of deception – has been based on the Allied point of view without due reference to, and corroboration with, the German decision-making process and related documentary evidence. By failing to undertake an in-depth study of the German perspective, many writers may have fallen prey to the *post hoc ergo propter hoc* fallacy. A closer examination, he believes, may persuade the historian that in many instances, German mistakes or moves previously attributed to the effectiveness of Allied deception were in fact the result of autonomous German decisions. He argues that simply because deception was not exposed does not necessarily mean that it was successful.

If anything, Professor Müller forces anyone interested in deception in general, and the Second World War in particular, to re-examine the evidence and take a critical look at the existing literature in the field. From a heuristic point of view, Professor Müller has certainly per-formed an important service for all students of deception by causing them to reconsider many methodological issues and ideas that may have been taken for granted.

The following quotations are representative of Müller's criticism and major arguments.

Reading books by former intelligence officers on the subject one often gets the impression that some authors are obviously inclined to overestimate the effects of the activities they were involved in. . . . [t]hey have obviously influenced more than one professional historian to adopt this evaluation without further scrutiny.

A closer examination, however, reveals that very often such an exaggerated evaluation of the effects of deception operations is not well founded, and therefore not very convincing. Even where these stratagems were 'bought' by those they were sold to, their effect at the strategic level was minimal in many cases. Deception at the tactical level, however, was very often successful. At the strategic level there are many examples of deception operations being less successful or even failures. In some instances deception is counter-productive.

Montagu, for example, came to his optimistic evaluation of Mincemeat's effects by analysing a small number of captured German documents he happened to find. . . . From the methodological point of view it is grossly inadequate to analyse enemy documents collected at random and to base one's conclusions on such a meagre sample of sources. . . . Yet this is how not a few of the memoirs and other books on deception have been written.

An account, and especially an analysis isolating deception operation factors, inevitably misses the point. Deception history cannot really be written by dealing exclusively with intelligence operations. This approach leaves out factors essential for understanding intelligence itself.

The German evaluation of the strategic situation and of the expected Allied operation, was not *decisively* influenced by Allied deception activities – even if some German authors also put forward this hypothesis. Quite the contrary, it was determined by a multitude of factors: military, psychological, political, geographical and economic. . . .

According to the German military tradition of strategic thinking . . . the planners aimed at a quick and decisive operation – the destruction of the enemy forces as quickly and as radically as possible by one decisive blow at the right place [my emphasis]. . . . No doubt, this specific pattern of thinking and perceiving reality decisively determined . . . the German evaluation of the strategic situation in the summer of 1943.

The German High Command was well aware that the Allies were doing everything to deceive and mislead them. In February [1943] the *Wehrmachtfahrungsstab* (WFst) issued a warning in this respect. *Nobody in the Führerhauptquartier could really*

> distinguish between real or fictitious information. This contributed considerably to weakening the effect of Allied deception measures. The German analysts ... therefore had to rely on their own strategic ideas when anticipating future Allied operations [my emphasis].
>
> Within this strategic context [i.e., at what location would the Allies invade in southern Europe] the two problems – securing the Balkans, and *keeping Italy in the war* – became the essential preconditions for the continuation of the war by Germany [my emphasis].
>
> Sicily was where Hitler expected the next Allied landing operation to take place (not excluding secondary or diversionary operations elsewhere).
>
> Germany's reactions in the Mediterranean were ... predominantly determined by one single motive [Müller actually mentions two above] the fear of Italy's imminent collapse and/or defection.

At this point, it is useful to discuss briefly some of the problems raised by Professor Müller's methodology. In the first place, he relies on a very small and unrepresentative sample to make his argument.[104] This he does on two occasions; in his choice of authors representing those who wrote on deception, and in the sample of case studies from which he tries to prove his case.

Montagu's *The Man Who Never Was* is in fact a well-documented book for which the material was not chosen at random, but which represented important decisions and reactions of the German High Command. Furthermore, Montagu was writing a limited monograph that focused on only one episode of deception: Operation Mincemeat, which was actually part of a much larger deception cover plan, Barclay. Montagu may claim much for Operation Mincemeat (and rightly so) but he never suggests that Mincemeat was not complemented by many other deception operations (which at the time he wrote his book were all classified), nor would he deny that the German decision-making process involved an admixture of motives.

While David Mure's *Practice to Deceive* does contain its share of inaccuracies, it is nevertheless a generally reliable book based on first-hand knowledge and apparently also on advice from Dudley Clarke and Noel Wild. Unfortunately it is not an accurate or balanced account but documents released in the future as well as the official history will prove it to be largely correct. While Müller often chooses to argue over 'tangential' issues such as why Rommel was sent to Athens or whether the Panzer division sent to Greece was fully equipped, he conveniently ignores another very central matter – that of the notional order of battle created by 'A' Force in the Middle East and passed by special means to the German *Abwehr*. Implemented much earlier than Operation Mincemeat and never exposed by the Germans, this deception operation must have had considerable influence on the German decision to concentrate troops in the Balkans. Throughout the Second World War, the Germans believed that in addition to the British 8th Army there was also a 12th Army. This fictitious formation partially explains German fears of a threat to the Balkans. Similarly, he ignores the deception operation (as discussed by Mure and Cruickshank)[105] intended to convince the Germans that the British were considering an attack on the Balkans in co-operation with the Turks, who had become more and more sensitive to Allied pressure. Müller does mention possible plans of an Allied attack from Turkish territory, but he omits to mention that this threat, which was taken seriously by the Germans as he suggests, was primarily fabricated by the Allies.

While focusing on Operation Mincemeat, which was the object of much publicity, Professor Müller also omits to discuss the eastern Mediterranean order-of-battle deceptions which were less spectacular but far more important in diverting German forces to the Balkans.

As Sir David Hunt shows, other British deception operations started before, and continued long after, Operation Mincemeat had been terminated.

> Already at the time of Husky the cover plan drew attention to a supposedly imminent invasion of the Peloponnese which caused, among other reactions, the precipitate move of 1st Panzer Division from France to the beaches of Kalamata at the southernmost extremity of the Balkans. S.O.E.'s operation in Greece, codenamed Animals, made a useful contribution. The next year [1944], the cover plan was even more elaborate, pointing to landings in Bulgaria on May 9. German susceptibility to these suggestions was increased by acceptance of the spurious formations continuously fed to their specialists in the Allied order of battle. This created a firm belief in the existence of strong forces standing ready in Egypt and North Africa to be used at the right moment in the Balkans; coupled with their ignorance of the essentials of amphibious warfare, this delusion gave them reason to suppose that landings almost anywhere in the peninsula were within Allied capability. On 10 June 1944, for instance, Foreign Armies West forecast an invasion of Albania and Epirus from Apulia commanded by the [fictitious] 3rd Polish Corps. At the same time the Operations Branch of OKW considered that an

invasion of Istria was highly likely. These misappreciations multiplied the value of the forces in the Mediterranean theatre as an instrument for misdirecting the movements of German reserves.[106]

The most important works – that is, the British and American official histories and the official reports on deception like those by Hesketh and Masterman – make very modest claims for the success of deception. Apart from mentioning deception very briefly, the official histories tend to ignore its contribution to Allied strategy and military operations. Constrained by the need for secrecy, many were written in the 1950s and 1960s before disclosure of the existence of Ultra and the special means operators. Later volumes, such as Molony's Volume Six of *The Mediterranean and Middle East* published in 1984, unjustifiably continue to gloss over the role of deception. For example, the code-name of the cover plan for Operation Diadem (i.e., *Nunton*) is not even mentioned in the British official history, perhaps because of the decision to concentrate the discussion of deception operations in a special volume being written by Sir Michael Howard.

Roger Hesketh, one of the foremost practitioners of deception and also one of its ablest historians, goes to unusual lengths *not* to exaggerate the impact of deception. Indeed the epigraph chosen for his account of Fortitude, the most successful of all deception operations, cautions the reader against the *post hoc ergo propter hoc* fallacy of assuming that simply because deception existed it was also decisive:

> It was prettily devised of Aesop: 'The fly sat upon the axle-tree of the chariot-wheel and said, "What a dust do I raise!" ' So are there some vain persons that, whatsoever goeth alone or moveth upon great means, if they have never so little hand in it, they think it is they that carry it.
>
> Francis Bacon, *Essay on Vainglory*

He mentions this again in the preface.

> It is always tempting for those who set out to deceive and who see their objects fulfilled, to claim the credit for their attainment when, in fact, the motive force lay in another quarter. Every effort has been made to complete the chain of cause and effect so that the reader can judge for himself to what extent the Germans were influenced by the action of Allied deceivers and to what extent they were impelled by other considerations. At all times the writer has kept before him the boast of Aesop's fly as he sat upon the axle-tree.[107]

The second fundamental problem with Müller's argument is the narrowness of the sample he uses to caution historians against over-emphasizing the importance of deception. Had he chosen as his sample deception operations Cockade, Starkey, Wadham, and Tindall as well as Fortitude North, it would have appeared as though deception does not work at all. This is what David Hackett Fischer refers to as 'fallacies of statistical sampling or generalizations which rest upon an insufficient body of data – upon a "sample" which represents the composition of the object in question'.[108]

The material presented in this volume and other cases not mentioned which took place in North Africa, Italy, Normandy, El-Alamein, and the Russian front, indicates that deception was often very effective and, even if not always successful, was only rarely counter-productive due to the overall incompetence of German strategic intelligence. In this book, for example, Colonel Glantz reveals for the first time the very successful and large-scale Russian deception operations on the Eastern Front. Not a single systematic study has yet been published on Allied deception operations in Italy (the best discussion so far is still in Sir David Hunt's *A Don at War*, a book not dedicated to the study of deception and intelligence operations), nor has the post-war report written by Dudley Clarke for the British Cabinet been published. While it is doubtful that any of those projects will lead to excessive claims, they will probably show that deception was practiced on a much wider scale than previously assumed.

A number of other methodological questions also merit discussion, for instance, complexity (or why deception and intelligence cannot be separated analytically). Professor Müller first suggests that deception must be studied in a wider context, that intelligence history must be studied in combination with other 'non-intelligence' issues, then proceeds to evaluate the influence of Allied deception on German strategy by discussing the German decision-making process in general and more specifically how independent strategic factors shaped German strategy. While this certainly is a sound methodology for his own discussion, Müller studies deception in isolation from one important dimension – the performance of German intelligence. Yet deception cannot be studied apart from intelligence, since intelligence is critical in designing and implementing deception operations as well as exposing them. In this last dimension of exposing deception, German strategic intelligence failed completely; worse still, it unwittingly became an important instrument in Allied deception. German strategic intelligence was unable to provide its high command with any useful clues on Allied strategy, intentions, capabilities or deception.

If the Allies intended to invade Sicily, Normandy, the northern

FIGURE 4
DECEPTION ORGANIZATIONS IN THE MEDITERRANEAN – 1943

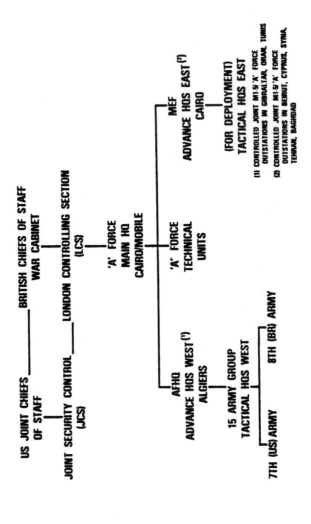

sector of El Alamein, or land in Anzio, *good* operational and strategic intelligence ought to have given the German High Command a more specific warning. This does not mean the task was easy or even possible, but it is an ideal which good intelligence services aspire to reach. Allied intelligence was certainly not perfect and suffered from many failures, but its overall record was far better than that of the Germans. In this it was helped to a large extent by Ultra.

This discussion can be related directly to Professor Müller's example, the invasion of Sicily. German intelligence could at no time give the High Command a clear-cut answer to the question of where the main Allied thrust was to take place. Sardinia, the Peloponnese, and even Spain, Corsica and southern France were added to the list of possibilities. Even if, as Professor Müller claims, it was eventually clear that Sicily was the real target, such a warning came much too late to be effective. In addition, the warning did not discount major attacks in other locations and offered no clue as to where in Sicily the attack would occur. Be that as it may, the reactions of the German High Command most assuredly indicate its hesitation and inability to determine that Sicily was the target. The extent to which this indecision can be attributed to deception or poor intelligence is impossible and unnecessary to determine, for Allied deception and poor German intelligence reinforced each other.

It is clear in retrospect, but should also have been clear at the time to a high-quality intelligence organization, that the Allies could not have simultaneously invaded Sardinia, Sicily and the Peloponnese. They simply did not have the necessary landing craft. At no time was this recognized by German intelligence, which assumed the possibility of numerous simultaneous operations or at least of one major invasion in conjunction with two diversionary operations. A major achievement of Allied deception was the gradual construction of a notional order of battle accepted by and large as genuine by German intelligence. Discussed, for example, by David Mure in *Practice to Deceive*, this long-lasting, effective stratagem – *not* Operation Mincemeat – was the most important Allied deception operation preceding the invasion of Sicily, for it catered to the German perception of a threat to the Balkans at a much earlier time than Mincemeat. Mincemeat only reinforced German fears awakened earlier by a more important deception operation (such as the creation of the fictitious Twelfth Army). This is ignored by Professor Müller. The Allies repeated the same order-of-battle (OB) type of deception *before* the invasion of Normandy with similar results. In both cases, German intelligence overestimated the Allied OB by 80 to 100 per cent. (See Appendix 2 for OKW Estimates of the Allied OB in May 1944.) Incorrect identification of a few non-existent divisions as real would have been forgivable, but to make the same mistake with dozens of divisions, whose existence *should* have been corroborated by material evidence, was disastrous.

Even worse, German intelligence never properly understood that one of the Allies' cardinal operational principles was never to operate outside the range of air cover, particularly when one was planning a highly dangerous landing operation. This excluded Sardinia, Greece or Norway from any major landing operations. Yet the Allies themselves did not always agree on this principle right from the start. In 1941, 1942 and even later, Churchill seriously considered an invasion of Norway and was only dissuaded from this 'Gallipoli of the North' project by virtue of Alanbrooke's strenuous efforts. Sardinia was also considered as a target for invasion but in each case the impossibility of providing air cover was a major factor in the decision not to proceed. On the German side, Field Marshal Kesselring was one of the few to consider this possibility, which eventually enabled him to determine that Sicily was the Allies' true objective.

Müller also discusses two other factors that seriously undermined the quality of German intelligence as well as the German approach to strategic analysis in general. One can be described as German *ethnocentrism*, the other as the *whistling in the dark* syndrome. In the quotations cited earlïer, Müller repeatedly explains that the Germans tried to predict the course of Allied strategy on the basis of how they themselves might have acted. This approach would be rational only if the intelligence organization had absolutely no knowledge of the adversary. Otherwise, it is a poor substitute for good intelligence. Projection of one's own fears, procedures or expectations on an adversary is one of the cardinal sins of intelligence and strategic analysis in a world where strategy is neither purely rational nor symmetrical. The fact that Germany considered the Balkans to be a critical source of raw material did not mean that it was a top priority for the Western Allies. Germany may have been convinced that Sardinia was the key to victory in Italy, while the Allies did not necessarily consider it to be as important if it was out of range of their fighters or if their strategy in Italy was to divert and tie down German troops rather than seek a decisive victory. The fact that Norway was of critical value in Hitler's own mind did not bring it within Allied range of fighter cover or transform it into the most effective avenue of attack in north-west Europe. Similarly, to assume that the Pas de Calais would be the chosen location for the Allied invasion because that is how the Germans would have done it, is hardly a sound way to make intelligence estimates or strategic decisions. Just as almost every strategist can correctly determine the most obvious and rational course of action, he can also assume that the enemy will be equally aware of this possibility and prepared to counter it. While to a certain extent unavoidable, projection and ethnocentrism are very dangerous biases that must be overcome as much as possible. They facilitate self-deception as well as deception by the enemy. The combination of German staff methods, ethnocentrism, racism, and early victories rendered German intelligence and its high command very susceptible to the projection of its own strategic logic and preferences on others.

Müller mentions at least three times that the Germans knew they were the target of Allied deception. They circulated a memorandum by the *Wehrmachtführungsstab* to this effect; and at one point Hitler asked one of his military aides, 'Christian, couldn't this be a corpse they have deliberately planted on our hands?' This was 'whistling in the dark', because knowing that one is being deceived without knowing *how* is not always an advantage. Even if the police know that a crime is going to be committed every evening, they may not be able to prevent it unless more specific information is obtained.

A general warning to watch out for deception can be counter-productive because it places every piece of information in doubt, which may lead to paralysis and paranoia. The only constructive way to deal with deception is to unmask it – to find out how it is being implemented. This is the duty of intelligence and counter-intelligence. The Germans rarely succeeded in discovering deception. On occasions when deception failed to convince them, it was not because they had exposed it, but because they failed to pick up the bait. Mincemeat may not have been an important factor in determining German strategy but at least it was never exposed. Had the Germans recognized Operation Mincemeat as part of an Allied ruse, the results would have been quite different, for they would then have been able to identify Sicily as the Allies' true objective.

By dwelling on Operation Mincemeat and ignoring the more important notional order-of-battle deceptions, Müller appears to view deception as an *ad hoc* policy not as part of a continuing strategy; but since Mincemeat was only one scheme designed to reinforce the whole fabric of earlier deception operations, there is no justification for dealing with it in isolation. Viewing deception as a continuous policy may lead to a different evaluation of its worth. Indeed, after the invasion of Sicily, the Allies managed to protect and hence continue their deception operations in Italy (and elsewhere) with great success.

Professor Müller argues that because Operation Mincemeat was implemented only *after* the German strategy had already been formulated, those who credit this Allied ploy with so much success have fallen for the *post hoc ergo propter hoc* fallacy. This, however, is not a convincing argument. He cannot prove that it failed to have any influence simply because it came after the strategic decision had already been made. As is well known, a dog that does not bark can provide as much evidence as one that does. According to Professor Müller's line of argument, only a visible change in German strategy would constitute sufficient proof that the stratagem had succeeded. Yet the deceivers were not interested in bringing about any changes. Quite to the contrary, their deception was intended to *reinforce* – not contradict – existing German strategic concepts.[109] All that Müller can logically claim is that German strategy in southern Europe was decided before Operation Mincemeat. The evidence from German documents demonstrates rather convincingly that Mincemeat did indeed strengthen the existing German concepts and was therefore effective to at least some degree. The only positive way to prove that Mincemeat was a failure would have been to expose it as deceptive. Furthermore, Operation Mincemeat could only be effective because the Germans made earlier decisions that in turn were also influenced by Allied deception. It is very unusual and very difficult for deception to create new concepts for an enemy. It is much easier and more effective to reinforce those which already exist. For example, with or without deception, Hitler might have decided to identify the Pas de Calais as the Allies' chosen point for the invasion of Europe. All the deceivers did was to reinforce this concept and try their best to perpetuate it. How much of the success of Fortitude depended on Hitler's earlier decisions or on Allied deception is difficult to say. Without the kind of definitive proof provided by Garbo's 9 June message which was passed all the way up to Hitler and prevented German Panzer reinforcements from being sent to Normandy, Müller might have used the same reasoning to argue that deception was irrelevant because the Germans had decided long before to concentrate their troops in the Pas de Calais area; instead, he might have attributed the decision to Hitler's irrational obsession with the Pas de Calais and so on. In the light of the information acquired courtesy of the Allied deceivers, Hitler in fact made a very rational decision from his point of view.

Müller sets forth an array of independent strategic arguments to demonstrate that other factors, and not deception or Mincemeat, formed German strategy. Using his own arguments, it is possible to show why this is not convincing; had the Germans not been deceived or had their intelligence functioned better (two inseparable factors) they would have pursued a very different course of action! Effective strategy rests on a foundation of reliable intelligence. Had German intelligence warned Hitler that on 10 July at 0430 the Allies would invade Sicily from the south and southeast, he would have made very different decisions.

Müller himself supplies the best argument when quoting Wallach to the effect that German military planning always sought the most decisive battle of annihilation. If Hitler had known the place, time and date of the invasion, he could have decisively beaten the Allies on Sicily's beaches by replacing two weakened German divisions with four strong ones, thereby saving Italy, and significantly delaying the re-entry of the Allies to Europe. In a message to Churchill on 28 March 1943, Eisenhower warned of this risk:

> . . . if substantial German ground troops should be placed in the region (Sicily) prior to the attack, the chances for success become practically nil and the project should be abandoned.

In another message sent on 7 April 1943 he was more specific:

> . . by the term substantial is meant more than two German divisions.[110]

The validity of my argument is supported by Hitler's actions. This is how Sir Michael Howard commented on Hitler's actions immediately after the invasion of Sicily had begun:

> Hitler's own reaction was immediate. He ordered two more German formations, *1st parachute* and *29th Panzer Grenadier Division* to be hurried into Sicily to throw the invaders into the sea.[111]

The will to be decisive was surely there – but not the necessary intelligence to support it. The combination of Allied deception and poor German intelligence reduced Hitler's incentive to send more troops to Sicily before the attack started; indeed, as in Normandy, even after the invasion was under way, German planners at the OKH did not rule out the probability that it would be followed closely by another landing in Greece.[112] This is an excellent example of the decisive, if not always visible, role played by intelligence (and deception) in strategic planning.

Professor Müller argues that German strategy in southern Europe in 1943 was determined by the desire to secure the Balkans and keep Italy in the war. 'German reactions in the Mediterranean were . . . predominantly determined by one single motive, the fear of Italy's imminent collapse and/or defection'. The Germans should therefore have made it their first priority to defend Italy in Italy, not in the Balkans. After all, the occupation of Sicily or Sardinia was of more direct concern to Italy than the Balkans. It could be expected that the invasion of Sicily would bring about a more rapid Italian decision to defect. Why then did Hitler not send more troops to Sicily? This was not due to the consideration of Italian 'sensitivities' as much as it was a sign of uncertainty regarding the location of the Allied invasion. As long as Sicily did not appear to be threatened, Hitler could afford to consider Italian wishes. That the Germans viewed the Balkans as important for the defense of Italy makes sense only if they perceived no immediate threat to Italy itself. After all, invasion of Italy and Sicily was more of a direct threat to Italy's continued alliance with Germany. In sum, either Hitler and his generals made a mistake or they viewed a threat to the Balkans (and via the Balkans also to Italy) as more imminent. If the latter choice were correct, then their strategic priorities in the first half of 1943 would make more sense. In reaching such conclusions they were no doubt convinced in part by the Allied notional threat to the Balkans.

As Müller claims, Montagu may have analysed only a small number of documents. What matters, however, is the importance of the documents rather than their number. To begin with, Montagu selected two very important German Naval War Staff documents which unmistakably indicate the German reliance on Major Martin's documents. This led to changes in German dispositions and increased direction of attention to Sardinia and the Peloponnese with a corresponding reduction of troops in Sicily. Montagu also furnishes a facsimile of a document from the German Naval Archives in Tambach which evaluates one of Major Martin's documents that went all the way up to Dönitz. (The evaluation accepted the document as authentic.) Müller goes on to assert that the German Naval Command and the Naval Conferences with Hitler were not important. Perhaps this was so, although it is difficult to see Dönitz, the Führer's last heir, as an unimportant decision-maker. The Führer's Naval Conference of 14 May 1943 tells us that Hitler, having 'discovered the key to Anglo-Saxon order' (*sic*) did not consider Sicily as the target but rather Sardinia and the Peloponnese.[113] Even if he eventually changed his mind, as Professor Müller claims, he did not view Sicily as the target in mid-May 1943. Implementing strategy, building fortifications, laying minefields, transferring troops and the like are all time-consuming procedures. Therefore, even if by the first week of July Hitler had changed his mind and recognized Sicily as the main target (which is possible), the warning came too late. To be of value, strategic warning must be provided in time for the recipient to take appropriate action. Ironically, what may have finally given the Germans their first solid clue that Sicily was the real Allied invasion target, was the capture of Pantellaria on 11 June 1943. This operation appears not to have been co-ordinated with the deception cover operations and was not carefully evaluated as risking the disclosure of Sicily as the real target of the

Allies' next offensive. It was only after the seizure of Pantellaria that Kesselring ordered the Hermann Göring Division to move to Sicily.

Sir David Hunt contributes the anecdotal, but apparently genuine, information that Lieutenant Colonel F.K. Von Plehwa, who served as the Assistant Military Attaché under General von Rintelen, said that, '. . . he well remembered listening in to a telephone conversation between his chief and Alfred Jodl, Chef der *Wehrmachtführungsstab*, some time in the second half of May 1943. Von Rintelen was talking about the imminent invasion of Sicily, when Jodl shouted impatiently, "You can forget about Sicily, we know it is Greece". Jodl was, of course, on the record to the same effect in OKH documents'.[114]

All of this evidence was discovered after the war in German archives. The Allies, however, knew at the time from Ultra intercepts that their bait had been swallowed, 'hook, line and sinker by the right people'. This is the Ultra intercept:[115]

REF: 779   MIL 1955 CO
REF: CX/MSS/2571/T4   IN TWO   Parts Part One
                    XX

INFORMATION FROM SUPREME COMMAND ARMED FORCES, OPERATIONS STAFF, ARMY TO AIC IN C SOUTH AND C IN C & C IN C SOUTH EAST ON TWELFTH. OPERATIONS STAFF OF SUPREME COMMANDS NAVE AND GAF & GAF INFORMED. QUOTE ACCORDING TO A SOURCE WITH [sic] MAY BE REGARDED AS ABSOLUTELY RELIABLE, AN ENEMY LANDING UNDERTAKING ON A LARGE SCALE IS PROJECTED IN THE NEAR FUTURE IN BOTH THE EASTERN AND THE WESTERN MEDITERRANEAN. ((MIL 1955 & 1955 CO 876 & 876 IN TWO PARTS PART ONE)) THE UNDERTAKING IN THE EASTERN MED & MED HAS AS ITS OBJECTIVE THE COAST NEAR KALAMATA & KALAMATA AND THE COASTAL SECTOR SOUTH OF CAPE ARAXOS & CAPE ARAXOS (BOTH PLACES ON THE WEST COAST OF THE PELOPONNESE & PELOPONNESE). THE LANDING NEAR KALAMATA & KALAMATA IS TO BE CARRIED OUT BY FIVE SIX INFANTRY DIVISION, AND THAT NEAR CAPE ARAXOS & CAPE ARAXOS

                    33
EMJ/   15//Z/15/5/43
KVB

BY THE REINFORCED FIVE INFANTRY DIVISION. IT IS NOT CLEAR WHETHER BOTH DIVISION [sic] WILL OPERATE AT FULL STRENGTH OR ONLY WITH ELEMENTS. ((ML 1955 & 1955 TWO/AND FINAL)) IF THE FORMER WERE THE CASE ABOUT TWO OR THREE WEEKS WOULD BE NEEDED BEFORE THE BEGINNING OF THE LANDING. SHOULD ONLY ELEMENTS OF

THE DIVISIONS OPERATE, THE LANDING COULD TAKE PLACE
AT ANY TIME. THE COVER-NAME FOR THE LANDING IS
HUSKY & HUSKY. A FEINT AGAINST THE DODECANESE &
DODECANESE MUST BE RECKONED WITH UNQUOTE.
COMMENT COLON KNOWS THAT FURTHER INFORMATION
(PRESUMABLY DEALING WITH WESTERN MEDITERRANEAN
& WESTERN MEDITERRANEAN) NATURE OF WHICH
UNKNOWN THERE, WAS TOO [sic] BE SENT TO OTHER
ADDRESSEES NAMED ABOVE, BUT NOT & NOT TO CHARLIE IN
CHARLIE SOUTH EAST

1551Z/15/5/43

The documents cited by Montagu, Howard and others may not prove
conclusively that deception was decisive in influencing German
strategy in 1943, but they do provide strong circumstantial evidence
that it worked. In the final analysis, Müller's evidence is not more
direct.

What about Müller's Norwegian example? Here he is correct in the
sense that the Allied deception, while again not exposed, failed to have
a direct effect on German strategic decisions. This is evident from a
German intelligence document of 4 March 1944 cited by Hesketh.

> Since the operations of the enemy command in the present
> stage of the war all mean the tying up of German forces on
> subsidiary fronts, or alternatively their removal from the decisive
> Atlantic front to subsidiary fronts, and as the enemy has already
> been successful in this sense in Italy, it seems thoroughly possible
> that he has come to a like decision in the Scandinavian area. The
> hitherto inadequate data do not allow us to call this certain or even
> probable.
>
> It seems nevertheless that henceforward enhanced prepared-
> ness on the Norwegian coast and above all on intensification of
> air reconnaissance over the whole of the North Sea area are
> indispensable. This measure appears to constitute the only
> means, which has any prospect of success, of avoiding surprises
> such as those of the Sicily and Nettuno landings.[116]

It is worth noting that even a German intelligence officer believed that
the Germans had been surprised in both Sicily and Anzio.

Again, deception and intelligence work in general cannot be
separated. Without air cover support and sufficient troops, the Allies
had no intention of invading Norway. Good intelligence ought to have
exposed the notional order of battle projected from Scotland. In the
absence of adequate intelligence, however, the Germans could not
afford to ignore the possibility of a diversionary threat to Norway,

particularly given Hitler's obsession with the idea. In the end, Hitler and the German High Command deceived themselves and tied down an average of 250,000 soldiers in Norway.

What about the possibility that the Allies and some authors overestimated the contribution of Fortitude North? The most telling and relevant conclusions regarding this are in the Hesketh Report:

> Inasmuch as FORTITUDE NORTH aimed at convincing the Germans that certain forces were located in Scotland for a certain purpose when in fact those forces either were not there at all or at least were not there for the purpose stated, the plan, through the operation of Special Means, will be seen to have succeeded. The Germans accepted the danger of a diversionary attack against Scandinavia. They also accepted the presence of most of the formations which we had created or appropriated for the purpose of exercising that threat. To what extent did FORTITUDE NORTH succeed in tying down additional forces in Norway and Denmark? We have it from Jodl that Hitler had always been obsessed by the fear of an Allied attack on Scandinavia. It would not have required more than 100,000 troops to garrison the two countries and keep the native population in subjection. *In fact the average number of occupational troops had been in the region of 250,000 ever since Norway was first occupied.* The balance of 150,000 was to be regarded as an insurance against invasion. In these circumstances any minor troop movement that may have occurred in the spring of 1944 (and it is true that the garrison was increased at that time by one formation, the 89th Infantry Division) loses its significance, and one is thus forced to the conclusion, if one accepts Jodl's view, that FORTITUDE NORTH, though successful as a deceptive operation, had no influence upon the course of the war. It was, in fact, a case of the fly on the axle-tree.[117] [My emphasis].

Playing the role of devil's advocate, Professor Müller challenges his readers to reconsider much that has been written to date on deception as practiced during the Second World War. His argument that deception has almost always been examined with an overemphasis on the Allied viewpoint and that its success has often been taken for granted without a thorough study of the German decision-making process certainly merits very serious consideration. His methodological insistence on the fact that deception cannot be studied in isolation is well taken. The history of deception as well as the role of intelligence in general during the Second World War will require much more thinking by those seeking to determine its actual importance.

Throughout the history of warfare there has been no other period in which intelligence and deception occupied such a crucial position. Furthermore, the existence of detailed documentation on the Allied side regarding its total intelligence effort also makes it the first time in history that one can trace the role of intelligence in war with some measure of detail. Yet, as Professor Müller suggests, there is not always a direct linear connection between intelligence effort and success or failure in war. Such a methodological caveat should serve to provide the impetus for further detailed research and reflection on this subject.

The preceding detailed analysis which addresses Professor Müller's argument at length is the best tribute to its elegance and explanatory power. Professor Müller has made an important and stimulating contribution by causing those interested in the history and influence of deception in the Second World War to re-examine their views on the subject. After much thought, I cannot avoid the conclusion that, if anything, the role of Allied deception in the Second World War has been underestimated to date.

NOTES

1. All quotes are from Carl V. Clausewitz, *On War*, edited and translated by Michael Howard and Peter Paret (Princeton, N.J.: Princeton University Press, 1976), Book
   3, Chapter 10, 'Cunning', p.202.
2. Cyril Falls, *Military Operations Egypt and Palestine* (London: H.M.S.O., 1930) Vol. I, p.32.
3. Quoted from R.F. Hesketh, 'Fortitude: A History of Strategic Deception in North Western Europe April, 1943 to May, 1945', unpublished after-action history of deception operations in north-west Europe, primarily those preceding the invasion of Normandy. February 1949, 259 pages, to be cited below as the Hesketh Report.
4. I have suggested elsewhere a somewhat different definition: 'Deception can be defined as a purposeful attempt by the deceiver to manipulate the perceptions of the target's decisionmakers in order to gain a competitive advantage.' Michael I. Handel, *Military Deception in Peace and War* (Jerusalem, Israel: The Leonard Davis Institute for International Relations, 1985, Jerusalem Papers on Peace Problems, Number 38, 1985), p.3.
5. Sun Tzu, *The Art of War*, translated by Samuel B. Griffith, (New York: Oxford University Press, 1982), p.66. Sun Tzu adds:

   > Therefore, when capable, feign incapacity; when active, inactivity; when near, make it appear that you are far away; when far away, that you are near. Offer the enemy a bait to lure him; feign disorder and strike him. Pretend inferiority and encourage his arrogance. Attack where he is unprepared; sally out when he does not expect you (pp.66–7). Now war is based on deception. Move when it is advantageous and create changes in the situation by dispersal and concentration of forces. (p.106).

6. Clausewitz, *On War*, p.202.
7. For a comprehensive discussion of the principles of the art of war, see: John I. Alger, *The Quest for Victory: The History of the Principles of War* (Westport, CT.:

Greenwood Press, 1982). The basic principles of war differ from period to period and from army to army. A typical list of such principles will include: The Principle of the Objective; The Principle of the Offensive; The Principle of Mass; The Principle of Economy of Force; The Principle of Maneuver; The Principle of Unity of Command; The Principle of Security; The Principle of Surprise; The Principle of Simplicity (Alger, *The Quest for Victory*, p.XI.)

8. G.P.R. James, *The History of Chivalry* (New York: A.L. Fowle, 1900), p.28.

9. From the introduction of Neal Wood to Niccoló Machiavelli, *The Art of War* (Indianapolis: Bobbs-Merrill, 1965), pp.XXIV–XXV.

10. This attitude is reflected in a quote from Admiral De Roebeck's observance of the landing in Gallipoli. It is used by Liddell Hart in his book, *Strategy* (New York: Praeger, 1968). (Sec. Rev. Ed.) 'Gallant fellows those soldiers, they always go for the thickest place in the fence' (p.15).

    In Renoir's film, *La Grande Illusion*, the dialogue between the French and German commandants, who wish they could still continue fighting according to the old rules and agree that in fact they have more in common with each other than with their own soldiers, is also representative of the chivalrous ethic of war.

11. For ideological and racist tension that eliminates all the traditions of chivalry and moderation see, for example, John W. Dower, *War Without Mercy: Race and Power in the Pacific War* (New York: Pantheon, 1986). Also Omer Bartov, *The Eastern Front, 1941–1945* (London: Macmillan, 1986), and 'The Barbarisation of Warfare, 1941–1945', Ph.D. thesis, Oxford University, 1983.

12. C.W.C. Oman, *The Art of War in the Middle Ages A.D. 378–1515* (Ithaca, NY: Great Seal Books, 1963), p.34.

13. Ibid., pp.43–4.

14. 'Generally in war the best policy is to take a state intact; to ruin it is inferior to this. To capture the enemy's army is better than to destroy it; to take intact a battalion, a company or a five-man squad is better than to destroy them. For to win 100 victories in 100 battles is not the acme of skill. To subdue the enemy without fighting is the acme of skill'. Sun Tzu, *The Art of War*, p.77. See also *Maurice's Strategikon: Handbook of Byzantine Military Strategy*, translated by George T. Dennis (Philadelphia: University of Pennsylvania Press, 1984).

15. On the changes in the international system as a result of the French Revolution and the influence of ideological considerations on the level of tension and attitudes of states to each other see, for example: Kyung-Won Kim, *Revolution and International System: A Study for the Breakdown of International Stability* (New York: New York University Press, 1970), and Richard N. Rosecrance, *Action and Reaction in World Politics: International Systems in Perspective* (Boston: Little, Brown & Co., 1963).

16. Clausewitz, *On War*, p.204.

17. Ibid., p.282.

18. Ibid., p.203.

19. See Michael I. Handel, (ed.), *Clausewitz and Modern Strategy* (London: Frank Cass, 1986), pp. 51–95: 'Clausewitz in the Age of Modern Technology' by Michael I. Handel.

20. See Falls, *Military Operations in Egypt and Palestine*, Chapters I–II, pp.1–44. For an excellent article also Yigal Shefi, 'Stratagem and Deception in the Third Battle of Gaza', *Maarachot* (Hebrew) IDF Journal, Nos. 302–303, (March/April, 1986), pp.56–61.

21. For the importance of utilizing real troop formations whenever possible for the creation of a notional order of battle, see: the *Hesketh Report* and David Mure, *Practice to Deceive* (London: William Kimber, 1977).

22. For Operation Mincemeat, see: Ewen Montagu, *The Man Who Never Was* (Philadelphia: J.B. Lippincott, 1954), and *Beyond Top Secret ULTRA* (New York: Howard McCann, 1978), Chap. 13, pp.143–51. For a balanced account, see: Michael Howard, *Grand Strategy* (London: HMSO, 1970), Vol. 4, August 1942 – September 1943, p.370; F.H. Hinsley, *British Intelligence in the Second World War* (New York: Cambridge University Press, 1984), Vol. III, p.78; F.W. Deakin,

The Brutal Friendship (New York: Harper and Row, 1962), pp.346–57; Roger Morgan, 'The Man Who Almost Is', *After the Battle*, No. 54, 1986, 1–25.

23. On Meinerzhagen's 'haversack ruse' see: Falls, *Military Operations Egypt and Palestine*, Part I, pp.30–31; Colonel A.P. Wavell, *The Palestine Campaign* (London: Constable, 1936), (3rd ed.) p.106; Anthony Cave Brown, *Bodyguard of Lies* (New York: Harper & Row, 1975), pp.280–81; Meinerzhagen, *Army Diary, 1899–1926* (London: Oliver and Boyd, 1960); Sir, Major General George Aston, *Secret Service* (New York: Cosmopolitan Books, 1930), Chap. 16, pp.201–16; Shefi, 'Deception and Stratagem in the Third Battle of Gaza'.

24. Wavell, *Palestine Campaign*, pp.106–7.

25. See Charles Cruickshank, *Deception in World War II* (New York: Oxford University Press, 1980), pp.19–33; Mure, *Practice to Deceive* pp.130–47; David Fisher, *The War Magician* (New York: Howard McCann, 1983).

26. Wavell, *The Palestine Campaign*, pp.107–8.

27. Ibid., p.112.

28. Ibid., p.201.

29. Shefi, 'Deception and Stratagem in the Third Battle of Gaza'.

30. Falls, *Military Operations Egypt and Palestine*, Part I, p.43.

31. Wavell, *The Palestine Campaign*, p.124.

32. The best discussion on deception in the Italian campaign is still Sir David Hunt, *A Don At War* (London: William Kimber, 1966), particularly Chap. 15, p.252; Brigadier L.J.C. Molony, *The Mediterranean and the Middle East* (London: HMSO, 1984), Vol. 6, part I, Chap. 2.

33. See Wavell, *The Palestine Campaign*, p.203. Also B.H. Liddell Hart, *Colonel Lawrence* (New York: Halcyon House, 1937), new and enlarged ed., Chaps. 17–18, pp. 248–79; Falls, *Military Operations Egypt and Palestine*, Part II; W.T. Massey, *Allenby's Final Triumph* (New York: E.P. Putton, 1920), Chap. 8, pp.95–111.

34. Liddell Hart, *Colonel Lawrence*, p.249.

35. From General Wavell's introduction in Dudley Clarke's book, *Seven Assignments* (London: Jonathan Cape, 1948), p.7. Wavell's early deception initiatives and contribution to the use of deception in the Second World War have not as of now received the attention they deserve. Wavell issued a short order in July 1942 on 'Ruses and Stratagems of War' which can be found in General Sir Archibald Wavell, *Speaking Generally: Broadcasts and Addresses in Time of War, 1939–1943* (London: Macmillan, 1946), pp.80–83. See also his *The Palestine Campaign* and his biography by John Conell Wavell, *Scholar and Soldier* (London: Collins, 1964).

    David Mure goes so far as to suggest that: '. . . the General's lifetime conviction and mastery of the value of strategic deception of which he, and not Sir Winston Churchill as has sometimes been suggested, was the originator in World War Two' (*Practice to Deceive*, p.19).

36. Major General I.S.O., Playfair, *The Mediterranean and Middle East* (London: HMSO, 1954), Vol. I, p.362.

37. See Leonard Mosley, *The Cat and the Mice* (London: Arthur Barker, 1958); Major A.W. Sansom, *I Spied Spies* (London: George Harrap, 1965); Mure, *Master of Deception* (London: William Kimber, 1980), Chap. 7, also *Practice to Deceive*, pp.30–31.

38. Mure, *Practice to Deceive*, p.23.

39. Playfair, *The Mediterranean and Middle East*, Vol. I, p.274.

40. See Dennis Wheatley, 'Deception in World War II', *RUSI*, Vol. 121, No. 3 (September 1976), p.87.

41. Hesketh Report, p.17 (Noel Wild is not mentioned by name).

42. Wheatley, 'Deception in World War II', 87.

43. J.C. Masterman, *On the Chariot Wheel* (Oxford: Oxford University Press, 1975), p.22.

44. Insufficient co-ordination can lead to conflicts of interest and contradictions between different deception agencies in different regions – or with other interests

of other organizations and activities. In the winter of 1915, Admiral Blinker Hall and Lt. Col. Drake of MI5 initiated a notional threat invading the Belgian coast and Schleswig Holstein through a double agent system controlled by MI5. The information received and accepted as genuine by German intelligence led to German reinforcement of the threatened areas and to a large scale concentrated movement of the German Navy which was interpreted by British Military Intelligence – which was not aware of the original deception plan – as a possible threat of invasion of England. Better co-ordination between various intelligence authorities in England could have avoided unnecessary confusion and alarms. As was mentioned above, however, until the end of the First World War deception was still primarily an activity left to the uncoordinated initiative of individual commanders. See Patrick Beesly, *Room 40: British Naval Intelligence 1914–1918* (New York: Harcourt, 1982), pp.67–9. Also Admiral Sir William James, *Eyes of the Navy* (London: Methuen, 1955), pp.72–3.

45. Hesketh Report, p.174.
46. Mure, *Practice to Deceive*, Chap. 6, pp.93–104.
47. Cruickshank, *Deception in World War II*, Chaps. 6–8, pp.85–124.
48. Ibid., p.19.
49. The goals of the double-cross system were defined by Masterman as:
    1. To control the enemy system, or as much of it as we could get our hands on
    2. To catch fresh spies when they appeared
    3. To gain knowledge of the personalities and methods of the German Secret Service
    4. To obtain information about the code and cypher work of the German Services
    5. To get evidence of enemy plans and intentions from the questions asked by them
    6. To influence enemy plans by the answers sent to the enemy
    7. To deceive the enemy about our plans and intentions
    Masterman, *The Double Cross System*, p.XIV, pp.8–9, also *On the Chariot Wheel*, p.221. As can be seen from this list, the use of double agents as a major link in the deception process came only as a last priority and was not contemplated when the system was originally created.
50. Hesketh Report, p. 22.
51. Beesly, *Room 40*, pp.67–9.
52. Brigadier Dudley Clarke, quoted by Mure in *Practice to Deceive*, p.14.
53. See Juan Pujol, *Garbo* (London: Weidenfeld & Nicolson, 1986). See also, Dusko Popov, *Spy/Counterspy* (New York: Grosset & Dunlap, 1974).
54. Hesketh Report, pp.175–6.
55. See David Kahn, *Hitler's Spies: German Military Intelligence in World War II*, pp.523–47.
56. See Kahn, *Hitler's Spies*. Also Peter R. Black, *Ernst Klatenbruner Ideological Soldier of the Third Reich* (Princeton, NJ: Princeton University Press, 1984), Chapter 6, pp.176–217.
57. In his long political career, Churchill played a critical role in the founding and development of the British intelligence community. Of particular importance was his support of Ultra and all deception activities. A special study dedicated to Churchill as an intelligence consumer remains to be written. Much information can be found in his official biography by Gilbert and in books written by, among others, Andrew, Beesly, Roskill, and McLachlan.
58. Michael I. Handel, *The Diplomacy of Surprise* (Cambridge, MA: Harvard Center for International Affairs, 1981).
59. Hesketh Report, p.171. The conclusions of the Hesketh Report are also reprinted in Donald C. Daniel and Katherine Herbig, (eds.), *Strategic Military Deception* (New York: Pergamon Press, 1981), pp.233–45.
60. Michael I. Handel, 'Intelligence and the Problem of Strategic Surprise', in *The Journal of Strategic Studies*, Vol. 7, No. 3 (Sept. 1984), 229–81.
61. Richard J. Heuer, 'Strategic Deception: A Psychological Perspective', *International Studies Quarterly*, Vol. 25 (June 1981), 294–327.

62. Donald McLachlan, *Room 39: A Study in Naval Intelligence* (New York: Atheneum, 1968), p.366.
63. See Pujol, *Garbo*; Popov, *Spy/Counterspy*. See attached schematic chart of Garbo's notional network of spies 'recruited' by him in England. (Source: *Hesketh Report*, p.24 and *Garbo*.)
64. See Hesketh Report, Appendix 14, JOSEPHINE and FUSAG, pp.245–6.
65. Michael I. Handel, 'Quantity versus Quality: Numbers do Count', *The Journal of Strategic Studies*, Vol. 4, No. 3 (Sept. 1981), 225-70. Also in Samuel P. Huntington, *The Strategic Imperative* (Cambridge, MA: Ballinger, 1982), pp.193–228.
66. Hunt, *A Don At War*, pp.254–6.
67. On technological deception, see Michael I. Handel, 'Technological Surprise In War', *Intelligence and National Security*, Vol. 2, No. 1 (January 1987), 5–53.
68. Clausewitz, *On War*, p.42.
    LCS made the following comments on the teaching of deception in an answer to U.S. inquiries:

> Here we actually tried at the end of the war to write a manual and completely failed. The answer seems to be given in the first five chapters of the 'History'. Military deception is based on certain main principles, but the methods to be used in gaining the objective depend upon developments in warfare, the circumstances of each case, and the character and organization of your enemy. All these change, and all you can do is to study what was done in the past so that you may apply the lessons of the past to the problems that may arise. You may in fact have to devise entirely new methods. I think the comparison made by Brigadier Dudley Clarke when discussing this with Colonel Sweeney puts it best. You can study a masterpiece by Rembrandt to see how he deals with a certain subject, but nobody attempts to lay down firm rules based on Rembrandt's painting technique and materials as to how anyone should paint, shall we say, a street scene in New York today.
>
> The first thing in developing deception techniques must be a study of your potential enemy, his characteristics and the terrain in which you may have to fight him. As a result of this study you may come to certain conclusions and the lessons of the past will be valuable in showing how adaptation, improvisation and ingenuity can cope with the most baffling problems. One need only mention deception in the Middle East, North West Europe and the Far East. The methods were in many cases quite different, adapted to the different terrain and character of the enemy.
>
> From File RG 319 *Cover and Deception*, Folder 77, Box 4, entry 101, Modern Military Records, National Archives, Washington, D.C.

69. Hesketh Report, p.3.
70. Mure, *Master of Deception*, p.273.
71. Hesketh Report, p.3.
72. Ewen Montagu, *Beyond Top Secret ULTRA*, pp.140–41.
73. Hesketh Report, p. 173.
74. Mure, *Master of Deception*, p.274.
75. Hesketh Report, p.17.
76. Mure, *Master of Deception*, p.274.
77. Hesketh Report, pp.12–13.
78. Ibid., p.13.
79. Ibid., p.15.
80. Ibid., p.175.
81. See Mure, *Master of Deception* for a critical analysis of Cockade/Starkey, pp. 220–24; Cruickshank, *Deception in World War II*, Chap. 5, pp.61–84; *Hesketh Report*, Chap. 2, pp.5–6; Pujol, *Garbo*, pp.95–100.
82. Cruickshank, *Deception in World War II*, p.80.
83. Ibid., p.84.
84. Ibid., p.72.
85. Ibid., pp.62–3.
86. Mure, *Master of Deception*, p.222.

STRATEGIC AND OPERATIONAL DECEPTION

88. See Alvin Coox, 'Flawed Perception and Its Effect Upon Operational Thinking: The Case of the Japanese Army 1937–1941', in Michael I. Handel, (ed.), *Intelligence and Military Operations*, forthcoming in 1988 as a special issue of *Intelligence and National Security*.
89. Richard K. Betts, *Surprise Attack: Lessons for Defense Planning* (Washington, D.C.: The Brookings Institution, 1982).
90. Clausewitz, *On War*, p.158.
91. Ibid., p.183.
92. Karl Popper, *The Poverty of Historicism* (New York: Harper and Row, 1964), p.12.
93. David Hackett Fischer, *Historian's Fallacies: Toward a Logic of Historical Thought* (New York: Harper & Row, 1970), p.172.
94. From an additional typed introductory letter to the Hesketh Report, by Roger Hesketh, p.5.
95. Major General de Guingand, *Operation Victory* (New York: Charles Scribner's Sons, 1947), pp.146–7.
96. Winston S. Churchill, *The Second World War*, Vol. 4, *The Hinge of Fate* (Boston: Houghton Mifflin, 1950), p.546. See also John North, (ed.), *The Alexander Memoirs, 1940–1945* (London: Cassell, 1962), p.25.
97. Captain Basil H. Liddell Hart, *The Tanks* (London: Cassell, 195), Vol. II, p.219.
98. F.H. Hinsley, *British Intelligence in the Second World War: Its Influence on Strategy and Operations* (New York: Cambridge University Press, 1981), Vol. 2, p. 416.
99. Correlli Barnett, *The Desert Generals*, second edition, (London: Allen & Unwin, 1983), p.263.
100. Michael Carver, *Al Alamein* (New York: Macmillan, 1962), p.39.
101. Cruickshank, *Deception in World War II*, p.23.
102. Sir David Hunt, in a letter to the author, 21 January 1987.
103. See Mure, *Practice to Deceive*, pp.30–31 and *Master of Deception*, pp.118–23.
104. On the dangers of using a small sample in cases of deception see 'Deception Maxims: Fact and Folklore,' (Princeton: Machtech and ORD/CIA, April 1980), pp.9–11. 'The law of small numbers'.
105. Mure, *Practice to Deceive*, Chap. 6, pp.93–105; Cruickshank, *Deception in World War II*, Chap. 4, pp.50–61.
106. Quoted from a paper entitled, 'Military and Political Planning and Aims in 1944', presented by Sir David Hunt to a conference in December 1984 as a representative of the British National Committee of Historians of the Second World War, p.7.
107. Hesketh Report, Preface, p.VIII.
108. Fischer, *Historian's Fallacies*, pp.104ff.
109. See, for example, 'Deception Maxims: Fact and Folklore', pp.5–9. Magruder's principle – the exploitation of perceptions. This maxim has been chosen as the most important, i.e., number 1, by the authors of this monograph.
110. Michael Howard, *Grand Strategy*, August 1942 – September 1943, Vol. 4, (London: HMSO, 1970), p.368.
111. Ibid., p.468.
112. Ibid.
113. Führer conferences on Naval affairs in *Brassey's Naval Annual 1948*, ed. Rear Admiral H.G. Thursfield, (New York: Macmillan, 1948), p. 327.
114. Letter written by Sir David Hunt to Constantine Fitzgibbon dated 16 May 1977.
115. The original Ultra message can be found at the U.S. Army Military History Institute (MHI) at Carlisle Barracks, PA. Reel 127 5 to 15 May 1943 ML dated 15 May 1944. See also F.H. Hinsley, *et. al., British Intelligence in the Second World War*, Vol. 3 (New York: Cambridge University Press, 1984), pp.78–9 (Chapter 3).
116. Hesketh Report, p.81.
117. Ibid., p.83.

APPENDIX I

From a letter written by Brigadier Dudley Clarke
to Major General Lowell Books of the U.S. Army*

The first concerns the scope of the organization's activities and, in particular, the directions in which they should be focused. Until this is properly understood there will be a tendency to muddle Deception with Psychological Warfare and even to suggest that the same instrument can serve both purposes. A moment's examination of the aims of the two will show this to be fundamentally unsound, and any attempt to mix both in practice will be highly dangerous. Nevertheless that danger is often present and is sometimes curiously difficult to dispel. The essential difference lies of course in the audience for whom the two organizations cater. Psychological warfare starts at the apex of a triangle and endeavours to spread its arms as wide as it can to embrace the broadest possible base. It matters little if many of its audience can detect the origin of their messages, nor if a privileged few can recognize distortion of the truth; its appeal is to the masses and it is unlikely to influence the thought or actions of the enlightened inner circles of the General Staff. Deception, on the other hand, works in exactly the opposite way. It starts at the base of the triangle and concentrates its influence towards a single point at the apex; its essential aim is to conceal the origin of its messages by directing them upon this single point from as many different directions as possible. It cares little for the thoughts and actions of the masses, but it *must* penetrate directly into the innermost circles of all. Its audience is narrowed down to a small handful of individuals, as represented by the senior members of the enemy's Intelligence Staff, and sometimes even to a single individual in the person of the Head of that Intelligence Staff. If they can influence him to accept as true the evidence they have manufactured for his benefit, then they have accomplished their entire aim, since it is only through the Head of the Intelligence that any enemy commander received the impression of his opponent upon which he has to base his plan of operation. It is necessary, therefore, that the single-purposeness of any deception machine should be recognized from the start and its shape dictated by the overriding need to concentrate every ounce of its diverse efforts upon that one ultimate target. As a corollary it follows that those who direct the deception machine must have an adequate knowledge of the small group of men on whom all their activities are focused, of their national characteristics, their languages, thoughts and professional methods with all their strengths and their weaknesses.

It is this note on personalities which leads to the next principle, which is a foundation stone in the successful application of deception. Deception is essentially an Art and not a Science, and those who practise it must be recognized as falling into the category of artists and not of artisans. This is difficult to accept in professional military circles where it is widely believed that the Art of War can be taught to the average educated man even though he may have little aptitude for it. But, nevertheless, it is true that frequently highly qualified and highly intelligent staff officers fail completely to cope with the work, although they do brilliantly

* File RG319, *Cover and Deception*, Folder 77, Box 43, Entry 101, Modern Military Records, National Archives, Washington, D.C. Letter from Lt. Col. E.J. Sweeney to Col. W.A. Harris, 18 December 1946.

afterwards on the Operations and other staffs. What they may lack is the sheer ability to create, to make something out of nothing, to conceive their own original notion and then to clothe it with realities until eventually it would appear as a living fact. And, since that is precisely what the Deception Staff must do all the time, it follows that the art of creation is an essential attribute in all who are charged with such work. To expect those who have not this art to produce the required results will lead to risks beyond that of mere failure.

If this thesis is accepted it is easy to see why one brain – and one alone – must be left unhampered to direct any one deception plan. It is after all little more than a drama played upon a vast stage, and the author and producer should be given a free hand in the theatre of war as in the other theatre. (Also, of course, in both they must have the necessary qualifications to justify that confidence.) It is not a bad parallel to compare a Commander in the Field with the Impresario who wants to mount a successful play at his theatre. He decides on the type of play he wants – drama, comedy, musical, etc. – and instructs an author to produce a script. Having accepted the script, he appoints a producer to mount the play. From that point onwards he may well leave everything else to those two, and look only to the results obtained. Provided these are satisfactory, the impresario who is not himself an author or producer wisely leaves them to rule the cast, scenery, costumes and all else that goes to make the play. The wise Commander-in-Chief will follow the same example. In his case the matter is simplified by the fact that the head of his Deception Staff doubles in the roles of author and producer. The Commander therefore tells him what sort of Deception he needs, examines the plans produced for him with the required aim in view, and, once the final version is approved, watches only the results and leaves all else to his specialist. In both peace and war, however, the Chief is the best judge of the results: in both cases he assesses them by the reactions of the audience (or the enemy), and should interfere in proportion to the degree in which they fail or succeed to achieve the object he himself has set. . . .

And it is this mention of the 'object' which brings me to the last of the principles I have tried to enunciate. For the theatrical impresario this presents no difficulty – all he wants is to see the audience moved to tears, laughter or rhythm in concern with the play – but to the General it is a problem which merits most careful thought. His audience is the enemy and he alone must decide what he wants them to do – to advance? to withdraw? to thin out or to reinforce? Whatever he chooses, the main point is that his 'object' must be to make the enemy do something. It matters nothing what the enemy THINKS, it is only what he DOES that can affect the battle. It is therefore wrong, and always wrong, for any Commander to tell his Deception Staff to work out a plan 'to make the enemy think we are going to do so-and-so'. It may be that the Plan will succeed but that the enemy will react to it in a totally unexpected way, upon which the Commander will probably blame the Deception Staff who have in fact produced exactly the results they set for. It is this boomerang effect which has made many people apprehensive of using the Deception weapon, and it cannot be stressed too strongly that, if used in the wrong way, it can prove a real danger. But there is one sure way to avoid any possible risk and that is to get the OBJECT right. Given a correct 'object' the Deception Plan may fail but it cannot in any do harm. Give it a wrong 'object' and it will invariably give wrong results. Our theatrical impresario after all will not attempt to dictate to the author the plot of the play, but that is precisely what the General does who tells his Deception Staff that he wants the enemy to be made to 'think' something. It assumes a knowledge of the enemy's likely reactions which the Deception Staff should know from experience very much better than the General. It is for the latter to say what he wants them to do, and for the specialists to decide what the enemy must be made to think in order to induce them to act in the manner required. Perhaps an illustration will explain this best. In the early part of 1941 General Wavell wanted the Italian reserves drawn to the South in order to ease his entry into Northern Abyssinia. He considered this might be done by inducing them to reinforce the captured province of British Somaliland, and he gave instructions for a Deception Plan to be worked to persuade the Italians that we were about to invade Somaliland. Deception was new then and on the surface that appeared to all concerned to be a perfectly laudable object. The Plan, innocently ignoring the real object of influencing the location of the enemy reserves, was entirely successful; but the results were totally unexpected. In face of the threatened invasion, the Italians evacuated British Somaliland. Not only had General Wavell to draw upon his own meagre forces to re-occupy the country, but the Italian garrison was freed to swell the forces in the North which were to block our advance at Koren. Had a different object been chosen, quite a different deception plan would have emerged and perhaps a quite different effect produced upon the actions of the enemy.

That concludes this brief review; and I will end by summarizing that to be successful any Deception Organization needs:

1. To be so organized that it directs the whole of its efforts to influence the enemy's Intelligence Staff – and that alone.
2. To be composed of senior officers with a real knowledge of the Intelligence Staff that is to become their audience.
3. To be directed, as specialists in an Art, by a Commander and Staff who tell them what results they require and who leave them unhampered to arrange the best means of obtaining those results.
4. To be given an object in terms of the manner in which the enemy is required to ACT in order to further the operational plan of their own commander.

Provided these four principles are faithfully observed, it matters little how the organization is shaped and it can best take the form most suited to the nationality concerned and the theatre of war affected.

APPENDIX 2

ANALYSIS OF ALLIED ORDER OF BATTLE
MEDITERRANEAN THEATRE
MAY 1944

	ACTUAL	BOGUS	OKW ESTIMATE
Divisions in Italy			
British	12	12	13
Polish	2	4	4
U.S.	7	7	7
French	4	4	4
	25	27	28
Western Med outside Italy			
British	1	4	3
U.S.	1	1	3
French	3	6	9
	5	11	15
Eastern Med including Persia and Iraq			
British	4	13	13
Defensive Formations			
British	0	8	10
French	4	5	5
	4	13	15
Grand Total	38	64	71

PART THREE

Ending War

9

The Problem of War Termination

War does not carry in itself the elements for a complete decision
and final settlement.[1]

The object of war is a better state of peace – even if only from
your own point of view. Hence it is essential to conduct war with
constant regard to the peace you devise.[2]

THE LITERATURE

In 1916, in the preface to his book, *Termination of War and Treaties of
Peace,* Coleman Phillipson wrote on war termination: 'There is no
publication in any language that deals with this most important branch
of international law and practice in a systematic and comprehensive
manner'.[3] While this statement could not be accepted at face value (and
Phillipson's own extensive bibliography qualifies it), it has nevertheless
been frequently and faithfully repeated in today's literature on the same
subject. Fred C. Iklé writes, for example: 'How are wars brought to an
end? Historians, students of military strategy, and experts on foreign
affairs have tended to neglect this question. Much attention, by contrast,
has been devoted to the question of how wars begin'.[4] Has so little really
been written since 1916 on such an important subject, and if so, why? Why
do so many scholars who themselves write in this field believe that the
research is insufficient?

To begin with, and in contradiction to this widely held opinion, the
literature on the subject of war termination is prodigious, if not overwhelming. An impression of the scope of this literature can be gained from
the incomplete bibliography attached to this essay. In addition, at least
two journals devote much of their space to pertinent issues: *The Journal of
Conflict Resolution* and *The Journal of Peace Research.* In fact, the
amount of literature on the termination of wars and on peace compares
favorably to other fields of interest within the study of the theory of
international relations. Thus, the persistent belief in the inadequacy of the
research on war termination is all the more puzzling.

I will try to offer in this context two interrelated explanations to this phenomenon: the lack of clarity concerning the subject matter and the semantical and epistemological confusion; and the misleading comparison of peace studies with the much better researched war studies.

The major reason for dissatisfaction with war termination studies stems from the lack of a clear definition of the subject. While scholars tacitly assume that they are working under a common definition, they have in fact different or only partially congruent concepts in mind when they approach the issue of war termination. The absence of a careful definition results, in part, from the difficulty in distinguishing between peace studies, in general, and war termination, which is a sub-category within the more general field of peace studies. (Moreover, it is even difficult to differentiate between peace studies and war studies.[5]) While peace studies cover such subjects as the prevention of war and the maintenance of peace, disarmament and arms control, peaceful change, and the behavior of states before, during and after war, war termination refers to the narrower problem of how to end wars once they have erupted, and is less concerned with its antecedents. Ambiguity has blurred the distinction between the two overlapping areas of interest, as is manifested in the literature on war termination, which has come to include nearly every topic under the more general term 'peace studies'.

It is true that in war termination research the focus of attention tends to revolve around the cessation of hostilities, an imaginary (or not so imaginary) point that marks the transition from a state of war to one of peace or, to be more precise, to one of non-war. War termination does not necessarily imply that a 'normal' peaceful situation has been created between two or more warring states. All that it can logically imply is that war has been stopped; it does not inevitably entail conflict reduction or resolution.[6] We must therefore conclude that war termination is a necessary but not sufficient condition for peace, since the discontinuation of hostilities does not perforce include positive progress towards peace.

Two possible definitions of war termination emerge, one narrower and one broader. The first focuses on the questions of when and why at a particular point war is terminated, on whether or not this point is predictable and if so, how. The broader interpretation, on the other hand, treats the termination of war within a longer span of time – a process that does not begin or end at any given, identifiable point in time.

It must be emphasized that of the two approaches to the study of war termination, the narrower one entertains greater pretensions or hopes of establishing a rigorous, quantitative, scientific and predictive theory explaining how wars end (discussed below as the 'rational' model of war termination). By contrast, the broader approach, while empirical and comparative, is nevertheless more impressionistic in nature and makes fewer claims of exactitude and predictive power. Under this broader heading we can group not only the question of the specific time and reasons why the warring parties agree to terminate hostilities, but also questions regarding the success and ultimate nature of the ceasefire. Will it, for example, be merely a pause followed by a resumption of the fighting, or will military arrangements lead to conflict reduction and eventually to conflict resolution and real peace? In order to attempt to answer these questions more must be known about the history of the conflict between the belligerents, about their values and motivations, their post-war economic and political stability, and not only about complicated cost-benefit calculations that cause the belligerents to stop the war but reveal little about what will happen after the war has ended.

Scholars would have been correct in deploring the scarcity of literature had they considered the narrower definition. In actuality, though, as we have seen, this misperception is due in part to the ambiguity over the meaning of 'war termination'.

A second cause for this frequently expressed disgruntlement might be that those involved in war termination research were, like Molière's Tartuffe, unaware that they were speaking prose all their lives. Just as deterrence was not 'invented' in the 1950s with the advent of nuclear weapons, but has existed ever since man first began fighting, so too has every war ever fought ended in one way or another. As a matter of fact, the subject of war termination, in one form or another, has received comparatively more attention than did the issue of deterrence prior to Hiroshima. Literature on war termination existed long before our time in the studies of diplomatic history, economics, international law, political theory, and even in the theory of international relations. For example, in the theory of the classical balance of power, it was invariably agreed that a war should be terminated without the elimination of the enemy. Morton Kaplan underscores this traditional axiom: 'It is necessary to limit one's objectives and not to eliminate other essential national actors so that one may be able, if necessary, to align oneself with them in the future'.[7] This old rule was apparently forgotten by those who formulated the Versailles agreement and shattered the post-war European balance of power, in effect setting the stage for the Second World War.

Therefore, although the theory of war termination was less explicit, less systematic and more diffuse than it currently is, it nonetheless existed and held a prominent place in philosophical and political thought.

The frustration over the lack of literature may also be traced to the frequent comparison between the study of war termination and war studies. Any such comparison is bound to be depressing for peace scholars, since war is, without doubt, the most written about subject in history: 'For every thousand pages published on the causes of wars there is less than one page directly on the causes of peace'.[8] While little has been written on the study of war termination relative to the study of war itself, a great deal has been written, in absolute terms, when compared to other aspects of international relations.

The research on war termination has been sufficiently extensive to classify it under five groupings:

1. 'Normative studies' of war termination and peace; political theory; philosophy; religion; pacifism, and so on.
2. Economic theories of war termination and the maintenance of peace.
3. International law.
4. Diplomatic history.
5. Theory of international relations.

First we have the 'normative studies' on war termination and peace. Generally, this type of literature is emotional in tone, utopian in nature and rarely empirically solid. Hitherto, the more theoretically oriented scholars have not found this literature to be of value in their studies on war termination. However, in the future, they should avail themselves increasingly of the useful ideas presented in some of these theoretical works.[9] For instance, works such as those by Kant, Abbé Saint-Pierre, Rousseau and Bentham on perpetual peace could give significant impetus to these studies. Kenneth Waltz's classical study, *Man, the State and War*, illustrates the fruitful incorporation of this type of literature into a work not unrelated to some aspects of war termination and highly relevant to the general study of peace. Waltz discusses the domestic form of government and its impact on international stability and the maintenance of peace. President Wilson believed, for example, that the war with Germany could be terminated only after a change from autocracy to democracy within Germany had been secured. While Waltz is only marginally concerned with the issue of war termination, there is no reason why an analysis similar to his cannot be made of this issue. Likewise, the literature on pacifism and the pacifist movement is vast and much can still be learned from it.

Second, a large number of studies has been published on the 'best' resolution of war from the economic point of view. Such works flourished between the two world wars and after the Second World War, when the shape of the recently concluded peace was of paramount concern.[10] This literature attracted considerable attention after the First World War, since it was believed that the economic consequences of the treaty of Versailles were disastrous, preventing, as it did, the creation of a stable peace, and eventually contributing to the outbreak of the Second World War.[11]

These economic interpretations are part of the broader approach to war termination studies, as they focus on the conditions and long-range effect of peace. For example, they address themselves to the problem of economic blockades and their impact on decisions to terminate a war, and calculate, to the extent possible, the comparative war potential of nations. In addition, they analyze questions of post-war employment, free trade and international trade in general, reparations, and financial problems of reconstruction.

More recently, the idea of positive economic incentives to induce a ceasefire has been implemented in efforts to terminate wars. America employed this technique in the Paris negotiations for the resolution of the Vietnam War. This was also the United States' approach in the Middle East, where it has promised extensive economic and military aid both to the Arabs and to Israel in order to induce a cessation of hostilities. Further research into this economic area could prove very profitable.

International law, the third class of war termination studies, has, in its narrower form, primarily explored the formal arrangements leading to a war's conclusion: the conditions that lead to the terms of a ceasefire; armistice and truce agreements; the legal position of the belligerents; recognition of parties to the dispute; the form of peace agreements; and the methods of enforcing the peace terms by the signatories to the agreement.[12] In its more comprehensive form, it is also interested in the role of third parties as contributors to the delicate process of war termination. Similarly, it is concerned with the role of international organizations in the process of war termination, organizations such as the League of Nations, the UN, the OAS, and the International Court at the Hague. In fact, some studies in international law approach the studies of a more utopian nature, for they examine the role of law in peaceful change, world government, world federations and the like.

In concentrating for the most part on the procedural factors of war termination, international law has neglected other and potentially more productive areas of focus, such as change in the laws regarding the ending of war, and problems of their enforcement. Yet the literature of international law is clearly fertile and relatively untouched ground for scholars of international relations who investigate the resolution of wars.

Diplomatic history, an integral part of the study of international politics and the theory of international relations, constitutes a fourth area of interest for the investigator of war termination. The amount of research on this subject conducted by diplomatic historians alone is overwhelming. No serious theoretical study of war termination can be undertaken without detailed reference to and use of this literature, for these works supply the scholar of international relations with all the empirical data and other information necessary to his work.

These works often include detailed analyses of the full process of the resolution of war. They usually treat a single peace conference and the policies preceding the decision to terminate a war. The weakness of these historical studies stems from their descriptive nature and the dearth of a more generally theoretical and comparative approach. This omission of the theoretical is due, in part, to the Rankian-Actonian tradition ('let the facts speak for themselves'), as well as to the fact that historians prefer to center on an in-depth study of a single historical case, avoiding comparative studies of larger scope. Thus, those who study war termination in the context of international politics can refer to this enormously rich and unexploited literature in order to draw comparisons, indispensable to their topic of interest. This process was begun only very recently.[13]

The fifth category of war termination literature, the study of the theory of international relations, can be divided into three separate levels for analytic purposes – the individual, the state, and the international system. A similar division can be made in the theoretical study of war termination *per se*. First, we can analyze the role and impact of specific political and military leaders and their attitudes towards the termination of war. Second, the influence of domestic politics, including the opinion of the political and military elites as well as public opinion, must be explored. This would cover questions such as the national morale and the termination of civil wars and revolutions, etc. Finally, we can examine the issue of war termination as an interaction between two or more warring states in the international system, their perceptions of each other, their problems of communication, power relations, and so on.

At a later point, research efforts should be directed at the more ambitious undertaking of large-scale, integrated and multi-level studies. At this stage, however, it would be more beneficial to conduct partial studies, such as psychological and psychoanalytical case studies of leaders' behavior under the pressure of defeat or victory in war, comparative studies of the position of military elites in different countries during victory or defeat, examinations of the impact of states' perceptions and misperceptions of one another's positions (in terms of military strength, morale, the will to continue fighting, their internal cohesion, etc.) and the importance of such interacting perceptions on the decision to terminate war.[14] Separate investigation of each level should sharpen our insight into the complex process of war termination, as the following analysis attempts to do.

THE FIRST LEVEL – A NON-RATIONAL MODEL

Most studies of war termination have either tacitly or explicitly assumed that the decision to stop fighting and start negotiating is a rational, well-calculated, cost-benefit type of decision taken by the states involved in conflicts. This premise ignores the important and often central role of individuals (rather than the state) in the war termination process, as can be demonstrated by some vivid illustrations.

The case of President Woodrow Wilson has stimulated the best available discussion of an individual's fatal involvement in the negotiations to end a war.[15] Both Nicolson[16] and Keynes,[17] neither of whom can be accused of being unsympathetic to Wilson's ideas, agree that Wilson's 'presence in Paris ... constitutes a historical disaster of the first magnitude'.

Wilson is best described as a theocratic and uncompromising agitator:

> It is not a sufficient explanation to contend that President Wilson was conceited, obstinate, non-conformist and reserved. He was also a man obsessed; possessed. He believed, as did Marat, that he was the physical embodiment of 'la volonté générale'. He was obsessed by the conviction that the League Covenant was his own revelation and the solution of all human difficulties. He was profoundly convinced that his new Charter of the Rights of Nations could be framed and included in the Peace Treaties; it mattered little what inconsistencies, what injustices, what flagrant violations of his own principles those Treaties might contain. He was able, as are all very religious men, to attribute to God the things that are Caesar's ...

> ... He possessed no gift for differentiation, no capacity for adjustments of circumstances. It was his spiritual and mental rigidity which proved his undoing. It rendered him as incapable of withstanding criticism as of absorbing advice. It rendered him blind to all realities which did not accord with his preconceived theory.[18]

These are hardly the best qualifications for long and cumbersome peace negotiations. The prophet may be admirably suited to the difficult task of leading his state with all the zeal and determination he possesses during war, but he is a dismal failure at conducting the delicate and complex process of peace negotiations. The prophet is not a man of compromise and patience – qualities that are *sine qua non* conditions for the prolonged process of peace negotiations.

Moreover, Wilson's unwillingness to incorporate the advice of his colleagues considerably undermined the negotiations at Paris and diminished the bargaining power of the American delegation. His determined refusal to collaborate in any way, shape or form with either the American delegation or the team that Colonel House made available to him resulted in a 'mutual isolation of the President on the one hand, and his staff on the other'.[19]

The end result was that:

commission discussions generally revolved about French and British drafts [and this] was of great significance in terms of the final text of the treaty. For, as usually happens, the initial concrete proposals more or less established the context of debate and tended to carry except where there were serious objections. Changes in the proposed drafts could be made only by amendments, which are not only relatively difficult to obtain but, too incessantly demanded, make a negotiator seem obstructionist. In these circumstances the American negotiators allowed a host of formulations representing the British and French points of view to pass unchallenged into the Treaty.[20]

Lacking a team to aid him in decision-making, President Wilson found himself overburdened with work, much of which was trivial, which further diminished his already unimpressive capacity to bargain effectively. Not as quick-witted as Clemenceau or Lloyd George, he placed himself at an even greater disadvantage by his self-imposed isolation, making him more vulnerable to manipulation by the other allies than he would otherwise have been. 'This sense of being always a little behind the others affected the confidence and nerves of every American negotiator'.[21]

Wilson's case offers a clear-cut example of the influence an individual leader may have on the resolution of a war, and emphasizes the possible intervention of non-rational elements in the delicate process of peace negotiations. Had the president preferred 'Wilsonianism' to Wilson the man, European history might have taken a more favorable turn.

From the foregoing discussion, several possible conclusions may be drawn. First, in such a fragile and complicated process as taking the decision to terminate a war and consummate peace negotiations, it is always better to rely on well-coordinated teamwork, rather than on the individual.[22]

Second, if negotiations are to proceed, and if peace is indeed the desired outcome of negotiations, the negotiators must be flexible, open-minded and capable of teamwork. Dogmatic or messianic-type negotiators will easily obstruct and block any successful negotiations. While these are obvious and by no means innovative conclusions, they emphasize the need for careful attention in the choice of negotiators as well as to their possible pattern of interaction with the other side's delegates. This has never been an easy task, and has all too often been neglected.

Third, it is likely that different types of leaders are needed for the various stages of war termination. Although the person who decides (or leads the movement) to terminate war may seem best-suited to participate in the peace negotiations themselves, this is not necessarily the case.

Non-rationality in the process of war termination can not only determine the outcome of the peace negotiations, but worse still, can obstruct a decision to stop the war itself when such a decision becomes inevitable. In times of war, the influence of a single individual is accentuated, and the possible damage he may inflict by delaying or evading a decision to end war is even greater than that caused by hesitancy in times of peace. When leadership is concentrated in fewer hands, it becomes more important to take into account non-rational elements.

An extreme example of the non-rational behavior of a leader regarding the termination of war is, of course, that of Adolf Hitler. Because Hitler's case demonstrates the partial predictive capacity of the non-rational model, it is an especially interesting example in the discussion of war termination. In 1943, Walter C. Langer predicted that Hitler would fight to the bitter end, *Götterdämmerung*-style, rather than surrender, and that he would rather commit suicide than end the war:

> Hitler may get killed in battle. This is a real possibility. When he is convinced that he cannot win, he may lead his troops into battle and expose himself as a fearless and fanatical leader. This would be most undesirable from our own point of view because his death would serve as an example to his followers to fight on with fanatical, death-defying determination to the bitter end. This would be what Hitler would want for he has predicted that: 'We shall not capitulate ... no, never. We may be destroyed, but if we are, we shall drag a world with us ... a world in flames. But even if we could not conquer them, we should drag half the world into destruction with us and leave no one to triumph over Germany. There will not be another 1918.' At a certain point he would do more toward the achievement of this goal by dying heroically than he could by living. Furthermore, death of this kind would do more to bind the German people to the Hitler legend and insure his immortality than any other course he could pursue.[23]

Hitler knew, perhaps before any other person in the world, that the war was lost; but he nevertheless entertained completely irrational hopes that the course of history might be changed. Such hopes reinforced his intransigence. The totally irrational and macabre atmosphere surrounding the *Fuehrer* is best described by Shirer:

> [Hitler] and a few of his most fanatical followers, Goebbels above all, clung stubbornly to their hopes of being saved at the last minute by a miracle.
> One fine evening early in April Goebbels had sat up reading to Hitler from one of the Fuehrer's favorite books, *History of Frederick the Great*. The chapter he was reading told of the darkest days of the

Seven Years' War, when the great King felt himself at the end of his rope and told his ministers that if by February 15 no change for the better in his fortunes occurred he would give up and take poison. This portion of history certainly had its appropriateness and no doubt Goebbels read it in his most dramatic fashion.

> 'Brave King! [Goebbels read on] Wait yet a little while, and the days of your suffering will be over. Already the sun of your good fortune stands behind the clouds and soon will rise upon you'. On February 12 the Czarina died. The Miracle of the House of Brandenburg had come to pass.

> The Fuehrer's eyes, Goebbels told Korsigk, to whose diary we owe this touching scene, 'were filled with tears'.[24]

Hitler then sent for a special horoscope to Himmler's 'R and D office', and was informed that 'In the second half of April we were to experience a temporary success. Then there would be stagnation until August and peace that same month. For the following three years Germany would have a hard time, but starting in 1948 she would rise again'.[25]

Fortified by Carlyle and the 'amazing' predictions of the stars, on April 6, Goebbels issued a ringing appeal to the retreating troops. No Czarina died in this instance, but on Friday, April 13, President Roosevelt died and the anticipated turning point of the war seemed to have arrived. This is, of course, an extreme case of refusal to come to terms with the hard facts of reality, and of wishful thinking that contributed to the unnecessary prolongation of the war. In retrospect, Hitler's behavior appears extremely irrational; however, when examined against our Western tradition and the behavior of the allies themselves in the earlier stages of the war, some of his irrational behavior can be better understood.

The 'Protestant ethic', demanding that the individual, and by extension the state, never abandon the struggle, even when hope seems lost, does not necessarily lead to rational behavior; it was not, after all, exactly rational for England not to yield and to seek peace in 1940, after the defeat and surrender of France and before the United States and Russia had entered the war. Similarly, it was not necessarily rational for the Soviet Union to continue fighting when the Germans stood ten miles outside of Moscow in 1941.

However, Hitler had some pseudo-rational justifications to delay the end of the war:

1. The hope that the grand coalition of the Allies would crumble and that England would sue for a separate peace. At a conference on January 27, 1945, the following discussion between the *Fuehrer* and Goering was recorded:

> *Hitler:*   Do you think the English are enthusiastic about all the Russian developments?
>
> *Goering:*   They certainly did not plan that we hold them off while the Russians conquer all of Germany. ... They had not counted on our holding them off like madmen while the Russians drive deeper and deeper into Germany, and practically have all of Germany now. ... If this goes on we will get a telegram [from the British] in a few days.
>
> On such a slender thread, the leaders of the Third Reich began to pin their last hopes. In the end these German architects of the Nazi-Soviet Pact against the West would reach a point where they could not understand why the British and Americans did not join them in repelling the Russian invaders.[26]

Yet despite mounting internal tensions, the Allies were still united in their common desire to defeat Germany, and managed to repress the conflict among themselves until the close of the war.

2. The psuedo-rational hopes in the development of new miracle weapons, weapons such as the V-1, V-2 rockets and the newly developed Me-262 jet fighters. While, indeed, the Allies possessed no comparable weapons, the German weapons appeared too late and in quantities too small to have the desired effect. Similarly, Hitler's hopes for the increased production of a newly designed battle tank were shattered. Fewer tanks were produced than predicted, and even had they been produced according to the expected schedule, the lack of tank (and jet) fuel would have rendered them immobile.

By the same token, it is also possible to find examples of a leader's positive influence on the course of war termination. For example, both Churchill and Bismarck took into account the long range and the shape of the peace to come. Therefore, both were willing to offer the enemy, once defeated, relatively lenient terms. As Churchill wrote, as the epigram to his work on the Second World War, 'In Victory: Magnanimity; In Peace: Good Will'. What Montesquieu called the moderation of the aristocratic form of government and the more secure and self-confident nature of members of the aristocracy may, in fact, have been at play in their policies of comparative moderation. In Churchill's case, the fact that he was also an historian gave him a wider than usual perspective and made him more conscious of the need for long-range considerations in the design of peace.[27]

Clearly, the enemies' perceptions of each other play a central, if not the most crucial, role in a decision to end a war (especially in a stalemate), and here, too, non-rational elements emerge (see discussion below). In creating a more balanced account of the process of war termination, non-rational factors must thus be given serious consideration. Yet one must be careful not to overemphasize their influence, since rationality is, after all, most essential to survival and success in war.

THE DOMESTIC LEVEL

The decision to terminate (or continue) a war can always be seen as a combination of both external and internal pressures. Neither of these can be completely controlled by any government at war. Usually there is much less control over external forces (i.e., the enemy's and any third party's behavior) than over internal affairs. Hence, the primary concern of the following pages will be the internal forces.

Most of the historical accounts of the process of war termination refer in great detail to the inner struggles between those who want to continue the struggle and those who advocate its conclusion. Among the forces that participate in this process, we can cite the government and its leaders, the opposition parties, the military elite and the rank-and-file armed forces, and public opinion.

The theoretical literature has devoted increasing attention to the domestic sources of peace, but it is still too general and impressionistic to suggest interesting generalizations. Much room remains for comparative monographic studies on various subjects related to the domestic sources of peace. For example, civil–military relations and the termination of war offer grounds from which interesting new insights can be drawn, through a comparative study of the position of the military under conditions of victory, stalemate and defeat. Other important comparative studies could be made of public opinion and its impact on war termination under democratic and authoritarian regimes; the development and effectiveness of public opinion under different circumstances; the morale of the population and the armed forces; the problem of domestic stability/instability during war, revolutions, coups d'état; changes in leadership and their impact on decisions to end a war.

The position of the military elite (as compared with that of civilians) regarding war termination has received scant treatment in the major theoretical studies in that field.[28] Much, however, has been written on the attitude of the military towards the issue of war termination in historical studies – especially in the case of the First and Second World Wars – and in special historical-political studies of armies in various countries.[29] Once war has begun, the military seems reluctant to agree to its termination on anything but favorable terms, preferring instead to continue fighting as best it can. Often it even refuses to admit that a war has been lost or cannot be decisively won. This was, to a certain extent, the case with all the armies of the First World War, the Japanese military elite in the Second World

War (to cite an extreme case), the French army in the Indochinese and Algerian wars, and the American army in Vietnam. Because the professional honor of the military leaders is at stake, they are loath to accept defeat and continue to hope for a military breakthrough; there is no substitute for victory. It is all the more important to study the attitude of the military leaders during war, for, unlike most politicians, they come to acquire a much more important position in the decision-making process.

The case of the German High Command in the First World War is an extreme but excellent example. When the campaigns of 1914–15 demonstrated that a decisive military victory for Germany was unlikely, the German government was forced to consider an end to the war through negotiations, in an attempt to obtain the best possible terms. However, the Army High Command stubbornly refused to make any of the concessions necessary to facilitate such negotiations. With the support of powerful interest groups, as well as that of a poorly informed public, Hindenburg and Ludendorff established a 'silent dictatorship' and their will prevailed over that of the civilians. They alone determined the objectives and strategy of Germany. Gordon Craig summarizes the impact of the German High Command on the war:

> Stubbornly rejecting any suggestion that total victory might not be possible, the army chiefs sacrificed all other considerations to that of military expediency, generally discovering belatedly that their most inspired strokes of policy aided and comforted the enemy without bringing Germany any of the military advantages they had expected. Finally, having destroyed the last hopes of negotiations, they bolted into a desperate and ill-conceived campaign without making any attempt to coordinate their strategical thrust with a political offensive or to prepare public opinion in Germany for the possibility of failure. The result was not only defeat but revolution; and the classic illustration of the truth of Clemenceau's dictum that war is too serious a business to be entrusted to the direction of soldiers.[30]

Similarly, in the spring of 1945, when Japan was literally losing the war faster than the United States and its allies were winning it, the Japanese Military High Command rejected surrender and considered a renewed war effort, with the possible help of the Soviet Union. Such plans were absurd both from the military and the political points of view.

Military men are customarily less aware than anyone else of the fact that war is fought to achieve political ends, namely, a better peace. For them, war is an activity with an independent momentum and logic. They have neither the desire nor the time to consider the shape of the peace and the aftermath of the war. When successful on the battlefield, they press for further advance and total victory. 'Victorious power should be pushed to its limit. The enemy must not only surrender unconditionally, but he must be made to realize how extensive and irreversible is his defeat. Triumphs on the battlefield must not be squandered in negotiation'.[31] This is precisely why the Allied High Command objected to the German request for an armistice towards the end of the First World War. Pershing argued that the military situation favored the Allies and that an armistice would enable the German High Command to gain time to withdraw from a critical situation to a more advantageous one, and that the effect of an armistice on the Allies would be dangerous since it 'would lead the Allied armies to believe this was the end of the fighting and it would be difficult, if not impossible to resume hostilities with our present advantage in morale in the event of failure to secure at the peace conference what [they] fought for'.[32]

At the peace conference, military men frequently endeavor to translate military success into a one-sided monopoly of power over the enemy, by supporting the policy of annexing strategically important territories and by imposing serious limitations on the size of the enemy's armed forces. Thus, in perpetuating the enemy's military inferiority, they also perpetuate his bitterness and desire for revenge. If the enemy refuses to accept the harsh conditions, the refusal is usually countered by the threat of immediate renewal of war (e.g., the German High Command during the negotiations at the end of the Franco-Prussian War of 1870 at Brest–Litovsk, and the Allied High Command in 1918–19). A potentially successful peace settlement is thus turned into a truce, an introduction to the next round of war.

The impact of public opinion on the termination of war is another subject which has not been studied on a comparative basis. It would be of great interest, for example, to discover at what stage of the war American public opinion began to have a serious impact on United States' decision-makers in the case of Vietnam. What was the role of French public opinion in Algeria? It would be interesting, in these cases and others, to learn why public opinion turns against a war, what role the mass media plays in a democracy in shaping public opinion, how the public reacts to developments in the battlefield, and what the time lag is between the beginning of military setbacks and a shift in public support.

Obviously, public opinion in autocratic and totalitarian regimes holds less sway. This gives leaders in totalitarian countries more time to delay, if they so wish, the decision to halt a war; once they have made this decision, of course, they need not worry so much about public opposition. The fact that public opinion was completely controlled in Nazi Germany and Japan during the Second World War undoubtedly contributed to the prolongation of the war.

If the Japanese masses had been told that the bulk of their navy and a fifth of their air navy had been destroyed in the Leyte action [end of October 1944], and that the United States had three times as many ships and planes in the Pacific as Japan has ever produced, popular sentiment in favor of surrender would have swelled mightily. The masses were not told, however – neither by Hirohito on domestic radio, nor by President Roosevelt in shortwave broadcast.[33]

Public opinion can play a significant role in peace negotiations. The British and French publics, who were promised, during the First World War, that Germany would be made to pay for the war, insisted that Germany be 'squeezed like a lemon'. Lloyd George, who wanted to win in the coming elections, had to please his public and in the process ruined the chances of securing a stable and lasting peace for post-war Europe.

The absence of public influence, on the other hand, can enhance the bargaining position of countries, as in the cases of North Vietnam and North Korea, both of whom chose to ignore the suffering of their peoples during the prolonged process of bargaining. The United States government, however, was under public pressure to complete the process as quickly as possible.

There are many excellent single-case historical studies of the impact of domestic political instability on a country's decision to end a war; yet no comparative study of this subject is available. Theoretical studies must therefore direct their questions at the issues of political unrest or popular revolutions during a war, and the need to eliminate or change the leadership of a country before peace negotiations become possible (e.g., the abdication of the Kaiser, Marshall Pétain's call to power, De Gaulle's return to power during the Algerian rebellion). The investigation of the political stability/instability question and the termination of war can be said to integrate all the issues included in this 'second level of analysis' (including civil–military relations, public opinion, and all other issues relevant to domestic affairs and war termination). This is the more general approach.

It is not my intention to enter into a detailed discussion in this context of the more general approach. Suffice it to say, as an obvious conclusion, that often an elite that is responsible for the opening of a war or military failure is reluctant to withdraw and pay the price of its activities.[34] Such withdrawal can be the physical end for such a leadership, or can necessitate the admission of its failures and mistakes.

The termination of a long and stalemated war is frequently preceded by a drastic political change in leadership in the country of one of the belligerents. A peaceful change in leadership occasionally occurs, but this often takes the form of the recall of a former military hero in order that he lend his prestige to ease the burden of surrender or compromise (e.g., Pétain in 1940, Mannerheim in 1944, and De Gaulle in 1958).

The possible subjects that can be discussed on this level are still far from being exhausted, including policymaking and planning for war termination,[35] bureaucratic politics and intra-governmental struggles concerning war termination (such as foreign offices and state departments vis-à-vis the military high command and/or prime minister and/or other influential governmental agencies according to specific circumstances).[36] One important conclusion emerges related to the theory of war termination within the discipline of international politics: It is probably much too early and much too ambitious to aspire to construct and develop general theories of war termination – as long as the number of lower-level type of generalized comparative studies, such as those mentioned above, is insufficient. The long and hard road to a more generalized theory of war termination must be erected on a larger number of comparative studies that have yet to be written.

> Wars usually end when the fighting nations agree on their
> relative strength, and wars usually begin when fighting nations
> disagree on their relative strength.[37]

THE INTER-STATE LEVEL – THE RATIONAL MODEL FOR THE TERMINATION OF WAR

The central problem in the theoretical study of war termination is that of the optimal time to cease fighting or to surrender. Who fared better in 1939, the Czechs who decided not to fight (i.e., to surrender) or the Poles who decided to fight?[38] Was it rational for the British to continue fighting alone in 1940 against the Germans while the United States and Russia were not yet involved in the war? Would it not have been more rational for them to start negotiating for peace, as the Germans expected they would? Why did the Russians not surrender when the Germans were within sighting distance of Moscow in 1941 and the situation appeared hopeless? Why did the Germans and the Allies only start to negotiate during the First World War in 1918, and not as early as 1914 or 1915? Why did the Korean War continue until 1953, and not stop in 1951, when negotiations had started and it seemed that neither side could improve his position on the battlefield? Why did the United States not quit the war in Vietnam immediately after the Tet offensive of 1968 instead of fighting until 1973? All these important questions imply that, at least in retrospect, the wrong decisions were made (as often as the correct ones) regarding the 'optimal' point at which a conflict should be terminated.

Much of the theoretical literature discusses the attempts to predict and develop criteria for identifying in advance this point in the war. Hereafter, the attempt will be referred to as the 'rational' model.

The rational approach assumes that the belligerents have sufficient information available to make the necessary cost-benefit calculations concerning the decision of when to terminate a war. The classic statement of this approach remains that of Clausewitz:

> Still more general in its influence on the resolution to peace is the consideration of the expenditure of force already made, and further required. As war is no act of blind passion, but is dominated by the political object, therefore the value of that object determines the measure of sacrifices by which it is to be purchased. This will be the case, not only as regards extent, but also as regards duration. As soon, therefore, as the required outlay becomes so great as that the political object is no longer equal in value, the object must be given up, and peace will be the result.
>
> We see, therefore, that in wars where one side cannot completely disarm the other, the motives to peace on both sides will rise and fall on each side according to the probability of future success and the required outlay. If these motives were equally strong on both sides, they would meet in the center of their political differences.[39]

As an ideal model, the rational approach may be summarized as follows:

1. One or both of the sides are referred to as uniactors (*states*) with one identifiable center of decision-making.

2. One or both of the sides knows precisely the *values and goals* and their respective value for which they are fighting, as well as the *exact values and goals* of the enemy and their worth to him.

3. They have *all* the *necessary information* to evaluate their power and that of the adversary, to continue fighting, and therefore each (or one) of the sides can calculate the *relative present and future* power of each other and its effects on the continued battle.

4. One or both of the belligerents can identify and compare the anticipated costs of all available courses of action.

It immediately becomes clear that a completely rational decision to terminate war is non-existent. The rational calculation of a war's conclusion is virtually impossible, for numerous reasons.

1. As we have seen above, states do not act as uniactors. Any decision to terminate a war is the result of complicated internal struggles among leaders, conflicts between the army and other organizations such as the foreign office, public opinion, and so on. This is an extended bargaining

process that often results in a compromise decision that is not always completely rational, but must answer the needs of various groups and reflect their relative influence and political power. Because such a process is often too slow, a decision may be reached only after the 'optimal' point for terminating a war has passed.

2. No side has complete and perfect knowledge concerning his values and goals. Opinions within each country are often divided, while the goals of fighting a war change with the fortunes of battle.

3. In order to make a perfectly rational decision, complete information concerning the values, goals and power of the enemy is necessary. Such information is often unobtainable or only partial, at best. Much of the evaluation of the enemy's values, goals and power is a question of perception and, therefore, of misperception as well. Warring enemies rarely have correct mutual perceptions of each other. Even if it is rational for one side to initiate unilateral peace negotiations, there is often fear that this will be misperceived as a sign of weakness and will result in worse terms as a basis for negotiations, or in the strengthening of the enemy's military efforts. Such reciprocal fears lead to modifications in rational behavior.

4. Many human values, such as freedom and honor, defy rational evaluation. One of the basic tenets of the Western view of war can be expressed in the cliché, 'Don't give up the ship'. Historical experience, such as the 1940 British decision and the 1941 Russian decision not to surrender, demonstrates that the decision to delay surrender can pay off. But this is discovered only *ex post facto* and is not a totally rational decision at the time that it is made. The risk involved is enormous. Iklé suggests that, 'It often happens in wars that the weaker party makes no attempt to seek peace while its military strength can still influence the enemy, but fights until it has lost all its power to bargain'.[40]

This problem is, of course, less relevant when a state is threatened with total destruction or is faced with an enemy's policy of *delenda est Carthago – guerre à outrance*, and thus is not left with any choice. Fighting to the end may make sense, though belligerent countries rarely make such declarations so as not to stiffen enemy resistance.[41]

5. The comparison of the cost-benefit calculations that Clausewitz recommends is impossible. The goals and values of each of the sides are not measured (if they can be measured at all) by the same means as the costs of war (i.e., the political benefits of freedom, the acquisition of more territory, the issues of security, honor, etc., cannot be compared with the financial price of war, the human losses and other costs which can only be measured by different means). The absence of a common denominator to measure costs and benefits renders such a rational

calculation impossible. Were calculations possible, war itself would
become unnecessary because:

> With perfect foresight, the potential loser would know before
> the conflict started that he must lose, even if his forces were
> initially superior. In this case, if he were rational, he would not
> initiate hostilities. In the absence of perfect foresight, however, the
> belligerents have to make the best estimates they can about the
> future shape of the war. Early in the conflict the data permit
> many different estimates. The actual outcome reveals itself only
> gradually, so that there is no way for the loser to guarantee himself
> against superfluous losses; he cannot know in advance whether
> further resistance may not reverse the trend. What the loser can
> certainly avoid, if he is rational, is that amount of attrition that he
> would suffer by fighting on when the available evidence definitely
> excludes everything but defeat.[42]

The following diagram illustrates some of the theoretical problems
involved in locating the 'optimal' point in the process of war termination.

DIAGRAM 1

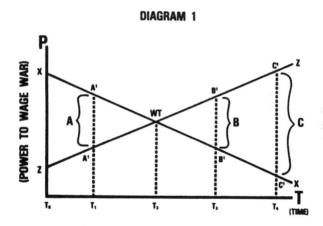

Such a diagram can be constructed only *ex post facto* and therefore has
little or no predictive value. Its main utility is not in any exact policy
directions or forecasts but as an analytical tool helping to clarify some of
the dilemmas involved in the process of starting to negotiate during a war.

The power of each country (X and Z) is the sum total of all the forms of
power that can be made available to it for war at any given time. In other
words, it takes different countries varying periods of time to translate their
potential power into actual power. In reality, the power of each country
would be represented by a curve instead of a straight line.

At the beginning of a war, country X can have much greater actual power than Z, whose power is still not converted from potential to actual power (e.g., Germany and the United States in the Second World War). When X first attacks, it might win the war, or at least gain a considerable advantage: gap A favors country X. If country X can decisively defeat country Z in the opening phase of the war and prevent it from translating its potential power into actual power, it can win. Thus, for example, if Germany had occupied Moscow and Russian territory as far as the Urals, including Russia's industrial base, it could have won the war – this was within its reach. When Japan attacked the United States, it had no chance of eliminating the United States' industrial base and, in the long run, it stood no chance of winning the war decisively. Its best hope was to establish an immediate bargaining advantage which might have induced the United States to recognize some of its conquests. In short, the interesting question regarding gap A is whether it can become sufficiently decisive so as to enable the adversary to reverse and maintain the situation.[43]

For the weaker country, Z, the questions that present themselves are: (a) is the gap decisive and irreversible, and (b) can it hold out long enough to equalize its power with the enemy's at point T_2 and surpass him at points T_3 and T_4? (For instance, Britain and Russia, in 1940 and 1941, respectively, had to make this calculation.) The problem lies precisely in the difficulty of making such calculations in advance, and hence, it can often be seen as rational for country Z to surrender at the first stage (again, Britain and Russia in 1940 and 1941, respectively).

Point WT (war termination) is, in retrospect, the optimal point for terminating the war, since the two sides are equal in power. This, however, is not the case in this particular diagram, and is frequently not the case in reality. At point WT (T_2), country Z is growing more powerful than country X and the former therefore has no reason to stop fighting until it has reversed its earlier defeats. The optimal war termination point at T_2 is therefore only an intersection (cutting point) at which the powers of the two opposing sides are temporarily equal or balanced. Country X usually perceives its situation as deteriorating only when it reaches point T_3 or T_4, and consequently has only a weak incentive to open negotiations. If, on the other hand, both countries, and especially country X, understand the direction of events (i.e., that time is working in favor of country Z), it would be in the interest of country X to open negotiations somewhere between points T_1 and T_2, while it is still in a better bargaining position.

In the case of a stalemate, point WT can also become a real equilibrium point and not simply an intersection (e.g., the First World War or the Korean War). The situation might then look like Diagram 2 below.

The next question posed by Diagram 1 concerns the point at which

DIAGRAM 2

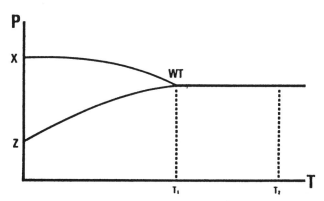

country X decides that the tide has turned against it. Will it be at point T_3 or point T_4? Surrendering or starting to negotiate at point T_3 would then be more rational than at point T_4, since at point T_3, X is still in a relatively good bargaining position and has not yet reached the critical gap C, where it is devoid of all bargaining power. The difficulty lies in the fact that countries generally estimate the shape of the curves (i.e., historical trends) incorrectly. Is Israel presently at point T_1, T_2 or T_3 of these curves (Diagram 1)? What is the best rational decision? Can it influence compromise while it is still at point T_1? Or do the Arabs think that they are at point T_2 (WT) and will they therefore be able to dictate their terms when the power gap turns in their favor at point T_4?

The different sides of a conflict naturally perceive the curves in different shapes at the same time and hence have divergent incentives for terminating the war.

DIAGRAM 3

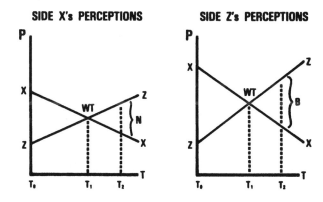

Countries X and Z both realize that the power of X is declining in relation to the power of Z. Yet at point T_1, X views his situation as declining only slowly until T_2. Z, on the other hand, believes at point T_1 that his power is rising at a comparatively faster rate toward point T_2. Consequently, X possesses a weaker incentive than Z realizes to enter negotiations. Had the anticipated developments been forecast by the two parties with similar results, X's incentive to open negotiations would have been far stronger.

It would be instructive to investigate the incentive of countries, given their conflicting perceptions of the power gap, to terminate a war. What kind of expected gap leads which side to initiate negotiations? The table below illustrates the possible combination of power relations and the corresponding incentives to terminate a war.

1. When both sides experience a rapid growth in power (as in an arms race, or when both receive massive weapon supplies in the beginning of a war from external powers – e.g., Spanish Civil War; Arab–Israeli War, 1973), the incentive to negotiate is non-existent in either camp.

2. When both parties continue to grow, although one increases in power more rapidly than the other, the incentive for war termination or negotiations remains nil or very low for both. (Israel possesses a small advantage in the rate of military growth ratio, but the Arabs enjoy political and economic advantages that balance the situation.)

TABLE 1

Possible Perceptions of Relative Power Trends by Countries X and Z and their Impact on their Incentive for Terminating War or for Negotiating

State Z ↘ State X	Rapid Rise in Power	Slow Rise in Power	Slow Decline in Power	Rapid Decline in Power
Rapid Rise in Power	no (1) no	low/no (2) no	low/strong (3) no	strong (4) no
Slow Rise in Power	no (2) low/no	no (5) no	low (6) no	low/strong (8) no
Slow Decline in Power	no (3) low/strong	no (6) low	low (7) low	low/strong (9) low
Rapid Decline in Power	no (4) strong	no (8) low/strong	low (9) low/strong	strong (10) strong

no   = no incentive for WT or negotiation
low   = low incentive for WT or negotiation
strong = strong incentive for WT or negotiation

3. When one side rises rapidly and the other declines slowly, the party whose power is declining slowly has an incentive, not necessarily strong, to open negotiations (Germany, 1942–43; Japan, 1942–43).

4. When one side experiences a rapid rise in power, while the other experiences a rapid decline, the stronger side will request an unconditional surrender and the weaker side will have a strong incentive to start negotiating an end to the war (Finland–Russia, 1944; Japan, 1945; Germany, 1918).

5. When the power of both parties grows slowly during a war, the incentive to halt the fighting is weak (First World War, 1915–16). This is a situation of stalemate and both sides are potentially able to muster further power.

6. When one side is slowly rising in power and the other is slowly declining, a delicate situation exists in which no decision has been reached, since the trends are not fully clear (Second World War, at the end of 1942). This is probably the point which, in retrospect, is viewed as the equilibrium – the 'optimal' point for terminating the war. In this case, the stronger party may be interested in terminating the war and in initiating negotiations for a favorable settlement. The weaker side can still fight, but has a strong incentive to negotiate (Finland–Russia, in the early stages of the 1940 war).

7. When both sides decline slowly (mutual gradual attrition), the incentive to terminate hostilities is increasing, but is not yet sufficiently strong for both sides to quit (First World War, 1917; and Korea, 1951).

8. When the power of one side is slowly rising and the other is declining rapidly, the incentive for negotiations can be low for the slowly rising side and strong for the rapidly declining state, before the other side's power starts to grow rapidly (e.g., Finland and the USSR in the later stages of the Second World War).

9. When both parties are declining but one declines faster than the other, both may develop the desire to negotiate, although the latter may evince a stronger desire to do so. The terms of the eventual settlement will slightly favor the more slowly declining side (Arab–Israeli war, end of 1973).

10. When the power of both parties declines rapidly, a situation of mutual attrition and exhaustion arises (Korea, 1953; the Egyptian–Israeli War of Attrition, 1970; possibly the First World War, which might have taken a different course without American intervention). In this instance, both develop a strong incentive to initiate negotiations.

This type of analysis can have some heuristic value. It emphasizes that the inclination of states at war to start negotiating is a function of their relative power relations. This analysis is, however, bound to be very inaccurate as a practical measure of each state's incentive to open (or not to open) negotiations for war termination, as the difficulties in estimating the power trends remain. In other words, the table attempts to explain what each side's action will ideally be if it perceives its relative strength as corresponding to each of the ten possibilities.

In short, the preceding analysis illuminates some of the important limitations and weaknesses in the application of a rational model to the process of war termination. Like many other political activities, this process is complicated, dialectical, and involves a high degree of uncertainty, including complex psychological elements. Nevertheless, this does not imply that the decision to terminate a war is an irrational one, nor does it abrogate the responsibility of leaders to behave as rationally as they are able.

The decision to terminate a war does, in the final analysis, comprise numerous rational elements. War is, after all, the human activity in which rational action considering the stakes involved is more vital and more necessary to achieve than in any other area of human concern.

The circumstances that must be taken into account by any country that is deciding whether or not to terminate hostilities can be summarized as in Table 2 on the following page.

The steps and possible calculations involved in the decision-making process leading to the termination of war and/or negotiations can be schematically represented by the flow chart.

The rational approach (model) to the study of war termination is also indispensable when applied to the often lengthy and tedious bargaining process which takes place between the belligerents in trying to settle the dispute and/or agree on the terms of war termination. The literature on bargaining theory in general (collective bargaining in labor disputes, for example),[44] but more specifically in the theory of international relations, can be of great interest here.[45]

It is beyond the scope of this paper to apply or develop the potential utility of this area of research to our subject, but a few examples are in place. Bargaining theory is of great help in explaining the tactics of the belligerents during their negotiations to terminate war. How does the weaker side try to compensate for its weakness by various bargaining skills and tactics? How does the threat of third-party intervention on behalf of one (or both) of the sides influence negotiations? How does one of the sides try to gain time during the negotiations in order to improve its relative position? Why do other sides insist on continued fighting while negotiations are carried out? How do stronger sides use threats to renew hostilities, to escalate or open new frontiers in order to press their adversary to accept their position? How do sides agree to give up after hard and tiresome negotiations on trivial points in order to demand later

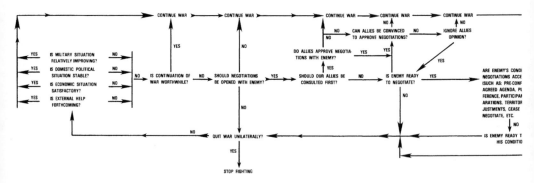

YES — IS MILITARY SITUATION RELATIVELY IMPROVING? — NO
YES — IS DOMESTIC POLITICAL SITUATION STABLE? — NO
YES — IS ECONOMIC SITUATION SATISFACTORY? — NO
YES — IS EXTERNAL HELP FORTHCOMING? — NO

CONTINUE WAR

NO — IS CONTINUATION OF WAR WORTHWHILE?

YES

CONTINUE WAR

NO — SHOULD NEGOTIATIONS BE OPENED WITH ENEMY? — YES

NO

CONTINUE WAR

SHOULD OUR ALLIES BE CONSULTED FIRST? — NO

YES

DO ALLIES APPROVE NEGOTIATIONS WITH ENEMY? — YES

CONTINUE WAR

NO

CAN ALLIES BE CONVINCED TO APPROVE NEGOTIATIONS? — NO

CONTINUE WAR

NO

IGNORE ALLIES OPINION?

CONTINUE WAR

YES

IS ENEMY READY TO NEGOTIATE? — YES

NO

ARE ENEMY'S CONDI... NEGOTIATIONS ACCE... (SUCH AS: PRE-CONF... AGREED AGENDA, P... FERENCE, PARTICIPA... ARATIONS, TERRITOR... JUSTMENTS, CEASE... NEGOTIATE, ETC.

NO

IS ENEMY READY T... HIS CONDITIO...

NO — QUIT WAR UNILATERALLY?

YES

STOP FIGHTING

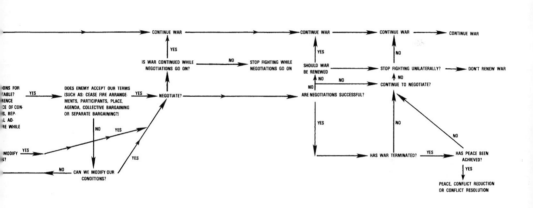

CONTINUE WAR ——————— CONTINUE WAR ———→ CONTINUE WAR ———————→ CONTINUE WAR

YES ↑

IS WAR CONTINUED WHILE ——— NO ——→ STOP FIGHTING WHILE
NEGOTIATIONS GO ON? NEGOTIATIONS GO ON

YES ↑ SHOULD WAR
BE RENEWED

DONS FOR
ABLE? ——— YES ——→ DOES ENEMY ACCEPT OUR TERMS ——— YES ——→ NEGOTIATE? ———————→ NO ↑ STOP FIGHTING UNILATERALLY? ——→ DON'T RENEW WAR
RENCE (SUCH AS: CEASE FIRE ARRANGE-
CE OF CON- MENTS, PARTICIPANTS, PLACE, NO ——→ NO ↑ NO
S, REP- AGENDA, COLLECTIVE BARGAINING CONTINUE TO NEGOTIATE?
L AD OR SEPARATE BARGAINING?) ARE NEGOTIATIONS SUCCESSFUL?
RE WHILE NO YES

MODIFY ——— YES ——→ YES

NO ——→ CAN WE MODIFY OUR YES
CONDITIONS? YES ↓ NO ↑ NO

HAS WAR TERMINATED? ——— YES ——→ HAS PEACE BEEN
ACHIEVED?

YES ↓

PEACE, CONFLICT REDUCTION
OR CONFLICT RESOLUTION

TABLE 2

Decision in Favor of Termination	Decision Against Termination
Expectations that:	Expectations that:
— the situation is deteriorating politically, militarily or economically	— circumstances are in our favor or show signs of improving politically, militarily or economically
— time is on the enemy's side: minimize or cut losses while it is still possible	— time is on our side or the enemy's situation is deteriorating more rapidly than ours
— military setbacks, defeat, stalemate or attrition; the limits of war potential have been reached or exhausted	— gains can be maximized and/or a continuation of the fighting will help cut losses; military situation is improving (or will) and our war potential has not been fully actualized
— no external support is forthcoming or expected	— external support is being received or will soon arrive
— domestic situation unstable: social and political unrest, morale low or declining, economic problems	— domestic situation stable: morale high and public continues to support war effort
— little or nothing can be gained even if victory is possible; war goals are unattainable	— a "time out" will work to our enemy's benefit
— the enemy offers convenient, reasonably lenient terms for conclusion of war	— terms the enemy offers are tough, excessively demanding and unacceptable
— a break for negotiations will work to our advantage	— initiating negotiations will weaken our bargaining position.

concessions on important issues? How do sides warn, threaten, bluff and commit themselves? How are propaganda and public opinion used during the negotiations? In the tactics concerning the pre-negotiation agreements, should the agenda be agreed upon prior to negotiations? Should the sides adhere to an agreed agenda or make the agenda the first subject of discussion? How is such an agenda to be structured – should topics on the agenda be discussed sequentially or should all topics be discussed simultaneously? What states, and with what status, should participate?

These and many other questions concerning the bargaining process between belligerents are of great importance. They have been discussed in great detail by diplomatic historians and in memoirs of participants in such negotiations. But such works are usually devoted only to one specific conference – such as the termination of the Balkan Wars, Brest–Litovsky, the Paris Peace Conference, the Munich Agreements, Finland 1940, Korea 1951–53, Geneva 1954 (the Indo-China War), the Separation Agreements 1973–1975, between Israel, Egypt and Syria.[46] Few attempts have been made to write a more general comparative study on bargaining tactics during negotiations to terminate war.[47] There is enough readily available material to supply both the theoretical background as well as the empirical data necessary for such a study.

CONCLUSIONS

In this chapter, I have taken a critical look at some of the problems of war termination and their treatment in the existing literature. Many of the studies on this subject have been written by diplomatic historians examining a single case study of war termination in detail (e.g., the peace of Westphalia, the Vienna peace conference, and Versailles); the number of theoretical and comparative studies was quite small. However, the number of such general studies has shown a marked increase in recent years. It is much too early to aspire to write a definitive general comparative study on war termination – if such an undertaking is possible at all. There is still a great need for more specific monographs to be written on more limited subjects within the field of war termination before the basis for a more general study can be established. Such subjects, for example, are the position of the military on war termination; mutual perceptions and misperceptions of belligerents during war and their impact on war termination; a general study of bargaining tactics and the termination of war; and many similar subjects.

The theory of war termination so far has had little impact on the policy-making and the decision-making process and on the behavior of states trying to end a war. This need not be the case, as the literature includes many insights and useful information which can be of great utility for leaders, negotiators and states considering the termination of war. With the growing accumulation of such studies and the teaching of courses on war termination at universities, more attention will be paid to past experience, and with the slow and gradual development of theoretical literature on war termination, it might be of great help to policymakers.

I have emphasized or demonstrated also the importance of non-rational aspects of the behavior of states and statesmen on the termination of war. These aspects have been neglected, in my opinion, in the theoretical studies on war termination. It must be remembered, however, that the termination of war and the establishment of peace have often been tied very closely to the political *Weltanschauung* and character of a few leaders. Some leaders have been more prudent, more responsible than others – Bismarck, Atatürk, Churchill, Kennedy in Cuba – and have not pressed their victories and successes to the extreme; they have been moderate and tried to secure a lasting peace and had a developed long-range vision. Above all, they tried to put themselves in the position of their enemy. Others – Lloyd George, Woodrow Wilson, Hitler, and perhaps Roosevelt – were short-sighted, immoderate or fanatical. They had no long-range view and did not stand up to the problem of building a stable lasting peace. It usually makes a difference if the leaders are Nasser and Golda Meir, Sadat and Begin, Kennedy and Khrushchev. Sometimes it happens that the force of circumstances, combined with the unique psychological environments – often even pathological – of leading decision-makers, locks the belligerents in a process over which they have little control.

These non-rational elements undermine and limit our possibility to understand or make predictions about the termination of war. The study of war termination is not an exact science and never will be. Nevertheless, these non-rational elements by no means excuse us from examining the processes involved in the termination of war. It is our duty as students of international politics to study how to prevent wars through deterrence, avoid wars by miscalculations, accidents and escalation – but also to learn how to bring wars to an end in the fastest possible way, once they have started.

NOTES

1. C. von Clausewitz, *On War* (London, 1968), p.123.
2. B.H. Liddell Hart, *Strategy* (New York, 1964), p.351.
3. C. Phillipson, *Termination of War and Treaties of Peace* (New York, 1916), p.v.
4. F.C. Iklé, *Every War Must End* (New York, 1971), p.v.
5. 'War and peace are more than opposites. They have so much in common that neither can be understood without the other' (G. Blainey, *The Causes of War* [New York, 1973], p.245). See also G. Schwartzenberger, ed., *International Law*, Volume 2: *The Law of Armed Conflict* (London, 1968), p.723.
6. For the distinction between conflict reduction and conflict resolution, see Janice Stein, 'War Termination and Conflict Resolution', in G. Schwartzenberger, *The Law of Armed Conflict*, pp.15–25. The concept of 'conflict reductionism' is also suggested in H. Schmid, 'Peace Research and Politics', *The Journal of Peace Research* 5 (No. 3, 1968), pp.217–231, 224ff.
7. M.A. Kaplan, *System and Process in International Politics* (New York, 1967), pp.23–24.
8. G. Blainey, *The Causes of War*, p.245.
9. For a bibliography, see *The Garland Library of War and Peace* (New York, 1971).
10. E.H. Carr, *Conditions of Peace* (London, 1943), pp.67–101; K.E. Boulding, *The Economics of Peace* (London, 1946); O. Dutch, *Economic Peace Aims* (London,

1941).

11. J.M. Keynes, *Essays on Persuasion* (New York, 1963), pp.3–77; idem, *The Economic Consequences of Peace* (New York, 1971); P. Birdsall, *Versailles Twenty Years After* (Hamden, Connecticut, 1962), pp.238–264; O. Dutch, *Economic Peace Aims*; E. Mantoux, *The Carthaginian Peace or the Economic Consequences of Mr. Keynes* (London, 1946).

12. See G. Schwartzenberger, *The Law of Armed Conflict*, pp.723–783; L. Oppenheim, *International Law: Disputes, War and Neutrality*, Vol. 2, ed. H. Lauterpacht (London, 1965, 7th ed.). For the termination of war, see chap. 7, pp.596–624. See also J. Stone, *Legal Controls of International Conflict*, ed. I. Silver (New York, 1973), Part V: 'Abatement of Hostilities, Termination of War, and Termination of Hostilities', pp.635–650. In the theory of international relations, a more complicated typology of possible ways to end wars is used. See, for example, K.J. Holsti, 'Resolving International Conflicts: A Taxonomy of Behavior and Some Figures on Procedures', *Journal of Conflict Resolution* 10 (No. 3, September 1966), pp.272–296.

13. P. Kecskemeti, *Strategic Surrender* (Stanford, 1958); F.C. Iklé, *Every War Must End*; R.F. Randle, *The Origins of Peace* (New York, 1973).

14. One such attempt is that by Randle, *The Origins of Peace*. He ignores almost completely the first level and the role of the individual in the termination of war.

15. A.C. George and J.L. George, *Woodrow Wilson and Colonel House* (New York, 1964); S. Freud and W.C. Bulitt, *Thomas Woodrow Wilson, Twenty-Eighth President of the United States: A Psychological Study* (Boston, 1967). For shorter but very interesting sketches of Wilson and his devastating influence on the course of the Paris Peace Conference, see H. Nicolson, *Peacemaking 1919* (London, 1937); and J.M. Keynes, *The Economic Consequences of Peace*, chap. 3.

16. H. Nicolson, *Peacemaking 1919*, pp.36–37, 71, 73.

17. J.M. Keynes, *The Economic Consequences of Peace*, p.36.

18. H. Nicolson, *Peacemaking 1919*, pp.52–53, 178.

19. A.C. George and J.L. George, *Woodrow Wilson and Colonel House*, p.221.

20. Ibid., p.222.

21. Nicolson, *Peacemaking 1919*, p.72.

22. There are many dangers in Henry Kissinger's 'lonely cowboy' shuttle diplomacy. Too much revolves around his own personality, and too many 'understandings', 'tacit agreements', as well as formal agreements, can collapse with his departure.

23. W.C. Langer, *The Mind of Adolf Hitler* (New York, 1972), pp.209–210.

24. W. Shirer, *The Rise and Fall of the Third Reich* (New York, 1960), pp.1108–1109.

25. Ibid., p.781.

26. Ibid., p.1098.

27. For an interesting psychoanalytical study of Churchill, see A. Storr, 'The Man', in A.J.P. Taylor, ed., *Churchill Revised* (New York, 1959), pp.229–277, especially pp.254–255.

28. S. Huntington, *The Soldier and the State* (New York, 1969); S.E. Finer, *The Man on the Horse Back: The Role of the Military in Politics* (London, 1967); B. Abrahamsson, *Military Professionalization and Political Power* (Beverly Hills, 1972).

29. Only a few of the more interesting examples can be mentioned here. The literature on the German army is immense: C. Craig, *The Politics of the Prussian Army 1640–1945* (New York, 1964); W. Görlitz, *The German General Staff 1657–1945* (New York, 1961); G. Ritter, *The Sword and the Scepter* (Coral Gables, Florida, 1970–71). For the French army, see J.S. Ambler, *Soldiers Against the State: The French Army in Politics* (Garden City, New York, 1968); G.A. Kelly, *Lost Soldiers: The French Army and Empire in Crisis, 1947–1962* (Cambridge, Massachusetts, 1965). For Japan, See R. Butow, *Tojo and the Coming of the War* (Stanford, 1969); and idem, *Japan's Decision to Surrender* (Stanford, 1968).

30. G. Graig, *The Politics of the Prussian Army*, p.300. See also G. Ritter, *The Sword and the Scepter*; D.J. Goodspeed, *Ludendorff* (Boston, 1966).

31. D. Thompson, E. Meyer, and A. Briggs, *Patterns of Peace Making* (London, 1945), p.48.

32. Ibid., pp. 48–49.
33. After the war US Strategic Bombing Survey teams conducted a poll to find out when the misinformed Japanese public began to realize that its side had lost. They discovered, as might be expected, that every reverse which could not be concealed from the people increased the number of pessimists. Two percent of the population despaired of winning in June 1944 before the fall of Japan, ten percent in December after the first heavy B-29 attacks, 19 percent by March 1945 when the fire raids began, 46 percent by June after the collapse of Germany, and 68 percent by August when the atomic bombs fell. The will to fight decreased proportionately, and by the time of surrender 64 percent of the people had reached a point at which they felt they were personally unable to go on with the war. [D. Bergamini, *Japan's Imperial Conspiracy* (New York, 1971), p. 1031.]
34. This desire not to take responsibility is one of Daniel Ellsberg's explanations for American presidents' inability to stop the war in Vietnam and get out of the quagmire. Each president wanted to keep on investing only as much power as was necessary not to lose the war – and let the next president struggle with the complicated question of terminating the war.
35. R.F. Randle, *The Origins of Peace*, pp. 457–480; M. Halperin, 'War Termination as a Problem in Civil–Military Relations', in W.T.R. Fox, ed., *How Wars End*, The Annals, Vol. 392, November 1970; R. Rothstein, 'Domestic Politics and Peace-making: Reconciling Incompatible Imperatives', in W.T.R. Fox, *How Wars End*.
36. J. Wheeler-Bennett, *Brest–Litovsk: The Forgotten Peace, March 1918* (New York, 1966).
37. G. Blainey, *The Causes of War*, p. 122.
38. See A.J.P. Taylor, *The Origins of the Second World War* (London, 1974): 'In 1938 Czechoslovakia was betrayed. In 1939 Poland was saved. Less than one hundred thousand Czechs died during the war. Six and a half million Poles were killed. Which is better, to be a betrayed Czech or a saved Pole?' (p. 26.)
39. C. von Clausewitz, *On War*, p. 125.
40. F.C. Iklé, *Every War Must End*, p. 34.
41. C. von Clausewitz, *On War*, p. 109.
42. P. Kecskemeti, *Strategic Surrender*, p. 9.
43. Ibid., pp. 8–10; idem, 'Political Rationality in Ending War', in W.T.R. Fox, *How Wars End*, pp. 105–115.
44. J.A. Rubin and B.R. Brown, *The Social Psychology of Bargaining and Negotiations* (New York, 1975); R.E. Walton and R.M. McKersie, *A Behavioral Theory of Labor Negotiations* (New York, 1965); R.M. MacDonald, *Collective Bargaining in the Automobile Industry* (New Haven, 1963); C.M. Stevens, *Strategy and Collective Bargaining Negotiations* (New York, 1963); A.R. Weber, ed., *The Structure of Collective Bargaining: Problems and Perspectives* (New York, 1961).
45. W.H. Riker, *The Theory of Political Coalitions* (New Haven, 1962); T.C. Schelling, *The Strategy of Conflict* (New York, 1969); M. Deutsch, 'Trust and Suspicion', *Journal of Conflict Resolutions* 2 (No. 3, December 1958); F.C. Iklé, *Every War Must End*; A. Rapoport, *Fights, Games and Debates* (Ann Arbor, 1960); C. Bell, *Negotiations from Strength: A Study on Politics of Power* (London, 1962); A.B. Fox, *The Power of Small States: Diplomacy in World War II* (Chicago, 1959).
46. See, for example, on the Balkan wars, E.C. Helmreich, *The Diplomacy of the Balkan Wars* (New York, 1966); Brest–Litovsky: J. Wheeler-Bennett, *Brest–Litovsky*; the Munich crisis: idem, *Munich: Prologue to Tragedy* (London, 1966). I have not yet come across an analysis devoted solely to Hitler as a bargaining tactician; this could make a fascinating study. For Russian–Finnish negotiations, see M. Jakobson, *The Diplomacy of the Winter War* (Cambridge, Massachusetts, 1961); A.F. Upton, *Finland in Crisis* (Ithaca, New York, 1965); for Korea, see J. Turner, *How Communists Negotiate* (Santa Monica, California, 1970); W.H. Vatcher, *Panmunjim: The Story of the Korean Military Armistice Negotiations* (New York, 1958); D. Rees, *Korea: The Limited War* (Baltimore, 1970). The Korean armistice makes a fascinating story; little use has been made of this material to date for a more theoretical study. For Indo-China, see R.F.

Randle, *Geneva 1954: The Settlement of the Indo-China War* (Princeton, 1969).
47. Since I wrote this essay (in 1977) the following book was published on bargaining and negotiating for war termination (the book also includes an up-to-date bibliography): Paul R. Pillar, *Negotiating Peace: War Termination as a Bargaining Process* (Princeton N.J.: Princeton University Press, 1983).

10

The Future of War: The Diminishing Returns of Military Power

Although many of the traditional descriptions of relations between the strong and the weak in the period since 1945 seem to conform to the realist model, a new trend in this relationship has been evolving. Initially, changes in the international system during the late 1940s and early 1950s were so subtle that they could still be interpreted in light of the old paradigm of power politics; since the late 1960s many anomalies have surfaced that now raise serious questions about the continued validity of that paradigm. Despite having undergone numerous changes, the relationship between strong and weak nations can still be explained by the traditional analysis of power politics, but applying the same model today produces very different results. Relations between the strong and the weak are no longer determined by considerations of pure power. Military and even economic strength cannot, as in the past, simply be translated into or correlated with political influence, spheres of influence, or hegemonic control. While the decline in the direct utility of power is unmistakable today, its origins go back to the period following the Second World War, and its full implications will become evident only in the years ahead.

The concepts of *dominant* and *subordinate* have become relics of the past, as irrelevant as 'gunboat diplomacy', 'open door policies', and 'capitulations'. The evidence is in every daily newspaper. The dominant powers do not seem to dominate, and the subordinate refuse to obey. In fighting against France and the United States, the Vietnamese refused to behave according to the conventional wisdom, which would have had them bow to the logic of the superior power or the great powers. Just as the Soviets have not been able to impose their will in Afghanistan despite their superior military power, the Iranians occupied the U.S. embassy in Tehran with impunity (something a subordinate would not be expected to do, considering the power differential involved). The United States did not send its gunboats to the Persian Gulf, nor did it threaten major military action. The Greeks do not try to please the United States, nor do the Israelis, who depend upon the United States, exhibit the subordinate type of behavior expected of a client state. The Soviet Union could not control Yugoslav or Chinese behavior to accommodate its interests nor can it dictate Romanian or Albanian foreign policy. The United States could not prevent Cuba from becoming a communist client of the USSR or today modify the behavior of the Nicaraguan leftist government. Following the bombing of the U.S. Marine position at the Beirut airport, the United States quickly withdrew from Lebanon. Such experiences not only reflect the changing attitudes and behavior patterns of the great powers but also those of middle powers and smaller states. Israel had to leave most of the territory it occupied in Lebanon, still unable to impose its will on a much weaker state. These and many other examples seem to indicate that our frequent resort to the terms dominant and subordinate is unrealistic. If current trends in the relations between the powerful and weaker states continue, these terms will become even less relevant in the future. Perhaps we are reaching a stage in international politics in which the use of raw power is becoming more and more difficult, as it has within modern societies.

Why are the strong reluctant to use their power? Why has the use of raw military power become increasingly less effective in recent years? Why have direct intervention and dominance become so much more costly than indirect intervention or no intervention at all? In this chapter I will identify and briefly discuss five interrelated major trends that are helpful in answering these questions:

(1) Democratic values.
(2) The slow but steady decline in the importance assigned to foreign policy since 1945 and the gradual increase in the relative importance of domestic politics.
(3) The nuclear revolution.
(4) The increasing cost of direct dominance and use of power.
(5) The realization that almost all raw materials can be obtained without the necessity of having direct control over other states.

HEGEMONY AND THE RISE OF DEMOCRATIC VALUES

Since the beginning of the nineteenth century democratic values have become the accepted norm for a modern state, regardless of the degree to which they have actually been implemented. Democracy is considered the ideal form of government for constitutional monarchies, republics, socialist states, and communist states. It is interesting to note that from the nineteenth century onward, democracy flourished in the countries that were often also the most important hegemonic powers. In the long run this generated a considerable amount of tension between the values of the domestic political systems and the use of force and power in relations with other states. Inasmuch as democracy became the accepted ideal political system domestically, the contradiction between the patterns of domestic and foreign policy could only be modified in the long run by adjusting the pattern of foreign policy behavior to conform to the values of domestic politics. The right to self-determination, to freedom of choice and expression, had to be extended to the outside world. Before the Second World War the British, French, Belgians, and Dutch could maintain thriving democratic political systems at home and still control vast colonial possessions. The inherent tension in this situation was not evident. But after the Second World War the contradiction between these two worlds became too obvious to be continued for long. The Wilsonian diplomacy of self-determination was one of the earliest manifestations of this trend (although it did not prevent Woodrow Wilson or subsequent presidents from pursuing a form of gunboat diplomacy in the Caribbean and Central America). After the Second World War the great European powers found it impossible to continue their direct control of vast overseas colonial empires; having been weakened by the war, they needed to focus most of their energies on the reconstruction of their own economies. Aside from this decline in power, the principal explanation for the demise of the colonial era had to do with the mood of public opinion in Paris and London. France lost its wars with Vietnam and Algeria as much in Paris as it did on the battlefield. British public opinion was not prepared to support the Suez expedition and pay the price of maintaining British colonial possessions. Likewise, the United States lost the war in Vietnam not so much on the battlefield as in the prolonged fight involving American opinion, the mass media, and congressional support. As the war dragged on, the American public asked more and more questions. Finally, the choice was between breaking the fiber of American society and its national consensus, or continuation of the war. Since the United States preferred democracy to success in war, the choice became inevitable.

Israel had a similar experience in its war in Lebanon. Israeli democracy could accept a military operation on a limited scale – but not a prolonged war and the occupation of another country against the will of its people. Again the choice was between the survival of Israeli democracy and continuation of the war. Israel decided to withdraw from Lebanon. (Israel's control of the West Bank will ultimately create a clash between Israeli democracy on the one hand and continued control of the West Bank population against its will. Since many Israelis

view the West Bank as important to Israel's national security, it is not
clear that democracy will triumph in this case.)

The weaker states have learned that the key to victory is not on the
battlefield but in the enemy's capital. In fact, the campaign on the
battlefield is conducted and directed with an eye to its influence on the
adversary's domestic public opinion. This was very clearly understood
by the Vietnamese and Algerians and is increasingly understood by
Israel's Arab neighbors.

Both the black opposition in South Africa and the anti-Marcos forces
in the Philippines have come to understand that the best way to achieve
their goals is by an appeal to American public opinion, to American
democratic values. Indeed, the Philippine opposition to President
Marcos achieved a great and bloodless victory by winning the battle for
U.S. public opinion, by obtaining congressional support, and as a result
also the support of the U.S. President. The blacks in South Africa have
begun to make progress since they captured the attention of the
American mass media and hence U.S. public opinion. Similar policies
are being pursued by Central and Latin American states as well as
by other weaker states. The weaker states will increasingly rely on
manipulating and convincing public opinion within the great powers in
order to achieve their goals. In this respect, of course, the USSR cannot
be manipulated as easily (if at all) as the United States. This does not
mean that in the long run, as changes occur in the Soviet domestic
system, that the weaker states will not also develop access to Soviet
'public opinion'.

FROM THE PRIMACY OF FOREIGN POLICY TO THE PRIMACY OF
DOMESTIC POLITICS

The instability of the European system throughout history and until the
end of the Second World War gave rise to the Rankeian axiom that the
foreign interests of a state must take precedence over its domestic
affairs. Domestic affairs cannot be addressed as long as the survival of
the state has been placed in jeopardy by external threats. The Rankeian
insistence on *Der Primat der Aussenpolitik* can be traced back to
Machiavelli and Thucydides and to the beginnings of recorded European history.

All of this changed by the end of the Second World War for reasons
that will be discussed below, but the recognition of such changes in the
European system has come about very slowly because of the long
tradition of the primacy of foreign affairs and the centuries of continued
instability. As is always the case, human perception and the theories

reflecting these perceptions always lag behind the changes that take place in the environment.

It is not surprising that the major powers were forced to give foreign policy precedence over domestic politics in view of the instability of the European system and as a result also the global system before and after the First World War. During this period both balance of power and the traditional alliance systems of the League of Nations failed as Europe went through a transition from a homogeneous system to a tense antagonistic ideological-revolutionary system. The tensions over state borders in the 1930s, the revisionist and aggressive policies of the fascist countries, the inability to solve problems through compromise and negotiation, the frequent resort to naked force, and the rise of communism in Russia all indicated the need to view the external environment as being of paramount concern. States could and did disappear from the map of Europe (e.g., Austria, Latvia, Lithuania, Estonia, Czechoslovakia). If anything, events leading up to the Second World War, the war itself, and no less its aftermath and the subsequent Cold War, only further buttressed belief in the primacy of foreign policy and the implications flowing from this axiomatic assumption.

Although the seeds for the emphasis on domestic politics were already present by 1945, the great powers continued to implement policies based on the primacy of foreign affairs. The fascist powers had disappeared, but the communist regime in the Soviet Union not only remained in power, it exported the communist revolution to Eastern Europe and later attempted to export it on a global scale.

The imperatives of the emphasis on foreign policy are clear: create spheres of influence as broadly as possible in order to directly control the immediate environment and secure your own borders. Direct control is preferable, but where not feasible, supportive alliance systems must be created. These policies were premised on the prolonged traumatic events preceding the two world wars. After the Second World War significant changes in the international system were completely ignored for two or three decades. The result was the continued reliance on military power, heavy investment in military strength, the acquisition and control of territory (in particular by the USSR), and the development of the zero-sum game mentality. Past experience and fear led to a self-fulfilling prophecy – a tight bipolar system and the tensions of the Cold War.

The realization that the international system had undergone a radical transformation came about only very gradually and in many ways has not been fully recognized even today. The invisible grip of history and past experience is too tenacious to be dissolved through logical and rational analysis alone. Thus, as long as new generations of Soviet citizens are indoctrinated with accounts of the traumatic events of the Second World War they will continue to believe that the international environment has not changed since that time.

Objectively speaking, the great powers' need to directly control adjacent spheres of influence has diminished if not disappeared. Neither Germany nor Japan threaten the great powers, and there is no need for directly controlled spheres of influence or buffer zones. Poland or Finland certainly pose no threat to the Soviet Union. If any threat exists, it emanates from the other superpower, and it is primarily based on the existence of intercontinental ballistic missiles, not the danger of conventional war. Territorial acquisitions, spheres of influence, and buffer zones are all irrelevant to the mutual nuclear threat and do nothing to diminish it. Whether or not the USSR controls Cuba is immaterial to the direct security of the United States. The security of the superpowers rests increasingly in their relations with each other but not in the direct control of outside territories. Security as an excuse for pursuing hegemonic policies is irrelevant for the great powers. Other factors reduce the importance of direct or even indirect control over other states in enhancing the national interest. The British, French, Dutch, Belgians, and Portuguese suffered no harm whatsoever to their political, military, or economic interests when they lost control of their colonial empires. If anything, such disengagement strengthened rather than weakened those states. The same can be said for U.S. involvement in Vietnam and potentially for the USSR in Afghanistan and Eastern Europe. Indirect control is much cheaper and by far more effective. The great powers have discovered the hard way that their interests are best served by indirect involvement and, wherever possible, by no intervention at all.

In the final analysis, control of the external environment is intended to enhance a state's security and thereby add to its quality of life, economic development, material welfare, and political stability. Security is a means to an end, not an end in itself. The rationale for direct intervention in or control of the affairs of other states can only be justified if the cost of control and involvement is smaller than the benefits to be reaped. Since the end of the Second World War direct intervention has rarely paid off. The French wars in Vietnam and Algeria weakened rather than strengthened France. The U.S. war in Vietnam was not only a negative investment economically and militarily, but almost disrupted the whole fiber of American domestic politics. There is little sense in assigning priority to foreign affairs in the absence of a threat to the survival of the nation – if in the process the state destroys itself from within. In a democratic age when all economic and commercial benefits can be secured without direct control and in which the costs of war have become unbearable, the focus of attention must be on the domestic affairs of the state. Of what value is control by the USSR over Eastern Europe or Afghanistan if its price is retardation of the Soviet Union's economic development (and hence ultimately also its security)?

This new order of priority (i.e., the primacy of domestic over foreign politics) already dominates the policies of the European powers, is becoming more and more visible in the post-Vietnam policies of the United States, and is certain to influence the policies of the USSR in the post-Afghanistan era as we approach the end of this century.

THE NUCLEAR REVOLUTION AND THE PRIMACY OF AVOIDING A NUCLEAR CONFRONTATION BETWEEN THE SUPERPOWERS

Following the development of nuclear weapons by the USSR in 1949, and the subsequent development of fission bombs and intercontinental missiles, the superpowers gradually recognized that a nuclear war between them could only mean the end of civilization as we know it and that there can be no winners in any type of nuclear conflict. They have therefore reluctantly and independently come to the realization that the most important interest they have is the avoidance of nuclear war.

The emergence of this post-Second World War interest caused a shift in the paradigm of great-power relationships and to a lesser extent the relationships between the superpowers and the weaker states as well as among the weaker states themselves. Unlike the squaring off of Germany and France in 1914 and 1939, Germany and Russia in 1914, Germany and the USSR in 1941, and Austria and Russia in 1914, a direct confrontation and certainly war between the superpowers has become highly unlikely. The very possibility of a direct confrontation between the United States and the Soviet Union that could lead to war and hence to nuclear escalation is now unthinkable and could serve no rational end. In today's world we can in fact speak about the 'primacy of avoiding a nuclear confrontation', hence about 'the primacy of avoiding a direct confrontation between the superpowers', rather than about 'the primacy of foreign policy'.

Although it is clearly understood by most politicians and experts in the 1980s, awareness of the full danger of superpower confrontation was not in evidence during the 1950s and early 1960s, as indicated by the two Berlin crises, by the Quemoy and Matsu crisis, and by the Cuban missile crisis. The outcome in each of these cases indicates that the logic of 'the primacy of avoiding a nuclear war' was already pervasive, but that at the same time this understanding was tacit, subconscious, and not as yet clearly formulated.

The Cuban missile crisis was the turning point: it forced the logic of the situation to emerge from the background into the forefront of the relationship between the superpowers. They had finally, albeit reluctantly, arrived at the realization that they could not afford any direct confrontations and that therefore they must also avoid those direct interventions in other parts of the world that could lead to such a confrontation. The ramifications were clear: each could employ direct force only in areas that were not critical to the other side. In other words, the superpowers realized that they cannot intervene (as they did in earlier historical periods) in each other's hegemonial spheres of influence (i.e., the United States could not directly or even indirectly intervene in Poland, East Germany, or Czechoslovakia, while the Soviet Union could not risk a large-scale direct intervention in the Western Hemisphere, Western Europe, or the Middle East).

The development of this interest in avoiding a direct confrontation clearly explains why each of the Middle Eastern wars has ended in politically indecisive results. Each superpower had to intervene with its own clients and allies to stop the fighting short of a politically and militarily decisive outcome in order to prevent a superpower confrontation and the possibility of a nuclear war. This is one reason why the United States failed to support and in fact came out against the British, French, and Israeli attempt to take the Suez Canal in 1956. This is also why Israel was twice (in 1967 and 1973) forced to halt its military operations before reaching the culminating point of victory. Although slow to recognize this situation, the regional powers have gradually realized that there is a very definite limit to the utility of military power, and that even if they win on the battlefield, they will find it hard to translate military victories into political gains. The recognition of these constraints on their freedom of action may become more clear to them in the future and may be taken more into account in the formulation of their foreign policies as well as in the design of their military doctrines.

The superpowers could not intervene in each other's spheres of influence or in a region in which their interests are shared (e.g., the Middle East), but each could fight or intervene (outside its own sphere of influence) in Korea, Vietnam, Angola, Ethiopia/Somalia, and Afghanistan. In other words, the only wars they could afford to wage were precisely those that were not worth fighting and where the costs would exceed any benefits. In the modern world of the superpowers what is possible to fight for without risking a nuclear war is almost by definition not worth the effort.

Intervention in areas of secondary or tertiary importance was in many cases a knee-jerk response to the dictates of the zero-sum game of the bipolar world, in which a missed opportunity was automatically perceived as the other side's gain. In addition, each war was viewed almost exclusively as part of a global contest, rather than in the context of its immediate causes. Intervention was therefore seen as part of a signaling process, that is, part of a global deterrence policy. In the process of fighting these wars of secondary and tertiary importance, the superpowers lost more often than they won. The costs of each war weakened them in relation to the rival superpower instead of augmenting their strength. From its perspective, the Soviet Union could not devise any better policy than that of allowing the United States to waste its power in Vietnam, an involvement that curtailed U.S. ability to pay attention to the rest of the world and simultaneously weakened the popular consensus at home. In the end the Vietnam conflict reduced U.S. willingness to intervene in other areas. (The Soviet Union did indeed hope to cash in on the American intervention in Vietnam through a redistribution of power in the Middle East. This explains the Soviet policy of encouraging if not pushing the Arabs to go to war against Israel in 1967.)

Although the United States vehemently opposed the Soviet Union's intervention in Afghanistan, from a Machiavellian point of view nothing better could have happened. The Soviet Union has thereby alienated many countries in the Muslim world and has become mired down in a quagmire reminiscent of Vietnam.

THE INCREASED COSTS OF THE USE OF DIRECT POWER

The cost of conventional and irregular warfare has increased to such an extent that the readiness and incentive of the great powers to use force and intervene directly have been considerably reduced. The myriad reasons for this can be discussed only briefly in this context.

To begin with, the weaker states have learned that they need not fight to win, but rather not to lose; they must simply try to hold out long enough to win – not on the battlefield – but in their adversary's capital. They have learned that a political victory is more important than a military victory. This type of victory requires patience and time, ingredients that are not always the strongest suit of the great powers. The weaker states have learned that this goal can best be accomplished by penetrating the domestic system of their adversary. To do this they need time; in the process they are, paradoxically, helped by their adversary.

Given the secondary or tertiary importance of their country to the superpower, the military and political leadership of the superpower will find it very difficult initially to send a large number of troops to fight their weaker adversary. As a result, the number of troops first sent to fight in Vietnam or Afghanistan is never large enough to be decisive at the outset; in the meantime, the weaker state or guerrilla force can continue to hold out while the superpower decides whether or not to invest still more resources in an area of relatively little importance. In this sense, time is on the side of the weak.

One reason that the real or absolute power of the superpowers is irrelevant is that they can never apply all the power at their disposal at any given point in time against the weaker state. Concepts such as 'compliance capacity' are not applicable here because the superpowers can only commit their troops and employ their superior force in a piecemeal fashion. This is true not only because the weaker states are not of central importance to the superpowers' survival but also because they must constantly look over their shoulders and maintain power sufficient to support their interests in other regions as well.

A corollary is that this issue of lesser importance for the superpower is the single most vital interest of the weaker state. Thus the stronger power will always have less of an incentive to fight than the weaker state. What is a matter of survival for the weaker state is a matter of choice for the superpower.

Other explanations for the increased cost of direct military intervention are these:

(1) The superpowers' conventional forces are designed for war against each other, not against weaker and less-developed armies. The tanks, aircraft, electronic equipment, etc., procured by the great powers are meant for high technology warfare in Central Europe, not for jungle or desert warfare in difficult terrain. All of this sophisticated equipment is of little relevance in the jungles of Vietnam or the mountains of Afghanistan.

(2) As a result of their potential – though, as argued, not actual – superiority, quantitatively as well as qualitatively, the superpowers tend to dangerously overestimate their own strength and underestimate that of their opponents. This often unintended arrogance can produce tactical defeats and unpleasant surprises on the battlefield. To its detriment, the stronger side may indulge its predilection for straightforward quantitative calculations while ignoring the balance in morale and motivation. It is the very vulnerability of the weaker states that gives them the impetus to develop more creative military doctrines and employ innovative tactics; the more complacent powerful states are, in the meantime, usually content to fight according to existing military doctrines tailored for another type of warfare. Furthermore, the forces of the superpower are often controlled from a distant capital and limited by the political leadership in their choice of tactics and strategy.

(3) The great powers fight, on the whole, according to the accepted rules of the game (particularly the Western democracies, less so the Soviet Union and other authoritarian states), whereas the hard-pressed weaker state will frequently resort to any possible means: terrorism, attacks on civilian population centers, avoidance of combat, and other advantages provided by guerrilla and other types of irregular warfare.

In many cases the superpower (again, more so the Western democracies) will be much more sensitive to casualties and losses than their weaker opponents who are fighting for mere survival.

(4) The weaker states or indigenous forces are more familiar with the local terrain and climate as well as with the culture and languages of the region. By the time the soldiers and officers of the superpower have become acquainted with the local conditions, they are 'rotated' – that is, sent home for recuperation and other duties. More determined from the beginning, the local forces will stay and fight on a continuous basis.

(5) Another important factor that has increased the costs of military intervention is the support provided to the weaker state by the rival superpower, either directly as by the USSR in Vietnam, or indirectly by proxy, as by the United States in Afghanistan through Egypt, Pakistan, and other states. In this 'game' the superpower backing the weaker state can never lose. It is not directly involved, and the material support it provides comes with a low price tag relative to the benefits it produces. Normally, the rival superpower provides the weaker state with large quantities of obsolete weapons for which it has no more use. This type of support has an impressive multiplier effect. For every dollar's worth of weapons furnished to the weaker state by one superpower, the opposing superpower will have to invest ten to twenty times as many resources in weapons and manpower. Indirect intervention has made the costs of direct intervention unbearable, for it is not only much cheaper – it is the only cost-effective form of military intervention.

The post-World War era demonstrates that direct military intervention on a large scale is not a viable proposition and does not promote the interests of the intervening power. In the majority of cases the great powers lived up to their reputations – they did not lose the war militarily. They lost politically when the price being paid was considered too high, and public opinion turned against the war.

The French did not lose militarily in Vietnam or Algeria, the British, French, and Israelis did not lose militarily in the Suez campaign, nor did the United States in Vietnam or Israel in Lebanon. The Soviet Union cannot and will not lose the war in Afghanistan in a military sense, but it cannot win either. In the end Soviet intervention and imperialist hegemonic policy will suffer the same fate as that of the Western democracies. If there is a lesson to be learned from the British victory (to be sure, only by the smallest of margins) in the Falklands/Malvinas War, it is that the cost of success was much too high. Israel's victory over the PLO in Lebanon was a psychological victory. The only lesson that the Israelis can draw is that the direct application of force should be used only as a last resort.

Perhaps the best indication of the increased cost of direct military intervention can be found in the evolution of U.S. national security policy toward military intervention and the support of other nations. The United States has come a long way since John F. Kennedy's enthusiastic 'blank check' type of support for direct U.S. involvement in world affairs. Kennedy declared that the United States was willing to 'pay any price, bear any burden, meet any hardship, support any friend, oppose any foe to assure the survival of liberty'.

By 1969, at the height of the Vietnam trauma, President Nixon had formulated a radically different and more sober doctrine. According to the Nixon doctrine, the United States would avoid direct intervention whenever possible and instead provide military and economic support to those who were ready to help themselves. 'We shall furnish military and economic assistance when requested and as appropriate, but we shall look to the nation directly threatened to assume primary responsibility of providing the manpower for its own defense'.

The dangers and increased costs of direct military intervention abroad were also recognized by the U.S. Congress in November 1973 in its War Powers Resolution. Under this resolution, the President must consult with Congress 'in every possible instance' before introducing armed forces 'into hostilities or into situations where imminent involvement in hostilities is clearly indicated by the circumstances'. He must report to Congress on the status of American troops in such situations and is required to withdraw such troops within sixty to ninety days unless Congress authorizes their continued presence. The President must in any case immediately withdraw the troops if directed to do so by a concurrent congressional resolution, which is not subject to a presidential veto. The War Powers Resolution certainly makes it more difficult to get U.S. troops directly involved in military action abroad and clearly reduces the President's incentive to do so.

Oddly enough, this trend has been reinforced by none other than the Secretary of Defense, as representative of the interests and views of the U.S. military. The Weinberger doctrine, 'On the Use of Military Power', first enunciated on 28 October 1984, requires the fulfillment of six conditions before the United States should be ready to commit its forces to military action abroad:

(1) The vital interests of the United States or its allies must be at stake.
(2) Sufficient force should be applied to unequivocally reflect the intention of winning (i.e., no half-measures).
(3) Political and military objectives must be clearly defined.
(4) The U.S. involvement must be continuously reassessed to keep cause and response in synchronization.
(5) Before troops are committed, there must be a reasonable assurance of support from American public opinion.
(6) A combat role should be undertaken only as a last resort.

Strict adherence to the Weinberger doctrine would place insurmountable barriers in the way of any large-scale American military use of force abroad. Who would decide what a vital interest is? Who can calculate in advance the necessary size of a force required to win a war? Can political and military objectives be clearly defined and by whom? How can public support, even if initially favorable, be guaranteed to last as long as the war effort requires it? These and a multitude of other questions raised by the Weinberger doctrine indicate the obstacles in the way of using forces abroad in accordance with this doctrine. It is not surprising that such a doctrine originated in the Defense Department, for no one is more aware of the prohibitive costs of war and intervention than the U.S. armed forces. The pressure to resort to military force, as Richard K. Betts has shown, is stronger in the civilian than in the military community.

The trend against the direct use of force as reflected in U.S. law and policy doctrines is clear. The use of force is too expensive, too ineffective. Indeed, force has finally become the *ultima ratio*. Although no such declarations have been made by the Soviet Union, its cost of using force abroad is not very different from that incurred by the United States. Whether made public or not, a doctrine similar to the Weinberger doctrine will have to be developed in the Soviet Union after the war in Afghanistan has ended.

FREE TRADE: BENEFITS WITHOUT RESPONSIBILITY

Another relic of the mercantilistic age is the idea that a country will fare better if it has direct control over other states. Today the old mercantilist theories have been replaced by strategic theories declaring the need to secure direct access to raw materials in the name of national security. From an economic point of view as much as from the political and military points of view described in the preceding text, the costs of direct control of resources have become too high.

In the age of high technology there is no need to be in direct control of the silicon mines overseas. All raw material, as recent history has shown, can be obtained more easily and cheaply through free international trade. In the first place the greatest volume of trade by far is between the industrial, developed states. The volume of trade between the highly developed and less-developed countries is much smaller and much less vital. The United States, or for that matter any other great power or state, does not need to be in control of any other states in order to acquire all the raw materials or industrial goods it needs. All commodities, from oil to coffee, bananas, titanium, rubber, or gold, can be obtained most cheaply in the free market. The underdeveloped countries are in fact competing to sell their raw materials and goods to the great powers. This competition tends to push the prices of all raw materials downward. If oil cannot be purchased in Libya or Saudi Arabia, it can be bought in the USSR or produced in Alaska and Mexico.

The strategic argument for the need to directly secure access to raw materials is patently fallacious for the following reason: we have seen that the supreme interest of both superpowers is avoidance of a nuclear confrontation. Any attempt by one superpower to deny the other access to vital raw materials such as oil will inevitably lead to a direct confrontation and hence to a risk of nuclear war. For this reason, the possibility that either of the superpowers would be denied access to vital raw materials is unacceptable and virtually nonexistent.

For years it has been argued that South African raw materials are crucial for the United States. Since the system of apartheid has become a U.S. domestic political issue, very little has been heard of the importance of that country's raw materials. Even if South Africa were to become a Soviet republic, it would, in any event, still have to trade and sell its raw materials in the West. Furthermore, an increasing number of raw materials can be replaced by synthetic substitutes readily available to any industrialized country. Direct control of lesser-developed states forces the more developed and stronger state to take into account their needs and may even force it to subsidize their weaker economies by paying higher than market prices for their products. Responsibility comes with control, and such responsibility is not good for the maximization of profit.

The USSR can be said to control lesser states, yet it is not better off economically for doing so. Countries in Eastern Europe such as Poland and Romania might collapse economically, and the resulting political instability would force the USSR to bail them out in order to avert political disaster. Direct influence or control over Cuba or Poland may be politically advantageous for the USSR but is a net loss in economic terms.

In contrast, the USSR does not directly control Finland, with which it has developed excellent and profitable relations. Should the Finnish economy collapse tomorrow morning, the USSR owes it nothing. The USSR can have its cake (political influence) and eat it too (economic benefits). Indirect control or Finlandization are politically and economically more effective than direct control because under this arrangement both countries have a common interest. Poland and the USSR, on the other hand, have antagonistic interests. In Schelling's words, Poland can play the game of 'coercive deficiency'; it can threaten, having no positive incentive, to commit economic suicide, and the USSR will have to come to its rescue.

A similar type of logic can be applied to U.S. policies. U.S. responsibility for the economic well-being of Latin American countries will increase in proportion to the degree of direct control it assumes.

Given the wealth of the USSR in raw materials, there is little doubt that in principle the Soviet Union could do much better without the economic burden of Eastern Europe. Such benefits, however, could only materialize if the Soviet Union were able to concentrate all of its energy inward and develop an economic incentive for its population to work harder. The key to the strength and survival of the USSR lies in its domestic, not its external environment.

According to the analysis presented in this chapter, future considerations of power politics will rely less and less on direct intervention and the direct application of power. If, in the past, the best way to augment power was through its actual use, in the modern world, the safest, least costly, and most rational way to maximize power is by conserving it. Such a policy was adopted by the European great powers in the 1960s, and was adopted de facto by the United States (with minor exceptions) following the war in Vietnam. The Soviet Union's difficult economic situation and experience in Afghanistan will most likely lead to the adoption of a similar policy in the 1990s. Those states that might continue to resort to the use of raw power against one another are the weaker states, not the great powers. Wars between nations such as Iran and Iraq, Israel and her Arab neighbours, Somalia and Ethiopia, Egypt and Libya, and perhaps Greece and Turkey will probably continue to flare up.

Paradoxically, a rational cost-benefit type of analysis leads one to conclude that the days of direct use of power by the superpowers have almost come to an end. Unfortunately, the actions of states in the international system, like those of individual political leaders, are not always governed by standards of rationality; therefore, the trends I have identified could conceivably be impeded by illogical or fanatical behavior.